LARGE MAMMALS
OF THE **ROCKY MOUNTAINS**

LARGE MAMMALS
OF THE **ROCKY MOUNTAINS**

Everything You Need to Know About the Continent's
Biggest Animals—From Elk to Grizzly Bears and More

JACK BALLARD

Guilford, Connecticut

An imprint of The Rowman & Littlefield Publishing Group, Inc.
4501 Forbes Blvd., Ste. 200
Lanham, MD 20706

Falcon and FalconGuides are registered trademarks and Make Adventure Your Story is a trademark of The Rowman & Littlefield Publishing Group, Inc..

Distributed by NATIONAL BOOK NETWORK

British Library Cataloguing in Publication Information available

Library of Congress Cataloging-in-Publication Data

Names: Ballard, Jack (Jack Clayton), author.
Title: Large mammals of the Rocky Mountains : everything you need to know about the continent's biggest animals—from elk to grizzly bears and more
/ Jack Ballard.
Description: Guilford, Connecticut : Falcon, [2018] | Includes index.
Identifiers: LCCN 2017060629 (print) | LCCN 2017043495 (ebook) | ISBN 9781493029532 (paperback) | ISBN 9781493029549 (e-book)
Subjects: LCSH: Mammals—Rocky Mountains.
Classification: LCC QL719.R63 B35 2018 (ebook) | LCC QL719.R63 (print) | DDC 599.0978—dc23
LC record available at https://lccn.loc.gov/2017060629

♾™ The paper used in this publication meets the minimum requirements of American National Standard for Information Sciences—Permanence of Paper for Printed Library Materials, ANSI/NISO Z39.48-1992.

Printed in the United States of America

CONTENTS

ACKNOWLEDGMENTS

Many, many people were instrumental in the writing and production of this book. The work is a culmination of a project that began in 2011 at the request of John Burbidge, acquisitions editor for FalconGuides. He contacted me to request I write a "pocket guide" on elk. That project grew to include guidebooks for nine of the twelve species covered in this book, much of which is a compilation of those works. Early on in the series, John had the idea of producing an encyclopedic volume of the combined books and is the virtuously patient acquisitions editor responsible for this volume as well, the finishing of which required far more time and effort than I imagined.

Numerous biologists, many of them leading experts in their fields, have generously reviewed and commented upon the portions of the manuscript with which they have acknowledged expertise or have otherwise enlightened my perspective on a particular species. They are: Jamie Jonkel, Shawn Stewart (Montana Dept. of Fish, Wildlife & Parks biologists); Jon Rachael (Idaho Fish & Game Department biologist); Mike Jimenez (former Wolf Management and Science Coordinator, US Fish & Wildlife Service); Dr. Chris Servheen (Professor of Wildlife Biology at the University of Montana and former Grizzly Bear Recovery Coordinator for the US Fish & Wildlife Service); Dr. Bob Garrott (Professor of Ecology at Montana State University); Doug McWhirter (Wyoming Game & Fish Department biologist); Hank Edwards (Wildlife Disease Specialist with the Wyoming Game & Fish Department); Melanie Woolever (National Bighorn Sheep Program Leader, of the US Forest Service); Dr. Brendan Moynahan (former Lead Biologist, National Bison Range); Marilyn Cuthill (formerly of Beringia South, one of the leading mountain lion research centers in the United States); and Sarah Dewey (wildlife biologist at Grand Teton National Park) for reviewing and making helpful comments on the manuscript.

My wife, Lisa, has endured countless hours of hearing the manuscript read aloud and has given many suggestions to give the text clarity. Lisa and my son, Dominic, have generously lent many photos from their files for the book as well.

Swarovski Optics generously provided superb binoculars to aid my field observations of wildlife. Thank you!

INTRODUCTION

No author has the personal expertise to pen an encyclopedic volume of this nature and is thus obligated to obtain information from numerous sources. This is often a difficult task, not only in accessing relevant sources but in evaluating their objectivity. Advocacy groups are frequently in the news. One group may vehemently oppose the killing of carnivores for wildlife management purposes while another desires predator "control" in hopes of increasing game populations for hunters. Both claim that "science" is on their side, frequently making statements such as "the science says" or "the best science supports our position." It is certainly not impossible for advocacy groups to fund good research, but citizens should understand the many pitfalls of what is sometimes termed "advocacy science." Many groups, from gas and oil companies to environmental organizations, fund research. I would suggest that the public interpret the results of such studies very cautiously. For this book, I have relied upon studies published in peer-reviewed sources as much as possible, supplemented with research conducted by federal and state wildlife agencies.

The purpose of this book is to provide a rather comprehensive resource for both laypersons and professionals. The original marketing plan behind the Falcon Pocket Guides that spawned this book was to offer consumers a guide far more detailed than a few pages in a field guide, but avoid the technical jargon of some of the full-blown treatises published on some species. I have thus taken pains to eliminate or explain formal biological terminology as much as possible to communicate to the broadest possible audience. In some places this involves nothing more than personal preference. For example, "white-tailed deer" is the name more frequently seen in scientific literature, but I prefer the simplicity of spelling and saying the more colloquial "whitetail deer" and refer to the species as such in this volume. The species included in the book as "large mammals" conform to two criteria. First, adult animals of the species commonly weigh 100 pounds or more. Secondly, they are relatively common to the Rocky Mountains of the United States. However, the treatment of a particular species is not limited to its natural history as observed in the Rockies, but its larger range in the United States and to a lesser degree, Canada. The text is organized to first include members of the deer species, then other ungulates (in alphabetical order), followed by the carnivores (also in alphabetical order).

Sharp-eyed readers will notice some repetition of themes from species to species, such as the ongoing debate regarding the legitimacy of certain subspecies or the entire notion of subspecies. The chapters of the book devoted to each species are intended to serve as stand-alone treatments, which requires a certain amount of such repetition. The reader might also notice that the chapters on bison, wolves, and mountain lions contain fewer sections than the others. A separate section on diet and nutrition was eliminated for these predators on the basis of their more limited diet

compared to ungulates. The information offered on their diets and feeding habits was rolled into treatments on habitat and predatory activities.

Human civilization and the activities of *homo sapiens* are placing increasing pressure on the habitat and survival of wildlife species all over the globe. How these play out in our country (and elsewhere) will be the product of politics and the extent to which the public understands the economic and environmental worth of wildlife. The argument has been put forth from many leading biologists that what is good for wildlife, small species and large, common animals and obscure, is ultimately best for humans as well. This compelling position is predicated upon a sound understanding of wildlife by policy-makers and the public. That it serves such an end is my fondest ambition for this book.

CHAPTER 1
ELK

My earliest memory of a national park involved an elk. On a rare vacation, my family motored to Yellowstone National Park for a long September weekend. As we wound along, frost glittered on flaxen grass in the meadows, and stately, emerald evergreens stood tall and motionless on the hillsides. The sun shone brightly in a cloudless blue sky.

Suddenly, my head nearly banged the front seat when my father slammed on the brakes of our big 1972 Chrysler. With urgency in his voice, he commanded us out of the car. Confused, we bustled out behind him, wondering about the cause of this emergency. "Look," he ordered.

Gazing in the direction of his pointed finger, I beheld the first living bull elk I'd ever seen. Goring the earth in a tiny meadow with its antlers, the bull lifted its head. Tilting its muzzle, the resplendent animal shattered the morning's tranquility with a resounding bugle. Its breath froze as a great, billowing plume in the frosty air. Even as a second-grader, I knew I'd witnessed something spectacular.

Since that first encounter, I've observed elk for more than four decades. I've watched herds of wapiti (the American Indian word for elk) grazing alpine pastures in Colorado's Rocky Mountain National Park and glimpsed them in the dark timber of Olympic National Park in Washington. I've spied elk in both of the Dakotas—in Theodore Roosevelt National Park in the north, Custer State Park in the south—and in countless locations in our national forests.

I'm thrilled every time I see them. This chapter is written in hopes it will similarly inspire your own admiration and understanding of these magnificent creatures, no matter where you encounter elk.

The bugle of a big bull elk is a sound you'll never forget.
JACK BALLARD

Names and Visual Description

"Elk" is the name given to a large, hoofed animal of North America. Elk are predominantly brown in color, although their bodies exhibit varying hues. The neck and head of an elk are typically dark brown or chocolate colored. The back and flanks vary from a rich, light brown to tan. Males have antlers and often appear lighter than females on the body, with sides sporting a very pale tan variation or a noticeably yellow coloration. The legs and underbelly of elk are dark, corresponding in color to the hair on the neck and head. Elk rumps appear large and pale in comparison with the rest of their body. Thus, mature elk exhibit a three-toned appearance that lightens when viewed from the front to the rear of the body: dark brown on the head and neck, medium brown to tan on the sides, followed by a lighter, cream-colored or yellowish rump. During the few months of summer when elk are adorned with a shorter hair coat, their overall coloration is more golden or reddish than at other times of the year.

The coat of a fat and sleek bull elk appears reddish brown in summer.
JACK BALLARD

Misapplication of British or European names to North American wildlife was quite common when nonnative peoples began to settle this continent. Such was the case with elk. "Elk" is actually the word used by British and European people of the colonial era for moose. Incorrectly applied to the more widely distributed elk, the name stuck. Thus, there are currently two species of large, hoofed mammals in the world called elk. Moose, known by the scientific name *Alces alces,* are called elk in Europe. The elk of North America bear the scientific name *Cervus elaphus* or *Cervus canadensis.*

In assigning a scientific name to North American elk, some biologists prefer *Cervus elaphus,* the same title given to the red deer of Europe, a species that has a noticeably different appearance than North American elk. Proponents of this name note that elk and red deer can interbreed, producing fertile offspring. Scientists championing the *Cervus canadensis* nomenclature point out the obvious physical differences between red deer and elk that would indicate separate species. They further note that while many species of other animals can interbreed and produce fertile offspring (mallard ducks and pintails, for example), the mere fact that two species can interbreed isn't sufficient reason to classify them as a singular species. So much for the scientists agreeing on everything!

To avoid confusion, many European writers use the name "wapiti" to refer to North American elk. Wapiti is perhaps the most common secondary name or nickname for elk, and perhaps the most logical moniker when speaking of the species in an international context. Originating from the native tongues of the Shawnee and

Cree Indians, wapiti means "white rump" and refers to this conspicuous portion of an elk's anatomy.

Within the species, male elk are known as "bulls." Females are called "cows," and babies are referred to as "calves." Sounds just like domestic cattle, doesn't it? For the first several months of life, calves are easily distinguished from adults not only by their smaller size, but also by their buff, spotted coats.

Related Species in North America

Elk are the third-largest hoofed animal indigenous to North America. The largest, in terms of weight, is the American bison. The second largest is the moose. Both elk and moose are members of the deer family, which also includes caribou, whitetail deer, and mule deer as species native to North America.

Although casual observers sometimes mistake other species of the deer family for elk or vice versa, attention to the most basic details of identification will eliminate the errors. Moose are noticeably larger than elk. Even if observers are not familiar with the relative size of the two species, they can still easily tell them apart. Moose exhibit a more uniformly dark brown appearance across the body, which sometimes appears almost black. Adult moose have high, humped shoulders, a feature not seen in elk. The shape of their head is different as well. A moose's head looks large in comparison to

its body, tapering to a prominent, bulbous snout. Adult moose also have a sizable flap of loose skin that extends below their muzzle called a "dewlap." The shape of the antlers also differs in elk and moose. Mature bull elk sport antlers that appear as a single beam, interspersed with pointed offshoots known as "tines." The antlers of adult bull moose look more like oversized paddles with tines sprouting from their perimeter. Lucky outdoor observers in the Rocky Mountains, the northern United States, and western Canada might see elk and moose at the same time or close to each other as their ranges overlap in these locations.

Of the other three species with which elk share the deer family in North America, caribou are the closest to elk in size. The ranges of elk and caribou overlap in

Although also members of the deer family, species such as caribou can be distinguished from elk based on coat color, size, and antler shape.
© ISTOCK.COM/ RONSAN4D

some portions of western Canada. Caribou are smaller than elk and quite dissimilar in appearance. The neck of a caribou is very light tan or creamy in appearance in contrast to the dark brown of an elk. While the tail of an elk is very short, rounded, and a bit fluffy looking, caribou have tails that are a bit longer, narrow to a point, and are white on the underside. Both male and female caribou have antlers; cow elk do not. The shape of an adult male caribou's antlers is different from that of an elk. Viewed from the side, a bull caribou's antlers sweep back then forward in an arc shaped like a semicircle. An elk's antlers appear straighter, bending slightly backwards. Protrusions from the main beam of a caribou's antlers are palmated, with short tines looking a bit like fingers on a hand instead of the singular tines extending from the beam of an elk antler.

The range of mule and/or whitetail deer coincides with elk most places wapiti are found in North America. However, it's extremely difficult to mistake an elk for either of these species of deer or vice versa. Elk are much larger than deer. Both species of deer are uniformly colored across the body, appearing in hues of tan, reddish-brown, or gray, depending on the species and time of year. Neither has the dark neck and head of an elk or the yellow rump.

Subspecies of Elk

Depending on the sensibilities of the biologist, over twenty different subspecies of elk might be recognized worldwide. Some of these subspecies, in Europe and Asia, would not be immediately recognized as elk by someone acquainted with the North American species. Many of these subspecies are European red deer, which, although capable of interbreeding with elk, show significant variations in size, coat color, vocalizations, and also the general shape and size of the bulls' antlers. It is interesting to note, however, that subspecies an American or Canadian would recognize as elk inhabit other parts of the world, including China, eastern Russia, Mongolia, and Kazakhstan.

Within the United States and Canada, several subspecies of elk are recognized to varying degrees by the scientific community. Rocky Mountain elk are the most common, distributed throughout the Rocky Mountains of the United States and Canada. Males of this subspecies typically achieve both large body and antler size where nutritious forage is available. Rocky Mountain elk are abundant and readily spotted by visitors in Wyoming's Yellowstone National Park and Rocky Mountain National Park in Colorado. In Canada, Banff National Park is an exceedingly scenic place to consistently view this subspecies.

Tule elk are found only in California. They range in pockets across the central portion of the state known as the Central Valley, preferring grassy areas and marshlands. Tule elk are the smallest subspecies of elk, with a typical body mass roughly one-half as large as the Rocky Mountain elk. Bulls of this subspecies also develop the smallest antlers. Reduced to just thirty-two animals in 1895, these unique elk now number more than 4,000 due to conservation efforts. Point Reyes National Seashore and Carrizo Plain National Monument are two protected areas where visitors often encounter Tule elk.

Roosevelt, or Olympic, elk roam the damp, coastal forests of Washington, Oregon, and California. In 1928 Roosevelt elk were transplanted to the Afognak and Raspberry Islands of Alaska. Roosevelt elk have also been reestablished in portions of British Columbia in Canada. These elk sometimes grow to impressive sizes and are considered by many biologists to be the largest of the North American subspecies. A four-year-old bull Roosevelt elk killed on Afognak Island had an estimated weight of 1,300 pounds, an incredibly large animal considering bull elk don't normally achieve maximum weight for several years after their fourth birthday. The desire to preserve habitat for

Roosevelt elk was a significant factor in the creation of Washington's Olympic National Park (originally called Mount Olympus National Monument) in 1909. Olympic National Park is one of the best places in the nation to encounter this subspecies.

The final subspecies of elk commonly recognized in North America is the Manitoban elk, which historically ranged across the midwestern United States and plains provinces of central Canada. Manitoban elk are thought to be somewhat larger in body size than Rocky Mountain elk, but the bulls typically produce slightly smaller antlers. Manitoban elk kept on game farms in Canada have been bred to grow exceptionally large velvet antlers (described later in this chapter) and are also prized for the quantity and quality of their meat. The extent to which Manitoban elk remain a recognizable subspecies is debated, as they were essentially exterminated from their historic range. Most of the elk now roaming areas that were home to this plains-dwelling subspecies, such as Wind Cave National Park and Custer State Park in South Dakota, and Theodore Roosevelt National Park in North Dakota, are actually Rocky Mountain elk transplanted from Yellowstone National Park or other locations.

Two other historic subspecies of elk in North America, one inhabiting the eastern forests and the other roaming across the mountains of the arid Southwest and northern Mexico, are now presumed extinct. Eastern elk and Merriam's elk succumbed to habitat destruction and, more acutely, over-hunting.

In terms of subspecies, it's important to remember that, with perhaps the exception of Tule elk, it's extremely difficult for even a trained biologist to distinguish one strain of elk from another. Members of the presumed subspecies freely cross geographical boundaries in many places as well. The Cascade Mountains of Washington and Oregon are thought to separate the Roosevelt and Rocky Mountain subspecies, although elk intermingle and freely cross the crest of this range. The situation is clearly similar on the Canadian plains between wild Manitoban elk (if they're considered as an intact subspecies) and Rocky Mountain elk introduced in numerous areas. Thus, while contemplating the various subspecies may be an enjoyable academic exercise, for practicality, a North American elk is just an elk!

Physical Characteristics

Although they often appear larger, adult elk normally stand from around 4 to 5 feet at the front shoulder, depending on sex, age, genetic endowment, and habitat quality. Measured from the nose to the rump, an elk is actually longer than it is tall, with adult specimens generally stretching the tape from around 6 to 10 feet. Mature bulls are considerably larger than cows of the same age. Males typically weigh from 600 to 1,100 pounds. Normal adult females range in weight from 450 to 650 pounds.

Tule elk of California are noticeably smaller than those found elsewhere in North America, commonly weighing about 30 percent less than these averages. Elk of Alaska and coastal populations in the western United States and Canada may be somewhat larger. Unlike humans, who maximize potential for healthy weight within the first quarter of their lifespan, bull elk continue to grow much later in adulthood.

Elk begin life as spotted, reddish-colored calves who commonly weigh between 25 and 40 pounds. Birth weight depends upon the age and physical condition of the mother, whether the calf is born singly or as a twin, and genetics. Calves retain their spotted coats for about the first three months of age; they are shed around the onset of their first autumn. Thereafter, they exhibit the same appearance as an adult elk in a smaller package.

Antlers and Antler Development

For humans, from native peoples to modern-day hunters to families simply wondering at the majesty of a band of elk in a national park, perhaps the animals' most impressive characteristic is their antlers. These appendages, formed of solid bone and found only on males, begin to grow in the spring or early summer, depending on a bull's age. Male elk have two bony protrusions on their skulls known as "pedicles." Pedicles are found on the top of the head between the ears and well behind the eyes. Shaped like cups and covered with skin, pedicles are the "roots" from which antlers grow.

Growing antlers are called "velvet antlers" for their fuzzy, velvety appearance. This velvety skin is filled with an extensive system of blood vessels that provide nutrients to the rapidly growing antlers, which can grow over an inch per day. In late summer, shifting hormones cause the blood supply to diminish. The "velvet" then sloughs from the antlers, a process that is often aided by the elk rubbing their antlers on trees and shrubs. The hardened antlers that remain are composed of bone. Naturally colored white, they soon take on various shades of brown. The coloration comes from staining and foreign material on the antler; it occurs when bulls rub their antlers on trees or gore the earth with the antlers in preparation for the mating season.

For most bull elk, their first set of antlers appears as single, rather thin spikes protruding from the head. Sometimes they are forked at the top or have multiple tines. True to appearance, yearling bulls with antlers that do not branch are commonly known as "spikes." Those whose antlers bear a single branch at the end are often called "forkhorns." A bull's first set of antlers is usually a foot or two in length and varies in diameter from the size of a broomstick to the size of the handle of a shovel. The antlers begin to grow around the bull's first birthday (usually in June) or slightly thereafter. A growth period averaging around ninety days is common for bulls one year of age. Contrary to popular belief, the number of points on a bull elk's antlers is not indicative of its age. Some yearling bulls sprout antlers that are little more than oversized pencils. I've seen spike bulls with short, very slender antlers in both Wyoming and Montana.

When the bull elk is a two-year-old, its antlers begin to grow earlier in the year, around late April or early May. The growth period is also longer, extending to around 115 days. Antlers of a two-year-old bull are longer, slightly thicker, and more branched than those of a yearling. From the central beam of the antler, several tines or "points" develop. This set of antlers usually contains from three to five points per side. Compared to antlers of older bulls, the two-year-old's headgear is smaller and may also be more brittle toward the tops, resulting in frequently broken tines when these bulls fight for dominance during the fall mating season. Among hunters and residents of rural areas in the western United States, these bulls are often called "raghorns."

Four-year-old bulls normally develop a classic set of mature elk antlers. These usually carry six tines on each side, with the fourth tine generally attaining the greatest length and overall size. Bulls of this age begin growing their antlers a bit before the 2-year-olds. The growth phase also lasts longer, now extending to around 140 days. Less frequently, mature bulls develop antlers containing seven or eight points on each side. Antlers exhibiting abnormal configurations, with random tines sprouting perpendicularly to the normal ones or unusual groupings of tines are called "nontypical" antlers. Some nontypical antlers may have ten or more points on each side.

The size and overall mass of a bull's antlers increase steadily until sometime around its sixth set, which require about 150 days to fully develop. Thereafter, a bull's antlers will increase in size and mass for up to another half-dozen years (if it lives that long), depending on the habitat in which an animal lives, its overall health and body condition, and the amount and quality of forage available to it in a given year. Wild bull elk in their prime may develop antlers that weigh over 40 pounds and are more than 5 feet long. Viewed from the front, the antlers may easily be 5 feet wide. Farmed elk fed a diet for optimizing antler growth can carry antlers weighing up to 60 pounds, as much as the weight of an average third-grade boy!

Bull elk shed their antlers every year before growing a new set from the pedicles. Older bulls with larger antlers shed theirs first, usually in mid- to late winter. Complex

Antlers are composed of bone. Their color is derived from staining from bark, soil, or other materials.
JACK BALLARD

Elk shed their antlers each year. Shed antlers are sometimes chewed upon by rodents or even elk seeking calcium.
JACK BALLARD

hormone interactions regulate the shedding of antlers. The level of testosterone, a male hormone, declines dramatically in the winter. This causes the adhesion of the antlers to the pedicles to decrease until the weight of the antlers pulls them from the bull's head. Once one antler falls from an elk with a large rack, its head is immediately unbalanced. If the bull then shakes its head, the other antler usually falls as well. In most cases, the cast antlers of mature bull elk are found in close proximity to one another. Once, while hiking in the mountains of Wyoming, I discovered one antler from a large bull lying within a couple of feet of another. Evidently the bull had dropped both antlers in essentially the same instant.

As testosterone levels begin to rise in the spring, the adhesion of the growing antlers to the pedicles becomes very strong. This bond is so tenacious that hardened antlers will break before being pulled loose from the pedicle, a condition that persists until the antlers are cast the following winter.

It has been estimated that a fully mature bull elk expends as much energy to grow its antlers as a cow does to produce a calf. Antlers are the fastest growing animal tissue known to scientists. Because there are similarities between the rapid growth of antlers and certain types of cancer, antler growth has been studied as part of cancer research. Antlers are also the only known appendage of mammals that can regenerate spontaneously, making antler growth an area of study in stem cell research as well. For biologists, elk antlers are fascinating for far more than their magnificent appearance.

Hooves and Tracking

The size of elk tracks varies substantially depending on the age, sex, and body mass of the individual. Adult animals of average size leave hoof prints that measure approximately 4 to 5 inches long and 3 inches wide. The length of the hind print is somewhat shorter than the front, commonly ½ inch, and is slightly narrower, although variation may be difficult to discern by the untrained eye. Tracks of large bulls may exceed the average dimensions by 50 percent or more.

Distinguishing elk tracks from other ungulates is a function of both size and shape. Elk tracks are substantially larger than those of deer, smaller than moose. In comparison to both moose and deer, elk tracks appear more rounded in shape. In light snow, mud, or soft dirt, the dew-claws of moose are plainly visible in their prints, appearing as two indentations behind the hoof print. Except in unusual circumstances (deep snow or very soft mud), the dew-claws of elk do not show on their prints. When elk run, the space between the two "toes" on their hoof prints widens and the distance between the prints increases substantially. To determine which direction an elk is traveling, follow the pointed portion of the hoof print. The hooves of elk narrow toward the front, yielding a simple way to determine their direction of travel.

RANGE AND HABITAT

Historic Range

When Europeans arrived in North America, elk were widely distributed across most of the continent. Many modern folks believe that elk are creatures of the mountains. While it's true that in our times mountainous regions of the United States and Canada hold the most elk, these adaptable ungulates were historically at home on the short-grass and tall-grass prairies of the central plains. They also roamed freely across most of the hardwood forests of the East.

In fact it's a little easier to describe where elk were absent prior to settlement. Elk were found in the southern Rocky Mountains of Arizona and New Mexico, with some herds ranging quite far south into mountainous areas of Mexico. However, the animals generally avoided the very arid portions of the desert Southwest. With the exception of small populations in the extreme northern and western reaches of Texas, the largest state in the contiguous United States was devoid of elk.

Similarly, California and Nevada had significant areas uninhabited by elk, namely, the southern and eastern portions of California and much of western Nevada. A band of "elkless" country continued north from eastern California and western Nevada through central Oregon and Washington, a natural "no-elk" zone that likely isolated the Tule and Roosevelt subspecies from the Rocky Mountain subspecies.

In western Canada, elk ranged freely across eastern British Columbia, in all but the extreme northern reaches of Alberta and Saskatchewan, and southeastern Manitoba. Moving east, their historic range uncannily followed what would eventually become the border between the United States and Canada. Elk were frequently found on the south side of the border, but rarely on the north, except in eastern Ontario in the Great Lakes region. The easternmost outposts of historic elk populations ended on the eastern border of New York.

Elk roamed in varying numbers across all of the eastern, southern, and central portions of the United States with the exception of areas adjacent to the coastlines of the Atlantic and Pacific Oceans. They were absent in Florida, but possibly found in low numbers in northern portions of Georgia, Alabama, and Mississippi. Some elk were known to be present in northern Louisiana, which was almost certainly the southernmost extent of their range.

Elk are often considered animals of the mountains, but historically, they roamed the plains as well.
JACK BALLARD

Current Range

With the arrival of Europeans to North America, the world changed for elk. Previously, human predation involved native hunters, skilled in their methods, but not efficiently able to kill large numbers of elk. Settlers not only brought their own firearms, but also put them in the hands of Native American hunters. Increased taking for food by both native peoples and settlers began to decrease elk populations wherever these large, tasty animals could be killed. By the late 1700s, people were already noticing a decline in elk numbers.

On the plains, huge herds of elk mingled with the seemingly innumerable bands of bison. Both species came increasingly under the guns of subsistence and market hunters in the latter decades of the 1800s. Many

Elk from Yellowstone National Park and the National Elk Refuge were used to supplement populations in many areas in the early twentieth century.
JACK BALLARD

elk were killed simply for their two front, canine teeth, which are composed of ivory and were fashionable as adornments to watch fobs.

By 1900 elk were nearly wiped out across most of their historic range. Their strongholds remained in the Rocky Mountains and coastal ranges in the western United States and Canada, where they were afforded some measure of protection from hunters by terrain less hospitable to humans. The creation of national parks in the mountain states, beginning with Yellowstone in 1872, gave elk a needed buffer from human hunters, although hunting was allowed for a time in some parks. Poaching (illegal hunting) remained a problem for decades. Yellowstone's elk herd and animals from the National Elk Refuge in Jackson Hole, Wyoming, became extremely important for early efforts to restore elk to their native range in other states. In Colorado, for example, elk numbered just a few hundred animals in the entire state in 1910. This remnant population was supplemented with elk from Yellowstone National Park. Nowadays, Colorado has the largest elk population of any state.

Currently, the stronghold of the elk's survival, the Rocky Mountains of the United States and Canada, remains its core area of distribution. Rocky Mountain states and provinces have the largest numbers of elk. Colorado's herd is estimated at almost 300,000 animals, essentially twice as many as any other state. Roughly estimated, states and provinces with between 100,000 and 150,000 elk (ranked from most to least numerous) include Montana, Oregon, Idaho, and Wyoming. New Mexico, Utah, Washington, and British Columbia (again ranked in order of most to least numbers) hold between 50,000 and 80,000 elk. Arizona, Saskatchewan, Nevada, California, and Kentucky are home to between 10,000 and 25,000 elk. Around fifteen other states and provinces have smaller herds of elk. Like those roaming the woodlands of Kentucky, elk in these areas are the products of transplanting efforts.

Fossil records indicate that elk were present in Alaska at the end of the Pleistocene epoch around 10,000 years ago. The dating of one elk fossil in Alaska ages it as 9,300

No matter where they live, politics and public opinion affect the health and survival of elk.
JACK BALLARD

years old. In 1925 the state of Alaska deliberately transplanted Roosevelt elk to several islands. The most successful of these transplants was on Afognak Island. From a tiny herd of three males and five females in 1929, animals brought from the Olympic Peninsula of Washington, the population burgeoned to over 1,200 animals in 1965, more than the island habitat could support. Since then, the Afognak Island population has fluctuated between similar highs and lows of around 500 animals. Elk have also been successfully introduced to several other islands in southeastern Alaska and have been known to swim between islands.

Elk now roam freely across these Alaskan islands and elsewhere in their historic range due to human efforts to restore them after their distribution was so severely curtailed around the turn of the twentieth century. But elk have done their own part. In many areas in the western United States, elk have naturally expanded their range. When my grandfather homesteaded the ranch of my boyhood west of Three Forks, Montana, just after 1900, elk had been eliminated from this foothills area between two mountain ranges. Crammed into the cab of a pickup with my dad and two brothers, driving up a rough country road on the way to a section of mountain pasture, I watched as my dad slammed on the brakes. Crossing the road in a dusting of snow was a set of elk tracks. It was around 1975. The day after Thanksgiving in 1980, a friend and I spotted four elk, two cows and two calves, on a neighbor's property near the back side of the ranch. Two years later, we saw several cows with spotted calves in the low mountains on and around the ranch. Within a decade, a herd of over a hundred elk roamed the area, much to the delight of my father. With them firmly reestablished in historic habitat, it's now hard to imagine my boyhood neighborhood without elk.

Wapiti have similarly moved into new territory of their own accord in many places throughout the western states, a pattern now repeating itself in other locations in the United States and Canada, where they have been recently transplanted into their historic range by wildlife management agencies.

Wildlife observers have plenty of options for seeing elk, some of the most reliable of which are in national and state parks. In the United States and Canada, wapiti are regularly seen in the following national parks and monuments and other public lands: Rocky Mountain and Great Sand Dunes (Colorado); Crater Lake (Oregon); Olympic and Mount Rainier (Washington); Point Reyes, Carrizo Plain, and Redwood (California); Yellowstone and Grand Teton (Wyoming); Glacier (Montana); Theodore Roosevelt (North Dakota); Wind Cave and Custer State Park (South Dakota); Dinosaur (Utah); Grand Canyon—South Rim (Arizona); and Banff and Jasper (Alberta, Canada). Visitors desiring to see elk in eastern national parks should focus their efforts on Great Smoky Mountains (North Carolina) and Buffalo National River (Arkansas).

Elk Habitat

Top: Reliable sources of drinking water are an essential element of elk habitat.
Bottom: Elk are very flexible in their diet, a factor that accounts for their ability to live in many diverse habitats.
JACK BALLARD

Something to eat, water to drink, a safe place to rest, and room to roam are the basic components of "habitat" for all living things. Various species may have very specific needs in relation to the four basics of food, water, shelter, and space. A ground squirrel, for example, doesn't need lots of area in which to roam or a standing water source, because it can get its required moisture from the consumption of plants. Elk, by contrast, need reliable water sources and hundreds or thousands of acres over which to range in search of forage. Although they definitely prefer specific things to eat at various locations and times, elk are quite flexible in their diet, one of the factors that, historically, allowed them to colonize most of the contiguous United States.

Habitat types or ecosystems are variously classified by biologists, but certain recognizable areas that contain consistent types of plant life (due to such factors as temperature, annual precipitation, and elevation) are cited as differing types of habitat. In the United States and Canada, forests and prairie (grasslands) comprise the dominant types of habitat. Forests consist of deciduous or coniferous trees or a combination of both. Prairies vary from regions dominated by shorter grasses to a few remnants of tall-grass prairie in the central United States.

Elk are highly adapted to thrive in virtually every type of forest and prairie habitat, although certain areas, such as high-elevation forests, are inhabited only in the summer months. Foothill regions, often a mixture of deciduous and evergreen trees, along with brush and mixed grasses, are favored by many elk herds as wintering areas. Elk are seldom found there at other seasons of the year. Historically, elk thrived on the grasslands in the breadbasket of North America. However, with the exception of national parks and other reserves, few elk now inhabit the prairies. Areas of intense agricultural production and ongoing human disturbance make it difficult for elk to exist in these places. Like people, elk are happiest when they have the right things to eat and a generous measure of personal space!

Adult elk can easily consume 20 pounds of forage per day.
JACK BALLARD

FORAGE AND NUTRITIONAL REQUIREMENTS

Nutritional Requirements

Elk are large animals with correspondingly large appetites. Various sources estimate the total food intake of an adult elk differently. Some report 15 pounds per day, others as high as 30 pounds per day. However, no single estimate of mass (in pounds or kilos) adequately captures the nutritional requirements of an elk on a single day. The amount of food an elk needs to consume depends on a variety of factors such as its age, its weight, and the quality of forage it's consuming. Total nutritional demands for adult bulls and cows vary considerably over the year. Cows nursing calves require more food than those that are not. During the period of antler development, bulls need greater amounts of high-quality, high-protein forage. Elk on winter range tend to eat about half the amount they consume during the summer months. As a general rule, it's probably safe to conclude elk need about 3 pounds of forage per 100 pounds of body weight per day to remain healthy.

Elk often spend their resting time chewing their cud.
JACK BALLARD

Digestion

Ruminants are a class of animals that digest their food in a two-part process. After consumption, the food is partially broken down in the digestive system, and then regurgitated and chewed slowly to further enhance digestion. It's then swallowed and further digested in a manner similar to that of humans and other non-ruminant animals. Elk are ruminants. Watch a herd of resting elk on a grassy hillside in the summer at midday, and you'll probably see many of the animals chewing, though they haven't eaten anything for over an hour. These elk are chewing their "cud," which refers to the partially digested plant matter they regurgitate for further chewing.

An elk's stomach is composed of four compartments, one of which acts essentially as a storage chamber for forage that has been eaten, but not yet rechewed. The other three compartments regulate and complete the digestive process.

Although seemingly inefficient (who needs four stomachs?) the digestive system of elk is remarkably adapted to their diet and daily routines. The expansive digestive chambers allow them to consume large quantities of forage. As much of what elk eat would be difficult to break down into usable nutrients in a simpler digestive system, or might contain potentially toxic chemicals, the slow but tenacious digestive mechanisms of elk allow them to gain nutrition from a wide array of sources.

A Colorado bull elk chews bark from a fallen aspen branch.
JACK BALLARD

The product of digestion, elk scat, appears as oval-shaped pellets ½ inch to ¾ inch long with a nub on one end and a dimple on the other. When forage is moist, the pellets may be clumped together.

Food Sources

Ruminant species vary widely in their selection of suitable food sources, a factor that has some bearing on the shape of their muzzle. Bison and domestic cattle are sometimes known as roughage feeders or grazers, which refers to their ability to consume lots of grass and low-growing plants, a habit aided by their large, wide muzzles. On the other extreme are selective feeders or browsers. These animals, like whitetail deer, are quite selective in the types of plants they eat. They also like to nibble twigs, leaves, and berries from trees and shrubs. Small, narrow muzzles give them the physical ability to be very discerning in the types of plants they consume, and even in the parts of the plants they eat.

Elk feed actively in autumn, seeking to gain fat reserves for the coming winter.
JACK BALLARD

Elk fall somewhere in the middle. As intermediate or mixed feeders, elk can graze quite efficiently on grasses and low-growing plants in mountain meadows or on the prairie. They're also very adept at browsing, happily nipping tender shoots and twigs from a wide array of deciduous shrubs. Elk can even strip bark from trees for nutrition, similar to beavers. On many occasions I've observed fallen aspen trees in the fall and winter in elk country. The exposed portions of these trees have been stripped clean of their bark by elk. Elk will also chew bark from living trees, though much less efficiently than from those that have fallen. Lichens and the needles from evergreen trees can also be eaten by elk. Have you ever seen an elk chewing on a bone? Bones and shed antlers are sometimes gnawed upon by elk, a behavior believed by biologists to be motivated by a demand for more calcium in their diet.

Food sources high in nutrients needed by elk at certain phases of their life cycle or plants generally high in nutrition are favored by elk over less-nutritious forage. Elk certainly can't read nutrition information about the food they're eating, so how do they uncannily choose the best forage? Controlled tests indicate these preferences, at least in relation to unknown plants, aren't based on taste or smell. Rather, biologists believe elk select plants that don't cause gastric discomfort and quickly lead to a sense of satiety or feeling full. Elk have highly developed memories related to the location of excellent forage, sometimes returning to very small areas every year to consume seasonal plants. For three years in a row, I found an identifiable band of bull elk (recognizable by the unique antlers on two of them) grazing on a tiny bench on the side of a mountain in the very early days of July. Evidently there were plants in this tiny area that the bulls loved, and they remembered exactly what time of the year they developed.

Forage through the Seasons

The fact that elk can, and do, eat from a wide range of sources gives them great flexibility in their diets, enhancing their survival in habitats less friendly to ruminants with more specific dietary needs. This helpful adaptation is amply illustrated in the ways the eating habits of wapiti change during different seasons of the year.

When snow becomes deep or in areas of limited grass, elk readily turn to browse for winter nourishment.
JACK BALLARD

With the coming of spring, the low-lying areas upon which elk typically spend the winter become tinged with green. The greening of the hills spells early plant growth, usually in relation to early-season grasses. As the soil warms, other grasses and forbs (broad-leafed plants that aren't grasses) begin to grow as well. Elk love these greening plants due to their superior nutrition over the old, bleached grass from the previous summer. They probably also enjoy their tender texture and taste. Toward the end of spring, when all seasonal plants are green and growing, elk become more selective, choosing species such as various clovers and grasses containing very high nutritional value. Spring is a time of intense feeding activity for elk, the animals seeking to regain body mass lost during the rigors of the winter. Elk spend around thirteen hours per day foraging in the spring.

During the summer, elk continue to eat large quantities of grass and forbs, but browse (buds, twigs, and leaves) from deciduous shrubs and trees also becomes an increasingly important part of the diet. Cows with calves demand additional rations of high-quality forage to produce milk for their growing offspring at this time. The nutritional requirements of bulls also change. Extraordinary amounts of protein are required to nourish growing antlers. To adequately support growing antlers, bull elk must consume at least 100 grams (3.5 ounces) of protein every day. However, due to the abundance of food available during the summer and its generally high quality, elk spend considerably less time foraging than they do during the spring. On average, about ten hours of an elk's day in the summer is devoted to eating.

Autumn brings increased feeding activity among elk. The average feeding time per day is nearly thirteen hours. The animals evidently feel the need to maintain the fat reserves they gained during the summer or increase them if possible. Elk feed eclectically from grass, forbs, and browse during the fall, orienting themselves toward food sources containing the best nutrition. Some grasses, for example, will sprout new shoots during the fall if there's sufficient moisture and the temperature remains high enough to promote growth. Elk enthusiastically consume these tender, nutritious shoots. In areas of agriculture, elk are highly prone to invade alfalfa or wheat fields that contain green plants.

The snowy, cold days of winter represent one of the greatest challenges to an elk's survival. In most places, both the quantity and quality of forage available to wapiti in the winter are at their lowest points of the year. Elk need to conserve energy during the winter. On average, they spend just nine hours per day foraging. While it seems reasonable to conclude that elk should actually spend more time feeding during the winter to take in calories to stay warm, due to the decreased abundance and lower quality of winter forage, it's really more efficient for them to conserve their resources. Thus, elk pass about thirteen and a half hours of a winter day at rest in a bed, nearly four hours more than at any other season of the year. Elk readily consume grass, deciduous browse, pine needles, and lichens during the winter. To some extent, their winter forage preferences are determined by snowpack. Once snow reaches a depth of around a foot, it becomes easier for elk to browse from shrubs above the snow than paw through it to reach grasses underneath.

Due to local and regional habitat conditions, the forage patterns of some elk may vary significantly from those described above. Elk in northern Idaho, for example, routinely encounter deep snows. Their winter diet thus consists primarily of browse. Elk in prairie habitats have greater access to grass and forbs the entire year than browse. Browse is thus a less important part of their diet than it is for elk in western Oregon, where browse is often more abundant than grass. Eastern populations of elk exhibit similar foraging strategies that exploit the most readily available foods with the best nutrition. Elk transplanted to eastern states devour acorns during the fall, an exceptionally nutritious food source available only in areas containing oak trees and produced sporadically in relation to local growing conditions.

Migration

Many populations of elk inhabiting mountainous areas are migratory, a phenomenon directly related to nutrition. During midsummer, mountain-dwelling elk in the Rocky Mountains are often found at or above timberline. In addition to nutritious alpine grasses and forbs, wapiti favor the high country for its cooler temperatures and lower concentrations of biting flies and other parasitic insects. However, elk are not

equipped to deal with 6 to 10 feet of snow that might blanket these summertime haunts in the winter. Thus, they migrate to lower elevations with less snow.

However, unlike the more predictable migrations of many birds, elk don't descend to their winter range strictly in relation to the calendar. In fact they'll often stay in the high country long after most people think. Late one October in the Snowcrest Mountains of southwestern Montana, I spotted a herd of thirty elk bedded on a rocky knoll above timberline. To my surprise, a brace of burly mountain goats were bedded around 100 feet below these alpine-loving elk.

Elk in many mountainous areas use the alpine zone during the summer but migrate to lower elevations for the winter.
JACK BALLARD

What triggers the migration of elk from higher to lower elevations? A highly respected biologist with the Wyoming Game and Fish Department once told me he believes it's a variety of things. The depth of snow cover is perhaps the factor that contributes the most, probably followed by cold temperatures and declining forage availability at higher elevations. Some small bands of elk in Rocky Mountain National Park don't migrate at all; they stay in high-elevation areas where the wind blows the snow from the grass.

In the springtime, a reverse migration occurs as winter snowpack retreats to successively higher elevations. Elk follow the retreating snow (or greening grass) up the mountains. During both seasonal migrations, bull and cow elk behave somewhat differently. Mature bulls remain at slightly higher elevations during the winter, probably due to their longer legs and stronger bodies, which allow them to navigate deeper snow. They also tend to be the first to drift back toward higher elevations in the spring. These seasonal movements from summer to winter habitats occur among many elk populations. Other migrations are more spectacular. Elk in Montana and Wyoming sometimes move over 50 miles between their summer and winter range.

ABILITIES AND BEHAVIOR

Physical Abilities

Elk cannot sprint as fast as a pronghorn, nor can they leap as high as a whitetail deer or mountain lion. Nonetheless, in relation to their size, the physical abilities of these large animals are nothing short of amazing.

Bounding adult elk can cover up to 14 feet in a single stride. Bulls are thought to be a bit swifter of hoof than cows, capable of bursts of speed up to 45 miles per hour. However, evidence suggests that cows and older calves are capable of running longer distances at sustained speeds than bulls. This is certainly true in late summer, when bulls in good habitat have much higher percentages of body fat in relation to cows that have been nursing calves. Elk can maintain speeds of 30 miles per hour for extended periods of time.

Fleet of foot, elk can sustain speeds of 30 miles per hour over long distances.
JACK BALLARD

Although elk are very fleet of foot, their endurance is perhaps more exceptional than their speed. During the settlement of the West, hunters on horseback sometimes pursued elk. Historical records indicate that horsemen riding notably fast, well-conditioned horses could run down elk on the plains, which they sometimes lassoed for sport. However, in terrain broken by hills or in rocky areas, the speed, endurance, and agility of elk were greater than those qualities in the horses. Rarely could mounted hunters catch elk under these conditions.

On several occasions, I've had the good fortune of observing the running abilities of elk firsthand. One time, I frightened a band of several dozen elk in open, mountainous terrain. In a matter of a few minutes, the animals had descended a deep drainage divide, had crossed a sizable creek, and were trotting up a distant drainage nearly 2 miles away. A cousin and I once watched a herd of cow elk, caught between two parties of hunters in the mountains, scale an incredibly steep chute leading to a knife-edged ridge. Legs churning, rocks and gravel hurtling down the escarpment from their passage, the beleaguered elk finally scaled the ridge and plunged over the other side. Eyeing the chute afterward, it seemed a mountain goat might successfully ascend it, but had we not witnessed the spectacle, neither my cousin nor I would have believed elk could scale the route.

While hiking in the Black Hills of South Dakota, my older brother spotted a band of a dozen cow and calf elk feeding just below the brink of a hill beneath a scattering of large boulders. Suddenly the elk fled in alarm. A mountain lion leapt from the top of the rocks, intent on one of the calves. After just a few leaps, it abandoned the chase. Recounting the incident to me back at our campsite, my sibling reported he was much more impressed with the speed of the fleeing elk than the spectacular leap of the lion.

In addition to their running ability and endurance, elk are very comfortable in the water, easily fording streams and rivers. Their swimming prowess is outstanding. Hypothermia represents an extreme danger to humans in cold water, but body fat and hollow hair not only insulate elk in frigid water but also make them very buoyant. The spring migration routes of elk often include rivers. At this time of year, streams may be running out of their banks, swollen from snowmelt and very deep. Young calves are frequently confronted with crossing these swift rivers. Just a few days after birth, calves are highly capable swimmers, although young calves often take hours (sometimes days) of encouragement from their mothers before they'll attempt a difficult crossing.

The same notable endurance that allows elk to cover long distances swiftly and efficiently on foot also aids them when swimming large rivers or lakes. Elk on Afognak Island in Alaska have been documented swimming to Kodiak Island, 3 miles away.

In addition to swimming and running, another remarkable physical feature of elk is the strength of a mature bull, particularly in its neck. The neck muscles of a large-antlered bull must support heavy antlers throughout most of the year. (Just think how strong your arms would be if you had to carry 20-pound weights in each hand all day, every day.) During the mating season, or "rut," the circumference of a bull's neck increases dramatically. These overdeveloped neck muscles are used when it thrashes limbs from small evergreen trees and gores the earth so fiercely as to dislodge large clumps of soil. One fall, I watched a very large bull engage its antlers on the underside of a fallen tree trunk appearing some 8 inches in diameter. With a powerful thrust of its neck, the animal launched a section of the partially rotted log into the air. When bull elk fight, one of their primary strategies is to attempt to twist the head of the other animal and throw it to the ground, a task accomplished through the use of their powerful neck muscles. In rare cases, one bull exerts enough force on the other to break its neck.

Vocal Communication

Speech is thought to be one of the abilities that separates humans from the rest of the animal world, but many other species of mammals also communicate verbally. Elk are no exception. A diverse range of grunts, barks, and whistles are all used by elk for various purposes.

The mostly widely recognized and dramatic form of elk vocalization is the bugle. Bull elk "bugle" primarily during the mating season to announce their presence to other bulls and the cows a dominant bull gathers together in a group known as a "harem." The bugle of an elk is a drawn-out, rather high-pitched whistle that carries for remarkably long distances. Older bulls often punctuate the end of their bugle with a series of deep, guttural coughs or grunts. In general the bugles of younger bulls are more shrill and lack the resonance of a large bull, although the tonal quality of the

Top: The bugle of a bull is an iconic symbol of autumn in elk country. Bottom: Cow and calf elk communicate with a variety of vocal and bodily signals.
JACK BALLARD

bugle is not always indicative of the size of the elk. On a number of occasions, I've witnessed very large bulls with somewhat shrill-sounding bugles. No matter the specific tone, the bugling of a bull is one of the iconic symbols, in sound, of autumn in elk country.

Bull elk also communicate with another sound less easily heard during the rut. Large bulls attending a harem of cows keep the females from abandoning the group and other bulls from intruding upon their cows. To chase a yearling bull (spike) from the cow herd, the dominant bull will rush at the youngster with its lips curled back, nose up, and front teeth exposed in something of a snarl. These visual cues of aggression are accompanied by a distinct hissing sound. Cows that stray from the herd are prodded back toward the group, sometimes quite aggressively by the lord of the harem, who will hiss at unruly cows in the same manner as at small bulls. However, when another bull closer in stature to the herd bull approaches, the keeper of the harem announces its presence and displeasure with bugles and dominance displays rather than hissing noises.

Elk vocalizations aren't reserved just for the bulls. Cows and calves communicate with audible sounds as well. When alarmed, cows emit a very loud call that might best be described as a nasal bark. Depending on its intensity and the setting, the alarm bark creates instant alertness in an elk herd or sends them running in panic.

Cows also communicate with their calves. When separated, cows may call to their calves with a less strident, drawn-out "cow call" that has been described by Valerius Geist, an acclaimed elk expert, as a "nasal whine." Calves may respond to the cow calls with their own low bleats. When large herds of cows and calves are on the move, frequent communication of this type between cows and calves is quite common and apparently serves as a bonding and reassurance function as well as a locating call. Additionally, distressed or lost calves may emit a very loud bleat while attempting to locate their mothers. However, this communication strategy is not without risk. If predators hear the alarm bleat of a calf, they will respond as quickly as the mother, hoping to find an easy meal.

Since ancient times, exploiting the vocal communications of elk has been a strategy employed by human hunters. Most effectively used during the rut, the hunter may employ either a bugle or a cow call to attract the attention of elk. The bugle is an effective method of locating the general area of a bull. If the hunter imitates a bull's bugle and another bull responds, it is often a simple matter to ascertain the bull's position. Moving closer, the hunter tries to incite a herd bull to come out from its cows to confront this "rival." However, this strategy is not as simple as it seems. Many herd bulls, feeling pressured by a rival, may simply herd up their cows and move to new territory. Elk have an exceptionally keen sense of smell and acute eyesight. The slightest movement by the hunter or the barest whiff of human scent on an errant breeze will send the elk crashing into cover.

Another hunting tactic involves cow calling. Bulls not attached to a harem during the mating season spend most of their hours on the move, wandering about in search of unattached females. Hearing a cow call, a lone bull will often approach the sound, hoping to find a single female or small herd without a herd bull. Again, it takes a very skillful hunter to successfully employ this method of luring an elk within range of a bow and arrow or rifle. However, mimicking the natural noises of elk has been a favored hunting technique for its effectiveness and excitement since ancient times.

Herd Behavior

Elk are commonly known as herd animals. While this is true, it's also an aspect of elk behavior often misunderstood. Except during the mating season, mature bulls and cows live separately with notably few exceptions. Bull calves still nursing their mothers obviously stay with the cows. Yearling bulls and some two-year-old bulls also associate with cow herds during the summer season and throughout the winter. Only rarely are bulls of any kind found among the cows during calving time.

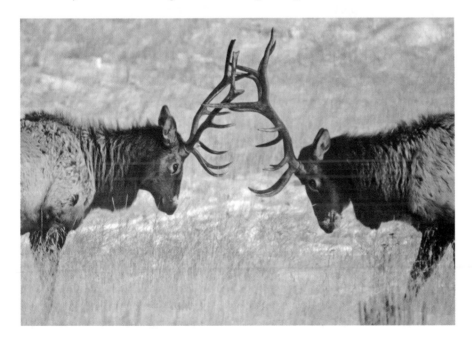

Sparring between bull elk establishes dominance without the exertion and risk of a full-blown fight.
JACK BALLARD

Cows live together in herds numbering a few animals or a few hundred animals, depending on the time of year. The largest herds tend to form in the late fall and winter. However, I've witnessed cow/calf bands of one hundred animals in July. Within these female bands, there exists a hierarchy. Older, dominant cows usually lead the herd. They also claim the best foraging spots and bedding areas. Conflict between cows is signaled by the laying back of the ears, often accompanied by the stomping of a front foot. If a rival isn't intimidated by these behaviors, the cow will rear on its hind legs and flail with its front hooves. Alternatively, a cow may expose its front teeth to a rival. This signals the elk is about to bite, another aggressive strategy used to assert dominance. These aggressive measures most often occur between cows in competition for food. The more crowded the elk and scarce the forage resources, the more commonly they occur.

With the exception of the breeding season, bulls also form groups. Sometimes known as "bachelor herds," these bands of mature bulls usually number from three or four animals to a couple of dozen. Huge bands of wintering bulls numbering fifty or more animals have been observed in Rocky Mountain National Park. Similar to the cow herds, bulls hold specific rank within the bachelor group. Rank is established between bulls in important, but generally peaceful, sparring with their antlers. Sparring usually occurs between bulls with antlers of similar size. The bulls carefully engage their antlers, pushing with their bodies and twisting their necks. These contests let bulls know which animal is the strongest and most likely to win should a full-blown fight erupt, a phenomenon witnessed between rivals during the rut. Like cows, bulls exhibit aggressive or competitive behavior with visual clues, most commonly by quickly bobbing their antlers forward toward an opponent. Bulls may also use exposed teeth as a warning, similar to cows.

Although they don't talk or wave good-bye, elk communicate vocally and with visual cues, just like humans. You'll know you're well on your way to becoming an expert observer of elk when you can predict behavior based on vocal or behavioral cues!

REPRODUCTION AND YOUNG

The Mating Season

Although baby elk are born in late spring, the reproductive cycle begins early in the fall. Somewhere around the end of August (varying slightly in relation to latitude, nutrition, and other local conditions), hormonal changes begin to prepare both bulls and cows for breeding. The necks of bulls swell considerably, and by early September, they begin to exhibit aggressive behavior such as raking their antlers on trees, goring the ground and small shrubbery with their antlers, and bugling. Overheated by the physical exertions associated with these activities, they sometimes take mud baths in bogs or wallow in damp areas or small springs to cool off. Within a week or so, they join the cow herds. Large herds of cows may become splintered, as even an extraordinarily large and imposing bull can seldom hold together a harem of more than two dozen cows, although, in some cases, dominant bulls may have harems of over forty females. Less dominant bulls may manage to gather a small band of a half-dozen cows.

The size and number of harems, and the age and strength of bulls required to hold a harem, vary depending on elk numbers in a region, the age and number of bulls in a population, and the ratio of males to females. In areas where the average age of bulls is just a few years old due to hunting pressure, a three-year-old bull might successfully defend a harem. In wilderness areas receiving little hunting pressure or areas where elk are protected from human hunters, such as national and state parks, a bull will have few breeding opportunities until it reaches a more advanced age.

Somewhere around the middle of September, approximately a week or two before the autumnal equinox, bulls enter the period of maximum reproductive behavior, which usually lasts from around twenty to thirty days. The "rut" technically refers to this season of intense reproductive activity. As individual cows within its harem come into estrus, the bull mates with them. Thus, an exceptionally robust bull may sire more than two dozen offspring. Cows that do not conceive a calf in this breeding period may come into estrus around a month later, in mid- to late October. Other cows might enter estrus slightly later than the rut due to lower body condition. Cows carrying low fat reserves will not enter estrus at all. Given all these variables, the entire breeding season for elk in a particular area might span six weeks or more.

Rubbing antlers, goring the ground, and wallowing in mud are all common behaviors of bull elk entering the rut.
JACK BALLARD

The rut is an intensely important part of a bull's life. Those males who compete successfully during the mating season pass their genes to subsequent generations of elk. However, being at the top of the reproductive heap doesn't come without cost. Bulls immersed in the frenzy of the rut spend very few hours per day feeding. Those tending cows expend incredible amounts of energy, not only in the act of reproduction, but also in repelling rival bulls and chasing wandering cows back into the herd, not to mention antler-rubbing, bugling, and other dominance displays. An active, mature male of the wapiti species may lose up to 20 percent of its body weight during a forty-day span in the breeding season. For a very large bull, this might represent a loss of 200 pounds. (Wouldn't fad diet programs for humans love to legitimately claim equally impressive results!)

Exhausted and alone, this large bull broke an antler tine in a fight during the rut, making it difficult for him to compete for a harem.
JACK BALLARD

Reduced body condition and injuries sustained during the infrequent fights occurring between evenly matched bulls during the rut can literally cost a stag its life. Unless they can regain weight quickly after the rut, a challenge due to poorer forage quality in late fall than during the summer, mature bulls often enter the winter with minimal fat reserves. During a severe winter, many of the bulls at the top of the dominance hierarchy during the rut are at the greatest risk of starvation. Puncture wounds, sprained limbs, or loss of eyesight incurred from the antlers of a rival during a fall fight may prove lethal to the winner due to infection, inability to forage efficiently, or predation later on in the winter.

Pregnancy and Gestation

Cow elk usually become fertile during the fall of their second year in life, the same time that their male counterparts are carrying their first set of antlers. However, unless these yearling cows have had access to quality forage and have attained good body condition, their first successful pregnancy is not likely to happen until the following year. Conception and carrying a calf to birth is also related to body condition in mature cows. Numerous studies of wild elk have shown that conception rates among cows are highly correlated to weight. Undernourished cows have difficulty both becoming pregnant and carrying a calf to birth. During years of poor forage conditions due to drought, cows nursing calves are often among those who fail to conceive next year's offspring. Cows in less than optimal body condition also tend to enter estrus later in the rut, delaying the birth of their calves by a month or more in relation to their healthier counterparts.

Cows in good body condition are more likely to conceive and birth a calf than those who are undernourished.
JACK BALLARD

Gestation, the length of time between breeding and birth, is usually given as 255 days for elk. At least one study under controlled conditions has placed elk gestation slightly shorter, at around 247 days. For naturalists, an approximate gestation of eight and a half months gives a good estimate of the time between breeding and birth for elk.

A cow elk requires a substantial increase in available energy and nutrition to successfully carry a fetus to birth. If the calf is growing inside the cow during the season when it's most difficult to obtain nutrition (winter), how can it hope to meet these needs? At least two important factors facilitate the development of the fetus during this demanding time. Under normal conditions, cows are at their fattest and healthiest going into the winter, giving them energy reserves beyond their daily intake of forage. Also, the fetus develops very slowly for the first 150 days of gestation. At this point, the developing calf weighs only about 5 pounds, or 10 to 15 percent of its birth weight. Beginning around the first of March or the last three months of a cow's pregnancy, the fetus develops much more rapidly. This increased growth normally coincides with rising temperatures and decreasing snow depth on elk winter range, reducing the amount of energy a cow needs to maintain itself and allowing more to be invested in the rapidly growing fetus. However, late winter and early spring nutritional stress on pregnant cows can cause them to abort their fetuses or birth weak, stunted calves with reduced potential for survival.

Birth

The birth of an elk calf is known as "calving." Normally, the first of June represents the pinnacle of calving activity among wild elk. However, some yearly and local variation in this date exists due to the nutritional state of cows during the breeding season and pregnancy, along with other local variables.

Most elk calves weigh from 30 to 35 pounds at birth, though some calves occasionally nudge the scale beyond 40 pounds. Weights vary in relation to numerous factors. Female calves weigh slightly less than males. More significantly, older, larger cows tend to produce larger calves than their younger, smaller counterparts. Good nutrition during pregnancy increases birth weight, but only to a small degree. Twins are relatively uncommon among elk, especially in relation to other members of the deer family, such as moose, mule, and whitetail deer. Biologists estimate that fewer than 1 percent of the calves born to elk are twins. Calves dropped by cows in poor condition may sometimes weigh as little as 15 pounds. Malnourished calves have little chance of survival. Research indicates that when birth weight drops below 25 pounds, calves have less than a 50 percent chance of survival, even in the absence of predators.

In many populations, nearly two in three births occur in a span of three weeks on the fore and aft sides of Memorial Day. Biologists refer to such a profusion of young born in a short period as "synchronous breeding." Research reported by the Wildlife Management Institute from a number of studies indicates that whether it's a herd in Canada's Banff National Park, the dense woodlands of northern Idaho, Montana's famed Madison River valley, North Dakota's Theodore Roosevelt National Park, or the lofty mountain vales of northwestern Wyoming, the majority of elk calves birthed in a given year fall to the earth moist and wriggling from late May to early June. Elk calves born later in the summer are more apt to starve their first winter than those born around the first of June. Later-born calves don't have as much time to grow and develop as those born earlier and enter the winter smaller and weaker.

Cow elk typically return to known "calving grounds" year after year. A few days before calving, female elk leave the cow herd. Calves are born in solitude, usually within a few hours of the onset of labor. Extremely vulnerable immediately after birth, the fate of the calf is often tied to the experience of the mother. Cows birthing their first calf or those enduring a difficult pregnancy may abandon the calf altogether, or fail to give it adequate maternal care during the first critical hours of life.

At birth, calves are nearly scentless. Their spotted coats blend with the sagebrush or tall grasses in which they're commonly born. Elk calves can stand within twenty minutes of birth, but for the first several days of life, they spend most of their time hiding from predators. Remaining motionless for most of the day, a newborn calf spends limited time with its mother. The pair is together only for several brief periods of nursing lasting just a few minutes at a time. Within a week, elk calves can run fast enough to elude most predators. About this time, the cow and its new calf rejoin the cow herd from which the cow departed to give birth.

For the first two months of life, the elk calf's growth is highly dependent on its mother's milk. The volume of milk available to the calf is greatly determined by the quality of forage the cow has to eat. In subsequent months, the calf becomes increasingly able and willing to forage on its own. By the end of its first summer, an elk calf's juvenile spots disappear. Although elk calves are nutritionally independent of their mothers by this time, they generally remain in a herd with their mothers through their first winter.

ELK AND OTHER ANIMALS

Elk and Other Ungulates

Wherever they live, elk share their world with other hoofed mammals (ungulates). Some of these, such as bison, are much larger than elk. Others, such as antelope, are relatively small. Elk compete with some ungulates for food; with others they merely share habitat at certain times of year and have little or no discernible relationship. Along with wild species, elk also share their range with domestic ungulates in many places, primarily cattle and sheep.

In relation to other wild ungulates, the interaction between elk and mule deer is probably the topic of greatest concern to biologists and wildlife managers. Over the past few decades, elk populations have risen dramatically in many places, coinciding with a decline in mule deer numbers, leading some to conclude that large numbers of elk have a detrimental effect on mule deer.

Overlap in diet between the two species certainly exists and may suggest competition for the same forage, in which case it is assumed that the larger elk would have an advantage over deer. Under typical conditions, mule deer consume more browse from shrubs than elk. However, it's important to remember that elk are very adaptable animals in terms of diet and will readily consume a wide range of foods. In locations where browse is the primary source of nutrition on winter range, some biologists believe elk compete directly with mule deer for forage and ultimately displace them.

Although generalizations about rising elk numbers negatively affecting mule deer are misguided, in certain locations there seems to be a legitimate concern. Research conducted on the Mount Haggin Wildlife Management Area in Montana demonstrated a significant amount of overlap between the two species with winter forage. Antelope bitterbrush, the shrub representing the highest percentage of mule deer diet during the winter, also composed the greatest percentage of elk forage. In mild winters, there's usually enough food to go around. But this study, and some others, indicates that in difficult winters, an abundance of elk may negatively affect the survival odds of mule deer.

In Yellowstone National Park and a few other places, elk share habitat with bison. Conflicts between the two species are rare.
JACK BALLARD

Competition between elk and other ungulates, such as whitetail deer, antelope, caribou, or moose, for food or space is unlikely. Occasionally, elk may face off with bison in meadows for pasture or passage. The diets of elk and bison overlap significantly, although with the exception of Yellowstone National Park and a handful of other refuges, bison do not exist in enough numbers to affect elk. When rare confrontations between elk and bison occur in these places, large bull elk are sometimes able to intimidate female and young bison. In most cases, elk give bison wide berth.

Similar diet overlap occurs between bighorn sheep and elk, both of which species consume large amounts of grasses. Direct competition on winter or summer range for forage would certainly favor elk, although little study has been undertaken concerning this potential relationship.

On both public and private land, elk frequently utilize the same range as cattle. For the most part, elk and cattle don't mix. Both casual observation and research support this notion. One section of mountain pasture on my family's ranch is grazed by both elk and cattle. When the cows are rotated to this area for grazing, the elk tend to move elsewhere. Elk often exhibit signs of anxiety or heightened alertness in the presence of cattle. Some biologists argue this behavior is more a function of cattle's proximity to people and the trappings of human civilization than the domestic cattle themselves. In certain areas, elk have developed a stronger tolerance for cattle than in others. However, it's unlikely you'll routinely observe elk in the same proximity to cattle as that which they comfortably maintain with other wild ungulates such as deer and moose.

Parasites and Diseases

Like other creatures, wild and domestic, elk are susceptible to numerous diseases and are occasionally plagued by parasites. The number and frequency of diseases among elk have doubtlessly increased since the time prior to European settlement of the United States and Canada. Growing contact between elk and domestic animals and reduction of their historic range have exposed elk to maladies not encountered by their forebears.

Among these diseases, brucellosis is perhaps the most widely recognized and exposes elk to the greatest controversy. Brucellosis is an infectious, very contagious disease that occurs in various forms depending on the infected species. In cattle and elk, brucellosis may cause infected females to abort their unborn calves. When infected, slightly more than 50 percent of cow elk will abort their first calf after contracting the disease. Crowding of elk on winter range is a major factor in the transmission of brucellosis among elk. The disease occurs among free-ranging elk only in Yellowstone and Grand Teton National Parks and surrounding areas. Brucellosis was almost certainly first transmitted to wild elk in the area by cattle around the turn of the twentieth century. Maintaining brucellosis-free cattle herds is of extreme importance to ranching in the Rocky Mountain states. The potential of elk infecting cattle with brucellosis may create political tensions in local areas where ranching and wildlife interests collide. Another disease of great concern to domestic cattle operations is bovine tuberculosis. This disease can, and has, infected elk but is quite rare.

Chronic wasting disease (also known as CWD) was first detected in elk at a research facility in Colorado. The disease plagues captive as well as wild elk. Assumed to be caused by an infectious protein, or prion, CWD invades the central nervous system. Extreme weight loss and chronic, heavy salivation are common systems of chronic wasting disease. Since its discovery in Colorado, CWD has cropped up in wild and domestic herds in many other states as well. The exact mechanisms of transmission of CWD from one animal to another are not clearly understood. What is certain is the outcome. Chronic wasting disease is always fatal in infected animals.

Early speculation surrounding the disease raised concerns that it might be transmissible to humans or that it might wipe out entire elk populations. Neither alarm has been warranted. The best medical evidence indicates humans who have physical contact with elk or eat their meat are not at risk of contracting the disease. However, state wildlife agencies often encourage hunters to handle elk carcasses in such a way as to minimize possible exposure to the disease—namely, by avoiding contact with tissue from the central nervous system of animals with CWD. CWD testing programs for animals killed by hunters are available in most states.

Along with diseases, elk are subject to numerous parasites. A variety of worms, mites, ticks, and other not-so-nice-to-contemplate creatures attach to elk as their hosts. Infections by parasites are sometimes fatal, but in most cases, elk have developed a natural resistance to the parasitic creatures in their historic habitat. However, parasites and the transmission of CWD are perennial concerns with elk reintroductions from one area to another. After a small herd of elk was transported from Wyoming to Michigan in 1918, for example, biologists observing the animals in later decades noticed severely ailing animals exhibiting signs of meningeal worms they likely contracted from the deer. This parasite commonly occurs among whitetail deer in the eastern half of the United States, animals generally unaffected by the parasite. Elk moved from one location to another are potential carriers of exotic parasites to the new location or may be exposed to parasites to which they are unaccustomed.

Elk and Predators

A variety of predators prey upon elk. In North America these include coyotes, wolves, mountain lions, black bears, and grizzly bears. Healthy newborn elk have much more to fear from fellow creatures than foul weather. In one research study in north-central Idaho, approximately 70 percent of the calves marked by researchers were killed by predators, mainly black bears. Although predation rates are normally lower than this, in certain areas predators claim a substantial percentage of the calf crop. Interestingly, well over half of the calf mortality occurred in the first ten days of life. Within just a couple of weeks of birth, elk calves develop the speed and endurance to elude all but the most tricky or tenacious attacks from their predators.

Given elk vulnerability in the days just after birth, biologists theorize that the synchronous breeding of elk ensures that some significant percentage of the calf crop will reach the age that makes them less susceptible to predation. Birthing numerous vulnerable prey in a short period of time makes it more likely that some of them will escape detection by predators until they're mature enough to successfully flee. To borrow an analogy from an Easter egg hunt, consider two different strategies. In one, five children have just twenty minutes to find 200 eggs hidden in a backyard. Across the street, egg hunting is a weekend-long affair. On Saturday and Sunday, twenty-five eggs are hidden four times each day. The five youngsters can search for the eggs as long as they like. In which case will the greater number of eggs be found? Conditions being equal, the children with more time to discover what amounts to the same number of eggs scattered over a longer period of time will be more successful. Similarly, synchronous breeding stacks predator evasion in favor of a larger number of elk calves, even though there are actually more vulnerable young on the ground at peak calving time than there would be if the birthing period was prolonged.

Although their role is hotly debated in public circles, the increasing number of predators in recent decades has placed pressures on reproducing elk not seen since settlers and market hunters overran their habitat, eliminating wolves, mountain lions, and grizzly bears in the process. As more natural populations of these predators have increased due to widespread legal protection, it has become more difficult for elk calves in many areas to survive until their first birthday.

Grizzly bears are major predators of elk in some areas, preying heavily upon newborn calves in the first few days of life.
JACK BALLARD

Elk calves, especially those of small size, are more easily taken by mountain lions and other predators than healthy adult animals.

JACK BALLARD

When wolves were introduced into the Yellowstone ecosystem in 1995, biologists had the opportunity to study the impacts they were having on elk populations. Initial research showed that the wolves routinely preyed on older and weaker animals, reducing the number of elk in the northern Yellowstone herd to levels more in line with management targets. Wolf advocates pointed out that grizzly bears, not wolves, were wreaking the most havoc on newborn elk.

While that conclusion is supported by a number of studies, it fails to note the impact of wolves on calves in their first winter. Cow/calf ratios among elk are an extremely important indication of a herd's viability. When the ratios fall below levels in the 20 to 30 calves per 100 cow range, most elk herds begin to decline in numbers, even if the hunting of antlerless animals by humans is severely restricted. Thus, surviving the first wave of vulnerability to predation in the first weeks of life isn't necessarily the most important hurdle calves must clear to reach the age of reproduction. Calves must also dodge predators throughout the rest of their first summer and winter.

For the past two decades, wolves have been increasingly multiplying throughout the Rocky Mountains. In some regions wildlife managers feel there are too many wolves. Abundant wolf populations have been linked to severe elk declines in Montana, Idaho, and Wyoming where elk are also hunted.

How many elk are enough? What share should go to wolves versus predators, including humans? These are highly contentious issues. To one extreme are pro-wolf groups who feel wolves should never (or rarely) be killed by humans. To the other extreme are anti-wolf individuals, including some hunters and livestock owners, who feel wolves should be completely eliminated wherever possible.

Increasingly, wildlife management agencies are caught in the middle of competing interests when it comes to wolves and elk. Surely there's a biologically sound solution somewhere in the middle that balances wolf and elk numbers. Given the emotions competing sides have around the issue, the "happy medium" is difficult to find.

Once winter hits, wolves become the dominant predator on elk calves, with coyotes also capable of picking off these smaller, weaker animals, which are less able to flee through deep or crusted snow than their adult counterparts. Several studies have found wolves prey heavily upon elk calves during their first winter. In fact wolves show their strongest selection, or preference, for elk calves versus adults when available. Winter wolf predation, in many areas, is a very important factor in limiting the percentage of calves that survive their first year. In addition to bears, wolves, and coyotes, mountain lions also target young elk. Where mountain lions are present in high numbers, they often exert a significant impact on elk survival in their first year of life.

Whether young or old, elk employ a number of strategies to elude predators. Faced with a single wolf, black bear, coyote, or mountain lion intending to kill a calf, a cow elk or group of cows may confront the predator with flailing front hooves capable of delivering a lethal blow to the would-be killer. Bull elk may also fend off single predators

Large herds of fleeing elk create confusion for predators, making it difficult for them to target a single animal.
JACK BALLARD

with their antlers. However, the best antipredation method employed by elk is flight. Few predators have the speed or stamina to run down a healthy elk, although wolf packs are highly capable of downing adult elk in good condition.

The herding instinct of elk also serves as a buffer against predation. In open country, elk often form large herds, especially in the winter. Many pairs of eyes and ears give them a better chance of detecting advancing predators. Once fleeing, dozens of elk in a moving herd make it harder for predators to target a single animal. The herd also tends to favor the strong and healthy in predator attacks. Old, young, or weakened animals typically fall behind the others when running, making them more easily taken by predators.

ELK AND HUMANS

Elk and American Indians

Interactions between elk and humans in North America extend back into history for a period of some 10,000 years. Artifacts from an archaeological site in Alaska, dated approximately 8,000 to 11,000 years ago, were accompanied by bone fragments from a number of animals including elk. A site in eastern Wyoming from the Folsom era revealed artifacts dated at 10,300 to 10,800 years ago. The Folsom people utilized a unique type of stone arrow point with a groove on either side. A portion of elk antler consisting of a tine from a large bull was recovered from this site. Archeologists believe the antler was used with a simple levering device to create grooves in arrow points.

For the next several millennia, ancient peoples of the North American continent continued to utilize elk for food and parts of the elk, most notably the antlers, for a variety of primitive tools. Elk antlers were used for digging instruments and as tips

Prehistoric peoples in North America used elk antlers to make a variety of tools.
JACK BALLARD

for fishing spears along with hammering devices. Shoulder blades were fashioned into primitive hoes for cultivation. Although the ability of these primal hunters to kill elk was probably limited, antlers picked up just after shedding were as strong and useful as those taken from a bull killed by arrows or other methods.

The record of interaction between elk and native peoples during the last 500 years is more complete than that of more ancient peoples. From 1500 to 1850, numerous American Indian tribes east of the Mississippi are known to have hunted elk. These include the Sauk, Cree, Chippewa, Huron, Winnebago, Iroquois, and a host of others. Elk meat was a welcome addition to the ordinary diet of these eastern Indians, although wapiti represented a secondary source of food. Elk were difficult for the native peoples to kill. Snares, arrows, spears, and deadfalls (traps consisting of an elevated log that would fall upon an animal when it dislodged a support-ing triggering device) are presumed to be methods used to kill elk. The animals were also hunted in the winter when Indians on snowshoes could efficiently overtake elk floundering in deep snow. Some evidence suggests the Indians also obtained elk by surrounding herds and driving them into strategically placed natural enclosures fortified with other materials.

In the mountainous and coastal regions of the western United States, Indian tribes also hunted elk. In addition to the methods commonly used by the eastern peoples, certain western tribes developed other methods of securing elk. Lewis and Clark observed Indians of the Pacific coastal regions effectively securing elk using pits. Large

Prior to being displaced by European settlers, elk were commonly found on the plains, where they were hunted by American Indians.
JACK BALLARD

holes were dug on trails, then carefully disguised with leaves and branches. Elk using the trails would fall into the pits. Some tribes planted sharpened sticks into the bottom of the pit to aid in securing their quarry.

The acquisition of horses by native peoples on the Great Plains dramatically changed their lifestyle. Occurring in the 1600s, this development gave the Indians greater mobility and also a more efficient means of killing large animals, namely bison. However, some of the plains-dwelling tribes, including the Comanche, Kiowa, Crow, and Cheyenne, also used their fleet horses to pursue elk on the prairie.

In various regions, American Indians developed other skillful and opportunistic methods for harvesting elk. Some tribes learned to chase elk herds toward rivers with thin ice, killing the animals that broke through and were trapped. Others deliberately surrounded and pushed elk into lakes and other large bodies of water where they could be more easily killed than in the forest. Some evidence indicates that Indians may have also used "jumps" to secure elk as they did with bison. Jumps were areas where highly orchestrated, communal drives ran animals over cliffs, where they were killed or sufficiently injured in the fall to be easily dispatched. Requiring much effort, well-executed jumps could secure large quantities of food for an entire band of Indians in a single day.

Along with the importance of elk as a food source, Indians prized the animals for numerous other reasons. As mentioned earlier, elk antlers and bones were used as tools. Antlers were also fashioned into clubs as instruments of war. The saddles of some Indians utilized portions of elk antlers for their framework. Antlers and bones became chisels, wedges, and cooking utensils. Some tribes in California even shaped small, elaborately decorated purses from hollowed elk antlers, which were used to store dentalium shells from mollusks that served as currency.

However, the hides were perhaps the most valuable commodity Indians took from the elk. Wapiti skins were especially prized for their durability. Thicker than the skins of smaller game animals, yet less bulky than the hide of a bison, elk hides were "tanned" by Indians to create exceptionally durable leather. Elk garments, such as jackets for men and dresses for women, were commonly worn in winter due to their weight. The leather from elk also made excellent, long-lasting moccasins. For most tribes, elk garments were not used for everyday wear but reserved for ceremonial purposes and special occasions. Elk skins were used by a few tribes for covering teepees, but this practice was not common and usually applied to the most wealthy and revered members of a tribe.

The canine teeth or "ivories" were used by many American Indian tribes to decorate dresses.
JACK BALLARD

Wapiti also factored prominently in the social and spiritual life of many Indian tribes. Hidatsa, Nez Perce, Hopi, Pawnee, Crow, Flathead, and a host of other tribes had elk societies or religious cults that variously revered and spiritualized the power

The rugged habitat of the northern Rocky Mountains may have saved elk from extinction in North America.
JACK BALLARD

of the elk. The canine teeth or "ivories" of elk were used as adornments in clothing and jewelry by many tribes. One of these practices involved the sewing of dresses adorned with elk ivories. Worn by women and sometimes children, these garments attested to the hunting prowess of a woman's husband or a child's father and were very valuable. Prior to the late 1800s, men apparently viewed elk tooth adornments as appropriate only for women. However, after the 1870s, men from a number of tribes began to adopt elk tooth jewelry, perhaps in relation to the increasing scarcity of the animals and their ivories. Elk tooth dresses are still fashioned by many tribes today, although the "ivories" are usually artificial.

Elk and European Settlers

Armed with muskets and rifles, European settlers had a much easier time killing elk than did native peoples. In fact the firearms of white explorers and homesteaders were too efficient. Elk were killed for food, but widespread slaughter of elk on the plains for their hides and the two ivory canine teeth hastened the demise of these animals from most of their native habitat.

Many biologists feel that had it not been for the rugged mountains of northwest Wyoming and similar areas in other states, elk might have been hunted to extinction. Protections afforded to the animals by the creation of Yellowstone National Park in 1872 were critical to their survival. Visitors to the park reported a scarcity of game animals in the first decade after Yellowstone's creation. By 1891, however, Yellowstone's gamekeeper reported that elk numbers had increased to an estimated 25,000 animals. In the early 1900s, elk from Yellowstone were relocated to create or augment elk herds in many locations throughout the Rocky Mountains. In Montana, nearly 1,000 elk from Yellowstone were distributed to various regions across the state in 1910. The future of Montana's elk became brighter in 1913 when hunting laws and closures were enacted to protect the animals, a situation that occurred across many western states at about the same time.

Elk and Us

With the development of hunting laws, concerted efforts to reestablish elk into many parts of their historic range, and greater concern for the preservation of habitat, wapiti numbers and distribution in the United States and Canada have increased steadily for the last century. Currently elk are commonplace throughout the Rocky Mountains and many other places, their health and habitat largely protected by the vigilance of wildlife and land managers at both the state and federal levels.

While estimates of the exact impact vary, elk probably have the greatest economic value for humans in relation to hunting, although elk viewing also brings substantial revenue to many national parks and adjacent communities. Numbers fluctuate annually, but nearly one million hunters take to the forests and prairies of the United States and Canada to hunt elk each fall. Interestingly, there's almost a 1 to 1 ratio between hunters and elk. For every elk in North America, there's one human hunter. As a rough estimate, hunters kill about 150,000 elk per year in the United States and Canada. Some hunters pursue elk strictly for their meat and may expend less than $100 for their hunt, including the cost of the permit, gas, and ammunition for their rifle. Others are highly motivated to obtain an impressive set of elk antlers to display in their home. These individuals, sometimes called "trophy hunters," often spend over $5,000 in search of a trophy bull. Employing guides and outfitters, trophy hunting is an important part of the local economy in many small towns across the western United States and Canada. In addition to hunting, the prospect of viewing wapiti lures tourists and wildlife lovers to various national parks and other reserves across the country, giving elk economic importance beyond hunting.

Elk are of extreme economic importance to local communities and state wildlife agencies in the West due to expenditures by hunters for licenses and other services.
JACK BALLARD

The current range of elk encompasses millions of acres of public lands, but the animals also range across extremely large tracts of private land, much of it found on ranches. But not all ranches are equal, at least from the standpoint of wildlife management by state agencies. In the latter decades of the 20th century, many, many ranches in elk country were bought as "trophy ranches" as opposed to "working ranches." In the case of a trophy ranch, ownership is motivated by hunting, recreation, privacy or other such aspirations. Raising cattle or crops may be part of the enterprise, but is not foundational to the economics of the operation. A working ranch sees the agricultural component as the primary means of ownership. Many working ranches have been passed down through families for generations, but it is an increasingly difficult way to make a living in many areas.

Numerous ranching communities are now a patchwork of trophy and working ranches, while some are dominated by one type of the other. This has spawned conflict regarding elk in some locations, a situation state wildlife agencies often find impossible to manage. Where trophy ranches prohibit hunting or allow very little harvest of elk, the animals soon learn to occupy these lands during the hunting seasons. Since human hunting is the most effective way to regulate elk populations in most areas, harvest goals by state wildlife agencies can be thwarted when elk utilize the refuge of trophy ranches to escape hunting. In addition to over-populating the habitat with elk, the situation can be troublesome to working ranches. Wintering elk can take a heavy toll on haystack. Fencing keeps the animals at bay, but the construction of a sturdy, 8-foot high fence sufficient to protect hay from elk is expensive. Elk may also congregate on hayfields, substantially reducing production. Even though the owners of working ranches might wish for a higher elk harvest in their area, if herds can find refuge on other private properties during the hunting season, there's little wildlife managers can do to reduce elk numbers and the negative impact excessively high populations might have on working ranches.

Elk are among the most popularly viewed and economically valuable wildlife species in the West. As such, their management on public and private lands is perpetually marked by some controversy.

CHAPTER 2
MOOSE

"Let's see how close we can get to those moose."

Not one to let a challenge pass, I eagerly accepted the invitation from my older brother. We were in our early twenties, hunting deer deep in remote drainage in Montana. Moments earlier we'd spied four bull moose bedded at the edge of the timber, about a half-mile from our position.

When we crept from cover, a scant 150 yards from the bulls, eight moose eyes were already focused in our direction. Though I didn't realize it at the time, the animals' keen ears had doubtlessly detected our best sneaking. The moose didn't seem alarmed, so we strolled closer. At 50 yards it suddenly seemed too close. Just then, the largest member of the bachelor band rose to his feet, cocked his antlers in our direction, and snorted forcefully. The fact both of us were carrying rifles didn't matter. Our retreat was mirthless and hasty.

Moose are abundant in Maine and have recently returned to New York's Adirondack Park.
© ISTOCK.COM/
KJMPHOTOGRAPHY

A couple of years later, while hiking in the same drainage, I happened upon a very large shed antler from a bull moose. In a lifetime of collecting a varied assortment of treasures from the wild, it is perhaps my most prized memento. It lay collecting dust in the garage for two decades. Struck with inspiration, I recently fashioned it into an elegant chandelier that now graces the table above a family retreat in New York's Adirondack Park.

Moose are fascinating creatures, both in appearance and behavior. At the present time, they're not thriving in the contiguous United States. Populations remain healthy in some areas and in the past decade have actually expanded in a few places. But across the board, moose are suffering. Populations have plummeted in states such as Minnesota and New Hampshire. More gradual but significant declines have occurred in the northern Rocky Mountains.

Are these decreases temporary setbacks in historically fluctuating numbers or the beginning of a serious downward spiral in American moose populations? More time and research are needed to answer that question. In the meantime, I hope this chapter will increase the reader's knowledge of this singular species and encourage a commitment to the conservation of moose.

NAMES AND FACES

Names and Visual Description

The moose is the largest antlered animal in North America. Bison are the only land animals on the continent that weigh more than moose. However, the average adult moose is as tall as a bison. Moose have very long legs. They exhibit a dark brown or black appearance overall, with lighter, grayish fur on the lower portions of their legs. The belly and inside of the legs are also grayish. On overcast days or in low light, the coat of some moose often looks very black. While their dominant coloration is similar, the coats of males and females differ in certain ways. Males have a very dark muzzle, while the muzzle of a cow is medium or light brown. Both sexes have a short, stubby tail. Cows have a light patch of fur just below their tail. In the spring, prior to shedding their winter coat, the fur on moose may appear lighter and more faded than at other times of the year.

The flap of skin below a moose's chin is called the "bell" or "dewlap" and is more pronounced on bulls than on cows.
JACK BALLARD

Viewed from the side, a moose is a lanky creature that may remind some people of a horse. Moose have a long face terminating in a somewhat bulbous snout. The upper lip of a moose overlaps noticeably with its lower lip. Their front shoulder is humped, while a curious flap of skin and hair dangles below their chin. The purpose of this strange appendage (if there is one), known as the "bell" or "dewlap," is unknown to biologists. The dewlap is larger and more easily spotted on mature males than on cows or young animals.

The term "moose" originates in the native Algonquian language of American Indians historically inhabiting the northeastern United States and southeastern Canada. In the native language, "moose" refers to these animals' habit of nibbling twigs and stripping bark from trees. Thus, the creature's name aptly captures its dominant eating habit in the native language. Linguists believe the term "moose" entered the English language from Algonquian very early in the seventeenth century. The scientific name for the moose is *Alces alces*.

Moose were confused with a related North American mammal, the elk, by early European immigrants. In Europe and Great Britain, the common name of the *Alces alces* species is "elk." In fact, the Latin term alces, whence the scientific name of the moose is derived, means elk. Early European settlers to North America may have never seen a Eurasian elk or moose (*Alces alces*), but they were aware of its existence as a large, antlered creature. When they arrived in the New World and encountered North American elk (*Cervus elephus*), they mistakenly named them for the Eurasian creature of the same name. Thus, the North American animal we know as the "moose" is commonly referred to as the "elk" in Europe.

Related Species in North America

The moose is the largest member of the deer family, a group of antlered animals with cloven hooves. Due to their massive size and unique color, competent observers are unlikely to mistake a moose for any other member of the deer family, although elk hunters have been known to accidentally shoot moose, thinking they are elk. Moose are much taller than elk, usually standing a foot or more higher at the front shoulder. While moose have an overall dark brown or blackish appearance, elk are tawny or light brown across most of their body, with darker brown fur on their neck and head and a prominent yellow or tannish colored rump. The face of an elk is noticeably shorter than that of a moose. An elk's muzzle tapers to a slender nose and mouth, while the nose of a moose appears round and bulging.

In Canada and Alaska, moose sometimes share range with another member of the deer family, the caribou. Moose are huge compared to caribou, with adult specimens of corresponding genders weighing at least three times as much as a caribou. Caribou and moose are also notably different in appearance. While moose

Top: Elk are tan or reddish brown in color compared with the darker moose. Bull elk also lack the palm-shaped antlers found on moose.
JACK BALLARD
Bottom: Unlike moose, caribou have a white neck and mane. Caribou are much smaller than moose, and their antlers are shaped differently.
© ISTOCK.COM/JAMCGRAW

are uniformly dark brown or black over most of their body, caribou have a mottled gray or grayish-brown look, with a white or light gray neck that is unlike anything seen on a moose. Caribou also have a longer tail than that of a moose, which is white on its underside.

Two other members of the deer family also share the moose's range in many parts of the contiguous United States and Canada. Both whitetail deer and mule deer are frequently found in proximity to moose. However, it's unlikely that even a novice observer would mistake either of these species for a moose. Both are much smaller than moose and colored very differently. Mule deer are predominantly gray in the fall and winter, with a reddish-brown coat in summer. Whitetail deer are brown or grayish brown in the winter, with a rich, reddish brown summer coat. Neither the size nor the overall color scheme of these species would create confusion with their larger cousin, the moose.

From a distance, bison might be mistaken for moose. Bison are large, brown herbivores (plant-eating creatures) whose height at the front shoulder is similar to moose. However, the characteristic shapes of bison and moose are dissimilar. An animal that primarily eats grass, the massive head of a bison is carried below its front

Moose sometimes share range with mule (above) and whitetail deer (below) but are much larger and colored differently than either species.
JACK BALLARD

Moose may appear similar to bison from a distance, but unlike moose, bison have horns and a much more massive head.
LISA BALLARD

shoulder. By contrast, the head of a moose protrudes above its shoulder. The muzzle of a bison is short and broad in relation to its head, while the muzzle of a moose is elongated. The short ears of a bison are found on the sides of its head, while the ears of a moose sprout from the top of its head. Moose have an overall tall, long-limbed appearance. Bison look more massive. Finally, both sexes of bison have short, curved horns. Male moose have antlers that are much longer and shaped differently than the horns of a bison. Cow moose have neither horns nor antlers.

Subspecies of Moose

Biologists speculate that moose arrived to the North American continent from Asia via the Bering land bridge 11,000 to 14,000 years ago. As such, they are a fairly recent addition to the continent's spectrum of wildlife. How moose moved from Alaska, where they first colonized after their arrival, to other parts of North America is a matter of debate. Some biologists speculate that animals scattered slowly from the seed population in Alaska. Others believe small numbers of moose expanded their range in long-distance dispersals, creating isolated populations in suitable habitats that were far from the nuclear population.

A term of biological classification, "subspecies" refers to distinct populations within a species that exhibit differing physical characteristics or behaviors from other members of the species. Subspecies most often develop as a result of geographic isolation. Mountain ranges, deserts, and oceans are among the geographical features that may keep populations within a species isolated from one another. In addition to natural geography, alterations to habitat by humans may further isolate population segments within a species. Fenced highways, for example, may create barriers that keep animals separate. Large tracts of land cleared for farming may also effectively isolate populations of forest-dwelling animals from each other.

Historically, moose roamed across northern Europe and northern Asia in addition to North America. Currently, four subspecies of moose are commonly recognized in Europe and Asia, although a few biologists believe Eurasian moose should be considered a separate species from North American moose. Four subspecies of moose also inhabit North America.

The largest subspecies of moose in North America is the Alaska moose (*Alces alces gigas*), sometimes known as the Yukon moose. This subspecies is found in northwestern Canada and Alaska. Generally speaking, mammals found in northern climates are larger than their southern counterparts. Such is the case with the Alaska moose. Massive bulls of this subspecies may weigh as much as 1,800 pounds and carry antlers spanning more than 6 feet wide. A bull moose of this subspecies killed by a hunter at Redoubt Bay, Alaska, in 1958 had antlers that measured 80 inches wide. Interestingly, moose of this subspecies in their northernmost distribution are not the largest. Animals found at around 65 degrees latitude (N) in Alaska and the Yukon are the largest, with body size diminishing in animals found north of 70 degrees latitude (N). Severe winters and poorer food sources likely account for the decreasing size of

Alaska moose found at the northern extremes of their range. Some observers believe members of this subspecies have coats that are darker (nearly black) compared to other North America subspecies.

A second subspecies of North American moose exists in much of the interior of Canada and portions of North Dakota, Minnesota, northern Wisconsin, and the Upper Peninsula of Michigan. Known as northwestern moose or western moose (*Alces alces andersoni*), this subspecies was proposed by a Canadian biologist in 1950. The scientific name of the subspecies, *andersoni*, was given in honor of Dr. Rudolph M. Anderson, an eminent Canadian zoologist and explorer. Northwestern moose are typically not as large of body or antler as their Alaska counterparts. Nonetheless, they are ponderous creatures, with some bulls carrying antlers spanning up to 70 inches. Some naturalists note that northwestern moose are slightly lighter in color than Alaska moose, with the body appearing more consistently deep brown than black.

A third subspecies of moose, the eastern moose (*Alces alces americana*), ranges across eastern Canada and the northeastern United States. Eastern states harboring this subspecies include Maine, Vermont, New Hampshire, Rhode Island, Massachusetts, Connecticut, and New York. Dispersals of moose from Maine, which holds large tracts of excellent moose habitat, are largely responsible for the growing moose populations in other northeastern states. Eastern moose aren't as large on average as those found in western Canada and Alaska. Nonetheless, they can grow to impressive size. In 1982, a hunter in Maine killed a moose that weighed 1,330 pounds after being field-dressed (gutted) by the hunter. State wildlife officials estimated that the animal had a live weight of 1,700 pounds. A Maine moose shot by a hunter in 1997 (which became the state record-holder for the largest antlers) sported antlers spanning over 60 inches.

The final subspecies of moose in North America is the Shiras moose (*Alces alces shirasi*). These moose are found in the northern Rocky Mountains of the United States, with populations occurring in Oregon, Washington, Idaho, Montana, Wyoming, Colorado, and Utah. The range of Shiras moose also extends slightly north into southern Alberta and British Columbia. In an odd twist of biology, the name for this subspecies traces to a Pennsylvania politician. George Shiras III served in the US House of Representatives from 1903 to 1905. He was elected from Pennsylvania's 29th congressional district. Shiras was an avid and pioneering photographer and was keenly interested in wildlife biology, particularly moose. In 1935 he published a volume of wildlife photographs that perhaps included the first wildlife photos lit with a flash. When E. W. Nelson of the US Bureau of Biological Surveys named this subspecies in 1914, he dubbed them in honor of his friend George Shiras.

Shiras moose are the smallest subspecies in North America, both in terms of body weight and antler size. A few extraordinary bulls have been recorded with antlers spanning over 60 inches. Male Shiras moose are sometimes described as weighing up to 1,400 pounds. However, any Shiras bull weighing over 1,000 pounds is an exceptionally large animal. Naturalists sometimes note that Shiras moose often exhibit lighter coloration along their backs that is lacking in the other North American subspecies.

Physical Characteristics

Unlike some small ungulates that appear much taller than they actually are, the perception of moose as a tall animal is very accurate. A mature Alaska moose male may easily measure 7 feet tall at the top of its front shoulders and weigh 1,300 pounds. Exceptionally large Alaska males may stand 8 feet tall at the shoulder. These outsize males may also span 9 feet in length from the tip of their nose to their stubby tail. By contrast, the average Shiras male in Utah weighs less than 750 pounds and stands shorter than 6 feet at the shoulder. Moose exhibit considerable variation in size between males and females (sexual dimorphism), with mature females being 30 percent to 50 percent smaller than corresponding males.

Nomenclature for species within the deer family follows one of two patterns. Mule deer, for example, are named "buck" for an adult male, "doe" for an adult female, and "fawn" for an immature animal less than a year old. Elk and moose follow a slightly different scheme of identity for the various genders and ages. An adult moose is called a "bull." An adult female is referred to as a "cow." A youngster less than a year old is dubbed a "calf."

Moose calves typically weigh 25 to 40 pounds at birth. In contrast to the young of elk and deer, which are covered with distinct white or creamy spots at birth, moose calves are uniform in color. They look like a cute, cuddly version of an adult moose with fur that is reddish brown and much lighter than that found on an adult. Maximum life expectancy of moose in the wild is about fifteen years, although they may live longer in areas containing ideal habitat with few predators. Several studies have found that cow moose, even in populations that aren't hunted, have a slightly longer life expectancy than bulls. Occasionally cow moose live to over twenty years in the wild.

Antlers and Antler Development

Bull moose have the largest antlers of any animal in North America, or the world for that matter. The weight of a pair of moose antlers can easily exceed 30 pounds for all subspecies. Moose found in Alaska and Canada may have antlers that weigh more than 70 pounds, with exceptionally large specimens achieving even greater weight. In 2012, a 73-year-old hunter in Alaska killed a gargantuan bull moose in the Brooks Range that weighed over 1,500 pounds. Its antlers spanned 73 inches in width, and were reported as weighing 98 pounds.

Carrying an extra 30 to 75 pounds of body weight on the top of an animal's head requires a notably strong neck. The neck muscles of bull moose are very thick and highly developed. Their antlers are sometimes used to ward off the attacks of predators and become potentially lethal weapons in battles with other bulls during the mating season. Not only must the neck muscles carry the antlers, they're also required to pivot and propel these bony weapons with great speed and dexterity.

Growing moose antlers are covered with a fuzzy skin known as "velvet." Bulls achieve their largest antlers at around 9 years of age.
JACK BALLARD

Moose antlers are composed of bone. They begin to grow in the spring or early summer, with the antlers of older bulls starting their development the earliest. Bull moose have two bony protrusions on their skulls known as "pedicles." The pedicles are located on the top of the head, above and slightly behind the eyes but in front of the ears. Pedicles are slightly cupped and covered with skin. They are the "roots" from which antlers grow.

Growing antlers are called "velvet antlers" for their fuzzy, velvety appearance. The skin covering the developing antlers is filled with an extensive system of blood vessels that provides nutrients. Rapidly growing moose antlers can increase over an inch per day. The blood supply to the antlers decreases in late summer, due to hormonal changes. At this time the antlers solidify as bone and the velvet skin covering starts to dry. The "velvet" then sloughs from the antlers, a process that is often aided by the moose rubbing its antlers on trees and shrubs. Antlers are naturally colored white, but they take on various shades of light brown or reddish brown. The coloration comes from staining by foreign materials when bulls rub their antlers. Variations in the hue and depth of antler color depend on what a bull rubs his antlers upon, and how much he rubs.

Developing moose antlers require an incredible amount of energy and minerals. The energy required by a massive bull to grow 70 pounds of antler is notably higher than that required by a cow to develop a fetus. Phosphorous and calcium are two minerals used in great quantities in developing moose antlers. Researchers modeling mineral requirements for moose antler development in one study found that bulls whose antlers weighed more than 44 pounds could not obtain enough phosphorous from food sources and that antler development absorbed (robbed) some of this mineral from the animal's skeletal system. Bulls with racks weighing in excess of 66 pounds also diverted calcium from the skeletal system during a six-week period of maximum antler growth. Researchers have also found that bulls younger than 4 years of age have smaller antlers in relation to their body size than older bulls. Biologists theorize that while the bodies of bull moose are still growing, more nutrition is utilized for weight gain than antler development. Such seems to be the case. Researchers in Alaska have discovered that bull moose achieve their maximum weight at an average of 8 years of age. Their largest set of antlers is normally grown as a 9-year-old animal. Antler growth then tends to taper notably in animals exceeding 10 years of age.

RANGE AND HABITAT

North American Range

The current range of many large mammals in North America is much smaller than the area the animals inhabited prior to European settlement of the continent. Elk and grizzly bears are two prime examples. Prior to the early 1800s, both species were abundant on prairie habitats east of the Rocky Mountains in places such as eastern Montana, and North and South Dakota. Overhunting and active persecution exterminated the animals in these areas. Current land-use practices and human population make it unlikely they will reclaim these historic habitats in any significant numbers.

Moose are common to the northern Rocky Mountains, although their populations have declined in some places such as Yellowstone National Park.
© ISTOCK.COM/BETTY4240

Moose range in North America contracted as a result of overhunting and habitat loss in the eighteenth and nineteenth centuries. However, the loss of range was not as dramatic as that experienced by elk and grizzlies. Protection of moose with the legislation of hunting seasons in the nineteenth and early twentieth centuries and reclamation of habitat, accidental and intentional, allowed moose populations to increase and their range to expand in the past century.

Moose are currently found in most of Alaska except for the far western portion of the state. They range across most of Canada, with the exceptions of the arctic region, the southern prairies, and the extreme southwestern portion of British Columbia.

In the contiguous United States, moose habitat occurs in three areas: the Rocky Mountains, northern reaches of the upper Midwest, and northern New England. Moose range across northeastern Washington, with a small population also found in northeastern Oregon. They're residents of the mountains of eastern Idaho and western Montana. Moose inhabit the western mountains of Wyoming, with populations occurring farther east in the Bighorn Mountains in the northern part of the state and the Snowy Mountains in the south. Moose are also found in the northern reaches of Utah and Colorado. Scant historical records indicate that a breeding population of moose was probably never found in Colorado. Transient animals may have occasionally roamed the northern mountains of the state, most likely wandering south from Wyoming. Moose were introduced into western Colorado in 1978 and 1979 near Rand in two groups of twelve animals each from the Uinta Mountains in Utah and northwestern Wyoming. They have since expanded their range across the Continental Divide and are regularly seen in Rocky Mountain National Park west of the Continental Divide, with some animals pioneering on the east side of the park as well. Additional transplants in

Colorado occurred in 1987, 1991, and 1992. Moose range is expected to expand in the future as animals move into the state's unoccupied but productive moose habitat. The Colorado moose population was estimated at 2,300 animals in 2013.

In the Midwest, moose range across portions of northeastern North Dakota and the woodlands of northern Minnesota. They occupy forested habitat in the northernmost reaches of Wisconsin and Michigan's Upper Peninsula. An isolated population of moose is also found on Isle Royale in Lake Superior.

Farther east, moose grace the woodlands of much of Maine. They also range across most of New Hampshire and Vermont in suitable habitats. Moose track forested areas in Massachusetts and have increased their habitation in northern New York. Absent from New York's sprawling Adirondack Park for decades, moose are now increasingly sighted by area residents and visitors.

The history of moose in the contiguous United States follows the same basic pattern of decline and recovery seen with other large mammals that had economic value in settlement times or were deemed pests. Early colonists happily killed moose for their meat and hides. Once abundant in the East with a range extending across all of New England and into northeastern Pennsylvania, moose populations declined precipitously, to the point it was believed only fifteen animals inhabited the entire state of New Hampshire in the mid-1800s. The situation repeated itself in the upper Midwest and the Rocky Mountains. Vast tracts of suitable moose habitat were lost to clearing for agriculture and logging, though timber harvest often improves forage for moose by stimulating the rapid growth of deciduous trees and shrubs. By the late 1800s, moose were found only in isolated pockets of their former range in the contiguous United States.

In most areas containing suitable habitat in the lower forty-eight states, moose numbers increased substantially from 1970 to 2000. However, moose populations in many regions experienced alarming declines from 2005 to 2013. In northeast Minnesota, for example, moose numbers dropped from an estimated 8,840 animals in 2006 to 2,760 in 2013. A full 35 percent reduction in the already compromised population occurred from 2012 to 2013, prompting state wildlife managers to suspend their moose hunting program. New Hampshire experienced a significant loss of moose during the same time period. In the five-year stretch ending in 2013, the state's moose number decreased to 4,500 from 7,500 animals. Total moose populations contracted significantly in stronghold states such as Montana and Wyoming during the same period as well. In a few areas, such as the eastern front of the Rocky Mountains in Montana, moose numbers increased slightly in the years that were so troublesome to the species in most of the United States. Biologists have yet to specifically identify the conditions that caused such a notable decline in moose country's moose population.

Moose Habitat

Moose are often classified as generalist browsers by biologists, meaning they receive most of their nutrition from the leaves, twigs, and bark of trees and shrubs. As such, they are primarily creatures of the forest. Over much of their northern range, moose are found in mixed timberlands containing both coniferous and deciduous species of trees. Although they prefer to forage in open areas or along the edges of timber, they routinely utilize heavier timber for escape cover from predators, for shade in the summer, and protection from severe weather in the winter.

Often found in the mountains, moose occupy a surprising range of elevation. In the Absaroka Mountains near my home in Montana, I've seen moose along lower-elevation creek bottoms at 5,000 feet above sea level to 9,500 feet, just below timberline, within the space of a few days. The mountains of eastern states aren't so lofty as those in the Rockies, but moose roam over a diverse range of elevations in the East as well. They can be found in the valleys or near the mountaintops, depending on the season and local conditions.

Within generally treed areas, moose occupy various habitat niches. In many regions, the best moose forage is concentrated in small areas. Riparian zones (habitat found along waterways) are perennially favored by moose. Some of their favorite food sources grow abundantly along creeks, rivers, backwaters, and boggy areas. These include young aspens, poplars, birch, and several species of willows. A much smaller creature, unrelated to the moose, is responsible for creating ideal moose habitat in many places. When beavers construct dams, ponds and marshy areas are formed behind the impoundments. These provide water for deciduous shrubbery and may also stimulate the growth of aquatic plants, another food source favored by moose. Even after the beavers leave, old beaver dams often maintain a boggy area along the watercourse, which promotes good moose habitat.

Moose are creatures of the forest, relying on woodlands for food and shelter.
© ISTOCK.COM/ URMASPHOTOCOM

Shallow lakes and other water bodies often create excellent moose habitat. This cow and calf were photographed in Glacier National Park, Montana.
© ISTOCK.COM/ WILDNERDPIX

In some areas of the country, shallow lakes and ponds also represent critical moose habitat. Lake waters less than 15 feet deep often support a profusion of aquatic vegetation during the summer months. These plants are often highly nutritious for moose. Aquatic vegetation growing in slowly moving streams may also be eaten by moose.

Within a given geographical area, moose occupy various habitat niches in relation to the season. In the spring and summer, they tend toward areas with easily accessed shrubs and trees that abundantly produce buds, flowers, and leaves. These may include subalpine shrublands, aquatic areas, and places that have been recently burned by a forest fire or cleared by logging operations. If it becomes very hot in late summer, moose will retreat to mature, dense forests for shade. They return to shrubby areas with readily available stands of shrubs and young trees in autumn and early winter. In mid- to late winter, when snow depths are at their highest, moose prefer areas of coniferous forest with large trees that shelter them from the snow and cold.

NUTRITIONAL REQUIREMENTS AND FORAGE

Nutritional Requirements

The bulk of a moose's diet comes from browse, primarily the leaves, buds, twigs, and bark of deciduous trees and shrubs. An animal weighing in excess of 1,000 pounds requires a considerable amount of food to maintain its body. Moose are no exception. Biologists in eastern states note that healthy moose in the region typically consume 40 to 60 pounds of browse per day. At an average of 50 pounds per day, this means a moose will munch over nine tons of plant matter each year. The amount of forage available to moose and required for body maintenance varies considerably through the seasons. Research conducted in Alaska has indicated that moose can survive during the winter on just over 10 pounds of dry mass per day, but will ingest considerably more when it's available. The metabolism of moose slows considerably during the winter, allowing them to subsist on less forage than at other times of the year.

Nutritional requirements for moose also vary significantly in relation to an animal's position in its life cycle. As noted in the previous section, mature bulls invest considerable resources developing their massive antlers. Lactating cows (those producing milk for their young) also require much more nutrition than females that are not nursing a calf. Available nutrition is a very important component in the reproductive efficiency of moose. Cows with higher percentages of body fat in the fall are much more likely to produce twin calves than thinner females. Additionally, cows in better body condition birth larger, stronger calves than those that don't receive adequate nutrition.

Digestion

The digestive system of a moose is large, long, and complex. Moose, like deer, do not have teeth on the front portion of their upper jaw. They use the teeth on their lower jaw and their oversized upper lip to efficiently strip branches of their leaves or to nip twigs. The tongue and lips of moose are strong and covered in thick skin, allowing them to rake leaves from branches without the aid of upper front teeth.

Digestion begins when the animal swallows its meal of twigs, leaves, aquatic vegetation, or whatever else has captured its interest as a browser. While eating, a moose doesn't follow the human rule of chewing food thoroughly before swallowing. It simply rakes the forage into its mouth, grinds it a time or two with its rear molars, and swallows. The newly eaten forage lodges in the first chamber of a moose's stomach. It is later regurgitated and re-chewed by the animal, usually while lying at rest during the day. After it's swallowed a second time, the forage passes beyond the first chamber of the moose's stomach and into additional digestive chambers. From there it travels through the animal's intestines and is finally expelled as waste in the form of oval-shaped pellets. Moose feces (sometimes called "nuggets") are uniformly oval-shaped in the winter, having the general appearance of small eggs. In the summer, when the animals are eating primarily green plant matter, the pellets may clump together, sometimes looking more like cow patties than pellets.

The lips, tongue, and front teeth of moose are highly adapted to removing leaves and twigs from trees and shrubs.
LISA BALLARD

Chewing plays a role in a moose's digestive process, but it's actually a complex mixture of bacteria and other microbes (known as microflora) in the animal's gut that is primarily responsible for digestion. Throughout much of the year, a moose eats large volumes of plant matter that have relatively low nutritional value. Its microflora breaks this material down into digestible nutrients. While the microflora works quite efficiently, it doesn't adapt quickly to change. During the summer, this digestive soup is optimized to handle moist, green forage. As summer fades into autumn, it becomes more specialized in breaking down woody browse.

While the digestive systems of bears and other carnivores can adapt quickly to changing food sources, the digestive mechanisms of ruminants like moose, elk, and deer aren't so flexible. The ability to digest plant matter of low nutritional quality gives ruminants certain survival advantages. However, it also necessitates a gradual customization to new types of food, a process that can be temporarily stressful or even deadly in demanding circumstances.

Food Sources

In the fanciful children's tale *Thidwick the Big-Hearted Moose*, an accommodating bull moose allows a host of other creatures to take up residence in his antlers. When the rest of the moose herd abandons Thidwick and swims across a lake in search of more moose-moss to eat, Thidwick is left behind to fend for himself. The story has a dramatic and amusing ending, but Dr. Seuss, the author and graduate of Dartmouth College, either didn't know much about moose or didn't care if his story accurately reflected

Willows are a preferred food source for moose in a wide range of habitats. This bull is browsing willows near Colorado's Rocky Mountain National Park.
JACK BALLARD

biology. For one thing, moose are seldom found in groups of more than a few animals except sometimes in winter and never in herds. Of all the things they might eat, moss is very low on the list. In a few locations, moose sometimes munch moss in the winter, but its normal contribution represents less than 1 percent of a moose's wintertime diet.

Because they occupy such a wide range (Alaska to Maine) and are found in many different ecosystems, the plant species upon which moose normally browse may be very different in one region than another. However, certain types of trees and shrubs are eaten by moose wherever they're found. Among these, willows are one of the dominant species. Alaska moose are known to feed on at least twelve varieties of willow. In the northern Rocky Mountains, in places such as Grand Teton and Yellowstone National Parks in Wyoming, moose are strongly associated with stands of willows that grow along small creeks and rivers. One study of moose in Rocky Mountain National Park found that six species of willows composed 80 percent or more of their summer diet.

Along with willows, moose dine on the leaves and twigs of aspen trees over much of their range. They consume many other types of deciduous trees, some of the more common of which are cottonwoods, birch, maple, beech, and alder. Shrubs are another important source of browse for moose in some areas. Depending on the habitat, elderberries, currants, high-bush cranberries, gooseberry, buffalo berry, red osier dogwood, and mountain mahogany are among the shrubs often eaten by moose. In the Jackson, Wyoming area, they are often seen on sagebrush flats where they feed on bitterbrush. Moose occasionally eat twigs and needles from evergreen trees as well. These may include Pacific yew, subalpine fir, Douglas fir, lodgepole pine, and other species. Balsam fir, an evergreen common in the northeastern United States, is a staple browse for moose in many areas, particularly during severe winters. Although moose consume a wide variety of forage that may include several dozen species of trees and shrubs, research in many different areas has found they typically focus on six or fewer key species at any given time of the year. For example, wildlife biologists in northern Minnesota have noted that 80 percent or more of a moose's diet comes from five or fewer plant species.

Browse composes the bulk of a moose's diet, but aquatic vegetation is a very important source of nutrition for these oversize ungulates in many locations. In the summer, aquatic plants grow quickly in shallow lakes and ponds, providing an abundant food source for moose. Slow-moving rivers also host various types of submerged vegetation, some of which are fed upon by moose. On several occasions, I've observed moose in Yellowstone National Park feeding on aquatic vegetation along lazy stretches of the Madison River near the park's west entrance.

The list of plants associated with aquatic environments and eaten by moose is quite extensive. Along the edges of lakes and streams, and in marshy areas, moose may eat sedges or swamp grasses. These are grasslike plants with fibrous roots, often sporting distinct, triangular stems. In shallow water, moose target reedy plants such as bulrushes and cattails. They also eat bur-reeds, pondweeds, water lilies, and pond lilies, aquatic plants that commonly grow in water 1 foot to 3 feet deep. Aquatic plants rooted in deeper water, such as water shield and milfoil, are also relished by moose. Moose have been observed completely submerging themselves in search of these plants, and may remain underwater for more than thirty seconds at a time.

Moose eat a wide variety of aquatic plants. This young bull is feeding in the Madison River in Yellowstone National Park.
JACK BALLARD

Why do moose spend so much effort to feed on aquatic plants? Similar to most other herbivores, moose love salt. Aquatic plants concentrate salt and other minerals, sometimes in astonishingly high quantities. Certain aquatic plants have sodium levels that are literally several hundred times higher than woody browse in the winter. Sodium and other minerals found in aquatic plants are important to healthy body functions in moose. Minerals and protein (also found in some aquatic plants in relatively high levels) are necessary for antler development. Sodium is required for proper functioning of the nervous system. These minerals can be stored in a moose's body but are depleted during the winter, when the animals eat smaller amounts of woody forage with low mineral levels. Come spring and summer, moose are actively seeking mineral-rich sources of forage.

Forage Through the Seasons

A moose's diet varies considerably depending on the season. With the coming of spring, the animals encounter newly budding trees and shrubs, and the greening of grasses and broad-leafed plants at ground level. Moose eat the tender shoots of some grasses during this time and may also ingest broad-leafed plants (forbs) such as fireweed and dandelion. Newly emerging vegetation on trees and shrubs is an important source of springtime nutrition as well.

Summer is a season of great bounty for the average moose. Leaves and new, tender growth on their favorite deciduous trees such as aspens, willows, cottonwoods, and birches are abundant. Summer also brings the season of maximal growth to aquatic plants. In many places inhabited by moose, beavers build dams of sticks and mud that impound small streams, creating ponds. Moose may find aquatic plants in the beaver pond and moisture-loving trees and bushes along their edges, making beaver ponds prime feeding areas for moose in the summer.

Green leaves turn to shades of red, yellow, and brown in autumn and eventually drop from the trees. Nonetheless, fall normally provides plenty of food for a hungry

moose. The small twigs sprouted by deciduous trees during the summer are easily cropped by moose in the fall and are quite nutritious. Moose may also find bushes loaded with berries, such as blackberries and raspberries. They're happy to strip both the leaves and berries from fruit-producing shrubs.

Winter is by far the leanest time of year for moose. Woody browse from deciduous trees makes up most of their diet across much of their range. Conifer needles and stems may also be eaten. During the winter the metabolism of a moose slows and its appetite is diminished. Research has shown that even when moose have abundant, desirable food sources readily available in the winter, they still eat less than at other times during the year.

Migration

Moose don't undertake such spectacular migrations as some other ungulate species, such as herds of caribou and pronghorn. Nonetheless, they frequently move significant distances from summer to winter range. These migrations normally take them from higher-elevation summer habitat to wintering areas in the foothills or along lowland streams.

ABILITIES AND BEHAVIOR

Physical Abilities

Certain characteristics of moose offer hints of their physical ability, but their general appearance is anything but athletic. Their legs seem too long for their bodies. Their front shoulders are higher than their rump, giving them a somewhat off-balance appearance. The large, bulbous nose of the moose looks out of proportion to the rest of its body, and the dangling dewlap lends the animal an almost comical appearance, even if it's a massive bull with spreading antlers.

But like the gangly kid who becomes downright impressive the moment his sneakers hit the basketball floor, moose have many physical abilities that are nothing short of exceptional. Consider their speed. Moose can run 30 miles per hour or slightly faster. Their long legs allow them to navigate fallen logs and other obstacles in the forest while trotting at high speeds, a strategy they sometimes use to elude predators. While hiking in the Absaroka Mountains in Montana one fall, I startled a large bull moose. It whirled and dashed up a steep slope, clearing the yonder ridge and disappearing from sight as fast as a whitetail deer or elk. Compared to other North America ungulates, moose are very adept at running through moderately deep snow, an ability resulting from the length of their limbs. Their taller front shoulders

The long legs of moose allow them to clear obstacles in the forest while moving at high speeds, one of the strategies they use to avoid predators.
JACK BALLARD

make their front legs longer in relation to their rear legs, allowing them to more easily step over objects when walking or moving swiftly through thick timber.

Moose are also very skilled swimmers. They can swim at speeds up to 6 miles per hour and are reported to swim up to 2 hours at a time. Their swimming speed and endurance are promoted by their long legs and buoyant fur. The hairs that compose a moose's coat are hollow, which help them float. Moose are known to swim across large lakes or to islands in search of food.

Although their swimming ability is known by most wildlife enthusiasts, it comes as a surprise to many people that moose can also dive. Moose sometimes dive below the surface of a lake to reach aquatic plants and can stay submerged for 30 to 50 seconds. The diving ability of moose, while real, is often exaggerated. Video footage has reliably shown that moose do attempt to dive. But due to their buoyant coats and air in their

Moose are very capable swimmers, sometimes swimming long distances across lakes or to islands in search of food.
© ISTOCK.COM/OVERSNAP

large lungs, they are not well adapted to diving, and their rear quarters tend to float as they dive. Some sources claim moose can dive up to 75 feet underwater, but these are certainly tall tales. Moose submerge themselves in search of aquatic vegetation, most types of which grow in water that is less than 15 feet deep. While feeding in shallower water, they often submerge their heads for similar periods of time, a bit like a grade-schooler bobbing for apples at a Halloween party. However, a moose is much more adept at underwater foraging than kids. Specialized tissues in its oversize nose create a seal that keeps water from entering its airway as it roots around underwater. Whether wading, swimming, diving, or foraging, the bodies of moose are well adapted to aquatic environments.

The senses of a moose are ideally matched to its woodland surroundings. It is commonly reported that moose have poor vision, but such a description depends upon what aspects of vision are most valued. Canines, such as domestic dogs and wolves, don't have nearly as keen eyesight as a human when it comes to differentiating colors or discerning detail. However, their eyes are much more adept at sensing motion. While the eyesight of moose doesn't appear to perform as well as that of canines or humans in relation to the above factors, their vision works well in other ways. The eyes of a moose contain many more rod cells in the retina than cone cells. Rods promote low-light vision and motion detection but do not allow for color distinction or clarity. Thus, moose probably perceive the world in shades of gray or have limited perception of color. They see well at night but don't have the ability to visually discern nearly as much detail as a human. Additionally, moose have a large "blind spot" in front of their head. This isn't a result of their poor eyesight but has to do with the position of their eyes on the head. The eyes of a moose are set on the sides of its head, which give it good peripheral vision but require it to rotate its eyes to see objects that are directly in front of it.

Moose have an excellent sense of smell, allowing them to pick up and discriminate scents at a considerable distance. Although little research has been done specifically to determine a moose's smelling ability, it's safe to say that certain odors can be detected from a mile away. The large, oddly shaped nose of the moose promotes its remarkable sense of smell. Moose have large nostrils located farther apart on the nose than the nostrils of other ungulates. Some biologists speculate that the oversize, widely spaced nostrils on a moose allow it to gather scent from a wider range than other creatures and may also create stereo-olfaction, a fancy way of saying that moose may be able to detect the direction from which a scent originates much better than most other creatures.

Moose use their sense of smell to detect danger and also identify food sources. For people, the taste of food is related to smell and to the perceptions we receive from our taste buds. While moose have a much more highly developed sense of smell than

The eyesight of moose excels in low-light conditions. The animals have a blind spot directly in front of them but have good peripheral vision.
JACK BALLARD

humans, it's interesting to note that their tongues contain far fewer taste buds than a human's. It's quite possible moose select food items based primarily on their smell, not their taste. This may explain why moose will happily browse on the strong-tasting needles of evergreens in the winter, such as balsam fir.

Along with their keen sense of smell, moose also possess excellent hearing. Their large ears are roughly sixty times larger than the ears of a human. Each ear can move independently of the other, making it possible for them to search for and locate sounds by manipulating their ears.

Like other mammals, certain senses of moose are more highly developed than others. Their eyesight is not as good as some other creatures, but in the forested environments they most commonly inhabit, sight distance is usually limited. However, their sharp senses of smell and hearing serve them very well. Due to these abilities, moose can often detect the presence of a predator long before it comes into view, giving them time to flee or prepare for an attack.

Vocal and Visual Communication

Compared to other North American ungulates such as elk, moose are very quiet animals. Elk communicate with each other in herds throughout the year with barking sounds and grunts. They become extremely vocal during the mating season, when bulls emit loud bugling noises and communication within cow herds increases due to mating activity. Moose, on the other hand, rarely vocalize, except during the breeding season. At that time, cows emit a very loud moaning noise that can be heard by bulls from up to 2 miles away. The call signals that a cow is ready for mating and is vigorously investigated by bulls. Some evidence indicates that cows may change the pitch of their calls when tended by young bulls. Some biologists believe this strategy is used to gain the attention of bigger, older bulls more fit for breeding, giving cows some ability to select their mates.

Bulls also vocalize during the mating season, emitting noisy bellows that alert cows and rival bulls of their presence. These calls are similar to a person making a drawn-out sound of a long "o" with a slightly guttural tone. Males may also make mating sounds that are

Moose do not vocalize as much as many other animals. Cows and calves sometimes communicate with grunts.
© ISTOCK.COM/ HEIDIMICHELLE

sometimes described as barks or croaking sounds. At other times of the year, cows may grunt more quietly to call their calves. This grunt sounds like a person making an "errh" sound. It is somewhat similar to the moans and grunts cows make during the breeding season, but much quieter and not as drawn out. Moose of both sexes sometimes make a very loud roaring sound when startled.

Although their vocalizations are infrequent during most times of the year, moose often communicate their intentions and internal state with body language. Cows may nuzzle and lick their calves, giving a visual indication of contentment and bonding. Bulls communicate dominance and aggression toward one another during the mating season by displaying their antlers and turning their heads. A moose that stops feeding to focus its eyes on a person or another object is communicating its alertness to a potential threat. Raised hackles and ears that are laid back are often preludes to a defensive or aggressive attack by a moose and may be used by both cows and bulls. Moose may also clack the teeth in their lower jaw against their upper gum just prior to violent behavior.

Herd Behavior

In many cases, the behavior of an animal species in one area provides a clue to its actions in another. Moose are the least vocal of the North American members of the deer family, giving some hint of their social structure as well. They do not form lasting herds and are seldom found in groups. However, moose do band together at certain times of the year and under specific conditions. They congregate in varying numbers during the breeding season, most often when several bulls are attracted to a cow.

Bulls themselves sometimes form small "bachelor" groups. These are most often found in proximity to desirable habitat during the summer and early winter. One summer I observed and photographed four magnificent males near a lake on the east side of the Continental Divide, just south of Rocky Mountain National Park in Colorado. The bulls had taken up residence in a sprawling stand of willows, upon which they browsed vigorously. In such cases, the apparent companionship of the herd is probably more a matter of attraction to a particular resource than a desire to remain in the company of other animals.

Bull moose may temporarily congregate in small bands at various times during the year. Moose are found in herds only under special circumstances.
JACK BALLARD

A similar situation occurs during severe winters with deep snow. Several moose may assemble in a yard. The term "yard" refers to an area where ungulates mass together in the winter at a site of abundant feed. In addition to forage, moose have an advantage in a yard due to the trails created by multiple animals tracking through the snow, requiring less energy for locomotion. Once the winter has passed, the herd of moose observed in the yard quickly disperses.

REPRODUCTION AND YOUNG

The Mating Season

During the mating season, the normally quiet moose becomes loud and talkative. Bulls roar, cows moan, and both sexes communicate to each other with a variety of grunting sounds. What is the purpose of all this noise in a typically silent, solitary species? Along with other communication strategies, the vocalizations of moose during the mating season, or "rut," is what brings bulls and cows together, often from distances of more than a mile.

However, sound is not the only way moose advertise their presence to potential mates during the rut. Scent marking is another. While it's easy to assume that bulls do most of the searching for cows during the rut, cows are also attracted to dominant bulls. Male moose sometimes gouge the soil with their front hooves to create "rutting pits" or "wallows." They urinate in these pits and paw the smelly soil onto the underside of their belly or roll in it. Cows may also visit rutting pits and wallow about in them. Although the thought of this activity isn't so appealing to people, it appears to serve an important function in bringing together cows and bulls for mating. Moose may also rub their heads on saplings during the breeding season, another way of distributing their scent to other animals. Although biologists don't understand the exact ways in which the various types of scent marking stimulate the activities of moose, it is obviously an important method of communication between the two sexes during the rut.

The peak of the breeding season for moose normally occurs in late September to early October, although some slight differentiation exists in relation to geographic region. Small variations in the timing of the breeding season have also been documented from year to year in localized moose populations. However, in most places the vast majority of the cows will be bred in a short window of time, about two weeks. For example, one study in British Columbia found that nearly 90 percent of the cows that bore a calf the following spring became pregnant in a ten-day period. Cows that do not mate during the normal span of the rut may conceive calves later in the fall, sometimes as late as November. Although rutting behavior tends to taper off rather quickly around the middle of October, bulls may stay on the lookout for cows and remain quite aggressive for several more weeks.

Scent is an important source of communication for moose during the breeding season. This bull is checking the smell of a nearby cow.
JACK BALLARD

For bulls, the mating season is a potentially risky and physiologically expensive time of the year. Preparation begins in late August, at which time the "velvet" covering dries and is rubbed from the antlers. Bull moose vigorously thrash their antlers against brush, saplings, and sometimes larger trees to rid them of the velvet. During the rut, antler rubbing also distributes a dominant male's scent.

As the breeding period of late September approaches, bulls become more aggressive toward one another. Confronted with a rival, males may turn sideways and circle one another, or tip their heads to display their antlers. As noted in the beginning of this chapter, antler and body size are correlated in moose. Older males with larger antlers are generally also bigger and stronger of body. Younger males are intimidated by the bulky bodies and spreading antlers of these dominant males and will not challenge them for the breeding rights to a cow.

Bull moose may engage in furious battles during the breeding season. However, dominance is often settled at other times of the year when bulls test each other through more friendly sparring matches.
© ISTOCK/PHOTOGRAPHYBY JHWILLIAMS

However, bulls of roughly equal size in terms of body weight and antlers sometimes engage in furious fights during the mating season. The conflict typically begins with the animals squaring off against each other and engaging in dominance displays. If neither disengages during the posturing, the encounter escalates with bluff charges and circling. The outright battle begins when the massive males clash their antlers together in a duel of strength, stamina, and agility. Protrusions (tines) on the outer portions of the antlers engage when the bulls begin their struggle. The combatants push and twist their heads in an attempt to reach the rival's ribs and flanks. If a bull is maneuvered sideways or loses his footing, he may be battered and gored by the pointed headgear of his adversary.

The winner of the battle claims breeding privileges to a cow or, in some cases, multiple females. However, he does so at a cost. Bulls in the prime of life (7 to 10 years of age) may lose 250 pounds of body weight or more during the rut due to their increased exertion. In populations including a healthy number of mature males, biologists have estimated that the average bull receives as many as fifty puncture wounds while battling during the rut. Bulls sometimes suffer wounds that prove fatal during or shortly after combat. However, infected, festering puncture wounds that heal slowly and rob an animal of health as winter approaches are more common. In rare instances, the antler tines of fighting bulls may become interlocked in such a way that the animals cannot disengage them. Without human intervention, this unusual situation usually leads to the death of both animals.

Moose in diverse regions pursue different rutting strategies, a rather unusual occurrence among North American ungulates. In most places, cows maintain their solitary lifestyles during the breeding season. These single animals are sought by bulls who remain with the cow until mating, then move on in search of other females. In Alaska and the Yukon, however, where moose inhabit open tundra areas, as many as two dozen animals may assemble on rutting areas that are used year after year. Here, a dominant bull guards a group of cows (harem) from rivals and mates with them as each becomes ready for breeding. Even the most lordly bulls can seldom maintain a harem of more than eight or ten cows. If the harem contains a dozen cows or more, multiple males may be associated with a single band of females. The most reproductively successful bulls may mate with twenty or more cows in a single season.

Pregnancy and Gestation

The time from the beginning of pregnancy to birthing (gestation period) varies from 215 to 245 days for moose, with 230 days the most commonly reported average. Most moose cows birth their first calf at 3 years of age. However, cows reared in habitat with abundant forage may birth a calf as 2-year-olds. Cows achieve their maximum reproductive potential from 4 to 7 years of age, although in good habitat cows as old as 12 years may consistently produce offspring. Habitat quality plays a very important role in the reproductive capability of females. In poor conditions, conception rates (the percentage of cows that become pregnant during the breeding season) may be very low in cows older than 7 years of age. Where habitat provides abundant, nutritious forage, cows may produce calves much longer. Cows of at least 18 years of age are known to have produced offspring in the wild.

Some evidence indicates that the gestation period of moose varies in relation to factors that promote calf survival. Cows that breed after the peak of the rut may have a shorter gestation, which puts their birthing time on the later side but within the normal birthing period of other cows in the population. Females in less than optimal body condition may experience a longer gestation, which spreads the physical demand of pregnancy across a longer period of time and results in a larger, stronger calf at birth.

Birth

Moose normally birth their young from mid-May to mid-June, depending on the region in which they live. From year to year, however, there is little variation of peak birthing times in local populations. One research study in Alaska documented calving for a five-year period and found that the season of peak birthing varied only by about a week, even during years of notably different temperature and precipitation. The vast majority of births (80 percent or more) occurred in about a fifteen-day span.

Moose may produce a single calf, twins, and sometimes triplets. In good habitat, births may be almost equally divided between singles and twins. Twins may be completely absent or account for birthing rates as low as 0 percent; as high as 90 percent has been reported in various moose populations in North America. Cows tend to use

Twin calves are commonly born to moose cows in healthy body condition.
© ISTOCK.COM/CHILKOOT

Moose calves are reddish brown at birth. They receive their adult coloration when their baby coat is shed at the end of their first summer.
© ISTOCK.COM/JOHAN10

established calving areas from year to year but birth their calves as solitary animals, not in herds. Birth weight varies considerably in relation to subspecies and other factors. The larger animals of Alaska and Canada birth bigger calves on average than their southern counterparts. Moose calves range from 24 to 40 pounds at birth. Cows receiving good nutrition during pregnancy have larger calves. Single offspring are usually about 20 percent heavier at birth than twins. However, there is no significant difference in the birth weights of male and female calves.

Newborn calves can walk within hours of their birth and can swim proficiently within days. Their reddish tan color is noticeably lighter than the pelage of an adult moose, but beyond the difference in color, they look quite similar to their mothers.

Nurturing Calves to Adulthood

For the first two months of life, baby moose receive most of their nourishment from their mother's milk. Statistically, this is the most highly dangerous period in a moose's life. Mortality among infant moose is often very high. In areas with abundant predators such as grizzly bears, black bears, and wolves, as many as 75 percent of baby moose may fall to predation in the first months of life. Those that survive grow rapidly, often increasing their body weight by 3 to 5 pounds per day. By autumn, most moose calves weigh 300 to 400 pounds.

Despite their size, young moose are still quite dependent upon their mothers during the first winter. They have yet to become adept at eluding or repelling predators and follow their mothers to wintering areas providing forage and shelter. Just prior to birthing her calf the following spring, the mother moose forcibly drives her yearling (1-year-old) offspring away. By this time, the young moose is ready to survive on its own but will often rejoin its mother and her newborn calf a few weeks after the young is born. Female moose reach physical maturity at around 3 to 4 years of age, but bulls may continue to increase in body mass until they are 8 or 9 years old.

MOOSE AND OTHER ANIMALS

Moose and Other Ungulates

Moose share their North American range with a broad complement of other ungulates. At the northernmost reaches of their habitat in Alaska and Canada, they may be in the neighborhood of caribou. In the Rocky Mountains, they track much of the same territory as elk, mule deer, and whitetail deer, where they may also occasionally encounter bighorn sheep. Most eastern populations of moose have frequent contact with whitetail deer.

For the most part, other species of ungulates exert little influence on the lives of moose, but there are some exceptions. In the wintertime, moose may browse on shrubs and trees also consumed by deer and elk. However, it's likely that where overlap in winter browsing occurs between the species, moose hold the advantage. Due to their long legs and overall height, moose can browse trees and shrubs at heights up to 9 feet, far beyond the reach of elk and deer. Nonetheless, biologists have speculated that in areas holding very high concentrations of elk, such as Colorado's Rocky Mountain National Park, moose and elk might compete for winter browse. Willows are an important source of winter feed for existing elk in the area. Moose introduced into Colorado are now populating the park in rising numbers. Some biologists are concerned that the additional impact to willow stands of wintering moose may limit the winter forage available to one or both species. Research in Canada's Banff National Park indicates high elk populations may negatively impact food resources for moose. Because elk are less specialized in their diet, they may be able to outcompete moose, which utilize a narrower range of food sources in the winter.

The relationship between moose and elk is complex in some places. Species such as willows are heavily used in the winter by both species.
JACK BALLARD

Predation is a major source of mortality for moose in many areas. With the reintroduction of wolves to the western United States and their subsequent dispersal to other areas, biologists are observing a complex set of interactions between predators, their prey, and the ecosystems they inhabit. What happens when wolves move into an area containing high numbers of elk and much lower numbers of moose? While it seems the moose might be buffered from wolf predation due to the greater availability of elk, such is not the case. Research on predation to elk and moose by wolves colonizing

Banff National Park in the latter decades of the twentieth century has told a different story. Wolf numbers in areas of abundant elk increase dramatically. Elk may constitute the majority of the wolves' prey, but due to their opportunistic nature as predators, they still kill moose, often in high numbers in relation to the population. Predator-prey relationships in regions containing multiple predators and several species of prey are multifaceted. Moose have direct relationships with other ungulates, but they are also associated with other hoofed mammals due to their shared role as prey.

Moose and Predators

The sheer size of an adult moose protects it from most potential predators. In North America, only two top predators, the grizzly bear and wolf, routinely prey upon adult moose. Many of their predation attempts on full-grown moose are unsuccessful. Moose can elude predators by trotting at high speeds through woodlands strewn with fallen logs, brush, and boulders, which their long legs carry them over more easily than the shorter limbs of a wolf or bear. Flight isn't the moose's only predator-avoiding strategy. Moose may elect to stand and fight, often choosing open areas or shallow water. These locations allow the animals to make the most of their long, powerful limbs. A blow from a moose's hoof can kill or maim a wolf and may even cause serious injury to a grizzly bear.

Young moose, however, are much easier targets for predators. Grizzly bears kill very high percentages of moose during their first month of life in many places, sometimes consuming over half of the annual moose crop. Wolves also prey upon significant numbers of moose calves in local areas. Black bears are another source of predation on baby moose, especially where wolves and grizzly bears are absent.

Although less frequent predators than grizzly bears or wolves, mountain lions (cougars) are also known to eat moose. One research project in Alberta, Canada, determined that moose are a very important prey animal for mountain lions in some places. In the study area, moose composed 12 percent of the winter diet for female cougars, while over 90 percent of the males' winter nutrition came from moose. The mountain lions preyed exclusively on sub-adult moose. Calves from 7 to 12 months of age composed 88 percent of their kills with the remainder targeted on yearlings, 13 to 20 months of age. Mountain lions in Utah have also preyed upon adult moose, although their threat to full-grown

Wolves and grizzly bears are the two North American predators that consistently prey upon moose.
© ISTOCK.COM/ANDREANITA
© ISTOCK.COM/NREFLECT

animals is usually very low. On rare occasions, coyotes may also kill newborn or young moose, although the extent to which coyotes can capably bring down moose is not well known. Nowhere in their North American range is coyote predation thought to be an important cause of moose mortality. If snow becomes deep and crusted in the winter, moose may be susceptible to predators unable to harm them in other conditions. The hooves of moose break through crusted snow, which impedes their movements, slowing their flight and tiring them quickly. The broad paws of predators like wolves and mountain lions allow them to run quickly on crusted snow, making it easier to bring down moose under such winter conditions.

Parasites and Diseases

Moose are indirectly but importantly related to other ungulates through predation. They are also affected by other ungulates in their roles as hosts of various parasites and diseases. Whitetail deer in eastern North America are often hosts of meningeal worms or brainworms. These parasites exhibit a complex life cycle that takes them from a deer's brain, to its lungs, to its digestive tract, where they are finally expelled in the deer's feces. Tiny snails and slugs transport the parasites to vegetation, where they are ingested by deer (and other animals). Larval worms migrate from the deer's stomach to its spinal cord and back into the brain, where the cycle begins anew.

While deer are normally unaffected by brainworms, moose aren't so lucky. Moose, elk, mule deer, and caribou are all considered "aberrant hosts" to brainworms, meaning these creatures can become infected, but aren't the ideal hosts of such parasites. Infections of brainworms in these species are typically fatal. Thus, high numbers of whitetail deer carrying brainworms (in some areas at least 80 percent of the deer host the parasite) greatly increase the chances of moose becoming infected and may be a limiting factor in moose populations. Some research indicates that areas with very high whitetail deer densities (more than ten animals per square mile) are seldom inhabited by moose in significant numbers.

A similar situation exists between moose and mule deer in the northern Rocky Mountains, though probably on a smaller scale. In the early 1970s, researchers in Montana documented moose infected with arterial worms, a parasite that takes up residence in the blood vessels of its host. Mule deer are the common host to these arterial worms, but the parasites can also infect moose, elk, bighorn sheep, and whitetail deer. Recent research in Wyoming has discovered that high percentages of moose in some areas carry arterial worms. The parasite is transmitted from one species to another by horseflies, and it is believed a prevalence of horseflies may up the risk of transmission of the parasites. While Wyoming researchers discovered moose can live with some level of arterial worm infections, the parasites are known to cause the death of moose and possibly play a contributing role in other types of mortality. Concentrations of arterial worms can decrease blood flow to the head of an animal, leading to impaired vision, hearing, and brain functions. The extent to which arterial worms may be a limiting factor in local moose populations isn't clearly understood, but they may be significant.

Moose are also hosts to lungworms, a type of roundworm that inhabits an animal's lungs. It has been known for some time that moose may be hosts to lungworms, but the infections were seldom obviously harmful or fatal to the animals. However, more recent study has raised the concern that young or unhealthy moose infected with lungworms are more likely to die as a result of other parasitic infections, such as those caused by the winter tick (which will be discussed later in this chapter). Recent research in Maine has also discovered a new type of lungworm, commonly found in red deer and fallow deer in Sweden, that is infecting moose. The degree to which this parasite may negatively influence moose populations is unknown, but some biologists believe it may be an important factor.

Other internal parasites also infect moose, with varying degrees of severity and harm to the animal. Moose can become intermediate hosts to hydatid worms (dog tapeworms), causing cysts in their lungs or other internal organs. Some research suggests that moose heavily infected with hydatid cysts are weakened and more susceptible to predation. Other internal parasites may also cause cysts in moose. Biologists have documented over twenty types of internal parasites capable of afflicting moose in North America.

External parasites such as ticks and flies can also be bothersome to moose. The most significant of these is the winter tick, or "moose tick." Winter ticks are frequently found on moose in the eastern United States and also occur in western populations. These parasites have a one-year life cycle that affects moose from autumn until spring. In late summer, larval ticks hatch from eggs on the ground and climb onto vegetation. They attach to moose and other hosts as the animals brush against shrubs, small trees, and tall grass. The tick larvae suck blood from the host, then remain dormant during the early winter. In January and February, the next stage of the tick's life cycle (the nymph) again feeds on the blood of its host. At this time the ticks enter the adult phase of their life cycle. The adult ticks again feed on the host around March and April. The ticks then mate and fall to the ground, where the females lay up to 3,000 eggs and then die.

Winter ticks can infest moose in such large numbers (up to 150,000 at a time) that they cause malnourishment and death. Severe outbreaks of winter ticks occur at various times and places in moose habitat in the eastern United State. Ticks directly drain moose of vitality by sucking their blood. They can also cause hair loss when moose rub their coats on objects in an attempt to rid themselves of the ticks. Moose with large areas of patchy fur due to heavy tick infestations have lost valuable insulation in addition to blood from the tick bites. Heavy winter tick infestations may also inhibit moose reproduction. Cows malnourished by ticks are in poorer condition and may not breed in the fall. Those that do are less likely to produce twins and may birth smaller, less vigorous offspring. Additionally, females in a reduced health state have fewer bodily resources to produce milk to nourish their calves.

While the magnitude and causes of global or continental warming trends may be debated, they will not be friendly toward moose. Warmer, shorter winters with shallow snowpack create more ideal conditions for winter ticks, an external parasite capable of killing moose and severely reducing reproduction. Cold, snowy winters mean fewer female ticks survive to lay eggs, giving moose a reprieve from these blood-sucking hordes of parasites.

Hotter summers create their own problems for moose, independently of parasites. The large bodies of moose do not dissipate heat very well. During torrid stretches of summer weather, the animals may simply hole up in the shade, refusing to eat. While this inactivity may not impact the survival of a moose itself, it almost certainly affects their reproduction. Cows that don't eat enough during the summer enter the fall with fewer fat reserves and may not breed. Females in optimal condition frequently birth twins; those with diminished reserves are more likely to produce a single calf. Thus, while moose may not be dying of heatstroke, their reproductive success may be compromised by climate change.

For many Americans, polar bears have become the "poster animal" of global warming. As research continues to unravel the complex lives of moose, it may prove that their health as a species in relation to climate change is equally challenging.

Along with winter ticks, moose may be hosts to other ticks, flies, and mosquitos. While apparently bothersome, these pests appear to have minimal impacts on moose in comparison to pervasive infestations of winter ticks.

Moose are also susceptible to a variety of diseases common to other wild ungulates and sometimes domestic livestock. Epizootic hemorrhagic disease (EHD) and bluetongue virus (BTV) are closely related diseases carried by biting midges and sandflies. Moose in Utah have tested positive for both diseases, but their effects on moose have not been extensively studied. Infectious kerato-conjunctivitis (pinkeye) has also been documented in moose in some places. This disease is most commonly associated with cattle and is normally contracted by close association with infected animals. Moose in the southern Rocky Mountains are known to occasionally become infected with pinkeye.

In addition to diseases caused by bacteria or viruses, moose can also contract white muscle disease. This condition is caused by a selenium or vitamin E deficiency and may cause excessive salivation, lameness, and heart failure. The extent to which it affects moose is not well known, but biologists in Utah have observed its presence.

MOOSE AND HUMANS

Moose and American Indians

Long before European settlers reached North America, native peoples hunted moose for their meat, hides, and antlers. Moose meat was an important source of nutrition for a variety of tribes in the northeastern United States. The meat was eaten on its own or mixed with fat and other ingredients to form pemmican, a portable food that formed a staple during the winter and times of travel. Some native peoples claimed that moose meat was more nutritious and would sustain a person in the midst of a journey much longer than the flesh of other creatures. Thomas Pennant, a biologist who lived in the 1700s, noted that Alaskan natives believed a traveler could cover three times the distance on a meal of moose than the meat of any other creature.

Along with the meat, moose hides were prized by many eastern tribes for clothing and moccasins. The skin of a moose is the largest and thickest of any animal found in the northeastern United States. Tanning (the process of converting an animal skin to leather) was very hard work. Tanning moose hides spanned several days of intense labor. Rawhide from moose skins was used to construct snowshoes, and Alaskan natives constructed canoes by covering a wooden framework with moose hides. Thomas Pennant also recorded indigenous peoples using the hair from the back and neck of moose in mattresses and saddles.

Large and impressive on a massive bull, moose antlers were used for practical and artistic purposes by native peoples. They were utilized for digging and fashioned into other tools. Pieces of antlers were sometimes carved to form decorative objects. Pennant documented native people creating ladles that could hold a full pint from moose antlers.

A handful of tribes had social societies named for the moose, and the animals appear in some native legends. But despite their importance to American Indians as a source of food and other products, moose were not afforded the same ceremonial or religious significance as some other creatures, including the grizzly bear, bison, raven, and coyote.

Moose were hunted using a variety of techniques depending on the region of the country and the season. Native hunters in areas where moose were relatively plentiful would use calls made of birch bark shaped like a cone to imitate the grunts of the animals during the mating season. This technique brought curious cows and bulls within range of the hunters' arrows. Some hunters also mimicked the calls of calves to lure protective cows. During the winter, hunters on snowshoes pursued moose in deep snow, easily overtaking animals when the snow developed a crust. Moose were opportunistically hunted in deep snow even in areas where their numbers were limited, such as northwestern Montana. Various tribes also set snares and devised deadfall traps capable of taking moose.

Moose and European Settlers

The history of moose in the United States parallels the fate of many other creatures. Where they were plentiful, moose were hunted by the colonists and settlers for their meat and hides. Elsewhere, moose were gladly killed as they were encountered as people went about their business hunting other creatures, prospecting, or ranching. Extensive clearing of woodlands for farming in the northeastern part of the country greatly reduced the amount of habitat available for moose and contributed to their declining numbers. By the end of the nineteenth century, moose range in what is now the contiguous United States had shrunk dramatically and the once common sight of a moose became a rare occurrence. In New Hampshire, for example, moose were plentiful prior to European colonization. By the mid-1800s their numbers had plummeted to an estimated fifteen animals.

Today moose are fairly common in the northern Rocky Mountains, in places like the mountains of Montana, Idaho, and Wyoming, although numbers there are far fewer than elk and deer. Unregulated hunting in the nineteenth century made moose quite scarce in these areas, but they were not plentiful prior to European exploration and settlement. The Lewis and Clark expedition traced routes across the northern Rockies taking them through hundreds of miles of productive moose habitat. However, their journals only contain two direct references to moose. In one, a hunter for the expedition wounded a moose on the return trip from the Pacific Ocean in western Montana, on July 7, 1806. The other journal entry is from five days earlier, and simply says Indians informed the expedition members there were "plenty of Moos" to the southeast of them (on the Salmon River in Idaho).

Journals from the Lewis and Clark expedition contain scant references to moose, although the corps traveled through excellent habitat on the rivers of Montana and Idaho.
© ISTOCK.COM/EYEZAYA

Across their historic range in the contiguous United States, moose numbers began to rebound substantially in the decades after World War II. A variety of factors led to growing moose populations. First, bans on unregulated hunting and the development of restrictive hunting (or no moose hunting at all) in many states buffered moose from a significant source of mortality. Maine's legacy with moose hunting is instructive at this point. In 1830, just ten years after Maine became a state, a law was passed setting the moose hunting season (with no bag limit) from September 1 to December 31. Further restrictions on the moose season were set by the 1883 legislature, shortening the moose season, enacting a possession limit of one moose, forbidding hunting on Sunday, and regulating hunting with dogs. The legislature also provided for strengthened enforcement of game laws. Several groups promoting ethical hunting and the preservation of natural resources became active in Maine in the late nineteenth century. Public support for wildlife conservation expanded, resulting in an 1891 law prohibiting the killing of cow and calf moose. Declining populations prompted the legislature to suspend moose hunting altogether in 1935. Maine did not reopen its moose hunting season until 1980. Since then, restrictive harvests have ensured hunting does not negatively impact the viability of local moose populations.

A similar pattern applied to moose management in other eastern states. New Hampshire, for example, opened a moose hunting season in 1988 after decades of strict moose protection. In the West, historical records of moose populations in the late nineteenth and early twentieth centuries are sketchy. However, it appears many populations actually expanded during these times. Moose are believed to have colonized Wyoming from Idaho and Montana around 150 years ago. In 1903 the Wyoming state legislature closed its moose hunt but reopened it in 1912 due to an expanding population estimated at 500 animals. Available data indicates moose fared better in the West than the East during the first half of the 1900s.

Protection from hunters ensured moose weren't being legally killed by humans. However, habitat enhancement was equally important to the moose population recovery in the West in the early decades of the twentieth century and in the East in the latter half of the twentieth century. Logging, wildfires, and changing land use all played a role.

In general, logging is beneficial to moose. Areas cleared of timber sprout deciduous trees and shrubs in prolific numbers when mature trees are eliminated, creating ideal browsing areas for moose. Where logging results in a mosaic of oases of mature timber interspersed with cleared areas in various states of recovery, moose find both excellent forage and sheltered wintering areas. Logging in the twentieth century in many regions of the country doubtlessly enhanced moose habitat.

Alterations in land use in the East also benefitted moose. Settlers cleared hundreds of thousands of acres in the New England states for farming, land that ultimately proved unsuitable for crops. As the pastures and fields were abandoned, they reverted to woodlands. Fast-growing deciduous shrub and trees were first to overrun the neglected fields, creating fine moose habitat in the process.

In the West, large-scale wildfires occurred in the early decades of the twentieth century. Fire activity again increased in the 1980s and 1990s. Management of fires on public lands has also undergone a shift in policy in the past several decades. Recognizing fire is often beneficial to wildlife habitat, land managers are more inclined to let some fires burn than attempt their immediate extinction. In some places, controlled fires are

Forest fires are often instrumental in regenerating habitat. Moose may benefit from fires for several decades after the burn.
© ISTOCK.COM/ALPTRAUM

deliberately set to rejuvenate habitat. Burned areas often result in increased forage for moose in the form of leaf-bearing shrubs and trees. Sometimes the habitat enhancement occurs within a few years; in other places the maximum benefit for moose takes a couple of decades. In either case, fire activity in the West has typically been good for moose.

Moose and Us

The scientific study of moose has lagged behind the depth of research devoted to many other North American species. However, the current decline in many moose populations has prompted an increased interest in these unique creatures. Some experts believe the contemporary contraction of moose numbers is simply an episode in the long-term history of a species prone to intense fluctuations in population due to changing habitat conditions and other yet-to-be-identified variables. Other biologists are more concerned, believing lengthy variations in climate conditions (drought, warming) and exposure to increased predation may put pressure upon moose populations from which the animals are less likely to recover.

Moose can be, and have been, domesticated. Tame moose have been broke to ride like horses and trained to pull carts and sleds. In bygone times, attempts to develop moose-mounted cavalry units were seriously discussed and experimented with on a limited basis in northern Europe and Russia. It was thought the animals would strike terror in the horses of opposing armies. Historical evidence indicates Tycho Brahe, an eminent Danish astronomer of the late sixteenth century, kept a pet moose. The moose was purportedly loaned to a nobleman for entertainment at a party. The moose consumed so much beer during the festivities that it became drunk and fell down the stone stairs of the castle, breaking a leg. Its injury eventually led to the creature's death.

Moose have been kept as pets in various locations in modern times, but you won't likely see one in a zoo. Hay and commercially produced feeds may keep the likes of elk and deer alive in an enclosure, but captive moose languish on such feeds. Their need for leaves, twigs, and fresh plant matter seems very important for their health, making them largely unsuitable as zoo animals.

At a more practical level, it's helpful for modern humans to be aware of hazards to themselves and the animals when traveling in moose country. Collisions with vehicles are a significant source of mortality to moose in some areas, sometimes killing vehicle occupants and resulting in extensive damage to automobiles. In Alaska, around 500 moose-vehicle collisions are reported annually. Highway officials estimate that over 20 percent of vehicle accidents on rural roads in Alaska involve moose collisions, and can double during severe winters. The Alaska Department of Fish and Game believes the number of moose-vehicle collisions may actually be up to 15 percentage points higher, since accidents are often unreported. In New Hampshire, around 250 moose-vehicle collisions occur annually, with most happening around dawn and dusk from April to November.

Drivers can reduce the possibility of a moose collision in many ways. Slowing down increases the odds of avoiding a moose, and also decreases the severity of impact and the likelihood of sustaining serious injury in a collision. Driving with greater vigilance in moose country, especially at dawn and dusk, also helps. Moose are hard to see at night. Utilizing high-beam lights when possible makes the animals more visible. Some evidence indicates moose are attracted to roadside "salt pools" that remain after highways have been salted to eliminate ice in the winter. Moose may frequent salty roadsides in the spring to obtain minerals.

Humans in vehicles pose a threat to moose, but moose may also be dangerous to humans. Bulls can become very hostile during the mating season. Cows are highly protective of their calves. Both sexes are known to engage in unpredictable, aggressive behavior at all seasons of the year. Moose most frequently attack by flailing their front hooves at a perceived threat or opponent. A blow from a moose's hoof can crush a human's skull or easily break other bones. Most people fear grizzly bears, but the danger posed by a belligerent moose is no less serious than a riled bruin.

Giving moose a wide berth, viewing them from a distance, and making noise to alert them of your human presence are the simplest strategies to avoid conflict. Surprised at close range, moose sometimes give physical signals of impending aggression before charging. Raised hair on the neck and back, laid-back ears, and agitated snorting all indicate a moose is upset. Exiting the area as quickly as possible (at a dead run if necessary) is advised by many wildlife officials when confronted with an upset moose. If the moose charges and you can't escape, ducking behind a tree or climbing it are other effective evasive strategies.

Moose can be dangerous and unpredictable, but most encounters with these creatures are quite the opposite. The opportunity to observe the behavior of this irreplaceable, intriguing member of the deer family is a real treat to wildlife enthusiasts. Whatever the future of these imposing creatures, human residents of North America inhabit a richer world in their presence.

Bull moose can be unpredictable and dangerous during the fall, and cows are very protective of their calves. Moose are best viewed from a distance and left alone.
© ISTOCK.COM/ PHOTOGRAPHY BYJHWILLIAMS

CHAPTER 3
MULE DEER

My head lolled from side to side as the aged Chevy pickup jounced slowly down a spit of a trail on a dusty ridge. It was hot. I was tired. A Saturday afternoon in September should be spent napping, or so my teenage brain told me. Instead, my dad had dragged my two brothers and me from the ranch house to repair fence on a wickedly steep slope on the back side of a mountain pasture. All I desired was sleep.

A quarter-mile from the terminus of the truck-trail, the driver inexplicably braked to a halt. Opening my left eye, I saw him squinting out the passenger-side window, intent on a yonder slope sprinkled with mountain mahogany, a smattering of junipers, and a few lone, stunted pine trees.

"See that buck?"

At his question, the optical organs in the heads of three adolescent hunters swiveled to look. I scanned the hillside for several minutes in silence, as did my elder siblings. None of us wanted to ask the inevitable, embarrassing question.

"Where is it?" I finally blurted in frustration.

"About two-thirds the way up, right under that big clump of buck brush."

"Buck brush" was dad's colloquial moniker for mountain mahogany. But there were dozens of "big clumps" of his buck brush on the upper side of the slope. I couldn't spy a buck under any of them.

"I still can't see it."

"All right. Can you see that little pine tree with the busted top?"

"Yep."

"Look about 20 yards below it."

Sure enough, there was the deer. Its body mostly concealed by a spreading mountain mahogany bush, a mule deer buck lay in its bed, peering in our direction. We didn't have binoculars, but Dad pulled his Model 70 Winchester .220 Swift rifle from the gun rack in the rear window of the pickup. We rested it on the hood and looked through the scope, taking turns to view the gray body of the motionless buck under the tiny, waxy leaves and dull branches of the buck brush. Its face was ashen with age, its antlers heavy, wide and dark. It watched us as intently as we viewed it but did

Mule deer are named for their over-size ears, reminiscent of those found on mules.
DOMINIC BALLARD

not bolt from hiding. Mule deer have a reputation as dimwits among hunters in many states, but those possessed of such sentiment have certainly never had the opportunity to witness the actions of a sagacious old stag.

"How did you ever see that deer?" I inquired as we clambered back into the cab of the three-quarter-ton pickup.

"Just have to know what to look for," came my father's reply, accompanied by a rare smile.

My dad was a devoted mule deer hunter and observer. He had an uncanny ability to know where deer would be at certain times of the year and day, and he aptly illustrated the fact that intimate knowledge of a certain species in a particular environment is based as much on patient observation as copious reading or formal study.

NAMES AND FACES

Names and Visual Description

"Mule deer" is the name given to a medium-size ungulate inhabiting the western United States, Mexico, and Canada. The name refers to the species' exceptionally long ears that reminded early observers of those found on mules. However, the species has also been known as the black-tailed deer.

Mule deer have an overall grayish color in the winter. Their distinctive white rump sports a slender tail with a black tip.
JACK BALLARD

The interchangeable names originated at least as far back in history as the Lewis and Clark expedition. The species was first seen in northeastern Kansas by an expedition member on September 5, 1804, noted in Clark's journal as "deer with black tales." Two mule deer were killed shortly thereafter, on September 17. Several members of the expedition commented on them in their journals. Clark failed to name the animal but noted it was "a curious kind of deer" and different from the whitetail deer, or "common deer" as he called them. Ordway refers to them as "2 Black tailed deer which differ from the other Deer." Whitehouse notes the animals as "2 black taild Deer." Gass first notes the animals as "two black-tailed deer," but a few sentences later adds a longer commentary and another name. "The black-tailed, or mule deer have much larger ears than the common deer and tails almost without hair, except at the end, where there is a bunch of black hair."

Later descriptions of the species in the journals kept by various expedition members refer to the species as "mule deer" and "black tailed deer." In some cases both names are used by the same individual at different times. Some commentators identify the name "mule deer" as originating with Meriwether Lewis. However, Gass's commentary in the above journal reference suggests otherwise. Various explorers of western America predating the expedition would have doubtlessly encountered mule deer and perhaps named them as such. The first person to tag the species with the "mule deer" moniker is thus a matter of speculation. A strain of mule deer found along the Pacific Coast of the United States and Canada is known as "blacktailed deer" or "blacktail deer." In some regions of the southwestern United States, mule deer are sometimes called "burro deer."

The scientific name for the mule deer is *Odocoileus hemionus*. *Odocoileus* stems from two Greek words meaning "tooth" (*odon*) and "hollow" (*koilos*). *Odocoileus* is the first term in the scientific name of both mule and whitetail deer and references the structure of their molars. *Hemionus* is derived from the Latin name for wild ass (donkey). A rather literal and humorous rendering of the scientific name for mule deer is thus "hollow-toothed wild ass."

The bodies of mule deer are gray or grayish brown in fall and winter. The summer coat is tan or reddish brown. Mule deer have very large ears in relation to their head. Their rump is white or cream, with the light coloration continuing down the inside of their rear legs. The inner sides of the front legs are also creamy or white. A light throat patch is evident on most animals. On some, the throat patch is divided by a band of darker hair. In the fall and winter pelage, the brisket and sternum are covered in dark gray hair. The tail of a mule deer is white, tipped in black. The blacktail strain of the species has a tail that is wholly or mostly black on the visible portions. The portion of white rump hair is smaller on blacktail deer, occurring mostly under the tail. Males of the species carry antlers; females do not.

Related Species in North America

The mostly closely related species to mule deer in North America is the whitetail deer. In some places, the two species infrequently interbreed. Genetic analysis of mule deer in Montana indicates some historic interbreeding of the two species.

Several physical features distinguish the species. Overall coloration is one clue at certain times of the year, but not completely diagnostic. During fall and winter, mule deer tend to exhibit a gray or grayish brown hue, while whitetails typically appear more tan or brown. More telling is the length of the ears and shape and color of the tail. The ears of whitetails are shorter than those of mule deer and look more proportionate to the size of their head. The tail of a whitetail deer is tan or brown on the outside, white underneath. It is wider at the base and tapers noticeably to the tip. The tail of a mule deer appears more ropelike (especially in summer), does not taper, and is white, tipped in black.

The antlers of mature mule deer and whitetail deer usually have different configurations, although exceptions are frequent. The tines, or points, on a whitetail buck's antlers sprout from a single main beam, similar to pickets jutting from a single top rail on a fence. The main beam of a mule deer buck's antlers forks, with each branch again forking toward the top of the antlers. Yearling bucks of both species often have antlers with a single fork.

Mule deer are closely related to whitetail deer, and the two species are sometimes confused. Whitetail have a more brownish coloration in winter, shorter ears, and a longer, brown, tapered tail than mule deer.
JACK BALLARD

Along with whitetail deer, mule deer share range with elk, moose, pronghorn, bighorn sheep, and mountain goats. Mule deer aren't easily mistaken for elk or moose due to their different coloration and size. However, exceptionally large bucks may briefly be confused with bull elk in silhouette at a distance when facing directly toward or away from the viewer. If the animal turns, the different configuration of an elk's antlers and body shape quickly differentiates the species. Pronghorn, bighorn sheep, and mountain goats are easily differentiated from mule deer because of differences in size and the fact that deer carry antlers and the other species have horns. At a distance, bighorn sheep and mule deer females might be confused, but a closer view that reveals horns readily distinguishes the species.

Subspecies of Mule Deer

At least ten subspecies of mule deer have been recognized since the 1930s. Like other mammals, current theories regarding mule deer subspecies are not all in agreement. Although genetic analysis of mule deer from various parts of the country has shown considerable variation, opinions on the exact genetic or more visible physical attributes upon which subspecies designations should rest are not shared by all experts. As of 2005 the taxonomic encyclopedia of world mammals published by Johns Hopkins University Press listed ten mule deer subspecies.

Two subspecies of blacktail deer represent what is thought to be a separate strain of mule deer occupying Pacific coastal regions. The Columbia blacktail deer (*Odocoileus hemionus columbianus*) occupies coastal mountain ranges and some interior regions of California, Oregon, Washington, and British Columbia, including Vancouver Island. The Sitka blacktail deer (*Odocoileus hemionus sitkensis*) is found in the coastal mountains of northern British Columbia and Alaska. They have also been introduced on some islands, most notably Kodiak Island in Alaska. Blacktail deer are notably smaller, on average, than other mule deer species. Their antlers are smaller as well.

The most numerous and widespread of the remaining eight mule deer subspecies is the Rocky Mountain mule deer (*Odocoileus hemionus hemionus*). This subspecies is found in the entire mule deer range in the United States and Canada (as described in the next section) except for the blacktail deer range noted above, most of California, western Texas, and the southern regions of New Mexico and Arizona. This subspecies produces animals with the largest bodies.

Desert mule deer (*Odocoileus hemionus eremicus*) occupy the second-largest area of any subspecies. They are found in southern Arizona and New Mexico, with their range extending into western Texas and north-central Mexico. Males of this subspecies in Mexico often carry exceptionally large antlers.

The remaining subspecies roam over much more limited range. The California mule deer (*Odocoileus hemionus californicus*) is found in portions of central and southern California. Inyo mule deer (*Odocoileus hemionus inyoensis*) are restricted to the Sierras of eastern California. Southern mule deer (*Odocoileus hemionus fuliginatus*), another subspecies, is found in a small portion of southwestern California and the northern part of the Baja Peninsula. The southern part of the Baja Peninsula is home to the Peninsular mule deer (*Odocoileus hemionus peninsulae*). Two subspecies are found on islands off the Baja Peninsula: the Cedros Island mule deer (*Odocoileus hemionus cerrosensis*) and the Tiburon Island mule deer (*Odocoileus hemionus sheldoni*).

Debate exists regarding the legitimacy of the Inyo subspecies. Some biologists also believe the two island subspecies are simply isolated populations of mainland deer. These and other issues, along with future information gleaned from genetic analysis, may well see the number of mule deer subspecies shrink, as has been the case for most large mammal species in North America in the past few decades.

Two varieties of blacktail deer are considered subspecies of mule deer. This Sitka blacktail doe was photographed at Kodiak National Wildlife Refuge in Alaska.
USFWS/STEVE HILLEBRAND

The classification of the blacktail subspecies of mule deer has left more than a few biologists scratching their heads for many years. These coastal deer are most obviously different from other mule deer. Taxonomists categorizing animals have often felt obligated to identify them as a distinct "race" or "strain" of mule deer, not merely a subspecies. At times people have wondered why they are not listed as a distinct species.

A genetic analysis of mule deer subspecies undertaken by university researchers and published in 2009 intended to analyze ancient glacial activity in relation to deer genetics found a notably high level of genetic variation between blacktails and other mule deer. The authors caution against making taxonomical judgments on the basis of a single study but conclude that the classification of blacktails as subspecies might warrant reconsideration. Depending on one's definition of "species" there may be enough evidence to classify blacktails separately from their mule and whitetail kin.

Physical Characteristics

The bodies of mule deer often appear blockier than those of their whitetail cousins. They are slightly larger, on average, as well. Bucks typically weigh from 130 to 250 pounds. Exceptionally large bucks can weigh more than 300 pounds, and a few cases of mule deer bucks exceeding 400 pounds have been recorded. A massive buck killed by a hunter in Colorado in 1938 is reported as having a dressed weight of 410 pounds, which would yield a live weight of a bit over 500 pounds. In hunted populations, few bucks reach an age to achieve maximum body size. Does are lighter than bucks of equivalent age. Weights for does normally range from 110 to 170 pounds. Sitka blacktail deer are notably smaller than other subspecies. Sitka bucks average around 120 pounds; does average about 80 pounds.

Mule deer typically stand between 32 and 42 inches at the shoulder. Their nose-to-tail length ranges from around 4 to 7 feet. The tail of a mule deer is usually 5 to 9 inches long.

Male mule deer are called bucks, females are called does, and their young are referred to as fawns.

Antlers and Antler Development

Mule deer bucks often grow massive antlers. Antlers begin growing in spring, sprouting from bony projections on the buck's skull known as pedicles. The developing antlers are covered in a skin-like tissue. Due to its fuzzy appearance, this tissue is often called velvet. The velvet contains a network of blood vessels supplying nutrition to the growing antlers.

Antlers are first noticeable on mule deer bucks about the time they reach their first birthday. A buck's first set of antlers are quite small. Most exhibit a "forkhorn" configuration that consists of a single fork in a slender beam, resulting in two antler tines. The horns of some yearling bucks are present as a "spike," which refers to an antler that does not branch at all. In some cases, yearling bucks may have antlers with more than two tines.

The antlers of mature bucks grow rapidly and are fully developed by mid- to late summer. A very large-antlered mule deer may carry antlers with a combined weight of more than 10 pounds. Mule deer bucks attain their maximum potential for antler growth at 5 to 7 years of age. Genetics, age, and nutrition are the three factors most widely believed to influence antler growth. Poor habitat conditions resulting from drought or overgrazing and the resulting nutritional deficiencies for mule deer is thought to reduce antler growth in mature bucks by up to 20 percent.

Large antlers on a mule deer buck require considerable nutrition to grow. Mule deer bucks usually grow their biggest antlers at 5 to 7 years of age.
JACK BALLARD

Mule deer bucks shed their antlers each year, usually in mid- to late winter. The antlers of small deer may be cast considerable distances and days apart. Large antlers often fall quite close together. The weight imbalance to a deer's head caused by the loss of one antler probably increases the likelihood that the other will soon fall.

RANGE AND HABITAT

North American Range—Historic

The actual historic range of mule deer can be estimated, but like other North American mammals, the species' status prior to European exploration and settlement is unknown. Journals and documents of early explorers strongly indicate that common ungulates like mule deer were not uniformly distributed across their range. Lewis and Clark, for example, found mule deer in abundance along the Missouri River once they entered Montana. The animals were scarce to the east, and once west of Three Forks, Montana, the captains again found game in short supply, although the habitat was certainly favorable. Similarly, mountain men in California in the early 1800s recorded few mule deer where the species thrived by the thousands in the late twentieth century. Some historians believe that hunting by native peoples exerted significant pressure on mule deer (and other ungulate) numbers even before the arrival of Europeans in North America. Captain William Clark asserted that the abundance of game along the Missouri River in Montana and elsewhere might be due to the region's status as disputed territory into which warring groups were reluctant to venture. His journal entry on August 29, 1806, makes such an assertion. "I have observed that in the country between the nations which are at war with each other the greatest numbers of wild animals are to be found."

Mule deer were historically associated with western North America. In the United States they occurred west of the Mississippi River. Their range likely covered the present-day western Canadian provinces of British Columbia, Alberta, and Saskatchewan, and the western and southern portions of Manitoba. A line drawn from the southeastern corner of Manitoba at the Minnesota border, continuing directly south through the middle of Minnesota and Iowa, then veering southwestward to the southern tip of Texas's western panhandle roughly delineates the eastern boundary of the mule deer's historic range in the United States. The western boundary is the Pacific Coast. However, the entire area was not occupied by mule deer, as certain areas did not contain suitable habitat.

Members of the Lewis and Clark Expedition regularly encountered mule deer on the Dakota and Montana prairies.
JACK BALLARD

North American Range—Current

Current mule deer range has probably shrunk somewhat in comparison to historic range on its eastern edge. However, mule deer probably range over most of the same area as they did in pre-colonial times. Although extirpated from some places in the late 1800s, mule deer have naturally recolonized much of their range and have been transplanted by wildlife management agencies to establish populations in others.

The approximate eastern edge of current mule deer range in the United States (starting in the north) runs through the middle of the following states: North Dakota, South Dakota, Nebraska, and Kansas. From there it run southwest through the Oklahoma panhandle to the southeastern corner of New Mexico and continues south-southeasterly to the Mexico border.

Mule deer are sometimes recorded east of this line. For example, mule deer have been killed by hunters in eastern Iowa and are occasionally reported in western Minnesota. However, these animals are not thought to be associated with resident, breeding populations. In 2015 a hunter killed a mule deer buck in Wisconsin. Whether the deer was wild or escaped from a game farm was not determined at the time it was taken.

West of the above boundary, mule deer roam the United States to the Pacific Coast. Certain large areas are devoid of deer, as are many smaller regions of unsuitable

Mule deer, like this doe in the rain forest at Olympic National Park, range from the central plains to the rain forests of the Pacific Coast.
© ISTOCK.COM/TAYA JOHNSTON

habitat. The valleys of central California between the Coastal Range and the Sierra Nevada and Cascade Mountains are one such area, as are the Mojave and Sonoran Deserts in southern California and southwestern Arizona.

In Mexico, mule deer are found in the north-central part of the country, about 300 miles south of the Arizona border and on the Baja Peninsula. Canada holds mule deer west of a line drawn from the southeastern to the northeastern corners of Saskatchewan and westward. Sightings of mule deer are sometimes reported in Manitoba. Mule deer habitat runs from the northern boundary of British Columbia into the south-central portion of the Yukon Territory, where the animals are occasionally harvested by hunters. Coastal populations of mule deer are also found in southeastern Alaska and on some islands off the Pacific Coast, including Vancouver Island in British Columbia and the Kodiak Islands of Alaska. Mule deer have also been introduced in Hawaii. (For information on the range of mule deer subspecies, see the discussion in the beginning of this chapter.)

Mule Deer Habitat

Mule deer are found in a diverse array of habitats, from the coastline of the Pacific Ocean to elevations higher than 13,000 feet above sea level in the alpine zones of Colorado. They tiptoe through dense, coastal forests in Washington and track semi-deserts in Arizona. Mule deer are also creatures of flatlands, thriving in both the low-elevation prairies of the western Dakotas and the high plains of Wyoming and Oregon.

The Western Association of Fish and Wildlife Agencies has identified seven "ecoregions" consisting of diverse habitat types that support mule deer: California Woodland Chaparral, Colorado Plateau Shrubland and Forest, Coastal Rain Forest, Great Plains, Intermountain West, Northern Forest, and Southwest Desert. Although the habitat contained in these various regions may differ dramatically in terms of plant species, annual precipitation, average temperature, amount of vegetative cover, elevation, and human use, they all provide mule deer the necessities of life and reproduction.

No matter what ecoregion they occupy, certain habitat elements are critical to mule deer. For all but the deer in the southernmost portions of their range, winter habitat is thought to be a limiting factor. Mule deer cannot survive severe winters (deep snow and cold temperatures) in the absence of range that provides access to consistent food sources, primarily woody browse on trees and shrubs.

Frenzied energy exploration and development in areas such as central and southern Wyoming in the 1990s and 2000s may have had considerable impact on winter range.

A recent, very long-term study of mule deer in Wyoming indicates that animals avoid energy development areas long after the initial exploration and drilling has

Adequate winter range is considered a limiting factor in the overall distribution of mule deer.
JACK BALLARD

ceased. The study examined radio-collared deer over a seventeen-year period, including two years prior to energy development and fifteen years during development. Mule deer were found normally to maintain slightly more than a half-mile distance from well pads during the development period, despite concerted mitigation efforts. This points to a significant loss of winter range, although the study noted that in times of particular severity and nutritional distress, deer might venture closer to energy infrastructure. Mule deer numbers dropped by 36 percent during the period of energy development, despite a 45 percent reduction in harvest by hunters.

Habitat also requires cover for birthing areas and escape from predators. Surface water is another limiting factor. Mule deer in arid regions can glean moisture from succulent plants, but they require some source of water to fully meet their needs.

In short, mule deer habitat must provide the species' demands for water, cover, and nutrition. Various ecoregions provide for these in different ways, with deer occupying different regions utilizing habitat in different ways.

NUTRITIONAL REQUIREMENTS AND FORAGE

Nutritional Requirements

Biologists have identified five components of mule deer nutrition: energy, protein, vitamins, minerals, and water. The specific requirements of these vary from season to season and in relation to the status of a particular deer. For example, a doe that failed to conceive a fawn the previous fall needs far less protein in her early-summer diet than a female nursing twins. Young animals also need sufficient protein levels to obtain maximal growth. Minerals are important to all deer, but older bucks need certain minerals

in abundance for maximum antler growth. With all mule deer, the availability of various nutritional components ebbs and flows with the seasons, with animals adapted to exploit seasonally abundant nutritional sources in relation to physical needs.

Energy is important throughout the year, but it's most available in plants during summer and fall. Insufficient energy in the diet can lead to low or no reproduction, weight loss, impaired growth, and compromised digestive function. A severe lack of nutritional energy can lead to starvation. Deer rarely find enough energy resources for daily maintenance during winter. Body fat stored from excess energy intake during summer and fall provides the necessary fuel to survive the

Mule deer rely on fat reserves from excess energy consumed during summer for winter survival.
JACK BALLARD

winter and, in the case of pregnant does, nurture a developing fawn.

Protein is required for body maintenance, growth, reproduction, and lactation (milk production). Plant protein levels are typically reported as "crude protein," or CP. Mule deer need 6 to 7 percent crude protein for minimal body health and to sustain the digestive function of the rumen. Robust growth, reproduction, and antler development demand 13 to 16 percent CP. Protein demands for pregnant does are highest

during the last 2.5 months of gestation and cannot be met through forage, which is at its lowest quality at this time of year (late winter, early spring). Stored protein is thus transferred from reserves in the doe's body to her developing fetus. She will regain protein during the spring and summer months, when it is most available from green plants.

Obtaining adequate protein is a nutritional issue for mule deer in many places and has been implicated in poor reproduction and declining numbers. One study of mule deer in the Texas panhandle found maximum CP levels of approximately 10 percent during spring, dropping to roughly 7 percent the rest of the year in one area. In another, deer had access to some agricultural crops that allowed them a diet including 13 percent CP in

Vitamins are essential for mule deer health and necessary for good antler growth in bucks. Green summer forage is an important source of vitamins.
JACK BALLARD

spring, and 8 to 11 percent at other times of the year. Even in the best study area, mule deer found minimal levels of protein for body maintenance and reproduction. Mule deer in other arid areas of the southwestern United States are frequently challenged by less-than-optimal protein levels in their forage.

Like people, mule deer need their vitamins. Deer require vitamin D, which they obtain from sunlight, just like humans who spend time outdoors. Vitamins A and E are the other two vitamins known to be very important for mule deer health. These are obtained primarily from leafy green plants and are most abundant in spring and summer. Vitamin A is essential for antler growth in mule deer bucks. Even after they begin to nibble green forage on their own, young fawns obtain much of their vitamin requirements from their mother's milk.

Minerals are required for body function in mule deer. Many of these are identified as "trace minerals" because they are needed in very low amounts. Trace minerals important to mule deer include chlorine, iron, magnesium, potassium, and zinc. These and other trace minerals are normally found at sufficient levels in mule deer forage. Two other minerals, calcium and phosphorous, are required at much higher levels and are not always readily available in forage. Adequate growth levels in mule deer require a diet including 0.4 percent calcium and 0.28 percent phosphorous. Higher levels of phosphorous are needed for maximal muscle and skeletal development of young bucks. Sufficient phosphorous is also believed to be necessary for maximum antler growth in older animals. In addition to basic levels, the ratio of calcium to phosphorous is instrumental in the absorption of these minerals. Equal levels or those containing up to twice the amount of calcium in relation to phosphorous are optimal. Ideal mineral levels for mule deer are best obtained when animals have access to a wide variety of plant species.

Water is the final component of mule deer nutrition. Availability of drinking water is an element of adequate habitat, but moisture intake from surface water for mule deer varies by region and season. Spring and early summer forage can contain up to 90 percent moisture. For young deer, with limited rumen (stomach) capacity, this may lead to excessive moisture volume in the digestive tract, which can impede nutrient intake. By midsummer, mule deer in most locations will certainly need some source of surface water to meet their requirements. A summer study of mule deer in the arid Picacho Mountains found animals visiting a man-made watering area at least once per day. Average consumption per drinking episode was 1 gallon. Bucks consumed an average of 0.94 gallon per watering episode in late summer, while the average intake of does was 1.1 gallons. The higher intake by does was perhaps due to increased moisture demands of lactation.

Mule deer acquire substantial moisture from succulent forage, but surface water is required to sustain them during dry seasons.
JACK BALLARD

A five-year study of summer water use by mule deer in western Utah supports the notion that mule deer need less surface water during wet years, when forage retains more moisture, and during cooler periods. Mule deer visited permanent water sources much less frequently during a summer following exceptionally high precipitation in spring. Deer drank, on average, about once every 1.5 days. The average might also be interpreted as a consumption pattern of two out of three days. Most visits to water sources occurred in late evening or at night. Bucks and does at some of the seventeen monitored sites showed strong preferences for water sources not shared by animals of the opposite gender, suggesting that differing home ranges of bucks and does may best be served by multiple water sources. One mature, identifiable buck used just one water source for four years of the study.

Digestion

The digestive system of a mule deer has the same basic configuration as that of other ruminants (animals that ruminate, or chew their cud). A deer has a four-chambered stomach or four stomachs, depending on one's terminology. Mule deer consume forage rapidly with virtually no chewing. The forage is swallowed and contained in the rumen, the largest compartment of the stomach. At times of inactivity, food stored in the rumen is regurgitated and chewed. "Cud" is the formal term for the regurgitated mass.

After the cud is chewed and re-swallowed, it enters the reticulum, which teems with microorganisms. The food is fermented in the reticulum, breaking down cellulose and producing methane gas. After further rumination, the food mass passes into the third chamber of the stomach, the omasum. Water is extracted in the omasum before the mass passes into the abomasum. The abomasum contains gastric juices similar to the human stomach, which further the digestive process. From the abomasum food passes into the deer's intestinal tract for extraction of nutrition. A mule deer's intestines may be 28 feet long. The final aspect of digestion is further extraction of moisture before waste is expelled in feces, most often formed into oval-shaped pellets.

The digestive system of a mule deer is adapted to extract nutrition from a wide variety of food sources, from grasses to twigs and leaves.
LISA BALLARD

The transition from dry, woody forage in late winter to lush grass and forbs can create a serious digestive challenge for mule deer. The microorganisms in the animal's gut are adapted to digesting various food sources throughout the year. A sudden "green up" in spring may find deer gorging on green forage their digestive system is not ready to handle. This may lead to starvation or scours, an illness spawning sometimes debilitating diarrhea. Actual death from winter malnutrition can occur at this point, with animals dying on a full stomach of green, highly nutritious forage.

Food Sources

An analysis of nearly one hundred studies of mule deer diets concluded that the animals consume nearly 800 different types of plants across their North American range. But the number can be deceiving. Mule deer are actually rather selective feeders compared to some other ungulates, such as elk. The smaller digestive system of the deer requires them to continually seek out the most nutritious food sources in their range at various times of the year. The myriad plant species eaten by mule deer are best understood as a function of the very wide array of their occupied habitats, not a testament to an animal that can consume almost anything.

Mule deer diets can be broadly analyzed in relation to three types of plants: grasses and grasslike species, forbs (broad-leafed plants), and browse (twigs, buds, and leaves of trees and shrubs). These types of plants are eaten by mule deer in varying ratios over their range. The mix of plant types in a deer's diet also changes with the season. Given the sheer diversity of mule deer habitat, it is nearly impossible to describe the "average" or "normal" diet of a mule deer except with regard to specific ecoregions and habitat types.

Grass is typically most important when it first sprouts during spring. Greening grass often represents the earliest source of new forage after the dormancy of winter. Grass may compose as much as 60 percent of a mule deer's spring diet or represent an insignificant amount of forage. In most habitats, grass drops to around 10 percent or less of the mule deer diet at other seasons of the year. Mule deer may feed heavily on grasslike small-grain crops such as wheat, barley, and oats where they are present. These are usually consumed in spring and summer, but fall-planted wheat is eaten as well. Grasses consumed by mule deer include both native and nonnative species that have naturalized or been planted for livestock pasture. Wheatgrasses, bluegrasses, bromegrass, fescues, and needlegrass are among the species commonly eaten by mule deer.

Many species of forbs provide outstanding nutrition for ungulates and are regularly sought by mule deer. Forb use typically peaks in summer, but forbs represent an important part of the diet for mule deer in many places in spring and fall as well. Forbs may constitute as much as 75 percent of the summer and fall diet for some mule deer; for others they make up less than 5 percent of the fare during these seasons.

Forbs commonly eaten by mule deer include arrowleaf balsamroot, lupine, certain types of thistle, dandelions, sagewort, fleabane, fireweed, yarrow, clovers, salsify, and many others. Alfalfa cultivated for hay or livestock pasture factors prevalently in the diet of mule deer where available. Other broad-leafed crops are also eaten in agricultural areas.

Forbs, such as the fireweed this buck is eating in Yellowstone National Park, often make up the majority of a mule deer's summer diet.
LISA BALLARD

Browse from trees and shrubs is foundational to the diet of mule deer over most of their range, particularly in winter. Deer can nibble twigs from trees and shrubs when cured grass and forbs are buried in snow. Over most of their interior range, healthy shrub communities and the presence of early succession (young) deciduous trees are assumed to be among the most critical components of quality mule deer habitat.

Sagebrush, mountain mahogany, bitterbrush, and quaking aspen are critical sources of nutrition for wintering mule deer in the foothills and high plains and are eaten at other times of the year as well. Gambel oak, Mexican cliffrose, wild rose, chokecherry, and skunkbush sumac are other important browse species. Mule deer also consume some coniferous trees and shrubs (especially in winter), such as creeping juniper. Conifer intake usually makes up a minor portion of the diet, as evergreen needles contain compounds that impede digestion. Catkins, buds, and leaves of trees and shrubs are eaten by mule deer in spring, summer, and fall. In many populations, browse represents about half or more of the mule deer diet in all seasons of the year.

Mule deer also favor berries and the fruit or seedpods of numerous trees and shrubs. Lichens are a significant food source for wintering deer in California's Sierra Nevada and may be eaten elsewhere. Mushrooms are a desired menu item for mule deer in certain areas of the Rocky Mountains. Mushrooms are a good source of protein and minerals.

Migration

Mule deer migrate in numerous locations, typically traveling from summer to winter ranges. These annual movements can cover just a few miles when deer complete elevational migrations, shifting between alpine or other mountainous areas in summer to foothills or other lower-elevation winter range. However, some mule deer herds follow ancient migratory routes spanning 150 miles that move them between winter-

Mule deer embark upon migrations of more than 100 miles in some places as they move from summer to winter range.
JACK BALLARD

ing areas and summer habitat. These dramatic journeys may find the animals crossing massive mountain ranges, fording rivers, and scaling man-made impediments such as highways and fences. Many seasonal migrations see changes in elevation from summer to winter range of 3,000 to 4,000 feet, sometimes more.

The longest known mule deer migration was discovered by accident. Researchers in Wyoming's Red Desert radio-collared several deer in winter 2011. When spring came, about half the collared deer left the area, embarking on a 150-mile migration that found them in the Hoback region (south of Grand Teton National Park) by midsummer. The animals returned to their wintering grounds on the Red Desert in the fall.

Since then, other long-distance migrations in Wyoming have been discovered. Some mule deer summering in Grand Teton National Park follow three impressive migration routes to wintering areas east of the mountains. One of these winds through the southeastern portion of Yellowstone National Park, leading deer to lower areas on the North Fork of the Shoshone River. The second traces through a series of mountain passes in two wilderness areas before scaling the Absaroka Range leading to the South Fork of the Shoshone River. The final migration takes deer up the Gros Ventre River drainage then over the Continental Divide before dropping to winter range in the Dubois area.

In fall 2015, Grand Teton National Park biologists discovered yet another area migration route. This one took a radio-collared mule deer doe in the opposite direction. The intrepid female crossed the northern flank of the rugged Teton Range on a westward journey, terminating on winter range south of Ashton, Idaho.

Similar mule deer migration routes have been documented elsewhere. Mule deer from the Paunsaugunt Plateau in southwestern Utah migrate from high-elevation areas to lower terrain, some of the animals heading south to winter in northeastern Arizona. Deer have been documented traveling from around 8 to 45 miles during the migration, with bucks frequently crossing hunting unit boundaries during the fall. Wildlife biologists in Montana have also tracked migratory animals that traveled in autumn from the western side of Yellowstone National Park to the Stillwater River drainage on the east side of the Beartooth Mountains.

Less-dramatic migrations take mule deer from alpine areas at timberline in the Rocky Mountains to wintering areas in the foothills. Such is the case in the Bighorn Mountains of north-central Wyoming, near the winsome community of Sheridan. Mule deer find ideal summer range on the peaks, plateaus, and hanging basins of the Bighorns. Come fall, they drop to the foothills and prairies on the east side of the range. Biologists have observed that the onset of bad weather as early as October may move these deer from the mountaintops to the lowlands in a matter of days.

ABILITIES AND BEHAVIOR

Physical Abilities

The mule deer's most unusual characteristic among North American ungulates is perhaps its gait (method of running). Mule deer walk and trot similar to whitetail deer and elk. But their maximum speed is gained by a gait known as "stotting." A stotting animal does not gallop like a horse or bound like a cheetah. Rather it propels itself forward with all four legs at a time, which creates a bouncing gait. Mule deer in full flight are sometimes described as having a pogo-stick bounce or hopping like four-legged kangaroos.

Despite the deer's odd and sometimes comical-appearing means of locomotion, stotting mule deer are no slowpokes. A California game biologist in the 1940s recorded a mule deer running at 36 miles per hour. After an initial burst of speed, the animal slowed to about 21 miles per hour and was soon short of breath. The same biologist measured the distance between stotting bounds of a mule deer and found the animal covering as much as 23 feet in a single bound on flat ground. A mule deer stotting down a 7-degree slope was able to propel itself 28 feet in a bound.

Mule deer can jump fences more than 6 feet high. They must frequently jump livestock fences over much of their range.
JACK BALLARD

Mule deer can carry speeds of around 18 miles per hour over distances of a mile or more. Their unusual gait is ideally suited for escaping predators in broken and brushy terrain. A stotting mule deer easily bounces over brush and rocks a running predator must go around. They accelerate very quickly when moving downhill and can easily leap over narrow gullies. The stotting gait also allows mule deer to change directions in a single bound, a very useful ability in evading predators and rapidly navigating rough terrain. Mule deer easily jump the livestock fences typically found on their range and are known to sometimes jump fences over 6 feet high.

Like their whitetail cousins, mule deer are good swimmers. They have been documented swimming across lakes on migration routes and crossing major rivers. Two young mule deer were once observed in a California lake, swimming back and forth and in circles much like dogs enjoying the water. Mule deer does have been reported swimming to islands in the Columbia River where they birth fawns. Their swimming ability is supported by very strong legs and buoyant, highly-insulating hair. Fat stored under the skin and around internal organs also helps mule deer float at times when animals are in good body condition.

Blacktail deer are sometimes observed swimming in the ocean off the Alaskan coast. One instance reported by a Juneau newspaper told of a family on a fishing boat pulling four exhausted young bucks on board. The ani-

A fawn lands then propels itself forward with all four feet in the "stotting" gait peculiar to mule deer.
JACK BALLARD

mals lay on the deck recovering while the boat motored to a dock. Three of the animals soon ran into a nearby forest, but the fourth required a lengthy rest before marshaling the energy to depart. Another account describes an Alaska State Trooper ferrying a tired buck to shore near Ketchikan after it attempted to crawl onto a patrol boat. State biologists believe these animals were likely chased into the water by wolves or other predators, or may be young animals attempting a water dispersion to find a new home range.

The sensory capabilities of mule deer are thought to be similar to those of whitetails. The eyeballs of mule deer function differently than those of humans. While people's eyes are especially adapted to discerning color and capable of discriminating fine detail, mule deer vision excels in low-light perception and the ability to detect motion. The horizontal slit of a mule deer's pupil contrasts with the round shape of a human's. This feature, coupled with the mule deer's highly developed ability to rotate its eyeballs, makes it capable of detecting distant motion while grazing or browsing at ground level, an extremely useful ability in sighting and eluding predators.

Another notable feature of mule deer vision is field of view. While a human's peripheral vision extends to about 180 degrees, a mule deer's spans more than 300 degrees, thanks to eyeballs mounted to the sides of its head versus the front.

Mule deer also have a very sophisticated sense of smell. It is believed they can detect odors up to 1,000 times better than a human. They are also able to discern and analyze more than one smell at once. The scent of *Homo sapiens* hunters or four-legged predators can be smelled by a mule deer at considerable distance and is an important survival mechanism, especially in areas of heavy cover where danger is not easily seen. One study in Montana of wintering mule deer concluded that the animals consistently alerted to human scent from an upwind position at 300 to 400 yards. Mule deer can reportedly smell water 2 feet below the soil surface and may excavate pits with their front hooves to obtain it.

The namesake ears of a mule deer are another of its sensory defenses against predators. Deer are assumed to have exceptional hearing, but little specific research on these and other sensory abilities has been conducted. One study of whitetail deer conducted by researchers at the University of Georgia found they were capable of hearing higher (ultrasonic) frequencies than humans. Their hearing was optimized at approximately the same tonal range or slightly higher than that of humans. Mule (and whitetail) deer have one notable hearing advantage over people: Their large ears can be moved independently, which allows them to pinpoint the exact source of a sound much more quickly than a person.

Vocal and Visual Communication

Mule deer communicate with several sounds, although the volume and frequency of such vocalizations are lower than with whitetails. Fawns and adults may bleat or make a barking noise when distressed. Low grunts are sometimes emitted by content animals or does tending their fawns. Bucks make a grunting sound during the mating season. Both bucks and does will sometimes be lured to the sound of clashing antlers during breeding season.

Among the more interesting research conducted on mule deer vocal communication is the way in which they may respond to calls made by other species. Researchers at the University of California found that mule deer became more vigilant after hearing the alarm calls of yellow-bellied marmots. A cooperative project by university researchers in the United States and Canada found mule deer does actively responding to the distress calls of several other mammal species, as long as they fell within the pitch range of fawn distress vocalizations. The does approached broadcasted recordings of anxiety cries of a range of other mammals, including humans, marmots, domestic cats, seals, and even bats. In some cases, the researchers manipulated the cries to fall within the pitch of the cries emitted by their own young.

A mule deer can move its ears independently, allowing it to quickly and accurately determine the source of a sound.
LISA BALLARD

Mule deer communication with one another through postures is more important on a routine basis than that of sounds. One of the most common indicators of this phenomenon is the transfer of the alert posture from one member of a herd to others. Biologists have observed that when one mule deer goes on alert, others usually respond to the visual cue, focusing their attention primarily on the direction they are facing until a specific threat has been detected.

A threat posture is another commonly used visual communication among mule deer. The aggressive animal thrusts its neck forward and lays back its ears, with its front feet spread widely apart. The threat posture might be followed by a lunge or hoof-strike if the animal at which it is directed does not yield to the aggressor. Aggression might also be communicated with a mule deer walking or trotting with its body held lower to the ground than usual and its neck outstretched.

An interesting form of nonverbal communication documented by a Montana researcher in the 1950s involves "displacement feeding." This behavior occurred when some intrusion on a mule deer (or a herd) caused mild arousal, but not enough to incite outright flight. Deer were seen nipping at forage but ingesting little to none. Displacement feeding often occurred for 10 to 15 minutes after arousal before deer settled.

Herd Behavior

Mule deer live in herds of a few to more than 100 animals for most of the year. Herds are typically largest during the winter months, when many deer, sometimes from diverse summer ranges, converge on wintering grounds.

Mule deer form the largest herds on winter range.
JACK BALLARD

During summer, does and bucks are usually found in separate bands, although bachelor bands of bucks sometimes contain an odd doe or two, and female herds may be joined by young bucks. Older bucks winter at higher elevations and segregated from larger, female-dominated groups in some places, but bucks and does frequently intermingle on winter range in other areas. Female herds in summer are often made up of animals related through an older matriarch or does sharing a maternal ancestor.

No matter what the herd composition, mule deer bands have a dominance hierarchy. Generally, older and larger animals dominate the younger. Fawns are always lowest in the pecking order. In groups of mixed genders, adult males (even yearlings) are dominant over females. Within bachelor herds consisting of a few or more than a dozen males, the largest male is almost always dominant. However, the social structure in buck herds can be altered when large-antlered dominant males cast their antlers before subordinates. If this occurs, males of a lower rank with their antlers intact may dominate higher-ranking bucks until they also have shed their antlers. Mule deer bucks with hard antlers (versus those still growing and covered with velvet) use antler swipes and hooking motions to maintain their dominance and as means of aggression. In the absence of antlers, mule deer bucks use their front hooves as weapons, similar to does.

REPRODUCTION AND YOUNG

The Mating Season

The mating season, or "rut," is a relatively short-lived phenomenon for mule deer in the northern and central Rocky Mountains, around twenty days—about the lifespan of a housefly. Does may conceive fawns in the weeks prior or subsequent to this primary breeding season, but in healthy deer populations occupying habitat in middle or northern latitudes within the contiguous United States, three out of four offspring birthed in spring are conceived during the approximately three-week period known as the rut. Year in and year out, the three final weeks of November span the major breeding period for mule deer from Colorado northward. One study in Montana found that 75 percent of the does that birthed a fawn the following spring conceived in the twelve-day period between November 21 and December 1. As is the case with other deer, the timing of the rut in southern mule deer populations typically occurs later (December to January) and is more drawn out than with northern animals. Considerable variation in the timing and intensity of the rut exists between various subspecies of mule deer and the region they inhabit.

For mule deer bucks, the hormonal shifts that culminate in a frenzied search for does with which to mate builds over time. Telltale signs of the rutting urge occur as early as mid-October, when aggression builds within herds of male deer and they began to go their separate ways. The hormonal shifts are most pronounced in older males, leading 3-year-old and older bucks to engage in the most intense and successful mating behaviors. By the first week in November, bucks are fully ready to breed, though few does are receptive to their courtship. Male mule deer are on the move at this time, actively seeking responsive does. They're often traveling at midday as well as during the traditionally active times of daylight and dusk.

Once he's discovered a doe that's ready to breed, a buck will remain with her for two or three days, waiting to sire his offspring. At this time his travels will mirror that of the doe. Whitetail bucks often herd the doe into seclusion, but mule deer bucks usually tend her in the presence of the doe herd with which she socializes.

Because a dominant buck is commonly spotted with a herd of does, some people conclude mule deer bucks gather a harem, similar to elk. This pattern of mating sees an ascendant bull elk gathering as many as a couple dozen cows to his company in early autumn. He stays with this herd throughout the breeding season, mating with each cow as she becomes receptive.

While a snapshot of a mule deer herd taken in mid-November with a regal buck in the company of multiple females appears to replicate this pattern, a more long-term

The breeding season for mule deer in the northern Rocky Mountain occurs primarily in late November. This buck tending a doe was photographed in Montana the week before Thanksgiving.
JACK BALLARD

Cooler weather may stimulate increased activity among rutting mule deer bucks, although decreasing daylight in autumn creates the hormonal changes in deer responsible for mating.
© ISTOCK.COM/TWILDLIFE

view illuminates a different program. A mule deer buck may keep company with a doe herd for more than a day or two, so long as there's a female in the group primed for breeding. However, in the absence of a receptive doe, the buck will abandon the herd to find another mate. This accounts for the "here today, gone tomorrow" pattern of mule deer bucks sometimes observed during the rut.

Buck activity can be quite variable from one week to the next during breeding season and can also seem inconsistent from year to year. This has led some observers to believe that cold temperatures or moon phases are important factors in the timing of the rut. However, the hormonal changes prompting mating behavior in mule deer have been definitively linked to photoperiod, or the diminishing amount of daylight that occurs during the fall. But while photoperiod induces the urge to rut, other factors may significantly influence deer behavior as well.

Among these, temperature is very important. By the time bucks are feeling the urge to seek does, their summer coat has been replaced with the dense, highly-insulating fur of winter. Cooler weather doesn't prompt the rut in a physiological sense, but it does make it more comfortable. Rubbing saplings with their antlers, sparring with other bucks, and traveling substantial distances are all high-demand physical activities. For a deer wearing its winter coat, 50°F is quite warm, even more so with exercise. Thus, when temperatures drop to freezing or below, bucks become more active during the rut.

Pregnancy and Gestation

Mule deer does typically conceive their first fawn as yearlings (approximately 1.5 years of age). Research indicates that yearling does breed around three to four weeks later than mature females. One eastern Montana study found that does from 4 to 6 years of age had the highest reproductive rates. Does more than 7 years old had fawn production rates around 15 to 20 percent lower than females of prime reproduction age. Along with age, other factors determine whether a mule deer doe will conceive a fawn. A strong relationship exists between body condition and pregnancy. Mature does in good body condition with sufficient fat reserves experience high conception rates. Those with less fat due to the nutritional stress of nursing fawns during drought years or other reasons are less likely to become pregnant. Does with less than optimal body condition that do conceive often do so later in the season than those in good health. Research in California found that pregnancy was much more likely in yearling blacktail does when lower deer numbers allowed access to better nutrition and boosted growth rates. Studies of reproductive rates and habitat quality in California and Utah documented fawn production nearly twice as high on productive habitat as in areas less suitable to mule deer. In arid regions toward the southern end of mule deer range in North America, low summer precipitation levels have correlated with low fawn production the following year.

The gestation period for mule deer is around 200 days. Variations have been reported as short as 183 days and as long as 218 days. Nutritional levels and local conditions are believed to affect the gestations period of individual animals.

Birth

Prior to giving birth, mule deer does isolate themselves in birthing areas that may be used in successive years. Ideal birthing sites include hiding cover for both the doe and her newborn fawn. Research in several states also indicates that ideal fawning areas are relatively close to water, although does in arid climates in the southwestern United States may not have the luxury of finding good birthing habitat close to a water source. One study in south-central Arizona concluded that does had to travel an average of nearly 2 miles to water from their fawning area.

Preferred fawning sites for does in the northwestern United States include cover consisting of shrubs or short trees dominating about half of the landscape. Habitat dominated by sagebrush tall enough to provide good cover is used as fawning sites for does in many areas. Although mule deer does generally avoid dense forests as birthing areas, they often drop their fawns adjacent to groves of quaking aspen or stands of juniper. Some research suggests that does inhabiting areas with abundant coyote populations may seek out steep slopes as birthing and fawn-rearing sites, as hunting coyotes prefer flat or modestly steep terrain.

Mule deer fawns average around 6 pounds at birth, but birth weights are quite variable within a range of 4.5 to 10 pounds. A multiyear study in Wyoming found a strong correlation between birth weight and survival, noting that an increase of 2 pounds of

A mule deer doe and her twin fawns are in fine physical condition in early winter. In good habitat, most does of peak reproductive age have twins.
JACK BALLARD

body weight at birth decreased a fawn's risk of predation by around 80 percent. Twins are commonly born to does during their prime reproductive years, while does birthing their first fawn are more likely to bear just one young. Incidence of twinning has also been linked to habitat conditions that may vary from year to year in the same location. A twelve-year study in prairie breaks habitat in Montana found that, on average, 55 percent of the does had twins, 44 percent had single fawns, and 1 percent birthed triplets. During years of abundant precipitation and mild winters, the twinning rate increased to 70 percent and the incidence of triplets to 3 percent. Single fawns are normally heavier at birth than twins, but no significant difference in average birth weight has been found between male and female fawns.

In northern populations, the vast majority of mule deer fawns (80 percent or more) are born within three to four weeks. Northern deer typically birth their young from late May to mid-June, though some later and earlier births may occur. Toward the southern end of their range, the birthing period occurs later, with most fawns born in July and August. Mule deer in Arizona have birthed fawns as late as October.

Nurturing Fawns to Adulthood

Once born, a fawn's primary survival strategy is to hide. Newborn mule deer fawns frequently spend considerable time away from their mother. Although they nurse frequently, nursing bouts typically last for just 10 minutes. The activities of both fawn and doe in the first weeks of the youngster's life are designed to minimize detection by a host of predators happy to prey upon vulnerable fawns.

Hiding is the main survival strategy for very young mule deer fawns.
© ISTOCK.COM/TWILDLIFE

At around 10 days of age, the fawn may follow the doe, but it continues its life of hiding for six to eight weeks. Mule deer fawns begin to supplement their mother's milk with other dietary sources quite quickly. At 2 weeks old, fawns begin ingesting green plants on their own where tender forage is available. Does usually remain on or near birthing areas for much of the summer. By fall, does and their fawns tend to congregate in female herds that consist of just a few deer to more than a dozen. Should they survive to fall, their first winter is routinely a challenge for fawns, especially during severe winters or those following a dry summer that yields poor forage for growing young.

Survival in the first year is an important benchmark for maintaining mule deer populations, as animals more than a year old are more winter hardy and old enough to begin their own reproductive life. Significant research has been conducted with radio-collared or otherwise monitored fawns to determine survival rates. The studies, while very valuable, typically do not consider fawn loss at birth, which might sometimes be substantial for poorly nourished does. One project in Wyoming documented that 15 percent of mule deer fawns were stillborn. In the first months of life, starvation, illness, and predation are the primary causes of fawn mortality. But natural accidents and vehicle collisions can be significant as well, accounting for 12 percent of fawns lost in the first few months of life in the Wyoming study. Researchers in west-central Colorado tracked fawns for six months shortly after birth (the average age was 3 days old when monitoring began) over a three-year period and found a 50 percent survival average. Of the fawns that died, three out of four had perished by 6 weeks of age, whether by predation or other causes.

Nutritious forage is critical to the growth of a mule deer fawn and its survival during its first winter.
© ISTOCK.COM/PHARMSHOT

However, six-month survival doesn't necessarily mean fawns will make it to a first birthday. Even during average winters, fawns are susceptible to starvation and predation. During severe winters, fawn mortality can be catastrophic. A recent study of mule deer in Wyoming found that 45 percent of fawns survived to be yearlings, with about one-fourth of the total mortality occurring during winter. The following year (2016–17) saw a very severe winter in which only one of seventy monitored fawns surviving as a yearling—a 99 percent mortality rate. The same winter saw very high winter mortality rates in portions of Idaho as well, essentially eliminating an entire age-class of animals from the population.

MULE DEER AND OTHER ANIMALS

Mule Deer and Other Ungulates

The wide distribution of mule deer in North America brings them into contact with a host of other hoofed herbivores. Their near kin, the whitetail deer, inhabits the same range in many places. Mule deer are commonly found in the same areas as elk in both mountain and prairie habitat. Mountain-dwelling deer may also track alpine uplands with bighorn sheep and mountain goats, while those on the prairie mix with bighorns, pronghorn, and sometimes bison. Mule deer subspecies common to forested regions of the continent mix with moose and even woodland caribou.

Where multiple ungulate species vie for the same resources, direct and indirect competition for physical space and forage sometimes occurs. Dietary overlap between species may be considerable, as can be the case for mule deer and other species (whitetail deer, elk, pronghorn) in certain regions and at specific times of the year. Thus, while the dietary overlap of several species may be small (perhaps 20 percent) when compared to one another, the overall reduction of a potential food source might have some population-impacting effect under certain conditions. For example, elk, mule deer, pronghorn, and bighorn sheep share portions of winter range in the northwestern corner of Yellowstone National Park and adjacent areas. Sagebrush is one source of winter forage in the area, a plant consumed by all four species. Does the sagebrush browse consumed by pronghorn leave less for bighorns? Do elk eat enough to deprive mule deer? While the obvious answer seems "yes," the extent to which dietary overlap might impact other species is thorny from the standpoint of research design and has not been widely studied.

There is, however, some evidence that abundant elk numbers might negatively influence mule deer, primarily on winter range. While mule deer numbers were generally decreasing across most of their range in the United States from the late 1960s through the close of the twentieth century, elk populations were often increasing, sometimes dramatically. In eastern Washington, researchers documented a corresponding decline in mule deer productivity when elk populations rapidly enlarged from 1980 to 2000. However, scientists are quick to point out that correlation does not necessarily imply causation. Mule deer numbers and fawn production also decreased in areas where elk were not present. Nonetheless, biologists in several states have tentatively identified competition with elk as a potential suppressor of mule deer populations.

Research at one wintering area in Montana found that elk consumed significant amounts of antelope bitterbrush, a winter staple for mule deer. Researchers at the Starkey Experimental Forest and Range in Oregon found that mule deer were generally leery of elk, which could cause them to be displaced when crowded onto winter range. Actual winter starvation of mule deer due to forage lost from elk on winter range is believed to be less of an issue than such factors as reduced fawn production due to nutritional stress on mule deer does. Many experts believe it is impossible to maintain super-abundant populations of even a single ungulate species on a range over a sustained period. The possibility of having enduring, extremely robust populations of mule deer and elk is unlikely anywhere. In response to current habitat limitations, some biologists believe certain areas should perhaps emphasize mule deer numbers with a deliberate effort to suppress populations of potentially-competing elk, primarily through hunting.

The relationship between mule deer and whitetail deer has received increasing interest in recent decades. Whitetails have expanded their range westward and northward west of the Mississippi River at the same time mule deer numbers have suffered. Many areas in Montana, Wyoming, Colorado, Idaho, and elsewhere now have substantial whitetail deer populations where they were absent or infrequent three decades ago. The bulging whitetail range has occurred noticeably along river bottoms and riparian areas, but the adaptable animals are also now found on native, semiarid prairies and at considerably higher elevations in some mountain ranges. I have personally observed whitetails at elevations up to 8,500 feet in the mountains of Montana and

Wyoming in the past two decades, in areas historically associated with only mule deer.

Some observers have concluded that whitetail deer may be responsible, at least in part, for mule deer declines in some areas. This, however, is an assertion based mainly on anecdotal evidence, inverse correlation of population levels, and theory, not research specific to the subject. Possible evidence for whitetail dominance includes anecdotal observations of whitetail deer "bullying" mule deer at common feed sources and on winter range. Whitetails may theoretically be more reproductively robust than mule deer—a substantial percentage of female whitetail fawns may conceive offspring in ideal habitat, while mule deer does rarely become pregnant their first year. The species also interbreed in some places, with most hybrid offspring being produced by the mating of a whitetail buck and a mule deer doe. This might also tip the reproduction equation toward whitetails, as a mule deer doe carrying a hybrid fawn doesn't add to the population of her species. Some evidence also suggests that mountain lions prey on mule deer at proportionately higher levels than whitetails where both species are present. These theories, while plausible on paper, may not be at all operative in the natural world. In the absence of more research, the answer to the question "Do whitetails affect mule deer populations?" is a very cautious "maybe."

Mule deer and whitetail occasionally interbreed in the wild. Offspring are typically from a mule deer doe and a whitetail buck (shown here).
CLAIRE O'CONNELL

Mule Deer and Predators

A host of predators prey on mule deer in varying numbers and at different points in their life cycle. A bobcat, for example, can be a surprisingly efficient predator of mule deer fawns, although an insignificant threat to adult animals. Black bears are similarly potent predators of fawns and of little concern to adults. Wolves and mountain lions, on the other hand, can capably kill mule deer at any time in their life cycle. Predators known to prey on mule deer include bobcats, mountain lions, black bears, grizzly bears, wolves, coyotes, wolverines, and golden eagles.

Predators accounting for the most annual mule deer mortality vary by region and ecosystem. Over much of their range, coyotes are the most significant predator, especially in the absence of mountain lions or black bears. Coyotes are responsible for very high mortality rates of mule deer fawns in some places. A study comparing predation rates on whitetail and mule deer fawns by coyotes in Colorado found that these canines consumed nearly 80 percent of the fawns that died early in life for both species. Total fawn mortality attributed to coyotes in various studies has ranged from 9 to 50 percent. Fawn predation by coyotes is influenced by several factors, including the presence of other prey species. Researchers have found that abundant populations of rodents, hares, and rabbits may reduce coyote predation on deer.

Mountain lions are highly efficient predators of both juvenile and adult mule deer. These felines may account for considerable fawn loss. Researchers in California in the early 1980s discovered that mountain lions accounted for half of the 50 percent mortality rate recorded among mule deer fawns. Of twenty-five radio-collared mule deer does, eleven were killed by mountain lions over a three-year period. A study in the Davis Mountains of western Texas found mule deer represented the highest percentage of mountain lion kills (24 percent) in an area where numerous species of mammals were available as prey, including mule deer, whitetail deer, elk, feral hogs, javelinas, and aoudads (a nonnative wild sheep). Other research suggests that mountain lions may disproportionately prey on mule deer than other ungulates in some places. Researchers in central Alberta, Canada, found that mountain lion predation was the leading cause of mortality among mule and whitetail deer in a multiyear study. Although whitetails were much more abundant, predation rates on mule deer by mountain lions were nearly twice as high as for whitetails.

Black bears are important predators of mule deer, primarily fawns, in some areas. Wolves also take significant numbers of mule deer, both adults and young, while bobcats prey mostly on fawns. One study in California of predation on mule deer fawns found that of the 50 percent of the fawn crop lost to predators, bobcats took 3 percent, black bears 22 percent, coyotes 27 percent, and mountain lions 49 percent. In a multi-predator environment, mule deer (especially fawns) may sustain significant losses from several major predators. However, the colonization of habitat by a major predator may actually be helpful to mule deer. Research indicates that the arrival of wolves can dramatically suppress coyote numbers and change habitat use of elk, which may result in mule deer being less frequently targeted by mountain lions. Such an occurence illustrates the often complex interactions between multiple predator and prey species.

A large body of research demonstrates a complex relationship between habitat, mule deer, and predators in which habitat, not predators, is most often the limiting factor in the total population. One study in Texas eliminated predators from a large fenced area. At first, deer numbers increased substantially, but then they declined to the point that they essentially mirrored population levels in the adjacent areas. Research suggests that predator removal may temporarily help compromised populations of mule deer under some conditions, but in normal circumstances it is habitat quality, not predators, that makes deer abundant or scarce.

Top: Mule deer are very vulnerable to predation as young fawns. It is not unusual for predators to take 50 percent of the fawn crop in some areas.
© ISTOCK.COM/CALINAT
Bottom: Coyotes prey on mule deer over much of their range, primarily on fawns in the first two months of life.
JACK BALLARD

Parasites and Diseases

Mule deer are hosts to an array of parasites and diseases across their range, some with insignificant physical consequences and others that are deadly under certain conditions. Parasites and diseases may be naturally occurring or, in many cases, originally transmitted to mule deer through domestic livestock or exotic animals. Most afflictions cause minor to moderate physical distress and pose minimal danger to healthy deer. Combined with malnutrition or mineral deficiencies, however, some diseases and parasites become a potent stressor of compromised deer and may contribute to mortality.

Internal parasites regularly occur in mule deer, usually in low to moderate infestations. Common parasites include flatworms, tapeworms, roundworms, and protozoa. Mule deer may also be plagued by nasal bots, larvae of the deer botfly (*Cephenemyia*). The larvae invade a deer's nasal cavity and may be found at the back of the mouth. Not an acute health threat, they are extremely bothersome and may stimulate aggressive sneezing or blowing when a deer tries to expel the pests. In some cases, localized infestations of certain intestinal parasites can be harmful or fatal. These often occur where deer are concentrated in a small area or come into frequent contact with livestock. For example, in spring 2011, residents near Roundup, Montana, reported numerous cases of mule deer with severe diarrhea, which appeared to have killed a number of them. The state's wildlife veterinarian found extreme concentrations of intestinal worms of the Trichostrongylidae family (roundworms) in the dead deer. The parasite enters mule deer through fecal matter on vegetation or other feed. High concentrations of deer around livestock feeding areas and scarce natural food sources after an exceptionally severe winter were assumed to be instrumental in in the parasite transmission.

Mule deer in some western states are infected with nonnative lice associated with western Eurasian fallow deer. The lice can create severe skin irritation, which causes deer to lick and rub themselves to the point they lose hair and weight. Numerous species of fleas, ticks, lice, and other winged insects may invade mule deer but seldom create major stress to individual animals and have not been identified as a cause of shrinking deer populations.

A variety of bacterial, viral, and other diseases regularly infect mule deer. While many aren't severe (much like a human catching a cold), some can be harmful—even fatal. One of these is chronic wasting disease (CWD), a variant of mad cow disease. It affects the brain and nervous system when proteins called prions alter the composition of a deer's brain. CWD is fatal to deer. Infected deer become malnourished, lose their ability to walk normally, and die. The disease is most readily spread by animal-to-animal contact, particularly in saliva. CWD became an acute concern among whitetail deer in the Midwest in the 1990s. It has since spread westward and now infects mule deer in numerous regions in the West. Interestingly, mountain lions hunting mule deer in CWD-infected populations prey upon infected deer much more frequently than those not carrying the condition.

Hemorrhagic diseases include epizootic hemorrhagic disease (EHD) and blue tongue, which includes several strains. These viral infections are spread among deer by biting midges. Severe infections cause swelling in the neck and head, respiratory distress, and can quickly become fatal. Some deer that recover from the illnesses may sustain damaged blood vessels in the hooves that makes them lame. These diseases are often associated with water and usually peak in late summer and early fall, when biting midges are most prevalent.

Mule deer are susceptible to several other bacterial and viral diseases. Papillomavirus spreads to mule deer through direct contact or biting insects. It may result in fibroma tumors, which are unsightly but usually not acutely harmful. Large scabby areas on the head and back of mule deer indicate a bacterial rain rot infection, a disease transmitted by flies and ticks. Other bacterial infections of mule deer include foot rot, black leg, keratoconjunctivitis, and occasionally leptospirosis, bacterial pneumonia, and Johne's disease.

Hemorrhagic diseases are carried to mule deer by biting midges, which often hatch profusely in stagnant water sources in late summer.
© ISTOCK.COM/ ASPENPHOTO

MULE DEER AND HUMANS

Mule Deer and American Indians

Mule deer were hunted by native peoples of North America for several millennia prior to the arrival of Europeans. An archaeological site near Dead Indian Creek in northwestern Wyoming provides evidence that natives were hunting mule deer in the area as early as 2500 BC. Mule deer skulls with antlers attached found at the site were arranged in a pattern indicating some ceremonial significance. Given their broad geographical distribution, mule deer served as a regular or intermittent food source for humans in numerous regions of western North America.

In more recent history, mule deer were hunted by American Indians with a variety of methods. Some tribes along mountains of the Pacific Coast regularly hunted mule deer (blacktail subspecies); others mostly ignored them, obtaining most of their meat from fish and marine animals. Natives of southeastern Alaska hunted Sitka blacktail, believed to be an important source of meat.

Mule deer were hunted communally or by individual hunters. Communal hunts involved driving deer into water, where they could be killed swimming; chasing them into various enclosures; or "herding" them into areas where hunters waited with spears or bows and arrows. Dogs were frequently used by coastal natives to hunt deer, aiding them in hazing efforts or sometimes running animals to exhaustion, when they could then be killed by hunters. Mule deer were also taken by ensnaring them in nets along trails or excavating pits that were covered with sticks and then spread with earth and leaves or other natural materials. Animals fell through the thin covering, impaling themselves on sharpened sticks driven into the bottom of the pit.

Skilled deer hunters were esteemed members of coastal tribes. Various peoples had different rituals and habits regarding preparation for hunting and the butchering and distribution of animals. Some tribes prohibited women from eating certain parts of the deer or occupying a dwelling containing a dead deer. At least one (the Sanetch, a tribe that occupied the area around Vancouver Island) did not allow the consumption of deer meat and fish in the same meal. Hunters were widely expected to be generous in distributing their kills. Squamish hunters of southwestern British Columbia were expected to hunt mule deer with great respect for the animals and abstain from consuming their kill until they returned to the village. It was believed those who did not generously share their deer would be shunned by the animal's spirit and impeded in future hunts.

American Indians hunting mule deer singly often used brush or other cover to get within close range of their quarry.
JACK BALLARD

Native peoples on the eastern flank of the Rocky Mountains and the plains also hunted mule deer. The Blackfeet occupied prime mule deer habitat along the Rockies in western Montana. Mule deer were hunted singly by skilled hunters with bows and arrows tipped with very sharp stone arrowheads. Hunters stalked within close range of the animals in brushy areas or other cover.

Mule deer, like other ungulates, were used by natives for more than their meat. Hides were tanned for leather clothing and other purposes. Antlers and bones were fashioned into elementary tools that could be used as digging instruments or as awls and spear points. Sinews were prepared as bowstrings or other cords. Though not as locally abundant as bison on the plains or salmon on the Pacific Coast, mule deer served as a significant source of food and other resources for a wide array of North American peoples prior to European settlement.

Mule Deer and European Settlers

The history of mule deer after the arrival of Europeans to North America and the rapid colonization of the West in the mid- to late 1800s parallels that of other large mammals. Overharvesting, whether for meat, hides, or other purposes, caused populations to decline. But the extent to which mule deer occupied their historic range prior to that time is a matter of debate. The animals were apparently abundant in places, but the writings of some early observers fail to distinguish between mule and whitetail deer, perhaps conflating their numbers. Journal entries and other written records and correspondence from the early 1800s suggest a pattern of local or regional abundance in some areas, scarcity in others.

Historical records from the early nineteenth century indicate that mule deer were abundant or at least common to many areas of Montana east of the Continental Divide, portions of Wyoming, and central Idaho. They appear to have sparsely populated areas such as California, much of Utah, Nevada, and southern Idaho. One indication of this is reports from hunting expeditions of the Hudson Bay Company that took place from 1826 to 1831 in northern Nevada. They fail to document any interactions with mule deer in a part of the country that 150 years later would support substantial numbers of the animals.

Where they were found, mule deer were happily slaughtered by hunters and homesteaders. By 1900 mule deer were scarce across the Western landscape. In Nevada, an official report estimated the number of mule deer in the Ruby Mountains at fifty animals in 1917. A decade later, a pair of biologists blamed the scarcity in this major mountain range on poor habitat, though current estimates place the population as high as 12,000, the state's largest concentration of mule deer.

The experience of residents in many states during the early 1900s amply underscores the rarity of mule deer. Seeing a mule deer or even deer tracks was considered a novel occurrence. One report documents a conversation with an individual in Utah who claimed to follow the tracks of a mule deer for four days as a youth around 1900 just to finally have a quick look at the animal. My father similarly described the experience of my grandfather, who homesteaded in western Montana just after the turn of the twentieth century. Even during their boyhood years in the late 1920s and early 1930s, Dad and my uncles asserted that seeing a mule deer was rare, though the family ranch was located in excellent habitat.

The severe reduction in mule deer numbers by the late 1800s was not unnoticed by state legislatures and fledgling game agencies. Arizona's territorial government enacted a four-month hunting season for mule deer in 1887, giving them some protection from indiscriminate killing. In 1893 the harvest of does by hunters was prohibited. A public initiative was passed in 1916 that reduced the hunting season to the

Mule deer numbers had declined sufficiently by 1900 that the sighting of even a single animal was considered a novelty over much of their historic range.
JACK BALLARD

month of October and limited the harvest to a single buck per hunter. Arizona's history with mule deer management reflects similar measures taken in other Western states to protect and restore ailing mule deer populations.

Mule deer numbers experienced a boom in numerous regions from the 1930s to the early 1960s. In addition to protection provided by regulated hunting, biologists analyzing the history of mule deer also believed land-use practices of the era benefitted the animals in many places. Local factors included logging, which provided a flush growth of deciduous trees and shrubs that created abundant browse. Access to crops offered deer a source of outstanding forage, and livestock grazing is believed to have regionally suppressed grasses in favor of the shrubs favored by mule deer. Active suppression of predators in many areas also may have contributed to the population boom. The gains in mule deer numbers were impressive. Populations in the Ruby Mountains of Nevada (referenced above) burgeoned from an estimated 50 animals in 1917 to between 25,000 and 30,000 by the mid-1950s. In 1916 some 8,500 mule deer were found in Utah. In the later 1940s they numbered around 375,000. The combined mule and whitetail deer populations in Idaho stood at approximately 45,000 in 1923 but grew to 315,000 in the next forty years.

Colorado, where this handsome buck was photographed in Rocky Mountain National Park, is home to the most mule deer of any state in the interior Rocky Mountains.
JACK BALLARD

However, the pervasive abundance of mule deer in the 1950s proved unsustainable. Estimates of mule deer numbers in the United States show a peak population of around 10 million animals at about 1960, which was perhaps similar to numbers roaming the landscape just prior to European settlement (pre-settlement numbers are highly speculative). Those numbers declined steadily during the next five decades to around 4.5 million animals in 2005. Population estimates compiled from state and provincial game agencies in 2016 found mule deer numbers of all subspecies in the United States and Canada at roughly 4.37 million animals. Of those, around 460,000 roamed the provinces of Canada. Two states, California and Colorado, claimed nearly 1 million mule deer of that estimate in the United States.

Mule Deer and Us

Precipitous declines in mule deer populations in multiple regions have led to a heightened level of research and habitat management among wildlife agencies in the past two decades. The Western Association of Fish and Wildlife Agencies formed a Mule Deer Working Group in 1997 to provide collaboration in addressing mule deer declines. A handful of mule deer advocacy groups, including the Mule Deer Foundation, formed in 1988, work to conserve mule deer and habitat.

Habitat loss and degradation are currently believed to be the leading causes of the shrinking populations witnessed in the latter decades of the twentieth century. Direct habitat loss through establishment of human habitation in both rural and suburban areas has gobbled up significant mule deer range in multiple states. Pervasive development for fossil fuel extraction has reduced and fragmented habitat on a considerable scale on both public and private lands. Habitat degradation is another issue. Mule deer range in numerous regions has experienced the loss of critical habitat components such as winter foraging areas and secure cover for birthing sites. Mule deer numbers appear to be stabilizing or actually increasing in some places but continue to decline in others.

Many hunters desire a return to the "glory days" of mule deer hunting in the 1950s and early 1960s. The abundance of the gray-faced ungulates during that time allowed for expansive hunting opportunity and the harvest of many large-antlered bucks. However, a burning question among biologists concerns the nature of those population highs in the post-settlement era. Were they sustainable? Many commentators believe that mule deer abundance contributed to their own decline. Overbrowsing, for example, causes suppressed reproduction and limited growth among shrubs. In more than a few locations, shrubs essential as winter forage aged, died, and failed to regenerate during the heyday years under the sharp incisors of mule deer.

There's no question that many mule deer habitats could be improved. Even if that happens, the issue of how many mule deer a region can sustainably support is largely unknown and has yet to be informed by sustained research.

CHAPTER 4
WHITETAIL DEER

At the beginning of my career as a writer, I worked part-time on a ranch west of Missoula, Montana, in exchange for housing for my family and a small herd of cattle. Early one morning, around the first of June, I was checking cattle in a pasture flush with a verdant cover of tall grass. Skirting the meadow, I happened upon a very new whitetail fawn, secreted by its mother at the base of a towering ponderosa pine.

My camera was in the pickup, so I made a hasty retreat to the vehicle. As I lay in a scratchy bed of pine needles 30 feet from the fawn, the rise and fall of its chest was the only thing betraying life in its otherwise motionless form.

For an hour I sprawled in the dirt, taking numerous photos of the newborn. Its rich cinnamon coat punctuated with milky spots was striking, and the camouflage of its form at the base of the reddish, scaly bark of the ancient pine was astonishing. For a brief period, the fawn raised its head, the dark pad on its tiny nostrils twitching, perhaps in response to my own scent.

Some hours later I returned with my young son, planning to show him the fawn. It was gone, whisked away by a mother who had likely detected my scent and taken her offspring to new quarters.

My encounters with whitetail deer have spanned four decades, numerous states, and two countries. Yet when I think of the species, it is that everyday encounter with the fawn that stands uppermost in my memory. Whitetail deer are commonplace to many residents of the United States. But within their familiarity resides a truly remarkable creature whose ability to adapt to human habitation is unrivaled by any other North American ungulate.

Whitetail deer are named for the milk-white fur on the underside of their large tail.
JACK BALLARD

Names and Visual Description

Whitetail deer are the most widespread hoofed mammal in both North and South America. They are an adaptable, medium-sized deer capable of thriving in a wide range of habitats. They can be found in ecosystems as variable as the burning deserts of Arizona, the swamplands of Alabama, the grasslands of the Dakotas, and the dense evergreen forests in the Rocky Mountains of Idaho. Perhaps it is their broad geographic range and association with people in all of the contiguous United States that leads to some confusion about their name. Scientifically, the species is known as white-tailed deer, but the name "whitetail deer" is also used in professional reference to the species. For example, South Dakota Game, Fish and Parks calls them whitetail deer. Montana, a neighboring state, labels the species as white-tailed deer. In verbiage common to rural areas of the country, these deer may also be referred to as simply whitetails. For the purposes of this book, they will be termed whitetail deer, a preference in nomenclature justified by no more compelling reason than the author's reluctance to endlessly hyphenate the description of the deer's tail. For simplicity's sake, they may also be called whitetails.

When Lewis and Clark returned from their epic journey across the West, they brought with them information regarding a host of animals unknown to folks in the settled portions of the United States. In their journals they often refer to whitetail deer, which they knew in the East as "common deer." At various places in their travels, they encountered and hunted whitetails but described them with different and sometimes confusing names. On the Missouri River in Montana, the expedition killed what Lewis described as "one common fallow or longtailed deer." This was certainly a whitetail, noted in the captain's journal in the same entry, which records the harvest of a mule deer, a separate species. At the Three Forks of the Missouri River (also in Montana) Lewis notes the company did not find any mule deer but hunted "longtailed red deer," which were obviously whitetails. Three decades prior to the Lewis and Clark Expedition, an employee of the Hudson's Bay Company referred to whitetails as "longtailed jumping deer." Other accounts of the species from the colonial period describe "Virginia deer." This latter nomenclature is reflected in the scientific name for whitetail deer, *Odocoileus virginianus*.

Whitetails are variously colored, with geographical and seasonal differences in their coat colors. Most animals exhibit a rusty-red appearance in the summer when their coats are short and sleek. In early autumn they acquire their winter pelage, which ranges from mostly tan to grayish tan. The slender legs and neck of a whitetail, along with its sculpted head and streamlined torso, give it an athletic appearance. Whitetail deer sport a coal-black nose and hooves. One of their most unique physical features is the appendage from which they get their name. Whitetail deer have a much longer tail than other members of the deer family in North America. The furry tail droops from the rump in an elongated V shape. The visible top side usually matches the color of the deer's body and is edged in white; the tail's underside is completely white. When alarmed, these deer raise their tail, displaying the characteristic white underside. This behavior is the source of the deer's name.

Although the overall impression of a whitetail deer's color is brownish, substantial portions of its body are white or cream colored, including its underside, the insides of the upper portions of its legs, and the rump directly under the tail. Whitetails also sport a patch of white on their throat that extends along the lower jaw in most animals. The insides of a whitetail's ears are white; the tips and edges of the ears are often dark brown or black. Most animals also display two dark spots on the lower jaw toward the rear of the mouth.

Names for whitetails of various ages and genders are the same as those of their close relative, the mule deer. Males are called bucks or less frequently stags. Females are known as does. Young whitetails, from birth to one year of age, are commonly referred to as fawns. Animals of both genders from one to two years of age are often dubbed yearlings.

The descriptive term for a male deer is the origin for certain other terms in American culture. A dollar is frequently known in slang as "a buck." This stems from the colonial era, when the hides of deer were highly valued and a staple of trade between Europeans, settlers, and Native Americans. In the late 1700s, a "buckskin," the hide of an adult male whitetail deer, sold for a Spanish dollar, thus the source of a dollar as a buck. The Ohio state tree, the buckeye, also owes its name to an association with whitetail deer. The nut of the buckeye is mostly shiny and reddish, but it contains a duller light-brown spot resembling the shape of a deer's eye. American Indians of the region called the tree *hetuck*, which means "the eye of the buck."

Related Species in North America

Whitetails are part of the deer family of North American mammals that also includes elk, moose, and caribou. They occasionally share range with a less closely related ungulate (hoofed mammal), the pronghorn or antelope. Whitetails are readily distinguished from antelope on the basis of color. Pronghorns exhibit a notable bicolor appearance with the upper part of their body and flanks adorned in reddish brown, their lower ribs, belly, and rump contrasting in white. Both male and female pronghorn have black horns, absent in whitetails, though the horns of female pronghorn are often small and difficult to see.

Moose are much, much bigger than whitetail deer and have a dark brown or blackish coat. The head of a moose is ponderous, highlighted by a large, bulbous nose, and that scarcely resembles the pointed nose and sculpted head of a whitetail. It is unlikely that anyone with a modicum of experience in the outdoors would confuse a moose for a whitetail. Whitetails live in almost all locations inhabited by moose.

Both elk and caribou are notably larger than a whitetail. The coloration is different as well. Elk in summer pelage may be rusty red in appearance, like a whitetail, but the coat on the front shoulders and neck is darker. Their rump is also yellowish in color,

unlike a whitetail, and sports just a stub of a tail. Elk and whitetails are found in the same habitat in portions of the East and in numerous locations on the plains and in the Rocky Mountains. Caribou are colored dissimilarly to whitetail deer: Their necks are creamy white while the rest of their body appears in gray tones. Caribou have long hairs along their throat that forms a mane, a characteristic absent in whitetails. Whitetail deer and caribou roam together in parts of Canada, but, with the exception of a few rare interlopers from Canada in the extreme northern reaches of Washington, Idaho, and Montana, whitetails in the contiguous United States never encounter caribou.

The closest relative and the animal most commonly confused with the whitetail is the mule deer. The two deer species share range in numerous locations west of the Mississippi River and sometimes interbreed. Bucks from both species carry antlers. On mature males, it is sometimes possible to distinguish the species by their antler configuration, although this is not a perfect diagnostic tool. The antlers of whitetail deer usually have tines that sprout from a single beam. Mule deer antlers sprout from the head with a main beam that normally forks, then forks again. However, bucks of both species sometimes carry antlers that do not match the common configurations.

Body color and appendage characteristics are the

Mule deer (above) and whitetail deer (below) are closely related. Tail size, color, and shape are the best ways to tell them apart. Mule deer have longer ears, a more grayish cast to their fall and winter coats, and usually differently shaped antlers.
JACK BALLARD

best way to differentiate mule and whitetail deer. The winter coat of a mule deer has a grayish cast, versus the more brownish appearance of most whitetails. In the summer, the two species may both look reddish brown. However, mule deer always sport a creamy rump, with a spindly tail tipped in black. This characteristic in itself is sufficient to distinguish mule deer from whitetails. Additionally, the ears of mule deer are much larger (nearly twice as long) than those of a whitetail.

Subspecies of Whitetail Deer

As with many other species of mammals in North America, the number and classification of various subspecies of whitetail deer is currently a matter of debate among biologists. Worldwide, thirty-eight subspecies of whitetail deer are traditionally recognized. Seventeen of those occur in the United States and Canada. The rest are found in Mexico and Central and South America.

Subspecies were historically classified based on separate geographical ranges and noticeable variations in physical characteristics such as body size, color, and other unique traits including length and shape of appendages or antler size. More recently, taxonomists (scientists who classify animals) have begun to investigate subspecies in relation to genetic differences versus physical characteristics that are sometimes a function of habitat conditions, not true species variation. For example, among deer in Mississippi assumed to belong to a single subspecies, animals from the delta region with fertile soils are 30 to 40 percent heavier than those found in the coastal flatwoods region, which has less productive soils.

Deer management practices during the twentieth century also confound current subspecies classifications. Whitetail deer were hunted to extinction, or nearly to extinction, in numerous regions throughout the United States in the late nineteenth and early twentieth centuries. Deer then were transplanted from one region to another to establish or augment local herds. In 1926, the state of Virginia embarked on an aggressive decades-long translocation program in which deer from other states were released at numerous locations throughout Virginia. Many other states engaged in similar restocking programs. The genetic interchange of these translocation projects has certainly diluted the genetic uniqueness of many supposed subspecies, if such genetic individuality existed in the first place. Research in the past decade has concluded there is no significant difference in the genetic makeup of at least six of the traditionally identified subspecies of whitetails in the United States.

As is the case with other identified subspecies of large mammals in North America, most subspecies of whitetail deer are associated with a specific geographic area. For example, whitetails inhabit several barrier islands along the Atlantic coast. The Hilton Head Island, Bull Island, and Hunting Island subspecies are all found on islands off the coast of South Carolina, isolated populations that presumably migrated at some point from the mainland. Farther south, the Blackbeard Island subspecies ranges only on Blackbeard Island and Sapelo Island near the Georgia coast.

Elsewhere in the country, subspecies have been identified that certainly interbreed due to a lack of geographic barriers between their ranges. The Northwest subspecies and the Dakota subspecies are both claimed to inhabit Montana, the Northwest species found primarily in the western portion of the state, the Dakota subspecies to the east. However, the river corridors favored by whitetail deer contain no natural or man-made barriers to deer dispersion from east to west, so it is safe to conclude these subspecies interbreed in many locations.

Two of the whitetail deer subspecies in the contiguous United States are currently protected under the provisions of the Endangered Species Act (ESA). The Columbian whitetail deer, *Odocoileus virginianus leucurus*, was originally identified along the lower Columbia River and its islands in western Washington. These deer were listed as endangered under the ESA in 1968. In 1978 another small population of Columbian whitetails was identified in southwestern Oregon's Douglas County, and these deer were also listed as endangered. Conservation measures in Oregon led to the growth and expansion of the Douglas County whitetail herd, which was removed from the endangered species list in 2003. In 2013, the United States Fish & Wildlife Service

Key deer are the smallest subspecies of whitetails. This young buck is grazing in the National Key Deer Refuge in Florida.
PHOTO COURTESY THE US FISH & WILDLIFE SERVICE

(USFWS) released a status review of the lower Columbia River population that recommended changing their ESA status from endangered to threatened. On October 9, 2015, the USFWS formally proposed the change in status. Since being listed as endangered, the population of whitetails on the lower Columbia River has doubled in number from around 450 animals to 900.

The subspecies of North American whitetail deer most distinct from other members of the species is the Key deer. These animals solely inhabit the Florida Keys, a series of tropical islands jutting from the southern tip of Florida. Key deer are notably different from other whitetails for several reasons. First, they are quite tiny in comparison to their northern relatives. While a mature buck in northern Minnesota might weigh over 300 pounds, a 100-pound male Key deer would be considered a giant; average weights for Key deer are 80 pounds for bucks and 62 pounds for does. Key deer fawns normally weigh less than 4 pounds at birth.

Other traits among Key deer are also unique among whitetails. Although they require freshwater to survive, Key deer are highly tolerant of salt water. They have much lower birth rates than other whitetails and tend to be more solitary. Their breeding age is older than that observed elsewhere in the species, and the antler development in bucks is slower.

By the early 1950s, Key deer were on the verge of extinction, with only an estimated twenty-five individuals left in the Florida Keys. Overhunting was the primary reason for the decline of Key deer. They received protection from hunting in the early 1950s. In 1967 they were listed as a federally endangered species and are currently listed as endangered by the state of Florida as well. Although the population of Key deer has rebounded significantly since their low, they are still considered vulnerable to extinction by many biologists. The population now numbers nearly one thousand animals, but most of those are found on just two islands, Big Pine Key and No Name Key. Hurricanes, rising sea levels, and disease outbreaks are all disasters that could conceivably wipe out this genetically and geographically isolated population of whitetail deer.

Physical Characteristics

Species that inhabit extended latitudinal ranges tend to exhibit a similarly large range in body mass. Whitetail deer are found from the southernmost portion of the contiguous United States (the Florida Keys) to its northernmost (northern Minnesota), a distance spanning 1,650 miles. Following a biological rule that body mass increases from south to north, Key deer are the smallest in the country; those dwelling in northern Minnesota are among the largest. Buck deer in Minnesota usually range from 100 to

300 pounds in weight; some males get even heavier. Minnesota does normally range from 85 to 130 pounds. Nationwide, the average weights for whitetail bucks and does are around 140 and 100 pounds, respectively. Occasionally, both bucks and does achieve sizes much larger than average. In 1926 a Minnesota hunter killed a whitetail buck that, after its internal organs were removed, weighed 402 pounds. Officials from the state's Department of Conservation estimated the buck had a live weight of 511 pounds. It is assumed by many to be the heaviest whitetail buck on record.

In most of their habitat in the United States and Canada, adult whitetail deer stand about 2.5 to 3.5 feet at the shoulder. The *length* of their body from nose to tail is commonly 6 to 7 feet. Because the neck and head of a whitetail extend above its shoulders, the typical adult deer's total height is about shoulder level to the average human female.

Antlers and Antler Development

Whitetail bucks grow antlers, bony appendages from their head that may be used for defense against aggressors, in dominance battles with other bucks, and as a symbol of a buck's vigor to both other males and females of his kind. In rare cases, does with hormonal abnormalities may also develop antlers; in wild populations, about one in three thousand does will have some form of antler development. Antlers sprout from bony projections on the frontal bones of the skull known as pedicles. Pedicles are similar in shape to a nearly rhyming word, "pedestal." In fact, the relationship between pedicles and pedestals can be helpful in understanding antler development. Pedicles appear as bony pedestals thrusting from a buck's skull. Similar to the common phrase "he fell off his pedestal," a buck's antlers detach from the pedicle every year. Antlers are thus described as deciduous, meaning they are regrown every year like the leaves on a deciduous tree.

Pedicles are noticeable on buck fawns by the time they reach four to five months of age. These bony nubs are often called buttons and are found on the top of the fawn's skull between his eyes and ears. As the buck ages, his pedicles tend to shorten but become broader, allowing subsequent antlers to achieve a larger diameter at the base.

Growing antlers are called velvet antlers for their fuzzy, velvety appearance. The velvet on the outside of the antlers forms a thin skin over the antlers, which are composed of bone. This skin is filled with an extensive system of blood vessels that provide nutrients to the rapidly growing antlers. At maximal expansion antlers on a whitetail buck may grow up to 0.5 inch per day. Antlers in the growth stage are formed of soft tissue that turns to bone through a process of calcification that occurs toward the end of yearly antler development. In late summer, shifting hormones cause the blood supply to diminish. The velvet then sloughs from the antlers, a process that is often aided by whitetail bucks rubbing their antlers on trees and shrubs. Naturally colored white, the antlers soon take on various shades of brown. The coloration comes from staining and foreign material on the antlers. Bucks that rub their antlers on various types of trees may develop antlers that range in color from nearly white to a deep, chocolate brown. In some habitats whitetail antlers are more reddish than brown.

This Smoky Mountain National Park buck's antlers are in the "velvet" stage. The deer was photographed in early summer.
LISA BALLARD

Antler size is a function of a buck's age, genetics, and nutrition. Studies on antler development indicate a buck will maximize his potential for antler growth at about six years of age. Some research suggests the timing of a buck's birth and the body condition of his mother during gestation also have lasting effects on antler size. Yearling bucks carry a set of antlers bearing about 30 percent of their maximal size. The antlers on two-year-olds achieve about 60 percent, three-year-olds 80 percent. From three to six years of age, antler size increases more slowly. Bucks may carry antlers at or near their maximum size for several years after their peak, if they remain free from injury and have access to adequate nutrition.

The overall size and number of tines (or points) on a buck's antlers increase with age. Can you tell a buck's age by counting the number of tines on his antlers? While some erroneously believe this theory, it is not true. Yearling bucks usually have spike antlers that consist of a single, elongated tine or exhibit two tines, in which case they are often called forkhorns. A few bucks may only carry two tines on each antler on their second set of antlers; others may have up to five. It is thus impossible to assess a buck's age based on his number of antler points. However, if an observer is familiar with the growth patterns of bucks in a particular region, age can be roughly estimated by antler mass (circumference) and overall length.

Whitetail bucks shed their antlers every year before growing a new set from the pedicles. Older bucks with larger antlers shed theirs first, usually in mid- to late winter. Complex hormone interactions regulate the shedding of antlers. The level of testosterone, a male hormone, declines dramatically in the winter. This causes the adhesion of the antlers to the pedicles to decrease until the weight of the antlers pulls them from the buck's head. Once one antler falls from a buck with a large rack, its head is immediately unbalanced. If the buck then shakes its head, the other antler often falls as well. In many cases, the cast antlers of mature whitetail bucks are found close to each other.

As testosterone levels begin to rise in the spring, the adhesion of the growing antlers to the pedicles becomes very strong. This bond is so tenacious that hardened antlers will break before being pulled loose from the pedicle, a condition that persists until the antlers are cast the following winter.

RANGE AND HABITAT

North American Range—Historic

Whitetail deer historically were animals of the woodlands and waterways of North America. They thrive in many geographical locations and habitat types but are found most consistently where woodland cover is interspersed with open areas. Whitetails are often described as animals of the edges, meaning places where forest cover intersects with meadows or other treeless space, offering them the best opportunity to thrive.

Whitetails are often described as animals of the edges. They thrive where cover is interspersed with more open areas.
JACK BALLARD

Prior to European settlement in what is now the contiguous United States, most of the territory east of the Mississippi River was forested and home to whitetail deer. American Indians hunted deer, utilizing their flesh for food, their bones for various implements, and their hide for clothing and shelter. These intelligent, enterprising hunters realized whitetails were found most frequently in transitional areas of the forest and sometimes deliberately set fire to the woodlands to create open areas with newly grown vegetation to attract deer and other animals. The diminutive Key deer of Florida were present prior to European settlement, their population already isolated by geography from deer on the mainland.

Whitetails were also found west of the Mississippi River during precolonial times, but the extent of their range and the density of their populations in this part of the country are often a matter of speculation. The species is known to have inhabited river corridors across the West in good numbers. They were also found on streams flowing to the Pacific Ocean on the west side of the Continental Divide.

In the Southwest, whitetail deer roamed across the Texas hills and river bottoms. Archaeological evidence shows deer were an extremely important part of the diet of the native peoples of Texas and Oklahoma for several millennia prior to European or Spanish settlement. The Coues whitetail deer of New Mexico and Arizona, one of the subspecies of whitetails identified in the United States, thrive in timbered areas at higher elevations than the desert scrub. These deer are notably small compared to their northern counterparts. They are believed to be the remnants of a whitetail population that became isolated when changing climate and habitat conditions eliminated forestlands at lower elevations, effectively separating these animals from their kin elsewhere in the region.

Historical biology of whitetail numbers and distribution in the United States indicates the species began to decline in the 1700s. Pressure from hunting by newly arrived Europeans and increased harvest by native hunters who acquired firearms both played a role in decreasing whitetail numbers in the East. Some biologists believe there may have been a short-term uptick in whitetail numbers in the early 1800s, a period of time when logging and clearing of land for agricultural purposes improved habitat for deer in numerous places east of the Mississippi River.

From around 1850 to 1900, whitetail populations contracted dramatically. It is impossible to know how many deer existed before Europeans came to North America. One common estimate puts the population in 1450 in what is now the United States at around thirty million animals. By 1900 that number had plummeted to less than three hundred thousand animals, according to some estimates. Regardless of the actual number, whitetail deer had been completely eliminated or their ranks drastically reduced in many parts of the country.

Two major factors contributed to the plunge in populations. First, an active market for deer meat and hides motivated people to hunt deer for profit. Secondly, improvements in firearms made killing deer more efficient. Repeating rifles, capable of firing several cartridges without being reloaded, allowed hunters greater capacity for downing multiple deer in a single episode or repeat shots at deer they missed. This technology, coupled with market demand, unregulated hunting, and an ever-growing human population in the United States prompted a crash in whitetail deer numbers in the closing decades of the nineteenth century.

Legal protections for deer were enacted in most states in the first two decades of the twentieth century. These consisted mainly of hunting seasons that made it illegal to kill deer outside of this time period and regulated how many deer and what sex could be harvested. Conservation measures, such as the creation of habitat reserves, were also gaining popularity with citizens concerned about whitetail deer and other wildlife.

But the dearth of deer was critical across many regions that now hold some of the nation's most robust herds of whitetails. By 1904, whitetails had been completely eliminated in the state of Ohio. Whitetail numbers in Missouri had plummeted to around four hundred, according to a 1925 estimate. In 1898 the state of Iowa completely closed its deer-hunting season because whitetails were rarely sighted and had been completely eliminated in most of the state. Whitetails were extinct in Kansas and Indiana by the early 1920s.

Whitetail deer populations began a slow recovery in most regions by the 1920s. Lands cleared for agriculture and logging created the edge and clearing habitat favored by deer. The Great Depression was also helpful for whitetails. As citizens fled small farms and rural areas to seek work in the cities, the abandoned land they left behind became refuges for wildlife.

From the 1950s to 2000, whitetail deer numbers increased about as rapidly as they dropped in the second half of the nineteenth century. Translocation programs (moving deer from one site to another) enhanced or established populations of whitetails in scores of locations. Management of deer numbers through hunting seasons and conservation efforts, often funded by revenue from hunting licenses, led to an increased amount of protected habitat. Today it is estimated there are some thirty million whitetail deer in the United States. Most experts believe there are now as many or perhaps more whitetails in the country as in precolonial times.

The historic range of whitetail deer covered much of North America and was probably similar to the species' range today. While the distribution of many North American ungulates (such as bighorn sheep) is currently much smaller than it was in historic times, whitetail deer have possibly increased the extent of their range in comparison to the presettlement era.

Many experts feel there are now as many or more whitetails in North America than in precolonial times.
JACK BALLARD

NORTH AMERICAN RANGE—CURRENT

Whitetail deer inhabit the United States and Canada to the extent that it is easier to describe their range in terms of where they are not found than where they are present. As of 2016, only two states are devoid of resident whitetail populations: California and Nevada. It is possible that deer from Oregon and Idaho occasionally make their way into these states, but there is no official record of a reproducing population.

Utah was also officially devoid of whitetails until the tail end of the twentieth century. Sightings of whitetail deer were reported in the northern part of the state beforehand, but the first documented whitetail was located in Cache County, in the north-central region, in 1996. In 2000, wildlife officials recorded the killing (legal) of a whitetail deer by a hunter. In the past two decades, whitetails have become permanent residents of the state in an expanding population occurring primarily northwest of the Great Salt Lake. It is expected that whitetails will continue to expand their range southward and into other river-bottom and agricultural areas of the state in the future. Wildlife officials estimate there are now over one thousand whitetail deer in Utah.

Whitetails are mostly absent in New Mexico and Arizona, with the exception of the Coues subspecies. Coues deer range across the mountains of southwestern New Mexico and are found in Arizona in mountainous territory in the south-central and southeastern portions of the states from the Mexico border northward through the Tucson area. The Flagstaff area represents the northern end of whitetail deer range in Arizona.

Oregon contains relatively few whitetail deer in three distinct populations. The Columbian whitetail (discussed under Subspecies of Whitetail Deer in the beginning of this chapter) is found in two rather small areas: the extreme northwest corner of the state along the Columbia River and in southwestern Oregon in Douglas County. Whitetails are also present in the northeast as part of a connected population to Idaho and Washington (Washington holds whitetails in most of the western half of the state). They are located primarily in Wallowa, Union, and Baker Counties.

In the remainder of the contiguous United States, whitetail deer are broadly distributed in relation to viable habitat. Overall, their range is expanding, particularly in western states. In the Rocky Mountains, whitetail deer now occupy higher percentages of mountain habitat and at higher elevations than seen in previous decades. For example, in November 2004, a park biology crew observed a whitetail doe in Colorado's Rocky Mountain National Park at an elevation of 8,630 feet. I have personally witnessed whitetail deer on the spine of the Continental Divide on the Montana-Idaho border at 6,600 feet and at nearly 8,000 feet in the Snowcrest Mountains of Montana. Whitetail deer have also increased their distribution in the semiarid prairie lands of several western states in the past few decades.

Perhaps the most dramatic aspect of whitetail deer range expansion is seen on Canada's northern frontier. Many biologists have noted the continuing northern movement of whitetail range in various portions of Canada in the last few decades. In western Canada, small bands of deer are now found in the southern portion of the Northwest Territories and appear to be moving slowly north. A hunter harvested a whitetail doe in good health about 65 miles south of the Arctic Circle in 1996. Climate change, and the habitat alterations it produces, will likely facilitate an even farther-northward expansion of the profoundly adaptable whitetail deer in the future.

WHITETAIL DEER HABITAT

Whitetail deer are considered one of the most adaptable ungulates in North America. They thrive in a broad range of geographic areas and habitats, but one necessity restricts their distribution: water. Whitetails will rarely be found more than a mile from a consistent water source.

A wide range of plants, shrubs, and trees can be utilized by whitetail deer for food. But a key component of their habitat is cover, generally composed of shrubs or trees that deer use to hide from humans and other predators. Whitetails also use cover for protection from winds and precipitation in the fall and winter, and they retreat to shaded areas to escape heat during the summer.

The necessity of cover for whitetails is readily observed in areas characterized by sprawling cultivation for agriculture. Crops such as soybeans, corn, alfalfa, and wheat represent attractive food sources for deer. However, if some woody cover is not present, deer will be found in low numbers or absent entirely. In heavily farmed areas, hedgerows and ravines unfit for cultivation that hold trees and shrubs provide deer enough cover to thrive. Numerous studies have shown that although deer can live with less, areas containing at least 30 percent cover represent the best habitat for whitetails.

"Forest succession" is the term used to describe the process of forest growth from infancy to maturation. Infant forests are those where some natural (fire, hurricane, flood) or man-made (logging, clearing for agriculture) occurrence has killed all or most of the trees in an area. In the early stages of forest succession, grasses, broad-leaved plants, and fast-growing shrubs and trees dominate the landscape. As larger deciduous and evergreen trees take over, the forest canopy closes, eliminating most direct sunlight from the forest floor. The understory becomes more barren. As the forest ages, fewer large trees dominate. The canopy opens somewhat, allowing enough sunlight to support a moderate level of lower-growing shrubs and plants to develop at ground level.

Whitetail deer thrive in habitats at the early stages of forest succession. These provide abundant food during all seasons of the year. They also benefit from mature, old-growth forests. In the East, the large trees of mature woodlands provide mast (nuts and fruit) that represent excellent food sources in the fall. Mature forests yield both protection from the elements during the winter months and woody plants upon which the deer may browse. Middle-aged evergreen forests, characterized by dense, light-blocking stands of species such as pine and fir, offer little for deer to eat. In woodlands, areas where infant forests are developing adjacent to mature timber offer whitetails the perfect mix of habitat.

In the past several decades, a novel habitat has seen an explosion in whitetail deer numbers. Urban and suburban areas are now home to thousands upon thousands of whitetail deer. The growth of deer populations in urban environments stems from two sources. First, as suburbs sprawl into forested and agricultural areas, they increasingly encompass land already inhabited by deer. Secondly, some deer have moved into suburban areas from the wildlands, apparently attracted to consistent food sources and protection from hunting and predators.

A few deer in town are usually seen as cute. Too many are destructive to landscaping, increase deer-vehicle collisions, and may contribute to the spread of disease, most notably Lyme disease, which is carried by the deer tick.

How to manage urban deer is often contentious. Lethal suppression through tightly controlled hunting or sharpshooting programs are most effective but are frequently protested by animal rights activists. Nonlethal removal through trapping and relocating is very expensive, as are programs that attempt to contain numbers through some form of birth control.

For over a century, state wildlife agencies focused their resources on managing whitetail deer in rural and wild environments. Increasingly, deer managers and biologists are being forced to deal with deer in their own backyards.

NUTRITIONAL REQUIREMENTS AND FORAGE

Nutritional Requirements

It is sometimes noted that the basic nutritional requirements for a grown whitetail buck are similar to those of an adult man. The buck needs about the same number of calories during a day as the man, but the food sources and the process by which they are digested are very different.

As a general rule, an adult deer consumes about 5 percent of its body weight in forage per day. Thus, a delicate adult doe in Florida's Everglades National Park weighing 90 pounds eats only about 4 to 5 pounds for forage per day, while a strapping buck in Virginia's Shenandoah National Park weighing 180 pounds eats around 9 pounds of food per day. However, food consumption for deer varies by nutritional quality and availability. When attractive forage is essentially limitless, as it is for whitetails with access to desired agricultural crops, animals may eat 7 percent of their body weight per day. Deer subsisting on woody browse will have to ingest more feed than those with access to nutritious broad-leaved plants.

The food requirements change over time, following a consistent pattern dependent on the age and reproductive status of the animal and the season of the year. An adult deer that is not pregnant, nursing a fawn, or growing antlers can maintain a healthy body with 6 to 10 percent protein in its diet. A growing fawn needs 14 to 18 percent protein for average growth; maximal growth for fawns is achieved when they receive 16 to 20 percent dietary protein.

Adult bucks that are growing antlers and pregnant does need nearly double the protein to maintain opti-

Does nursing fawns require higher levels of protein to maintain their health.
JACK BALLARD

mal health as they do at other times of the years. Lactating does (those nursing fawns) also require about twice as much protein, as they are converting protein from plants into the protein-rich, nutrient-laden milk that nourishes their fawns. Numerous studies have found that antler growth in bucks is highly related to good nutrition. One study of domestic deer found that two-year-old bucks eating a diet containing 16 percent protein grew antlers that had twice as much mass as those consuming 8 percent protein. In this case, the bucks needed protein for both antler growth and body development, as males normally do not reach their full body weight until four years of age.

Deer also need a variety of minerals in their diet. Two important minerals are calcium and phosphorous. These are needed for reproduction, bone development, and antler growth. Hardened antlers contain around 11 percent phosphorous and 22 percent calcium. Both does and bucks concentrate these minerals in their bones. At times when other parts of the body (such as growing antlers or a developing fetus) need more of these minerals than the deer consumes in food, the minerals may be temporarily "borrowed" from the bones, then restored later.

Bucks with developing antlers, like this one in Great Smoky Mountains National Park, need mineral- and protein-rich forage to nourish the growing tissue.
LISA BALLARD

Water is another crucial element in the nutrition of a whitetail. Deer may gain a significant amount of their needed moisture from plants, but in most places they still need surface water to survive, at least during certain times of the year. Water intake varies by season and geographic region. The exact water requirements of whitetails aren't fully understood, but most experts believe deer need 2 to 3 quarts of water per day for every 100 pounds of body weight. Most of whitetails' favorite foods are quite high in moisture. Apples, for example, are a treat for deer and hold about 80 percent moisture. Acorns, another favored food, contain about 70 percent moisture.

The water in forage reduces the amount of surface water a deer needs from a pond or stream, but most whitetails still drink water regularly. In arid environments, reliable water sources are a requirement for deer. Rarely will a whitetail go longer than forty-eight hours without drinking. In the winter, deer eat snow to obtain moisture. Deer that browse on vegetation moistened by rain or dew also gain moisture along with the feed.

Digestion

Deer belong to a class of animals known as ruminants or "cud chewers." Other ruminants include cattle, bison, elk, pronghorn, and sheep. Most ruminants have four stomachs, but some, like the camel, have three. Whitetail deer have four stomachs: the rumen, the reticulum, the omasum, and the abomasum. Ruminants eat quickly, minimally chewing their food before swallowing. At a later time, it is regurgitated and re-chewed to aid digestion. The food regurgitated from the rumen is called cud.

The first chamber of the stomach, the rumen, is the largest and normally holds about 80 percent of the solid mass in a deer's digestive system. Biologists theorize that deer consume most of their food in short bouts to counter predation. The distractive process of eating is minimized. Chewing, via the cud, usually takes place when the animals are resting and can be more vigilant to danger.

Whitetails consume forage, then regurgitate and chew it while resting. This bedded doe is chewing her cud.
JACK BALLARD

After the cud is chewed to a finer texture, it passes from the rumen through the other three stomachs of a whitetail, where it is further broken down. Nutrients are absorbed in the deer's stomachs, but the bulk of the energy and nutrition is extracted from the small intestine, where the food passes after leaving the abomasum, the last of the four stomachs.

Interestingly, the digestive system of the whitetail adapts to the type and amount of food it is eating. The rumen is essentially a fermentation chamber, where a multitude of microorganisms feed upon the forage a deer has swallowed, further breaking it down and converting it to more digestible molecules. The rumen is lined with tiny tendrils known as papillae. Papillae extend when the deer is eating nutrient-packed green forage in the spring and contract in autumn, when woody browse composes more of the diet. The composition of the "soup" in a deer's rumen changes with the seasons as well. In early spring, winter-stressed deer may starve to death with a full stomach because the digestive slurry has not yet adapted to breaking down green forage.

Food Sources

Whitetail deer take advantage of a dizzying array of food sources. If variety is the spice of life, there are few creatures that lead a more savory existence than deer. Studies of feeding deer in Missouri have revealed whitetails consume more than 600 different species of plants. Similar studies in arid climates in southwestern states have shown an equally high number of plants consumed by deer. Research in Arizona indicates whitetail deer eat at least 610 different plant species statewide.

Because it would take the entire contents of a book to catalog all the plants a whitetail might eat, it's easier to understand their food sources in broad categories that apply to different geographic regions and habitats. Probably the favorite type of forage for whitetail deer is forbs. In its widest definition, a forb is a flowering plant that dies aboveground each year and doesn't belong to the family of grasses or rushes. Forbs, like clover, occur in natural habitat and are also found as agricultural crops such as alfalfa. They develop at various times during the growing season, but most sprout and grow quickly during the spring. Many forbs are very nutritious and contain more protein than other plants.

In a natural habitat, browse is another extremely important and desirable food source for whitetails. Browse refers to the leaves, shoots, buds, and other parts of plants whose stems remains aboveground in winter. Browsing is most strongly associated with shrubs and trees. In many part of North America, browse is the primary food source for deer in the winter and plays an important role in whitetail nutrition at other times of the year. Deciduous trees such as maples, aspens, oaks, and dogwood are eaten by whitetails, in addition to many other species. Chokecherry, blueberry, snowberry, and honeysuckle are among a host of shrubs readily consumed by deer. Evergreen browse is also an important food in some places, especially during winter.

Grasses tend to be a lesser food source for whitetail deer, but they are eaten in fairly high quantities in some places at certain times of the year. The tender, greening grasses of spring are happily munched by whitetails. Sufficient rain also causes green regrowth of some grass species in the fall. These may offer a source of nutritious, tender forage for deer at a time of year when it is quite scarce.

"Mast" is a term used to describe the fruit and nuts from a variety of trees and shrubs. Mast is a preferred food for whitetails during the fall. Nuts and fruit provide large amounts of energy and nutrition, and they help whitetails develop fat reserves needed to survive cold winters. Deer love apples, berries, persimmons, grapes, and other fruits. In the desert Southwest, the pods of honey mesquite trees are an important mast crop, especially in drought years. Whitetails eat a wide assortment of berries when available, such as huckleberries, raspberries, and blackberries.

Whitetails sometimes eat aquatic vegetation. This doe is feeding on submerged vegetation at the National Bison Range in Montana.
JACK BALLARD

Acorns and other nuts are an exceedingly important mast crop for whitetails in many places. When abundant, acorns may compose more than 70 percent of a whitetail's diet in the fall. Studies in Tennessee and Georgia have indicated a strong correlation between the body weights of young deer and acorn production. Reproduction rates in young animals also appear to be higher in some regions when acorns are plentiful.

Other food sources less commonly eaten but sometimes locally important include aquatic plants, lichens, fungi, and ferns. Whitetails are even known at times to chew on dead fish and insects.

Migration

Mention the term "migration" and few people will associate it with whitetail deer. However, whitetails migrate regularly in some areas, sometimes for surprisingly long distances.

Whitetail migrations occur in two different patterns, with individual animals often following one or the other. Some deer are obligate migrators, meaning they migrate every year, no matter what the weather or habitat conditions. Others are conditional migrators, referring to animals that migrate some years but not others, depending on the conditions. In some populations, individual deer may be obligate migrators, conditional migrators, or nonmigratory. Researchers in southern Minnesota have found deer following all three patterns in the same area.

In the Midwest and other areas of widespread, intense agriculture, deer migrate in relation to crop growth and harvest. Growing crops provide whitetails with forage. Taller crops such as corn also give them a place to hide. Once the crops are harvested in the late summer or fall, the deer lose both their food source and cover. This prompts deer to move to areas where cover is present, sometimes triggering a migration of several miles.

Whitetails in northern habitats, including places like the Adirondack Mountains of New York or the forests of northern Minnesota and Michigan, are often migratory. In northern Minnesota, researchers have documented whitetail migrating over 30 miles. Migrations in these areas often lead deer to wintering areas known as yards, where many deer spend the winter in a relatively small area. As snow depth increases, travel becomes difficult. Yarding deer create trails that make for easier movement.

Deep snow and cold temperatures can prompt whitetail migrations. Some migrate every year; others move only during severe winters.
JACK BALLARD

In migratory populations, cold and snow depth—or more often, some combination thereof—are the triggers that spur deer to move from summer to winter range. A study conducted in the Dakotas concluded that whitetails may migrate 7 miles or sometimes notably farther between their summer and winter ranges. For these deer, temperature appears to the primary impetus for changing residence. Migration is initiated when daytime temperatures remain below freezing for three consecutive days, a situation that is often encountered during a major storm event.

If temperatures rise after an initial migration occurs, the deer remaining on summer range sometimes stay until another cold snap initiates another migratory wave. Another study in southern Minnesota documented whitetail migrations beginning when temperatures dropped below 20 degrees Fahrenheit. Some studies conducted in the Adirondack Mountains in northern New York have concluded that migrations toward wintering areas occurred with lowering temperatures but were also spurred when snow depths reached around 14 inches.

Spring migrations in whitetail deer populations tend to follow the development of food sources. As snow melts and seasonal plants begin to develop, whether naturally or via agriculture, deer follow these food sources between their summer and winter ranges.

ABILITIES AND BEHAVIOR

Physical Abilities

Whitetail deer are widely believed to be the most adaptable ungulate in North America. Their diet is unspecialized, and their bodies can adjust to the demands of living in a broad range of habitats. But another factor in their capacity to thrive in such a diversity of living quarters is their remarkable physical abilities.

Information regarding the running speeds of animals is readily available from online and other sources, but it is wildly inconsistent. Whitetails are commonly reported as reaching a top speed between 30 and 47 miles per hour. Which is it?

It appears that when reporting animal speeds, many sources provide unverified information from other sources that is based upon some assumed expert's best estimate. I know of no formal testing of wild animals' speeds. Probably the best information results in situations where a vehicle has inadvisably chased an animal or is driving parallel to a running animal. Several accounts report vehicles clocking whitetails at just over 40 miles per hour in maximum flight. Under most conditions, whitetail deer are probably capable of briefly sprinting at around 35 miles per hour. Normal running speeds are thought to be about 25 miles per hour.

Whitetails in full flight may reach speeds over 35 miles per hour. Recognizing their superior speed, predators seldom attempt to catch a fleeing deer from a distance.
JACK BALLARD

The gait of a whitetail is often described as bounding. With each bound the deer thrusts itself forward with the large muscles in its hindquarters. Its body extends until its rear hooves both leave the ground and are pointed directly behind the animal. At maximum extension in the bound, there is nearly a straight line from the deer's extended rear hooves along its belly to its front hooves, which are thrust forward in front of its body. The deer then engages its back and other muscles to arc its spine and pull its hind legs slightly ahead of its front hooves when they return to the ground. This allows a whitetail to propel itself incredibly long distances with each bound. Whitetail deer have been measured spanning over 25 feet in a single jump. The notable speed of whitetails enables them to elude all but the most enduring or stealthy predators.

Another remarkable ability of whitetail deer is their jumping prowess. Deer love many types of garden vegetables and ornamental plants. Will a 6-foot fence protect your corn and lettuce from whitetails? Probably not, if the deer is really craving a snack. Whitetail deer can clear an 8-foot fence with some effort. Dr. Leonard Lee Rue, one of the leading whitetail experts and authors in the United States, reports personally witnessing whitetails jumping 9.5-foot fences.

Their leaping ability, however, is not just used for raiding gardens. Whitetails fleeing a predator such as a coyote or wolf can use obstacles like fallen trees or brush piles to slow their pursuers. In such cases the deer bounds over the obstacle, forcing the predator to run around it. I have seen and observed the tracks of whitetails clearing tangles of downed timber measuring about 6 feet high and at least 6 feet wide.

The strength of the whitetail's limbs is put to another use when eluding predators. Whitetail deer are remarkably strong swimmers. It is commonly reported that they

can swim up to 13 miles per hour, though that figure appears to be based on a single, anecdotal incident when an individual purportedly clocked a swimming doe against his motorboat's tachometer. At that pace, a deer could cover a mile in the water in less than five minutes. Other estimates put the normal swimming speed of whitetails at around 4 to 5 miles per hour.

Regardless of their top speed, whitetails are very comfortable in the water and readily swim to elude predators. Where states or hunting district boundaries are separated by rivers, whitetail deer often swim from one location to another to avoid human hunters. Acclaimed naturalist Ernest Thompson Seton records an incident of a whitetail deer being found at sea, 5 miles from the coast of Maine in his book *The Life Histories of Northern Animals*, published in 1909. There are other accounts of whitetails swimming more than a mile off the Atlantic coast, and deer have been observed crossing large lakes in the United States and Canada.

Strong muscles help whitetails swim, but other aspects of their physical biology are also helpful. The hair of deer is hollow and buoyant, especially the longer, denser hair of their winter coat. Fat stored under the skin and around internal organs also aids in a deer's ability to float with ease. Fat and fur also combine to keep deer warm in cold water temperatures that would be debilitating to a human swimmer without protective gear.

As predator-avoiding strategies, the running and swimming prowess of the whitetail is only as good as the animal's capability in detecting a threat. Whitetail deer have superb senses that work together to inform them of the presence of other creatures in various settings. In open country, the keen eyesight of a whitetail is normally its best sense for identifying a predator. In dense forests, the deer may be more dependent on its ultrasensitive nose or excellent hearing to discern a threat. Singly or in combination, the acute, adaptable senses of whitetails are one of the reasons they are able to thrive in such an expansive array of habitats.

It is often said that the vision of deer is much better than the eyesight of people, but such a statement depends on one's definition of "better." The shape and composition of a deer's eyeball is quite different from a person's. It has been known for a long time that, compared to the round pupil of the human eye, the whitetail's pupil is shaped like a horizontal slit. A recent research project involving observations and computer modeling at the University of California–Berkeley demonstrates the shape of a deer's pupil is very effective in detecting motion and other visual cues at ground level, and helps in blocking overhead, dazzling light that sometimes confounds vision. The study also found that deer can rotate their eyeballs at least 50 degrees, about ten times farther than a human. This allows deer and other grazing animals with similarly shaped eyes to rotate their eyes upward when they drop their heads to graze or feed near the ground to maintain visual vigilance against predators.

Eyes set on the sides of their head give whitetails an expansive field of vision.
JACK BALLARD

Another aspect of whitetail eyesight that greatly assists them in evading predators is their exceptionally large field of vision. The eyes of a deer are set on the sides of its head, allowing for a field of vision spanning over 300 degrees. This allows deer to detect motion to the sides and even toward the rear of their bodies. Compared to a human's 180-degree field of vision, this aspect of whitetail eyesight gives them a much better ability to see objects a person or canine predator could detect only by swiveling its head.

In the past decade, several groundbreaking research studies have been conducted that indicate other significant differences between the vision of whitetail deer and humans. Deer have a poor capacity to discern detail. It is estimated that for general detail-oriented vision, whitetails are similar to a human with 20/200 vision or someone who can see but is legally blind because his or her vision is blurred. It also appears that deer have a horizontal band of sight in which they can detect greater detail. This might be likened to a computer screen where the middle 20 percent of the screen is in reasonably sharp focus but blurs quickly toward the top and bottom.

Whitetails also see color much differently than people. Research has demonstrated that deer detect only part of the color spectrum seen by humans. Whereas deer see blue tones exceptionally well (on the short wavelength side of the spectrum), they do not detect red (on the long wavelength side). Human eyes have a colored pigment in the lens that blocks ultraviolet radiation; deer do not. This has led some researchers to believe whitetails have the capacity for vision in the ultraviolet part of the spectrum. Regardless, the eyes of deer are highly adapted to low-light vision, much more so than people. They are also significantly more attuned to motion detection. A deer won't detect a person's presence on the basis of a bright orange shirt, even at close range; but if he or she so much as wiggles a finger, it will be seen immediately.

The extent to which whitetail deer rely upon the nose to detect predators and locate food sources is difficult to exaggerate. The nose of a wolf contains an estimated three hundred million olfactory receptors compared to six million in the snoot of the average human. Its brain dedicates forty times as much area to processing scent stimuli as a person's. Ungulate species, including whitetail deer and elk, are equally impressive in their olfactory abilities. It is estimated that the twitching black nose of a whitetail connects to a scent-sifting apparatus that is one thousand times more sensitive than a human's. What's more, a deer can detect and analyze multiple smells simultaneously.

Vocal and Visual Communication

Whitetail deer communicate with a variety of noises, sounds discerned by their fuzzy ears. Research performed on the auditory capabilities of deer has shown they hear best at the same tonal range as humans. However, they are capable of hearing high-pitched sounds undetectable to a person.

Whether listening for the grunt of a rival buck or the crunch of a hiker's foot on gravel, the ears of a whitetail are significantly more sophisticated than a human's. They are proportionally much larger. Their elongated dish shape makes them very effective in capturing sound waves. Whitetails can swivel their ears independently to maximize their hearing in a particular direction.

Alert to a noise behind her, this doe in Great Smoky Mountains National Park has swiveled her ears, an ability that helps whitetails pinpoint the source of sound.
LISA BALLARD

A deer's ears are important for detecting danger but also are used to receive communication from their own kind. Whitetails make a variety of sounds at various stages of life and at different times of the year. Does grunt softly to their newborn fawns. Fawns emit what is sometimes described as a murmuring sound when nursing. A fawn separated from its mother may signal its apprehension with a very loud bleating noise.

Bucks communicate vocally during the mating season, which occurs in the fall. Their calls are mostly grunt-like, with variations communicating certain activities or emotions. Bucks may grunt when following the scent of a doe. They also grunt to warn other bucks away when tending a doe.

Deer of both sexes may emit a loud snort when alarmed. A loud, lower-pitched snort alerts other deer to danger, but isn't an immediate signal to flee. If the snorting deer resorts to an even more intense, higher-pitched snort, other deer will instantly take flight, knowing a real threat is at hand.

The physical postures of whitetails communicate to other deer, similar to one person reading the body language of another. If a deer becomes alert, raising its head and staring intently in a particular direction, other deer in the area will also become alert. Deer may also stomp their feet when aroused by potential danger, a behavior that sends both an audible and visual signal to other whitetails. On one fall outing, I sat near a trail high in the mountains of Montana eating a sandwich. Between bites I heard the stomp of a hoof behind me. Although it was much higher in the mountains than I expected to encounter whitetails, I knew the sound. I turned my head very slowly to see a young whitetail buck staring at me from just a few paces away. My direct eye contact prompted a high-pitched snort and the buck bounded away.

Herd Behavior

Whitetail deer are not herd animals in the same sense as bison, which often form large, fairly intact groups. In the winter, many whitetails may be found together in a confined wintering area, but their proximity to one another is a function of habitat, not a herding instinct. However, whitetails usually spend much of the year together in one of two kinds of small groups.

The first is a maternal group. Does commonly stay in a small band with their mother and her other offspring until they are around three years of age. The does in this family group become solitary when birthing their fawns, but they rejoin the band once the fawns have reached a few weeks of age. When a person observes several doe deer together with their fawns, the odds are quite high that they are all related through the dominant doe or "grandmother" of the group.

The second type of whitetail "herd" is the male group or bachelor band. Except during the mating season, whitetail bucks normally live together in groups of a few animals up to a dozen or more, depending on the density of deer in a particular area. Bucks typically join these bands as yearlings and may associate with the same core group for several years. Biologists theorize that living together in small groups gives both males and females extra eyes and ears when it comes to predator detection. It's not terribly unusual to encounter single whitetails, but small-herd life is the norm.

Whitetails often raise their tail when alarmed and hold it erect when fleeing danger. Biologists believe this reaction alerts other deer to danger and discourages predators from pursuit.
JACK BALLARD

REPRODUCTION AND YOUNG

The Mating Season

For people intrigued with whitetail deer, whether photographers, hunters, or wildlife watchers, the mating season is one of the highlights of the year. Also known as the rut, the mating season creates a spike in deer activity. Bucks invisible at other times may show themselves during the rut. The whitetail world is alive with magnificent animals in prime physical condition, engaging in rituals of reproduction as ancient as the species itself.

The timing of the whitetail rut varies with location. In southern climates the start, length, and predictability of the mating season are less certain than in the north. The primary trigger for the rut is the photoperiod, or the length of daylight. As daylight

In northern climates, the whitetail deer mating season commonly occurs in November.
JACK BALLARD

diminishes during the fall in the northern United States and Canada, it stimulates hormonal shifts in whitetails that prompt reproductive behaviors. Seasonal changes in the photoperiod aren't as significant as one moves south, leading to a less-defined mating season. Near the equator, whitetail deer may mate and birth young at any time of the year.

For northern whitetails, the breeding season typically lasts around a month, with most of the mating occurring in a twenty-day period. Breeding may occur for several weeks on either side of the peak period, which commonly occurs in November. In my home state of Montana, mating behaviors tend to be most intense during the last two weeks of November.

In the southern United States, the mating season is longer and lacks the intense period associated with northern whitetails. Researchers have identified September as the month of peak breeding activity in portions of South Carolina. In Alabama and Mississippi, December is typically the peak month. Whitetails in northern Florida often mate most frequently in March, while deer in the southern portion of the state commonly breed in July.

Whitetails engage in a mating pattern known in biological circles as a tending-bond system. This simply refers to the habitat of a single buck courting a single doe until she is ready for mating. The buck will repel other bucks from her presence and will also attempt to keep the doe from fleeing his advances. Once the doe has been bred, the buck moves on, seeking another female with which to mate.

The actual mating season includes a prelude in which bucks advertise their status both to does and rival males. Increased testosterone levels cause the necks of mature bucks to swell to the point where they may look more like a thick-necked bull than a sleek deer. For several weeks before the rut and during the mating period, bucks rub their antlers vigorously on small trees and brush, creating what is often called a rub. As the buck thrashes his antlers on a tree trunk or willow brush, scent from a system of glands on his head and face are left on the bark. Other deer obtain information on this vigor based on the odor. The rub also serves as a visual signal to other animals. Bucks often create rubs that follow something of a trail or line, indicating their claim on the area as their home territory.

A similar form of communication is found in places where bucks paw the ground before or during the rut. These are known as scrapes and usually appear as a patch of bare earth amid a ground cover of fallen leaves, grass, or other vegetation. Scrapes are often located beneath an overhanging tree branch. In addition to pawing the ground, the buck rubs his head on the overhanging limb and may also nibble on its twigs. Scrapes are another way bucks advertise their territory during the rut. Other bucks, both subordinates and rivals, may visit the scrape of another. The scent and signals left after a visit serve as "business cards" identifying a buck's relative age and status. It is quite likely that deer can identify one another purely on the basis of scent. Confronted with the scent markings of the dominant buck in a territory at a scrape, a subordinate is probably quite aware of his superior.

Most often, bucks do not need to fight to establish which one is dominant and thus will have the mating rights to a doe. However, bucks evenly matched in size and perceived status will battle. The confrontation commences with the bucks staring directly at each other and circling, with each displaying his body and antler size to his opponent. Other signs of aggression include raised hair on the back and neck and ears laid back flat. If neither backs down during this mutual intimidation session, the fight begins when they clash their antlers together at close range.

If one buck substantially outmatches the other, the fight will last for just a few seconds before one male breaks away. Closely matched bucks may battle until they are nearly exhausted. Fighting strategies attempt to throw a rival from his feet or twist him sideways. Both tactics are designed to give a buck the opportunity to gore his opponent with his antlers. Intense battles may leave both victor and vanquished with lacerated ears, puncture wounds, joint injuries, and blinded eyes. Fights between bucks are spectator events in the whitetail world. Other bucks, and sometimes does, are attracted to the sound of crashing antlers during a fight and may travel considerable distances to witness the battle.

Pregnancy and Gestation

The gestation period, or time between breeding and birthing, for whitetail deer is around 200 days. Gestations between 187 and 213 days have been observed in whitetails. At a six-and-a-half-month average, this means a doe that mated in Montana's Glacier National Park in late November will birth her fawn in mid-June. The relatively brief mating season of northern deer means most fawns will be born within a short period of time that spans just a few weeks. This phenomenon, known as synchronous breeding, has certain survival advantages. Numerous predators are capable of killing a whitetail fawn. When most of the year's young are born in a short period of time, it contracts the period in which they can be successfully hunted, allowing more to survive.

The age and nutritional status of a doe are highly instrumental in her pregnancy. Whitetail fawns may breed before they reach one year of age, but they normally do so later in the mating season than adult does. Both female fawns and yearlings usually birth a single fawn. Adult does with good nutrition typically have twins, sometimes triplets. Does birthing up to five offspring have been recorded, though the birth of more than three fawns is very rare.

Caused by long, severe winters, summer drought, or marginal habitat, malnourishment is an important factor in pregnancy rates. Under normal habitat conditions, whitetail does in the northeastern United States have conception rates of 85 to 95 percent. Pregnancy rates are similar elsewhere in the country where deer have access to good forage. Does entering the breeding season in poor physical condition with low fat reserves are far less likely to become pregnant.

This buck is preparing to rub his antlers in Shenandoah National Park. Rubs serve as territorial markers for bucks during the rut.
JACK BALLARD

Birth

About a week before giving birth, whitetail does retreat to a birthing area. Does attempt to repel other deer from this territory, even their young from the previous year. Her most recent fawns, now yearlings, are forcibly removed from the area with kicks and other aggressive behaviors.

The birth of the fawn is preceded by her udder swelling with milk, around two days before the birth takes place. Birth usually begins with the doe lying on her side but is often completed in a standing position. Healthy fawns succeed in standing within thirty minutes of birth and nurse shortly thereafter. Fawns from undernourished does may lack the energy to stand and then starve. Does vigorously lick their newborn fawns, cleaning them of birthing fluids and tissues, and stimulating them to move and stand. Twin fawns born to healthy does are delivered within thirty minutes of each other. Whitetail fawns have white spots on their coats that disappear when their baby coat is shed in early autumn.

Some hours after birth, the doe will lead her fawns (or fawn) away from the birthing area. She then oversees them while they lie down in separate locations. Once the fawns are settled, the doe retreats to her own spot, some distance from the fawns. Biologists theorize this practice reduces the odds of a predator scenting the birthing area and finding the fawns. For the next few weeks, the doe will attend to her fawns for only a few times per day when they nurse. At a bit less than a month of age, the doe and her fawns will again mingle with her previous year's offspring and other members of the maternal group.

Top: Twins are commonly born to whitetail does. These healthy twins are prepared to face their first winter. Bottom: This doe and her young fawn have been joined by her previous year's offspring, which was briefly allowed to nurse, a rather unusual behavior. JACK BALLARD

Nurturing Fawns to Adulthood

One of the most critical periods in a fawn's survival is the first week of life. Very young fawns are easy targets for predators. However, due to their inactivity and the fact that they are nearly scentless, predators have a difficult time discovering them. A month-old fawn is fleet of foot. It can outrun many potential predators and may be defended by its mother if attacked. Its mobility is also a liability. Numerous research projects indicate fawns are most susceptible to predators between two and nine weeks of age. Young whitetails that reach three months of age are less likely to be preyed upon.

How important is it for a fawn to evade predators? In populations where natural predators are present in average or above-average numbers, predation is the leading cause of mortality in whitetail fawns. It is not unusual for predators to consume over 50 percent of the local fawn crop in a given year. Vehicle collisions, malnourishment, accidents, and diseases may also cut into the year's class of fawns. However, whitetails have a notably high reproductive rate. Whitetail populations that have declined due to disease or winter mortality can recover in a matter of a few years.

Once a fawn has reached the age where it is able to elude most predators, it still faces several challenges before reaching adulthood. A whitetail's first winter can be a major survival hurdle. If cold temperatures and deep snow persist, the youngest deer are among the first to succumb to starvation. Their smaller body size makes them less able to fight the cold. Where browse is scarce, young deer cannot reach as high onto shrubs and trees to nibble twigs. Fawns also find it more difficult to navigate deep snow. Once weakened, they are also easier targets for large predators such as wolves and mountain lions.

This two-month-old fawn is fast enough to foil most predators. It has survived some of the most precarious days of its life.
LISA BALLARD

Yearling deer, especially bucks, often disperse from the home range of their mother to live in new territory. These movements can create hazards, including highway crossings, unknown predators, and hostile members of their own kind. However, once a deer has survived its first birthday, it is well on the road to adulthood.

WHITETAIL DEER AND OTHER ANIMALS

Whitetails and Other Ungulates

In many parts of the country, whitetail deer are found on the same ranges as other North American members of the deer family: elk, moose, and mule deer. They may also inhabit prairie habitats shared with pronghorn, although whitetails normally select niche areas on the plains (creek bottoms, wooded draws) that are used less frequently by pronghorn. In a handful of locations, whitetail deer may come into contact with bighorn sheep on winter range and, to a lesser extent, mountain goats. However, their most regular interactions with other ungulates are shared with other members of the deer species.

Whitetails are incapable of directly challenging a larger moose or elk for forage or space. The interactions between these species are generally peaceful, with the smaller giving way to the larger. However, under some circumstances each may consume the same food sources, creating direct or indirect competition for forage. This most likely occurs in the northern portion of whitetail range in locations such as Idaho, Wyoming, Montana, and southern Canada.

In one study, researchers analyzed the winter diets of whitetail deer, elk, and moose in northwestern Montana. Dietary overlap was minimal during mild or normal winters, but one severe winter saw all three species consuming high percentages of the same forage. Under such circumstances whitetails are at a disadvantage compared to their larger relatives and may experience nutritional stress locally due to such competition. However, in general the long-term health of a whitetail deer population is not thought to be diminished by the presence of elk or moose.

Whitetails, though, may impact moose populations. Whitetail deer are often hosts to meningeal worms (brainworms). These parasites normally don't cause problems for deer but are deadly to moose. Moose are often absent in areas of high whitetail deer densities, even in good habitat. Many biologists theorize the presence of so many deer increases the odds of meningeal worm infection in moose to the point they are unable to survive.

Whitetails and their closest North American relative, the mule deer, share habitat in numerous regions throughout the United States and Canada. While mule deer are generally creatures of more open spaces and roam at higher elevations in the Rocky Mountains, there is considerable overlap in the range of the two species in both mountain, prairie, and river-bottom habitats.

Over the past few decades, mule deer numbers have declined in most places in the West. The reasons aren't fully known, but in some areas biologists speculate whitetail deer, whose numbers are generally increasing, may be instrumental in the decline. Whitetails are thought to be a more aggressive species and may displace mule deer in direct competition for food or other resources. It is important to remember, however, that correlation (observing two things are related) does not necessarily imply causation (one thing caused the other). While many people have pointed to increasing whitetail deer numbers as a cause for diminishing mule deer numbers, this hypothesis has not been confirmed or denied by scientific research.

An interesting twist in the relationship between whitetail and mule deer is their ability to interbreed. Crossbred animals of the two species are exceedingly rare in the wild, but in areas where they share the same range, some interspecies mating may occur. It is believed by many commentators that hybrids are usually the offspring of a whitetail buck and a mule deer doe, although that theory has not been verified by research on wild deer. What is known is that the survival of hybrid fawns is very low, even in captivity. Several captive breeding programs of these hybrid deer have a survival rate in fawns of around 50 percent.

Hybrids of the species inherit characteristics of both species and are extremely hard to identify in the wild. They generally have ears that are shorter than a mule deer's but longer than a whitetail's. Their tails are typically long, with dark fur on the outside and white hair on the underside in the pattern of a whitetail, but they often display much darker outer fur than is normally seen with whitetails. Survival of hybrids is possibly confounded by a mixing of the two gaits characteristic of each species. Mule deer run in a so-called stotting fashion, which means they bound with all four hooves hitting the ground at the same time in what appears as a pogo-stick or bouncing movement. Whitetails gallop similar to a running horse. Some evidence exists that hybrids inherit an awkward gait that may make them much less efficient in fleeing predators than either of their parents.

The only positive way to identify a crossbred deer is by examining the metatarsal gland on the outer portion of its lower leg. Mule deer have a metatarsal gland that sits high on the lower portion of the leg, measures from about 4 to 6 inches long, and is surrounded by brownish fur. The metatarsal gland of a whitetail is usually less than 1 inch in length, sits just below the midpoint of the lower leg, and is adorned with white fur. The metatarsal gland of a hybrid combines features of both parents. It is noticeably larger than a whitetail's, smaller than a mule deer's, and surrounded by white fur. To a skilled observer, this is the only way to differentiate hybrids, and it applies only to first-generation crossbreeds. First-generation male hybrids are usually sterile, but females are not. Genetic testing shows evidence of a small commingling of whitetail and mule deer genes in some places where their ranges overlap. A study in the early 1980s in western Texas found some evidence of hybridization in about 5 percent of deer from the two species. Results from similar testing in Montana revealed that somewhat less than 2 percent of the deer displayed evidence of hybridization.

Where their ranges overlap, the relationship between mule deer and whitetails can be complex, including interbreeding of the species.
JACK BALLARD

Whitetails and Predators

Whitetail deer are important prey for various predators. Predation is a leading cause of mortality in many areas, but the rapid reproduction of the species allows for high levels of predation without causing significant populations declines.

To understand the influence of predators on whitetail deer populations, it is helpful to distinguish between compensatory and additive predation. Compensatory predation occurs when animals of a species killed by predators would have died due to other causes. Deer cannot be stockpiled like canned food. A particular area can only support a finite number of whitetails. As their population increases, malnutrition, winter starvation, vehicle collisions, parasites, and diseases all claim varying numbers of deer each year. Compensatory predation occurs when predators such as wolves simply consume deer that would have been lost to some other factor. In good habitat conditions with normal numbers of deer and predators, biologists believe that predation is primarily compensatory.

Additive predation takes place when predators kill enough animals within a species that their influence adds to, instead of replaces, other types of mortality. Current research suggests this type of predation occurs with whitetails in areas with low populations, either as a function of habitat or after some dramatic event such as an exceptionally hard winter has severely reduced deer numbers. It appears predation can be a limiting factor in herd growth among whitetail deer in such instances.

The two species of predators that routinely prey on whitetails throughout the year in North America are mountain lions and wolves. Studies in both the northern and southern Rocky Mountains have shown deer (both whitetails and mule deer) compose the bulk of the typical mountain lion's diet. Some research indicates that where both species of deer exist, mountain lion predation on mule deer is disproportionately higher than on whitetails.

The predator-prey relationship between mountain lions and whitetails is complex. Female mountain lions consume more whitetails than males where other larger prey, such as elk and moose, are present. Biologists theorize that, because of the smaller size of the female cats, deer are a more manageable prey than bigger animals. Mountain lions prey heavily on whitetail fawns in the first few months of life, but other age classes of deer are vulnerable at certain times of the year. Research has shown that predation on does increases just prior to and after the birthing period. Older bucks are killed at higher rates after the mating season due to their physically stressed condition.

Top: Wolves are among the predators that routinely prey upon whitetails year-round.
LISA BALLARD
Bottom: Coyotes can capably prey upon whitetails, especially fawns, and are their number-one predator in many parts of the eastern United States.
JACK BALLARD

Wolves are another year-round and important predator of whitetail deer. Wolf predation on whitetails occurs primarily in the Great Lakes region, southern Canada, and the northern Rocky Mountains. Like other predators, wolves avidly consume whitetail fawns in the first few months of life. Their predation on whitetails may also increase during the winter. In open territory where deer can see for long distances, wolves have low odds of catching a whitetail. One study in Montana discovered wolves killed more deer in heavy cover and where deer densities were low. This possibly indicates that multiple deer are better at detecting wolves and more capable of escape in sparse cover.

Wolves prey heavily on adult deer as well as fawns in some places. A long-term study in Minnesota revealed that wolves killed between 4 and 22 percent of the doe deer in four study areas per year. The highest percentage occurred during a very severe winter when deep snows and weakened deer made them easy targets for wolves.

Coyotes may prey on whitetails (especially fawns) and are a significant source of deer mortality in many regions in the eastern United States. Coyotes were historically an animal primarily of the western plains but have colonized much of the East in the past five decades. Compared to their western counterparts, eastern coyotes are typically larger because of the genetic influence of coyote-wolf hybrids from eastern Canada and the north-central United States. Research in Pennsylvania concluded that the recently arrived coyotes had an additive predatory effect on whitetail populations, primarily in relation to fawn production. Human hunting is the primary means by which whitetail deer populations are kept from increasing to habitat-destructive levels in most parts of the country. Coyote predation in parts of the East has pressured populations to the extent that the number of doe deer harvested by hunters will apparently need to be reduced to accommodate the additional predation of coyotes.

A number of other predators have the ability to prey upon whitetails and may have a regional or local impact on mortality. These include bobcats and grizzly and black bears. In some places, bobcats are a significant predator of whitetail fawns. Studies in the southeastern United States have shown regional predation rates of bobcats at 7 percent (South Carolina), 8 percent (Alabama), and 9 percent (Georgia) of the total yearly fawn crop. Grizzly bears and black bears also opportunistically prey upon fawns and may be a substantial source of mortality in some places.

Other creatures such as red foxes, gray foxes, wolverines, Canada lynx, bald eagles, and golden eagles infrequently prey upon whitetails. Although predation of whitetails (mostly fawns) has been documented among these creatures, it is considered very rare.

Parasites and Diseases

Over one hundred different internal parasites have been recorded in whitetail deer in the United States. These run the gamut from tapeworms to lungworms to liver flukes. In most cases these parasites do not noticeably affect a deer's health. Heavy infestations of such parasites can lead to malnutrition or death, and they often occur when deer overpopulate their range. Heavy concentrations of lungworms, for example, are most common in young deer in stressed or poor habitat and can lead to weight loss or, in severe cases, death.

External parasites can be bothersome to whitetails and in rare cases can be fatal. Heavy tick infestations cause fawn mortality in some places. Along with ticks, deer are susceptible to biting flies, midges, and mosquitoes. They also serve as host to nasal bots, larvae of the *Cephenemyia* fly. The larvae invade a deer's nasal cavity and may be found at the back of the mouth. They are extremely bothersome and may stimulate aggressive sneezing or blowing when a deer tries to expel the pests.

Deer ticks, very small ticks common to whitetails, do not normally create problems for the deer. However, these are the carriers of Lyme disease, a malady that, if left untreated, is often fatal to humans. High numbers of whitetails in urban areas are thus a health concern in some places given their potential to host Lyme-spreading ticks. Other creatures such as rodents and birds can also carry the tick, so eliminating deer from an area may lower human exposure to Lyme disease but will not eliminate it.

Whitetails suffer from a host of diseases, most of which cause only temporary discomfort to the animal. However, some diseases are much more serious. In the United States, the most important of these are hemorrhagic diseases, chronic wasting disease, and bovine tuberculosis.

External parasites on this doe's head at Great Smoky Mountains National Park may be what prompts her scratching. Deer are bothered by many external parasites, but only in rare cases are they harmful to an animal's health.
JACK BALLARD

Hemorrhagic diseases include epizootic hemorrhagic disease (EHD) and blue tongue, which includes several strains. These viral infections are spread among deer by biting midges. They cause internal bleeding and are often fatal. Hemorrhagic disease occurs regularly in the southern United States and is becoming increasingly common in the north. Southern deer appear less susceptible to the disease. Farther north, outbreaks can cause severe losses of whitetail deer in some locations. These diseases are often associated with water and usually peak in late summer, when biting midges are most prevalent. The presence of deer carcasses near streams or standing water in late summer is a strong indication of a hemorrhagic disease outbreak.

Chronic wasting disease (CWD) is a variant of mad cow disease. It affects the brain and nervous system when proteins called prions alter the composition of a deer's brain. CWD is fatal to deer. Infected deer become malnourished, lose their ability to walk normally, and die. The disease is spread most readily by animal-to-animal contact, particularly in the saliva. Other means of transmission may also be possible.

Bovine tuberculosis (TB) is not present in deer in high numbers, but it is a concern in relation to its potential transmission to livestock. TB is a slowly progressing respiratory disease that deer or other animals may carry for years. It is not always fatal. TB may cause great economic loss among cattle operations, thus the intense concern regarding TB in deer. Whitetails in Michigan are known to host the disease, which may occur elsewhere in the country.

WHITETAILS AND HUMANS

Whitetails and American Indians

Whitetail deer were an important source of food, clothing, and tools for native peoples of North America for thousands of years before the arrival of European settlers. Archaeological evidence from Texas indicates native hunters pursued whitetails at least ten thousand years prior to the present era. Whitetail bones have been found in numerous archaeological sites. Near San Antonio, excavation for dam construction in the late 1970s uncovered a burial site. Whitetail deer antlers were carefully arranged over the graves, indicating some association with deer and the afterlife. Analysis of whitetail bones from archaeological excavations also suggests that the Texas whitetails of prehistoric times were significantly larger than they are today.

Before they acquired firearms from Europeans, American Indians used numerous ingenious methods to hunt whitetails. Perhaps the most basic technique was the still hunt, in which hunters moved carefully through deer habitat in an attempt to spot and stalk within archery range of deer. The bows and arrows used to hunt deer and other large animals were strong and deadly. One European hunter observed the bow of an Indian hunter propelling an arrow halfway through the body cavity of a deer at a range of 40 yards.

It is extremely difficult to approach a wary whitetail within archery range. To counteract their quarry's acute senses, native hunters often hid near established deer trails to ambush them. Stacked stones used to hide waiting hunters were placed within bow range of deer trails by Midwestern tribes. They also lured deer into archery range with various vocal calls and by clashing antlers together to simulate a buck fight. Native hunters sometimes wore stalks of grass on their heads to disguise their approach in grassy cover.

The Powhatan tribe that occupied territory in Virginia was among the first group of natives encountered by early settlers. Historical accounts of their hunting methods indicate deer were encircled by a band of torch-wielding hunters who drove the animals to the center. As the circle tightened, hunters were able to get close enough to kill them. Whitetails were also driven into water and then dispatched from canoes. Another method involved hunters draping themselves in a single deer hide with a stuffed head and stalking the quarry within bow range.

Native hunters hid along established deer trails, like this one in Montana, to ambush traveling whitetails.
JACK BALLARD

Whitetails and European Settlers

Colonists arriving in the New World found two ready uses for whitetail deer: Their meat and fat became an important source of food and their hides a valued item of trade. Some historians speculate that trade with the colonists in the seventeenth and eighteenth centuries prompted native peoples to kill more deer strictly for their hides than they had in previous times. Increasing numbers of European hunters and the acquisition of firearms by Indians eventually led to conditions in which whitetail reproduction could not keep pace with the harvest.

A plague among European cattle in the early eighteenth century prompted England to ban the import of cattle or their hides from Europe. To meet the demand for leather, deer hides from the American colonies became an extremely valuable commodity. Deer hides flowed to England primarily through the ports at Charleston, South Carolina, and Savannah, Georgia. Historical records indicate that from 1699 to 1715 the port of Charleston shipped around 54,000 deerskins to England per year. As demand increased, hunting of whitetails intensified. Shipping records from Charleston verify well over 5 million pounds of deer hides were exported from 1739 to 1761. From 1755 to 1772, around 2.5 million pounds of deerskins passed through the port

Deer hides were an important commodity in colonial trade with England. Hides from large bucks like this beauty in Shenandoah National Park commanded the highest value.
JACK BALLARD

at Savannah. In 1748 an estimated 160,000 deerskins were exported from the colonies. John Stuart, southern superintendent for Indian affairs, stated in 1764 that the number had grown to approximately 400,000 hides per year.

Before hunting pressure reduced whitetail numbers, trade in deerskins gave the members of various American Indian tribes access to a host of desirable goods. A 1717 agreement between the colonists and the Cherokee tribe specified the price of a musket (a primitive firearm) would be thirty-five deer hides. Bullets for the musket could be had at the rate of thirty per hide. A single deerskin could buy a knife, and three skins fetched a hatchet. A similar contract from 1751 underscores the increasing scarcity of deer hides. It specifies different terms for buck hides (larger) versus those of does (smaller). At that time, a gun could be acquired with seven buck hides or fourteen doe skins. A single doe hide could be exchanged for thirty bullets.

Market hunting for whitetails occurred at various levels of intensity and across numerous regions of the country until the close of the nineteenth century. By this time whitetails were very scarce or extinct over much of their historic range. But in 1900 the Lacey Act, a federal law prohibiting the interstate shipment of wildlife, including deer meat and hides, became law. Shortly thereafter many state legislatures created wildlife agencies and adopted hunting seasons or increased restrictions on deer harvests via existing seasons.

Whitetails and Us

Strict regulation of deer hunting, habitat changes involving timber harvest and clearing of forest for agriculture, and the reintroduction of deer to establish or bolster existing populations saw whitetail numbers increase throughout most of the United States during the early and mid-1900s. For example, by the 1930s deer numbers in northern Pennsylvania had increased to the point of intense habitat destruction in many locations. Unchecked whitetail populations can reduce or eliminate many plant species and desirable trees and shrubs. The middle decades of the 1900s saw overprotection of deer in numerous regions having substantially negative impacts on the ecosystem.

Throughout the early decades of the twentieth century, hunting seasons in most states generally protected does and allowed only the harvest of bucks. By the end of the 1970s, wildlife managers increasingly acknowledged the need for human hunters to kill does to keep deer numbers in check in the absence of major natural predators in most places.

Although no one knows for sure, many whitetail experts believe there are at least as many whitetail deer currently in the United States as there were in precolonial times.

Human hunting is essential to maintain healthy whitetail populations in most parts of the country.
JACK BALLARD

Estimates vary, but it is commonly believed around thirty million whitetails track the forests, fields, and even cities of the United States and Canada.

Human hunting is critical to keeping whitetail deer numbers in balance with their habitat capacity in most parts of the country. The return of wolves to the northern Rocky Mountains, the expansion of mountain lion populations in the West, and growing numbers of coyotes in the East have added a natural balancing component to whitetail herds in some places. However, without the harvest of whitetails by hunters, the deer would soon proverbially "eat themselves out of house and home" in most parts of the country.

Human hunters harvest around six million deer annually in the United States. In Texas, well over one million deer-hunting licenses are sold each year. Whitetail deer are the most popular big game animal in the United States, with over eleven million hunters pursuing the species each year. The sale of deer-hunting licenses is an integral component of most state wildlife agency budgets. It is estimated that whitetail hunting contributes $6 billion to the United States economy each year. Estimates indicate that nearly 300 million pounds of venison (deer meat) are consumed as a result of whitetail hunting each year.

However, the value of our most widespread large mammal isn't restricted to hunting. Whitetails are a popular part of the wildlife-viewing experience in many national parks such as Great Smoky Mountains and Shenandoah. They're a popular attraction at hundreds of state parks, national monuments, and other preserves across the country.

They also cause significant economic loss. A survey of thirteen northeastern states concluded whitetails caused $248 million annually in damages to landscaping,

Whitetails are remarkable in their ability to adapt to changing environments. The future outlook for the species, like this buck in Custer State Park, South Dakota, is excellent.
LISA BALLARD

nurseries, and crops. Degradation of habitat through overbrowsing by whitetails negatively affects plant communities and can suppress the presence of other wildlife species.

Although exact numbers are not available (as not all vehicle collisions with deer are reported), in 2008 the Insurance Institute for Highway Safety pegged whitetail collisions with motorized vehicles at around one million nationwide. It is generally accepted that deer-vehicle accidents cause around $1 billion in damages per year. Wildlife advocates have promoted deer-proof fencing with above- or below-highway crossings for deer and other species where highway collisions are numerous, but such solutions are expensive. However, weighed simply against the cost of collisions to both property and human life (150 people died in collisions with deer in 2008, some 29,000 were injured), projects to reduce vehicle accidents with deer and other wildlife may prove a worthwhile long-term investment.

Whitetails have been introduced in parts of Europe and are considered to be perhaps the most widely distributed ungulate in the world. They have shown a remarkable ability to adapt to human civilization and are considered to be one of the large mammals most capable of thriving in the future age of climate change and increasing pressure on natural resources.

CHAPTER 5
BIGHORN SHEEP

On a November elk hunt several decades ago, my older brother and I found ourselves sliding downward from an exceedingly high ridge on the flank of the Madison Range in Montana. Cresting a bulge on the vertiginous slope, the sight of three animals in a tiny, open basin found us scrambling for our binoculars. My initial impression of the animals assumed a small herd of mule deer, but even before I peered through my binoculars, I knew what they were. Three lordly bighorn rams lounged in the snow, the brown coats on their muscular bodies appearing thick and sleek under the midday sun. Their horns were much lighter, massive, and arcing from their heads like fence posts bent into a circle. The rams failed to detect our approach from above, allowing us to sneak within a distance of perhaps half a city block from the nearest sheep.

Bighorn sheep are named for the massive, spiraling horns found on males of the species.
JACK BALLARD

For some time we watched them in silence. I can still recall their white nose patches and the pale fur on their rumps, the grinding of their molars as they chewed their cud, and the dark, cloven hooves at the end of their outstretched front legs. Beyond the rams the landscape peeled away in an emerald mosaic of timber and an endless chain of barren mountain peaks melding into an ageless blue sky. The wildness of the space and the strength of life that seemed to radiate from the lounging bighorns will remain with me until erased by death or dementia.

Despite their apparent virility, bighorns are fragile creatures. They snort at -30°F temperatures, yet have less resistance to certain respiratory diseases than a newborn human. Perhaps more than any other species of hoofed mammal in North America, they need the care of thoughtful people to survive. After reading about them, I hope you'll be amply motivated to do your part.

NAMES AND FACES

Names and Visual Description

Bighorn sheep are creatures of the mountains and may also inhabit rough, badland regions of the plains. Their overall appearance is brown, varying from hues of rich chocolate to reddish or golden brown, depending on the region the animal inhabits and the time of year. Bighorns have stout, blocky bodies. Their tails are brown and stubby, and are only easily observed by the unaided eye from the rear at close range. The rump of the bighorn looks large, partly due to its highly developed muscles but also enhanced by its distinct coloration. In contrast to the brown body of the sheep, the rump appears cream-colored or pure white. Bighorns also have a pale patch of fur on the end of their nose, and varying levels of lighter fur on the inside of their legs and belly.

Although "sheep" in the truest sense of the word (bighorns can actually mate with domestic sheep in controlled conditions), observers expecting the long, woolly coat of the domestic sheep on a bighorn are mistaken. The bighorn's fur is sleek and much shorter than that of a domestic sheep. In late winter their coats may fade considerably. Their fur becomes patchy when shedding in the spring and early summer, but for most of the year, their hair-coat looks sleek and well-groomed.

Both female and male bighorn sheep have horns. The horns of a mature male dwarf those of a female. The horns grow from the top of the head and curl out and backward. Exceptionally large males may have horns that spiral into a full circle when viewed from the side.

American Indians inhabiting what is now the western portion of the United States utilized bighorn sheep for food and other purposes. Various tribes had different names for the sheep. The Blackfeet of northwestern Montana referred to the bighorn as "big head." The Mandans of the Dakotas called the animal "big horn," while the Crees of western Canada referred to the species as "ugly reindeer." Early European trappers and explorers sometimes adopted the names of the native peoples for bighorn sheep, but naturalists were often confused about the specific identity of the animal.

Such was the case with members of the Lewis and Clark expedition. The captains were aware of the presence of bighorns before they encountered or killed one, based on verbal accounts from other explorers and a spoon Clark observed in a village of Teton Sioux fashioned from the horn of a bighorn sheep. On May 25, 1805, Clark killed a female bighorn in the bluffs along the Missouri River in eastern Montana. The captain described the animal as "a female ibex or big horn animal," reflecting some of the confusion that surrounded the species in his day. Some American naturalists believed bighorns were a type of ibex, goatlike creatures that are native to central Europe, Asia, and northern Africa. Others believed them to be a strain of argali, wild sheep indigenous to eastern Asia. The confusion in the minds of Lewis and Clark is evident on their maps. In eastern Montana they named two separate watercourses "Argalia Creek" and "Ibex Creek" in the region where they first encountered bighorn sheep.

On Clark's eastward (return) journey down the Yellowstone River, he encountered a major tributary known by the Crow Indians as the "Bighorn River," the name he adopted on his map which persists today. After decades of confusion in the nineteenth century regarding the river's namesake animal, biologists successfully differentiated bighorn sheep from the argali and ibex of yonder continents and agreed upon the name "bighorn sheep," which the animals carry today. The scientific name for bighorn sheep is *Ovis canadensis*.

Related Species in North America

Bighorn sheep share summer and winter range with several other species of hoofed mammals, including elk, mule deer, and mountain goats. They may also be occasionally found in the proximity of moose and whitetail deer. Bighorns are kin to the "thin-horned" sheep of North America, the Dall's and Stone's sheep of northwestern Canada and Alaska.

Stone's and Dall's sheep are very close relatives to bighorn sheep—so close, in fact, that they have been successfully crossbred in captivity. However, the ranges of these northern-dwelling sheep and bighorns do not overlap, although both species exist in the mountains of British Columbia, Canada. In contrast to bighorns, Dall's sheep are completely white. Stone's sheep, technically a subspecies of Dall's sheep that inhabit the southern portion of its range, are found most abundantly in northern British Columbia. Compared to bighorns their coloration is more grayish than brown. While some Stone's sheep have a dark, solid charcoal appearance, most have a more mottled gray-brown coat. The horns of Dall's and Stone's sheep are somewhat thinner than those found on bighorn sheep, and tend to flare farther from the head as well.

In portions of their range in the western United States, bighorn sheep are found in proximity to mountain goats. Early European hunters and naturalists sometimes confused the identities of mountain goats and bighorns if they hadn't encountered both species. Once both animals had been viewed, they quickly realized they were seeing two different creatures.

The overall creamy-white appearance of the mountain goat contrasts sharply with the brown body of the bighorn sheep. Mountain goats sometimes exhibit a dirty coat of dingy gray, but are still lighter than bighorns. The fur of a mountain goat is longer than that of a bighorn sheep, especially in the cold months of the year when adorned in their winter coat. In comparison to the sleek coat of a bighorn, mountain goats appear shaggy. Like sheep, both male and female mountain goats have horns. However, their horns are colored and shaped differently than those on a bighorn. The smooth horns of a mountain goat are black, with bases that sometimes appear as gray when soiled. Their horns sweep up and back from the top of the head, ending in sharp, daggerlike points. In contrast, the horns of bighorn sheep are tan or auburn in color, slightly rough in appearance, and not nearly as pointed as those on a mountain goat.

Bighorn sheep also share habitat with several members of the deer family in some locations. Compared to moose or elk, bighorns are much smaller. Moose are darker in color and have much longer legs than a bighorn. Elk are also taller and heavier than bighorns, and their coats generally appear lighter and more reddish or golden brown than a bighorn. The neck of an elk is much longer. Female elk have neither horns nor antlers; male elk have antlers that are bony protrusions from the head, unlike the curling horns of a bighorn.

From a distance, mule deer may be the animal most likely confused for a bighorn sheep. They are roughly similar in size. Like bighorns, mule deer exhibit a light rump patch, and in the summer a mule deer's coat may be light brown or reddish in appearance. However, several details easily distinguish these species. First, a mule deer has a leaner, athletic look and longer neck than a bighorn. The name "mule deer" hearkens to their oversize ears that are much larger than those of a bighorn. Like elk, mule deer either have antlers if they are male, or lack horns or antlers if female.

Subspecies of Bighorn Sheep

Animals that inhabit range that is isolated from other populations of the same species often develop physical and/or behavioral characteristics that are different from other members of their own kind. For example, southern populations of many species are smaller than those in the north. Their coloration may differ as well. Regional variations within a species have led biologists to identify these different groups as subspecies.

In the twentieth century many naturalists were nearly subspecies crazy, sometimes identifying a dozen or more subspecies of a single North American mammal. Currently most biologists are much more conservative in their delineation of these distinct population groups. In most cases the number of subspecies for large mammal species on the continent has been whittled from many to a few. Such is the case with bighorn sheep. At various periods in history, as many as seven subspecies of bighorn sheep have been identified in North America.

Today most biologists recognize two or three subspecies of bighorns, while some might argue there is but a single species with no subspecies at all. Subspecies designations are sometimes muddled when biological and management classifications differ. Such is the case with bighorn sheep in the United States.

The two subspecies most commonly identified with bighorn sheep are the Rocky Mountain bighorn sheep (*Ovis canadensis canadensis*) and the desert bighorn sheep (*Ovis canadensis nelsoni*). The Rocky Mountain subspecies ranges across portions of western Canada and the western United States as far south as New Mexico. Desert bighorns are found in the southwestern United States. Occupied states include Utah, Nevada, Arizona, New Mexico, western Texas, and southern California, with a growing population also found in southwestern Colorado.

Distinguishing between Rocky Mountain and desert bighorns based on appearance alone is a difficult (some would argue impossible) task. In general, desert bighorns are thought to be smaller and exhibit a lighter coloration than their Rocky Mountain counterparts. Some believe the horns on female desert bighorns are longer than those on the Rocky Mountain subspecies. The horns of rams on the southern subspecies may be longer but less massive than those found on northern animals.

Desert bighorn sheep, like this ram in Utah's Zion National Park, are a subspecies especially adapted to living in arid environments. They are slightly smaller than Rocky Mountain bighorns.
© ISTOCK.COM/ NATURESTHUMBPRINT

In some biological circles a third subspecies of bighorn sheep is theorized, the California bighorn sheep (*Ovis canadensis california*). This subspecies is identified as those sheep historically occupying range west of the Rocky Mountains, including the Sierra Nevada of California and the Cascade Range in Oregon, Washington, and British Columbia. California bighorn males are thought to have smaller skulls and smaller, more widely flaring horns than Rocky Mountain bighorns. Whether these characteristics and geographical separation from most Rocky Mountain bighorn populations warrant subspecies classification remains a matter of debate among biologists.

When management and conservation enter the picture, the subspecies designations for bighorn sheep become even more muddled. The United States Fish & Wildlife Service (USFWS) has designated two population segments of bighorn sheep occurring in California with special status. The first is the population of desert bighorn sheep occupying the Peninsular Ranges in southern California from the San Jacinto Mountains south to the United States–Mexico border, and Baja California, Mexico. These are called Penisular bighorn sheep by the USFWS and are technically known as a Distinct Population Segment (DPS), not a separate subspecies. Under the provisions of the Endangered Species Act (ESA), geographically isolated populations of a species can be given status as an endangered species. Such is the case with the Peninsular bighorn sheep that were declared an endangered species via their status as a DPS in 1998.

The bighorn sheep subspecies discussion becomes even more convoluted in relation to the Sierra Nevada bighorn sheep (*Ovis canadensis sierrae*), a subspecies designated by the USFWS in 2008. In 2000 bighorn sheep in California's Sierra Nevada were granted endangered species protection by the USFWS after their population crashed to a low of around 125 animals. At this time the bighorns of the Sierra Nevada were considered

representatives of the California bighorn sheep subspecies as described above. Utilizing research indicating that the bighorns found in the Sierra are more closely aligned genetically with animals of the southwestern deserts than the northern mountains, but genetically different in some ways from both, the USFWS officially concluded these animals were a separate subspecies and named them Sierra Nevada bighorn sheep. However, a change in subspecies designation by a federal agency does not automatically make its decision accepted science, and not all biologists specializing in the natural history of North American wild sheep would agree with the position of the USFWS.

To conclude the subspecies discussion, it is interesting to note that some biologists would prefer to regard all bighorn sheep as members of a single species, no subspecies included. These scientists point out that historically interchanges between all populations now regarded as subspecies occurred on the edges of their range. They might further argue that even the most expert observer would be hard-pressed to identify individual animals as belonging to a particular subspecies in the absence of its known geographical range. Neither size nor horn shape, two physical characteristics often related to subspecies distinctions in bighorn males, is consistent. Small mature males from the Rocky Mountain subspecies on poor range may be similar in size to large desert males. The flaring horns offered as a physical characteristic of the California bighorn sheep subspecies are sometimes observed on Rocky Mountain animals. I have personally observed bighorn males in Montana with flaring horns that could easily be taken for the California subspecies.

If one wishes to push the issue even further, some biologists admit that all wild sheep of North America, both the bighorn and thin-horned varieties, might legitimately be classified as a single species, since they can interbreed and produce fertile, functional offspring.

Physical Characteristics

Bighorn sheep are not particularly tall or heavy animals. They are considered medium-size ungulates in comparison to others in North America. Average weights for bighorn males and females are comparable to those of the whitetail or mule deer. The overall dimensions of bighorns (height at the shoulder, overall length) are also similar between bighorns and deer.

Adult bighorn males normally stand from 2.5 to 3.5 feet at the shoulder, with a head-to-tail body length ranging from 5.2 to 6.1 feet. Males commonly weigh from 130 to 275 pounds. Females are substantially smaller, with normal weights varying from 80 to 150 pounds. Adult mass among bighorns is usually determined by habitat quality. Sheep with access to increased amounts of nutritious forage maximize body weight, while those in marginal habitats obtain smaller sizes as adults. An exceptionally large male weighing 301 pounds was once surveyed by biologists in Jasper National Park in Alberta, Canada.

Nomenclature for gender in bighorn sheep follows that of domestic sheep. Adult males are called "rams"; females are referred to as "ewes." Newborns or young of the year are known as "lambs."

Horns and Horn Development

Perhaps the most remarkable and distinguishing feature of the bighorn sheep is the massive, curling horns carried by an adult ram. The horns may weigh up to 30 pounds or slightly more, sometimes exceeding 10 percent of the animal's total weight. On the average, bighorn sheep horns increase in mass as one travels from south to north within their range. In the 1990s a number of rams were harvested by hunters in western Montana with horns measuring over 17 inches in circumference at the base of the horn near the skull. Measured from the base of the horn where it touches the skull around the outside curl, bighorn rams have been recorded with horns measuring over 49 inches in length.

The horns of bighorns are actually composed of keratin fibers, similar to the horns adorning other animals such as mountain goats, impala, bison, ibex, and some strains of domestic cattle. Keratin is the material also found in hair, hooves, and human fingernails. The horns of bighorn sheep form around bony projections on the top of a ram's skull known as "horn cores." Horns on bighorn sheep begin growing shortly after birth, and by its first birthday a bighorn ram may have horns that are 5 to 8 inches in length.

Each year another horn sheath grows from the horn core. The new sheath develops inside the previous horn sheath, expanding it and forcing it farther away from the horn core, which increases both the length and the circumference of the horn. A ram's horn is thus a succession of horn sheaths stacked one inside of the next, similar to a

Horns on bighorn sheep grow from the time the animal is born. Within a few months the horns on this lamb photographed in Badlands National Park, South Dakota, will be visible.
© ISTOCK.COM/KGRIF

bunch of empty ice-cream cones or paper cups placed one inside another. What is viewed on the outside of the horn is only the exposed portion of each horn sheath.

The annual development of a ram's horns creates a dark indentation where each new horn sheath begins to develop. These indentations create discernible growth rings, or annuli, that can be used to estimate a ram's age. Problems arise in this aging method for several reasons. First, rams may break off the entire sheath grown in the first year of life (sometimes known as "lamb tips") when fighting or rubbing their horns against trees. In extreme cases rams may lose up to three years of horn growth when the ends of the horns splinter in battle. Horns damaged in such a way are said to be "broomed." In such cases the total of the annuli is less than the ram's actual age.

Another aging problem arises in relation to the annuli found between the ram's first and second year. On many sheep this growth ring is less distinct than those found between successive horn sheaths. Additionally, some animals develop false growth rings. The horns of all bighorn sheep are rippled and indented in appearance. Extreme indentations are sometimes very difficult to distinguish from true annuli.

The length of a bighorn ram's horn increases most rapidly in the first years of life. Horns may lengthen at a rate of 6 inches per year for the first four years of life. Once a ram reaches nine years of age, its horns seldom add more than 2 inches of length from the base per year.

The horns of bighorn sheep develop dark lines know as annuli. Each line represents one year of growth.
© ISTOCK.COM/KOJIHIRANO

Development of the smaller horns found on ewes follows the same biological pattern as the massive horns carried by rams. Annuli on ewe horns are harder to distinguish due to their smaller size. Unlike the horns of rams that may be broomed during fighting, the horns of ewes generally remain intact.

RANGE AND HABITAT

North American Range—Historic

The occupied range of bighorn sheep has contracted dramatically since European settlers arrived in North America. Bighorn sheep, like elk, are now most strongly associated with the Rocky Mountains. However, unlike elk that once roamed over much of what is now the contiguous United States, the historic range of bighorn sheep was always confined to the western half of the continent. The reason for this is quite simple: Bighorns are animals of the open country. They do not live in dense forests. The eastern woodlands of the continent have thus never been home to bighorns.

Historically bighorn sheep occupied suitable habit as far south as the southern reaches of Baja California and northwestern Mexico. In the United States, a line drawn from the "Big Bend" of the Rio Grande in Texas northward to the intersection of the eastern border of Saskatchewan and North Dakota roughly approximates the eastern edge of the bighorn's historic range. They occupied mountainous areas jutting northward into Canada along the Rocky Mountains, primarily in southwestern Alberta and southeastern British Columbia. On the western side, the original range of bighorn sheep did not extend into the dense coastal forests of Washington, Oregon, and California. Bighorns ranged in drier, more open habitats in the interior mountains of these states.

Bighorn sheep were historically found in some habitats on the plains. This ram was photographed in the breaks along the Missouri River in eastern Montana.
JACK BALLARD

Although bighorn sheep are sometimes called "mountain monarchs," such a nickname tends to overlook the fact that historically the animals were creatures of the prairies as well as the mountains. Bighorn sheep were found in plains habitats in areas where steep slopes or cliffs gave them escape cover from predators. These places were often found along eroded river corridors, such as the breaks along the Missouri River, where Lewis and Clark first encountered bighorn sheep on their westward trek to the Pacific Ocean. Indigenous bands of bighorns tracked the soils of western North and South Dakota and western Nebraska, although most contemporary Americans do not conceive of them in such habitats.

Bighorn sheep faced the same perils from European homesteaders as other large ungulates and predators. They were killed for meat and for sport, the large, impressive horns of the rams considered a desirable trophy by hunters, including the great conservationist and president, Theodore Roosevelt. The meat of bighorn sheep has a delicate flavor, motivating early hunters to target them for their taste.

Hunting took a dramatic toll on bighorn sheep numbers in the later decades of the nineteenth century and early twentieth century, but other factors whittled their numbers as well. Domestic cattle and other livestock grazed on pastures in the foothills of the Rocky Mountains, leaving little for the mouths of bighorn sheep during the winter, sheep that often migrated to the mountaintops during the summer but passed the winter in the lowlands.

Fur trappers and explorers hunted bighorn sheep, finding the greatest success when targeting sheep on winter range.
LISA BALLARD

Competition for forage wasn't the greatest threat facing bighorn sheep from the newly arrived livestock of homesteaders. Diseases and parasites carried by domestic sheep are easily transmitted to bighorns. Lacking the immunity domestic sheep had developed during their centuries of domestication, bighorn populations in many areas were decimated by diseases from domestic livestock. To this day, disease transmission from domestic to wild sheep is one of the greatest perils to bighorn populations, and

on numerous bighorn ranges wildlife managers have worked diligently to keep wild sheep separated from their domestic kin.

How many bighorn sheep inhabited North America before the historic collapse in their population? No one knows for sure. In 1929, in his book titled *Lives of Game Animals*, Ernest Thompson Seton estimated there were 4 million bighorn sheep in North America prior to their decimation, 2 million in the contiguous United States and another 2 million in Canada. Seton's estimate has been widely accepted, although other biologists argue that the bighorn sheep population in North America has never climbed beyond 500,000 animals. However, eyewitness accounts from early explorers with a reputation for competence and accuracy point to abundance in many habitats.

Osborne Russell, a fur trapper, kept a journal while rambling through the Rocky Mountains from 1834 to 1843. He frequently notes that he and his companions, or the American Indians that they encountered, hunted bighorn sheep. He describes bighorns in terms of abundance in numerous places in his journals, and while in the mountains of northwestern Wyoming wrote that "thousands of mountain sheep were scattered up and down feeding on the short grass which grew among the cliffs and crevices."

Bighorns were the meal of choice for many early hunters, and the scant historical records of their presence in the nineteenth century indicate there were plenty to be found. For example, bighorns were abundant enough in the Southwest that sheep meat was available in markets in Tucson, Arizona, in the early decades of the twentieth century. An annual report from Yellowstone National Park in 1877 indicates nearly 2,000 sheep were killed in the region by hunters who pursued animals for their hides. Many biologists believe that bighorn sheep were the most abundant animal in the mountains of Idaho in the early 1800s.

However, despite their apparent abundance in places, unregulated hunting, habitat loss, parasites, and diseases were driving bighorn sheep to extinction over vast segments of their historic range. Their presence on the western prairies of North and South Dakota ended by 1905. They disappeared from California's Yosemite National Park around 1914. In eastern Montana, where Lewis and Clark first encountered them, a ram killed in 1916 is thought to be the last confirmed sighting of a bighorn sheep in the state's prairie habitat. Ernest Thompson Seton wrote in 1929 that bighorns were extirpated from the Black Hills of South Dakota in 1899. E. R. Hall, a naturalist who documented the mammals of Nevada in a book published in 1946, declared that bighorns were extinct in the state. In 1906 the State Game Warden of Idaho reported that a mere 300 to 400 bighorns were estimated to occupy the entire state.

North American Range—Current

Relegated to remnants of their historic range, most states where bighorns continued to exist banned their hunting around the turn of the twentieth century. However, disease and habitat loss continued to plague sheep herds even in the absence of hunting.

After World War II a number of states began transplanting bighorns from healthy herds into previously occupied habitats from which they had been eliminated. Sheep

Bighorns, including this young ram in Joshua Tree National Park, California, range over tens of thousands of acres of desert habitat in the southwestern United States.
© ISTOCK.COM/
RMIRAMONTES

returned to several states where indigenous bands had been completely wiped out. Numerous transplants were successful, resulting in the establishment of bighorns over increasingly broad portions of their native range. However, some transplanted animals failed to thrive in their new environments, and the introduced bighorns eventually died out. As of 1990 researchers had documented over 200 bighorn sheep transplants to their native range undertaken by fourteen different state wildlife agencies.

At the present time, bighorn sheep occupy fifteen states and two Canadian provinces, Alberta and British Columbia. Desert bighorns also roam across parts of Mexico, including limited areas in the extreme northwestern portion of the mainland, and on the Baja Peninsula.

In the United States, bighorn sheep are found in the following states, with some states inhabited by members of one or more recognized subspecies: Arizona, California, Colorado, Idaho, Montana, Nebraska, Nevada, New Mexico, North Dakota, Oregon, South Dakota, Texas, Utah, Washington, and Wyoming.

Cataloging the exact regional locations of bighorn sheep herds in each state is beyond the scope of this book. Suffice it to say that depending on the state, sheep have remained in, or returned to, varying percentages of their original habitat. In most states, wildlife managers have identified specific populations units, or herds, of bighorns that are separated from other members of their kind, most often by natural geographic or man-made barriers. Man-made barriers include fenced highways that sheep are unable to cross or habitat corridors now occupied by domestic livestock, croplands, or human inhabitation. These human-induced obstacles often impede genetic interchange between herds and prohibit sheep from expanding their range into unoccupied areas. Arizona, for example, has over thirty distinct herds or population units of desert bighorns, and a single herd of Rocky Mountain bighorns located in the east-central portion of the state. Where disease might be transmitted from one herd to another, wildlife managers sometimes deliberately attempt to limit interchange between bighorn sheep herds.

Some states have but a few population units of bighorns. Texas has around a half-dozen herds of desert bighorns. South Dakota's sheep are found in just four major herds, totaling around 300 animals in 2013. To the north, North Dakota's sheep also numbered around 300 animals in the same time period, with bighorns also confined to just a few population units. Nebraska's bighorns number around 340 animals in five herds.

Other states have relatively high numbers of bighorn sheep, creatures that occupy significant portions of their native range. Bighorns were never extirpated from Colorado. Intact herds and an aggressive transplanting program conducted since 1945 have increased the number of population units of Rocky Mountain bighorns to around eighty, with a handful of desert bighorn herds located in the west-central part of the state. Some 500 desert bighorns track Colorado; Rocky Mountain bighorns number nearly 7,000.

Northwestern Wyoming holds some of the most impressive herds of bighorns. Bighorn sheep were never extirpated from the Gros Ventre, Wind River, and Absaroka mountain ranges. The herds now inhabiting these areas have never been supplemented with sheep from other locations, making them true native survivors in the high country. In the sprawling Absaroka Range, over 4,000 bighorn sheep exist in one extended, connected population, many in bands that number just a few dozen animals.

No matter where they're found, bighorn sheep populations in the contiguous United States are fraught with frailty. Tough animals capable of withstanding bitter cold and extreme drought, catastrophic disease events frequently decimate entire herds, leading to what biologists call "all-age die-offs." An acute disease outbreak may take 80 percent or more of the sheep from a population unit. In some cases the remainder are so compromised that they fail to reproduce and eventually fade from existence. Understanding and managing disease among bighorns is perhaps the most critical factor in determining what their range will be in the future.

Bighorn Sheep Habitat

Bighorn sheep may be found in the mountains, the plains, or the desert. But within these vastly different ecosystems, several commonalities determine suitable sheep habitat. First, bighorns prefer open areas. Visual detection of predators and the ability to flee are critical to survival. Thus, bighorns range in areas where vegetation is neither too tall nor too thick to see clearly at a distance. Research indicates sheep are seldom found on gentle or moderate slopes where trees and shrubs cover more than 25 percent of the area. They also avoid brushy places where shrubs are more than 2 feet tall. On steep slopes they may venture into locations with somewhat heavier cover, but favor sparse vegetation at or above their line of sight in all environments.

Bighorns sometimes move through timbered areas on migrations or at other times, but do so with an apparent sense of danger. They tend to move quickly when traveling through forested habitats. Research on wild sheep has shown that their heart rate increases substantially when they enter forested habitats, attesting to the discomfort they experience in confined environments limiting their sight. Open timber is sometimes used by bighorns, but they are extremely reluctant to enter dense cover.

Another characteristic of bighorn sheep habitat consistent from alpine to arid ecosystems involves escape terrain. Bighorns are remarkably adept at traversing steep slopes and cliff faces. When danger threatens, sheep dash to the security of terrain where predators follow them with great difficulty or abandon the chase. Prairie badlands, canted mountain slopes, bluffs, rimrocks, and cliffs offer security to bighorns. Research indicates Rocky Mountain bighorn sheep are seldom found more than 0.5 mile from such escape terrain. Some research has shown that Rocky Mountain bighorns on winter range spend over 80 percent of their time within 110 yards of rocky terrain in which they can elude predators. Biologists have concluded that suitable escape terrain is a critical habitat component for bighorn sheep, something without which they cannot survive.

Water is another important component of bighorn sheep habitat, especially in desert environments. Bighorns obtain water from plant matter and dew, but may also eat snow. They are typically found within 1 mile of some type of surface water, be it a stream, pond, or spring. Sheep sometimes occupy habitat as far as 2 miles from a water source. Desert bighorns have an astonishing capacity to exist for extended periods without drinking. In extreme cases they may go up to fourteen days without water in dry seasons. However, some source of water is essential to their survival. Restoration efforts of desert bighorn sheep in many places have focused upon the construction of cisterns to catch rainwater or the development of seeps and springs to provide more water. When watering, bighorns show the same need for unimpeded vision and proximity to escape cover as at other times. Water sources surrounded by high vegetation or much farther than 0.25 mile from escape cover are seldom used by bighorns.

In mountainous areas many bands of bighorn sheep often occupy different habitat during the summer and winter. Summer finds them high in the mountains, grazing on alpine ridgetops where the elevation often exceeds 10,000 feet above sea level. During the winter these sheep descend to the foothills where snow cover is shallower and cured grasses from the previous summer provide forage. Some hearty bighorns in the Rocky Mountains spend their entire life in the alpine zone. These animals winter on very high ridges where the piercing winter winds clear the vegetation of snow. The winter range of these animals typically occurs on south-facing slopes where sun exposure warms their bodies and hastens snowmelt. All bighorns are remarkable animals, but many naturalists believe those sheep that winter on 10,000-foot ridgetops are the most extraordinary of all.

National parks are important refuges for bighorn sheep. This magnificent ram finds excellent habitat in Glacier National Park, Montana.
NPS/DAVID RESTIVO

Were it not for remote, inhospitable areas where they found refuge from human hunters and a buffer from the diseases carried by domestic sheep, bighorns may have been driven to extinction. National parks, where they received protection from hunting and existed away from domestic animals, were important reserves for bighorns in earlier times. Some prime examples of national parks important to the historical survival of bighorns include Yellowstone National Park in northwestern Wyoming, Rocky Mountain National Park in central Colorado, and Glacier National Park in northwestern Montana.

The passage of the Wilderness Act of 1964 created vast tracts of pristine habitat off-limits to vehicles, timber harvest, and other activities that disrupt and displace bighorn sheep. Domestic sheep grazed many wilderness areas in the past as one of these areas' legal uses, but the grazing allotments in some have been retired, giving bighorns a buffer from disease. However, a high percentage of bighorns are found on national forest and Bureau of Land Management (BLM) lands lacking wilderness protections. A variety of land-use practices on these public lands (grazing by domestic livestock, motorized recreation, and energy development) are direct threats to the continuation of the species in the contiguous United States. Wilderness areas and national parks continue to be very important refuges for bighorn sheep, although they nurture but a small percentage of the bighorns roaming public lands in the Lower 48.

NUTRITIONAL REQUIREMENTS AND FORAGE

Nutritional Requirements

Much less is known about the specific nutritional requirements of bighorn sheep in comparison to more intensively studied ungulates such as elk and whitetail deer. Captive bighorns have been recorded eating an average of 3 pounds of plant material per day, but the extent to which this intake approximates the rate of wild sheep isn't clearly understood.

Like other hoofed mammals wintering in cold climates, bighorn sheep lower their nutritional intake during the winter. While it seems the animals would graze or browse more during the winter because it takes more energy to stay warm in the cold, a different survival strategy is at work. Eating is an activity that burns energy in excess of what an animal requires in a resting state. One study found that bighorn sheep burned slightly over 30 percent more energy feeding than they did resting. Winter forage is typically of much lower quality than food items found on summer range. Burning substantial amounts of energy to ingest low-quality forage is a poor survival strategy. Thus, bighorns tend to rest more and get by on less feed in the winter than the summer.

The nutritional value of forage on a bighorn sheep's range is believed to influence a number of health-related factors in sheep herds. Ewes on range that provides poor nutrition do not have as high reproductive rates as those finding abundant, high-quality forage. Nutritional stress is also thought to be a potential influence in susceptibility to disease. Sheep unable to find enough suitable forage to meet their nutritional demands may succumb to diseases unable to overpower well-fed bighorns.

In addition to the forage required for energy and bodily maintenance, bighorn sheep, like other living creatures, need water to survive. Lakes, streams, springs, and other sources of surface water provide sheep most of their water demands in the majority of their habitats. However, bighorns may also obtain water from moisture contained in plants, snow, and ice. The ability of desert bighorn sheep to endure extended periods without water rivals that of most animals humans associate with existence in arid environments, such as the camel. Researchers have found that desert bighorns may not drink for periods up to two weeks long, sometimes losing 20 percent of their normal body weight due to dehydration.

Like camels, desert bighorns can restore water in the body in a single stint of consumption. A researcher measuring water consumption of desert bighorns in California documented a ram consuming 4.94 gallons of water in a single drinking episode, approximately 23 percent of his body weight. Other bighorns were recorded consuming up to 20 percent of their body weight in water after extended bouts of dehydration. Some biologists believe bighorns can exist for extended periods of time without any access to surface water at all, deriving enough moisture from plant matter to survive. If this is the case, it most likely applies to very few locations containing small herds of sheep.

Digestion

The digestive process begins with food intake. Bighorn sheep have developed the ability to ingest comparatively large amounts of forage in a hurry. This adaptation decreases the time they need to spend feeding. Feeding activity requires them to be less alert and may lead them away from rocky escape cover, two factors that increase their vulnerability to predators.

Bighorns frequently feed upon coarse, woody plants and tough, dry grass. A bighorn's front teeth are quite sharp, their rear teeth large and strong. A sheep's teeth grow throughout its entire life to counteract the wear involved in eating. Like other ruminants, bighorn sheep have a long, complex digestive system with a stomach composed of four chambers. Bighorns don't chew their forage while eating. Rather, it's bitten off and swallowed rapidly. After feeding, sheep retreat to secure areas where they lay down, or "bed," during the day. At this time they regurgitate food that has entered the first chamber of their stomach. It is then chewed thoroughly, re-swallowed, and passes through the remainder of the digestive tract. The digestive system of bighorn sheep is particularly efficient in digesting dry plant matter.

Food Sources

Ungulate species fall on a continuum between browsers and grazers. Browsers, like moose, generally specialize in the consumption of plant matter found on trees and shrubs. Leaves, twigs, buds, and evergreen needles compose a very high percentage of a browser's annual diet. Grazers, on the other hand, eat mostly grass. Animals like bison specialize in the consumption of grasses and other leafy plants known as forbs. They seldom feed on shrubs or trees. Some species, like elk, are generalist feeders that are happy to browse or graze, depending on the food sources available on their range. This explains why elk can be found in such diverse areas and habitat types across North America.

Bighorn sheep are often characterized as grazers, but such a description is not completely accurate. They browse extensively in some habitats and exhibit more flexibility in their diet than many observers realize. Desert bighorns, for example, obtain more of their annual nutritional intake from browsing than grazing in many places. Mountain-mahogany, brittlebush, false mesquite, desert holly, and ironwood are among the woody species browsed by desert bighorns. They are also known to eat saguaro, a tree-like cactus native to the Sonoran Desert of southeastern California and southwestern Arizona. Bighorns sometimes feed on the flesh of saguaro, in part to obtain its moisture in the absence of other water sources. In an odd twist of fate, a desert bighorn ewe was once observed with a spine from a saguaro penetrating her lacrimal bone (a small bone found between the eyes), causing her blindness and eventual death. The sheep had apparently contacted the spine in an inadvertent collision with a cactus. Desert bighorns are also known to eat prickly pear, barrel cactus, and pincushion cactus.

Bighorns in northern climates consume an eclectic diet, whose composition varies considerably by location and forage availability. Researchers have found that the bighorn sheep ranging from California to British Columbia consume over 260 different species of plants. Rocky Mountain bighorns show a preference for forbs (flowering plants with leaves and stems whose growth dies back to ground level at the end of the growing season). Of the 260-plus plants referenced above, 160 of them are forbs.

The diet of the typical bighorn is composed of grasses, forbs, and shrubs, with the relative percentage of each varying substantially by region. Research on bighorn sheep in Colorado indicates grasses compose 76 percent of their diet, with forbs accounting for 7 percent and shrubs 17 percent. The diet of Montana bighorns was found to be 41 percent grasses, 40 percent forbs, and 19 percent shrubs. Bighorns in California consumed 63 percent forbs and 37 percent grasses. It should be noted that these figures are statewide averages. Bighorns in various regions of states as large as California and Montana may exhibit considerable diversity in their typical diets.

Bighorns are very flexible in their diet. This ewe is grazing on grass near the Colorado River in Grand Canyon National Park. When grass is unavailable, desert bighorns readily turn to browse and may even eat cactus.
LISA BALLARD

Grasses commonly consumed by bighorns include various types of bluegrass, wheatgrass, fescues, and bromes. Forbs are represented by clovers, phlox, buckwheats, aster, lupine, balsamroot, and paintbrush, among many others. Shrubs often browsed by bighorns consist of chokecherry, several species of sagebrush, mountain mahogany, rabbitbrush, and bitterbrush.

Forage through the Seasons

The diet of bighorn sheep changes with the seasons, sometimes dramatically in relation to the relative percentage of grasses, forbs, and shrubs. Northern-dwelling populations of Rocky Mountain bighorn sheep experience seasonal variations in forage availability most profoundly affected by cold winters and their influence on the plant growth cycle. Seasonal availability of various forage types for desert bighorns is strongly influenced by rainfall. Unusually low annual precipitation or extended drought may alter plant growth and availability for bighorns no matter where they are found.

In the mountainous regions of the Rocky Mountains, forage selection by bighorn sheep follows a somewhat predictable pattern. Forbs are most abundant during the spring and summer, and are most highly represented in the diet of sheep during those seasons. Once they dry and decay in the fall, forbs offer little food value for bighorns.

For many Rocky Mountain bighorn sheep herds, grasses are a year-round source of forage. The first green shoots are eagerly consumed in the spring, as are maturing grasses during the summer. Seed-heads and cured grasses are eaten in the fall. Some species of grass experience a fall "green-up" if rain comes after they become dormant and temperatures are warm, providing a windfall of green forage to bighorns and other grazing animals. Dry grasses retain some food value during the winter months and are readily eaten by bighorns. Shrubs are most often consumed during the winter when forbs have become decadent and grasses may be covered in snow.

Shrubs are an important source of nutrition for some bighorns. This ram is browsing on sagebrush in Yellowstone National Park. Browse consumption increases during the winter in some sheep herds.
LISA BALLARD

Migration

Bighorn sheep migrations are usually associated with seasonal changes in the elevation at which animals are found in an ecosystem. Mountain-dwelling populations of bighorn sheep typically spend their summers in the alpine zone at very high elevations. Research on the nutritional value of grass species has compared high-elevation grasses with those growing in the foothills. Even within the same species, nutritional value is higher for plants found at lofty elevations. Many experts believe the availability of forage with superior nutritional value is what leads bighorns to their alpine haunts in the summer.

Increasing snow depth and cold temperatures are conditions thought to be instrumental in triggering the migration of bighorns from the highlands to winter range at lower elevations or in the foothills. The trek to winter range in most populations of Rocky Mountain bighorns occurs in October and November.

Rocky Mountain bighorns that spend the entire year at high elevation may move from one alpine area to another, diverse habitat niches that represent distinct summer and winter ranges. Females complete the fall migration before males. The spring return to higher pastures happens as early as April or as late as July, depending on the area and seasonal conditions. Bighorns tend to follow greening forage up the mountains, a phenomenon that may be accelerated or retarded by snow depth and temperature. A discernible pattern of spring migration between the sexes is not apparent.

Some desert bighorns also engage in migrations. These may be seasonal movements between various mountain ranges covering considerable distances, or elevation-related migrations occurring within a particular mountain range. Seasonal availability of water sources may also trigger migrations of desert bighorns. Like the migrations of Rocky Mountain bighorns, recurring movements of desert animals appear to be prompted by a motivation to exploit the most desirable swatches of habitat within a sheep's range.

Fall migrations from alpine environments to mountain foothills are common among bighorns. This small band was photographed in the foothills of the Absaroka Mountains in Montana in November after migrating from summer habitat on the mountaintops.
JACK BALLARD

ABILITIES AND BEHAVIOR

Physical Abilities

The physical traits of wild hoofed mammals are remarkably adapted to the habitats in which they live, including specialized abilities that help them escape predators. Pronghorn are exceptionally fleet of foot, so fast that no predator on the North American continent can match their speed in a chase. Moose have excellent hearing and can trot at high speeds through forests and over obstacles, which makes it difficult for would-be predators to catch them.

Bighorn sheep have neither the speed of the pronghorn nor the hearing of a moose. Nonetheless, they are extremely adept at eluding predators in the steep, rocky places they inhabit. The muscles on the hindquarters of a bighorn sheep are very developed. These muscles propel them in powerful leaps that may take them from ledge to ledge on a vertical rock face or in a quick dash from a grassy area to a jumble of stones. The relatively short, blocky bodies of bighorns aren't built for speed in the open country. Some historical accounts indicate bighorns caught in the open could

Top: Strong muscles in the rear quarters give bighorns the power to make incredible leaps in steep terrain.
© ISTOCK.COM/IRONMAN100

Bottom: Specialized hooves and spectacular balance allow bighorn sheep to traverse cliffs where predators are unable to follow.
© ISTOCK.COM/ANDREANITA

be easily overtaken by a pack of dogs or run down by a rider on horseback. However, when it comes to running up or down steep slopes, bighorns are very fast and agile.

The ability of bighorns to traverse seemingly impossible terrain is legendary. They are sometimes observed on cliff ledges or rocky promontories where it seems impossible to stand. However, bighorns have several physical adaptations that permit such abilities. First, their bodies are very strong and compact, allowing them to brace against the forces of gravity and maneuver in places creatures with larger limbs or bodies find it impossible to follow. Bighorns also possess hooves that lend them extremely efficient gripping ability on slick or steep rocks. The cloven hooves of bighorns consist of two digits that can move independently of each other. A spongy portion is found on the rear of each part of the hoof with a rubbery outer covering, yielding a substance that provides the bighorn with outstanding traction on hard, slippery surfaces. The front hooves of bighorns are slightly larger than the rear hooves, a characteristic thought to aid their exceptional climbing ability. Although bighorn sheep sometimes slip and fall from cliffs, occasionally sustaining serious or fatal injuries, these occurrences appear to be quite rare, indicating bighorns also possess an uncanny sense of balance and precision of movement in constrained space.

Of their perceptive organs, bighorns appear to rely on their eyes more than other senses to detect other animals, including predators. Some sources claim the eyesight of bighorn sheep is approximately eight times better than that of humans. Such claims, though common in relation to the vision of animals, are seldom scientifically tested. The ability of bighorns to discern motion at considerable distances has been documented, but definitive studies of their perceptual abilities are lacking. Bighorns can detect the movement of other creatures at a distance of 1,000 yards. The keen eyesight of bighorn sheep is also thought to be instrumental in the animals' prowess in jumping and perceiving footholds in perilous terrain.

Animals inhabiting dense, forested habitats, both predators and prey, often display exceptional hearing and sense of smell. These abilities allow them to discern other creatures where eyesight is impeded. The ears of bighorn sheep are quite small compared to those of elk, mule, or whitetail deer. While bighorns can probably detect sound as well as humans, their hearing is not nearly as developed as deer or elk. It is interesting to note that the other animal that shares the bighorn's affinity for cliffs and steep places, the mountain goat, also has small ears in relation to its size. The same holds true for the bighorn sheep's sense of smell. Bighorns sometimes detect predators via their nose, and rams have been observed following unseen ewes on the basis of scent. However, in the world of North American ungulates, the bighorn's sense of smell appears to be inferior to many of its kin.

One of the most remarkable physical abilities of bighorn sheep is their endurance of extremely cold temperatures. Bighorns wintering on high alpine ridges may encounter temperatures below 0°F for extended periods of time. How do they keep from freezing to death? Research has found that the bodies of bighorn sheep are extremely efficient at producing and retaining heat. At around 10°F bighorns achieve a state of thermal

Bighorns have an amazing ability to endure cold. Metabolic adaptations and a super-insulating coat allow them to conserve energy throughout the winter.
JACK BALLARD

neutrality. "Thermal-neutral" is a term used to describe the temperature at which an organism doesn't burn energy to stay warm or cool itself. The compact body of bighorns, an efficient metabolism, and a super-insulating coat are among the adaptations allowing sheep to thrive in low temperatures. However, when temperatures increase in the summer, bighorns spend considerable energy keeping their bodies cool. Desert bighorns seek out shade in caves or under trees to stay cool. Rocky Mountain bighorns move to high elevations to find forage, but may also be motivated by the cooler temperatures. The circulatory system becomes more active in higher temperatures to help the animals disperse heat.

Vocal and Visual Communication

Bighorn sheep, like other herd animals, frequently use vocalizations as a means of communication. Ewes and lambs often communicate with bleats that sound similar to the "baah, baah" noises made by domestic sheep. Newborn lambs and their mothers bleat back and forth frequently after birth, apparently to strengthen the mother-offspring bond and to familiarize each other with their voice. When the ewe needs to find her lamb within the maternal herd (or vice versa), she will not only look for her young but also bleat to get its attention. Once the lamb is found, the mother sniffs the youngster, in what appears to be a behavior that confirms its identity.

Research has indicated that young lambs rely more on sound to identify their mothers than sight or smell. Although ewes and lambs become attuned to each other's voices, the vocal means of identification isn't perfect. Occasionally ewes will respond to the bleats of a lamb in the herd that is not her own. However, the unique smell of the offspring is a more accurate way to recognize its individuality. Ewes will not accept a lamb that fails to pass the scent test.

One of the loudest and dramatic noises created by bighorn sheep is not used as a means of communication. During the mating season, rams clash their horns together in battles for dominance. The sharp cracking sounds made when the rams butt their heads

together can sometimes be heard at a distance of a mile, and may alert a person to the presence of bighorn rams.

Like other mother-offspring pairs in the world of ungulates, bighorn ewes and lambs communicate their bond with physical behaviors as well as vocalizations. They many nuzzle one another, or the mother may butt a pesky offspring or another lamb. However, perhaps the most complex and interesting forms of physical communication occur between adult rams. Throughout the year, rams assert or accept dominance of other males. Subordinate rams nuzzle their superiors. They may wag their horns at rams of equal or higher social status in a gesture that suggests submission, not a challenge. Dominant rams may place their head on the neck or back of a subordinate, or mount them from behind. To initiate a challenge to a dominant ram, an upstart subordinate may kick its belly to incite a confrontation.

Rams use many sophisticated means of physical communication. Older rams may rest their head on the back of a younger male in a display of dominance.
JACK BALLARD

Herd Behavior

Bighorn sheep may sometimes be found alone, particularly yearlings or old rams, but the vast majority live in herds whose composition shifts at various times during the year. Except during the mating season, older rams live in bands separately from ewes and lambs.

Juvenile rams stay in female bands composed of adult ewes and their offspring for up to three years, rarely beyond. Some research suggests young rams transition from female herds to groups of adult males when they become dominant animals in the female bands. Studies of bighorns in some locations also suggest young rams join herds of adult males as they travel to mineral licks, places where sheep deliberately ingest soil to obtain minerals that apparently enhance their health. The number of individuals in a herd of rams varies significantly in relation to habitat and the number of bighorns occupying a particular region. Ram bands may consist of just two or three individuals, or may hold over a dozen adult rams of different ages.

Female herds of bighorn sheep normally live in different places than the ram bands, except during the mating season when the separate groups intermingle. Like ram bands, the size of female herds varies dramatically, depending on habitat and sheep population in a given area. One interesting variation in female herds occurs when pregnant ewes depart the female bands to birth their young. At these times sheep may congregate in female herds led by barren ewes, often older animals beyond prime reproductive age. The barren ewes are accompanied by immature rams and yearlings of both sexes separated from their mothers for the first time. Young sheep that haven't learned independent living strategies greatly benefit from their association with these matriarchs as they transition to adulthood and enjoy greater survival rates than immature sheep forced to live on their own.

REPRODUCTION AND YOUNG

The Mating Season

The mating season, or "rut," for mammal species is understood by biologists as the period of time in which reproductive behaviors between males and females result in a large percentage of the offspring crop for a given season. As is the case with numerous other mammal species, the mating season for bighorn sheep in northern latitudes and high elevations is more circumscribed than those living in milder climates. The reason for this is simple: Offspring born on either side of an optimal period in cold climates have a substantially reduced chance of survival. For example, a bighorn lamb birthed too early in the spring in the northern Rocky Mountains may freeze to death in a late-arriving storm. Lambs whose birthdays occur in midsummer may initially benefit from warmer temperature and the presence of succulent forage. However, late-born bighorns are smaller and less vigorous entering their first winter than older offspring, reducing their odds of surviving to their first birthday.

In contrast, lambs born in warmer climates aren't at risk of freezing in a late storm or required to endure frigid temperatures or forced to navigate snowy terrain in their first winter. Thus, the mating (and birthing) season for desert bighorn sheep is much longer and less intense than for Rocky Mountain bighorns inhabiting northern portions of their range. Researchers have documented the birth of desert bighorns in various parts of their range on nearly a year-round basis. For example, bighorns in the Sonoran Desert of Arizona are known to have produced lambs in every month of the year except October. Some other desert bighorn sheep populations have mating and birthing seasons that are more circumscribed. Rocky Mountain bighorns in Canada

Rams clash horns in battles to determine dominance. These equally matched rams were photographed fighting in Custer State Park, South Dakota.
LISA BALLARD

and the northern United States typically mate in November and December, with some populations beginning the rut in mid-November and breeding activity persisting into mid-January.

Competition among rams for females represents one of the most dramatic seasons in the annual life-cycle of bighorn sheep. Males whose rivalry can't be resolved with dominance displays or intimidation settle their differences head-to-head. Rams battle by head-butting. Rival males clash their horns and skulls together in fierce butting bouts that may last for many hours. The most forcible battles involve fights that see two rams rearing at a distance of 10 yards or more, then lunging toward one another at speeds of 20 miles per hour. The force of the impact between battering rams is sufficient to crush and kill a human. Rams possess specialized skulls and muscular-skeletal structures in their necks that allow them to absorb such violent contact. However, the fights do sometimes result in serious injuries such as broken jaws or noses and eye trauma. The horns of adult rams often bear the marks of battle, including chipping and damage to the horn bases and splintered tips.

Contrary to some accounts of bighorn sheep natural history, the dominance battles of rams do not normally occur during the mating season, but before it. The pecking order among rams is established in bachelor groups before they join the ewe herds on mating grounds. During the rut, mature rams spend their time courting and repelling younger rams from females. Sexually mature but subordinate rams may expend considerable effort to chase a receptive ewe from the presence of a dominant ram. Although it is assumed by some observers that rams play the central role during the rut, observations by researchers have shown that ewes are selective in the breeding process, actively seeking the attention of rams on the mating grounds with the largest bodies and horns.

Rams may become fertile before they reach one year of age in the desert bighorn subspecies. Research indicates Rocky Mountain rams become capable of reproduction a bit later, but may attain such status by eighteen months of age. However, in most populations rams do not reproduce until much later. Observations of Rocky

Mountain bighorns show that in most populations rams will not play a major role in reproduction until their seventh or eighth year.

By this time males on good range will have attained both body weight and horn mass greatly superior to young rams. They are able to dominate immature males and are more readily accepted by breeding females.

Although younger rams can successfully impregnate ewes, in both captive and wild populations, the presence of massive, monarch rams plays a role in the health of sheep herds beyond reproduction. Young rams tend to be aggressive and overly energetic in their pursuit of females on the breeding grounds, not only depleting their own energy reserves but those of the ewes fleeing their untimely advances. Older rams, by contrast, are more reserved in their courtship. Their intolerance of young males creates a buffer between ewes and immature rams that allows ewes to conceive offspring without wasting energy and depleting body reserves running from inexperienced rams.

When it comes to the health of a bighorn herd, the presence of a few monarch rams is better than a dozen lesser males.

Pregnancy and Gestation

Research with captive bighorn sheep has shown that the period of time between the initiation of pregnancy and birth (gestation period) is around 175 days, over three weeks longer than the gestation period of domestic sheep. The reproduction efficiency of bighorn sheep females is highly correlated to body weight and forage availability and quality. Age also plays a role in reproduction. Ewes in Rocky Mountain populations typically bear their first offspring at three years of age, although some may reproduce as two-year-olds in expanding populations or under unusual circumstances. Desert bighorns are sometimes reproductive at younger ages than their Rocky Mountain counterparts. Researchers have observed yearling ewes with lambs in California and Nevada. Elderly ewes rarely breed and produce young.

Pregnancy rates among fertile bighorn sheep females are very high. Desert bighorn ewes typically conceive lambs at a rate of around 75 percent to 85 percent depending on the population. Among Rocky Mountain bighorns the conception rates are even higher. It is not unusual for females in local herds of the northern-dwelling subspecies to experience conception rates of 90 percent.

Birth

Lambs are usually born in May and June in most populations of Rocky Mountain bighorns. However, later births are known to occur in some herds occupying high-elevation habitat. Some lambs are born earlier in southern populations of the Rocky Mountain subspecies. April births have been documented in California and may happen elsewhere in southern ranges. The offspring of desert bighorns may be born at almost any time of the year, depending on the patterns of local animals. However, the typical birthing season is often reported as occurring between December and June, with most births taking place between February and May.

Bighorn sheep normally birth a single offspring. Twins have been documented, but the occurrence of multiple offspring is extremely low and is not considered to be a significant factor in reproduction rates or herd growth.

Prior to birthing their lambs, ewes retreat to rugged areas, most often among cliffs or exceedingly steep terrain. In northwestern Wyoming I have observed bighorn ewes with tiny lambs inhabiting navigable terrain between two sheer cliff faces. Protection from predators that mark lambs as easy prey is assumed to be the primary reason ewes birth their offspring in such places, but climate may play a role as well. In northern latitudes very steep, south-facing slopes afford baby bighorns increased exposure to sunlight, which may result in warmer surroundings and better survival in colder-than-average temperatures. Birthing sites may be used by individual ewes or females in a particular herd on a year-after-year basis.

The actual birthing process of wild bighorn sheep is seldom witnessed, but research with captive animals indicates actual labor is brief, averaging less than twenty minutes. Prior to labor, bighorn ewes show signs of the impending birth, including pacing and sometimes pawing at the earth. Newborn lambs usually stand and nurse very quickly, with most lambs starting their first nursing within an hour of birth. Lambs that receive frequent attention from their mothers, such as nuzzling or licking, stand and nurse earlier than those born to less-attentive females. Baby bighorns normally walk within the first hour or two of being born.

Rocky Mountain bighorn lambs typically weigh between 6.2 and 12 pounds. Desert bighorn babies are usually a bit smaller, with an average birth weight of about 6.4 pounds. Differences in birth weights related to the sex of the offspring are insignificant.

Top: Bighorn sheep normally birth a single lamb. Twins, like these born to a ewe in Badlands National Park, South Dakota, are quite rare.
© ISTOCK.COM/ TOMOLSON54
Bottom: Bighorn ewes use terrain where lambs are buffered from predation as birthing sites.
© ISTOCK.COM/DSSIMAGES

Nurturing Lambs to Adulthood

Although bighorn sheep exhibit high conception and birth rates, mortality among young sheep is very high. Occasionally as few as 5 percent of the lambs born within an area will survive to see their first birthday, especially among herds subject to disease or extreme weather conditions. Even among relatively healthy desert bighorns, first-year survival rates as low as 20 percent are not unusual.

A number of hazards account for deaths among young bighorns. Survival in the first year is profoundly influenced by weather events. Very young lambs born in alpine environments are susceptible to hypothermia (decreased body temperature caused by cold, wind, precipitation, or some combination thereof). It is not well known if hypothermia is a direct cause of death among bighorn lambs. However, the weakening effects of the condition are believed by many biologists to be instrumental in a decreased resistance to illness and impaired growth, both of which diminish a young sheep's prospects of survival.

The offspring of desert bighorns can be stricken when drought leaves its mother with too little forage for milk production, leading to malnutrition. Biologists theorize that in some cases young desert bighorns may be at risk when precipitation levels are much higher than average as well. Excess groundwater in the form of ponds and pools may spawn swarms of biting insects carrying fatal diseases.

In some areas significant numbers of young bighorns are killed in the first few months of life by predators, a topic we'll explore more fully later in this chapter. However, the dramatic and devastating effects of respiratory disease appear to be the number one factor that limits lamb survival and bighorn sheep numbers.

Bighorn lambs grow rapidly. By six months of age, many desert bighorns will weigh ten times more than their birth weight. Birth weight and subsequent weight gain are extremely important for survival in the first year of a bighorn's life. Research indicates lambs with lower birth weights have lower survival rates than their heavier counterparts. Lambs that fail to grow adequately may die directly from starvation or secondary issues related to malnutrition. Larger young with superior body condition are better prepared to endure the rigors of their first winter among northern populations. At one year of age, rams are noticeably bigger than ewes. Reported average yearling weights for the sexes in desert bighorns are 122 pounds for rams and 100 pounds for ewes.

In their second year, bighorn sheep face another survival challenge. Yearlings are separated from their mother when she prepares to birth the next year's lamb. Those that attach themselves to older, barren females have a leader to follow. Yearlings forced to live on their own may wander into habitats unfit for bighorns or areas where they are easily targeted by predators.

At around two years of age, the growth histories of rams and ewes diverge. Females reach their adult weight at around three or four years, but males continue to grow until age six or beyond. Researchers have recorded weight differences between the sexes in bighorns favoring rams by 18 percent at age two, 65 percent at age six. Among desert bighorns, survival rates increase dramatically once a sheep reaches two years, then begin to decrease at age seven.

BIGHORN SHEEP AND OTHER ANIMALS

Bighorns and Other Ungulates

Bighorn sheep share their range with a considerable number of other ungulates in various habitats throughout North America. Desert bighorns, for example, live in places uninhabitable to moose. Rocky Mountain bighorns in mountainous areas in states such as Montana, Wyoming, and Idaho may occasionally cross paths with moose. Bighorns in prairie habitats including eastern Montana, North Dakota, and

South Dakota may find themselves in proximity to pronghorn, while sheep dwelling in mountainous regions do not. Prairie and mountain herds of bighorns come into contact with mule deer. Both Rocky Mountain and desert bighorns are frequently found on the same range as mule deer. Sheep wintering in foothills locations in the Rockies can sometimes be seen in proximity to elk, and less frequently come into contact with whitetail deer.

Direct interactions between bighorns and the ungulate species noted above are probably uncommon and infrequently observed by humans. Biologists are generally unconcerned with the impact these ungulates might have on bighorns. One exception might concern utilization of winter range. In the case of elk, both bighorns and elk are generalist feeders that consume both grasses and browse in the winter. It seems reasonable to assume high numbers of elk on winter range might decrease the amount of forage available for bighorns, but research addressing this relationship is lacking.

Bighorn sheep share summer and winter range with mountain goats in many areas in the northern Rocky Mountains. In some places, such as Montana's Glacier National Park, bighorns and goats have tracked the same crags and alpine meadows for thousands of years. Elsewhere, native bighorns have come into contact with transplanted mountain goats in fairly recent times. Introduced, nonnative populations of mountain goats now share habitat with bighorn sheep in portions of Idaho, Montana, Wyoming, Nevada, Utah, and Colorado. Expansion of mountain goat range in those areas has brought increasing numbers of bighorns into contact with nonnative mountain goats.

Although it's well known that mountain goats and bighorn sheep can and do coexist without apparent harm to either species, the introduced populations of mountain goats in the above states are of concern to many biologists involved in bighorn sheep management and research.

In the era when goats hit the ground in Montana, Colorado, and Idaho, the desirability of relocating animals to establish populations for hunting provided the impetus for the transplants. Little thought appears to have been given to the broader questions of the animals' impact on native ecosystems, including the other mammals with which the newcomers would interact. Such was the case with mountain goats.

From a wildlife management perspective, two issues have emerged in relation to transplanted mountain goats and bighorn sheep. The first has to do with habitat. In the extreme environments the two species occupy, palatable forage is sometimes at a minimum. Will a herd of fifty mountain goats reduce the feed available to bighorn sheep, particularly at times of the year or in habitat niches where sheep are most vulnerable?

It is disease, however, not forage or competition for other valuable habitat commodities like secure birthing sites, that is of greatest concern to many state and federal biologists observing the growing and expanding mountain goat presence in bighorn sheep habitat. Bighorn sheep are notoriously susceptible to diseases, especially pneumonia. Disease transmission from domestic sheep to bighorns is invariably disastrous. Is it possible that colonizing mountain goats are also carrying diseases to bighorns?

In fact, biologists and wildlife disease specialists in Wyoming have concluded that mountain goats carry all of the pathogens that are potentially lethal to bighorns. Even though researchers haven't tested as many goats as sheep, research indicates goats are capable of carrying and spreading pathogens to sheep. Most biologists aren't particularly concerned about goats causing catastrophic collapses in sheep herds. For the most part, it appears bighorns currently sharing range with mountain goats already carry some mix of the pneumonia-causing bugs so fatal to bighorns under certain conditions. However, if goats continue to expand into other mountain ranges, they may eventually come into contact with sheep herds that are disease-free. If the ranges of goats or sheep change, the disease issue may become much more problematic.

The presence of nonnative mountain goats and their potential to compete with native bighorn sheep for forage or to transmit disease is becoming a thorny issue in several national parks. In 1977 President Jimmy Carter signed Executive Order #11987, which restricted the introduction of nonnative species on federal lands. The order has been largely ineffectual, but the National Park Service (NPS) is one of the federal agencies that has developed policies that prioritize the health and preservation of native species over nonnatives. Thus, fisheries management in places like Yellowstone and Grand Teton National Parks favors endemic cutthroat trout over introduced rainbow trout.

If NPS policy frowns upon the presence of nonnative wildlife, even species inhabiting similar habitats in other parts of the United States, the presence of mountain goats in several national parks is a cause for concern. Currently, NPS is grappling with how to handle colonizing mountain goats in Grand Teton National Park, Wyoming. Grand Teton isn't the only national park where biologists are warily watching a growing goat presence. Yellowstone shares the issue, and it is likely to occur in Colorado's Rocky Mountain National Park as well. Olympic National Park in Washington is also home to nonnative goats.

Like many other nonnative species that have become naturalized in an area, mountain goats in national parks are regarded as native creatures by many observers who relish the sighting of one. Most hikers in the Tetons, for example, are happy to report the presence of goats. Should the NPS move to eliminate mountain goats from national parks, a certain amount of public backlash is the most predictable result. Additionally, eradicating goats from parks is probably not feasible. If the present population is removed, others will almost certainly recolonize from outside.

However, the NPS policy that prohibits the introduction of nonnative species and prioritizes the preservation of natives recognizes a simple but far-reaching biological principle. Nonnative plants and animals are often detrimental to indigenous species, sometimes through interactions that take decades to document and determine. Mountain goats and bighorn sheep have coexisted in Glacier National Park, Montana, for centuries. How transplanted goats may affect bighorns in other national parks remains to be seen.

Bighorns and Predators

Living among cliffs and badland environments gives the powerful, agile bighorn sheep an effective means of escaping predators. Nonetheless, a wide array of predators have the ability to prey upon bighorns, though few predators routinely target sheep as prey. Among those, mountain lions (cougars) and coyotes may be the most potent predators. Mountain lions are capable of killing adult bighorns of both genders. Mountain lion predation has been recorded virtually everywhere the two species coexist.

The killing of bighorns by cougars appears to be a significant factor in the establishment and maintenance of desert bighorn herds in a number of areas. Desert bighorn introductions in New Mexico, Utah, Texas, and Arizona have been abandoned or severely hampered by mountain lion predation. Biologists theorize that introduced populations may be particularly susceptible to predation by the big cats until sheep discover and learn to use preferable escape terrain. In California, mountain lion predation is considered to be an impediment to the recovery of the endangered Sierra Nevada bighorn sheep in and around Yosemite National Park.

Mountain lions are perhaps the only predator in North America capable of consistently preying upon adult bighorn sheep. Predation by mountain lions has impeded bighorn transplant projects in several southwestern states.
© ISTOCK.COM/SANDMANXX

Mountain lion predation on bighorn sheep is a complex phenomenon. Research on the relationship is sparse, but two factors appear to increase predation on sheep by these formidable feline predators. First, predation on bighorns by mountain lions is thought to be most acute where sheep share range with mule deer. Mule deer are a primary prey species for mountain lions in many regions. In such places bighorns may become frequent targets of cougar predation if mule deer numbers are depressed or at times of the year (primarily winter and early spring) when sheep are more vulnerable to predation. A second important factor involves prey specialization by mountain lions. Within a cougar population, certain cats may focus on particular species of prey. Such is seemingly the case with bighorns. In most areas where mountain lions prey on substantial numbers of sheep, it is relatively few of the cougars that do most of the killing.

Coyotes, like mountain lions, take considerable numbers of bighorn sheep in some areas. Lambs are most vulnerable to coyote predation. In British Columbia, researchers have documented predation rates by coyotes as high as 80 percent on lambs in the first year of life. Some biologists theorize that coyote predation is higher in places lacking adequate escape terrain, most notably in areas where bighorns have been introduced outside their native range. Coyote packs are also capable of killing adult bighorns, although coyote predation on adult sheep is not considered a principal source of mortality.

A number of other mammalian species are either known or assumed predators of bighorn sheep, though none are thought to exert any instrumental effect on bighorn numbers. These include black and grizzly bears, wolves, wolverines, lynx, bobcats, jaguars, ocelots, and some species of foxes. Evidence of predation or actual predation on bighorns by most of these species has been infrequently observed.

A final bighorn sheep predator worthy of note has feathers, not fangs. Golden eagles are known to be regular predators of bighorn lambs in some places, although they take relatively few young. Eagles may be capable of killing older sheep in certain circumstances. Some observational evidence suggests golden eagle predation becomes more acute after severe winters when these imposing raptors have fewer prey choices. Eyewitness accounts have shown that bighorn ewes will actively defend their young against eagles or sometimes take them into heavier cover when eagles are present, one of the few instances in which bighorns will deliberately choose denser vegetation over more open slopes.

Golden eagles prey upon bighorn lambs in a variety of habitats. Ewes are frequently successful in repelling the attacks of eagles against their lambs.
JACK BALLARD

Parasites and Diseases

In appearance and in relation to the demanding habitats they frequent, bighorn sheep might easily be assumed to be one of the toughest mammalian species on the planet. When it comes to diseases, nothing could be further from the truth. Entire herds of a hundred or more animals may be decimated by disease in less than a year in epidemics killing 80 percent or more of the animals in a short period of time. Many herds never recover from the maladies and eventually become extinct.

Pneumonia is the disease most often associated with plague-like decimation of bighorn sheep herds. At the present time, wildlife disease specialists have implicated several strains of bacteria in widespread bighorn die-offs associated with the disease. However, the specific pathology of pneumonia in bighorns is poorly understood. Healthy bighorns can carry the pathogens that spawn pneumonia for years without appearing or acting sick. Some wildlife disease specialists believe some combination of stress, nutritional deprivation, and invasion by various pathogens trigger disastrous pneumonia outbreaks in herds already carrying pathogens. During the 2009–10 winter, dramatic pneumonia epidemics afflicted bighorn sheep herds in four states (Montana, Nevada, Washington, and Utah). The disease events caused from 33 to 95 percent die-offs among bighorns. Lamb survival is typically low in herds experiencing pneumonia outbreaks for three to ten years after the event, making population recoveries very slow. In many cases bighorn sheep herds never recover to previous levels after a pneumonia epidemic.

Contact with domestic sheep is often the cause for pneumonia in bighorns. Domestic sheep have evolved to harbor the pathogens that cause pneumonia in bighorns without harm to themselves. The abundance of bighorn sheep in the contiguous

United States prior to European settlement, and their inability to recover to the extent of other species such as elk and bison, gives some indication of the degree to which contact with domestic livestock makes them vulnerable to disease. Reducing contact between bighorns and domestic sheep is considered by biologists to be essential to the survival of the *Ovis canadensis* species.

Along with pneumonia, diseases common to other ungulates also afflict bighorn sheep. Bighorns may contract paratuberculosis (Johne's disease), contagious ecthyma (sore mouth), bluetongue, chronic sinusitis, and mandibular osteomyelitis (lumpy jaw). These diseases are not believed to be instrumental in suppressing bighorn sheep populations, but may intermittently inhibit production in some areas. Capture myopathy, a syndrome brought about by extreme stress or exercise and sometimes associated with trapping of bighorns for transplantation or research purposes, is also sometimes listed among bighorn sheep diseases. The condition affects bodily systems of bighorn sheep in sudden, disruptive ways that may lead to severe shock and death. Capture myopathy appears in other ungulate species including elk, deer, antelope, moose, and mountain goats. Minimization of stress during handling and the appropriate administration of immobilizing drugs greatly reduce the possibility of animals succumbing to the condition.

Ungulates in North America are often hosts to a broad range of external and internal parasites. Bighorn sheep are buffered from certain parasites due to the harsh environments they inhabit but nonetheless may be inflicted with dozens of parasites. Ticks, fleas, biting midges, and other external parasites may cause discomfort to sheep, but are little threat to the welfare of healthy bighorns receiving adequate nutrition. A variety of internal parasites, including intestinal worms and flukes (many of them introduced to wild populations of ungulates via livestock), are also known to invade bighorn sheep. Little research has been done to determine how these parasites might influence the health of bighorns, but it is assumed that high densities of such parasites might weaken sheep, perhaps making them more vulnerable to winter starvation or predation. One internal parasite, lungworms, are of greater concern. Lungworm infestations in bighorns have been implicated in pneumonia outbreaks and high lamb mortality.

A pneumonia outbreak can strike bighorns like this ram, the picture of health and vigor, in a matter of weeks.
JACK BALLARD

BIGHORN SHEEP AND HUMANS

Bighorns and American Indians

Images of bighorn sheep painted or etched on rocks are found in numerous locations across the western United States. Created long before the arrival of European settlers, the origins and dates of the rock art are unknown, but are thought by some archaeologists to be at least 3,000 years old. The purpose of the primitive artistic endeavors

Petroglyphs of bighorn sheep are found in many places in the southwestern United States. Some are thought to be at least 3,000 years old.
© ISTOCK.COM/ BELFASTEILEEN

is a matter of speculation. Some experts believe the images, which are often found in places bighorns lived and could have been hunted, were seen by their makers as good luck charms to ensure the success of sheep hunts. Others feel the representations of sheep had a religious purpose, while some scholars admit they may have been merely artwork, similar to modern drawings with sidewalk chalk or roadside graffiti.

While the role of bighorn sheep in such ancient artwork is unknown, history validates the utilization of bighorns in numerous American Indian cultures. Bighorns were hunted for food and their horns were used in the construction of various implements, such as spoons and bowls. One of the most fascinating connections between bighorn sheep and native peoples of North America involves a clan of Shoshone Indians who inhabited the region in and around Yellowstone National Park prior to European settlement.

The horns of bighorn sheep were used by American Indians to create utensils such as spoons. Bows fashioned from rams' horns were very valuable to native peoples.
LISA BALLARD

The name "Shoshone" hearkens to a loosely confederated group of American Indians that is thought to have migrated from the Great Basin area between California and Nevada northward to the Salmon River region of Idaho and northwestern Wyoming. Subgroups of the Shoshone were linguistically classified by their primary diet. The Shoshones included "eaters of pine nuts," "eaters of salmon," and "buffalo eaters." A relatively small group of Shoshones known as the "sheep eaters" inhabited the Greater Yellowstone region. Although their diet also consisted of roots, berries, and other game animals such as elk, this singular people depended heavily on the bighorn sheep for its sustenance. The mountainous ungulates provided meat and clothing.

Sheep-eater artisans also fashioned beautiful bows from the sweeping horns of bighorn rams through a process that possibly involved heating the horns in local hot springs. It took the native craftsmen up to two months to complete the construction of a horn bow. The hunting implements were quite compact, typically measuring just under 3 feet in length, and very strong. Sheep-eater bows were highly prized by other tribes as well. Some historians believe sheep-horn bows had a value similar to that of ten horses in regional trade. While many native tribes readily assimilated the horse and European firearms into their culture and hunting practices, the sheep eaters found little use for them. They relied on pack dogs to carry their possessions, creatures much more suited to travel in rugged mountains than horses, and highly sophisticated hunting methods to kill sheep that didn't require the use of a long-range rifle.

The Crow Indians, native to Montana and Wyoming, revered the bighorn sheep. Little Big Horn College, a two-year tribal college located on the Crow Indian Reservation in Montana, is specifically named in honor of the bighorn sheep in Crow legend. According to the legend, a young Crow boy was cast over a cliff in the Big Horn Mountains (in northern Wyoming) by his stepfather.

His family assumed him dead, but the youth was saved by seven bighorn rams who raised him to adulthood. Along the way the rams instructed him in the principles of the bighorn's way of life. As an adult, the boy returned to the Crow people and became known as Big Metal. Tribal tradition attributes the wisdom of the people to Big Metal and the seven bighorn rams who mentored him. The mascot of Little Big Horn College is the Ram. Numerous geographical features in Crow country bear the name of their beloved sheep, including the Big Horn Mountains and the Big Horn and Little Big Horn Rivers.

Bighorns and European Settlers

Spanish explorers encountered bighorn sheep in southwestern regions of North America as early as the sixteenth century. Jesuit missionaries in what is now the northern part of Mexico and the southwestern United States were aware of the bighorn prior to 1700. European experience with bighorns in the Rocky Mountains accelerated in the early decades of the nineteenth century with exploration of the region and the increasing forays of fur trappers. Bighorns dwelling in rough country along the rivers of the plains and mountain foothills were sometimes hunted by pioneering trappers and explorers, especially in the winter when found at low elevations. Bighorns occupying mountainous areas were often viewed as quarry whose effort to obtain them was not worth the outcome.

As more Europeans flocked to the West for various economic purposes including mining, logging, and agriculture, bighorns faced increased hunting pressure and habitat loss. In the late nineteenth century, bighorn sheep were pursued by market hunters who sold their meat and hides. However, death by disease transmitted from domestic sheep to bighorns was probably more instrumental in the widespread collapse of bighorn sheep populations that occurred across the western United States from the late

Domestic sheep graze on an alpine ridge in Colorado. Diseases from domestic sheep have been implicated in numerous die-offs of bighorns that led to population collapses in the late eighteenth century.
© ISTOCK.COM/PATRICKPOENDL

1800s to around 1960. In Idaho, for example, ranchers introduced domestic sheep by the thousands in the 1860s and 1870s. Shortly thereafter, homesteaders witnessed massive die-offs of bighorns in the central part of the state to the extent that the bones of sheep were scattered across their winter range for several decades. A similar pattern plagued bighorns in many other Rocky Mountain states. Oregon was historically home to bighorns, but disease reduced their numbers to less than fifty animals by around 1910. The feeble population rallied slightly in subsequent decades, but by the mid-1940s the species had vanished from the state.

Around 1900 most states passed legislation prohibiting the hunting of bighorn sheep. But the species continued to languish due to habitat loss and disease outbreaks. Bighorn sheep persisted in the high mountains of Colorado into the twentieth century, but experienced one of the most dramatic die-offs in the post-settlement era in the United States. In 1953 disease swept through one of the largest herds. A single winter saw sheep numbers in the region (central Colorado) plunge from around 1,000 to 30, representing a population decline of roughly 97 percent in a period of a few months.

Bighorns and Us

The plight of the desert bighorn sheep received substantial publicity in 1936 when Boy Scouts in Arizona began a program aimed at preserving bighorns. Major Frederick Russell Burnham, an outspoken conservationist, became concerned that less than 200 bighorns persisted in the mountains of Arizona. Burnham enlisted the help of Boy Scout leaders to spread the word about the magnificent sheep and their precarious existence. A poster contest with a "save the bighorns" theme was conducted in schools across the

Conservation efforts by the Boy Scouts of America in Arizona in the 1930s led to the creation of two national wildlife refuges intended to protect bighorn sheep.
© ISTOCK.COM/WSLINES

state. The winning entry was used on a special neckerchief slide distributed to some 10,000 Scouts. Other publicity efforts included radio programs and school assemblies documenting the plight of the state's bighorns.

Several prominent national conservation groups including the Izaak Walton League of America, the National Audubon Society, and the National Wildlife Federation rallied to the cause. As a result, two national wildlife refuges were created in Arizona with the specific intention to conserve habitat for desert bighorn sheep and other wildlife. The total area of the refuges (Kofa and Cabeza Prieta) covers 1.5 million acres, or 23,437 square miles. In 2012 the desert bighorn population in the smaller Kofa refuge was estimated at nearly 500 animals.

Efforts to reestablish bighorn sheep on their native range began as early as 1922, when South Dakota senator Peter Norbeck acquired eight bighorns from Canada that were released in Custer State Park. The same year, Canadian bighorns were released in Montana on the National Bison Range. Bighorns were transplanted in New Mexico from Canada in 1932. In Colorado, native bighorn sheep numbers were sufficient to provide seed stock for transplant efforts elsewhere in the state. Sheep captured in the Tarryall Mountains (a sub-range of the Front Range) were moved to the Mount Evans area in 1945. In the next seven years, 223 bighorns from the Tarryall Mountains were relocated to thirteen other sites in Colorado. The transplants were timely. The 1953 disease epidemic (referenced above) that virtually wiped out Tarryall's bighorns put an end to the transplant program from the Tarryall population, but animals from many of the previous transplants thrived in their new environments.

Across the western United States, transplant programs returned bighorns to native range in many areas in the 1960s and 1970s. Since that time, relocation efforts have remained active. Numerous transplants have been successful, resulting in growing bighorn populations of both the desert and Rocky Mountain subspecies. However, acute disease outbreaks continue to plague bighorns in many places. As noted previously, a high percentage of these are known or suspected to originate from contact with domestic sheep. Young bighorn rams are sometimes seen investigating domestic sheep herds, and individual domestic sheep occasionally wind up in odd places on bighorn sheep range.

During a severe disease epidemic in Colorado in the Tarryall and Kenosha Mountains that began in 1997, a single domestic sheep was discovered among a band of bighorns in remote habitat. The domestic sheep was promptly removed, but numerous bighorn mortalities due to pneumonia occurred in the vicinity where the domestic sheep was discovered. Natural interchange between bighorns was suspected of transmitting the disease to other sheep in the area. The final result was a loss of approximately 50 percent of the bighorns in the two mountain ranges.

Accidents claim the lives of bighorn sheep in numerous habitats. Bighorns have drowned in the Colorado River and been struck by trains. The skeleton of a young ram was found in Nevada, its horns encircling a cable. Sheep occasionally fall from cliffs or become trapped in sinkholes.

In some places collisions with automobiles claim disturbing numbers of wild bighorns. One research project near Hoover Dam in Arizona focused on forty-nine adult animals. During the study period, twelve sheep were killed. Six of the mortalities occurred when bighorns were struck by automobiles, a full 50 percent of the mortality, accounting for exactly twice as many deaths as predation.

A substantial herd of bighorns inhabits the area around Georgetown, Colorado, adjacent to I-90 and other roads. Vehicle collisions have claimed many bighorns from the Georgetown herd, where biologists once witnessed the death of five bighorn rams in a single vehicle accident.

Bighorn/automobile collisions have also claimed substantial numbers of sheep in Montana. A single week in the summer of 2013 saw seven bighorns killed by vehicles in three different locations. From 2008 to 2012, 107 bighorns were killed in the Thompson Falls area. Biologists concluded mortality from motor vehicle accidents during the period was instrumental in an overall decline of sheep population in the area. A 2012 vehicle incident in the Rock Creek drainage east of Missoula, where bighorn sheep were recovering from a 2010 pneumonia outbreak, killed seven bighorn lambs in a single collision. The lambs represented a full one-third of the year's reproduction within the struggling population.

Management response to vehicle accidents that may claim human life as well as bighorns is growing. State wildlife agencies and highway departments have increased signage and protected crossings for bighorns in many locations. Motorists can do their part by heeding signs and slowing their travels where highways and sheep habitat intersect.

Successful recovery programs have shown that new bighorn sheep populations can be established in suitable habitat. But the vulnerability of wild sheep to pneumonia and other diseases and habitat loss or disturbance appears more acute than with other North American ungulates. Funding for transplant programs and bighorn research is an essential component of the continued health of the species. The greatest share of funding for sheep management and research comes from state wildlife agencies, primarily in the form of revenue from hunting licenses and excise taxes on the sale of sporting equipment including firearms, ammunition, archery tackle, and arrows. Several conservation organizations devoted to bighorn sheep have also been instrumental in funding transplant programs, habitat improvement projects, and research. Hunters comprise the majority of membership in such organizations.

Some commentators have suggested that a broader investment by state and federal governments, not so heavily dependent on hunting dollars, is warranted for bighorn sheep conservation. Whatever the sources, bighorn sheep are a unique and valuable species worthy of considerable economic and management investment to ensure their future survival.

Theodore Roosevelt National Park in North Dakota provides excellent habitat for several hundred bison, like this massive bull.
JACK BALLARD

CHAPTER 6
BISON

On a warm July afternoon, I sat on a hard wooden bench with a host of other tourists, waiting for the eruption of Old Faithful Geyser, one of Yellowstone National Park's premier attractions. The bench was one of many arrayed in semicircular rows, affording a front row seat to one of nature's unique spectacles.

As the estimated time for the eruption neared, the benches filled to capacity. But there was a distraction. A bull bison grazing between the arena and the geyser slowly lumbered toward the audience, its head down, teeth grinding, apparently oblivious of the seated humans. The bull came closer to the benches. People yielded their seats in deference to the hulking animal, though it seemed to sense only the earth between its hooves, the stems of grass between its teeth. All the humans yielded to the bison, save one.

One chubby, middle-aged man with a sunburned countenance, safari-type shorts, and a camera slung over his shoulder wasn't about to be buffaloed. He kept his front row seat as the bison edged closer, though the ring of empty seats around him steadily grew. Smugness radiated from his erect posture, no doubt emanating from his superior courage in the face of all those other cowardly tourists.

Some 50 feet from Mr. Smug, the bison charged without warning. In the blink of an eye, as hundreds of people gasped in alarm, the immense creature went from a mindless, grazing hulk to a wild-eyed, snorting behemoth. Faster than I could contemplate the consequences, its massive head and curved, dirt-stained horns confronted the previously defiant human at a distance measured in inches.

The animal's intention was clearly to intimidate its challenger, not injure him. It succeeded masterfully. Limbs flailing, the terrified gentleman fell backward from his seat, scrabbling about in the dirt like a frenzied centipede. He proceeded to crawl frantically under the benches away from the bison, standing only when he reached the host of people with sense enough to give the bull its space. The mood of the crowd instantly changed from consternation to mirth. When the geyser erupted minutes later, the previously truculent fellow was noticeably absent from the crowd.

A humorous instance, that experience forever changed my attitude toward bison. The knowledge that they are unpredictable, powerful, and supremely athletic beasts when provoked was emphasized in spades. But a curiosity about their natural history and behavior awakened as well. In the three decades since that idle summer afternoon, I've had the opportunity to observe bison in dozens of habitats in numerous locations, most often in state and national parks. Their life seems one of boring routine, occasionally punctuated with notable events and memorable behaviors. It is in those moments that they are among the most fascinating creatures in North America.

I hope while you read about them your respect and appreciation for these iconic creatures of the Old West will grow with the turning of each page.

NAMES AND FACES

Names and Visual Description

Bison or *American bison* is the formal name of the largest terrestrial (land-dwelling) animal in North America. In the common language these animals are more often called *buffalo*.

Which name, *bison* or *buffalo*, is correct? Although some individuals make a fuss over referring to these animals as *bison,* either term is acceptable. In scientific circles and formal biological contexts, *bison* is the preferred term. However, most experts agree that in common conversation either *bison* or *buffalo* is an appropriate name for these imposing animals.

With an average height at the humped shoulder that interestingly equals about the average height of an adult human in the United States, bison are tall, but bulky-appearing animals. Bison are brown, but their coloration is not completely uniform. Their head, neck, and lower legs are usually quite dark, frequently the color of strong black coffee. Their shoulders and hump are sometimes tan or even golden in appearance. Their ribs and hindquarters are medium brown. However, coloration on an adult bison's body may vary from animal to animal and can change from season to season. Some adult bison exhibit a consistent medium brown color that doesn't change much over their entire body. Other animals have tan hair that extends from the base of their neck all the way to their rump. I've seen bison with very dark brown legs and heads that display golden brown hair on the rest of their massive frames.

Male bison are called bulls. Bull bison are the largest land animal in North America.
JACK BALLARD

Male bison are known as *bulls,* females are called *cows.* Viewed from the side, bison have a noticeable hump that extends above their shoulders. Seen from the front, their head appears broad and massive. Both bulls and cows have horns that sprout from the sides of their skull near the top and curve upward. The horns of cows tend to curve up and in, while the horns of bulls curve up and out. Their tail extends from their rump about halfway to the ground or around the level of their hocks (the prominent joint at the midpoint of hoofed animals' rear legs). The hair at the end of their tail is often thicker or tufted. Bison have a prominent "beard" of hair that hangs below their chin. They also sport long hair below their neck and on the rear of the upper portion of their front legs. The hair on their head, neck, and shoulders is longer and curly in comparison to the hair found on the rest of their body. This is especially noticeable on large bulls during the summer months.

Related Species in North America

To the trained eye, there is no other wild animal in North America easily mistaken for a bison. The animals' sheer size, characteristic shape, and prominent hump give them a profile that is much different from the other herbivores with which they share their range. However, novice wildlife watchers, like early settlers to the eastern United States, might confuse bison with two of the continent's other large hoofed animals.

The ranges of moose and bison overlap in some places in the Rocky Mountains, Canada, and Alaska. Moose are similar in height to bison and somewhat the same color, although moose usually appear more uniformly dark brown or black across their bodies when compared to bison. Bison lack the prominent, round ears that thrust from the top of the moose's head. Moose look lanky, with legs that are long in comparison to the bulk of their body. By contrast, bison appear to have shorter legs that seem stubby in relation to their behemoth bodies. Although moose have an evident hump on their shoulders similar to bison, the top of a moose's rump is just slightly shorter than its shoulders. By contrast, the hump over a bison's shoulders sits much higher than its rump. The bison's massive head is carried lower than its shoulders when standing; the top of a moose's head is higher than the apex of its shoulders. Male moose (bulls) carry flattish, branched antlers for much of the year; female moose (cows) have neither horns nor antlers. The shorter horns of the bison, which taper to a pointed tip, look very different from the antlers of even a small bull moose, which usually broaden as they extend from the animal's skull. A moose's tail is stubby and hardly noticeable, unlike the longer tail of a bison.

Elk, another hoofed mammal of notable size, share ranges with bison in many places, such as Yellowstone and Grand Teton National Parks in Wyoming, Theodore Roosevelt National Park in North Dakota, and Custer State Park in South Dakota, to name a few. Elk are significantly shorter than bison. Like bison, the elk's body is covered in hair in shades of brown. However, elk have a large, prominent patch of fur on their rump that is quite yellow. Elk have a very short tail, more like a moose than a bison. Young male elk (bulls) have antlers that are over a foot long; mature bull elk

Moose and elk might be mistaken for bison at a distance. The towering hump and noticeably lower hindquarters of the bison contrast with the straighter backline of elk and moose.
JACK BALLARD

have antlers that sport multiple tines and are commonly 3 to 4 feet in length. Female elk (cows) lack the horns seen on both cow and bull bison.

Musk oxen—a large, hairy animal of the far north—could potentially be mistaken for bison. Musk oxen are creatures of the Arctic tundra. Their range is more than 500 miles to the north of the nearest bison found in Alaska or Canada. The musk oxen's horns are larger than a bison's and curve downward instead of up. Musk oxen have exceptionally long hair that extends nearly to the ground, obscuring most of their front and hind legs.

Of the animals in North America, bison are most closely related to domestic cattle. American bison share the *bison* genus with one other species of European bison. However, they are also very closely related to members of the *bos* genus, which includes domestic cattle, gaur, yak, kouprey, and banteng. Banteng, gaur, and kouprey are wild cattle-like creatures that are native to southern and southeastern Asia. Yak are a long-haired cattle-like species of south central and eastern Asia. Because bison can mate and produce fertile offspring with every species of the *bos* genus, many biologists feel that bison and these other cattle-like species should be included in a single genus. Ranchers who captured and maintained bison with their cattle herds sometimes deliberately interbred bison and cattle to the extent that most "wild" bison found in the United States at the present time carry some (generally very small) genetic influence from domestic cattle.

Subspecies

American bison are near relatives of the wisent or European bison. The scientific or Latin name for American bison is *Bison bison*. European bison bear the formal name *Bison bonasus*. Like their North American counterparts, wisent are the largest land-dwelling wild animal in Europe. The bison of North America and Europe are generally similar in appearance. However, European bison are a bit taller on average. They also have slightly longer horns and tails. The hair on the frontal portions of the North American bison's head, neck, and shoulders tends to be longer than that on the wisent. Additionally, wisent carry their heads higher—a feature that better enables them in browsing on shrubs and woody plants—than the low-slung head of the American bison, which feeds almost exclusively on grass and sedges.

In addition to their biological similarities, American and European bison share a common history with humans. Both species were hunted to near extinction, with surviving populations originating from remnant herds that numbered a tiny fraction of

Some biologists believe wood bison, like this one in northern British Columbia, should be classified as a separate subspecies. Others believe wood bison and plains bison are the same.
© ISTOCK.COM/ MTNMICHELLE

their historic numbers. Wisent have been reintroduced into the wild in select areas of several countries in Europe, a pattern similar to the reintroduction of bison at various national, state, and provincial parks and wildlife refuges in the United States and Canada.

Within North America some biologists recognize two subspecies of bison: plains bison (*Bison bison bison*) and wood bison (*Bison bison athabascae*). Others believe that wood bison and plains bison should not be recognized as separate subspecies. Wood bison are found in Alaska and Canada. Plains bison are found primarily in the contiguous United States.

Historically, wood bison roamed throughout much of the boreal forest regions of Alaska and western Canada. Genetically pure wood bison were considered by many to be extinct by the early twentieth century, due to interbreeding with plains bison. In 1957, however, a herd of around 200 animals was discovered in Alberta, Canada, that was thought to be an isolated, genetically pure strain of wood bison. The Canadian government developed and implemented a program to preserve and propagate these bison. Today free-ranging wood bison are found in a limited number of areas in Alaska and Canada.

The largest specimens of North American bison belong to the wood bison subspecies. Wood bison bulls are usually about 10 percent heavier than plains bison bulls. Large wood bison bulls can weigh over 2,200 pounds and stand over 6 feet tall at the shoulders, making them the largest land animal in North America. When viewed from the side, the prominent hump on a wood bison sits in front of its shoulders. Wood bison have thick, woolly hair on their head and shoulders. They are commonly believed to have thicker hair, longer legs, and a more pointed beard than plains bison.

Plains bison are the subspecies that originally inhabited the vast grasslands of North America. The current existence of plains bison can be traced to a remnant herd in Yellowstone National Park and a few private herds that were kept from extinction in the late 1800s. The plains bison's hump sits slightly behind its front shoulders when viewed from the side. Plains bison are often described as being somewhat shorter than wood bison with a slightly blockier appearance.

Virtually all bison in the United States can be traced back to two sources of animals in the late nineteenth century. A tiny herd of some thirty bison persisted in the mountains of northwestern Wyoming after receiving protection from hunting through the creation of Yellowstone National Park. Elsewhere, as bison were nearing extinction on the plains, a handful of ranchers captured wild bison and began breeding them in captivity. Historical records indicate five such captive herds were established with a total of around eighty animals.

While these ranchers loved their bison, they also saw them as a means of improving their domestic cattle herds. Bison and cattle can interbreed, although with difficulty. Mating between the two species does not normally occur under natural conditions and often requires considerable effort by ranchers seeking to produce bison-cattle offspring. A bison-cattle crossbred animal, the ranchers speculated, would be much more hardy and better able to survive the harsh winters that sometimes decimated cattle herds on the prairies. Thus, some of the cattlemen tinkered with various crossbreeding schemes between their bison and cattle.

Ultimately, the experiments went nowhere from a commercial or agricultural standpoint. However, they did introduce cattle genes into these bison herds in varying degrees. Animals from these five sources were used to populate various state and national parks, along with other governmental reserves where bison began to flourish. Bison that can ultimately be traced to these five sources were also brought to Yellowstone to supplement its herd.

Advances in genetic testing over the past few decades reveal that most free-ranging and captive bison display genetic markers of domestic cattle. The extent of this genetic "introgression" varies from place to place. In no case is it significant enough to change the appearance of the bison. In fact, a crossbred bison-cattle animal bred back to a bison will lose readily identifiable features of a cow in just a generation or two. However, scientists wonder if the tiny, but persistent genetic influence of cattle makes a difference in existing bison.

Perhaps it does. One study compared bison from two herds, one in a nutritionally rich environment and another in a nutritionally stressed environment. Researchers found that bison displaying traces of cattle genes in their mitochondrial DNA did not weigh as much and had a smaller frame than bison whose DNA did not contain cattle genetics.

To the human eye, the trace cattle genes intermingled in bison herds in our state and national parks is undetectable. Typical viewers of bison in the likes of Yellowstone, Wind Cave, Badlands, Grand Teton, or Theodore Roosevelt National Parks have no inkling of the cattle genes present in the large animals in front of them. Maybe it doesn't matter. But if new herds are established on additional public reserves in our nation, the issue may cause debate between some biologists who would like to see only "pure" bison introduced in new public areas and those who feel the greater genetic diversity offered by animals that exhibit slight introgression of cattle genes is ultimately better for the species.

Physical Characteristics

Reported averages vary somewhat depending on the source, but most bison bulls mature at around 1,800 to 2,000 pounds. Bison are a species that displays significant sexual dimorphism. *Sexual dimorphism* is a fancy biological term that simply refers to the fact that one gender within the species (usually males, but sometimes females) is significantly larger than the other. In the case of bison, the variance in weight between bulls and cows is extreme. Bulls are about 75 to 100 percent heavier than cows. The average cow matures at around 900 to 1,100 pounds. Most adult bull bison stand approximately 6 feet at the shoulders. Cows are about a foot shorter.

Baby bison are called *calves*. A bison calf begins life a much different color than its parents. Bison calves are reddish in color, with lighter, nearly cream-colored hair on their bellies and the inside of their legs. The unusual-colored coat of the young bison is shed at around 2 months of age. After shedding, youngsters mostly appear as smaller versions of adults, with much tinier horns.

Bull bison (on right) are nearly twice as heavy as cows (on left).
JACK BALLARD

RANGE AND HABITAT

Historic Range

Bison once ranged over much of North America, from northern Mexico to Alaska. Prior to the middle of the second millennium (around 1500), most of the contiguous United States held bison herds. Bison were absent from heavily forested areas along the Pacific Coast and the desert regions of the Southwest. They did not inhabit Maine and were found only in the southern portion of the other New England states, probably in small numbers. There was something of a bison buffer along the Atlantic coast. The range of bison was normally found at least 50 to 100 miles from the coastline. Bison were found in the Southeast, perhaps as far south as northern Florida, but some debate has existed regarding the historic range of bison in this area for over a century. As early as the late 1800s, experts argued whether bison actually inhabited southern portions of Louisiana or Georgia. They also squabbled over the historic status of bison in Florida and Alabama.

Estimating the historic range of bison illustrates an interesting aspect of history. Eyewitness accounts of various animals by early explorers are a common way to establish that a certain species lived in a particular area. However, in the case of Europeans exploring North America in first few centuries following the "discovery" of the New World by Christopher Columbus in 1492, they didn't always know what they were viewing. Many North American wildlife species are absent from Europe. The names given to North American animals in the journals of early observers weren't always consistent, nor were there differentiations among species. For example, suppose an intrepid traveler saw an animal that he described as large, dark, hairy, and cloven-hoofed. The creature could be a bison, but it could also be a moose.

Historical records of nonnative adventurers encountering bison in North America during the fifteenth and sixteenth centuries are few, but they do help to establish the nearly coast-to-coast historic range of these large, imposing animals. Alvar Nuñez Cabeza de Vaca, a Spanish explorer, was shipwrecked in the Gulf of Mexico around 1530. He journeyed inland through what is now Texas, observing large herds of bison at least three times. He ate bison, commenting favorably on the taste of the meat. Members of Coronado's Spanish expedition viewed bison on the southern plains about a decade later, somewhere in the region of the Texas panhandle.

Perhaps the first encounter with bison by nonnative peoples on the East Coast occurred in 1612. On March 18, Captain Samuel Argoll, an Englishman, anchored his ship off the coast of Virginia. He then presumably traveled up the Potomac River. Somewhere not too far from the present-day location of Washington, DC, he happened upon a herd of bison. His Indian guides killed two of the animals for meat. In a letter to a friend back in England, Argoll commented on the pleasant taste of the meat and the fact that the buffalo weren't as wild as other animals he had encountered in the American wilderness.

In December 1679, Father Louis Hennepin saw bison on the Illinois River in the vicinity of what is now Peoria. The French priest had journeyed along the Saint Lawrence River and across the Great Lakes region on an exploratory trip of the area. He killed an old bull buffalo and noted the difficulty his party had in retrieving the animal from the mud.

As scouts traveled westward from the settlements along the Atlantic coast in the 1700s, they increasingly came into contact with bison. Buffalo were discovered in North Carolina and Virginia, and as Europeans began exploring the Appalachian Mountains, they found bison from southern New York to Georgia. After the Revolutionary War westward settlement accelerated. Pioneers discovered bison with each westward expansion, gladly killing them for food or their hides. As they went, the settlers quickly exterminated the bison.

The story of the decline of American bison from their historic range has often been oversimplified. A common estimate of the number of bison in North America prior to European settlement is sixty million animals. However, recent scientific estimates of the carrying capacity of bison range based on such variables as rainfall, grassland types, competition with other grazers, and historic US Department of Agriculture (USDA) livestock census data indicate a maximum figure of around thirty million. One scholarly source merely reports that bison in the tens of millions historically roamed North America.

Unbridled hunting by market hunters and extermination campaigns intended to eliminate the major food supply for Native American peoples during the mid- to late 1800s are the most frequently cited reasons for the near extinction of the bison. But the equation isn't quite so simple. Prior to widespread killing by Europeans, native hunters had already exerted some pressure on bison populations. When American Indians acquired horses in the 1600s, cultures soon developed that depended heavily upon bison for food, shelter, and other necessities of life. The horse gave the native peoples increased efficiency in killing bison. Historians note that by 1800, Comanche Indians were starving for a lack of bison on the southern plains and that soon thereafter bison disappeared from the region west of the Rocky Mountains. Biologists variously cite pressure from native hunters, exotic bovine diseases, competition with wild horses, predation, drought, and other natural phenomena as instrumental in the decline of the bison. However, most agree that the widespread elimination of herds by market hunters supported by railway development in the latter decades of the 1800s was the most significant cause of the near-extinction of the bison.

By 1835 bison had disappeared east of the Mississippi River. Two buffalo were killed by Sioux Indians in northern Wisconsin in 1832, perhaps the final chapter in the animals' history east of this great riverine dividing line in America. However, bison were still wildly abundant on the Great Plains and westward to the Rocky Mountains. Competent observers in the 1860s in Kansas claimed to have been within viewing distance of 100,000 or more bison from a single hilltop.

The Lamar Valley in Yellowstone National Park was home to some of the last surviving bison in the late 1800s.
JACK BALLARD

By 1880 the innumerable herds of bison on the plains had nearly vanished. Unbridled hunting of bison for their hide, meat, and bones, along with aggressive efforts to suppress bison numbers as a means to subdue American Indian tribes, wiped out buffalo by the hundreds of thousands per year. Naturalist William Hornaday estimated in 1913 that no more than 1,300 bison existed in the wild or captivity by 1889 in the United States and Canada. In 1975 a respected biologist theorized that only 85 bison remained in the wild in the United States in 1888. Shortly thereafter, the only free-ranging vestige of the tens of millions of bison once found in the United States was a tiny herd of some 30 animals eking out a precarious existence in the mountain valleys of Yellowstone National Park.

Current Range

Describing the current range of bison in North America is difficult. It's not that bison are hard to locate or live in terrain inhospitable to human observers. Rather, one's assessment of the buffalo's current range depends on how the author handles the numerous bison that are private property, classified as livestock, and range exclusively on private lands. Bison "ranches" are found all over the country. In some states small herds are owned by universities or conservation organizations. In other places bison are raised and slaughtered for their meat as an agricultural product. Around 30,000 bison are kept as wildlife or for conservation purposes in public and private herds in North America. Approximately 400,000 bison are owned by private individuals as livestock.

For our purposes in describing the bison's current range, let's stick with the major state and national parks where visitors are quite likely to observe them. The most logical place to begin is Yellowstone National Park in northwestern Wyoming.

Yellowstone National Park

In 1902 President Theodore Roosevelt appointed Charles "Buffalo" Jones as game warden in charge of Yellowstone's bison. Jones arranged for 21 bison (3 bulls and 18 cows) from private herds in Montana and Texas to supplement the approximately 30 bison remaining in Yellowstone. The bison population increased quickly, fluctuating dramatically over the next sixty-five years depending on prevailing management sentiments. In 1967 the park adopted a policy of limited management, where bison would range on their own without supplemental feed or significant management. The bison population in Yellowstone currently fluctuates between around 2,300 to 4,500 animals, depending on such factors as drought and winter severity.

Antelope Island

Antelope Island is the largest island in Utah's Great Salt Lake. In 1893 two Utah residents, John Dooley and William Glassman, transported 12 bison to the island by boat. The descendants of these bison are now managed to maintain a population of around 550 animals. A bison roundup occurs on the island each fall, when excess animals are sold at an auction. Limited sport hunting is also used to control the island's buffalo numbers.

The Wichita Mountains National Wildlife Refuge

In 1905 the Wichita Forest and Game Preserve was created in Oklahoma (later renamed the Wichita Mountains National Wildlife Refuge). Naturalist William Hornaday personally selected 15 bison from the New York Zoological Park to establish a buffalo herd here in 1907. By 1923 the herd had increased to nearly 150 animals. The bison population is currently maintained at about 650 animals on this 59,000-acre refuge in the southwestern portion of Oklahoma.

The National Bison Range

The National Bison Range in western Montana was established specifically for bison preservation. Created in 1908, this 18,500-acre refuge was originally stocked with 36 animals from the Conrad Kalispell herd in Montana. Four more bison were added from other private sources in its first year of operation. The herd grew rapidly, expanding to around 700 animals by 1924. To add genetic diversity, bison from other areas have been added to the herd at various times since its creation. The US Fish & Wildlife Service (USFWS) administers the National Bison Range. Bison are currently maintained at a level of around 350 animals.

The Fort Niobrara National Wildlife Refuge

The Fort Niobrara National Wildlife Refuge was created in 1912 by an executive order of President Theodore Roosevelt "as a preserve and breeding ground for native birds." Its mission soon expanded to the preservation of bison. In 1913 a private rancher in Nebraska gifted 6 bison to the refuge. Yellowstone National Park sent 2 more. A few bulls from the National Bison Range and Custer State Park were added on at least three occasions to limit inbreeding. This 19,131-acre refuge in north-central Nebraska maintains its bison herd at approximately 350 animals.

Custer State Park

Custer State Park in western South Dakota also became home to bison in 1913. The State of South Dakota purchased 36 bison from a private ranch and released them into the park. Since that time, Custer State Park has grown in size and now sprawls over 71,000 acres of grassland and low mountain (Black Hills) habitat that is ideal for bison. Around 1,300 bison roam the park, with the population varying somewhat depending on conditions. The herd is checked from overpopulation by culling excess animals through an auction sale and limited sport hunting.

Wind Cave National Park

In 1913 yet a third public bison herd was established, this one at Wind Cave National Park in western South Dakota. The New York Zoological Society donated 14 bison to create this herd, supplemented by another 6 animals from Yellowstone National Park in 1916. In the 1950s bison from Wind Cave were baited into Custer State Park, which adjoins the national park to the north. At about the same time, brucellosis, a disease harmful to domestic cattle, was discovered in the Wind Cave bison herd. For the next several decades, park management worked to eradicate the disease. The herd was declared brucellosis free by the State of South Dakota in 1986. Currently about 400 buffalo range across Wind Cave National Park. The herd size fluctuates due to natural conditions and culling of excess animals when numbers exceed the carrying capacity of the range.

The Henry Mountains

Along with Yellowstone National Park, the bison in the Henry Mountains of southeastern Utah are a truly free-ranging herd. The animals roam across approximately 300,000 acres. The federal government and the State of Utah administer more than 98 percent of the land the animals inhabit; private individuals own about 1.5 percent.

In 1941, 18 bison (3 bulls, 15 cows) were transplanted from Yellowstone National Park to the Henry Mountains. Another 5 bulls were relocated the following year. Since that time, no further additions have been made to the Henry Mountain herd. Disease (brucellosis) was discovered in the bison in 1962. The following year an extensive corralling operation was undertaken to test the bison for brucellosis and cull infected animals. As a result of their experience with the capture, the bison shifted their range. Prior to the 1963 capture, the buffalo used the Burr Desert as winter range and the Henry Mountains as summer range. Since that time, the bison have maintained a home range in the Henry Mountains. The Henry Mountain herd fluctuates in size from around 200 to over 400 animals. Sport hunting is the primary mechanism for population control. The Utah Division of Wildlife Resources manages the Henry Mountain bison.

Grand Teton National Park

Twenty bison were relocated from Yellowstone National Park to Grand Teton National Park in Wyoming in 1948. Disease in the herd hampered the struggling population, which was augmented by 12 bison from Theodore Roosevelt National Park in1964.

Prior to 1969 the buffalo were kept in a large enclosure. After being released from the enclosure to become free ranging, the bison herd expanded. At the present time around 600 bison live in Grand Teton National Park. The bison winter primarily on the nearby National Elk Refuge, where they receive supplemental feed, along with elk.

Theodore Roosevelt National Park

Theodore Roosevelt National Park in western North Dakota was originally established as a national monument in 1947 and consists of two separate areas, the North Unit and the South Unit. Bison were transplanted from the Fort Niobrara National Wildlife Refuge to the South Unit in 1956. The 29 bison reproduced rapidly in this prairie environment. In 1962, 20 bison were moved from the South Unit of the park to populate the North Unit. Due to their health and reproductive success in this excellent bison habitat, the herds are culled periodically to avoid overpopulation.

Excess animals are sent to zoos, other national parks, and Native American tribes. The buffalo herd in the North Unit is maintained at 150 to 250 animals, the larger South Unit is managed for 200 to 500 animals, depending on range conditions.

Badlands National Park

South Dakota's Badlands National Park received 50 bison from Theodore Roosevelt National Park and 3 from the Fort Niobrara National Wildlife Refuge in 1963. Twenty additional bison from the Colorado National Monument joined the herd in 1983 as part of the decision to remove bison from the national monument. Centered in the bison's historic plains environment, the animals thrive in Badlands National Park. The herd generally grows at a rate of 15 percent or slightly more each year. Excess animals are culled as necessary to avoid overpopulation. The herd is managed to stay below the 600-animal carrying capacity of the park, although numbers occasionally exceed this target.

Caprocks State Park

In 1878, at the urging of his wife, a Texas cattleman name Charles Goodnight captured 2 bison calves. He added a few more in subsequent years, establishing a bison herd with seed stock from wild bison from the southern portion of the animals' native range. The herd grew to 125 animals by 1910 and to over 200 animals by 1920, its peak population. Stock from the Goodnight bison herd was used to populate several other public and private herds. After Goodnight's death his buffalo were sold several times. In 1997 the State of Texas took ownership of this genetically isolated bison herd and relocated them to Caprocks State Park. The herd has grown considerably from the 36 animals that came to the park.

Bison Habitat

Hoofed mammals fall along a continuum between species that are "grazers" and those that are "browsers." Grazers eat grass and other leafy plants; browsers eat plant material

Top: Buffalo normally receive over 95 percent of their nutrition from grazing.
Bottom: In the winter bison move snow with their massive heads to reach the grass underneath.
JACK BALLARD

from trees and shrubs. Some animals, like elk, graze on grasses and other leafy plants, but they also browse on trees and shrubs.

Bison are grazing animals. Research indicates that bison do browse in some places, but browsing seldom exceeds 5 percent of their annual diet. In certain locations, however, bison do sometimes browse. In the Lamar Valley in Yellowstone National Park, researchers have discovered that bison frequently browse on willows along the Lamar River, both in the summer and the winter.

However, the bulk of the bison's diet comes from grasses and sedges (narrow-leafed plants similar to grass or rushes). As such, bison are found in habitats that support various species of grasses. Historically, the open grasslands of the central portion of North America were the finest bison habitat on the continent. However, bison were also found in remote mountain valleys and along river bottoms in the West. They roamed woodlands in the East, in areas where there was enough grasslike forage to maintain them.

In the Henry Mountains in Utah, bison range up to 11,000 feet in search of subalpine grasses in the summer. Bison are also found in high mountain valleys and along elevated ridges in Yellowstone National Park. Their massive size and thick coats make them very winter hardy and able to withstand cold temperatures. As such, they can winter in harsh environments, as long as there is grass to eat. Bison forage in the winter by moving snow with their massive heads to reach the grass underneath.

ABILITIES AND BEHAVIOR

Physical Abilities

The bison's large size and awkward-appearing shape betray an animal that is deceptively agile and swift. A bull bison can accelerate a ton of flesh and bones from a standing position to 30 miles per hour in a matter of seconds.

In 1986 a rodeo contestant and animal trainer named TC Thorstenson brought a trained bull bison to a horse race at a track in Gillette, Wyoming. The 2,700-pound bison swept the field by 2.5 lengths, easily winning a race spawned by a bet between parties debating the speed of a bison versus a horse. "Harvey Wallbanger," the male bison, was subsequently entered in numerous exhibition races around the United States, winning seventy-six of ninety-two contests against racehorses. Although he certainly wasn't competing against the top racehorses in the nation, his record amply illustrates the speed of a buffalo.

In the days when American Indians hunted bison with bow and arrow on horseback, hunters mounted themselves on "buffalo runners." Buffalo runners were horses that were exceptionally swift, sure-footed, and courageous. Only the Indians' finest mustangs could capably match the speed and maneuverability of a fleeing bison. While the native hunters usually aspired to kill more than one bison as they followed a herd dashing across the prairie, very few of their horses had the speed and endurance to run down more than one bison in a single chase, although historical records indicate Indian hunters sometimes killed two or three. Not only are bison fast, they can carry their speed for considerable distances. Observe a massive bull bison closely, and it's possible to detect some hint of its endurance. The hindquarters of the animal are narrow and lean. Disguised by the long hair descending from its front quarters, the shoulders power forelegs that are actually quite long. These physical features give bison a long stride that carries them efficiently across the prairie at high speeds.

Along with their straight-ahead speed, bison are very athletic in other ways. Bull bison have been observed jumping 6 feet from a standing position to clear obstacles. Cattle guards, a series of parallel poles or pipes set in a roadway a few inches apart, are often used to keep domestic livestock in a pasture. They are placed above a shallow pit where fences intersect a roadway, making it possible for cars to pass over, but prohibiting wandering cows to cross. Cattle guards are usually about 8 feet wide. In the case of bison, it takes a much wider cattle guard to check their movements. Bull bison are known to simply hop across an 8-foot cattle guard, clearing a span of some 14 feet considering that a bull bison is about 6 feet long.

When American Indians hunted bison on horseback and in current-day roundups, much of the danger involved stems from the buffalo's agility. These animals can change direction in the blink of an eye. When this happens, the mounted pursuer is in grave danger if the bison attempts to gore the pursuing horse. The amazing maneuverability of a bison comes from its physical structure. Much of its weight is centered over its front hooves, allowing it to pivot quickly without moving an extended amount of its mass. Bison also have specialized vertebrae above their shoulders with blades of bone that extend about a foot above their spine. These bones attach to large muscles and a tendon that extends to the base of the skull, allowing their massive head to turn very quickly and with considerable force.

Normally, however, bison go about their living at a slow plod. They move quite leisurely when grazing and spend long periods of time lying down, chewing their cud, and digesting their food. Herds of bison tend to travel at a measured pace, whether feeding during the cool hours of a summer day or moving from one snowy pasture to another in the winter. Biologists believe the unhurried movements of buffalo help them maximize their energy efficiency. Moving such a large body at high speeds requires burning a considerable number of calories. The normally slow pace of a bison helps it conserve energy.

Bison are very comfortable in water and are good swimmers.
JACK BALLARD

Along with their speed and agility, bison are also good swimmers. They are known to regularly swim across rivers spanning a half a mile or more. Researchers studying wood bison in Canada's Northwest Territories concluded that bison can also handle swift currents. Wood buffalo were observed swimming in currents with speeds up to 10 miles per hour without difficulty. In some areas, however, drowning is a significant source of bison mortality. Along the Liard River, a large stream in the Northwest Territories in the Nahanni area, bison commonly swim to forage on both sides or on islands within the river. Animals may be swept away and drowned attempting to cross the river or from the islands when the river rises rapidly. This most often occurs in the spring, when snowmelt raises the river to its flood stage.

When swimming, bison calves and bulls sink low in the water. Some biologists speculate that this makes them more vulnerable to wave action or strong currents. Bison calves are sometimes drowned or swept downstream and abandoned by their mothers shortly after birth in areas where bison herds range on both sides of streams. In Yellowstone National Park buffalo congregate in the Lamar Valley at calving time. The Lamar River is easily waded by bison in midsummer, but can become a raging torrent due to snowmelt in the spring. Buffalo herds in the valley cross the river frequently. It is not unusual for a few calves to be swept away from their mothers when swimming the river at flood stage, sometimes drowning. At other times they wind up on islands in the river or in isolated areas downstream. These unattended calves are often discovered by predators such as grizzly bears, black bears, and wolves and are easy prey. Occasionally, however, diligent female bison search the riverbanks and are reunited with their flushed away calves.

Vocal and Visual Communication

Bison lack the range of vocal communication observed in canine predators, such as wolves and coyotes. However, at certain seasons within the yearly life cycle, bison are quite noisy. After calves are born in the spring, mothers and babies often maintain contact vocally. The basic call between cows and calves is a grunt that sounds somewhat similar to the grunting of a domestic hog. Cows and calves also grunt occasionally when grazing, a call that has a contented tone. The frequency of their communication increases when a herd is on the move in search of better grass or on the way to water. After a herd has stampeded, a period of intense, more frantic grunting often ensues, as if the cows and calves are saying to one another, "Here I am. Where are you?"

Once separated, cows and calves use their grunt calls to get back together. Sometimes, however, they get fooled. A cow and calf may move toward one another from opposite sides of the herd, attracted by each other's voice. When they approach, they may sniff each other and then move away. Although their ears might mistake their grunt for that of another bison, their nose never lies. I have observed similar behavior in herds of domestic cattle during a roundup. Evidently the ears of cattle-like mammals aren't capable of perfectly discerning between the calls of different animals.

Bull bison become very vocal during the mating season, which occurs in late summer. Described as a "bellow" or "roar," bull bison breathe out a loud, rolling sound that announces their presence to rival bulls in the herd and the cows with which they wish to mate. On calm days the bellows of a bison bull can sometimes be heard from over a mile away. When many bulls are roaring in a large herd of buffalo, people who are not familiar with this peculiar noise may mistake the sound for the rumbling of thunder. When two bull bison are in conflict over a cow, their bellowing becomes more frequent and intense.

Along with vocalizations, bison communicate in other ways as well. They use body language, such as postures and movements that signal their "mood" and intentions to other buffalo, predators, or humans. When nursing, bison calves often vigorously wag their tails like a happy dog. This wagging appears to signal its pleasure, similar to a mutt having just received a treat. Bison cows sometimes nuzzle their nursing calves, a gesture that indicates the bond between a mother and her offspring. Cows are also known to rest their heads gently on the back of their calves and lick their calves, especially when they are very young.

Bison signal aggressive intentions in a variety of ways. Bulls have an elaborate series of behaviors they use to communicate aggression, dominance, or submission during the mating season, a subject we'll explore later in this chapter. However, buffalo communicate agitation at other times during the year through several common behaviors. A raised tail is one of the most widespread signals of a defensive or aggressive attack. Bison also snort, stamp their feet, and shake their heads to communicate their displeasure. Where trees are present, they may also gore the trunk or branches with their horns. While one or more of these physical signals usually precedes aggressive activity, bison sometimes charge a perceived threat without any prior behavioral cue.

Herd Structure and Dynamics

Bison are gregarious animals that spend most of their lives in herds that may range in size from a half dozen to several hundred. Except during the mating season, cows and mature bulls are found in distinct herds. Cow herds are larger and more diverse than smaller bands of bulls. Cows, their most recently born calves, and adolescent animals of both sexes congregate in the cow herds.

A cow herd of bison moves toward better pasture in early spring. Cow herds are composed of cows, calves, and young bulls.
JACK BALLARD

The close bond between a mother bison and her calf persists until she no longer has milk for her offspring, at which time it is weaned. Weaning generally occurs around 7 or 8 months of age or shortly thereafter, a condition that is somewhat influenced by the availability of forage for the mother, her age, and body condition. After weaning, bison calves stay in the cow herd with their mothers but don't spend as much time in close proximity to them. By the time they are yearlings (1 year old), bison calves are essentially independent of their mothers, although they remain in the same herd. Female bison may remain in the same herd as their mother for many years, perhaps as long as both mother and daughter are alive. Bison bulls usually depart their mothers' cow herd at 3 to 4 years of age.

Once they leave the cow herd, bison bulls join groups of other males that form smaller bands than the cow herds. They remain in these bull herds or bachelor groups from fall to midsummer. During the mating season the bull herds splinter, with various males joining cow herds that share a similar range. Although bison cows are rarely found alone, bull bison may become solitary creatures. Many observers believe that lone bull bison are the older members of the male population, animals that may have been driven from a cow herd by dominant younger bulls and retained a solitary lifestyle afterward. In some cases lone bison bulls do not participate in the breeding season at all. I have observed large, single bison bulls apart from cow herds during the breeding season in several national parks.

Bison appear to form herds primarily for protection. Both bulls and cows participate in repelling a predatory threat from animals such as wolves. When confronted by predators, buffalo may form a defensive position around calves. Having multiple animals within a herd makes it more likely that some member of the group will detect danger. If the herd flees, being a member of a large group increases the odds that any single animal will be targeted for predation.

There are dominance hierarchies within both bull and cow herds. Dominance hierarchies simply refer to the idea of a pecking order or a structure in which certain animals will yield to others during competition for food, water, mating, or other biological resources. Researchers have found that where forage is abundant, the dominance structure in cow herds revolves most predominantly around age. Cows that are 3 years old dominate those that are 2 years old. Cows that are 6 can push around those that are 4. Intense competition for food might disrupt this basic pattern, but otherwise cow bison tend to follow the idea of "respect your elders."

The situation is similar for bulls in their early years of life but changes as they grow older. Research on bison bulls kept in captivity indicates that some bulls may become capable of reproduction at around 1.5 years of age. However, most experts feel that wild bison bulls reach fertility at 2 to 3 years of age. Nonetheless, these younger bulls aren't normally able to reproduce until a few years later in life. Bulls in the 6- to 8-year-old range, or those slightly older, dominate the breeding hierarchy. One observational study in Yellowstone National Park concluded that bulls over the age of 8 years are most successful in mating. Once bulls reach their prime around age 6, they must rely on their strength, size, and fighting ability to maintain their rank in the bull herd and at breeding time.

Young bison are buffered from predators by the herd. Biologists believe bison form herds primarily for protection.
JACK BALLARD

BISON AND OTHER ANIMALS

Bison and Other Ungulates

In an age before humans factored predominantly in the history of the bison in North America, these animals shared their habitat with a host of other plant-eating mammals. On the prairies where they were most numerous, bison lived alongside large herbivores such as elk, pronghorn, and eventually wild horses. However, they also interacted with smaller plant eaters, including many species of ground squirrels and prairie dogs.

Bison and Elk

Although the diets of elk, bison, and pronghorn overlap somewhat, the species do not compete directly for food. Bison and elk are occasionally viewed in proximity to one another, but if their paths cross directly, elk yield to bison. Elk graze more than deer or pronghorn, giving them more dietary overlap with bison. Biologists at the National Bison Range have historically considered elk as equivalent to .70 bison, deer as .40 bison, and pronghorn as .25 bison in relation to forage consumption in that area. In a few areas bison might impact elk browsing on willows and other deciduous plants commonly consumed by elk in the winter. However, most biologists believe that

competition between elk and bison for forage is not a limiting factor in local populations of either animal.

In some places elk may buffer bison from wolf predation. Where elk and bison are both available prey to wolves, the canines prefer elk. In the years since wolves were reintroduced to Yellowstone National Park, bison numbers have increased on the northern range, an area once heavily populated by elk. Some researchers believe wolf predation on elk has improved overall habitat conditions for both elk and bison in terms of available forage. With wolves targeting elk far more often than bison, more buffalo than elk are allowed to take advantage of the improved range conditions.

When both species are available, wolves prefer to prey on elk rather than bison. An abundant elk population may buffer bison from predation.
JACK BALLARD

It is estimated that millions and millions of bison once roamed the Great Plains. How many prairie dogs do you suppose tunneled into the sod beneath them? If the thought of thirty million bison taxes your brain, what about five billion prairie dogs? That's exactly how many of these rodents some biologists believe once lived in North America. Although they weigh only about 1.5 pounds, the astronomical number of prairie dogs made them an animal that had considerable impact on prairie ecosystems. Prairie dogs were an important food source for countless predators including foxes, coyotes, black-footed ferrets, eagles, hawks, and rattlesnakes.

Bison and prairie dogs historically existed in a mutually beneficial relationship that persists today in places like Custer State Park, Badlands National Park, and Theodore Roosevelt National Park in the Dakotas. Prairie dogs do not exist in tall grass. Instead, the rodents and bison feed on the grass in a prairie dog town (a place where many prairie dogs live together in an extended colony), keeping it short. Bison are attracted to prairie dog towns by the tender new shoots that arise from the closely cropped grass in the spring or after rainfall in the summer. Feeding bison keep the grass from growing too tall for the prairie dogs. Their dung and urine add nutrients to the dirt around the prairie dog town, enhancing the productivity of the soil. In an odd twist of ecology, one of the prairie's largest mammals benefits from a small, burrowing rodent.

Although they may weigh less than 1/1,000th of an adult bison, prairie dogs are actually beneficial to bison.
JACK BALLARD

Bison and Predators

The list of predators in North America capable of killing bison is very short. Under normal circumstances only gray wolves and grizzly bears can successfully prey upon adult bison. Predation attempts by grizzly bears on adult animals are very rare. Black bears, mountain lions, and coyotes have the ability to kill bison in their first few months of

The massive size of adult bison (especially bulls) makes them highly immune to most predators.
JACK BALLARD

life, but it would be highly abnormal for these predators to target an adult or even yearling bison.

Bison and Wolves

When Europeans began regularly exploring the central portion of the United States in the late eighteenth and early nineteenth centuries, they encountered seemingly innumerable herds of bison. Along with buffalo they also observed gray wolves in great numbers. The predator-prey relationship between wolves and bison was recorded in the writings of numerous early explorers. On their epic journey to the Pacific Ocean, Lewis and Clark encountered "vast assemblages" of wolves. The explorers noted in their journals that large packs of wolves constantly accompanied the great herds of bison (and elk) they encountered along the Missouri River in Montana.

Other pioneering journalists noted more specific interactions between these bands of prey and predator. In 1834 Charles Joseph Latrobe, an English explorer and mountaineer, made an expedition through North America with Washington Irving. Latrobe observed wolves and bison in many areas, including present-day Oklahoma. He noted in his writings that wolves "hunt the straggling cows and calves in packs."

Historically, wolves were the primary predator of bison. Today, in places where they are both found, this historical relationship has reasserted itself. Its basic pattern is similar to what Latrobe recorded nearly two centuries ago. Wolves regularly kill bison in some areas, almost always targeting immature animals or females.

Where do wolves prey upon bison in modern times? In the United States Yellowstone and Grand Teton National Parks in northwestern Wyoming are the only places the two species frequently come into contact with one another. Both national

Wolves regularly prey upon bison in some areas. Most of the bison killed by wolves are taken in the winter.
NPS

parks are home to moose and elk, animals that wolves generally target for predation before attempting to bring down bison, which are larger and normally more difficult to kill. Biologists have recorded very few bison predation attempts by wolves in Grand Teton National Park, perhaps due to the relatively low number of bison and large number of elk that winter in the area.

In Yellowstone wolves have been observed killing bison since shortly after their reintroduction to the park in 1995. Although bison do not constitute a major portion of a wolf's diet within the park as a whole, in certain areas they are very important prey. On average, bison account for less than 5 percent of the gray wolf's prey in Yellowstone. However, in the central portion of the park from which elk migrate in the winter, bison are the wolf's major prey during the snowy months. Bison are also the most important prey for wolves in areas of northern Canada, most notably Wood Buffalo National Park and the Slave River Lowlands. In these areas bison may account for 80 to 90 percent of a wolf's annual diet. In Alaska wolves sometimes kill bison. Due to the remote nature of much of the habitat occupied by Alaskan bison, little research has been done to document the extent to which they are preyed upon by wolves.

In places where wolves consistently prey on bison, biologists have recorded certain trends and behaviors in this fascinating interaction between predator and prey. For example, winter is the season when wolves bring down the majority of the bison. Other prey animals are more commonly available in the summer months, including other hoofed animals and smaller quarry such as birds and rodents. In Yellowstone National Park over 90 percent of the bison killed by wolves are taken in the winter. Buffalo brought down by wolves at other times of the year are typically young calves separated from their mothers or animals that have been injured.

The wolves of Yellowstone and northern Canada that routinely prey upon bison in the winter show a distinct preference for juvenile animals and cows. Unless injured or severely weakened by nutritional stress in late winter, bison bulls are too large and dangerous for wolves to attack. Wolves most commonly target animals that are enduring their first winter, but can also kill adult cows.

Successful predation of bison by wolves tends to follow a consistent pattern. A pack of wolves confronts a bison herd. In some areas they use trees or brush to conceal their approach, but they often move directly toward a bison herd without any attempts at stealth. The wolves then harass the herd, hoping to separate vulnerable animals from the band. When bison stand their ground, wolves most often abandon the attack unless they are extremely hungry. As pack members harass the buffalo with lunges and biting, the bison may panic and begin to run. When this occurs, the wolves follow in pursuit, targeting vulnerable animals from the rear, biting and holding their hind legs and flanks. Bison that are slowed or held by a wolf or two are then overcome by the rest of the pack. Wolves in the interior region of Yellowstone National Park often attempt to chase a bison herd into areas of deep snow, such as drifted ravines, where the entire pack can swarm upon a floundering buffalo.

Wolf packs that are consistently successful in killing bison have several characteristics in common. On the whole, wolf packs with higher numbers are more capable of killing bison than those with fewer hunters. Packs that regularly hunt bison often number ten or more wolves. Along with increased numbers, wolves that must bring down buffalo to survive are some of the largest of their kind in North America. Bison-eating wolves of northern Canada are notably big, as are their counterparts in Yellowstone. The largest wolves observed in Yellowstone most commonly belong to the packs that hunt bison in the winter. Additionally, these packs also contain more adult male wolves than usual. The central Yellowstone wolf pack that accounts for the most bison kills in the park frequently contains several large adult males. The superior size and strength of these wolves helps them bring down buffalo that may weigh ten times as much as any single wolf in the pack.

Bison and Grizzly Bears

Adult grizzly bears are capable of killing adult bison. However, grizzly bear predation on adult bison is very rare. In the fall of 2000, a park employee in Yellowstone National Park observed a female grizzly bear pursue a young adult bison that the bear startled at close range. When the bull buffalo ran, it was pursued and knocked from its feet by the bear. It then slid down a steep embankment and was repeatedly attacked by the bear. The bison was apparently injured when it slammed against a tree in the slide. The attack terminated in an area where the bear was driven from the badly wounded bison to protect the safety of park visitors and construction workers. Wildlife managers euthanized the bison. Experts believe the grizzly bear would have completed its predation in the absence of human interference.

Historical records indicate one other credible reference to a grizzly bear bringing down a cow bison. Circumstantial evidence in Alaska (grizzly bears discovered on adult bison carcasses) may also suggest that the grizzlies prey upon adult bison

on rare occasions. Biologists believe that when grizzly bears do kill adult bison, it is most likely in late winter or early spring when hungry bears emerging from hibernation encounter buffalo that have been substantially weakened from malnutrition after a severe winter.

Bears don't frequently target bison calves, but grizzly bears have been observed killing bison in the first few months of life in Yellowstone National Park. When bison cows bunch together to protect their calves, they can normally repel the investigations of bears. However, if the herd stampedes or a grizzly bear discovers a lone cow and calf, the bear can successfully run down the young bison. Some evidence also exists of black bears killing very young bison calves. Nonetheless, bison predation by bears of either species is highly unusual.

Grizzly bears occasionally prey upon young bison. Predation attempts on adult bison by grizzly bears are very rare, but they have been recorded.
© ISTOCK.COM/JILL RICHARDSON

Bison and Coyotes and Mountain Lions

Under similar circumstances, coyotes and mountain lions might successfully kill young bison calves. In one very unusual incident, several coyotes were observed assisting a wolf in killing a young bison. After the bison was brought down, the wolf chased the coyotes from the kill. Suffice it to say that wolves frequently prey upon bison in some places. Otherwise, bison mortality from predation is a very rare occurrence.

Parasites and Diseases

Bison and cattle share many common parasites and diseases. However, due to their physiological differences, infection rates and physical symptoms of parasites and diseases are not always similar in the two species, even where they share habitat. Research in the Henry Mountains in Utah has shown that even where they occupy the same range, the parasite prevalence between buffalo and cattle is different.

The exposure of bison in public herds to parasites and diseases depends on where they live. Bison of the far north in places such as Canada's Wood Buffalo National Park may be exposed to very different parasites and diseases than those roaming the Wichita Mountains National Wildlife Refuge in Oklahoma. Because much of the bison research involving parasites and disease has been conducted in private herds, it is difficult to establish with certainty the extent to which animals in public herds might be affected.

Internal parasites that are known to afflict bison include lungworms and tapeworms. These parasites are not normally a significant cause of bison mortality, but they may weaken or kill individual animals that are severely infected. Bison are also sometimes plagued by a variety of external parasites, such as mosquitoes, ticks, and biting flies. The long, dense hair of bison makes it difficult for ticks to reach their skin. Bison also roll in the dirt (wallow) and groom themselves by scratching with their hind feet or rubbing on trees and rocks. Both activities help dislodge ticks from the body. When their coat is short during the summer months, bison are sometimes harassed by biting flies to the point that they abandon feeding areas where fly infestations are

Rubbing on trees and rocks helps bison rid themselves of ticks and other external parasites.
JACK BALLARD

particularly acute. Some researchers believe bison found at very high elevations in the summer may be avoiding biting insects more prevalent at lower elevations.

Bison are susceptible to a number of diseases that are also found in domestic cattle. Domestic animals such as cattle and sheep may transmit certain diseases to bison and vice versa.

Brucellosis is a disease common to bison in Yellowstone National Park. Brucellosis is caused by bacteria of the *brucella* family and can infect a variety of animals including cattle, bison, elk, goats, pigs, camels, dogs, and humans. Bison are affected by the strain known as *brucella abortus*. As the name implies, severe brucellosis may cause a female buffalo to abort her fetus. Other symptoms of brucellosis include swollen joints and testicles, infertility, lameness, and reduced milk production. In most cases, however, bison that are infected with the bacteria do not exhibit readily observable symptoms of the disease.

Over the past century the livestock industry has spent considerable resources to eradicate brucellosis from domestic livestock. Brucellosis is of concern to ranchers due to its economics. Aborted fetuses cost ranchers calves. The disease also requires ranchers to spend money on testing and vaccinations, and it causes weight loss and other factors that adversely affect cattle production.

The potential for bison to transmit brucellosis to cattle in areas adjacent to Yellowstone National Park is a very contentious political and economic issue. Some groups believe Yellowstone bison should be allowed to migrate to adjacent public lands without interference. Others believe the bison should be kept away from area cattle even if it requires lethal control. At the present time the State of Montana uses hunting as a means to control bison that wander beyond the boundaries of the park.

Hunters take the animals for meat, but the state also hopes to keep bison from mingling with cattle by hunting them. However, elk in the region of Yellowstone also carry brucellosis, making it impossible to stymie the threat of spreading the disease to cattle by keeping them from bison without addressing the issue of brucellosis in elk.

Bovine tuberculosis is another bacterial disease that is sometimes found in bison. The disease causes lesions in the lungs and lymph nodes and may be fatal to infected animals. Outbreaks of bovine tuberculosis have occurred in various public and private bison herds during the past century. Research indicates that some bison inhabiting Wood Buffalo National Park are infected with both bovine tuberculosis and brucellosis.

Anthrax is another bacterial disease known to occasionally infect public bison herds in North America. Bison may also be susceptible to other bacterial and viral infections found in cattle and other ungulates.

REPRODUCTION AND YOUNG

The Mating Season

Bison calves are born in the spring, but the reproductive cycle of these massive grazers actually begins the previous summer. The bison mating season occurs in midsummer, usually spanning the weeks of late July and early August. Cows that do not conceive a calf during the normal breeding season may mate a month or so later. Within some bison herds half of the cows may become pregnant in the span of a week.

As the breeding season approaches, the bachelor herds of mature bulls splinter. Bulls join the cow herds, moving through the females in search of cows that are preparing to breed. Throughout the rest of the year, the massive males live together with very little conflict, resting and grazing in their bull groups. During the mating season, however, bulls that have achieved sufficient size and status in the herd to claim cows find themselves in competition with other males.

This bison bull is "tending" the cow, keeping himself between her and potential rivals in the herd.
JACK BALLARD

Public bison herds from which animals are not culled often have a nearly equal number of breeding-age bulls and cows. The majority of the cows become ready for breeding in a short span of time, creating intense competition among the mature bulls. Shortly before a cow is ready for breeding, she is joined by a "tending" bull. The bull often attempts to separate the cow a short distance from the herd or keeps her at the edge of the buffalo band. He positions his body between the cow and rival bulls, communicating his intention to mate with the cow to both the female and other competitive males. This tending behavior persists for several hours until the cow is bred or a rival bull drives the bull from the cow. In some cases the cow breaks from a tending bull and bolts back into the herd, apparently attempting to motivate the advances of a bull that is superior to the one courting her.

Two dramatic displays of bison athletics occur during the breeding season, one that involves cows, another that takes place between bulls. While it's easy to assume that the big, bold bison bulls are the fastest animals in the herd, it's the cows that are swiftest of feet and more agile. If a cow isn't sufficiently impressed with the bull tending her, she may attempt to dash away from him. Bulls respond to these maneuvers by their own rushes as they try to keep themselves between the cow and potential rivals. This action appears very similar to the activities of a cowboy on horseback who uses his mount to cut a cow away from the herd for roping. Many biologists believe that bison cows are nearly always capable of escaping a tending bull. A cow's attempts to evade him might simply be part of her assessment of a bull's desirability as the sire of her calf. If a cow really decides to escape from a tending bull, her speed and agility are impressive. Equally inspiring is the number of rival bulls that come rushing from the herd to claim her.

Most of the conflict between bulls during the mating season is settled with aggressive displays that result in one bull backing down from another when they contest the breeding privileges of a cow. Confronted with an older, larger bull, a young male just coming into breeding age is most likely to back away without a contest. Mature bulls that are evenly matched in size and rank within the herd aren't so easily intimidated. Whether challenging one another over a receptive cow or jostling for dominance in the breeding hierarchy, bulls of roughly equal stature engage in a variety of threatening behaviors intended to intimidate their rivals into submission. The vocal aspect of the threat involves bellowing. As a bull approaches a rival, his bellows usually become louder, more frequent, and more intense. However, one university research study on the Fort Niobrara National Wildlife Refuge in Nebraska found that the volume of a bull's bellows was inversely correlated to his breeding success. The truly dominant animals seemed to adopt more of a policy of "walk softly but carry a big stick" than their loudmouthed rivals.

Along with the vocal menace, a threatening bull relies on a number of physical behaviors to communicate his intentions. Bulls stomp their feet as they walk toward a rival. They also urinate in a wallow (a patch of bare ground where bison roll in the dust to relieve itching or rid themselves of insects), then wallow in the damp soil. Some biologists believe this seemingly random act gives rival bulls some indication of a male's fitness that can be detected by his opponent's keen sense of smell.

If the threats of bellowing, stomping, and wallowing don't resolve the conflict, bulls engage in a series of closer postures that may lead them to a full-blown battle. Bulls may approach each other directly with their heads cocked slightly to one side. If one of the animals turns aside, he is admitting the dominance of his rival. They may also confront one another from a parallel position with their bodies broadside to one another. The confrontation may also lead to the two hulking males coming nearly within touching distance of each other, then simultaneously bobbing their heads in a threatening manner.

Full-blown fights between mature bull bison often begin as head-to-head confrontations. When one bull attempts to hook the other with a horn or rams his head, the battle begins.
© ISTOCK.COM/ JEANNETTEKATZIR

When none of these threats or postures successfully intimidates a rival, a battle ensues. The confrontation begins with the butting of heads or one bull attempting to hook the other with his short, pointed horns. Some fights are momentary, ending when one bull signals his submission by turning his head sideways and backing away between clashes. Others are lengthy tests of strength and courage that end with the injury of one or both bulls. Fighting bison repeatedly clash their massive heads together, pivoting swiftly about on their front feet in an attempt to reach their opponent's ribcage or flank. If a bull is successful in pressing such an attack, he may gore his rival in the ribs, abdomen, or hindquarters. Ribs may be broken when this occurs, or the horn of one bull may pierce the hide of another. Legs may be fractured or joints dislocated as well. In rare instances a bison bull may kill his opponent on the spot. More frequently, bulls die from infected puncture wounds or injuries that make them unable to travel and feed.

Bison bulls may lose over 10 percent of their body weight (sometimes over 200 pounds) during the breeding season. The weight loss stems from calories burned during stressful threatening displays and fighting. During the mating season bull bison spend more of their time confronting rivals and mating, and less time eating. Their lower nutritional intake and high output during this time may cause dominant bulls to lose so much weight that they are at increased risk of starvation in a severe winter.

Pregnancy and Gestation

In bison herds that have access to highly nutritious forage on a consistent basis, as many as 90 percent of the mature cows may conceive a calf. Conception rates in public herds that do not receive supplemental feed are more variable. Drought, winter severity, and other environmental factors affect the percentage of cows that bear calves in the spring. Historical records from Yellowstone National Park from 1931 to 1966 show pregnancy rates that fluctuate from around 50 to 90 percent depending on the year. Other public bison herds have experienced pregnancy rates as low as 35 percent in times of nutritional stress.

Bison females are most reproductively successful from around 4 to 12 years of age. Older cows occupying good habitat frequently birth calves as well. One cow on the Wichita Mountains National Wildlife Refuge in Oklahoma lived to be 31 years old and raised a calf at age 28. Other females in the Wichita Mountains herd have birthed calves beyond age 20. However, calving rates appear to decline sharply in females over 15 years old.

The gestation period (the time between conception and birth) for bison is similar to that of domestic cattle and slightly longer than humans. The most commonly reported gestation length for bison is 9.5 months or 285 days. Various scientific studies indicate that gestation may vary from 270 to 300 days. Within 6 months of pregnancy, a bison fetus weighs around 25 to 30 pounds, or about 60 percent of its birth weight. The last 3 months of gestation result in the most rapid growth of the unborn bison calf.

Birth

Under natural conditions most bison calves are born between late April and early June. The calving season can be manipulated in buffalo herds kept as livestock. Both the timing and duration of the birthing period vary somewhat by region. Research at the National Bison Range in western Montana has recorded as high as 97 percent of the births occurring in a three-week period from the last week in April to the second week in May. Researchers have observed a significantly longer calving period at Wind Cave National Park in South Dakota and the Fort Niobrara National Wildlife Refuge in Nebraska. A small percentage of bison calves may be born later in the summer.

The high concentration of bison births in a short period of time is part of a biological phenomenon known as "synchronous breeding." Young bison calves, like other newborn ungulates, are much more vulnerable to predation in the first few weeks of life than they are later in the summer. Evolutionary biologists theorize that synchronous breeding increases the odds of some bison calves achieving an age at which they're less susceptible to predation. When predators encounter such a large number of potential prey, "predator satiation" occurs, making it more likely that some of the prey will survive.

Birthing normally occurs on the bison's winter range. Individual cows leave the herd to birth their calves in solitude, rejoining the maternal band a short time later. The birthing process lasts but a few minutes, with the cow usually lying down but

Young bison calves are similar in appearance to the offspring of domestic cattle, lacking the characteristic hump, horns, and coloration of their parents.
JACK BALLARD

sometimes standing. The mother vigorously assists the newborn in freeing itself from the birthing membranes and urges it to its feet with licks and nuzzling. Calves normally attempt to stand just a few minutes after birth and can move in a clumsy run within an hour. For the first few days of life, the calf spends most of its time lying down, standing to nurse. Bison females do not produce as much milk as a domestic cow, but it is incredibly rich.

Newborn bison are very similar in appearance to newborn domestic calves, lacking the hump of their parents that will develop within a few months. The brick red or cinnamon color of the bison calf also transitions in its first months of life to the dark brown of an adult. Baby bison weigh around forty to fifty pounds at birth, with birth weights varying noticeably in some locations. Average birth weights at the Fort Niobrara National Wildlife Refuge in Nebraska are reported at fifty to sixty pounds. Newborn bison on Antelope Island in Utah average twenty-five to forty pounds. Bison cows normally birth a single offspring. Twin bison calves are quite rare.

Nurturing Calves to Adulthood

On the whole, bison cows are very attentive mothers, although in rare instances they may abandon their newborn calf. A few days after birth, the cow rejoins the cow herd with her young calf. Although cows within the herd care for their individual calves, the young buffalo also receives the protection and care of the entire maternal herd. Bison cows have been observed banding together to repel predators. In a unique instance in Yellowstone National Park, a cow was photographed deliberately nudging a group of calves to their feet during very cold, snowy weather in early May, reducing their chances of freezing to death.

Some research indicates female calves remain with their mothers longer than male calves. In either case bison calves can survive in the herd without direct maternal care by their first winter.
JACK BALLARD

Bison calves nurse for about the first seven or eight months of life, sometimes a bit longer. Bison calves have been observed attempting to graze within a week of birth and will drink water after their first week. Once weaned from mother's milk, a young bison stays in the cow herd of its mother, but the close association between female and offspring begins to fade. Some research indicates that female calves remain in closer proximity to their mothers within the herd for a much longer period after weaning than male offspring. In either case young bison are able to forage and survive within the herd after weaning.

BISON AND HUMANS

Bison in Prehistoric Times

The bison of the current era were preceded by several related species. Although imposing animals, modern bison are actually smaller than their predecessors. The first bison in North America are believed to have been Steppe bison or Ice Age bison (*Bison priscus*), which arrived on the continent from Siberia.

In a fascinating twist of history, miners discovered a frozen intact carcass of a Steppe bison near Fairbanks, Alaska, in 1979. The animal was a mature bull, perhaps 8 or 9 years old, that had been killed by American lions, large cats similar to today's African lions that once roamed North America. Radiocarbon dating indicates that the bison was killed some 36,000 years ago. Its death came in late fall or early winter. The lions fed on the animal's hump and flesh that covered the ribs on one side, but scientists believe the carcass froze shortly thereafter. They theorize the bison remained frozen and inhospitable to scavengers during the winter and was perhaps covered by a mudslide in the spring. It then became entombed in the permafrost, remaining in remarkably good condition until it was exposed by the miners. A reaction between chemicals in the bison's tissue and minerals in the surrounding soil created a compound that produced a bright blue color when exposed to the air. This phenomenon earned the bull the nickname "Blue Babe," in reference to the mythical Paul Bunyan's blue ox.

The horns of Steppe bison were much longer than those of today's bison, but a later species that descended from the Steppe bison sported even longer horns that sometimes spanned more than 6 feet from tip to tip. Sometimes called Giant Ice Age bison (*Bison latifrons*), these giant creatures were 20 to 25 percent larger than today's bison. Bulls would have weighed nearly 3,000 pounds, with exceptionally large specimens possibly exceeding 1.5 tons by a few hundred pounds. Both of these species became extinct some 10,000 years ago. Several smaller-bodied, smaller-horned descendants of these bison also ranged across portions of North America. But by the time the first Europeans set foot on the continent and the native peoples acquired horses, only the American bison (*Bison bison*) remained.

Bison and American Indians

The vast herds of buffalo on the central grasslands in North America nurtured human cultures intimately tied to their presence. Some historians believe that the connection between the plains tribes of American Indians and bison illustrates the strongest dependence on one animal by any human society from prehistoric times to the present. Bison provided these native peoples with food (meat), shelter (hides), and tools (bone, sinew, and other body parts). Red Cloud, a former chief of the Sioux tribe, purportedly listed twenty-two uses of the bison by his people. Others have placed the number as high as eighty-seven.

The image of plains Indians hunting bison on horseback factors significantly in our understanding of the history of native peoples. However, the relationship between native hunters and bison stretches much further into the story of American Indians and is very poorly appreciated. Plains Indians pursued bison on horseback for some two centuries, or slightly longer, before the buffalo's near extinction. Their ancestors hunted bison on foot for nearly 10,000 years prior to their acquisition of horses.

How could humans, propelled by legs capable of sprinting at speeds of around 20 miles per hour, successfully kill 1,000-pound animals able to run 30 miles per hour? Not only were these people able to bring down bison, they were remarkably skilled and efficient in doing so. Like their mounted successors, many of these tribes depended upon bison for the necessities of life. Their methods of killing such large, swift ungulates amply illustrate the extent to which human intelligence is able to dominate the superior physical abilities of animals.

One such technique was known as the "surround." This method involved many hunters surrounding a bison herd, or just a portion of the herd if they believed the entire band was too large to manage. The hunters would run and shout on the perimeter of the surrounded bison, slowly closing in on them from all sides. When they came close enough to the encircled animals, they shot arrows and flung lances at the bison. Animals killed on the perimeter of the trapped herd further impeded the flight of those on the inside. In a very successful surround, a few dozen or even a few hundred bison might be killed without a single escape.

A variation of the surround that involved fire was also used in some places. Fires were strategically ignited on three sides of a bison herd, leaving them a single path of escape. The ring of fire pushed the bison to waiting hunters, who blocked their flight from the flames. American Indians who inhabited the upper regions of the Mississippi River most commonly used this technique.

Early hunters also brought groups of bison within the range of their killing implements by driving them into enclosures. In some places natural features such as box canyons or steep-sided washes served as primitive corrals. Enterprising hunters also fashioned stout pens from rocks or wooden poles. These corral-like enclosures, sometimes called a "pound," were most often used in areas where bison inhabited rocky or somewhat wooded terrain on the flanks of the mountains or in mountain valleys. Archaeologists have discovered enclosures that were used by tribes for many years.

Working together, the party first incited a herd of bison to run, then used lines of hunters to direct buffalo into the enclosure, where they were then dispatched with arrows and spears.

Large numbers of bison were also killed at places known as *pishkuns* or buffalo jumps. A buffalo jump was simply a cliff over which a herd of bison could be driven. Animals not killed in the fall were brought down by hunters who waited at the bottom of the cliff while others caused and directed the stampede above. Some tribes were extremely diligent to kill every bison that came over the jump, believing that any survivors that escaped might warn other bison to avoid the precipitous trap in the future. Buffalo jumps occurred most frequently on the eastern front of the Rocky Mountains. The sites of hundreds of buffalo jumps are found in northern Wyoming, Montana, Saskatchewan, and Alberta.

In addition to these communal efforts to kill multiple bison, in the period prior to hunting on horseback, native hunters developed methods of stalking and killing individual animals. One widely employed technique involved a hunter draping himself in the skin of a wolf and approaching a bison herd on all fours. Buffalo were accustomed to the sight of the wolves, which were a constant presence in their world. The wolves sometimes attacked vulnerable animals, but more often simply shadowed the herds

American Indians hunted the vast herds of bison on the plains and foothills of the Rocky Mountains for thousands of years before they acquired horses.
JACK BALLARD

or went about the business of being a wolf. A mature bull or cow had little to fear from an individual wolf and would scarcely interrupt its grazing if such an animal came close. Native hunters used this knowledge to disguise themselves as a skulking canine and approach bison. Once within range, the hunter clad in a wolf's skin would shoot his target with an arrow.

Although the final generations of American Indians who hunted bison on horseback have most vividly captured our imagination, their skilled forebears feasted on bison for many centuries prior to the arrival of the horse. Horses gave the native peoples more mobility, developing cultures that were more nomadic than those preceding them. But Indians had hunted bison efficiently for perhaps as long as 10,000 years before taking to the back of a mustang.

The Great Eradication

As discussed earlier in this chapter, much conjecture exists regarding the number of bison in North America prior to the arrival of Europeans. The widely published figure of sixty million animals most likely traces back to estimates of bison observed by Colonel Richard Dodge on a wagon trip in Kansas in 1871. Dodge estimated both the number of the herd of bison he observed and the land area it covered. Ernest Thompson Seton, a later naturalist, extrapolated these figures to his calculation of bison range in North America, arriving at the sixty million estimate. As noted previously, more recent, scientific calculations based on range capacity, competition with other grazers, and fluctuations in precipitation and winter severity have concluded that half that many (or fewer) bison actually occupied the continent.

Exceptionally severe winter weather and epic storms can be fatal to even healthy adult bison.
JACK BALLARD

Whatever their historic numbers, the collapse of the bison population in the late 1800s (particularly the 1870s) was truly dramatic. Millions of animals dwindled to a population in the United States of a few hundred in a matter of a few decades. What triggered the decline?

Much has been written about the extensive market slaughter of bison, particularly in the 1870s. Bison were killed by the tens of thousands, not for their meat, but for their hides. Leather was an important industrial commodity of the day. Buffalo leather was particularly thick and durable. It found its way into a host of products, including the broad belts that powered industrial machinery. Buffalo hides became an incredibly valuable commodity, important enough to create a rush to slaughter in the 1870s that might fruitfully be likened to the Alaskan gold rush. Most biologists and historians believe the massive slaughter of bison for their hides was the primary culprit in the population collapse.

For several decades prior to the 1870s, both American Indian and European hunters actively sold bison hides to traders to procure luxuries for themselves, such as flour, tobacco, and molasses. Although their harvest failed to rival that of the later hide boom, it exerted pressure on the bison population.

Some experts believe that bovine diseases introduced by domestic cattle also claimed substantial numbers of bison. Subsistence hunting by American Indian tribes possibly played a role as well. Native hunters on horseback most often targeted cows with their arrows, potentially reducing the reproductive capacity of the herds they hunted. Nonetheless, subsistence hunting probably played a minor role in the bison decline in comparison to the number of animals killed for leather and other purposes.

Mother Nature was not always kind to the bison, either. Weather events and drought in the 1800s exerted downward pressure on bison numbers in some areas. For example, in 1841 a warm wind during the winter melted the top layer of snow in bison habitat in Wyoming. A cold snap followed, turning the softened snow to a rock-hard crust of ice. Unable to reach the grass underneath, bison died in untold numbers. In the spring of 1844, an unusually heavy snowstorm in eastern Colorado was responsible for a massive die-off of bison.

Bison and Us

Bounding back from the brink of extinction not much more than a century ago, about 430,000 bison are estimated to now live in the United States and Canada. While their survival is no longer a question, their dual status as livestock and wild animal makes them unique among North American mammals. Other wild ungulates such as elk and whitetail deer are kept on farms, yet their numbers in the wild vastly outnumber those in domestic operations. Bison are just the opposite. Over a dozen times as many bison are contained in livestock operations than are kept for conservation purposes or roam public lands as "wild" herds.

Over the past few decades, the number of bison kept as livestock has expanded rapidly. Sales of bison meat at retail outlets and in the restaurant market totaled around $278 million in 2011. Bison meat is normally marketed as a natural meat free of growth hormones. Buffalo meat has less fat, cholesterol, and calories per ounce than beef, pork, or even skinless chicken. Many consumers thus regard bison as a healthier alternative to these traditional meats. However, it is substantially more expensive. Bison may sell for twice as much as beef for equivalent cuts of meat. Most agricultural economists view the buffalo livestock industry as a business

Many wildlife advocates believe the restoration of the bison will not truly be complete until more free-ranging herds of these iconic animals have been established on public lands in the contiguous United States.
JACK BALLARD

in its infancy. Whether or not demand for the meat will sustain the current numbers of bison kept as livestock remains to be seen.

Public bison herds at national wildlife refuges, along with state and national parks, are presently very healthy and generally expanding. Numerous American Indian tribes now have bison herds of their own that graze on tribal lands. The Crow tribe in south-central Montana has a substantial free-ranging herd that roams the northern flanks of the Bighorn Mountains. Most publically kept bison herds produce more offspring than their range can support. Excess animals are often sold at public auctions.

Despite the success of bison restoration over the past century, many biologists feel the comeback of these animals in the United States is still lacking. Just two truly free-ranging bison herds occupy public lands in the Lower 48, those in Yellowstone National Park and in the Henry Mountains in Utah. Although bison in such large reserves as South Dakota's Custer State Park may range over 71,000 acres, these wild animals are ultimately confined behind a towering woven-wire fence. In the minds of some, the restoration of bison in America will not be complete until additional free-ranging herds track more of their native habitat on public lands.

CHAPTER 7
MOUNTAIN GOATS

A hanging basin just below the crest of a high ridge in the Absaroka-Beartooth Wilderness harbors a modest lake, a tarn with deep blue waters when viewed from above, the home of some of the healthiest cutthroat trout on the planet. The fish are fat, beautiful, and loads of fun to fly-fish. There is no trail to yonder lake. The first time I aimed my boots toward its shoreline in an ascent from a boulder-strewn jeep trail, the expedition lasted about 1 hour. Panting upward along the edge of an elongated clearing in the company of a brindle greyhound, I looked up to see a grizzly bear digging casually at the upper end of the meadow. The retired racer seemed supremely confident in her ability to dodge the predator. Not so optimistic myself, I retreated down the mountain. Two years later I reached the lake. The only evidence of previous human visitation was a weather-checked, rotting piece of the cinch strap from a saddle.

The overall white coloration of the coat is one of the most distinguishing features of mountain goats.
JACK BALLARD

The third time I set out for the lake, a new route seemed in order. Instead of bush-whacking through the jungle of lodgepole pines below the lake, I hiked up a trail that crossed the ridge and then followed the drainage divide for a couple miles before descending to the lake. The new route nearly doubled the distance but certainly reduced the effort.

Along with an easier passage, my newfound path routinely placed me in the presence of mountain goats. The sighting of a herd of females and their playful kids was always adequate reason to shuck my backpack and rest. On one occasion, I was startled to see what appeared to be a dead goat lying on an expansive snowbank on the north side of the ridge. Curious to view the carcass, I skirted the snowfield's lower edge to get close to the goat. When I was a stone's throw away, it lifted its head at the sound of my footsteps crunching on gravel. It stood but seemed reluctant to leave its naturally air-conditioned parlor. Before dropping from the ridge toward the lake, I looked back toward the billy. It was again sacked out on the snow. I have long since learned that his behavior is fairly common to goats in alpine environments, which sometimes cool themselves on snow. Mountain goats are probably the least researched and under-stood ungulate in the United States. I've learned much about them researching this book and am confident you will find them a fascinating subject as well.

NAMES AND FACES

Names and Visual Description

"Mountain goat" is the name given to a large white ungulate occupying alpine and steep mountain habitat in western North America. Mountain goats, however, are not goats. They are not directly related to domestic goats or the wild goats of the genus *Capra*. Ibex and other wild goats range across portions of Europe, Asia, Asia Minor, and the Middle East. By contrast, mountain goats are found only in North America and are the sole species in the genus *Oreamnos*.

The full scientific name for the mountain goat is *Oreamnos americanus*. "*Oreamnos*" is composed of Latin terms that trace to ancient Greek words for "mountain" (*oros*) and "lamb" (*amnos*). It is somewhat odd that the scientific name references *amnos*, the ancient term for a baby sheep versus *capra* ("goat") or *eriphos* ("baby goat," "kid"). Perhaps this is an attempt to distinguish mountain goats at a species level from other goats. However, the reference to "lamb" is just as confusing, as it suggests a relation-ship with sheep, a genus of animals also unrelated to mountain goats. The *americanus* portion of the scientific name is used with other species with which the mountain goat shares its continent of residence and merely references "America."

Colloquial terms for the mountain goat are not commonly used among wildlife professionals or the human residents of the mountainous regions the animals call home. "White goat" and "Rocky Mountain goat," however, are sometimes referenced as other names for the mountain goat. In Spanish the species is known as *capra delle nevi*, which means "snow goat" and forges a poetic relationship to both its color and the winter habitat in which it lives.

Mountain goats are often described as being white in color, but a close examination reveals a coat that is not pure white but slightly yellow or cream. During the mating season, male mountain goats sometimes wallow in the dirt, giving their coat a dingy gray color. Throughout the year their coat has a shaggy appearance, much more so from late fall to early summer, when they are carrying their exceptionally long, luxurious winter coat. Both male and female mountain goats have beards of hair jutting from their lower jaw. Mountain goats have a short, furry tail matching their coat. Goats of both sexes have dark, stiletto-like horn sprouting from the top of their skull.

Male mountain goats are called "billies," females are "nannies," and a baby mountain goat is called a "kid."

Related Species in North America

Due to the consistent, overall cream shade of their coat and the mountain environments in which they live, mountain goats are unlikely to be confused with any other species of animal in North America. The pronghorn has a light-color body and dark horns like the mountain goat. However, pronghorn are creatures of the plains, an animal whose presence in goat country is highly improbable. Additionally, pronghorn have large portions of reddish-tan hair on their coats in addition to hair similar in color to the mountain goat. The horns of female pronghorn are much shorter than those of an adult mountain goat, and male pronghorn sport horns with the distinctive "prong," or short fork, for which the species is named.

Bighorn sheep share range with mountain goats in many areas. The horns of this female bighorn in Glacier National Park, Montana, are shaped and colored much differently than a mountain goat's.
NPS/TIM RAINS

The ungulate whose habitat often overlaps with the mountain goat is the bighorn sheep. Although generally similar in size, sheep are colored differently than goats, having an overall gray or brownish appearance. The massive, spiraling horns of male bighorns quickly differentiate them from mountain goats. Although female bighorn sheep have shorter, thinner horns than the males, their horns are also different than a goat's. A female bighorn's horns are light brown versus the overall black coloration of a mountain goat's. From the rear, a bighorn sports a distinctive white rump and small, almost indistinguishable tail that contrasts with a darker body. A very light gray or white wolf wandering high-mountain habitat might momentarily be mistaken for a bighorn, but a closer appraisal would quickly reveal the error.

The animal most likely to be confused with a mountain goat is the Dall sheep, a species of white sheep found in northwestern Canada and Alaska. Dall sheep and mountain goats are roughly similar in size and occupy similar mountainous terrain. However, the large, spiraling horns of a Dall ram quickly distinguish it from a mountain goat. Female Dall sheep have horns superficially similar to those

The shaggy musk ox is believed to be the closest North American relative of the mountain goat.
USFWS/TIM BOWMAN

of a mountain goat, but the black horns of a mountain goat immediately differentiate it from the tan or brownish horns of the sheep. Additionally, mountain goats have an overall shaggier appearance compared to the sleeker coat of the Dall sheep.

The animal perhaps most closely related to the mountain goat in North America looks nothing like *Oreamnos americanus*. The musk ox is a large, shaggy, ox-like ungulate of the far north. Recent molecular genetic studies indicate mountain goats and muskoxen may share evolutionary ancestors.

Subspecies of Mountain Goats

There are no currently recognized subspecies of mountain goats, although that has not always been the case. In 1904 Dr. J. A. Allen identified four subspecies of mountain goats in the annual *Bulletin of the American Museum of Natural History*. The subspecies designations were made primarily on the basis of overall size differences and varying skull dimensions of goats found in different geographical regions. These differences are today explained largely in terms of available nutrition that promotes or inhibits mature body mass rather than subspecies distinctions. Along with its identification of four subspecies that were abandoned in 1970, the book also tags mountain goats with the scientific name *Oreamnos montanus*. For some time, different taxonomists used competing names for the same species. The mountain goat was identified as *Oreamnos americanus* as early as 1816, but other scientific designations were used until later in the twentieth century.

Physical Characteristics

The dense hair coat of the mountain goat disguises the actual shape and size of its body to a large degree, even when adorned in its shorter summer coat. Adult mountain goats are a substantial animal. Fully grown females commonly weigh from 130 to 185 pounds, depending on their habitat. Mountain goats display significant sexual dimorphism (difference in size base on gender). Males weigh from 195 to 300 pounds. In exceptional cases, they may grow even heavier. A billy weighing 385 pounds was recorded by biologists in the Haines, Alaska, area; but any billy weighing more than 300 pounds is considered a very large animal. Billies are around 10 percent heavier than nannies at 1 year of age. At 5 years they outweigh corresponding females by around 30 to 60 percent. Nannies normally achieve their maximum body mass at about 6 years of age, but billies may increase in mass for several years thereafter. Sexual dimorphism and overall size are greatest in northern populations. In extreme cases, massive billies may be nearly twice as large as the nannies with which they mate. Adult mountain goats stand about 3 to 3.5 feet at the shoulder. Their total body length is 4.5 to 5.5 feet.

Mountain goats possess numerous physical adaptations allowing them to thrive in harsh alpine environments. Their winter pelage consists of a long, luxurious outer coat covering an inner layer of dense, highly-insulating fur. This gives them the ability to withstand the low temperatures and harsh winds common to their winter range in the mountains.

Underneath their shaggy coat, the skeletal structure of a mountain goat is quite narrow. Their hooves are black and quite large in relation to their body mass. The ears of a mountain goat are narrow and pointed, measuring 4 to 6 inches in length. A goat's ears appear much longer when carrying its summer coat as opposed to the heavy coat of winter. The nose of a mountain goat is black; its eyes appear dark against its creamy coat. Goats have black glands located at the rear of the base of their horns that are sometimes visible, especially on mature billies.

The hooves of mountain goats are adapted to give them traction on a variety of mountain environments, such as the summer snowfield this goat is crossing in Washington's North Cascades National Park.
NPS/BRUMAND-SMITH

Horns and Horn Development

Both sexes of mountain goats grown horns that are used for both aggression and defense. The upper portion of the horns usually appears very dark or black, but the bases may appear grayish or brownish. Tiny horn nubs are observable on kids within three months of birth. Horns continue to grow throughout a goat's lifetime, although growth slows considerably after around 5 years of age. Researchers in Canada have concluded that 93 percent of maximal horn growth occurs by 3 years of age, and that horn length (not mass) is similar for nannies and billies over 6 years of age.

Differences in horn characteristics are one of the ways to differentiate the sexes of mountain goats, a difficult task for the amateur observer. The horns of male goats normally display more mass at the base and greater overall heft than those of females. Horns on a billy also tend to sweep backward in a consistent arc. A nanny's horns, by contrast, usually sprout almost straight from the head and then bend sharply backward about two-thirds of the way from the skull. These variations in horn shape become more distinct as animals age. Goats can be aged by the "growth rings" on their horns, fissures that ring the horn and indicate the annual break between growth and dormancy in horn development.

The age of a mountain goat can be determined in relation to the "growth rings" on its horns.
NPS/TIM RAINS

Goats do not butt heads during intraspecies combat like bighorn sheep or bison do. Instead their horns are used for stabbing. Horns taper to a sharp point and are thus formidable weapons. Perhaps due to the potential for horn thrusts creating harmful, even fatal, wounds, mountain goats seem reluctant to fight one another, but they will readily use their horns for protection when cornered.

RANGE AND HABITAT

North American Range—Historic

Mountain goats share their range with bighorn sheep in many places, but unlike big-horns, which historically claimed a broad range including prairie breaks as well as alpine haunts, mountain goats are strictly creatures of the mountains. Their historic range was much smaller than many other large mammals of the Rocky Mountains, limited to high-elevation haunts in the western and Pacific coastal mountain ranges of North America.

The historic range of the mountain goat was bounded on its southern end by the Columbia River in Washington and eastward into Idaho and western Montana, west of the Continental Divide at an approximate latitude of 44°N. These three states are currently believed to be the only areas in the contiguous United States that historically contained mountain goat populations. However, some commentators speculate that mountain goats are also native to northeastern and north-central Oregon. Scant archaeological evidence and a few references in the journals of Lewis and Clark from April 1806 have sometimes been (disputably) interpreted as referencing mountain goats on the south side of the Columbia River in Oregon. One 1905 natural history of mountain goats references mountain goats in Oregon as far south as Mt. Jefferson, a major peak in the Cascade Range about 60 miles south of the Washington/Oregon border.

Historic mountain goat range extended northward into Canada and Alaska. Goats were found in the coastal and interior mountains of western Canada. Goats were present from the eastern edge of the Rocky Mountains in western Alberta to the Coastal Range in British Columbia. They tracked the mountains of northern British Columbia into the mountains of the Yukon and Northwest Territories. Mountain goats were present in the Cassiar, Coast, Logan, Selwyn, and St. Elias Ranges of the Yukon Territory and the Mackenzie Range of the Northwest Territories.

The extreme northwestern boundary of the mountain goat's range is found in Alaska. Historically, mountain goats were present along the coastal mountain ranges of Alaska to Prince William Sound and the Kenai Peninsula. They were also found in northern portions of the Chugach Mountains and southern portions of the Talkeetna and Wrangell Mountains. A latitude of 63°N is considered the northern terminus of historic mountain goat range.

Mountain goats have never been as popular a game animal for eating as species such as elk, bison, or moose. However, the arrival of European immigrants to the Rocky Mountains created increased pressure on mountain goat populations due to hunting for meat, sport, and their hides, which were quite valuable. This led to extirpation of mountain goats in portions of their historic range.

North American Range—Current

Mountain goats remain in much of their historic range. Toward the middle of the twentieth century, goats were transplanted from existing populations to areas within their historic range from which they had been eliminated. These transplants occurred in portions of Alaska, Montana, Idaho, Washington, and Alberta, Canada.

Along with reintroducing goats where they had been extirpated on historic range, relocations of mountain goats occurred from the 1950s onward to establish populations in other suitable habitat, primarily for sport hunting. These relocations have expanded the current range of mountain goats southward and eastward many hundreds of miles beyond their historic range.

Mountain goats were introduced to Washington's Olympic Peninsula in the 1920s, an area to which they are not native. Olympic National Park was created in 1938 in the decade after approximately a dozen mountain goats were released in the Olympic Mountains. The goat population has grown dramatically in the area. In 2004 an estimated 240 mountain goats were found in the Olympic Mountains. By 2011 the number had grown to 350. The population continued to increase dramatically, with 584 goats counted in 2016. Beginning in the 1960s, mountain goats have also been transplanted to the Selkirk Range in northeastern Washington.

A mountain goat crosses a slope in Olympic National Park, Washington, one of numerous places where goats have been introduced outside their native range.
NPS

More than half of Montana's mountain goat population inhabits nonnative range, including this animal photographed from the Beartooth Highway southwest of Red Lodge.
JACK BALLARD

Mountain goats were released in the Wallowa Mountains of eastern Oregon in 1950, where they quickly established a permanent population. Additional transplants have made it to other areas. In 2010, forty-five mountain goats were released on Mount Jefferson in the Cascade Range.

In Idaho, mountain goats occur at intervals at high elevations from the panhandle southward to the central portion of the state. They are found in numerous mountain ranges and are considered native animals in this region. One notable transplant occurred in eastern Idaho in 1969 and 1970. The 1969 transplant occurred in the Palisades Creek drainage of the Teton Range several miles from the Wyoming border west of Jackson, Wyoming. Although the transplant occurred in an area of ideal mountain goat habitat, mountain goats were historically absent from the area.

Mountain goats inhabit numerous mountain ranges in Montana. Historically they were limited to mountainous areas west of the Continental Divide. The white denizens of the crags have been transplanted to many areas east of the Divide, to the point that more than half the mountain goat populations in Montana are animals introduced into areas to which they were not native. In the 1950s mountain goats were relocated from western Montana into the Elkhorn Mountains south of Helena and the Sleeping Giant (Gates of the Mountains) area east of Helena. A 1969 transplant took goats from the Sleeping Giant area to the Big Belt Mountains, another range east of the Continental Divide to which mountain goats are not native.

Other Montana mountain ranges east of the goat's historic range hold substantial populations. The Crazy Mountains received mountain goats in the 1940s; the animals have established a robust population. Mountain goats were transplanted into the Absaroka Range in the 1950s. Other transplants occurred in the Madison, Gallatin, and Tobacco Root Ranges, all east of the Continental Divide.

Mountain goats were introduced into Colorado from the 1940s to the early 1970s, and herds have become established in several mountain ranges. The first eight mountain goats came from western Montana and were released on Mount Shavano in 1943. Mount Shavano is in the Sawatch Range of central Colorado, which holds eight of the twenty highest peaks in the state. In the late 1950s and early 1960s, goats were released on Mount Evans, where a stable herd is now located. Mountain goats have also colonized portions of the Gore Range and the San Juan Mountains, where they were released in 1971. Although mountain goats were categorized by the Colorado Wildlife Commission as native wildlife in 1993, that designation was based on questionable historical evidence. More recent research by biologists at Colorado State University has concluded it is very unlikely mountain goats were found in the state prior to introduction.

Utah pioneered its mountain goat transplant program in 1967, when six goats from Olympic National Park in Washington were released in the Lone Peak area of the Wasatch Range east of Salt Lake City. Mountain goats have also been introduced in the Uinta and Tushar Mountains. In 2013 and 2014, thirty-five mountain goats were released in the La Sal Mountains near the Colorado border. At this writing, this is the southernmost mountain goat population in North America.

Nevada claims mountain goat populations in two places. Twelve mountain goats were transplanted from Washington into the Ruby Mountains southeast of Elko in the mid-1960s. In 1981 another eleven goats were received from Washington and freed in the East Humboldt Mountains east of Elko. Both populations have become well established.

The easternmost population of mountain goats in North America is found in the Black Hills of South Dakota. Mountain goats were brought from Alberta, Canada, to Custer State Park in 1924. The first night at their new home, a nanny and kid escaped from the park's enclosure, leaving behind four of the six translocated animals. The other four goats also escaped in the next few years, and the entire group moved into the rugged country around Black Elk Peak, the highest point in the Black Hills. The mountain goat population in the Black Hills has seen several boom-and-bust cycles. Lack of genetic diversity in the herd is seen as one potential culprit in the population declines of the early 2000s. Additional transplants to increase genetic diversity were made with nineteen goats from Colorado in 2006 and twenty-one goats from Utah in 2013.

Wyoming holds mountain goats in two areas, but the state has never deliberately introduced them. One herd is in the Beartooth Mountains southwest of Red Lodge, Montana. These goats originated from the release of fourteen animals in the Rock Creek drainage of Montana in 1942 that have since expanded their range into Wyoming. The other goat population is in the Teton Range in and adjacent to Grand Teton National Park. These animals colonized from a transplant (noted above) of goats on the opposite side of the Teton Range in Idaho.

Mountain goats are found throughout the southeast panhandle of Alaska. Their range extends west and north along the coastal mountains to Cook Inlet. The Wrangell and Chugach Mountains hold goats in south-central Alaska, with a smaller population in the Talkeetna Mountains. Mountain goats also have been introduced to several islands where they are not native, including Kodiak, Baranof, Revillagigedo, and Chichagof Islands (where they failed to become established). The Mount Juneau area (adjacent to the city of Juneau) has also received transplanted goats to replace a vanished herd.

The above sketch of mountain goat range in the contiguous United States and Alaska is by no means exhaustive. Goats have been planted in other areas not noted, and their range has grown in many places as well due to their colonization of available habitat in areas where they were found historically and in others where they were introduced. Mountain goats are found over much of their historical range in Canada, as described previously. Wildlife management officials in Alberta have concluded that mountain goats did not suffer substantially in relation to overhunting and habitat loss that plagued elk and bighorn sheep in the late nineteenth and early twentieth centuries. Mountain goats were not actively managed or researched (at least in that province) until the 1960s. At least fifteen transplants of goats originating in Alberta or released in the province from other parts of Canada occurred from 1924 to 1995.

British Columbia holds the most mountain goats of any state or province in North America. Mountain goats have remained in most of their historic range in this province. Several transplants have moved goats from one part of the province to another, most occurring in the latter 1900s. Most of these were undertaken to augment or introduce mountain goats to portions of their native range from which they had been extirpated or to bolster existing populations. Only one of these was intended to introduce mountain goats to suitable habitat outside their known, native range.

Based on the available data, it appears there is a notable difference in mountain goat management strategies between the United States and Canada. State wildlife agencies in the United States seem much more willing to translocate mountain goats to areas outside their historic range than their Canadian counterparts.

Mountain Goat Habitat

Mountain goats are creatures of the cliffs and crags. Their primary defense against four-legged predators is to retreat to broken cliffs and narrow ledges, where wolves, mountain lions, and bears are unable to follow, much less overtake a goat that traverses such formidable terrain with ease. Despite their dependence on rock formations for security, goats cannot climb sheer cliffs, requiring some texture in the rock face for footholds. A Montana research project concluded that mountain goats are rarely found more than a quarter-mile from such terrain. However, researchers have also observed that fidelity to rocky escape cover varies in relation to predators. Where mammalian predators are scarce, including some goat habitat in Colorado, the animals are much more willing to wander away from escape cover and may be found more than one-half mile from cliffs.

Mountain goats may spend time literally at sea level, where these nannies and kids were photographed at Kenai Fords National Park, Alaska.
NPS/JIM PFEIFFENBERGER

The location of the precipitous escape cover with which mountain goats are associated varies dramatically. At certain times of year, mountain goats may be found literally at sea level in British Columbia and Alaska or 13,000 feet or more above sea level on mountain ridges in Colorado. The altitude zone inhabited by mountain goats varies widely. In coastal British Columbia and Alaska, they winter from sea level to around 4,500 feet, with most animals wintering above 1,000 feet. Mountain goats in interior mountain ranges are often found at or above tree line. In some places they retreat to lower elevations during winter, but in others they remain in the alpine zone, occupying habitat niches where wind and very steep terrain keep snow cover to a minimum.

Mountain goat habitat is strongly tied to slope, or the steepness of the terrain. Studies of mountain goats in several regions have found that they prefer slopes with a 30-degree or higher incline. In some places their preferences are for extremely steep terrain. One study from Washington found goats favored slopes with a 50-degree or more slope. A research project in southeastern Alaska concluded that most wintering goats were found on slopes between 31 and 50 degrees and avoided areas with less than a 30-degree slope. To put these in perspective, researchers using a specialized treadmill for an evaluation of human performance on steep inclines found that even elite athletes could not balance while walking on slopes above 40 degrees with ideal traction conditions. Another study found that most people failed to walk upright when the slope angle exceeded 25 to 30 degrees. Thus, mountain goats use terrain humans find challenging to traverse on two feet but are most happy on slopes where a person would need some sort of handhold to move upon.

NUTRITIONAL REQUIREMENTS AND FORAGE

Nutritional Requirements

Mountain goats survive on a variety of food sources. In summer they readily consume grass and leafy plants. Winter finds them eating more browse, woody twigs from deciduous trees and shrubs as well as conifers. In one study, biologists estimated that mountain goats ingest nearly 5,000 calories per day during the summer, almost 40 percent more than is needed to maintain their body condition. This allows them to store the excess calories as fat reserves which will be used to survive the winter.

The same study reported that goats on winter range obtain slightly less than an estimated 1,600 calories per day. This provides just under 90 percent of their required energy. The energy balance in winter must come from fat reserves. If those are depleted, energy is "cannibalized" from muscle and other body tissues and eventually compromises the animal's survival. However, it should be noted that the above estimates were extrapolated from research done with deer and should be interpreted with caution. Research specific to the nutritional requirements and digestive efficiency of mountain goats is virtually nonexistent.

Generally, the nutritional value of forage increases with elevation. Even plants of the same species show disparate nutritional qualities based on elevation, with those

Summer is normally a time of plenty for foraging mountain goats. Fat reserves gained during the summer are needed for winter survival.
NPS/TIM RAINS

Summer habitat near melting snowfields and springs gives mountain goats adequate access to surface water over most of their range. This goat is drinking from a small seep on Mount Evans in Colorado. If these resources dry up, goats may relocate to other areas.

JACK BALLARD

growing at higher haunts packing a greater nutritional punch than those found in the lowlands. This factor is significant in mountain goat health. Research has determined that goats living in higher elevation areas tend to grow faster and maintain better overall health than those at lower elevations.

Mountain goats rely on surface water, snow, and moisture in the plants they consume to obtain liquid for body function. Research regarding water intake requirements specific to mountain goats is lacking. Based on their size relative to other creatures, it might be estimated that an adult mountain goat needs no more than 1 to 2 gallons of water per day. When grazing on succulent plants in summer, much of a mountain goat's water intake probably comes from forage. Access to water is not an important issue in mountain goat nutrition. During summer, goats are most often found in the vicinity of snowfields and drifts that provide ready access to water in the form of runoff. Snow probably gives them most of their needed moisture in winter. Researchers in Montana have observed mountain goats eating snow in summer and drinking from streams and alpine lakes. In periods of drought or above-average summer temperatures, mountain goat distribution is sometimes affected by water resources. One study of mountain goats of the Pasayten Wilderness in Washington's northern Cascades found animals shifting their summer range toward water when resources dried up. Under most conditions, mountain goats live in habitat that gives them relatively easy access to water.

Digestion

As noted earlier, research specific to mountain goat digestion is lacking. Mountain goats are ruminant animals, meaning their food is regurgitated after eating and chewed further to facilitate digestion. Like other ruminants, mountain goats have four digestive compartments, or stomachs, that play different functions in the absorption of nutrition. Upon exiting a ruminant's fourth stomach, the digestive mass passes

Mountain goats do most of their cud chewing when lying down in an area that allows them to easily see and flee predators.

USFWS/DAVE GRICKSON

into the small and large intestines, which function similarly to those in a human or other animal. Mountain goats, like other ruminants, spend considerable time grinding their "cud" (food regurgitated for chewing) with their molars to promote digestion. The digestive system of a ruminant is thought to allow rapid consumption of forage in considerable quantities without time lost to chewing. This digestive strategy (eat quickly and chew later) decreases the time the animal is distracted by eating and more vulnerable to predation. Cud-chewing occurs when the animal is bedded, typically in a location that allows easy detection of approaching predators. For mountain goats, this is often a rocky ledge or perch on an alpine slope close to rugged escape cover.

Food Sources

Mountain goats are among a group of ruminants known as "generalist feeders." These animals show preferences for certain types of plants at various times of the year but readily switch between plant species to capitalize on a wide range of nutritional sources. The number of plant species on which mountain goats forage over their entire range is thus a dizzying array of grasses, forbs, shrubs, and trees. Mountain goats are also known to consume sedges, ferns, mosses, and lichens. The variability of mountain goat diet is highlighted by the fact that in southeast Alaska alone, more than 170 different plants have been cited as mountain goat forage.

Given the broad geographic and elevational range of their distribution and their confirmed status as creatures that will happily consume a dizzying array of forage items, generalizing about mountain goat diets is difficult. That said, one review of ten studies of mountain goat diets from various parts of the continent concluded that the "average" summer consisted of 16 percent browse, 30 percent forbs, and 52 percent grass (the other 2 percent apparently from other sources). The winter diet saw the intake of forbs drop to 8 percent and the amount of browse increase to 32 percent. However, it is imperative to note that due to the plant communities available in various geographical areas where mountain goats are present, intake of plant types may depart dramatically from the average. For example, a 1983 review of research on mountain goat diets found that grass may compose as much as 82 percent of the summer diet or as little as 12 percent, and that browse might be completely absent in the summer diet or represent as much as 70 percent. Winter forage habits are similarly disparate. Depending on their location, conifer browse might account for 70 percent of a goat's forage or none at all. Some goats don't eat any lichens in winter; others may rely on them for as much as 28 percent of their forage.

Certain plants are favored by mountain goats for forage no matter where they are found. Hairgrass, bluegrass, and wheatgrass are all grasses with species that thrive in alpine environments and are readily eaten by mountain goats. Fescues are another type of grass with alpine species relished by mountain goats. Bluebell (*Mertensia*) is a flowering plant native to the Rocky Mountains often consumed by goats, as is alpine sagewort, a dwarf flowering shrub often found in mountain goat range in Alaska. Grasses and forbs are primarily summer diet items for many mountain goats, but where winter range occurs on high, windswept ridges, cured plants are also eaten in winter.

The summer diet of mountain goats, like this grazing animal in Glacier National Park, consists primarily of grass and forbs (broad-leafed plants).
NPS/TIM RAINS

Deciduous trees and shrubs are also important food sources for mountain goats. Green alder is a low-growing tree or shrub found in mountainous habitat in the northern Rocky Mountains of the contiguous United States through Canada and Alaska. It sprouts readily in avalanche chutes and other vertiginous terrain partial to mountain goats. Sprouting leaves and flowers of alder are an important source of nutrition for mountain goats in many places in spring. Certain species of willows are similarly important to mountain goats, both as spring and winter forage.

Lichens and conifers are seldom eaten by mountain goats in summer (less than 3 percent of the diet) but are important nutritional items in winter in many areas. Lichens may be gnawed from rocks by wintering goats or nibbled from old-growth trees in sheltered wintering areas among the coastal mountain ranges. Conifer browse is an even more crucial component of winter mountain goat diet in numerous areas. Mountain goats are reported to browse on a host of evergreens, including Alaska cedar, Douglas fir, Engelmann spruce, junipers, lodgepole pine, mountain hemlock, ponderosa pine, subalpine fir, western yew, western hemlock, and whitebark pine.

Despite mountain goats' widespread consumption of evergreen needles and twigs, conifer browse represents a rather poor source of winter nutrition. Mountain goat intake of conifer browse increases with deep snowpack that limits their access to other food sources. Although mountain goats in some locations eat substantial amounts of conifer browse, animals forced to consume it exclusively in winter may be in dire straits nutritionally. Analysis of the stomach contents of mountain goats that succumbed to malnutrition during a difficult winter in Montana revealed that most had a stomach filled with conifer needles. The extent to which mountain goats can subsist on conifer browse is affected by the nutritional value of the specific species of conifers they consume and access to other food sources that may augment the nutrition of the evergreen forage.

In some areas, mountain goats visit "mineral licks" to obtain such minerals as sodium, magnesium, and sulfur from certain soils. Mineral licks occur naturally, but in some places goats use man-made licks, where minerals may be scattered on the ground or made available in block form. This behavior can occur at any time of the year, but the frequency of goats at lick sites increases during spring and summer. Both billies and nannies (with or without young) use mineral licks. However, males typically seek licks earlier in spring than females. A study of goat behavior in southeastern British Columbia discovered that visitation to mineral licks by most billies occurred from early May to late June, while most nannies came to the sites from early June to mid-July. Researchers in Colorado found that males frequented a man-made lick two weeks earlier, on average, than females.

The drive for minerals prompts some unusual behaviors among mountain goats. They generally avoid dense forest cover where predators might easily ambush them, but goats have frequently been observed traversing such habitat to reach mineral licks. Goats typically remain on a relatively small home range that provides their food and shelter requirements, but may travel miles to reach a mineral lick. Biologists

Mountain goats may travel considerable distances to reach mineral licks, especially in late spring and early summer. This goat was photographed nearing a well-used lick in northwestern Montana in late May.
NPS/JON RINER

theorize that the nutritional benefits of the minerals outweigh the energy expenditure and predation risks that are sometimes involved in reaching the licks.

Migration

Mountain ungulates may undertake two types of migrations that can be simply understood as occurring on either the vertical or horizontal planes of their world, or both. Vertical migrations involve seasonal changes in elevation, triggered by changing habitat conditions of forage availability, temperature, and exposure to the elements. For example, mountain goats may drop from ridgetops to timbered edges during a windy September snowstorm. Other migrations involve animals moving horizontally, perhaps crossing several drainage divides when traveling from summer to winter range. These migrations most often involve elevational shifts as well.

Mountain goats are frequently engaged in elevational migrations. The most basic pattern has goats dropping to lower elevations during winter to avoid the deep snow and severe weather in the highlands. Goats on the Alaskan coast commonly pass the summer at elevation of 5,500 feet or higher. Most drop to lower elevations in winter, with some found on rocky outcroppings near sea level. A similar pattern exists in the coastal mountains of British Columbia, where snow accumulation increases, sometimes dramatically, in relation to elevation. Along Idaho's Salmon River, mountain goats descend to lower elevations in winter and are frequently found at the lowest point in April and May to access forage that first greens in the low-lying areas.

An opposite pattern is seen in some goat populations, particularly during winters of high snowfall. These elevational shifts see animals moving up from mountain flanks onto peaks and ridges where howling winds keep snow cover absent or to a minimum. Modest ascents of this type have been observed in numerous locations, such as Montana, Colorado, and interior mountain ranges of British Columbia.

Horizontal migrations also occur with some mountain goat herds that use distinct summer and winter ranges. Mountain goats in several Montana mountain ranges travel from 2 to 15 miles between summer and winter ranges. Similar movements have been documented with goats in southeastern Alaska, where animals may move more than 15 miles to access seasonal ranges.

ABILITIES AND BEHAVIOR

Physical Abilities

On a hiking trip in Montana's Absaroka-Beartooth Wilderness, a partner and I once watched a younger companion scramble up a steep, rocky slope to peek into the next drainage. Upon his return my companion remarked, "Geez, you climbed up there just like a mountain goat." No explanation for his analogy was needed. To climb "like a mountain goat" is a comparison well understood by humans even vaguely familiar with the legendary ability of goats to scale seemingly impossible terrain.

Another excursion into backcountry terrain in my home state found me observing a lone, apparently young mountain goat traversing a sheer cliff face, broken here and there by ledges scarcely the width of a windowsill. The goat seemed intent on traveling from one side of the cliff to the other, its chosen path a series of broken ledges. When one petered out, it leaped to another above or below. My breath caught each time the goat, suspended some 100 feet above the base of the escarpment, made a jump between the narrow shelves of stone.

Mountain goats have developed numerous physical adaptions that allow them to casually navigate inhospitable terrain.
NPS/BOB FUHRMANN

Midway to its assumed destination, the goat encountered a dished-out chute in the cliff, which afforded no possible passage. I watched in utter amazement as the goat, seemingly trapped in the chute, managed to reverse itself by heaving its body up and around, all the while balanced on its hind legs on a ledge that appeared not much wider than a human hand.

Many of its Rocky Mountain relatives are fleeter of foot, but none climb like a mountain goat. With a body supremely adapted for locomotion in terrain that keeps would-be predators at bay, mountain goats have numerous physical characteristics that buttress their climbing ability. Their cloven hooves consist of two parts that can spread and contract, each portion of which contains a hard outer horn enveloping a softer, rubbery pad. The two portions of each "toe" on the hoof work in conjunction to provide superb traction on loose soil (from the horn) or unbroken stone (from the pad). A mountain goat's center of mass is low and its skeleton narrow, limiting the amount of space it needs to maneuver on sheer slopes.

At a very young age, mountain goats develop superb confidence in jumping from considerable heights. The leap of this kid was captured in Glacier National Park.
LISA BALLARD

In an intriguing research project, two experts in biomechanics from the University of Calgary analyzed the movements of a young mountain goat scaling a 45-degree rock face. They concluded that the goat's initial "push-off" was facilitated by the very forceful propulsion of its hind legs. Its subsequent bounds were enabled by exceptionally strong muscles in its shoulders and neck that powered its forelegs. They also observed the goat's apparent ability to "lock" its humerus (the bone between its shoulder and elbow) to keep its center of mass close the cliff and maintain its vertical progress. Mountain goats can easily leap 10 feet from a standing position and are very comfortable jumping from similar or greater heights onto uneven terrain.

Mountain goats are also notable for their ability to withstand bitterly cold temperatures and frigid winter winds. Underneath their long, shaggy outer winter coat is an inner layer of dense, highly-insulating wool. Biologists have estimated that adult mountain goats do not experience cold stress until air temperatures drop below -5°F. Exposure to wind or direct sunlight may increase or decrease cold stress in relation to air temperature.

Research investigating the perceptual abilities of mountain goats in relation to vision, hearing, and sense of smell is lacking. Anecdotal evidence from observers suggests that mountain goat have adequate hearing but not as developed as deer or elk. Their sense of smell appears to be quite good, and they will readily react to human scent. However, due to the variable nature of air currents in their habitat, smell is probably an unreliable way for them to detect danger. Most commentators believe mountain goats rely on their eyesight to detect predators. Like other mountain ungulates, the eyes of mountain goats are very adept at sensing movement. At least one researcher has noted that the hairy white cliff-dwellers do not readily discern motionless humans in their environment.

Vocal and Visual Communication

Mountain goats are not very vocal creatures. One summary of the species published by the American Society of Mammalogists drawn from numerous research sources concluded that vocalizations among mountain goats are infrequent. When they do

Mountain goats seldom vocalize but frequently communicate with a variety of body postures indicating submission or aggression.
NPS/JON RINER

emit noises, the calls are typically soft and difficult to hear from a distance. Known vocal communication among mountain goats occurs during the breeding season, with males emitting low-pitched grunts and soft bleats. Adult mountain goats may snort when surprised. Nannies and kids sometimes bleat to locate each other when separated, the bleat of the kid having a higher pitch than that of the nanny.

A variety of body postures are used to communicate between mountain goats. Several displays indicate an aggressive intent to greater or lesser degrees. One goat may stare at another in an act of mild aggression. Another more obvious aggressive posture involves a goat dropping its head forward to display its horns. An even more belligerent display occurs when one goat rushes at another, lowering its horns as it approaches. Fights or aggression between mountain goats occur somewhat frequently. A prelude to an actual battle often involves goats circling each other in a head-to-flank position. The intent of aggressive displays is to assert dominance over another mountain goat in relation to forage, mates, or some other desirable resource. A goat indicating its submission to a dominant animal may stretch itself low to the ground.

Herd Behavior

Throughout most of the year, nannies and mature billies normally maintain separate herds or bands. Biologists sometimes use those terms separately for management and research purposes. In technical terminology, a "herd" consists of the entire number of goats that share an identified seasonal range but may be found in multiple groups. A "population" refers to the mountain goats in some defined geographical area, perhaps an entire mountain range or a portion thereof. Populations are thought to be mostly genetically and geographically isolated from one another. A "band" is group of goats that maintain a close physical association with one another. In less-formal language, "herd" and "band" may be used interchangeably to describe an identifiable group of goats, as they are in this book.

Herd behavior is influenced by the particular habitat in which goats live, but as a general rule, bands of nannies and their offspring are typically larger and inhabit more open terrain than billies. Nanny, or maternal, herds mays consist of a few animals or several dozen. Maternal herds numbering more than seventy individuals in late summer are not unusual for a goat population in prime alpine habitat. "Bachelor" bands of billies are smaller, usually consisting of two to six individuals. One multiyear study in Alberta found that the size of bachelor herds in the area decreased from an average of around five animals in May to two in September. This seems to indicate that billies become less friendly with one another as the late-fall breeding season gets closer.

There are, however, some exceptions to the rule of segregation between males and females. Mountain goats in one portion of Glacier National Park, Montana, frequently mingle in bands consisting of both sexes during summer. Biologists theorize

that good forage, coupled with limited range and high population density, account for this important exception. It should also be noted that young billies normally stay with a maternal herd for the first few years of life. Most yearling and 2-year-old males remain in the company of maternal herds. But by age 4, most billies pass the summer on their own or in bachelor bands.

Dominance hierarchies, or "pecking orders," exist in both male and female groups of mountain goats. Those in maternal herds may be more complex simply due to the size of the group and the disparity of age, size, and the aggressive tendencies of individuals. However, female-to-female dominance interactions are highly determined by age. In one study, researchers concluded that older nannies dominated their younger counterparts in more than 90 percent of their encounters. The same study found that interactions between adult females and young males were mixed. Confrontations between adult nannies and young billies from 3 to 4 years of age saw the males coming out on top twice as often as the females.

The size of maternal mountain goat herds varies in relation to habitat. Goats using open terrain, most commonly alpine areas above tree line, tend to form larger bands than those living in places where scattered trees or brush provide cover. Males are also more often found in partially timbered areas than females, either as small bachelor bands or individuals.

Biologists theorize that these herd behaviors are related to predation. In open country, the many eyes and ears of a large maternal band are more likely to detect predators. This allows individual animals more time to feed, as the shared vigilance of the group requires less time on the lookout for each goat. In timbered habitat, where members of a herd may be screened from one another by vegetation, this anti-predation strategy is compromised, as the alarm of one animal may not be detected by other members of the group. It is believed that large billies are substantially less susceptible to predation than females and young. Their larger size and formidable horns probably discourage predation attempts except by the boldest of predators. This perhaps allows them to utilize the superior forage sometimes found in lightly timbered areas at much lower risk than females, either singly or in a herd.

The home ranges of billies are larger than those of females in some places, smaller in others. This is perhaps due to the nutritional demands of large female bands versus those of smaller bachelor herds or solitary males. Some biologists suggest that a female band with many animals needs to use a much larger territory to obtain sufficient forage than a few males. One review of measurements from numerous geographical locations concluded that home ranges for mountain goats may cover as many as nearly 20 square miles or slightly fewer than 3 square miles.

Summer ranges are typically larger (sometimes much larger) than winter ranges. Researchers in southeastern British Columbia and Colorado found that winter range for mountain goats was less than 15 percent of summer range. Winter ranges are very small in some cases. A band of mountain goats in western Montana was observed

Male mountain goats may pass the summer in small herds or alone. This mature billy was photographed as a loner on a snowbank in Montana's Absaroka-Beartooth Wilderness in August.
JACK BALLARD

wintering on less than 10 acres. The size of winter range is highly influenced by snow depth that impedes the movements of mountain goats. Winter ranges for both nannies with kids and billies average more than twice as large during years of light versus normal snowpack.

REPRODUCTION AND YOUNG

The Mating Season

The mating season, or "rut," for mountain goats commences in late fall, but billies begin a series of mating behaviors much earlier. As summer progresses, bachelor bands of males break up. With the onset of September, most mature billies are found alone, or perhaps in the proximity of one other male.

Late September sees billies undertaking several rutting behaviors. One of these involves pawing out a depression in the ground known as a "rutting pit." The male goat scrapes out the pit with his front hooves, urinates in the loose dirt, then uses his front feet to kick the loose earth onto his body. Billies engaged in this pre-mating behavior are often noticeably dirty, with dirt-stained coats visible at a considerable distance. Males may also rub their horns on shrubs and vegetation as the mating season approaches. This perhaps disperses scent from a large dark gland found at the rear of the bases of a billy's horns, though the exact function of the gland is unknown.

This solitary billy in Olympic National Park was photographed in late September. His dirty beard and stained rear flanks are indications of rutting behavior.
NPS/KLAHANE

As the actual mating season approaches, young billies (2 to 3 years old) still associated with the maternal bands begin approaching females in attempted courtships. These gestures are rebuffed forcefully by the nannies. By the time nannies are ready to breed, dominant older males have moved into the female herds, displacing younger males. Mountain goats most often use a "tending" pattern of mating, whereby a dominant male keeps company with a single female that is ready to breed and repels other males. Mating completed, the male moves on to seek other females. Thus, the most prevailing billies mate with numerous females during the rut, while subordinates may not mate at all. In most mountain goat herds, males between 5 and 10 years of age sire the vast majority of kids. However, the proportion of males to females in a population and the average age of males are highly determined by the age of mating billies. In a population in Alberta with rather high numbers of mature males, billies did not reproduce until at least 4 years of age (about 54 months of age at mating). A population in Montana, by contrast, that had a low male-to-female ratio saw some 2-year-old billies (about 30 months of age at mating) producing offspring.

The mating season comes with several hazards for mountain goat billies. One of these involves fights with other males. The horns of mountain goats are very destructive weapons, sharper than the antler points on moose and elk, as well as most deer. Battling mountain goats do not clash their heads together like bighorn sheep or lock horns and shove like male ungulates with antlers. They instead circle and parry, attempting to gore the ribs or flanks of the opponent. The hide on a mountain goat's flanks is exceedingly thick, an adaptation believed to protect it in conflict with its own kind. It's not uncommon to observe puncture wounds in rutting mountain goats when there's a robust number of mature billies in the population, and researchers have observed penetrating thrusts that proved fatal.

Billies may reach sexual maturity earlier, but in most populations most breeding is done by older males.
© ISTOCK.COM/CHILKOOT

In addition to the perils of battle, the mating season takes a toll on billies in other ways. Male goats in Alaska and other areas may undertake travels between female bands that lead them through heavy forests, where they are at higher risk of ambush from skilled predators such as mountain lions and wolves. The rigors of the rut, with or without the added physical demands of healing wounds, exacts a nutritional toll on large billies, which lose substantial weight during the mating season. Ironically, older, dominant billies that have reached their reproductive zenith are at risk of starvation during a severe winter.

Pregnancy and Gestation

Female mountain goats (and males) become fertile by 18 months of age. But very few individuals of either gender mate this early in established populations. Under most circumstances, female mountain goats first reproduce much later in life and at lesser frequency than females of other ungulate species in the Rocky Mountains.

Female mountain goats experience their first pregnancy later and have lower reproductive rates than other North American ungulates.
JACK BALLARD

The age of first reproduction for nannies is heavily influenced by population densities and habitat. On historical range where large herd numbers are stable or declining, nannies first reproduce at 5 or 6 years of age. Introduced populations in an expanding stage find nannies birthing kids much earlier. Research in Washington with a newly introduced population found kids born to a few 2-year-old nannies with births to 3-year-olds quite common. Another study with an introduced herd in Alaska concluded that almost 40 percent of 2-year-old females birthed kids.

Along with a later age of first reproduction, nannies also birth kids with less frequency than most North

American ungulates. Research in Alberta and British Columbia indicates nannies in highly occupied habitat may give birth only every three or four years. Mountain goats newly introduced to ideal habitat may experience much higher initial reproduction rates that decline once animals become established in suitable areas. Reproduction rates also appear to be related to age. Nannies in the 5-to-10-year age group generally experience higher birth rates than younger or older females.

Dates vary somewhat by location, but most female mountain goats conceive their kids in November or early December. The gestation period for mountain goats is variously stated, most likely due to a lack of specific research in this area. Based on available data, the gestation period for mountain goats is approximately 175 days.

Birth

It is commonly reported that nannies birth their kids on cliff ledges and related inaccessible terrain. While this may be the case in most populations, its prevalence may be overstated. One Canadian study found that just 30 percent of births occurred in such terrain, while the others took place near tree line or in forested terrain. The extent to which nannies retreat to difficult terrain to birth their young may be limited by topography. Cliffy areas may be preferred but apparently are not instrumental to reproductive success, although some biologists theorize that the presence of such terrain may enhance kid survival in the presence of predators.

A more potent anti-predatory adaptation may be seen in the dispersal of nannies before their young are born. Female mountain goats are highly social for most of the year. Those preparing to birth young, however, disperse long distances from one another and often retreat to habitat niches unused by goats at other times of the year. It is postulated that this behavior may thwart predation by vastly increasing the area a predator must cover to discover multiple mountain goat young. In the Kenai Fjords area of Alaska, nannies descend precipitous terrain to birth their kids at sea level, in secluded pockets of habitat surrounded by cliffs too steep for predators to navigate.

The birthing process for mountain goats occurs quickly, involving a short period of labor. Kids normally stand and nurse in less than an hour. The mother and her newborn remain close to the birthing site for a few days, possibly in the company of her previous year's offspring if giving birth in successive years. Mountain goat kids often display a brownish streak in the fur along their backbone that fades over time. Little specific research has been conducted in relation to mountain goat birth weights, but available data indicates that kids weigh between 5.5 and 7.5 pounds at birth. There is no significant size difference between the sexes at birth. Two newborn mountain goat males captured at approximately 3 days of age in a 1955 study in the Crazy Mountains of Montana weighed around 6.5 pounds.

Most mountain goat kids are birthed from late May to mid-June. Researchers in Canada observing mountain goats from 1993 to 1999 found that, on average, 80 percent of the births occurred within a span of sixteen days. In some years, 80 percent of kids were born within one week. The earliest birth in the seven-year study was May 14, the latest July 2.

In established populations, single offspring are the rule for mountain goats, while twins are quite rare.
JACK BALLARD

Twins are common to many ungulates, but in long-occupied mountain goat habitat, multiple births are quite rare. Two studies of mountain goats in highly populated areas of Alberta and Washington saw twins representing just 2 percent of total births. However, in expanding or newly-introduced populations, twins may account for as many as one-third of the births. In rare cases, nannies may have triplets. Multiple research projects indicate triplets are more typical to introduced populations (though still rare). Newly introduced populations also have a higher number of twins and reproduce more frequently than is typical for native populations.

Nurturing Kids to Adulthood

Mountain goat kids mature quickly, perhaps on an accelerated pace to grow large and strong enough to survive their first winter. Kids can walk well enough to follow their mothers at a few days of age. They can nibble vegetation as early as a week old. After a couple of weeks in seclusion, nannies lead their new kids to join a female band that may initially consist of a few mothers with young but often swell to several dozen animals by midsummer.

By 1 month of age, kids weigh about 20 pounds. Toward the end of summer, at 4 months of age, most weigh around 60 pounds. The kids are normally weaned from their mother's milk by this time and rely on vegetation for their sustenance. Mountain goat kids are very social during their first summer, actively playing with one another in apparent games of "king of the hill," mock fights, and chasing.

Mountain goat kids are social, cute, and playful. Much of their play prepares them for the rigors of adult life.
© ISTOCK.COM/ ARINAHABICH

Similar to other young ungulates, mountain goats are at their highest risk of predation in the first few months of life. Most predation on kids is probably incidental, meaning the predator was not specifically hunting mountain goats but took advantage of a predation opportunity on a young goat as it arose. It is possible that some predators (bears in particular) might learn to target young mountain goats in certain habitats; however, research or authoritative observations in this area are lacking. It is known that both airborne (golden eagle) and land-bound (mountain lion, wolf, bear, wolverine, etc.) predators kill mountain goat kids, but the extent to which such predation occurs is largely unknown. The available evidence is sparse but indicates predation is a much lower source of mortality among mountain goat kids than for other Rocky Mountain ungulates. Mountain goats have relatively high survival rates to 1 year of age, with harsh winter conditions being their greatest challenge to surviving to their first birthday. Two studies in Montana found that winter mortality of kids was approximately two to three times higher during severe winters than when conditions were mild. Extreme winters may see more than 75 percent of kids succumbing to nutritional stress and exposure.

Yearling mountain goats are frequently found in the company of their mother, whether she has new offspring or not. Two-year-old goats are occasionally associated with their mother as well.

Mountain goats frequently "disperse" when they reach young adulthood (2 to 3 years old). This involves the young goats making exploratory or permanent relocations to areas beyond their normal home range and most often occurs in midsummer. Billies are more likely to disperse than nannies, although bother genders frequently undertake such travels. A handful of mountain goats may disperse as yearlings. More unusual is the occasional dispersal of nannies who have already reared a kid. This phenomenon has been observed in Washington and is considered a very rare occurrence in female mammals.

Dispersal may take mountain goats many miles from their birth area, across rivers and other natural and man-made barriers, and through substantial tracts of heavily forested, hostile habitat. While hiking in the extreme southwestern portion of Yellowstone National Park, I once encountered a young mountain goat on the trail in an expansive tract of lodgepole pines, dozens and dozens of miles from the nearest occupied goat habitat. A similar experience occurred in my boyhood when a goat took residence in a narrow canyon in the foothills country west of Three Forks, Montana, not far from my family's home. The goat stayed in the area for a month or so, then disappeared. The nearest goat population was located at least 20 miles away and on the opposite side of a river.

Documented dispersals have been recorded covering more than 150 miles in Canada. Mountain goats from Olympic National Park in Washington have moved more than 60 miles. Dispersals more than 10 miles are common and are assumed to be instrumental in maintaining genetic diversity among mountain goats and may serve as seed stock in establishing new populations in unoccupied habitat.

MOUNTAIN GOATS AND OTHER ANIMALS

Mountain Goats and Other Ungulates

Because of the unique habitat they occupy, mountain goats are usually isolated from other ungulates. Mountain goats may share a broad swath of habitat with other

ungulates but are normally found in niches used for extended periods of time. By contrast, most of the other hoofed creatures venturing into mountain goat habitat range over a much broader area. Due to the inaccessibility of goat habitat and the infrequent contacts between goats and other ungulates, very little is known about if, and how, they interact.

Mountain goats may encounter mule deer, elk, and bighorn and Dall sheep on both summer and winter range in certain parts of their current range. Whitetail deer, moose, and woodland caribou are also known to sometimes venture into areas also used by mountain goats. I have witnessed mountain goats and elk bedded within 200 yards of one another on the flank of a high ridge in the Snowcrest Mountains of Montana in late October. During a backpacking trip in August, I also observed mule deer and mountain goats in the same alpine basin at approximately 10,000 feet elevation in the Absaroka Mountains.

Lush alpine grass brings other ungulates, including elk, onto mountain goat summer range in some places.
JACK BALLARD

Some dietary overlap probably occurs between mountain goats and deer, elk, and bighorn sheep. Goats are unlikely to compete directly with deer or elk for forage, except perhaps in spring, when greening grass, forbs, and shrubbery just below the snowline are consumed by each species. It is not believed that direct or indirect competition for nutritional resources among these species has any effect on population dynamics or survival.

The situation between mountain goats and bighorn sheep is more complex. In some areas, the two species are found on the same range in both summer and winter and use similar environmental resources for food, comfort, and cover. Observations by researchers indicate that mountain goats dominate bighorn sheep in most direct interactions. A research team on Caw Ridge in Alberta has watched bighorns and goats (both native to the area) that share similar but normally segregated alpine habitat. At the edge of the creatures' mostly separate ranges, the two species sometimes come into contact with one another. The few interactions observed by the researchers saw mountain goats aggressively displacing the sheep in most cases, but sometimes ignoring them.

In some places, wildlife managers are becoming increasingly concerned about the potential for introduced mountain goats negatively affecting bighorn sheep populations. Mountain goats are not native to the Greater Yellowstone Area (GYA), the region of contiguous mountain habitat in and around Yellowstone and Grand Teton National Parks in Wyoming, Montana, and Idaho. Goats are now present in several GYA areas that also hold native bighorn sheep. A similar situation exists, or may arise, in several locations in Colorado.

Two points of concern are present in relation to mountain goats and bighorns. Some bands of bighorns in the GYA winter at very high elevations, on windswept ridges where they find forage and bedding sites kept free of snow. Mountain goat presence in these relatively small wintering havens has increased in the past two

decades, while sheep herds in some places have dwindled. Some biologists theorize that direct competition on this limited winter range is detrimental to the bighorns.

Disease transmission is the other focus of concern. Both mountain goats and bighorns can contract a variety of diseases from domestic sheep and goats that cause pneumonia and blindness. Bighorn sheep are acutely susceptible to pneumonia. Outbreaks of the disease cause severe declines in bighorn numbers and have been responsible for the eradication of the majestic sheep in some areas. Population declines of 80 percent or more are common with pneumonia infestations among bighorn sheep.

Mountain goats, on the other hand, appear much more resistant to these diseases (though not completely immune) than bighorns. Some wildlife managers speculate that mountain goats that carry disease may transmit them to bighorns where the two species exist in proximity. In the GYA and Colorado, this potential has led wildlife managers to question the wisdom of maintaining nonnative mountain goat populations in areas where they may transmit disease to native bighorns with calamitous results.

Mountain Goats and Predators

The list of predators known and purported to claim mountain goats as prey is quite long. Ground-based predators include mountain lions, grizzly bears, black bears, wolves, Canada lynx, bobcats, coyotes, and wolverines. Golden eagles occasionally attack mountain goat kids from the air, and some sources in Alaska also list bald eagles as a predator, with at least one reported sighting of a flying bald eagle clutching a small kid.

Of those potential mountain goat predators, evidence that the smaller of them (bobcats, lynx, coyotes, and wolverines) actually kill mountain goats is sparse, and the vulnerability of a healthy adult mountain goat to these animals is highly questionable. Mountain goat fur has been found in the scat of at least some of these species, but whether it originated from a goat killed in a predation event or came from the scavenged carcass of an animal that succumbed to other circumstances is unknown. Predation by black bears is also poorly documented and assumed to be quite rare. Golden eagles have been observed taking or attempting to take mountain goat kids, though this is also an uncommon occurrence. Researchers have documented small kids running to hide under their mother when eagles are present. Due to the widely dispersed birthing habits of mountain goats, golden eagles are believed to be the only predator capable of efficiently scouting for very young, vulnerable kids. A few incidences of golden eagles attempting predation on yearling and adult mountain goats have also been reported.

Predators apparently do not focus on mountain goats as prey like they do other ungulates, such as elk, moose, and deer. Biologists theorize that mountain goats generally represent a poor prey base for any predator. However, it is also noted that the mountain lion, the predator most capable of routinely killing goats, could prey more heavily on mountain goats in some situations. Individual mountain lions often become specialists in seeking certain types of prey in habitats where multiple prey species are present. For example, some mountain lions specialize in killing feral horses in places where other prey species are common. A few mountain lions have also accounted for the majority of bighorn sheep consumed by their species in the southwestern United States.

Mountain lion predation on mountain goats is well documented in multiple areas. These athletic cats can capably stalk mountain goats in quite difficult terrain and are masters of ambush. Predation attempts on mountain goats by mountain lions (and other predators) most often occur when goats are in or near habitat that offers concealment for the predator, including forests of brushy areas. The scarce available data indicates that kids and yearlings are by far the most susceptible to mountain lion (and other) predation. An adult mountain goat's piercing horns are a considerable hazard to any predator and probably serve as something of a deterrent to predation attempts. However, some biologists believe that a single mountain lion focusing on goats as prey could inflict population-compromising pressure on an individual goat herd, although this occurrence has not been documented.

Mountain lions are widely considered the predator most capable of regularly preying on mountain goats.
© ISTOCK.COM/EVGENY555

Wolves are also known to prey on mountain goats. Some biologists monitoring mountain goats in southeastern Alaska believe wolf predation may be a significant source of mortality that affects goat numbers, but specific information is lacking. In one such area, a study found wolves visiting mountain goat habitat about once every two weeks and documented goat remains in more than 50 percent of the wolf scat in the area but could not determine whether it was consumed by wolves actually killing goats or scavenged from goat carcasses. The little that is known regarding wolf predation on mountain goats strongly suggests that kids and yearlings are most often taken. An Alberta study recorded eight known or suspected mountain goat kills by wolves over an eight-year period. Of these, 75 percent occurred with yearlings and kids, the remainder on older (9+ years) animals. The study also documented goats rebuffing predation attempts by wolves on two occasions. Some biologists postulate that wolf predation may suppress mountain goat populations in certain areas, but studies have not been undertaken to analyze such a relationship.

Grizzly bears roam across mountain goat habitat in some areas and are a documented predator of goats. I've observed grizzly bears in goat habitat on several occasions in Montana and Wyoming, though not in the immediate proximity of mountain goats. Grizzly bears are highly effective at hunting very young offspring of ungulates such as moose, elk, and deer, and they annually return to known birthing areas in some places to search for this vulnerable prey. Mountain goat kids born away from steep, rocky terrain are probably most exposed to grizzly bear predation. The sparse existing evidence of the mountain goat–grizzly bear relationship as prey and predator shows a similar relationship to that of wolves and mountain lions, as kids and yearling have been most frequently documented as grizzly bear prey.

Parasites and Diseases

As noted previously, mountain goats can contract a variety of diseases, some of which originate in domestic livestock. They may also harbor a range of internal and external parasites.

There has been little study of disease and parasites among mountain goats, but it is widely believed that both may contribute to poor health and mortality in some situations. Mountain goats are sometimes infested with roundworms at very high levels. Officials in Washington have observed heavy loads of this internal parasite in hunter- and road-killed mountain goats. Roundworm infestations may also suppress mountain goat reproduction. In one instance in Washington, salt blocks containing a deworming compound were placed in an area suspected of high parasitism. The following spring, 80 percent of the nannies produced a surviving kid while goats in an adjacent, untreated area saw 0 percent survival of kids. Other factors may have been at work, but some commentators suggest this episode gives evidence that high parasite loads negatively affect the health and survival of goats in some places.

Mountain goats are sometimes infested with lungworms. These parasites are usually not fatal to the animal but are considered a factor in mortality when combined with respiratory diseases. Researchers have observed other internal parasites of the digestive tract and the muscles, such as tapeworms, in mountain goats. An analysis of parasites from one sample in Washington discovered bowel worms found in the large intestine of domestic sheep in numerous mountain goats. Internal parasites are probably most influential in mountain goat mortality when the nutritional drain robs the host of resources needed to survive environmental stress, particularly severe winters.

Mountain goats in Washington given salt blocks with a deworming agent experienced greatly increased reproduction rates, indicating that internal parasites may locally suppress populations.
© ISTOCK.COM/GACOOKSEY

External parasites such as ticks and lice are often found on mountain goats. They are a nuisance but are not thought to routinely reduce the vigor of goats. However, goats experiencing very high tick loads are believed to suffer some level of nutritional stress in addition to exhibiting such signs of discomfort as hair loss and scratching.

The prevalence and consequences of disease among mountain goats is another poorly understood aspect of their biology. Mountain goats can carry a host of diseases common to other ungulates. Pneumonia is one of these and may cause death in some cases. Mountain goats can also contract a range of fungal infections and viral diseases. One viral disease, contagious ecthyma (sore mouth), is somewhat common in domestic sheep and goats. The disease is highly contagious and causes blister-like lesions on the skin, most obviously around the mouth and nose but also found on other parts of the body. Death is rare in domestic animals, but infected wildlife often have trouble feeding normally and lose body condition. Contagious ecthyma has been found in mountain goats in Kootenay National Park, British Columbia, and may be present in other populations. But the prevalence and results of this condition, like other mountain goat diseases, are poorly understood. Given the general lack of knowledge in relation to specific parasites and diseases of mountain goats, several wildlife experts advocate extreme caution with relation to the potential comingling of domestic livestock and mountain goats. Some pathogens, such as those causing contagious ecthyma, can survive for years in the environment before being transmitted to another creature. Thus, the elimination of potential sources of disease transmission in mountain goat habitat is advised.

MOUNTAIN GOATS AND HUMANS

Mountain Goats and American Indians

Mountain goats are not thought to have been a widespread source of food for American Indian tribes prior to the arrival of Europeans to North America. This was due in part to the difficult terrain mountain goat hunters were required to navigate and the species' relative scarcity in relation to other game animals such as bison, caribou, deer, and elk. However, mountain goats were regularly pursued by some tribes and locally very important resources, not only for their meat but also for their hides and horns, which were used for clothing and utensils. Some native groups favored mountain goat meat, and its consumption was largely restricted to those with high social status in some tribes. Others apparently pursued goats only when other game was scarce.

Coastal tribes from Washington to Alaska hunted mountain goats. Mountain goats were also pursued by native peoples in interior regions of the continent, from Idaho and northwestern Montana to southeastern

Due to the difficult terrain wild goats inhabit and their relative scarcity in relation to other game animals, they were not widely hunted by American Indians.
© ISTOCK.COM/CHILKOOT

Alaska. A variety of effective and ingenious methods were used to harvest this challenging quarry. Some tribes used dogs to help drive mountain goats toward hunters hidden in natural escape terrain. Others used woven willow snares to capture goats or chased them over cliffs. Mountain goats were also arrowed from blinds made of natural materials or stalked, most often from above, since the animals focus more on threats from below. Some bands of Tlingit peoples are reported to have hunted goats with sharpened sticks instead of bow and arrows, as bows were frequently damaged on treacherous terrain.

Due to the danger and skill involved in killing mountain goats, hunters from several coastal tribes performed various rituals thought to protect the hunters and bring success. According to some sources, locations offering the opportunity of high success and safety while hunting mountain goats were esteemed and regulated by the leaders of some Tlingit groups.

Mountain goats were used for much more than meat by native peoples. Goat fat was highly prized and sometimes rendered and stored for sustenance in times of scarcity. Goat kidney fat is said to have been rubbed on the face as protection against severe cold or burning sun. The hides of mountain goats were tanned with the hair on for use as ceremonial and other clothing by numerous groups. The Kootenay people who inhabited southern British Columbia and northern portions of Idaho and Montana were famous for the quality of their tanned mountain goat hides. Nez Perce warriors, a tribe native to the mountain region covering western Montana to eastern Washington, wore leggings sometimes made from mountain goat hides.

Mountain goat horns were fashioned into various tools, such as highly ornate spoons. The sinews served as cord for a variety of uses. Though mountain goats were not an abundant commodity for most native peoples, they were used for numerous purposes when available.

Mountain goats also provided "wool" used for weaving blankets. Under the long outer coat of the mountain goat is an inner layer of fine hair. The fibers from the inner coat were collected from clumps of hair left on the ground or clinging to bushes after animals shed their coat in summer or were gleaned from the hides of animals killed by hunters. Intricate designs were woven into blankets that were dyed and infused with cedar bark. Blankets were crafted on a simple loom and entirely woven with the weaver's fingers. A magnificent blanket spun from mountain goat hair sometimes took a year to complete, and such blankets were extremely valuable. This wool was also used to fashion pillows for baby cradles.

The weaving of mountain goat wool into blankets probably reached its apex with the creation of the "Chilkat Blanket." The Chilkats were a group of Tlingit Indians inhabiting the region of the Chilkat River in Alaska. The Chilkats developed their weaving skills into an art form. Highly decorated blankets with intricate designs, fringes, and colors became the hallmark of Chilkat weaving. These Chilkat blankets were one of the most valuable items of trade among native peoples prior to the introduction of firearms and currency.

By the early 1900s making Chilkat blankets was a dying art, with just a dozen or so knowledgeable weavers remaining. In the latter portion of the twentieth century, interest in preserving the art form increased. Currently, a handful of dedicated weavers have retained this remarkable historic skill.

For the past hundred years, most weavers have relied on commercial wool to create their blankets. But the appeal of working with authentic mountain goat wool to create a Chilkat blanket is high among some weavers. In 2008 the Alaska Fish and Wildlife News published an article apprising hunters of opportunities to donate whole or partial mountain goat hides to weavers. A state biologist also became active in sourcing mountain goat wool for weavers, either from hides or shed goat fur. Personnel at Glacier Bay National Park have also assisted weavers in gathering shed wool. Thanks to their efforts, it appears an age-old art wedding mountain goats and humans will persist for decades to come.

Mountain Goats and European Settlers

The general pattern of east-to-west settlement and their habitat far from areas favored by humans buffered mountain goats from the market hunting and hide trade that decimated populations of bison, deer, elk, and even bighorn sheep. One of the first known encounters between Europeans and mountain goats occurred during Captain James Cook's third voyage. This final voyage of the renowned British seafarer took him to the coast of British Columbia and Alaska, where he traded with native peoples. Along with valuable sea otter pelts, he acquired tanned hides adorned with luxuriant white fur. The captain believed they were the pelts of white bears, but they were mountain goat hides.

Members of the Lewis and Clark Expedition first recorded mountain goats on August 24, 1805. The journals of Meriwether Lewis on that date note the skins of an animal in the possession of Shoshone Indians while at the headwaters of the Beaverhead River in Montana, just below the Continental Divide. Although the hides had been in use so long they were worn and Lewis could not satisfactorily determine the color, he wrote that the natives told him they were from a white animal with curved horns they hunted high in the mountains to the west and southwest of the camp (the Bitterroot Mountains on the Montana-Idaho divide, where mountain goats persist to this day). The journal notes that Captain Clark saw one of the creatures at a distance on the same day. When ascending the Columbia River on April 10, 1806, the expedition traded for the skin of a young mountain goat with the head and horns attached. Two days later, another goat skin was acquired from another band of natives, and both captains mention garments worn by natives fashioned from mountain goat hides.

Mountain goats were first recorded in a natural history write-up in 1816, but little was actually known about the animals. Knowledge of these unique creatures expanded through the nineteenth century, though there was little focused research on the species until after World War II. Mountain goats are almost certainly the least researched and understood ungulate species in the United States.

Mountain Goats and Us

Mountain goats survived in the backwater of wildlife management through the first several decades of the twentieth century. Efforts to introduce goats to new areas were undertaken sporadically, perhaps most notably the transport of mountain goats to Washington's Olympic Peninsula. Mountain goats were hunted with few restrictions during this time in portions of Alaska and Canada.

The 1940s and 1950s saw burgeoning interest in mountain goats as a big game species. Mountain goats were transplanted to numerous areas, primarily to increase hunting opportunities. Motivation and methods for the transplants reflected the less-formal wildlife management of the time. For example, mountain goats were introduced to the Crazy Mountains in Montana at the request of Barney Brannin, a dude-rancher on the east side of the range. His interest in establishing a goat population in the mountains near his ranch inspired him to raise half of the funds needed for the transplant from area residents. He also helped state wildlife management personnel trap goats in northwestern Montana in 1941 and 1943 to accomplish the transplant. Brannin took a keen interest in the soon-thriving mountain goat population, keeping a diary of birthing activities and supplying the goats with salt.

Visitors motivated to view mountain goats, like this one in Glacier National Park, spend money in local communities and increase the species' economic value.
NPS/TIM RAINS

Introductions of goats to nonnative range occurred regularly throughout the latter decades of the twentieth century. Hunting seasons were enacted in many places. Permit-only hunting first occurred in Washington in 1948. Mountain goat hunting in the Kenai Mountains of Alaska was mostly unregulated prior to 1971. Excessive harvests in the 1950s and 1960s caused sharp declines in goat numbers in some areas, especially those easily accessed by hunters. In the 1980s the state moved to more intensively manage hunter mortality on mountain goats, establishing hunting units covering distinct geographical areas and strict quotas for harvest in each unit. Currently, mountain goat hunting is similarly regulated by states and provinces across their range.

Mountain goats have considerable economic value from the standpoint of both wildlife viewing and hunting, not to mention their intrinsic worth as one of the most unusual wildlife species on the continent. The prospect of seeing and photographing a mountain goat brings visitors to places like Mount Evans in Colorado and Glacier National Park, Montana. Licenses to hunt mountain goats are quite limited and in some cases very expensive. In 2017 a nonresident hunter paid $1,518 for a mountain goat license in Utah, $2,149 in Colorado, and $2,152 in Wyoming. Nonresident hunters often hire guides and outfitters to hunt mountain goats, further enhancing their value to state and local economies.

In some places, recreational interactions between mountain goats and humans have become problematic. Aggressive goats, seeking a handout from hikers or wanting to lick soil where humans have urinated, are a problem in Olympic and Glacier National Parks. Goats looking for food or minerals may invade backpackers' camps and damage equipment. In 2010 a mountain goat attacked, gored, and killed a 63-year-old male hiker in Olympic National Park. Recreationists in areas where mountain goats have become habituated to humans should remember that the sharp horns of the animals can be very dangerous and give them plenty of space.

Mountain goats in some portions of national parks and other areas heavily traveled by humans on foot or in vehicles can become quite tolerant of such activities. Animals occupying remote habitat are easily displaced by motorized activity, a factor associated with population declines where such use is persistent.

One motorized craft causing severe stress to mountain goats is the helicopter. For decades biologists had witnessed extreme fright by goats in the presence of choppers. But a lack of real research left questions as to whether individual goats had a helicopter phobia or the phenomenon was species wide, and to what extent goats might become habituated to nearby choppers.

An intense study in Alberta documented goat reactions to helicopters for a three-month period during the summer. The observers witnessed frequent panicked reactions from mountain goats in an area where helicopters were flown frequently for resource exploration and other activities, and had been for many years. Goats were not habituated to helicopters and were seen racing from feeding areas and dashing over cliffs when helicopters approached within 550 yards. One nanny sustained a broken leg while fleeing a chopper.

This research suggests that more attention should be paid to helicopter overflights in mountain goat habitat. Helicopters are frequently used in resource extraction efforts, sometimes in goat habitat. Recreational applications of helicopters, especially for skiing, may occur over mountain goats on winter or spring range. Such activities represent a potential for severe stress at times of the year when goats are least equipped to deal with the energy expenditures related to flight. Based on the results of this study, it appears mountain goats are indeed afraid of helicopters, and it's in the species' best interest to keep them at a distance.

Like other ungulates, mountain goat populations undergo ups and downs. However, declining herd numbers in some places are a cause for concern. Research efforts have expanded in the past decade, in part to determine whether such factors as human encroachment on habitat (particularly motorized), climate change, disease, and overhunting are exerting downward pressure on mountain goat populations.

Pronghorn are named for the pointed protrusion, or "prong," on the horns of males of the species.
JACK BALLARD

CHAPTER 8
PRONGHORN

The shortgrass prairie on the foothills west of Three Forks, Montana, gives way at last to sagebrush, junipers, and austere limber pines as the landscape juts upward. Alternately seated and standing at the helm of a weary John Deere "R" tractor, I steered it round and round a field at the terminus of the prairie along the eastern flank of what was locally christened "Mother's Mountain." The tractor towed 14 feet of chisel plow, its two broad cylinders coughing a *pop-pop-pop* of seeming protest through its upright muffler.

I was as miserable as the machine. A midsummer ridge of high pressure pushed daytime temperatures into the high 80s. Shirtless, shrouded in dust, I piloted the tractor's slow cycles around the 60-acre wheat field with as much enthusiasm as a convict sledgehammering large stones into gravel.

As I approached the upper end of the cropland on one round, I spied two pronghorn bucks locked in combat at the field's edge. They jostled each other mercilessly, their forked horns locking and stabbing, each assailant attempting to twist the other to the ground or drive a horn into his flank. As the tractor ground closer, I expected the battle to end. It did not. Some 30 yards from the panting pair, I disengaged the hand clutch on the tractor and throttled the diesel engine to an idle to watch.

The desperate contest raged as time paused. Neither would yield, though their frothing mouths gaped open in exhaustion and tufts of fur, gouged from neck and face, were tilled into the dusty soil by their flailing hooves. When it seemed they might both collapse from exhaustion, one at last broke from the battle, yielding his claim as territorial viceroy. The victor staggered a few strides in pursuit then simply eyed his vanquished foe with tired, ebony eyes before unsteadily departing in the opposite direction.

Pronghorn were among the wildlife species intimately associated with my childhood and youth. I nearly tripped over a tiny fawn one spring while hunting ground squirrels. We sighted the animals frequently while harvesting, working cattle, or repairing barbwire fence. With a Kodak "Instamatic" film camera, I once crept within a few body lengths of a bedded pronghorn buck in an attempt to take its picture. The first wild game I provided for the family table was a pronghorn buck I harvested on the north end of the ranch. Pronghorn are supremely fascinating creatures. My technical biological knowledge of the species has expanded far beyond my youthful understanding of them. But my childhood observations remain among the finest in my experience with this one-of-a-kind species.

Names and Visual Description

"Pronghorn" is the scientifically accepted name for the fleet, tan-and-white mammal of the prairies of North America. However, the species is also widely referred to as "antelope," especially by state wildlife management agencies in the western United States, where the species is hunted as a game animal. In some cases, state management agencies maintain essentially a dual naming scheme. For example, in Montana's hunting regulations, this prairie mammal is called "antelope"; the state's official field guide names it "pronghorn." In most contexts these names are interchangeable, and both are deemed acceptable. For the sake of clarity, it seems "antelope" is the preferred moniker in relation to hunting and game management, while "pronghorn" is the title of choice for those concerned with natural history and wildlife biology not specifically related to hunting. In this book, both "antelope" and "pronghorn" will be used to describe the species.

In some regions, pronghorn are known by other names. "Pronghorn antelope" is sometimes used as a descriptor, a compound term that incorporates both common names of the species. Other names sometimes given to pronghorn include "prong-buck" and "American antelope." The scientific name for pronghorn is *Antilocapra americana*. "Antilocapra" is a compound term consisting of Latin words for "antelope" (*antilo*) and "male goat" (*capra*). Thus the scientific name literally means the "goat antelope of America." But as will be described in the next section of this chapter, pronghorn are neither goat nor antelope.

Pronghorn are creatures of the prairie and other open country. They are usually quite easy to view, with tan-and-white coats that often contrast with their surroundings. The back of the pronghorn is tan, and this coloration extends downward on the front and rear quarters and outer legs. The lower part of the body and belly are white, as are the inner portions of the legs. White and tan intersperse on the neck. The chest and rump of the pronghorn are white. Hair on the rump can be flared when a pronghorn is alarmed, a behavior that signals danger to other animals.

The pronghorn's body is streamlined for speed. A slender neck holds a narrow head, and the legs are thin. A mane of erect hairs adorns the back of the neck, though this feature is diminished or absent in some southern populations. The face of the pronghorn is dark brown or black. Males typically have a darker face than females and display a patch of dark hair below the ears.

Both male and female pronghorn have horns, although those on females may be only a few inches long and indiscernible at a distance. Horns on some females consist of little more than buds obscured by hair on the animal's head. The horns of a mature male are usually black but sometimes appear gray or brownish due to staining from earth or plant material. A distinct prong, or triangle-shaped protrusion, extends from the main stem of the horn, usually around the midpoint.

Male antelope are called "bucks," females are "does," and their young are called "fawns."

Related Species in North America

Pronghorn have no close relatives in North America. In fact, they have no near kin in the entire world. They are somewhat similar in appearance to the antelopes of Africa, but the development and shape of their horns are much different. Although their scientific name references goats, antelope are not closely related to any goat species. Again, the horns and other physical features differentiate them from goats. Some genetic analysis suggests pronghorn may be more closely related to the Giraffidae, the family of animals consisting of giraffes and okapi, although most people would think the association between a spotted, long-necked giraffe of Africa and the sleek American pronghorn not particularly strong.

Historically, pronghorn shared their prairie homelands with bison, elk, and mule deer. Along river bottoms, they would also sometimes encounter whitetail deer. Of these animals, antelope are most likely to be viewed in the proximity of mule deer today. Their interactions with bison on public lands are limited to a few refuges where both species occur, including Yellowstone National Park (Wyoming), Custer State Park (South Dakota), Badlands National Park (South Dakota), Theodore Roosevelt National Park (North Dakota), Grand Teton National Park (Wyoming), and the National Bison Range (Montana).

Antelope are found on the same range as mule deer across much of the western United States. Elk are their neighbors in some locations on the Western prairies and in high mountain valleys. Whitetail deer numbers have expanded on the plains in the

Mule deer are the ungulate species most likely to share range with pronghorn. This buck was photographed with mule deer does on Little Mountain in Wyoming.
JACK BALLARD

past century on both native prairie habitats and in agricultural areas they sometimes share with pronghorn. Due to their smaller size and markedly dissimilar coloration, it is virtually impossible for any informed viewer to confuse an antelope with any of its ungulate neighbors.

Subspecies of Pronghorn

Earlier taxonomists (biologists who classify organisms) identified numerous subspecies for mammals in North America. Subspecies were usually distinguished based upon populations of the same animal living in different locations that sometimes displayed either noticeable or almost indistinguishable variations in size, coloration, or other physical characteristics. Current taxonomical theory tends toward recognizing fewer (if any) subspecies for large mammals. The language of the Endangered Species Act (ESA), which allows for conservation of a Distinct Population Segment (DPS) of a species, independent of its status as a subspecies, is perhaps a better conceptual framework for viewing animals of the same species that live in different areas or may tend to separate themselves from others due to behavioral differences. For example, some herds of antelope inhabit high mountain valleys in states such as Wyoming and Montana, from which they migrate to lower range in winter. On their winter range they may mingle with resident, nonmigratory antelope. While it is very helpful to recognize these two separate segments of the population from the standpoint of natural history and wildlife management, few would argue for describing them as different subspecies, despite their profound behavioral differences in relation to migration. By the same token, antelope from northern and southern ends of their range in North America that have been identified as separate subspecies display only slight differences in physical characteristics and genetics. They are certainly distinct populations, but their status as a separate subspecies may be unwarranted.

Currently, four subspecies of pronghorn are commonly recognized in North America. A fifth, the Oregon pronghorn (*Antilocapra americana oregona*), which was thought to contain some populations in California, Idaho, and Nevada, is no longer considered a subspecies by most taxonomists.

The American pronghorn (*Antilocapra americana americana*) is the most widely distributed subspecies. It ranges from southern Canada in the prairie provinces throughout the western United States in suitable habitat to the Mexico border. A second subspecies, the Mexican pronghorn (*Antilocapra americana mexicana*) is identified with some antelope of the southwestern United States and northern Mexico. However, the status of this subspecies has been questioned in recent years and is no longer recognized by some biologists and conservation organizations, including the International Union for Conservation of Nature and Natural Resources (IUCN).

The remaining two pronghorn subspecies seem to be more warranted based upon genetic differences, geographical isolation, and modest differences in physical characteristics. The Sonoran pronghorn (*Antilocapra americana sonoriensis*) ranges across the Sonoran Desert in southern Arizona and northern Mexico. This subspecies is protected as an endangered species under the provisions of the Endangered Species Act. Current population estimates in the United States number between 150 and 200 animals, up from just two dozen in 2002. Another 200 to 300 animals inhabit Mexico.

The Sonoran pronghorn faces survival threats from multiple sources. Habitat loss due to the damming of rivers, loss of other natural water sources, disturbance from illegal human and drug trafficking, and poaching have all been identified as threats to this subspecies. The fact that much of the current Sonoran pronghorn habitat is on an active US Air Force bombing range (the Barry M. Goldwater Air Force Range) adds complexity to their recovery and management. A captive breeding program for Sonoran pronghorn began in 2004 with the capture of animals from the wild for seed stock.

The final subspecies of antelope is the Peninsular or Baja California pronghorn (*Antilocapra americana peninsularis*). This subspecies is considered critically endangered. A 2012 estimate showed just 50 antelope in the wild, with an additional 400 in captivity at the Vizcaino Biosphere Reserve in Mexico. The breeding program began in 1998 with the capture of five wild pronghorn. The captive animals are kept as survival insurance of the subspecies should the wild herd become extinct.

Physical Characteristics

Pronghorn are small in relation to most other North American ungulates. Mature bucks typically weigh between 100 and 140 pounds. Does are considerably smaller, normally weighing between 80 and 110 pounds. An adult antelope stands around 3 feet tall at the shoulder. Body length is around 4.5 feet.

Pronghorn have a host of physical characteristics that make them unique among the world's animals. They are the only horned species in the world with horns that fork or branch. Branches are common on antlered animals, whose headgear is composed of bone and shed each year, versus horns, which are composed of keratin fibers. Pronghorn horns are distinctive in that they are shed every year; they are the only horned animal in the world that sheds its horns.

Antelope have a gall bladder like sheep and goats but unlike deer and elk. Sheep, goats, deer, and elk all have dewclaws (two small hooflike appendages on the back of

Pronghorn, unlike members of the deer family (e.g., deer, elk, moose), do not have dewclaws. Look closely to observe the lack of this feature on this buck in Yellowstone National Park.
DOMINIC BALLARD

the leg just above the hoof), but antelope do not. The singular status of several physical features of the pronghorn stems from the fact that it is the sole surviving species of a family of animals that contained at least nineteen species in prehistoric times. Fossil remains indicate other species of extinct pronghorn shed their horns as well.

Horns and Horn Development

The horns of antelope are composed of keratin fibers, like the horns of mountain goats, impala, bison, ibex, and some strains of domestic cattle. Keratin is also found in hair, hooves, and human fingernails. A close examination of an antelope's horns reveals their association with hair. Coarse strands of hairlike material can be seen on the horns of many pronghorn, especially toward the base of shed horns.

Antelope horns consist of two parts: a bony core that protrudes from the animal's head as a permanent part of its skeleton and an outer sheath composed of keratin that is grown and shed each year. As noted previously, pronghorn does also have horns, but they are very small compared to bucks'. Research indicates that about 70 percent of pronghorn does develop visible horns. Thus, our discussion is focused on the headgear found on bucks.

Pronghorn bucks develop horns that are noticeably larger than does by the time they are 1.5 years old. Horns attain maximum growth by midsummer, at which time horn development ceases. Research in northern latitudes (Montana) demonstrates that this occurs in August. During the breeding season (rut), which takes place in mid- to late September in northern populations, a new horn sheath begins to develop under the existing one. The upward and outward pressure of the developing sheath loosens the existing horns, which are usually cast in late October to the middle November in these populations.

A seasoned observer can still distinguish bucks with recently cast antlers from does. The darker face and pronounced dark patches below the ears and behind the jaw distinguish bucks from does. A close-up view of a buck's head also reveals the remaining bony cores around which its new horns will develop.

Unlike deer, elk, and other animals whose antlers develop in spring and summer, the horns of a buck antelope grow substantially during winter. By midwinter the prongs and the pointed portion of the horn above the prong are developed. The horn continues to lengthen and swell during spring and summer.

Males of antlered animals tend to develop their maximum potential for antler mass between 5 and 10 years of age. Although comprehensive research is lacking, anecdotal evidence and a few studies suggest that the horns of an antelope buck are fully developed by 3.5 years of age and that subsequent horns are more likely to decrease than increase in length and overall mass.

RANGE AND HABITAT

North American Range—Historic

Historically, the greatest concentrations of pronghorn occurred on the shortgrass prairies of the Great Plains and the shrub steppes of the Rocky Mountain states, though they were present in other regions as well. But the genealogy of the pronghorn in North America extends far into the continent's history and contains many branches, some of which extend into other portions of the country.

As briefly noted in the beginning of this chapter, more than a dozen species of animals originally composed the Antilocapridae family in North America. Like modern antelope, these prehistoric pronghorn were animals of the open country, relying on their keen eyesight and incredible speed to elude predators such as the long-extinct America cheetah. Fossil remains discovered in Florida indicate that several species of pronghorn once roamed at least portions of the southeastern United States. Some archaeologists theorize that the development of scrub timber along the Mississippi River eventually closed the corridor that may have allowed these animals to migrate westward to open habitats. Other *Antilocapra* species ranged across western North America with today's American pronghorn. Some of those had four horns, each growing from a separate bone core on the animal's head. Why *Antilocapra americana* survived but all other species became extinct (some may have persisted as recently as 16,000 years ago) is a matter of speculation.

Analysis of historic documents referencing pronghorn in various parts of the country during European settlement indicates that their historic range was much larger than their present distribution. The eastern border of the historic range (from north to south) of antelope

Pronghorn have always been most numerous on the shortgrass prairies of the West, like the habitat occupied by this buck in Montana.
USFWS/RYAN HAGERTY

approximates the border of Minnesota and the Dakotas, continuing south along the border of Nebraska and Iowa. In southwestern Minnesota and northwestern Iowa, antelope occurred approximately 100 miles east of this line. From the southeastern corner of Nebraska, the historic range of pronghorn veered in a southwesterly direction to the middle of Texas then ran south to around the eastern border of Texas and Mexico. In central Mexico, antelope were found as far south as around 20°N latitude, about 100 miles northwest of Mexico City.

In addition to central Mexico, antelope were found in Baja California. In the United States, their historic range included all areas west of the above-described border, with the exceptions of northwestern California, western Washington and Oregon, and the northern Rocky Mountains. Their range extended a couple hundred miles into Canada on the prairies of Saskatchewan and Alberta. However, it must be clearly noted that pronghorn did not inhabit all areas within the limits of their range. Antelope are creatures of open country, absent from woodlands and scrub forests. Thus they were absent from the southern Rocky Mountains, for example, and other portions of the West containing habitat unsuitable for their environmental adaptations.

How many pronghorn roamed the prairies, deserts, and sagebrush steppes of the West prior to European settlement is a matter of speculation. Ernest Thompson Seton, an esteemed naturalist of the early twentieth century, developed population estimates for various ungulates. He theorized that some 40 million antelope inhabited North America in the early 1800s. Seton's estimate was based in part on reports of vast herds of wintering pronghorn and an extrapolation of those numbers to the whole of their range.

More recent estimates of antelope numbers prior to the settlement era have been based on theoretical carrying capacities of range in the western states. A 1978 estimate concluded that 10 to 15 million antelope inhabited eleven western states. Many biologists believe that pronghorn numbers in the pre-settlement era fall somewhere between the extremes of these two estimates (10 million and 40 million). However, some historians believe pronghorn were more numerous than bison, whose numbers have been estimated as high as 60 million animals. Current numbers of antelope in North America represent 10 percent or perhaps much fewer than the legions of pronghorn tracking the continent at the time Christopher Columbus "discovered" the New World.

North American Range—Current

Pronghorn range has shrunk dramatically in the past 150 years. Unbridled hunting in the latter half of the nineteenth century, disease and parasite transmission from livestock, fencing, and conversion of native habitat to agriculture have all played a role in reducing pronghorn range and numbers.

Although pronghorn numbers and distribution are dramatically lower than they were prior to European settlement, antelope are still found over much of their native range. Pronghorn numbers in the United States are believed to have reached a low point of around 13,000 animals in 1915. The establishment of hunting seasons, protected reserves in state and national parks, and relocation efforts caused nationwide

populations to increase in subsequent decades. A century after their low, pronghorn numbers in the United States were estimated at around 1 million. In many places, antelope populations experience substantial periods of growth and decline due to winter mortality, drought, and disease. For example, data compiled by the USDA Forest Service indicates that the nationwide pronghorn population increased by about 50 percent from 1980 to 1985.

Currently, the largest contiguous region of occupied pronghorn habitat on the continent extends across eastern Montana and into western North and South Dakota. From there it ranges southward through eastern Wyoming and western Nebraska. It narrows to include the eastern third of Colorado and a small portion of western Kansas, terminating in northeastern New Mexico. Another large expanse of contiguous pronghorn country includes much of southern Idaho and southwestern Oregon, extending into smaller portions of northwestern California and northern Nevada. Elsewhere, pronghorn occupy smaller parts of Nevada, Utah, Colorado, Arizona, New Mexico, Texas, Oklahoma, and Kansas.

Deep snow and frigid temperatures during a severe winter can dramatically reduce pronghorn numbers in local areas or across large regions of habitat.
JACK BALLARD

Pronghorn Habitat

Pronghorn are creatures of open country. They sometimes bed in the shade of trees, such as singular ponderosa pines and junipers on the prairie or aspens in open, high-mountain valleys. However, pronghorn consistently shun forests or shrubby habitat that impedes their vision. Research indicates that antelope found in shrublands prefer areas with a maximum vegetation height of 30 inches.

Historically, antelope were most numerous on the shortgrass prairies east of the Rocky Mountains, a pattern that persists today. These grasslands also sprout forbs (broad-leafed plants) and various types of shrubs such as sagebrush, bitterbrush, and other species, all of which are important nutritional items for antelope. Pronghorn tend to favor flatter areas but may be found in hilly expanses of prairie, so long as the topography allows a broad visual field and room to flee.

Pronghorn also roam extensively across the sagebrush steppes of the Rocky Mountains and their foothills. This habitat is characterized by a preponderance of sagebrush and similar species, interspersed with grass and forbs. In such habitat, pronghorn may range to surprisingly high elevations. Mountain valleys in such locations as Yellowstone and Grand Teton National Parks hold pronghorn as high as 7,000 feet or more. A similar situation exists in mountain valleys of Idaho, Montana, and Colorado. In most cases, pronghorn migrate from these lofty elevations to winter range in lower valleys, foothills, or prairie.

Pronghorn also track some portions of the deserts in the American Southwest. However, desert populations account for less than 1 percent of the antelope found in the United States. Desert pronghorn rely on succulent vegetation, including some species of cacti, for most of their nutritional needs.

Pronghorn can survive in desert environments, though not in large numbers. This one tracks arid habitat in the Buenos Aires National Wildlife Refuge of south-central Arizona, about 20 miles from the Mexico border. USFWS/STEVE HILLEBRAND

No matter what type of ecosystem they occupy, access to water is a critical component in pronghorn habitat, especially in desert areas. Antelope can absorb significant amounts of moisture from leafy plants, to the extent that they may not require surface water. On dry range, however, access to reliable water sources is considered a limiting factor for pronghorn. An aerial survey of antelope on the Red Desert of southwestern Wyoming revealed that 95 percent of the observed pronghorn were recorded within 4 miles of water.

NUTRITIONAL REQUIREMENTS AND FORAGE

Nutritional Requirements

A leading pronghorn biologist once concluded that the same amount of fodder on native rangeland required for a single domestic cow could maintain as many as three dozen pronghorn. This conclusion, however, overlooks a very important difference in the foraging habits of the two species. Pronghorn select highly nutritious plants when available and consume little grass during most of the year, while cattle feed primarily on grass, which may be nutritionally inferior to other plants.

One research study found that male yearling pronghorn needed to consume about 560 food calories per 10 pounds of body weight per day to maintain their body condition. Thus a 90-pound yearling male would require a bit more than 5,000 calories per day. Although pronghorn can subsist on low-quality forage for a time, their highly tuned bodies require high levels of protein and other nutrients for optimal performance. Research has shown that antelope consistently select plants high in protein and vitamins. Pronghorn tend to have less body fat than other North American ungulates, making it more difficult for them to survive extended periods of nutritional distress. Their smaller body size is also less efficient at retaining body heat. Exceptionally cold, snowy winters can therefore lead to extensive stress, even starvation, among pronghorn in the northern portions of their range.

The study referenced in the preceding paragraph found that yearling male pronghorn in captivity consumed 0.012 gallon of available water per 10 pounds of body weight. Given free access to water, a 90-pound pronghorn male consumed slightly less than 1 gallon per day. Water requirements for free-ranging pronghorn are a subject of some debate. Some biologists believe pronghorn can ingest most of their required moisture from water contained in plants and have limited need for surface water. Others believe access to drinking water is a critical component in viable pronghorn habitat. Researchers in one study concluded that antelope did not drink water when the moisture content of their forage plants was greater than 75 percent. (For reference, bananas contain about 74 percent water, green peas around 79 percent.) However, moisture content of plants on pronghorn range seldom exceeds these levels, especially in summer and early autumn.

Other studies have found that antelope do show a reliance on drinking water, especially during dry periods of the year. An Arizona study discovered that antelope does consumed approximately 0.18 gallon of water per day in March, increasing to 0.82 gallon in June. Like other animals living in arid environments, antelope have several adaptations for preserving body moisture. Their kidneys are large, allowing them to concentrate bodily moisture. Long nasal passages promote the retention of moisture as they exhale and help trap water vapor from the outside air when they inhale. Pronghorn also decrease the output of urine and feces during times of water stress, which also helps them preserve body fluids.

Digestion

Antelope are ruminants, a type of animal with a digestive system that specializes in breaking down plant matter for nutrition. North American ruminants such as pronghorn, elk, bison, mule deer, and bighorn sheep have four stomachs (or a four-chambered stomach): the rumen, the reticulum, the omasum, and the abomasum. Ruminants eat rapidly, chewing their food little before swallowing. It is later regurgitated and rechewed to aid digestion. The food regurgitated from the rumen is called "cud."

The first chamber of the stomach, the rumen, is the largest and normally holds most of the mass in a ruminant's digestive system. Plant matter regurgitated for chewing comes from the rumen. Cud-chewing normally commences when the wild ruminant is resting and can be more vigilant to danger.

After the cud is chewed to a finer texture, it passes from the rumen through the other three stomachs. Nutrients are absorbed in the stomachs, but the bulk of the energy and nutrition is extracted from the small intestine, where the food passes after leaving the abomasum, the last of the four stomachs.

In relation to larger ruminants whose diet is often dominated by grass (bison) or woody browse and leaves (moose), antelope select less-fibrous, more nutritionally dense forage. Their digestive system is specifically adapted to maximize these foods. The pronghorn has a relatively large abomasum and small omasum. This lowers the need to absorb water from fibrous forage and speeds the digestive process. Antelope also have an elongated colon, which promotes water absorption from digestive matter and reduces moisture lost in the excretion of feces.

Food Sources

The slender muzzle and narrow mouth of pronghorn identify them as an animal capable of high selectivity in its diet. For example, a pronghorn can delicately nip the fruit

Top: Pronghorn, like these does in Wind Cave National Park, South Dakota, are known as "selective feeders," animals that focus on the most nutritious plants in their environment.
NPS
Bottom: Pronghorn can ingest significant moisture from green plants but rely on surface water for fluid, especially during hot, dry seasons of the year.
JACK BALLARD

of a wild rose bush (rose hips) or its leaves while avoiding the thorns. Such a feat is virtually impossible for a wide-mouthed ruminant such as a bison or domestic cow. Additionally, the digestive system of an antelope is especially adapted to quickly absorb nutrients and energy from the most nutritious plants on its range and the parts of plants (leaves versus stems, for example) containing the greatest food value.

The typical pronghorn diet consists of forbs (broad-leafed plants), shrubs, and grasses. When available, antelope select heavily for forbs, which are most strongly associated with spring and summer. Autumn and winter see their diets transitioning toward shrubs, which have been described by some biologists as the pronghorn's "survival food." Grasses usually compose but a small portion of the diet and are most readily eaten as newly emerged, tender blades in spring. In some locations and at specific times, cacti may be an important component in the pronghorn diet. One study concluded that antelope may consume up to 20 percent of their diet in prickly pear cactus for periods of time during dry winters. Research on the diets of pronghorn in the Sonoran Desert has identified jumping cholla (a large cactus) as representing as high as 27 percent of antelope food intake for brief periods. The moisture and nutrition in the fruit of jumping cholla are believed to be especially important to pronghorn during droughts.

Grass is typically most significant in pronghorn diets in late spring and early summer, when it is most tender and nutritious. This buck was nipping grass in Custer State Park, South Dakota, in mid-June.
LISA BALLARD

Research on the specific makeup of pronghorn diets in various parts of the country have substantiated the animal's preference for forbs but also indicate a considerable range of adaptability and variation through the seasons. An analysis of more than a dozen studies of pronghorn diet in various parts of the country found that forbs average 62 percent of the annual pronghorn diet.

However, antelope diets show a high degree of local and seasonal variation. In northwestern South Dakota, one study found that forbs composed 65 percent of the pronghorn diet in midsummer but only 4 percent in winter. The same study observed a winter diet consisting of 96 percent shrubs, while shrubs accounted for just around 10 percent of the summer diet. Grasses made up roughly 35 percent of the diet in June and July but were nearly indiscernible as a food item from November to February.

Pronghorn prefer nutrient-packed forbs in their diet, but in certain areas they are forced to choose other foods. A study in northern Arizona comparing the diets of two antelope herds on different ranges found the animals predominantly consuming forbs on one, grass and shrubs on the other. Although adult animals appeared healthy in both places, reproduction rates were significantly lower for the herd eating primarily grass and shrubs. Nutritional levels are extremely important during all phases of reproduction, and some studies suggest that antelope with limited access to forbs may experience population declines due to lower birth rates and fawn survival.

Migration

Numerous ungulate species in North America are migratory. Migrations consist of relatively short, elevational migrations, where a species such as elk or mule deer descends from summer habitat on mountaintops and high ridges to winter range in the foothills or adjacent prairies. Other movements include more dramatic, overland travels from summer to winter range that span more than 100 miles. As tracking techniques and technology have improved in the past decade, researchers have discovered more of these epic migrations.

Pronghorn claim the lengthiest of the major migrations discovered to date. A herd of around 300 antelope that inhabits Grand Teton National Park during summer departs eastward over the mountains to winter in the upper Green River basin. The migration spans about 150 miles and is fraught with numerous natural obstacles that may include deep snow and raging streams. Man-made obstacles prove even more challenging. Wyoming pronghorn must find their way through numerous wire fences and cross an extremely busy highway along the way. Gas and oil development on their winter range threatens habitat and creates other obstacles to migration, such as the subdivisions that have sprung up on the migration route as the area's human population increases.

Another dramatic pronghorn migration occurs in south-central Idaho, where pronghorn move northeastward along the base of the Pioneer Mountains through Craters of the Moon National Monument to winter on a plain at the base of the Beaverhead Mountains, whose spine makes up the Continental Divide. The maximum distance between these summer and winter ranges is about 160 miles. These pronghorn migrations are currently the second-longest known migrations of any land animal in the North America, only exceeded in distance by the migration of Arctic caribou.

This herd of migrating pronghorn was photographed near Craters of the Moon National Monument in Idaho, along a 160-mile migration route. Pronghorn undertake some of the longest seasonal migrations of any mammal in North America.
JACK BALLARD

Physical Abilities

The most remarkable physical ability of the pronghorn is its speed. It is commonly reported that pronghorn can hit speeds of 60 miles per hour or slightly higher, although some credible sources cite a maximum speed of around 50 miles per hour. Antelope are believed to be the second-fastest land animal in the world, their sprinting velocity exceeded only by the cheetah. (The other creature with speed rivaling the pronghorn is the greyhound. I have personally observed a greyhound overtaking a pronghorn; although it should be noted that the incident occurred on a cultivated field where the running surface favored the spreading paws of the canine versus the pointed hooves of the pronghorn.) However, in contrast to the fleet African cat or the specially bred dog that can maintain their speeds over short distances, the pronghorn can flee danger at about 45 miles per hour for several minutes, enough time to carry them 4 miles from their point of fright in short order.

Pronghorn possess a variety of physical adaptations promoting both sprinting speed and endurance, characteristics probably originating in their ancient ancestry at a time when North America was inhabited by an array of efficient and fearsome predators, including extinct saber-toothed tigers, large wolves, and cheetahs.

An antelope's speed comes from the length of its stride and the rapid cadence of its hoofbeats. Long limbs are hallmark traits of fast runners. Antelope have long legs characterized by muscular upper sections tapering to thin shins and feet. The spine of the pronghorn is very flexible, allowing it to bend under the animal's body as it runs. At high speeds, the rear hooves of an antelope reach beyond its front feet. Pronghorn do not have a collarbone, an adaptation allowing their front legs a broad range of movement that further lengthens their stride. In full flight on flat, obstacle-free terrain, a grown antelope covers about 20 feet with each bounding stride.

Pronghorn, like this galloping buck in Yellowstone National Park, can cover more than 2 miles in a matter of minutes. No other animal in the world is capable of the sustained speeds of an antelope.
JACK BALLARD

The quick cadence of a pronghorn's flight is promoted by the structure of its legs. Propulsion of the legs comes from muscular quarters that appear as part of the body. Lower portions of the legs consist of light but very strong bones, minimal muscle structure, and dense, specialized ligaments. One such ligament extends from the hooves to the back of the shinbone. The weight of the animal "loads" this ligament, much like a stretched rubber band. When the pronghorn springs forward, the ligament contracts, its stored energy propelling the animal forward. A pronghorn's hooves are narrow and light, but spread to absorb impact on hard ground. Antelope hooves also lack dewclaws (small, secondary, hooflike appendages located above the hoof on the rear of the foot), further lightening their feet for rapid locomotion. The front hooves of an antelope bear most of its weight while running and are slightly larger than the rear. Both the front and the rear hooves are serviced by a gland that produces an oily substance, which serves as a conditioner that helps prevent hoof cracking and wear.

The remarkable endurance of the pronghorn is supported by numerous physiological traits. Compared with other hoofed mammals, the heart and lungs of an antelope are oversize. Its trachea (windpipe) is exceptionally large as well, promoting increased oxygen intake. Research on pronghorn oxygen consumption indicates that antelope can consume three times as much oxygen as the average for animals of similar body weight. The pronghorn's relatively small stomach allows it to run with less weight, enhancing endurance. A slender neck and slim, narrow head and lightweight horns (versus heavy antlers) are additional weight-saving features that heighten the antelope's stamina.

Sensing danger is as critical to prey species as the ability to flee it. For pronghorn, notably acute eyesight serves as the primary means of detecting danger. The eyeballs of antelope are larger in proportion to their body than any other ungulate in North America. Situated on the sides of the head, the eyes of an antelope detect a visual field encompassing nearly 300 degrees. Pronghorn are extremely capable of detecting movement, able to discern moving objects at a distance of 4 miles under ideal sighting conditions. The visual acuity of pronghorn is thought to be the equivalent of a human peering through 8× to 10× binoculars, though such estimates have not been scientifically tested to this author's knowledge. It is known, however, that the physical structure of the pronghorn's eye is especially suited to motion detection, a powerful defense against predation in the open habitat in which the creatures thrive.

Keen eyesight with exceptional motion-detecting ability is the pronghorn's primary means of sensing danger.
LISA BALLARD

Pronghorn are powerful, efficient swimmers, a trait that comes as a surprise to some people. Why would an animal of the plains, peculiarly suited to running, be a good swimmer? Physiologically, the strong limbs of an antelope create forceful propulsion in water as well as on land. The hair of antelope is hollow, promoting both insulation and heat dispersion. It is also very buoyant, aiding the animal's swimming ability. Although pronghorn don't normally need to swim, migratory herds must cross rivers in some places. During the spring migration, these streams may be flowing at high, dangerous levels.

Despite the leaping potential of their extremely powerful hind legs, pronghorn are reluctant or unwilling to jump over obstacles, preferring to duck under impediments such as fences. On two occasions the author has witnessed antelope (both bucks) easily leaping over a barbwire fence. However, on countless other occasions he has seen entire herds of antelope duck under the lowest wire or refuse to jump a woven wire fence too low for the animals to crawl under.

Although keen eyesight is the pronghorn's primary mechanism for detecting danger, they also possess a capable sense of smell. Their ears are small in comparison to members of the deer family such as elk, mule deer, or moose. The sense of hearing is not as developed in pronghorn as these animals, but the ears of antelope are still important for detecting danger and responding to vocal communication of their own kind.

Vocal and Visual Communication

Compared to canines such as coyotes or wolves, or even herbivores like bison, pronghorn are a noticeably quiet species. The most widely witnessed antelope vocalization is a loud call, best described as a combination of a snort and a wheeze. Pronghorn emit this call when alarmed by forcefully expelling air from their lungs. An initial alarm call is often followed by a series of three or more loud snorts. Antelope within hearing of this call become instantly alert. Movement or other indications of danger following an alarm call usually have pronghorn racing from the perceived threat.

The flared white rump hair on this fawn indicates that it is aroused. This posture is used to communicate alarm among members of a pronghorn herd.
LISA BALLARD

Pronghorn fawns sometimes bleat when distressed or to gain their mother's attention. During mating season, bucks occasionally emit a repetitious wheezing sound that some commentators describe as having a slightly metallic characteristic. Bucks may also use a high-pitched whining noise as a courtship call to does.

Antelope bucks use a variety of visual displays during the breeding season, including pawing, exaggerated urination postures, and staring directly at a rival. They may also twist their raised head to the side when attempting to court a doe, a posture almost appearing as though the male is showing off his horns to his potential mate.

Probably the most common form of visual communication for the pronghorn is an alarm signal. Antelope can flare the hair on their rump into an erect position that is noticeable from a considerable distance. Alarmed antelope often use this signal in conjunction with their vocal alarm call. When mildly alerted, a pronghorn might flare its rump hair then drop the posture when it returns to a more relaxed state. In some cases, certain animals within a herd may assume this alarm posture while others do not, giving credibility to the notion that certain antelope are more naturally skittish than others.

Herd Behavior

Antelope bucks sometimes lead a solitary existence at certain times of the year, and does retreat to private portions of their habitat when birthing fawns. Beyond these two exceptions, antelope are normally found in herds of a few to a few hundred animals. During spring, summer, and into early autumn, herds usually comprise somewhere between a half-dozen and thirty or so animals. As autumn fades to winter, pronghorn herds increase in size, especially toward the northern reaches of their range. Severe winters sometimes see larger than normal herds that may number as many as 300 animals.

Herds of mixed sexes are usually observed, but at certain times of year the composition may favor one gender or the other. From late spring to midsummer, after does have rejoined the herds with their fawns, females dominate larger congregations of pronghorn. Males are often found in separate herds, some of which contain a dozen or more members. By late summer, dominant males begin to expel rivals from herds within their territories. During this period, other bucks may be found in bachelor bands primarily composed of younger males. As the breeding season subsides by mid-autumn, herds become comingled with bucks and does. Mature males of the elk and deer species typically winter in areas separate from females and young males. However, wintering pronghorn herds contain members of both genders and exhibit little separation by sex.

Pronghorn develop a dominance hierarchy, or "pecking order," within a herd, although this organization may be difficult to discern in large bands. Antelope herds are most often led by a mature doe, the identity of which may not be obvious to all but the most expert human observers. But on at least one occasion, the author has sighted a buck leading a very large herd of wintering pronghorn as they fought through deep snow descending a long hillside in Idaho.

Antelope herds spend from 40 to 60 percent of their time feeding, a number that varies in relation to the season and forage availability. They rest for extended periods, time often devoted to chewing cud. Pronghorn herds are seldom bunched tightly when resting or feeding. The slightly dispersed character of their herds allows for better detection of danger, particularly on uneven terrain. Antelope herds typically move a half-mile or considerably less during foraging bouts in spring and summer. Fall and winter find them searching more widely for food, sometimes traveling 2 to 5 miles while foraging.

Pronghorn herds composed of females, males, and mixed sexes are governed by dominance hierarchies. The sparring of these bucks in the summer months will help determine their rank.
JACK BALLARD

REPRODUCTION AND YOUNG

The Mating Season

Pronghorn follow a mating pattern similar to that of other North American ungulates in that northern populations have a shorter, more prescribed breeding season than southern populations. Northern pronghorn typically engage in a breeding period, or "rut," of approximately three weeks in mid- to late September. Southern antelope may mate from September to October, although breeding behavior is sometimes witnessed in southern herds before and after this period.

Several months before actual mating begins, bucks engage in dominance behaviors that position them to mate with a maximum number of does, provided they can withstand challenges from other males. Pronghorn bucks begin establishing dominance and breeding territories in spring. The mating strategies of pronghorn are more fluid than those normally employed by deer and elk. Depending on the health and type of habitat, number of pronghorn in an area, and ratio of males to females, mating may follow one of several known patterns.

A vigilant buck keeps watch over his harem of does. This mating strategy occurs most frequently in places where bucks are highly outnumbered by does.
JACK BALLARD

A territorial approach to mating occurs when a dominant male establishes a circumscribed territory within a larger expanse of antelope habitat. The buck defends this territory and the does within it against rival males. Territories containing water and desirable forage (primarily succulent forbs) are held by the most dominant males. Bucks mate with the females in their territory (usually found in a single herd) and spend considerable time watching for and expelling intruding males.

Where habitat contains widely dispersed forage and water or low numbers of pronghorn, bucks may attach themselves to a herd of does known as a harem. However, the selection process is not one-sided; does may abandon a lesser buck to join the harem of a more virulent male. In the harem breeding pattern, the buck stays with his band of females, which may wander widely in search of forage and water, regardless of a smaller, defined territory. A harem pattern of breeding is also commonly observed in pronghorn populations when the ratio of females to males exceeds 10:1.

A third breeding strategy occurs when available resources are quite consistent across an expanse of habitat and the ratio of males to females is several bucks for every ten does. Under these conditions, antelope often develop a dominance system of breeding. Herds consist of both bucks and does during the rut. However, a clear dominance hierarchy is established among the bucks wherein the most dominant male mates with the most does.

Prior to and during the breeding season, antelope bucks exhibit two primary behaviors to mark their territory or advertise their dominance, both of which can be readily observed by a

This handsome buck is rubbing scent glands on his cheeks against vegetation, a territorial marker of dominant males during the mating season.
JACK BALLARD

watchful human. In the first, the buck sniffs at the ground then paws forcefully with a front hoof; he then urinates and defecates in the pawed earth. Each portion of this behavioral sequence is highly exaggerated, perhaps to better call attention to the activity. Bucks also rub scent glands located on their cheeks against tall grass, sagebrush, and sometimes other shrubs to announce their presence via sense of smell.

Pregnancy and Gestation

Antelope, like other large ungulates in North America, engage in synchronous breeding. This term refers to the fact that most pronghorn does conceive their fawns in a relatively short period in early autumn and birth their offspring in a correspondingly short time frame in spring. Biologists theorize that synchronous breeding serves as a survival mechanism in relation to predation. Antelope fawns are most vulnerable to predation in the first few weeks of life. When most fawns are born close together on the calendar, more of them reach the age at which they can elude predators, as opposed to a breeding pattern where fawns are birthed over a longer period.

Unlike whitetail deer, where a small percentage of females conceive offspring in their first fall, pronghorn does do not normally reach sexual maturity until around 16 to 17 months of age. They typically birth their first fawn about the time of their second birthday. Males achieve reproductive capability at around 1 year of age, but unless older bucks are lacking in a population, they normally don't sire offspring until 3 or 4 years of age.

As a very rough rule of thumb, the gestation period (the time between breeding and birth) for mammals decreases in relation to size. Antelope, however, have a gestation period of around 250 days, longer than both whitetail deer (about 200 days) and moose (about 230 days). Toward the northern end of their range, fawns are born in May or June. The birthing period of southern populations is around a month later. The "birth pulse" for pronghorn normally lasts around ten days, at which time most mature females in a local population will have given birth.

The body condition of a pronghorn doe significantly determines her reproductive status. Does in good condition conceive fawns at higher rates than those that are

Twin fawns are the rule among healthy pronghorn on good range, an important factor in the ability of pronghorn numbers to bounce back a few years after a substantial winter die-off.
LISA BALLARD

nutritionally stressed. Fawns born to does malnourished by difficult wintering conditions or poor habitat have lower survival rates. Evidence from Texas also suggests that high loads of certain parasites in does may substantially reduce fawn birth weight and survival rates.

In most cases does birth twin fawns. Antelope does typically develop a separate embryo in each branch, or horn, of their uterus (womb). Multiple embryos are implanted in the uterus after breeding, but only two normally survive to develop into the fetuses.

Birth

Pronghorn fawns weigh 7 to 9 pounds at birth. The combined weight of the twin fawns normally born to an antelope doe represents about 18 percent of her body mass. This would be the equivalent of a 130-pound human mother birthing twins weighing well over 10 pounds each. Antelope fawns are born large in relation to their mother

Hiding is the primary survival strategy for newborn antelope fawns. Sufficient hiding cover is necessary to conceal very young fawns from predators.
USFWS/TOM KOERNER

because they need to mature quickly to elude predators and gain enough body mass to survive their first winter.

Some days before their fawns are born, pronghorn does make a solitary trek to fawning grounds, portions of their range best suited for fawn survival. Antelope does tend to use the same fawning areas year after year. Although pronghorn avoid habitats with vegetation tall and dense enough to impede their vision, does favor areas with more cover than normal as fawning areas. Research has shown that does seek habitat with taller and denser than average vegetation to birth their fawns. On the shortgrass prairie of Colorado, researchers concluded that depressions (used for hiding), sagebrush, and other vegetation over 10 inches tall enhanced fawn survival.

The actual birthing of pronghorn fawns occurs quickly. The entire birthing process of antelope twins typically takes about 1 hour. Does vigorously lick and clean their fawns immediately after birth. Newborn fawns stand and nurse soon after birth. In some cases, the firstborn of twin fawns may wobble to its feet before its sibling is born. After nursing and tending her newborn fawns, the doe will bed them in a hiding place.

Nurturing Fawns to Adulthood

Once born, a pronghorn fawn's survival is highly dependent on its mother's milk, her watchful eyes, and its ability to hide. For its first week of life, a pronghorn fawn remains motionless for most of the day, concealed beneath a sagebrush, tucked into a tiny swale, or hunkered in a swath of tall grass. Does keep watch on their offspring from a distance, visiting them several times per day to let them nurse. Research has shown that pronghorn does stay about 70 yards away from their newborns, far enough to disguise the location from predators, close enough for the keen-eyed mothers to watch over their offspring.

At 1 week of age, a healthy pronghorn fawn can easily outrun a human and elude most predators. Once their fawns are around a week old, does band together in maternal herds formed of females and their new offspring. Twin fawns begin bedding together between 2 and 3 weeks of age.

Pronghorn fawns develop rapidly. Their dependence on their mother's milk fades more quickly than many other mammals. By 3 weeks of age they can nibble and digest plants. At 6 weeks of age their teeth have develop sufficiently to eat a wide variety of plants and they begin transitioning to a diet of vegetation. Antelope fawns are social and playful. Play often consists of running, appearing to a human observer as games of tag or races. Fawns typically remain with their mothers through their first winter and into spring, until she births her next fawn. However, they are completely weaned (nutritionally independent from their mothers) at 5 to 6 months of age.

Predation and malnutrition are the primary threats to pronghorn survival and are often intertwined. Fawns that are smaller and weaker at birth are slower to develop the running ability necessary to elude predators. Those whose mothers lack enough nutrition to supply adequate milk in the first weeks of life are similarly at greater risk from predators. Coyotes, bobcats, and golden eagles are the primary predators of antelope fawns in most places. A single doe or several does may band together to chase coyotes, kicking at them with their front feet. Does may also attempt to incite a four-legged predator into chasing them if the carnivore strays too close to their fawns. Research in Alberta, Canada, revealed that fawn mortality over a ten-year period averaged around 50 percent. In one study, coyotes and bobcats accounted for the death of just over 40

Pronghorn fawns are very social. Here an older fawn (identified by its larger size) pals with a set of younger twins in South Dakota.
LISA BALLARD

percent of marked fawns. Predation rates were highest on fawns 4 days to 2 weeks of age, but fawns 2 to 8 weeks old were also taken by predators. In some locations, predation rates on fawns is much higher. One study at the Hart Mountain National Antelope Refuge in Oregon saw 84 percent of monitored fawns killed by predators in a two-year period, primarily by coyotes. Interestingly, this study concluded that fawns born at the peak of the birth pulse had higher survival rates than those born toward the beginning or end of the birthing period, lending credibility to the theory that synchronous breeding gives a survival advantage to the young of many ungulate species.

Once old enough to be generally safe from predators, antelope fawns face another survival challenge before becoming adults: winter. Pronghorn, as a species, are more susceptible to winter mortality due to starvation than larger ungulates such as deer or elk. Research in Montana during a severe winter indicated that fawns succumbed to starvation at higher rates than adult antelope. Animals that were more than 1 year of age but less than 3 years old had the highest survival rates.

PRONGHORNS AND OTHER ANIMALS

Pronghorns and Other Ungulates

Pronghorn are found on the same range as several other ungulates. Depending on the location and season, antelope might locate in proximity to mule deer, elk, whitetail deer, and bighorn sheep. In some places they also roam among bison herds, both wild and domestic.

Due to their small size, pronghorn are apt to come out on the losing end of any direct conflict with larger ungulate species. But the relationship between antelope and other ungulates isn't restricted to direct interactions, such as a mule deer displacing a pronghorn from a sagebrush on winter range. Biologists sometimes categorize "competition" between wildlife species in two ways. One involves space and pertains to competition in relation to a place to live. This might involve one species yielding to another when forced into close association due to high population numbers or limited habitat. The second form of competition involves forage. Dietary overlap exists between a number of ungulate species to a greater or lesser extent. This impacts smaller animals such as antelope most profoundly on winter range. Pronghorn, mule deer, and elk, for example, may all utilize various species of sagebrush for winter forage. Is it possible that antelope populations are negatively influenced by the presence of these other, larger ungulates where their ranges overlap?

Research specifically investigating competition between antelope and other native ungulates is sorely lacking. When discussing the issue, biologists agree that in healthy habitat antelope and their hoofed neighbors have little impact on one another. On limited winter range or in drought conditions, however, it is possible that mule deer and elk might sometimes consume forage that would otherwise sustain antelope. One

Sagebrush is a plant widely consumed by elk, mule deer, and pronghorn on winter range. Some research indicates that very high elk numbers may infrequently suppress pronghorn herds, perhaps due to competition for limited resources on winter range.
LISA BALLARD

study suggested that excessively high elk populations in the northern portion of Yellowstone National Park prior to wolf reintroduction may have been responsible for declining pronghorn numbers. A similar conclusion was reached by researchers in northern Arizona. While such local influences may occur, the presence of other native ungulates is not believed to be an influential factor on pronghorn populations over most of their range.

Pronghorns and Predators

The superior speed and endurance of a healthy adult pronghorn makes it nearly immune from predation. However, certain conditions make them vulnerable to a variety of predators. Winter-weakened pronghorns are vulnerable. Those that stray close to predator-concealing cover also may succumb to predation. Similar to other ungulate species, fawns in the first few weeks of life are most vulnerable. Where multiple predators exist, fawn survival can be severely impacted by predation. For example, one study of twenty radio-collared fawns in Texas witnessed eighteen of them (90 percent) being killed by predators. If such high fawn mortality rates continue year after year, a pronghorn population cannot be maintained. Some research indicates that fawns in habitats including expansive stands of tall or dense shrubbery are especially vulnerable to predation.

Although small animals, bobcats are a surprisingly efficient predator of pronghorn fawns. This sizable bobcat in Badlands National Park, South Dakota, is capable of taking large fawns.
NPS/TERI STOIA

Coyotes, mountain lions, wolves, bobcats, bears, and eagles are known to kill antelope. Of these, coyotes are the most consistent predators. Several research projects have documented coyotes as significant predators of both adult and young pronghorn in some areas. One of these studies examined predation on a herd of approximately 200 antelope found in Yellowstone National Park and adjacent habitat. Of thirteen documented predator mortalities on adult pronghorn, five were attributed to coyotes, the most in the study. Fourteen tagged fawns were taken by predators, six by coyotes, also the most in the study. Significant predation by coyotes on pronghorn fawns has also been documented in Arizona and other states.

Mountain lions are also capable of catching pronghorns. In the study referenced above, mountain lions took three of the thirteen adult antelope killed by predators. Habitat in the northern reaches of Yellowstone and just outside the park where pronghorn were found offers stalking cover in some areas sufficient for a cat to closely approach antelope. Research in Arizona has also documented mountain lion predation on pronghorn in areas where ambush cover exists. The explosive speed of mountain lions over very short distances allows them to overtake a pronghorn surprised at close range.

Wolf predation on adult pronghorns has been documented in Yellowstone National Park and elsewhere. In Montana's Madison Valley, state biologists have observed wolf packs running pronghorn into fences through which they cannot easily pass and catching them. Such instances illustrate the effect that man-made impediments may have in rendering some ungulate species more susceptible to predation. The Madison Valley consists primarily of very open habitat where the keen eyesight and speed of antelope would make it extremely difficult for wolves to prey on pronghorns under natural conditions.

Wolves, however, may be more beneficial than harmful to pronghorn in the predator-prey equation. These apex predators have little tolerance for coyotes in their territories. In the first few years after their reintroduction to Yellowstone National Park, wolves killed or displaced numerous coyotes, drastically reducing their numbers. Coincidentally, pronghorn numbers began to rise. At the time of reintroduction, the park's pronghorn herd numbered about 200 animals. Some fifteen years later, the number had grown to around 350. Wolf suppression of coyotes is believed to have decreased coyote predation on fawns and increased fawn survival, allowing the population to grow.

Black and grizzly bears may opportunistically take pronghorn fawns. Black bears have also been observed (unsuccessfully) attempting to stalk and pursue adult antelope. Bears are not believed to be a significant predator of pronghorn.

Bobcats are also known to prey on pronghorn fawns. Although small animals, bobcats can be extremely efficient predators of very young antelope. One five-year study in western Utah found that bobcats took by far the most young pronghorn of any predator. The cats killed fawns ranging from 3 to 104 days of age. Adult bobcats in the area generally weigh from 12 to 30 pounds. The largest antelope fawn killed

Regardless of the predator, antelope fawns are far more susceptible to predation than adult animals.
LISA BALLARD

by a bobcat in the study weighed 48 pounds, substantially larger than the average bobcat in the area. Bobcats have also been documented preying on adult Sonoran pronghorn in Arizona, although these occurrences are undoubtedly rare.

Eagles also take pronghorn fawns. In the previously referenced study of predation on pronghorns in Yellowstone National Park, one fawn was killed by a large bird of prey, presumably a bald or golden eagle, as both are found in the study area. Golden eagles are common to the open prairie habitat favored by pronghorn. Research projects have documented golden eagle predation on antelope fawns in Utah and other states.

In addition to fawns, golden eagles may infrequently prey on adult pronghorn. A month after an article I had written on golden eagles was published, I received a handwritten note from a man in Wyoming. In it he described in detail a successful predation episode in which a golden eagle dove on a pronghorn buck running at the rear of a fleeing herd. The impact of the eagle knocked the animal from its feet, the bird also being thrown to the ground. Upon regaining its footing, the buck attempted to overtake the herd but soon fell with blood streaming from puncture wounds on its ribcage. The author surmised that the raptor's talons had sufficiently penetrated the antelope's lungs to cause fatal bleeding. Communicating a fabricated story seemed unlikely, and in a subsequent telephone conversation, I concluded that he had witnessed an exceedingly rare, dramatic act in nature's drama. Given that golden eagles have been observed attempting to take adult mountain goats, his account is certainly plausible.

Parasites and Diseases

Pronghorn are susceptible to many of the same parasites and diseases as other North American ungulates. In some situations, these can seriously influence both short- and long-term declines in antelope populations.

Internal parasites known to plague pronghorns include roundworms and tapeworms. Research suggests that pronghorn sharing range with domestic sheep have higher incidences of internal parasites than those living where sheep are not present.

Pronghorns, like other animals, can carry low to moderate loads of internal parasites without apparent ill effects. However, in some cases internal parasites have been implicated in diminished reproduction and contracting pronghorn numbers. A substantial die-off of pronghorns in western Texas in 2009 coincided with several years of extremely low fawn production. Among a handful of other factors, biologists discovered that antelope in the region were carrying extremely high loads of barber pole worms, a type of roundworm. Researchers also found antelope afflicted with abnormally high numbers of bloodworms, a parasite that ingests blood from the intestinal walls of its hosts. Pronghorn in the study area had six times more bloodworms, on average, than antelope sampled in the Texas panhandle.

External parasites known to infect pronghorns include several kinds of ticks and flying insects. These may be temporarily bothersome to the animals but are not believed to have detrimental effects on their health.

Pronghorn are resistant to some wildlife diseases but very susceptible to others. Brucellosis, a disease found in elk and bison, is of concern when it is communicated to domestic cattle. The disease causes pregnant cows to abort their calves. Although pronghorn mingle with bison and elk in Yellowstone National Park, one of the areas where brucellosis is present, they do not carry the disease.

A similar situation occurs with chronic wasting disease (CWD) and hair loss syndrome. CWD is found throughout many areas of the United States. Both diseases occur in deer in the West and are of concern to wildlife managers. Neither has been found in pronghorn.

However, pronghorn are very susceptible to bluetongue and epizootic hemorrhagic disease (EHD), two hemorrhagic diseases carried by biting midges. Several strains of these diseases cause massive internal bleeding in infected animals and are often fatal. The disease-carrying midges commonly breed in standing water, and pronghorn are bitten by the midges at water sources. Ironically, years of abundant rainfall that produce good forage also may increase the amount of standing water on pronghorn range and up the odds of an EHD or bluetongue outbreak. These diseases plague pronghorn in many areas. Significant die-offs due to hemorrhagic diseases have occurred in northeastern Montana. Outbreaks in Wyoming have caused the loss of thousands of animals. Hemorrhagic diseases tend to occur at lower elevations. Pronghorn inhabiting areas above 7,000 feet elevation are unlikely to be exposed to the diseases.

PRONGHORNS AND HUMANS

Pronghorns and American Indians

Pronghorn evolved on the North American prairies with a host of formidable predators. Long-limbed lions, fleet-footed hyenas, and cheetahs all roamed the grasslands of the continent eons ago. It is believed that antelope developed their keen eyesight and legendary speed as adaptations for eluding such predators.

In more recent history, pronghorn have been routinely hunted by humans. American Indians pursued pronghorn for many centuries prior to the arrival of Europeans. At Trappers Point, west of Pinedale, Wyoming, archaeologists have excavated a site where ancient peoples drove pronghorn into a sophisticated enclosure.

In prehistoric times, pronghorn shared habitat with fast, formidable predators. This is thought to be the evolutionary mechanism that led to their amazing speed and eyesight.
JACK BALLARD

The site sits near the Green River on a migratory route pronghorn have perhaps used for 10,000 years. Three layers of tools, projectiles, pronghorn remains, and charcoal were uncovered in the excavation. The lowest and oldest of these layers dates from approximately 6,000 to 8,000 years ago. Pronghorn still migrate along the route from wintering grounds around Pinedale to summer pastures in Grand Teton National Park.

Similar pronghorn harvest corrals have been discovered elsewhere. A construction of two stone walls consisting of some heavy rocks has been found in central Nevada. Pronghorn were apparently driven along the fences and ambushed at the opening between the two stone walls. The site is believed to have been used in the early 1000s. Hopi Indians successfully drove antelope onto flat-topped mesas, where a narrow bridge of land connected the mesa to the surrounding territory. Trapped on the mesa, pronghorn were killed by hunters or driven over the sheer sides of the landform, falling to their death. The Northern Paiute Indians inhabited the Great Basin region of western Nevada, southeast Oregon, and the eastern reaches of California. They hunted pronghorn in drives employing numerous hunters and assisted by small dogs.

Along with communal drives and trapping operations, American Indians used a wide variety of methods and weaponry to kill pronghorn. Historian George Bird Grinnell wrote extensively about the Cheyenne and Blackfeet cultures. He records an incident in which a Cheyenne acquaintance killed an antelope by hurling the most primitive of weapons, a stone, at the animal's head. He also noted that older Cheyenne youths hunted pronghorn fawns. The boys would form a line, with hunters spaced at regular intervals, and travel across the prairie in search of hiding antelope fawns and other game.

Early native peoples in America may have used spears, slings, and atlatls (a wooden handle used to throw darts or spears with surprising velocity) to take pronghorn. But the hunting implement most suitable and widely used for pronghorn hunting was the bow and arrow. It was very portable, had reasonable range in skilled hands, and could be shot accurately and with sufficient force to send a stone-tipped arrow into the vital organs of an antelope.

American Indians used archery equipment to hunt pronghorn in a variety of ways. Stone blinds have been found adjacent to regularly used pronghorn trails in California. Hunters used the piled stones for concealment while ambushing antelope. Pronghorn were also lured within bow-and-arrow range by a variety of methods appealing to their innate curiosity. Hunters from some tribes tied articles of clothing onto sticks that were waved above grass tall enough to conceal the archers. Antelope investigating the novel objects were shot when they came within range. Another quite common method involved hunters draping themselves with the skin of an antelope or wearing a headpiece crafted from the horns, skull, and hide of a buck. These concealments allowed a patient hunter to creep within bow-and-arrow range of his quarry.

Pronghorn were hunted by native peoples for their meat and hides. The skin of the pronghorn is thin compared to those of other ungulates such as deer, elk, and bison. While not as durable, antelope hides were probably easier for natives to preserve and desirable for certain types of clothing.

Other parts of the pronghorn were used for practical, decorative, and ceremonial purposes. Pronghorn bones were used as awls. Dried hooves were fashioned into necklaces, and the headdresses of high-ranking chiefs and medicine men in some tribes were adorned with antelope horns. Pronghorn also held important spiritual and representational powers for many tribes. Pictures of pronghorn were painted onto the shields of some tribes of the northern plains. The images were probably thought to protect the shield-bearer through the animal's uncanny ability to see predators. The Hopi and Zuni Indians utilized six points of direction. Animals were assigned to correspond with each; pronghorn were associated with the south.

Pronghorns and European Settlers

Spanish explorers in the early sixteenth century were probably the first Europeans to encounter pronghorn in what is now the United States. Like other early European explorers, the Spaniards were sometimes confused by this animal that had no counterpart in their native country. Is it a goat, a sheep, or some type of deer?

French explorers penetrated numerous historical pronghorn habitats from the 1500s to the 1700s. Their travels inland from the coast of California, up the Mississippi River, and across Canada would surely have brought them into contact with pronghorn.

Early European explorers encountered pronghorn in the Dakotas and elsewhere. These antelope roam the badlands of Theodore Roosevelt National Park in western North Dakota.
NPS/LAURA THOMAS

A party of French explorers reached Mandan Indian villages on the Missouri River after traveling southward from Canada in 1738. The leader of the party noted that there were many antelope in the area.

The Lewis and Clark Expedition first recorded pronghorn on September 5, 1804, in the vicinity of Niobrara, Kansas. Less than two weeks later, William Clark killed a pronghorn buck that he described in detail, noting the animal was more like an antelope or gazelle from Africa than any known sheep or goat. The journals of the expedition contain numerous references to antelope in their travels both to and from the Pacific Coast.

Sustained settlement of the West in the decades after the Civil War saw intense pressure placed on pronghorn herds for market hunting. Antelope were killed by the thousands. Butchers in Kansas bought pronghorn meat for as little as 2 or 3 cents per pound in 1873. In the era of rapid railroad construction, pronghorn frequently provided a significant portion of the workers' diet.

Harsh winters in the 1880s and 1890s took a toll on pronghorn numbers. The winter of 1886–87 was particularly severe, resulting in extreme losses of livestock on ranching operations in Montana, the Dakotas, and elsewhere. It was doubtlessly devastating to pronghorn as well. Not only the severities of winter worked against the animals; their movements were hindered by snowdrifts and an ever-expanding network of fences on the open range. Hunters and settlers took advantage of their vulnerabilities, sometimes killing them in astonishing numbers. One account from the Texas panhandle asserts that 1,500 pronghorn trapped against a fence were killed by area residents.

Antelope played several intriguing roles in Custer's infamous Battle of the Little Big Horn in 1876. Custer himself once kept a pronghorn for a pet. It is believed that Indians in the massive encampment he attacked included pronghorn among their primary sources of meat. Thomas Lafarge, leader of the Crow scouts employed by General Terry (Custer's superior officer), was thrown from his horse after being startled by a pronghorn. The scout's collarbone was broken in the fall. Some historians believe this may have spared Lafarge from the battle—and death.

In addition to market hunting, vast numbers of pronghorn were shot indiscriminately to eliminate their supposed competition with livestock and to protect agricultural crops. By the 1890s antelope were rapidly disappearing from the Western landscape. Indians on some reservations told agents they could no longer find pronghorn, which had previously been a somewhat reliable source of meat.

The downward spiral of pronghorn numbers in the United States toward the close of the nineteenth century and the first decades of the twentieth is comparable to that of most other North American ungulates. Arizona closed the state to pronghorn hunting in 1905; the state's pronghorn population was estimated at less than 1,000 animals in 1922.

Arizona's history with pronghorn was similar to that of other states. The US Biological Survey in 1908 estimated pronghorn numbers in the United States and Canada at 20,000. The number had shrunk to 15,000 by 1915. A nationwide hunting ban prompted a slow but steady recovery in antelope numbers by the 1920s. By the 1950s populations had rebounded sufficiently to allow limited hunting.

Pronghorns and Us

By the 1980s, pronghorn had increased to abundance over much of their historic range. Numbers were estimated at 1 million animals in North America in 1984, the highest number since the mass reductions of the previous century. However, populations began a slow slide thereafter. At the close of the second millennium in 2000, population estimates included 765,200 pronghorn in the United States, 32,000 in Canada, and 1,200 in Mexico, for a continent-wide population of just under 800,000.

Antelope populations were probably susceptible to dramatic local and regional fluctuations prior to European settlement of North America. Their relatively high vulnerability to winter mortality and rapid reproduction rates set the stage for notable population swings over fairly short periods. However, several human-caused influences are driving these population fluctuations today.

The impact of fences on pronghorn is sometimes considerable. One problem has to do with "exclusionary fences," fencing that forms an essentially impassable barrier to wildlife. Some fencing designs are exclusionary to some species of wildlife but can be passed by others.

Pronghorn are perhaps the species most highly impacted by exclusionary fences in the West. In ranchers' vernacular, "sheep fence" commonly refers to a type of fencing that includes woven wire on the bottom with two or three strands of barbwire on the top. This fence design is very effective for keeping sheep in a pasture. Deer and elk readily jump over fences; pronghorn typically do not. In nearly fifty years of observing wildlife, I have seen pronghorn jump a fence on only two occasions. Because they're

A moratorium on hunting and the development of parks and refuges as protected areas for wildlife helped pronghorn numbers rebound from a nationwide low around 1915. This doe was photographed in a national wildlife refuge in Wyoming.
USFWS/TOM KOERNER

reluctant to jump barriers, the woven wire on the bottom of a sheep fence usually proves exclusionary to pronghorn.

Fences can trap antelope on roads, making them susceptible to vehicle collisions. Fences may also slow them down when fleeing predators. Due to their superior speed, pronghorn aren't normally targeted as prey by wolves. But wolves are sometimes successful in bringing down antelope stuck against fencelines.

Impediments to movement across habitat are an even larger problem. In severe winters, pronghorn in northeastern Montana may travel southward 100 miles or more to avoid extreme cold and deep snow. Fences may hinder or completely halt their progress.

There are myriad solutions to pronghorn problems with fences. Some are simple and cost-free. Others are more complex and costly. Simply leaving gates open when livestock isn't on the range provides an avenue of passage. Removing unused fencing (especially along highways) eases stress and difficulty for antelope. More challenging projects involve replacing or modifying existing fence. In some states, landowners can receive information, assistance with design, and sometimes cost-sharing for fence improvement projects.

Fences and roads are among the human-erected barriers pronghorn must navigate on seasonal migrations or significant relocations prompted by severe winters. Pronghorn are struck by vehicles at all times of the year, but in some locations these collisions are most prevalent in winter.

However, trains may be the most dramatic human instruments of antelope carnage during severe winters. Pronghorn tend to congregate on railroad tracks to escape deep snows. They may also be attracted to grain spilled from railcars or be trapped on rail corridors by fences that may provide a way in but no easy way out.

Migrating pronghorn confront a fence in Idaho. Fences are substantial impediments to antelope movement across their range and may contribute significantly to winter mortality.
JACK BALLARD

Refuges on public lands continue to be instrumental in pronghorn conservation. These areas, such as Wind Cave National Park in South Dakota, the location of this image, provide the species a buffer against habitat destruction.
NPS

When a train comes roaring through, the results can be devastating. A 2003 train collision claimed forty-one pronghorn near Green River, Wyoming. In 2017 twenty-three antelope were killed by a train near Sage Junction, also in Wyoming. A train wiped out 270 pronghorn in a single collision in northeast Montana during a severe winter in 2011. Pronghorn congregated on open highways also fall victim to human transportation, at times in large numbers. Large trucks in southern Wyoming have killed as many as twenty pronghorn in a single collision.

Deep snow makes open highways attractive to antelope during severe winters. Fencing that keeps the animals off the road but provides movement corridors via overpasses is one way to reduce collisions. Motorist awareness and reduced speeds (especially at night) are others. Trains and other modes of transportation can cause pronghorn losses at any time of the year; during difficult winters they can be devastating.

Livestock on pronghorn range are thought to be the primary reservoirs of EHD and bluetongue, diseases capable of decimating local pronghorn herds under certain conditions. Habitat alteration caused by livestock grazing that converts shrub-grasslands to primarily shrublands renders them uninhabitable to pronghorn and is thought to be a major factor in population declines in some areas. Although antelope are thriving over much of their historic range, populations in Arizona and New Mexico have declined. Drought, disease, and habitat loss are thought to be the primary culprits.

Along with disease and habitat conversion, outright loss of habitat due to subdivisions, gas and oil development on private and public lands, and agriculture are also chewing into prime pronghorn range. Antelope benefit from farming, such as the cultivation of alfalfa for hay and the planting of small grains (wheat, barley, etc.) at certain times of year. These crops may provide good forage for pronghorn in spring and summer, but they offer little in the way of winter nutrition. Increased human activity around gas and oil development sites is known to push pronghorn from important habitat resources (such as good birthing areas) in some places. Extended drought, thought to be a product of climate change, also takes a toll on pronghorn and their habitat. Pronghorn currently are thriving over much of their historic range, but populations in some areas are stressed by an array of environmental factors.

Black bears are curious, good climbers that live in a wide variety of habitats.
ISTOCK.COM/EEI_TONY

CHAPTER 9
BLACK BEARS

The neighborhood was astir. Telephones rang, engines turned, and kids scrambled from their houses toward the vehicles. In less time than it takes to summon a take-out pizza, a cavalcade motored down the dusty gravel road, intent on entertainment, Montana-style.

The occasion was not a party or something as sensational as a shooting. A black bear sow and two cubs had wandered into the foothills ranching community of my childhood. When approached by a neighbor's pickup truck, the bruins scrambled up a towering cottonwood tree overshadowing an abandoned homestead.

A youth of 6 or 7 years, I peered eagerly out the window as we turned from the county road toward the sagging cabin and a gathering group of onlookers. High in the branches, partially obscured by the tree's waxy green leaves, I spied a large black form and two smaller ones. The sow was easier to see, but my gaze focused more acutely on the cubs. They were fuzzy and cute. One had a small patch of white on its chest.

A decade would pass before I sighted another black bear, this one high in the Bridger Mountains. Hiking with two brothers and friends, we paused to rest on a rocky outcropping above a clearing that we'd just passed through. A glance down our back trail set my senses on alert. An immense, coal-black bear with a shining coat came lumbering out of pines and into the meadow. Even to my untrained eye the bear was huge. Visions of snarling bears on the covers of sporting magazines plagued my imagination. Suddenly the entire hiking party was aflame with energy. We covered the next mile in record time.

Three decades later, black bear sightings have become a more common part of my outdoor experience. As I write this, I can see a band of open slopes dotted with aspen trees along the eastern face of the Beartooth Mountains. Should I train my spotting scope on the mountainside, I might spot a black bear, for I've seen them there in my ramblings. Like most other regions of the country, the number of *Ursus americanus* occupying Montana has risen substantially in the past few decades.

Years of observation and study have changed the vision of black bears I held as a youth. Those open-mouthed bruins on the magazine covers, I've come to realize, were trained grizzlies and black bears that a handler induced to snarl while a photographer snapped a photo. With black bears in particular, these portrayals do not reflect reality. They are normally shy beasts and rarely aggressive—animals deserving our respect, not fear.

As black bear numbers in North America continue to rise and their range expands, more and more people will have the opportunity to observe them firsthand. I write this chapter with the desire it will help the reader better understand and appreciate these intriguing creatures.

Names and Visual Description

The "black bear" is the name given to the most widespread and common species of bear in North America. However, this name is somewhat misleading. Not all black bears are black. In the northwestern United States, a significant percentage of black bears are brownish or reddish-brown in color. "Cinnamon bear" is a term sometimes used to describe black bears with coats exhibiting brownish or reddish hues. Elsewhere, black bears may sport coats intermixed with black and lighter hairs, giving them a bluish appearance. Black bears in some areas may also rarely be cream-colored, or have small to quite large patches of white hair on their chests. The black bear's scientific name, *Ursus americanus,* is derived from *ursus,* the Latin word for "bear" and *americanus,* a term that refers to the species' home continent. In some respects, adopting the English version of the black bear's scientific name as "American bear" might help dispel notions about the animal's color based on its common name.

However, if you consider the origin of the species' moniker, it's easy to understand why they became known as black bears. When Europeans began colonizing North America, their first explorations and settlements were in the eastern part of the country. At that time, black bears were abundant in the eastern forests. Black bears in the eastern United States are normally black in color and rarely exhibit the variable hues noted above. Thus, the term "black bear" was very appropriate for the species as encountered by colonists in the east.

Compared to more streamlined predators such as wolves, foxes, mountain lions, and bobcats, black bears appear bulky and slow, although they are deceptively fast and agile.

Black bears were named for their coat color as most commonly seen in the eastern United States, but not all black bears are black.
© ISTOCK.COM/ SEVENTHDAYPHOTOGRAPHY

Viewed from the side, black bears have a large, rounded rump. The highest part of the rump on a black bear may be taller than the point of its front shoulders. Like other bears, the skull of the black bear is broad but tapers quickly in the region of its eyes to a narrow jaw and nose. The side profile of a black bear's face is straight or slightly convex (rounded outward). Animals with darker coats sometimes have tan hair on their snouts that contrasts with their black noses. Bears with black coats may also display small patches of tannish hair on the forehead near the eyes.

Black bears have fairly large claws that, unlike the claws of a cat, cannot be retracted into their toes. The claws of a black bear are often visible at close range, but may not be readily observed at a distance. A very short, stubby tail is found on the rump, but has no readily known purpose.

The taste and texture of bear meat has been historically likened to that of pork. Perhaps that is why male black bears are known as "boars" and females are called "sows." Baby black bears are referred to as "cubs."

Related Species in North America

Black bears share the North American continent with two other species of bears: polar bears and grizzly bears. Polar bears, *Ursus maritimus,* are creatures of the far north, ranging across the frozen regions of Alaska, Canada, and the Arctic islands. In Alaska, the range of black bears does not extend as far north as the polar bear's habitat. Polar bears are white or nearly white in color, and much larger on average than black bears, making it unlikely that any competent observer could confuse the two species.

Polar bears are also much different from black bears in their foraging habits and diet. While black bears are omnivorous, eating grass, nuts, insects, berries, eggs, and nearly anything else that has nutritional value, polar bears are carnivores. The diet of the great bears of the north consists primarily of seal. Polar bears have longer necks than black bears so that they can more efficiently thrust their heads into holes in the ice to capture seals.

The grizzly bear, *Ursus arctos,* is the black bear's other relative in North America. Black bears inhabit much of the same range as the grizzly, making it probable the two species might be encountered in proximity in the northern Rocky Mountains of the contiguous United States, over much of Alaska, and in numerous areas of Canada. Because black bears and grizzly bears share many characteristics, biologists often remind recreationists and wildlife watchers to avoid using any single characteristic to distinguish between the two species. Instead, laypeople are advised to focus on several identifying features to determine if an animal is a black bear or a grizzly bear.

Color variations may be helpful in some situations, but color is not a reliable way to tell the two species apart. A bear that is uniformly jet-black in color is probably a black bear. However, grizzly bears can have coats that are a dark, dullish brown color, making them appear black in certain lighting conditions. Just because a bear is blonde or brown doesn't make it a grizzly. As noted previously, black bears may have coats that are similarly colored.

Although similar in size to a black bear, the dished face, prominent hump, short ears, and grizzled appearance identify this young bear as a grizzly.
JACK BALLARD

Adult grizzly bears are substantially larger on average than adult black bears. However, many full-grown black bears are just as big as immature grizzly bears. Where their ranges overlap, big black bear males may be as large as smaller grizzly bear females. Thus, although a 600-pound bear is almost undoubtedly a grizzly, variations of mass in the two species in relation to age and gender make it very difficult to separate the two North American bears based upon size.

Beyond color and size, several other traits can be analyzed to distinguish a black bear from a grizzly. First of all, in contrast to the straight or convex profile of the black bear's head, the head of a grizzly looks slightly concave or dished. Additionally, a grizzly bear's claws are very long, light-colored, and readily observable compared to the shorter, dark claws of a black bear. Grizzly bears usually exhibit a noticeable hump on their front shoulders, which is absent in black bears. However, depending on the posture of the bear, grizzlies may appear to lack the shoulder hump and a black bear's shoulder may seem humped. In most cases, the ears of a black bear appear longer in relation to its head and body than those of a grizzly, although the season and the length of an animal's coat may confound such an evaluation.

Although voracious consumers of nuts, berries, and other plant matter, grizzly bears are more likely to consume large prey than black bears. Grizzlies don't often target healthy animals in their predation attempts, but will readily kill weak or injured animals as large as caribou, elk, or moose, and are capable of bringing down much bigger animals than all but the largest black bears.

Subspecies

Biological literature commonly reports sixteen different subspecies of black bears in North America. However, many contemporary bear experts question whether there is enough genetic, behavioral, or morphological variation among the historically identified subspecies to warrant such classification. In some cases, subspecies were identified on the basis of dominant hair color. Other subspecies were designated in relation to populations of black bears inhabiting certain regions that might have slightly different physical characteristics, such as bigger teeth or larger average body size, than bears observed in other areas. However, the extent to which such variation is caused by local factors, such as nutrition, versus distinct genetic lineage is not well known. Some research on black bears suggests that at least in terms of genetics, just a few subspecies inhabit the continent, certainly not sixteen.

Interestingly, the confusion surrounding how to classify bears with different sizes and color schemes from various parts of the continent is not a recent problem. On May 31, 1806, while camped with the Nez Perce in Idaho, Lewis and Clark appealed to the natives to help them distinguish a number of bear hides they had accumulated. The Nez Perce separated the "Hoh-host" (grizzly bear) hides from the skins of the "Yack-kah" (black bear). They went on to explain to members of the expedition that grizzly bears have long claws and are much more ferocious than black bears. Separately in their journals, though apparently after consultation, Lewis and Clark concluded that the predominantly black-haired black bears they encountered along the Pacific Coast were the same species as the black bear or "common bear" that they were familiar with in the eastern part of the country. They believed that the reddish or cinnamon-colored black bears they encountered in the interior Rocky Mountains of Idaho and Montana were a separate species, distinct from both grizzly bears and the black-colored bears found along the Pacific and Atlantic Coasts.

Rather than catalog sixteen debatable subspecies, it seems more helpful to point out trends in coat colors among black bears and highlight several unique populations. A comprehensive study identifying the location and coloration of more than 40,000 black bears in the United States and Canada revealed several definite trends. In the eastern United States and Canada, the vast majority of black bears are black, with other color phases increasing as one moves westward toward the Great Lakes region. In western Ontario and Minnesota, approximately 5 to 10 percent of black bears exhibit non-black coloration. Black bears in the northern Rocky Mountain regions of Montana, Idaho, and Wyoming show the greatest diversity in color. More than 80 percent of individuals in local populations may have coat colors other than black. Biologists in Washington's North Cascades National Park found that of 1,586 bears observed, more than 30 percent had fur that ranged from nearly white to dark brown. In the Rockies, the percentage of bears with black coats increases from north to south and from east to west. Many more bears living in the mountains near the Pacific Coast and in the southern Rockies have black coats.

Lewis and Clark mistakenly identified the brown and reddish black bears of the central Rocky Mountains as a distinct species from black or grizzly bears.
© ISTOCK.COM/HTRNR

Although variations in coat color are a fascinating element of black bear biology, they generally play a minor role in subspecies identification. However, one subspecies of black bear, the Kermode bear or spirit bear *(Ursus americanus kermodei),* contains individuals that display a very unique coloration. Kermode bears inhabit dense rain forests along the British Columbian coast and nearby islands. The term "spirit bear" stems from the fact that a percentage of these black bears are colored exactly the opposite—they are white, but not albinos. The white fur represents a genetic mutation similar to that found in red-haired humans. A recessive trait, white fur in bears occurs when two adults (who may both be black) transfer the recessive gene to their offspring. Where the Kermode bears range on the mainland of British Columbia, only about 1 to 2.5

percent of the bears are white. That percentage increases dramatically on some of the islands inhabited by these unique black bears. On Gribbell Island, one of many islands located near the mainland, white-colored bears represent some 30 percent of the population.

Other subspecies of the black bear are not identified on the basis of such dramatic physical features as the Kermode bear. Instead, they're usually distinguished by geographic isolation from other populations of black bears. The Mexican black bear *(Ursus americanus eremicus)* is found only in western Texas and northern Mexico. It is currently listed as a threatened species by the state of Texas. Potential bear habitat also exists on the eastern side of Texas, which may one day be occupied by the Louisiana black bear *(Ursus americanus luteolus),* which is presently found in Louisiana and southern Mississippi. Not far to the east, the Florida black bear *(Ursus americanus floridanus)* ranges across Florida, southern Georgia, and portions of Alabama. Many Florida black bears display a patch of white hair on their chests. Both the Louisiana and Florida black bear subspecies are currently listed as threatened under the Endangered Species Act. Their status as subspecies is due to their geographic isolation and limited habitat. The extent to which their genetic makeup differs from northern populations of black bears has not been extensively researched.

In Alaska, the Haida Gwaii black bear or Queen Charlotte black bear *(Ursus americanus carlottae)* is a subspecies found on the Haida Gwaii or Queen Charlotte Islands near the coastline of British Columbia. These bears tend to have notably large skulls and molars. Genetic studies of the Haida Gwaii bears have attempted to determine the extent to which this subspecies might have been isolated from other black bear populations during prehistoric periods of glaciation. At least one of these studies provides some evidence of a coastal lineage of black bears in western North America that differs from bears found on the mainland.

Will the widely publicized designation of sixteen subspecies of black bears persist in the future? Intense study and genetic analysis of creatures such as the grizzly bear and gray wolf have sharply reduced the number of subspecies in relation to those theorized in earlier times. It is likely that further genetic research and biological study of the black bear will reduce the sixteen to less than a half-dozen.

Physical Characteristics

Black bears show a remarkable variation in size. Due to differences in available nutrition and the energy bears must use to obtain it, black bears in one part of the continent might be considerably bigger or smaller than those found elsewhere. Within specific populations, however, mature males are notable heavier than females on average. Research studies in Idaho and Pennsylvania have found males to be nearly twice as large as females. Some of the size variation between the sexes is due to maturational patterns. While females normally obtain maximum weight by the time they are 4 years old, males may continue to grow to age 8 or beyond. A New York study of black bears revealed that the average 3-year-old male weighed as much or more than the typical 8-year-old female. In addition to its greater weight, the skull of a black bear boar is about 10 percent larger than the head of a female of similar age.

The weight of a black bear may fluctuate by 30 percent or more depending on the season. Bears are heaviest just prior to entering hibernation and lightest when they emerge from their dens in the spring. Bears in the eastern part of the contiguous United States tend to be larger than those found in the West. Northern bears obtain weights that are usually a bit higher than those found in more southern climates. However, the tendency of north-dwelling members of a particular species to be larger than their southern counterparts (Bergmann's Rule) is not as pronounced in black bears as many other species, including their grizzly bear cousins. Thus, determining an average weight for the two sexes of black bears that is consistent across the continent is very difficult. Males probably range from around 130 to 550 pounds at mature weight in various parts of the country. Corresponding females reach weights of about 90 to 360 pounds.

How large can black bears grow in the wild? Mammoth specimens have been recorded in a variety of locations. Numerous boars killed by hunters or vehicles in the fall have topped the scales at 800 pounds and beyond. In December 2011, an 829-pound male was shot in New Jersey. An 879-pound boar was taken by a hunter in Pennsylvania in 2010. The same bear weighed 700 pounds when captured by biologists in New Jersey in June 2009. In 2001, a black bear was struck by a vehicle and killed near Winnipeg, Canada. The huge animal depressed the scale to 856 pounds. Biologists estimated its live weight at nearly 900 pounds.

Like weight, other physical dimensions of black bears are highly variable. The animals range from about 4 feet to 6.5 feet in length from nose to tail. Adult bears may stand from 26 to 42 inches at the front shoulder. The rear paws of a black bear are longer than its front feet and may measure from around 5.5 inches to 9 inches. A black bear's rear paw prints look something like the barefoot track of a human with noticeable claw marks in front of the toes. The bear's front paws are broader and more squarely shaped than the rear.

RANGE AND HABITAT

Historic Range

Black bears may occasionally roam across open areas where trees are absent or limited, but are primarily associated with forests. They're equally at home in the deciduous woodlands of eastern North America and in the evergreen timberlands found in the Rocky Mountains and coastal regions of the West. Black bears may also inhabit the more arid scrub forests and shrublands of the Southwest. But rarely are they year-round residents of regions lacking some type of forest cover.

Prior to European settlement, much more of North America was forested or contained significant patches of timber and shrubland. Exceptions included the far north, in the tundra regions of Alaska and northern Canada. Desert areas in the Southwest,

Black bears are found in Alaska as well as the contiguous United States. This bear is standing in Alaska's Russian River.
© ISTOCK.COM/SORINCOLAC

including most of Nevada and portions of California, Arizona, and Utah, were also largely devoid of trees. Significant forested regions were also absent in Baja California and southern Mexico. But otherwise, varying levels of tree cover were present across the continent.

Highly adaptable and omnivorous, black bears were historically able to survive nearly any place that had timber, making them residents of almost all of North America. Except for the desert Southwest, the bruins inhabited virtually all of what is now the contiguous United States. Their clawed footprints scratched the soil of the entirety of mainland Canada south of the Arctic Circle. They also inhabited essentially all of Alaska except for the arctic regions. Black bears ranged well into the northern reaches of Mexico, primarily in the mountains. The animals were also found on most islands along the Pacific Coast capable of supporting bear populations. Black bears probably colonized various islands by swimming from the mainland or perhaps by crossing ice bridges during periods of glaciation.

Settlement of North America by Europeans occurred rapidly in the 200-year period from the beginning of the 1700s to the early 1900s. Several trends associated with this settlement greatly reduced black bear numbers and range. First of all, bears were actively hunted for their meat, hides, and fat. The fat was rendered into bear grease, which was sometimes used as shortening for cooking, as leather dressing, in cosmetics, and for other purposes.

However, the destruction and elimination of black bear habitat probably exerted more negative pressure on bear numbers than hunting. Logging cleared vast tracts of forest, converting it into treeless farmlands inhospitable to the timber-loving bruins. Black bears, like other predators, were also actively persecuted with traps and poisons ro remove their perceived threat to humans and livestock. On the plains of the Midwest, where black bears were associated with treed areas along major river corridors and other riparian areas, cutting timber for homesteads degraded their habitat and also brought them into association with humans happy to kill them for food or to simply eliminate the possibility that a black bear might dine on a sheep or raid a hen house for eggs. In the contiguous United States, hunting, persecution, and habitat loss extirpated black bears from most of the southern and central portions of the country. They persisted in remote, timbered areas of the Northeast, upper Midwest, and Rocky Mountains, primarily in places unsettled or avoided by humans.

Current Range

Clearing forested lands for timber and agricultural use, along with unregulated hunting, were the primary culprits in black bear decline. Nationwide, black bear numbers probably hit their lowest levels between the 1920s and the 1950s. During this time, however, societal changes slowly occurred that made it possible for bear numbers to increase and populations to reclaim segments of habitat from which they'd been eliminated. Hunting seasons were enacted in most states that protected bears from unregulated and year-round killing. North Carolina, for example, enacted its first bear-hunting season in 1927. Over time, this season became restrictive to maintain bear populations. In 1927 the season spanned two-and-a-half months and had no limit on the number of bears a hunter could kill. In 1947, a yearly bag limit of two bears per hunter was enacted. The limit was reduced to one bear in 1971. Arizona instituted a bear-hunting season in 1927, which converted to year-round hunting throughout much of the 1940s, an era in which agricultural interests believed the only good bear was a dead bear. Restrictive seasons were re-established in 1954, leading to a gradual increase in the state's bear population.

Along with protections from unregulated hunting, black bears began to benefit from changing land use practices during the twentieth century. In the East, in places such as New York's Adirondack Mountains, designation of land as state or national parks protected bears from hunting and preserved their forested habitat. Numerous areas where farmers cleared and attempted to raise crops were abandoned due to soils that were too rocky or infertile to sustain grains or vegetables. Mountainous areas across the country, heavily logged for large, old-growth timber, began the process of reforestation. Fast-growing deciduous trees and shrubs are often the first species to recolonize cleared timberlands, resulting in dense undergrowth that creates fine habitat for black bears and providing them with the fruit, nuts, and berries that make up a large portion of their diet.

Black bears now roam throughout most of their historic range in Canada, except for the expansive farmlands of southern Saskatchewan, Manitoba, and Alberta. In 1937, black bears were extirpated from Prince Edward Island and have not been reestablished. They range across most of the forested regions of Alaska, but are absent on the Seward Peninsula, in the Yukon-Kuskokwim delta, and north of the Brooks Range. They're abundant on many of the islands of southeastern Alaska, but are absent on many of the large islands that are occupied by grizzly bears.

In the contiguous United States, the largest segments of habitat harboring black bears occur in the northern portion of the country and extend along forested mountain ranges to the south. Elsewhere, bears occur in fragmented and isolated pockets of habitat. In the northeast, black bears are abundant in Maine and are found as far south as Virginia and West Virginia. Bears are most abundant in the Appalachian Mountains, where their range extends as far south as the northern border of Georgia. More isolated populations of bears are found along the coastal regions of southern Virginia and

Small populations of black bears are found in the southwestern United States. This bear was photographed in New Mexico.
© ISTOCK.COM/JJMILLER11

North and South Carolina. They also survive in rural, forested tracts in varying numbers in Florida, Georgia, Mississippi, Alabama, Louisiana, and eastern Oklahoma. The Ozark Mountains of Arkansas and southern Missouri represent the largest intact area of currently occupied black bear habitat in the South.

The dense, secluded forests in the Great Lakes region were an important refuge for black bears prior to the enactment of hunting seasons and the era of wildlife conservation. Today, bears are plentiful in the timberlands of the northern reaches of Minnesota, Wisconsin, Michigan, and the entire Upper Peninsula of Michigan. Farther west, their primary range is found along the Rocky Mountains from the Canadian border southward through Montana, Idaho, western Oregon, Wyoming, Utah, and Colorado. They also occupy the large expanses of forest in the coastal mountains of western Washington, Oregon, and California. Black bears inhabit the Sierra Nevada mountains of central and north-central California. More isolated, sometimes very small populations are located in various regions of New Mexico, Arizona, and western Texas.

Due to the large ranges they inhabit, reliable estimates of black bear populations in North America are difficult to obtain. Various sources differ substantially in their assessments of how many bears live on the continent. Best estimates indicate some 100,000 to 200,000 black bears inhabit Alaska. The Canadian population includes another 320,000 to 400,000 animals. Approximately 285,000 to 350,000 bears track the forests of the contiguous United States. It is not known for sure how many black bears occupied North America prior to European settlement, but some experts believe the current population is nearly equal to presettlement numbers.

Black Bear Habitat

Black bears are avid consumers of plant matter, much of it from trees and shrubs in the form of fruit, nuts, and berries. Some black bears also find suitable habitat in swamps or desert scrub. The small population inhabiting western Texas is one example of black bears existing among scrub vegetation in an arid climate. Swamp-dwelling black bears occur in the South and boggy areas of the north, including a population in the sprawling Okefenokee Swamp that covers portions of Florida and Georgia.

Depending on the location, the forested habitats with which the black bear is most strongly associated may be quite different. In Arizona, for example, black bears are found among several different types of forest including pinyon-juniper woodland, oak woodland, pine and mixed conifer forest, and chaparral (stands of woody, drought-tolerant, evergreen shrubs). These habitats contrast markedly with the moist, deciduous forests of the Great Lakes region or the rain forests along the Pacific Coast, where black bears make their homes in very different surroundings.

Bears may exist in many types of woodlands, but the best black bear habitat offers the creatures both a buffer from human habitation and access to a variety of nutritious foods. Bears in northern climates hibernate for extended periods of time during the winter. Hibernation requires the animal to gain substantial fat reserves in the fall to provide the energy needed to survive winter. Deciduous forests containing trees

that produce mast (nuts or berries) represent excellent habitat for black bears. The oils found in acorns that fall from oak trees, for example, allow bears to quickly gain fat reserves when the nut crops become available in autumn. Although oak trees are absent from the northern Rocky Mountains, coniferous forests are often interspersed with fruit-bearing shrubs such as huckleberries, chokecherries, and raspberries. Regions containing berries or other fall-ripening fruits represent superior habitat to forested areas lacking such richly nutritious food sources.

FORAGE AND NUTRITIONAL REQUIREMENTS

Basic Food Sources and Digestive Biology

Technically classified as carnivores, black bears have strong, stocky bodies more suited to overturning rocks, swimming, or tearing apart rotting logs than pursuing prey. Wild canine and feline predators such as wolves, red foxes, mountain lions, and lynx feed almost exclusively on the meat of the prey. Black bears, by contrast, often receive 90 percent of their annual nutrition from plant matter.

Although black bears tend toward a vegetarian diet, their digestive system is not as specialized as that of an elk or whitetail deer when it comes to breaking down plant material. The ungulates have very long digestive tracts in which several compartments with specialized bacteria and functions aid the digestion of plant material. The digestive tract of a black bear is longer than that of a wolf or mountain lion, but shorter than that of ungulates. This makes it possible for bears to gain substantial nutrition from plants, not just meat. But they are unable to capably digest the woody twigs of shrubs and trees, or the mature grasses commonly consumed by hoofed mammals.

Black bears receive most of their nutrition from plant matter. This bear is eating berries and foliage.
JACK BALLARD

Thus, black bears are quite picky about the types of vegetation they eat and must ingest large amounts of plant matter to acquire sufficient energy and nutrients.

Because they inhabit such a broad geographic range in North America, and occupy so many different types of woodlands, scrub forests, and swamps, summarizing the diet of black bears is a nearly impossible task. However, it is possible to characterize their food sources in general terms. Certain types of foods are consumed by black bears nearly everywhere they're available, be it Denali National Park in Alaska or Great Smoky Mountain National Park in Tennessee.

When it comes to plants, black bears usually target specific species at the period in the growth cycle when they are most tender and nutritious. Researchers in New York's Adirondack Park have concluded black bears consume more than thirty different types of plants in the park. Succulent shoots of grasses and sedges are eaten by bears. They also relish broad-leafed plants such as alfalfa, clover, and dandelions. Certain parts of plants, such as flowers and roots, are also eaten by black bears. In comparison to grizzly bears, however, whose massive claws and exceedingly powerful forelegs make them very adept at digging, black bears are less likely to expend considerable effort in unearthing roots, bulbs, and tubers. Other ground-growing food items for black bears include mushrooms and the newly emerging heads of some fern species.

Low-lying shrubs that produce berries or other edible seeds and nuts are important sources of nutrition for bears in a broad range of habitats. In the Rocky Mountains, in places such as Yellowstone, Grand Teton, and Glacier National Parks, these may include wild raspberries, huckleberries, and rose hips (the fruit from wild rose bushes). In the

Blueberries and rose hips are commonly eaten by black bears.
LISA BALLARD

Adirondacks or other locations in the Northeast, black bears feed on wild cherries, elderberries, blackberries, and other species. Nearly anywhere they're found, black bears have at least some access to fruit produced by low-growing shrubs.

Moving into even taller vegetation, black bears glean nutrition from many different types of trees. They happily consume many varieties of nuts, including the nuts found within the cones of some evergreen trees and deciduous species. Apples, plums, and other fruits, domestic or wild, are highly prized by black bears. Bears may also eat the fuzzy catkins of trees in the poplar family.

Black bears supplement the vegetarian diet with a wide array of other foods. They're large animals, but most of the living things they eat are quite small. Bears are known to eat a surprising range of worms and insects, including earthworms, ants, various grubs, grasshoppers, moths, caterpillars, beetle larvae, and even some species of bees and wasps. Insects are often caught by the black bear's long, sticky tongue. The nests of multiple bird species, from geese and ducks to forest-dwelling grouse, are raided for eggs or to catch newly hatched birds unable to escape. Nests in trees are sometimes raided, but most of the eggs and hatchlings taken by bears are from the clutches of ground-nesting birds. In the swamps of Florida and elsewhere in the deep South, bears may also raid alligator nests, sometimes confronting female alligators when they steal their booty. Black bears may also eat frogs, although their consumption of amphibians and reptiles is rare.

Some species of mammal are also preyed upon by black bears, depending upon the geographic region and habitat in which the bears live. The newborn young of hoofed animals, including mule and whitetail deer, elk, caribou, and moose, are sometimes eaten in significant numbers by black bears. In some locations, roaming bears happen upon the young creatures and kill them opportunistically. Researchers also believe black bears deliberately hunt young ungulates, such as elk calves, in areas where females are known to birth their young year after year. Black bears may also kill adult and subadult individuals, almost invariably targeting the injured or weak. Beavers, ground squirrels, mice, and voles may also be taken by black bears. Infrequently, bears may kill and consume smaller predators (often the young), such as bobcats, wolves, red foxes, and coyotes. Historical records also indicate that adult black bears (typically males) may kill and eat members of their own kind.

Fish is another notable source of nutrition for black bears in some places. Like grizzly bears, many populations of black bear on the Pacific Coast rely upon runs of spawning salmon for food. Inland bears may also learn to catch fish, most often preying on the spawning runs of species that use smaller streams for reproduction, such as trout. Black bears may also ambush other types of fish, especially those found in shallow water where the bruins

Black bears are capable fishers. On the Pacific Coast, fish are an important part of the diets of some bears.
© ISTOCK.COM/RONSAN4D

can easily catch them, including catfish, carp, and suckers. When berry and nut crops are sparse, some biologists have concluded, bears put more effort into fishing.

Forage Preferences by Season

The black bear's diet is perhaps the most flexible of any animal in North America. At any given time of the year, bears may have a dozen or more local food sources available to them. That said, black bears display strong seasonal preferences to various types of food.

In the springtime, black bears emerge from their dens lean and hungry. After enduring months of winter dormancy, it takes their digestive systems a couple of weeks to regain their full function. In most places, the end of hibernation coincides with the beginning of the annual growing season for trees and plants. Springtime forage for black bears thus includes the soft, new shoots of grass and sedges. They also seek broad-leafed plants that sprout early in the season, such as dandelions and skunk cabbage. Budding vegetation on certain trees, including quaking aspen catkins, offers another source of nutrition for bears in the spring.

While black bears are snoozing away in their dens during the winter, the conditions outside may challenge the survival of hoofed animals sharing the bears' habitat. Each winter, old or weakened ungulates such as deer, elk, moose, caribou, and bison succumb to starvation. If the winter is very long or includes extended periods of intense cold and deep, crusted snow, other segments of the ungulate population are also susceptible to winter kill. Deer enduring their first winter are more vulnerable than adult animals. Aggressive males may lose most of their fat reserves during the frenzied activity of the fall breeding season or be recovering from battle wounds, making it more difficult to survive a brutal winter. Tough winters that take a heavy toll on ungulate populations provide a bounty for bears emerging from hibernation. The bruins are able to scavenge the carcasses of winter-killed animals, giving them access to high-protein forage in large packages. Bears in some areas, such as Yellowstone National Park, dig small rodents like pocket gophers from their shallow burrows. They may also snack on insects and worms that become active in the spring, including night crawlers and earthworms.

As spring transitions to summer, bears encounter a broadening food base. Ungulates often birth their young in June. Black bears are able to add newborn deer and the offspring of other hoofed animals to their diet in many regions. Summer-flowering plants are consumed by bears that may eat the blossoms, stems, and roots. Fireweed, a broad-leafed plant with pinkish-purple flowers, grows abundantly in mountainous areas in the Northwest, especially after forest fires, as its name implies. Black bears eat fireweed and other flowering plants, including spring beauty and glacier lilies, and cow parsnip. Mushrooms may also become part of a bear's summertime diet.

Some black bears gain a surprising amount of nutrition from insects. Since most bugs are active and abundant during the summer, that's when bears are best able to key on them for food. One of the continent's smaller insect species, the ant, is actively hunted by the bears of the Great Lakes region and in other parts of the country. Bears don't normally dig ants from ground-dwelling colonies, but instead seek those living in rotted logs. They tear the logs apart and adeptly eat the insects in the pupal and larval stages of development, along with the worker ants that may be tending them. When berry and nut crops fail in locations such as northern Minnesota, ants become a very important food source for bears. A bear may not put on fat by eating ants, but these high-protein morsels allow them to maintain their body condition in the absence of other foods.

Perhaps the most important source of summertime nutrition for black bears is berries. Raspberries and other early ripening species become available in July in many locations. As the summer progresses, other fruit species mature, allowing bears to move from one berry to the next. The calorie-rich berries help bears develop their fat reserves for the winter. In turn, the seeds of the berries are distributed to new locations in the scat of the berry-munching bears. Researchers have concluded that some Minnesota black bears may eat more than 30,000 berries a year.

Berries and other fruits may persist as food options for bears in the fall. But in many parts of the country, nuts are the preferred menu item for bears wherever they're available. Hazelnuts are relished by bears. Black bears may travel substantial distances, 20 miles or more, to reach habitat niches flush with nuts. Sharp claws enable black bears to climb trees in search of nuts, giving them an advantage over ground-bound creatures that also eat mast. The cones of the whitebark pine tree are collected by squirrels in huge caches in the northern Rocky Mountains. Nut-bearing cones of other evergreen species are similarly horded by squirrels elsewhere in the country. Black bears often discover and raid the caches to eat the nuts from the cones. I once observed a black bear in Montana eating pine nuts from a squirrel cache. The enraged rodent would descend down the tree above the cache, chattering fiercely at the robber. It would drop to a branch just inches above the ears of the preoccupied bear. The bruin intermittently raised its head or lifted a paw toward the squirrel, sending it scampering back to the treetop. An amusing incident for the watching human, it wasn't nearly so appreciated by the upset squirrel.

ABILITIES AND BEHAVIOR

Physical Abilities

Black bears are large, shaggy animals that may be rolling in fat in autumn. To the untrained eye, they look neither swift nor athletic. However, black bears are surprisingly quick and very strong.

Over short distances, black bears can sprint to about 30 miles per hour, nearly as fast as a fleeing deer or roughly the same pace as a galloping horse. Their dense fur and compact bodies overheat rapidly, limiting the distance over which black bears can fully exert themselves. Nonetheless, they can vanish in a heartbeat when alarmed, or make an effective predatory chase on other mammals when given the opportunity. A

Black bears are excellent swimmers and will cross rivers and lakes in search of food.
LISA BALLARD

black bear can easily outrun the fleetest human. Thus, if confronted by a bear, it is futile to attempt flight. Instead, experts advise people to stand their ground and appear as imposing as possible, a subject we'll explore later in this chapter.

Along with their speed, bears are impressively strong. Researchers have observed young black bears easily overturn large, flat rocks weighing 350 pounds to unearth the insects underneath. While hiking in early summer in western Montana, I once happened upon a hillside where a black bear had been eating insects living under stones. The bear had flipped over a dozen or more rocks, each as large as a coffee table. It had also pried up several boulders that were nearly buried, stones that were about twice the diameter of a basketball. Black bears commonly use their powerful shoulders and forelegs to rip apart fallen logs to expose ants, grubs, and other insects. Their claws are shorter than those of a grizzly bear, but still very effective in demolition when coupled with their stout forelegs and paws.

Black bears are also very strong and efficient swimmers. Although they don't look like Olympians slicing artfully through the water, two physical characteristics help bears swim with ease and a surprising amount of grace. The same strength that powers their forelegs in turning over rocks and ripping logs apart allows them to propel their bulky bodies through water. Black bears are also quite buoyant, meaning they float rather than sink. Air trapped in their dense fur provides the buoyancy, as does body fat, which is less dense and provides more flotation than muscle. While canoeing one summer on a mountain stream in central Montana, I watched a young black bear splashing about in the shallow water at the river's edge, apparently enjoying the cool pool on a hot July afternoon. When it spotted the canoe, it swam effortlessly across the strong current, then scrambled up a towering Douglas fir tree along the bank, dripping enough water from its coat, it appeared, to fill a bathtub. Various sources report that black bears can swim 3 to 5 miles per hour and have been recorded swimming as far as 5 miles. While that distance is certainly exceptional, black bears are extremely comfortable in the water and will readily swim across rivers, to islands along the seacoast, or on freshwater lakes in search of food.

Can bears climb trees? A certain amount of confusion exists regarding this question, and such misconceptions sometimes factor into other erroneous beliefs. Some people think bears are unable to climb trees and that shinnying up the nearest trunk is a potential means of escape in a bear confrontation. While it's true that large grizzly bears are generally unwilling to climb trees, young grizzly bears sometimes do so.

But what about black bears? In fact, black bears are much more adept tree climbers than grizzlies. Young black bears are extremely agile in trees. Faced with danger, black bear cubs (and often their mothers) will scurry up a tree for safety. Large black bears probably use trees less often than smaller bears. Yet even robust adult males may climb a tree to break off branches bearing nuts or fruit, or to investigate a beehive in a hollow tree for honey. The tree-climbing prowess of black bears can be traced to their sharply pointed claws and dexterous paws. Their claws can dig firmly into the bark of a tree, while the sophisticated touch of their paws allows them to grasp branches somewhat like a human. Once up a tree, black bears do not turn and descend face first as some creatures do, but "back down" like a person would.

Black bears walk "plantigrade," a scientific way of stating that the entire foot has contact with the ground. Bears share this physiological feature with humans. Plantigrade locomotion allows a creature to maintain superb balance while moving and to traverse challenging terrain with ease. Due to their plantigrade rear feet and unique skeletal structure, black bears can stand on their hind legs for extended periods of time, unlike hoofed animals that can "rear up" on their hind legs but are unable to balance that way for more than a second or two. While moving in search of food, black bears often pause to stand on their hind feet. Biologists speculate the bears assume such a posture to give them a better view of their surroundings and perhaps to aid their sense of smell. In the presence of an unidentified danger, black bears will often stand on their hind feet and actively scan their surroundings to pinpoint the threat. A similar strategy may also be used when a bear detects potential prey.

The sense of smell is often touted as the black bear's most highly developed perceptual ability. In 1991, researchers from the North American Bear Center in Minnesota observed a black bear sow with twin cubs sniffing the air. Her nose led her on a remarkable journey spanning three days and covering 41 miles. Her trek ended in an area with a high density of hazelnut bushes, drooping with a bumper crop of nuts. Five weeks later the family returned to their home range, the mother shepherding two of the heaviest cubs the researchers had ever seen.

Specific tests of the smelling abilities of various animals are difficult to design and perform. However, biologists widely believe that the olfactory sensitivity of bears ranks among the greatest of any mammal in the world. Inside a black bear's nose is a very large nasal cavity enclosing a complex system of mucus membranes. The scent-detecting mucus membranes of a black bear are up to 100 times larger than those of

Sharp claws and strong legs make black bears very adept at climbing trees. They may shinny up a tree in search of food or to escape predators.
JACK BALLARD

a human. Some scientists theorize that a black bear's sensitivity to smell may be 1,000 times greater than that of the average person. Black bears use their exceptional smelling abilities to find food, but scent is also extremely important for detecting animals that might represent a threat, gathering information about other bears in their territory, and bringing boars and sows together for mating.

For decades, folklore pertaining to bears assumed that because their smelling abilities were so developed, their other senses were weak. Black bears are sometimes characterized as having poor vision and hearing. However, researchers have demonstrated that bears have a capacity for hearing and vision equal to or better than humans. One study found that black bears were very capable of discriminating between different colors. Their ability to distinguish color and their good close-up vision, along with their uncanny sense of smell, are now believed to be important to their foraging strategies. Observing the color and shape of berries on a bush, for example, may give bears important visual cues concerning their desirability as food items.

Black bears are sometimes characterized as having poor vision and hearing, but they see and hear as well or better than humans.
JACK BALLARD

Research concerning the hearing abilities of black bears is lacking, but our continent's most numerous bear probably hears as well as humans and may be capable of detecting pitches beyond the range of people. Naturalists and casual wildlife watchers have seen grizzly bears and black bears reacting to noises at ranges well beyond what would be expected of an animal with stunted hearing capability. Of the three species of bears in North America, black bears have the largest ears in relation to their body size. This may indicate that black bears have the most highly developed sense of hearing among the three.

Black bears may appear large and clumsy, but certain parts of their bodies are capable of precise movement. Their claws are attached to large paws, but can be used skillfully to find a crack in a hollow log with an insect colony inside, or to slide under the lid of a closed garbage can to pry it off. The long tongue and front teeth of a black bear are also very sensitive and adept. Bears can lick up ant larvae while ingesting few of the adult insects, or nip individual blackberries from a vine. Despite their bulk, black bears are capable of surprisingly refined tactile skills and also have a superb sense of balance.

Vocal and Visual Communication

Black bears have a wide range of vocal communications and body postures by which they signal their intentions. Along with scent-marking, these are the primary ways by which they communicate with their own kind and give verbal and visual signals that can be interpreted by knowledgeable humans.

The sounds made by black bears are not typically as loud as those commonly emitted by some other creatures, such as a bugling bull elk, a bellowing bison, or a honking flock of Canada geese. However, bears make several types of noises that indicate whether they're content or disturbed. In the den, newborn cubs may make a noise similar to a cat's purring. Cubs most commonly use this sound when they're nursing, but may also emit the motorlike hum when in close proximity to their mother and very content. A loud screaming sound, very similar to the cries of a terrified human child, is associated with a bear cub in distress. In rare instances, female black bears have investigated the sound of a crying child, evidently thinking it was a cub in distress.

Cubs may also seek to attain a sow's attention with a bawling noise, which may indicate they want food or may communicate displeasure with other aspects of their world. Sows respond to the vocalizations of cubs with their own noises, sometimes grunting to gain their

Cubs are often more vocal than adult black bears. This frightened youngster has climbed a tree and is bawling for its mother.
© ISTOCK.COM/DSSIMAGES

offsprings' attention, such as when they want the cubs to descend from a tree. Adult bears may greet one another by clicking their tongues or emitting a high-pitched, friendly grunt. Agitated black bears often blow air forcefully from their lungs in a woofing sound and may clack their teeth together. A frightened bear, such as one cornered by a dominant animal or one that has climbed a tree to avoid danger, may emit a moaning noise, indicating its fear.

Along with vocalizations, black bears communicate their mental states with body language. A bear standing on its hind legs is usually alert and may be looking for something or reacting to a sight or scent it has yet to identify. Upright ears and a fixed gaze also signal alertness. Ears laid flat on the head may indicate submission or potential aggression. Conflict between black bears usually occurs in relation to competition for mates or food. Black bears are normally solitary creatures, most frequently encountering one another during the mating season or at food-rich areas when nutritional resources are concentrated, such as during the spawning run of fish or on a hillside flush with berries. During these encounters, conflict is usually settled in relation to the dominance hierarchy or "pecking order" of bears in the area, with larger bears intimidating smaller ones. However, sows can act abnormally fierce when protecting food resources for themselves and their cubs, sometimes successfully repelling boars twice their size. During these encounters, complex behavioral cues, including foot stomping, jaw popping, and circling may be part of how a bear evaluates the threat posed by a rival.

Hibernation

It's commonly known that black bears hibernate during the winter. But when does hibernation begin, and what happens to bears as they snooze through the long, cold nights of winter in a den?

Preparation for hibernation begins long before a black bear excavates a hole in the earth or crawls into a hollow log for its winter slumber. During late summer and autumn, black bears enter a behavioral phase known as "hyperphagia." In people, hyperphagia is fancy way to say they're overeating and likely to become obese. Hyperphagia describes essentially the same process for black bears, but instead of resulting in an unhealthy condition, becoming fat is absolutely essential. A bear's metabolism slows dramatically during hibernation, but it still needs enough energy to sustain itself through the winter.

In the northernmost portion of their range, black bears may spend up to seven months of the year in hibernation. In the northern portions of the contiguous United States, they commonly pass four to five months in hibernation. Fat reserves gained during the hyperphagia period, during which bears gorge on nuts, berries, and other food sources, are essential to winter survival. Large black bears may add 150 pounds of fat to their frames before denning for the winter. Black bears normally lose 15 to 25 percent of their body weight during hibernation, necessitating a considerable increase in weight before winter. Nursing females may lose even more body mass, sometimes emerging from the den 30 to 40 percent lighter than when hibernation began.

The hibernation of black bears is different from that of other hibernating animals, such as marmots. While the body temperatures of rodents drop drastically during hibernation (sometimes more than 60 degrees F), the temperature reductions in bears are quite modest (5 to 10 degrees F). Rodents also awaken occasionally during hibernation to eat and pass body waste. Bears may go without expelling waste for months. Their urine is recycled and their digestive functions come to a halt. While rodents are incapable of arousing to perform coordinated physical functions during hibernation, bears can "wake up" quite quickly.

Black bears are often portrayed as hibernating in caves, but large underground caverns are not used as dens. Bears instead seek out smaller quarters. They may hibernate in crevices between rock slabs or in holes created by overhanging shelves of stone. More frequently they excavate an abandoned badger hole or coyote den, or simply dig a hole of their own. Black bear dens excavated in soil generally consist of a short shaft, just large enough to allow the bear's body to pass, ending at a slightly larger "room" with just enough space for the bear to turn its body. Hibernating bears may also use hollow logs as dens, and smaller bruins are fond of dens located in tree cavities located 10 feet or more above the ground. These dens protect the young bears from predation. Both wolf packs and larger bears are known to prey upon denning black bears.

With all the effort it takes to locate or dig a den, it seems bears would return to the same winter resting spot year after year. Such is not the case. Black bears seldom reuse a den, although some dens may be used for years by different bears. I personally observed a den in Montana utilized by various bears over a ten-year period. While it's possible that a few of the dennings were by the same bear, variations in track size indicated multiple animals.

Some people believe that black bears hibernate in caves, but they're more likely to dig a hole or a den under logs.
USFWS/KAREN LAUBENSTEIN

Some bears don't hibernate in a den at all, but make a nest of grass, leaves, or other plant material and sleep above ground. Scientists believe the plant matter in the nest keeps the bear's body above moisture that might collect on the ground. Black bears also sometimes opt for more sophisticated dens. They're known to sleep in crawlspaces under rural cabins, or to slip into the crumbling foundations of abandoned buildings. In western Montana, a sizeable black bear once invaded a lakeside cabin, ransacking the interior. When the owners visited their retreat on New Year's Day, they thought it had been burglarized, but noticed the only thing missing was bedding. Imagine their surprise when they found the bear snoozing amongst their pillows in the crawlspace under the floorboards of the cabin!

While denning, a black bear commonly curls up with its head tucked firmly against its chest. Thermal imaging of the bodies of hibernating black bears shows the greatest heat loss in the area of their eyes, noses, and foreheads. A bear tucking its head against its chest evidently isn't just assuming a cute sleeping posture, but is reducing its heat loss during hibernation.

The duration of a bear's hibernation increases in northern latitudes. Black bears in northern Canada and Alaska usually spend two months longer—or more—in hibernation than bears in the lower 48. The season of hibernation decreases even further as one moves south. Pregnant sows and females with cubs den earlier and become active later in the spring than males. Big boars are the last to enter their dens in the fall and the first to exit them in early spring.

In the deep South, in Florida and Alabama, some black bears may not hibernate at all if food sources are plentiful. Conclusive research has yet to settle the matter, but some biologists believe female black bears in Texas hibernate (at which time their cubs are born), but the males do not. If such is the case, a similar pattern is probably also at work among black bears in Mexico.

Certain physiological characteristics serve important functions in some places, but not in others. Weasels living in northern climates turn white in the winter, while their southern kin remain brown. Hibernation is often viewed as the black bear's most unique adaptation, facilitating its survival. But like the notable adaptations of other animals, its presence may decrease or disappear when it no longer serves a purpose.

REPRODUCTION AND YOUNG

The Mating Season

Black bears mate in June over much of their range, but the mating season can begin in May and persist into July. Some biologists speculate that preparation for mating begins much earlier. As noted earlier, large males are the first to emerge from their dens in early spring. Why do they come above ground before springtime plant growth has begun, when there's still very little forage available? It's possible that their early break from hibernation gives them more time to range across large territories and scout for females. In fact, the home range of black bear boars is much larger than sows. In Michigan, the home range of males covers an average of 335 square miles, while females' home range averages 50 square miles. Researchers in Minnesota have concluded the mating range of dominant males can cover 80 to 160 square miles and may encompass the home range of a dozen females. While the home range of a female sometimes overlaps the ranges of other females, dominant males repel other males from their territories during the breeding season.

Although boars commonly reach sexual maturity at age 3, they usually don't have an opportunity to breed in good habitat until much later. Older, larger males prevent them from breeding. Females may reach reproductive capability at age 2, but don't normally breed until age 3. In poor habitat in the far north, where food resources are limited, females may not breed until 6 or 7 years of age.

Black bears are promiscuous, meaning a male may mate with more than one female during the breeding season, and a female may mate with more than one male. Black bears often have twin cubs and triplets, and due to their promiscuous mating habits, the cubs within a single litter may all have different fathers.

Males locate females during the breeding season primarily through their sense of smell. They also announce their own presence within the home range through scent-marking. Boars utilize "bear trees" as signposts. They gouge the trees with their claws, usually reaching as high onto the tree as possible, a behavior that probably gives other bears an indication of their size. They also rub their bodies on the trees and may leave bite marks as well. While boars are highly tuned to the scent of females during the breeding season, their attention is very selective. Females nursing cubs will not breed and are avoided by males, as are females too young to breed.

Pregnancy and Gestation

After breeding in early summer, a female no longer tolerates the company of males. Her focus turns to food—to ingesting enough forage to sustain her during hibernation and to nurture a litter through pregnancy. Black bears (along with grizzlies and polar bears) are among a number of species that experience delayed implantation. For most animals, an egg attaches to the uterine wall of the female shortly after fertilization and begins fetal development. The process is different for bears. The fertilized egg (or eggs in the case of multiple offspring) experiences a limited amount of development (cell division) but does not attach to the uterine wall. It "floats" in the uterus for the remainder of summer and into the fall. If the sow has gained the necessary fat reserves to nourish herself and maintain a pregnancy during hibernation, the embryo attaches to the uterine wall and gestation begins. If not, the embryo is simply absorbed into the body of the female.

Defining the gestation period (the amount of time between the beginning of pregnancy and birth) is somewhat confusing for bears. Although the female's egg may be fertilized in June, significant embryotic development may not begin until November. Thus, the gestation period could be defined as beginning when the egg is fertilized (in late spring or early summer) or when it attaches to the uterine wall and embryotic development begins (in late fall). Biological reference works typically report the gestation period of the black bear at around 215 days, the time from mating until cubs are born. However, it's important to remember that a considerable portion of this time includes delayed implantation. An embryo's uninterrupted development, from implantation until birth, takes only eight to ten weeks.

Birth

Most large mammals birth their young in the spring or early summer. The birthing period usually occurs just prior to a season when food is plentiful. Canines and felines, such as wolves and mountain lions, birth their young just before hibernating rodents emerge and before baby deer and elk are born. This allows the adult predators to nourish their young with easily caught prey. Hoofed animals birth their young at about the time plants become very green and nutritious in spring, enabling females to produce abundant milk for offspring.

Why then are black bear cubs born in January or February, in the weeks that uncannily coincide with the coldest days of the year? Biologists speculate that birthing very small cubs allows a sow to avoid the nutritional demands of a pregnancy that produces much larger offspring at birth. Newborn black bear cubs are very tiny. Most weigh less than a pound, coming into the world at around eight ounces and 9 inches in length. The average wolf pup is twice as large as the average black bear cub at birth. Although the average adult coyote weighs only thirty pounds, their newborns are nearly identical in size to those of the much larger black bear.

Birthing such tiny offspring in January rather than May actually gives young black bears a survival advantage. Like their parents, baby black bears need to gain lots of weight before hibernation. Their midwinter birthday allows them to be older and larger when they confront their first physically demanding season of hibernation, increasing their odds of survival.

The birth of her cubs occurs around the midpoint of winter dormancy, but the sow is awake during the birthing. Black bear litters range from one to six cubs, but twins are

By the time they emerge from the den, the eyes of baby black bears have opened and their bodies are covered with fur.
© ISTOCK.COM/GKUCHERA

most common. Cubs are born blind and covered with sparse, gray fur. They are immediately cleaned of birthing tissue and fluids by the sow. While this behavior, common to most mammals, is also thought to imprint the scent of her offspring on the mother, the process is probably different for bears. Researchers have found that hibernating sows will readily accept an orphan cub, but once fully awakened in the spring will reject or even kill an unknown cub. This behavior has led some biologists to conclude that even though a sow is alert while birthing her offspring and aware of their movements and needs, her sense of smell may be limited or dormant during hibernation.

The first few weeks of the cubs' lives are spent nursing and snuggling closely to the warm, furry body of their mother. Cubs nurse at two- to three-hour intervals, with each nursing session lasting but a few minutes. At around 6 weeks of age the eyes of black bear cubs open. By this time they are mobile and have grown considerably, weighing four to seven pounds. Cubs born to larger females and those in smaller litters tend to receive more milk and grow the fastest. The milk of the black bear has a very high fat content (around 25 percent) compared to the milk of other mammal species, allowing cubs to easily quadruple their body weight in the space of a few weeks. Though not an appetizing topic for dinnertime conversation, it's worth noting that female black bears lick their tiny offspring to stimulate defecation. They then eat the feces, probably to keep the den clean. Maybe that's the real reason the sense of smell of sows remains dulled until they finish hibernation!

Nurturing Cubs to Adulthood

Black bear cubs are 2 to 3 months old when they emerge from the den with their mother. By this time they weigh eight pounds or more. Their ears look large in relation to the rest of their body, and the thin, gray fur they had at birth has thickened and become darker. While the mother is still somewhat lethargic in the days after exiting the den, and her digestive system needs some time to accept solid food, the cubs are full of energy. They run and play in the new outside world, but are watched carefully by their mother.

Cubs fresh from the den can rely on their mother's milk for nourishment, but it's a demanding time of the year for the sow. Perhaps that's part of the reason females with cubs are the last black bears to emerge from their dens. For a period of time the mother will subsist primarily on leftovers from last year's food crop, or perhaps on the carrion of animals that died during the winter. Once the first shoots of green vegetation begin to emerge, the sow has more food options. Cubs begin testing solid foods and are eating them alongside their mother by midsummer, but will continue to nurse for about five months after emerging from the den.

Black bear cubs are very active, wrestling with one another, engaging in activities that appear to be impromptu games of tag or follow the leader. They also toy with objects. They're skilled tree climbers, a behavior that serves them well as youngsters.

Few predators pose a threat to black bear cubs protected by a vigilant mother. One of the most serious dangers cubs face is the male black bear, which sometimes kills cubs. Sows often tend their offspring near a "refuge tree," a large-trunked, tall tree that the cubs can climb. If danger threatens, the cubs scramble quickly up the refuge tree. In the case of a predatory black bear male, the larger animal is not likely to expend the effort needed to climb the tree in pursuit of the cubs. In the Great Lakes region, sows often choose broad, towering pines as refuge trees.

In late summer and fall, cubs undergo the same process of hyperphagia as adult bears. They voraciously consume all the food their mother discovers. If berry and nut crops are sparse and other food sources dwindle, this becomes a stressful and sometimes highly competitive period for sows with cubs. The sow must not only ingest enough forage to fatten herself, but must also produce milk for the cubs and find enough food to feed them as well.

Sows with cubs are among the first bears to den in the fall. The cubs hibernate with their mother (otherwise black bears rarely share a den). When the family surfaces the following spring, they'll stick together for a few months, until the mating season begins. Just prior to mating, the female will drive her young (now called yearlings) away. Yearling black bears usually wander away from the home range of their mother in a journey known as "dispersal," at which time they seek territories of their own.

Dispersing yearlings may become attracted to human sources of food, or may be struck by vehicles while crossing roads. They must find enough forage to fatten up for their first solo hibernation, and must avoid other dangers, including predation by large bears and, in some areas, wolf packs. If all goes well they'll secure a den and hibernate. When they emerge from hibernation as 2-year-olds, they've successfully transitioned to adult life.

Yearling black bears must learn to live on their own. Their success in finding a territory and managing their first solo hibernation are critical to long-term survival.
© ISTOCK.COM/CCHOC

BLACK BEARS AND OTHER ANIMALS

Black Bears and Other Predators

Black bears share their world with a variety of predators, depending on the part of the continent they occupy. These predators include carnivores as large as their grizzly bear cousins, which sometimes weigh more than 1,000 pounds, as well as sleek, petite weasels whose weight is measured in ounces. Black bears will gladly usurp the prey of smaller predators, but may also be the targets of predation under unusual circumstances.

The ranges of grizzly bears and black bears overlap across much of Alaska and northern Canada. National parks in southwestern Canada, such as Banff and Jasper

National Parks, are also home to both creatures. In the contiguous United States, the tracks of both species dot the soil in Yellowstone and Grand Teton National Parks in Wyoming, Glacier National Park in Montana, and other wilderness locations in Wyoming, Montana, and Idaho. Almost without exception, black bears give grizzlies a wide berth. Grizzly bears are not only much larger, on average, than black bears; they are also more naturally aggressive, and far more likely to counter a perceived threat with an attack of their own. Large black bears may occasionally dominate smaller grizzlies when competing for food sources such as spawning fish or berries, but in most cases grizzly bears are the dominant bruin.

Predation of black bears by grizzlies is very rare, but has been documented. In Yellowstone National Park, researchers have found the carcass of a big black bear boar that had apparently been killed by a hulking male grizzly. The black bear's massive skull showed puncture wounds consistent with the crushing bite of a larger grizzly. Another Yellowstone incident involved the discovery of a dead black bear sow that was also presumably killed by a grizzly bear boar.

Black bears share their range with grizzlies in places like Yellowstone National Park, the home of this grizzly. Black bears generally give grizzlies a wide berth.
© ISTOCK.COM/JILL RICHARDSON

However, in most situations, black bears can foil attempted predation by grizzlies. Avoiding a grizzly's space is their preferred means of dodging attacks, but if caught in close quarters, black bears will readily climb trees. Although young grizzlies can and do climb trees, and an adult grizzly may be able to reach 10 feet or more to pull a black bear from the branches, bear researchers believe grizzlies won't expend the energy needed to remove a "treed" black bear.

Wolf packs also constitute a threat to black bears, especially immature bears or sows with cubs, although aggressive interactions between the two species are rare. Again, a black bear's very best defense against a wolf pack attack is a speedy retreat up the nearest tree.

But even if caught in the open, a mature black bear can capably repel a small wolf pack if it stands its ground. However, under certain circumstances, wolves have been known to kill black bears and vice versa. Adult black bears have killed individual female wolves that were protecting the wolf's den site and pups. A study of the interactions between wolves and black bears in Minnesota over a ten-year period concluded that single wolves normally give way to black bears—even subadult black bears similar in size to the wolves. Incidents of wolves killing female and immature black bears have been recorded in the Canadian provinces of Ontario and Alberta.

Wolves sometimes prey upon denning black bears, with predation most likely successful on immature bears. However, in 1977 biologists recorded the killing of a 16-year-old sow and her cubs in northern Minnesota. The bear's den site consisted of a shallow depression under several midsize logs. In mid-February, a pack of wolves that had previously been observed as containing nine members attacked the bear from both sides of the den. The sow escaped the den, then fought the wolves as she fled some 25 yards to a large aspen tree. The wounded bear escaped up the tree, but later descended and returned to her den site, where she was either killed by the wolves or died from her wounds. Wolves were observed feeding on her carcass for some three weeks after the attack. Biologists speculate that a very light snowpack during the winter made the bear more vulnerable to predation. Additional snowpack would probably have made the bear's den much more difficult—or impossible—for the wolves to penetrate.

Hefty black bears dwarf even the largest mountain lions (cougars). On average, adult black bears are roughly twice as big as their cougar counterparts of the same sex. Nevertheless, mountain lions are fearsome predators capable of downing hoofed animals many times larger than themselves. Solitary, elusive creatures, mountain lions are seldom seen by humans in the wild. Recent studies have shed more light on the habits and behaviors of the mountain lion, but very little current evidence exists regarding interactions between black bears and cougars. Given their population densities and range, however, it is certain that the species frequently encounter one another.

A study of the interactions of mountain lions and bears in the northern Rocky Mountains documented numerous instances in which mountain lion kills of deer or elk were usurped by bears. Most of the bears chasing cougars from the carcasses were grizzlies. But black bears were also documented claiming mountain lion kills. A single instance of a mountain lion preying upon a black bear cub in Arizona has also been documented. A surprising number of historical accounts from the eighteenth and early nineteenth centuries tell of ferocious battles between mountain lions and bears (both black and grizzly). Most of these end with the death of the bear at the teeth and claws of the mountain lion, but several record the deaths of both combatants. As interesting as these accounts may be, current observations seem to indicate that, for the vast majority of time, black bears and mountain lions leave one another alone.

Black bears comingle with a host of smaller predators across their North American range. Lynx, bobcats, coyotes, and red foxes are found in black bear territories in a variety of regions. These smaller predators might kill an orphan cub or challenge an immature black bear. They pose little threat to cubs protected by their mother. While it's quite likely that an adult black bear would displace these species from their prey if the opportunity arose, competition for food or other resources between black bears and these smaller predators is extremely rare.

Parasites and Diseases

Black bears are frequently bothered by a wide array of internal and external parasites. Their exposure to parasites depends upon the habitat and region of the continent they occupy, and is also somewhat determined by their diet. In Yellowstone National Park, for example, one research study concluded that grizzly bears had a much higher rate of infection by intestinal parasites than black bears. The researchers concluded the grizzlies were more often exposed to those parasites because their diet included a higher percentage of the carrion and prey animals that would host them.

Common internal parasites of black bears include roundworms and tapeworms. They may also be infected with parasites that live in other parts of the body, including the trichina worm. Some evidence indicates that black bears expel intestinal parasites just prior to hibernation, ridding themselves of organisms that could potentially drain energy reserves needed to survive the winter. Although high percentages of black bears in some areas host internal parasites, biologists have found little evidence that the infections typically become fatal or even cause significant health problems for the bruins. However, black bears are known to succumb to severe parasitic infections on occasion. University researchers investigating the death of a young bear in northern Idaho, which was thought to have succumbed to rabies, discovered the bear's brain, sinus tissues, and lungs were riddled with a tiny parasite from the fluke/flatworm family. The parasites were responsible for the rabieslike symptoms the bear exhibited shortly before its death.

In addition to internal parasites, black bears may be plagued with fleas, ticks, mosquitos, and biting flies. Ticks are common on bears but don't seem to cause any noticeable harm. Mosquitos have a difficult time reaching the skin of a black bear, but may attack exposed skin on its ears, nose, and face. Bears don't appear bothered by mosquitos and seldom exert much effort to rid themselves of the pests. They're much more aggressive toward biting flies. The bruins will swat incoming flies with their paws or snatch them with their teeth in lightning-quick bites.

North American black bears are remarkably free of diseases. The primary disease known to sometimes infect black bears is rabies. Several cases of rabid black bears have been recorded in a variety of places, but even this disease is quite rare.

Predation

The diet of the average black bears consists of more than 90 percent plant material. The remaining 10 percent, which is made up of animal protein, mostly comes from insects. Thus, the characteristic black bear is a casual carnivore at best.

However, those facts tend to minimize the black bear's potential as a predator. In some places, their predatory impact is notable. Certain animals, most possibly large, adept males, are much more predatory than the average bear. A study in central Idaho involving predation and elk calves is instructive. In an area with substantial populations of two large predators (black bears and mountain lions), 59 percent of all the elk calves researched in the study were killed by predators. Nearly 40 percent of the calves eliminated by predators were killed by black bears. Interestingly, black bear predation was highest on calves 5 weeks old and younger. Mountain lions also took many calves in the first month of life, but were far more effective than bears after the calves attained an age of 6 weeks.

Although the predation rates of black bears in this study are higher than those in studies conducted in other locations, the results demonstrate the predatory efficiency of black bears. Cow elk birth calves in identifiable, traditional "calving grounds" that are used year after year. It appears that individual black bears remember these

enticing late-spring food sources and deliberately hunt newborn calves. Very young elk calves are nearly odorless and employ a hiding strategy to escape predation. By diligently searching calving areas and using their incredible senses of smell and eyesight, black bears are able to discover the secreted calves. Once the young calves are discovered, the quick, agile bears can easily run them down. Within weeks, however, elk calves become very fleet and can outrun all but the most persistent bears.

Moose, white-tailed deer, and mule deer do not gather at traditional birthing grounds like elk, making their young typically more dispersed and harder to find. Nonetheless, roaming black bears also prey upon deer fawns and moose calves in significant numbers in some places. Caribou calves may be similarly targeted by black bears in northern habitats.

Black bears occasionally prey upon adult ungulates, though these instances are rare. The animals they bring down are normally weakened by injury or malnutrition. Under such circumstances, a large black bear can kill deer, caribou, elk, or even moose.

Smaller prey is also taken by black bears. They dine on burrowing rodents with some frequency, although the methods of capturing them are different from those used by grizzly bears. Grizzlies often dig ground squirrels or other rodents from their burrows, using their massive claws as astonishingly efficient excavators. The claws of black bears are shorter and more sharply curved than those of grizzlies, making them more useful for climbing trees than for digging. Thus, black bears tend to ambush rodents that have wandered from their dens. A research study of predation on yellow-bellied marmots in Colorado found that black bears killed fewer marmots than coyotes or badgers did, but more than hawks and eagles. Similar to elk calf predation, black bears probably have higher success preying upon rodents in the few weeks after young, inexperienced animals have emerged from their burrows in the spring.

Black bears are significant predators of young ungulates in some places. In the contiguous United States, they most often target elk calves and white-tailed deer fawns.
JACK BALLARD

Primarily plant eaters, black bears are very capable predators under the right circumstances.
© ISTOCK.COM/ SEVENTHDAYPHOTOGRAPHY

The predatory instincts of black bears sometimes motivate them to attack livestock. Full-grown cattle or horses are at little risk of predation, but the bruins sometimes consume young calves. Black bears are more apt to prey upon sheep, and occasionally kill several sheep in a single predation event. Although the predation of livestock by black bears has little economic impact on the livestock industry on a nationwide scale, sheep farmers in some areas may lose a significant portion of their flock to bruins. A bear that repeatedly attacks livestock may be relocated or shot by wildlife officials.

Though the diet of a black bear consists primarily of plant matter, they're scientifically classified as carnivores. But perhaps the carnivore designation is helpful as a reminder that under the right circumstances, black bears are very capable predators.

Black Bears in History

Long before the arrival of Europeans on the North American continent, indigenous peoples lived in proximity to black bears. Many American Indian tribes organized themselves into clans bearing the names of animals. For example, the Ojibwa (Chippewa) people in the Great Lakes region were originally organized into five clans named for various animals. Of these, the Bear Clan was by far the largest. The black bear (called "muckwa" in the native language) was sacred to the Ojibwa, but was also hunted and eaten by them.

Native peoples of the Pacific Northwest were aware of the Kermode bear, the creamy white color phase of the black bear, centuries before these unique bruins came to the attention of settlers. To the indigenous people the white bears, or "spirit bears," were sacred. One legend of indigenous origin recounts a bargain that was struck between Raven, the creator, and Black Bear. Raven wished for something to remind him of the primal age, when the land was covered in white glaciers and snowfields. After receiving Raven's word that he could lead a life of peace until the end of time, Black Bear consented to having one in ten of his people turn white. The white bears would serve as a reminder to Raven of the bygone era when the world was white and unhappy. For years, the native peoples did not speak of the Kermode bears to outsiders, a tradition that may have insulated this black bear population from European hunters.

American Indian hunters pursued black bears using a variety of methods. Bears were killed with the bow and arrow, but were also taken in deadfall traps. These consisted of a log that was supported by a stake with some type of bait attached. A bear that snatched the bait would topple the stake and be crushed under the log. Indigenous peoples in North America utilized the meat, hides, and fat of black bears. Bear hunts were often preceded by ceremonial rituals, with another ceremony following the successful hunt. Many tribes viewed the black bear's hibernation as evidence of its potent spirit and mystical powers.

Black bears were both revered and hunted by American Indian tribes.
© ISTOCK.COM/
SEVENTHDAYPHOTOGRAPHY

Settlement of the East Coast and the subsequent westward expansion of European immigration in the eighteen and nineteenth centuries spelled trouble for the black bear. As forests were converted to croplands and livestock brought onto farms on the edge of the wilderness, conflicts between bears and humans were inevitable. Black bears sometimes preyed upon livestock, and also took a liking to pioneers' vegetable gardens and crops. In New York state for example, almost 75 percent of the land was cleared for farming by 1900. Bears were killed as pests throughout the state, but were also diligently hunted for their hides, meat, and fat, which was rendered into bear grease.

Black bear hides were considered more valuable than those of grizzly bears, and for a time an active market for bear hides flourished in North America. In the 1700s thousands of black bear hides were exported to Europe. A bearskin was as valuable as a beaver pelt. The late 1700s and 1800s saw many states enact bounties (cash payments for dead animals) for black bears and other predators. Maine began offering a black bear bounty in 1770. Two counties in Maryland began offering bounties around 1750. Vermont's state legislature approved a $5 bounty on black bears in 1831. The bounty was increased to $15 in 1868, a handsome sum in an era when laborers might receive $1 as a day's wages. In New York state, a bounty was paid on black bears from 1892 to 1895.

Indiscriminate killing was one factor in the rapid decline of black bear populations across the contiguous United States in the nineteenth century, but habitat loss was a more acute problem. Wide-scale clearing of forests for agricultural purposes and timber eliminated mature nut-bearing trees in many locations, and deprived the bruins of the forested haunts in which they're most at home. Further compounding habitat loss in the East was the near-complete destruction of the American chestnut tree, which took place from the 1920s to the 1940s. American chestnut blight, a disease caused by a fungus, killed most of the chestnut trees in the United States, depriving black bears and other wildlife species of one of the most bountiful nut crops of eastern forests.

Black Bears in Modern Times

Several "modern" movements in American culture contributed to a broad recovery of black bear population, some beginning as early as the late 1800s. In 1885, New York state created the Catskill and Adirondack Forest Preserves, which later became Catskill Park and Adirondack Park. The preservation of wilderness habitat in these areas buffered black bears from further habitat loss. In the same time period, the federal government began creating national parks. In the West, Yellowstone and Yosemite were designated national parks prior to 1900, preserving critical habitat for black bears and other species. Shenandoah National Park and Great Smoky Mountains National Park were created in 1926 and 1934, respectively, providing black bears important refuges in the East.

However, cultural and economic trends during the same time period were also instrumental in renewing black bear populations across much of their range. Industrialization brought human populations to the cities. Much of the land enthusiastically deforested for farm fields was found to be too rocky or not sufficiently fertile to profitably grow crops. Marginal farmlands were abandoned across much of the East from 1900 to 1950. The land reverted to forest, increasing habitat for black bears.

The creation of hunting seasons and the protection of black bears as a game animal were also important to the species' recovery in the United States. Unregulated bear hunting ceased in New York state in 1903, when black bears were given status

Parks and wildlife refuges provide black bears with protected habitat and have been instrumental in their recovery. This bear was photographed at the Alligator River National Wildlife Refuge in North Carolina.
USFWS/STEVE HILLEBRAND

as a game animal and protected from being hunted in July and August. A more structured hunting season and bag limits were established in 1923, the same year Montana designated black bears a game species. Michigan gave black bears protection as a game animal and instituted a hunting season in 1925. By the 1950s, black bears were protected by hunting laws that strictly regulated harvest rates and hunting season dates throughout most of the United States.

It is largely accepted among biologists that black bear populations in North America reached their lows sometime around 1950, or perhaps a decade or two before. Since then, *Ursus americanus* has staged a remarkable comeback, both in numbers and distribution. State wildlife agencies often classify the status of animal species as "declining," "stable," or "increasing" in relation to population. In the vast majority of locations where their numbers and range are recorded, black bears are classified as "stable" or "increasing." The growth of black bear populations and range in some areas is quite dramatic. The number of square miles of habitat occupied in North Carolina by black bears showed a seven-fold increase from 1971 to 2010. Bears are believed to inhabit more habitat in North Carolina at the present time than they have for 150 years. Even in southern states, where bears were eradicated and have been classified as endangered or threatened species, populations appear to be thriving. In Georgia, for instance, black bears were nearly eliminated in the 1930s. Currently, some 5,100 bears roam the state in three population areas.

Limitations to black bear range expansion are primarily related to small, fragmented portions of habitat where bears are poorly buffered from human disturbance and dangers posed by human activity. Roads, for example, can be perilous to black bears. Death caused by collisions with vehicles is a significant factor in bear mortality in some places. Researchers have found that boars are more often killed by vehicles than sows. Young males dispersing into new territory in the spring appear particularly vulnerable to roadkill. However, biologists have also determined mortality from vehicle collisions also claims a noteworthy number of females, particularly in southern states. Both sexes are at higher risk on roads during the late summer and autumn, when they cover more territory in search of food.

Humans and Black Bears: Current Interactions and Precautions

Black bears have no natural predators in most areas of North America. They are also notably resistant to disease and are seldom harmed by parasites. Although their reproduction rates are quite low compared to other large animals, such as white-tailed deer, these factors allow populations to persist and thrive wherever they find suitable habitat.

At the present time, humans are the dominant source of black bear mortality in the contiguous United States. They are killed both deliberately and indirectly by humans.

Hunting is the number one source of human-caused mortality. The International Union for Conservation of Nature (IUCN) estimates that 40,000 to 50,000 black bears are harvested annually by hunters in the United States and Canada. The majority of biologists agree that carefully regulated hunting poses little or no threat to black bear populations. Boars are taken more regularly by hunters than sows, which reduces the reproductive impacts of hunting. Collisions with vehicles and lethal removal of "problem" bears are the other primary sources of human-caused mortality to black bears, though those impacts are much smaller than hunting.

Given their omnivorous eating habits, it should come as no surprise that black bears will happily eat human and pet food. In the days of open, unfenced garbage dumps, black bears were frequent visitors to refuse heaps, scrounging through the rubble for vegetable peelings, bread crusts, rotting meat scraps, and whatever other morsels might attract their attention. The 1950s and 1960s saw a curious tourist industry develop in relation to the bears (black and grizzly) in Yellowstone National Park. Motorists fed begging bears along the roadsides, with the freeloading bruins sometimes crawling into automobiles and trashing the interiors in search of more grub.

Roads represent a peril for black bears. Collisions with vehicles are a significant source of bear mortality in some areas.
© ISTOCK.COM/ WERGODSWARRIOR

Black bears were
treated as novelties—
almost pets—in
Yellowstone National
Park prior to the 1960s.
Here, in an undated
photo, President Calvin
Coolidge strolls past
begging black bears on
a visit to Yellowstone.
NPS

Although the deliberate feeding of bears is now illegal in state and national parks, visitors sometimes unwittingly create "nuisance" or "problem" bears that actively seek human food. Unattended food baskets and coolers may be raided by black bears at picnic areas. Campers who fail to store food beyond the reach of bears sometimes discover their larders consumed by bruins. People cooking in the outdoors who leave behind scraps and crumbs also create a potential association between humans and food in the consciousness of bears. Additionally, bears will gladly gobble dog food and other pet foods, especially during periods of hyperphagia. In many areas, the most common complaint received from wildlife officials regarding black bears is their destruction of bird feeders and consumption of birdseed.

Bears that frequent human habitation in search of food are a difficult problem for wildlife managers. In early times, nuisance bears were often trapped and relocated to remote areas with proper habitat. However, bears have an uncanny homing instinct. Research studies from a number of areas demonstrate that about 50 percent of relocated black bears return to their homes within a few days, traveling distances up to 40 miles. Relocation also potentially puts the transported bear into competition with local bruins. When relocation is ineffective and a bear continually invades human habitation in search of food, wildlife managers often have little choice but to lethally remove the bear.

Keeping black bears from exploiting human food sources is usually as simple as removing the attractant. This includes utilizing "bear-proof" trash containers and dumpsters in rural areas, cleaning up after cooking outdoors, and storing food out of the reach of bears when camping.

Despite these precautions, people may still encounter black bears when recreating outdoors. Some folks worry that such experiences may be dangerous, that black bears may maul or kill them. While a handful of humans have been killed by black bears in the past century, lightning strikes and attacks by domestic dogs have claimed far more lives than black bears. Members of the *Ursus americanus* species are generally shy of humans. When confronted at close range, black bears may huff and stomp the ground with their forepaws. However, these behaviors are more an indication of the bear's discomfort than the prelude to an aggressive attack.

In the rare cases when black bears do attack people, their intentions are most often predatory. Experts advise recreationists to "play dead" if rushed by a grizzly bear. A black bear attack should be handled in the opposite manner. Biologists encourage people to fight back, punching, kicking, and yelling at the bear. Blows to the bruin's sensitive nose may be particularly effective in repelling an attack. The idea is to present the bear with a formidable foe versus an easy meal.

The largest carnivore in the region, a black bear at an eastern state or national park is a thrilling sight for most visitors. Bruin behavior is fascinating to observe, and the animal's presence is a compelling reminder that its species' history and future are an important part of our own.

A bear that learns to associate humans with food may take up residence around homes and cabins. This situation is never beneficial to the bear.
© ISTOCK.COM/COYSTCLAIR

Grizzly bears are named for the light hairs on their head and shoulders and the light highlights in their darker coat that give them a "grizzled" appearance.
KEVIN RHOADES

CHAPTER 10
GRIZZLY BEARS

"Hey, Jack, come check this out."

At my companion's urging, I poke my head from the zippered door of a backpacking tent deep in the Absaroka-Beartooth Wilderness in Montana. It has snowed overnight, one of the hazards of camping in the high-elevation portions of the wilderness in September. I pull on my boots and a jacket and then scramble out of the tent. The sky above is blue and unclouded, the ground beneath my feet carpeted in 2 inches of snow. Weathered alpine grass pokes from the pale mantle. The gnarled evergreens behind our camp droop with snowflakes, sparkling, pure, and cheerful in the day's first bashful rays of sunlight.

As beautiful and pristine as are the surroundings, it isn't the scenery that Brad is so impatient to show me. Waving his arm from the open meadow 100 yards from our tent, he beckons me with an expression somewhere between a smile and a scowl. I jog toward him, noticing a line of tracks leading from the edge of the timber across the clearing. Silently he points at the prints. They appear somewhat similar to fat, barefoot tracks of a human, but one feature indelibly sets these apart from the footprints of any naked, deranged individual cavorting about the alpine zone in a snowstorm at 2 a.m. In front of the toes on the prints are claw marks measuring several inches in length. The identity of the nighttime visitor is obvious. Our camp was closely bypassed by a grizzly bear.

But the bruin had no interest in us, or in the food cache we suspended from a tree 150 yards from our camp, although with its keen sense of smell it was most certainly aware of the presence of both. Instinctively I shiver, with both fascination and fear.

Grizzly bears arouse similar emotions in other humans to whom they are known. Many of the terrors and trepidations aroused by these indomitable predators are unfounded or greatly overestimated. However, only a fool treads unthinkingly into their domain without a large measure of respect and preparation. For a century or more, grizzly bears in North America have been maligned and misunderstood. Misinformation has been haphazardly distributed by both individuals who would have people believe grizzlies are bloodthirsty man-eaters and those who have falsely portrayed them as gentle giants. I offer this chapter in hopes that it will expand both your appreciation for and knowledge of these iconic creatures of the American wilderness.

NAMES AND FACES

Names and Visual Description

Names of certain animals are based on their appearance. Such is the case of the "grizzly bear." Its coat is usually medium to dark brown in color. Long hairs, known as "guard hairs," adorn grizzly bears along the back and shoulders. Protruding beyond the dense undercoat, the guard hairs of a grizzly bear are pale or white-tipped, giving the animals a grizzled look. A term historically used for the graying of hair on the human head, "grizzle" means to become gray or white. Early observers apparently likened the light guard hairs on grizzly bears to gray highlights in human hair. Thus, the name "grizzly bear" stems from the pale highlights in the dark coat of this large bear. In some locations this unique coloration on grizzly bears gave rise to another name, the "silvertip bear," a historical term not commonly encountered in modern terminology. Captain Meriwether Lewis of the Lewis and Clark expedition sometimes referred to the grizzly bear as the "white bear" in his journals, evidently in reference to the light hair on upper portions of a grizzly bear's body.

As previously mentioned, the typical coat of a grizzly bear appears as brown. However, individual bears can exhibit color variations ranging from light tan to nearly black. The extent of the grizzling varies as well. Some bears, viewed in the sunlight, almost seem to shine with radiance, a spectacle that gave rise to one of the grizzly bear's nicknames, the "silvertip." Other bears show minimal grizzling. These animals appear more solidly colored in whatever shade of brown is exhibited by a particular animal. For the purposes of species identification, the trademark pale hairs on the back and shoulders of a grizzly bear are one clue of its species, but not a definitive field mark.

Adult grizzly bears are large animals with a noticeable hump over their front shoulders when viewed from the side. The hump is composed of a muscular mass that facilitates the animals' excellent digging capabilities with the forepaws and their running speed. Their rump slopes away from the back in a rounded arc. Like other bears, grizzlies have a small tail that is often unnoticeable except when viewed from certain angles. Grizzly bears have massive front paws. Large claws extend from each foot and are often easy to see on the front paws. The claws of grizzly bears are longer and straighter than those of black bears, usually measuring 2 to 4 inches in length.

The face of the grizzly bear appears large and rounded when viewed head-on. Seen from the side, the face of a grizzly looks slightly concave or dished. Grizzlies have short ears that often look tiny in relation to the mass of the head on adult animals. The end of a grizzly bear's nose is black.

Naming of genders within grizzly bears follows the pattern of a poorly esteemed barnyard animal. Male grizzlies are known as "boars." Females are called "sows." Despite their iconic status as wilderness creatures, male and female grizzlies carry the same gender identities as pigs. However, youngsters of these regal predators fare much better in the naming category. They're not called piglets, but are referred to as "cubs."

Related Species in North America

Three species of bears are indigenous to North America: grizzly bears, black bears, and polar bears. Black bears *(Ursus americanus)* inhabit much of the same range as grizzly bears, except in the extreme northern reaches of Alaska and Canada, where grizzlies are present but not black bears. The two species are often confused by uneducated observers. Not all black bears are black in color. Like grizzlies, their coloration can vary quite dramatically, from nearly white to coal black. Although black is the dominant color of black bears, other colorations that are highly similar to the basic color scheme of grizzly bears occur. "Blonde" and "cinnamon" color phases of black bears are virtually identical to the hues found on the coats of many grizzlies. And remember, grizzly bears can be very dark. Thus, coloration is a very poor way to distinguish black bears from grizzly bears.

To the trained eye, the size of adult bears is one means of separating black bears from grizzlies. The average mature grizzly bear commonly weighs twice as much as the normal black bear, or even more. However, there are more certain ways to distinguish the species than color and size. Black bears lack the noticeable hump on the front shoulders that marks the grizzly. Their ears appear much longer in relation to their head than those of a grizzly bear. Viewed from the side, the concave appearance of the face of a grizzly bear is absent from a black bear. A black bear has a face that is straight or somewhat convex or slightly rounded outward. The claws of a black bear are not nearly as large or easily seen as those on a grizzly. When startled or alarmed, black bears may bolt up a tree, an evasive strategy not likely employed by an adult grizzly bear. Rather than relying on a single trait such as color to distinguish between black bears and grizzlies, one can make a more certain identification by analyzing a particular animal for a variety of distinguishing features.

In addition to black bears, grizzlies share the North American continent with polar bears *(Ursus maritimus)*. Residents of the far north, polar bears are found on the ice packs in the extreme northern reaches of Canada, Alaska, and the Arctic Islands. In a few places the range of polar bears and grizzly bears overlap. In the areas of overlap, the habitat is usually not ideal for grizzlies. Few grizzly bears have historically ranged into areas also inhabited by polar bears.

In addition to the obvious differences in range, the appearance of polar bears and grizzly bears is quite distinct. Polar bears are uniformly white in color, often mingled

Grizzly bears share portions of their range in North America with black bears and polar bears. Grizzly bears have a prominent shoulder hump and dished face not seen on black or polar bears.
© ISTOCK.COM/LUCAAR (TOP)
© ISTOCK.COM/JOHNPITCHER (BOTTOM)

with yellowish tones. A polar bear has short ears like the grizzly, but its profile exhibits a straight face more like the black bear than the dished appearance of the grizzly. Their claws are sharp, allowing them excellent traction on ice, but are much smaller and less noticeable than those on a grizzly bear. On average, polar bears are larger than the grizzly bears that inhabit interior regions of North America.

Polar bears are even more carnivorous than grizzly bears. While grizzlies contentedly dine on a variety of plants, nuts, and berries, such food sources are absent on the frozen ice packs. Polar bears dine primarily upon seals, young walruses, and fish.

Subspecies

Discussing the subspecies of grizzly bears raises an interesting point. Technically, there are no subspecies of grizzly bears. In fact, the grizzly bear is thought to be a subspecies by many biologists. Grizzly bears belong to the species *Ursus arctos,* which also includes the Alaskan brown bear. From a scientific standpoint both Alaskan brown bears and grizzly bears belong to the *Ursus arctos* species.

Subspecies of mammals are defined as unique, identifiable populations with genetic, physical, or social characteristics that separate them from the species as a whole.

In North America the brown bear is sometimes described as consisting of two subspecies, the Alaskan brown bear or Kodiak bear *(Ursus arctos middendorffi)* and the grizzly bear *(Ursus arctos horribilis)*. In the past century other categories of subspecies have also been proposed, some identifying a half-dozen different subspecies. However, the nomenclature relating to the brown bear species is often confusing. Some authoritative biologists refer to the entire *Ursus arctos* species as "grizzly bears," while others stick with "brown bears." For common folks it appears this is one species where you can choose a name. Take your pick. Whether you refer to these dominating predators as brown bears or grizzly bears, you're on sound scientific footing.

What distinguishes Alaskan brown bears from grizzly bears? For most biologists Alaskan brown bears, or the subspecies *Ursus arctos middendorffi,* refer to the population found along the coasts and islands of southern Alaska. Members of the robust population of these bears roaming Kodiak Island are sometimes known as Kodiak brown bears or Kodiak bears. While these coastal-dwelling bears were once deemed a separate species, biologists now recognize them merely as a subspecies of brown bears or make no distinction at all between this coastal population and bears ranging the interior of the continent.

Access to a rich diet of fish at certain times of the year, primarily spawning salmon, allows the Alaskan brown bear to reach an extraordinarily large size. Males often weigh in excess of 1,000 pounds, with exceptionally large specimens attaining over 1,500 pounds in weight. These gargantuan creatures are roughly equivalent in size to huge male polar bears, making them (along with male polar bears) the most massive land-dwelling carnivores on earth. Purported weights of both male Alaskan brown bears and polar bears have exceeded an incredible 1,700 pounds, nearly as large as a fully mature male bison or domestic bull!

Brown bears roaming the interior of the North American continent belong to the *Ursus arctos horribilis* subspecies and are commonly known as grizzly bears. As for some other mammals, the size of grizzly bears generally follows Bergmann's rule, a biological postulate that concludes that the mass of animals within a species increases in colder or more northern climates. Thus, the largest specimens for species such as moose, whitetail deer, and gray wolves come from the northern populations. While this rule (more like a trend) doesn't apply to all creatures, it holds quite true in relation to grizzly bears. Animals found in the northern interior of Alaska and Canada are considerably larger, on average, than those roaming the grizzlies' southernmost range in Idaho, Montana, and Wyoming.

Physical Characteristics

Grizzly bears, depending on their sex and range, exhibit a remarkable range in size. Smaller females in the southern portion of the bears' range may weigh just slightly over 300 pounds, while northern or coastal females can attain over twice that weight, up to nearly 800 pounds. Males usually weigh from 500 to 1,000 pounds. As noted earlier, exceptionally large males in coastal Alaskan populations may burgeon to over 1,500 pounds. Measured at the front shoulder, grizzlies range from around 3.5 to 4.5 feet in height when on all fours. Their body length commonly stretches from about 6 to 8.5 feet from tail to nose. Large males sometimes exceed these measurements for both height and length by considerable margins. Grizzlies sometimes stand on their hind legs, apparently to obtain a better perception of the world around them. An erect adult grizzly often stands from 7 to 8 feet in height. Standing height of the largest males can exceed 10 feet, with some individuals estimated as having heights greater than 12 feet. For the sake of comparison, the regulation height of a basketball rim is 10 feet. If bears were taught to play the game, I doubt any human all-star alive could dunk over a big boar grizzly!

The hind foot of a very large grizzly may measure 16 inches long by 10 inches wide, although most prints are somewhat smaller, around 10 inches long and 6 inches wide, depending on the location and size of the bear. A grizzly's hind feet are slightly larger than its front feet. The tracks are wide but elongated, appearing somewhat like a broad bare-foot human print with noticeable claw marks.

Utilized for digging, defense, and subduing prey, the claws of an adult grizzly bear may reach 4 inches in length. Although awkward appearing when walking with its head swinging lazily from side to side, a mature grizzly is remarkably swift and agile. The bears can sprint at speeds of 30

Grizzly bear tracks are elongated, with noticeable toe prints and claw marks.
KEVIN RHOADES

miles per hour or slightly faster, a speed that rivals the pace of the average horse in full gallop. Historical information from Yellowstone National Park from the late 1930s records grizzly bears comfortably running for over 2 miles at 25 miles per hour. The same record notes that grizzly bears can keep up with horses running downhill, but are outdistanced when following horses uphill. This observation might have given rise to the erroneous notion that humans attempting to flee from a bear are better served running uphill instead of downhill. In fact, grizzly bears are so much faster than humans that fleeing in any direction is futile.

RANGE AND HABITAT

Historic Range

Ask the average person where grizzly bears live and you'll probably hear some variation of a three-word answer: in the mountains. While that observation is true, grizzlies also roam across open expanses of tundra in the far north. Although it may come as a surprise to many people, grizzly bears are as suited to living on the plains as in the mountains. Prior to European settlement of North America, these great bears were common residents on the Great Plains, where they hunted bison and elk alongside wolves.

Members of the Lewis and Clark expedition encountered grizzly bears far east of the Rocky Mountains on their westward trek to the Pacific Coast. In April 1805, as the explorers journeyed through central and western North Dakota along the Missouri River, they discovered tracks of "the white bear of enormous size" and sighted a few grizzlies. After subsequent encounters in eastern Montana, where the corps learned that grizzlies were incredibly fast, unpredictable, and extremely hard to kill, grizzly bears became one of the most feared hazards of the journey. The US Fish & Wildlife Service (USFWS) estimates that around 50,000 grizzly bears roamed the western United States at the time of the Lewis and Clark expedition, ranging from the Pacific Ocean to the Great Plains.

As settlers moved onto the plains and into the Rocky Mountains, grizzly bears were eliminated through hunting and trapping. Prior to the animals' extermination by humans, the large, clawed footprints of grizzly bears marked the soil in the interior of what is now the United States as far east as Ohio. Grizzlies were also present in the coastal mountain ranges along the Pacific Ocean, ranging southward through California and into northern Mexico. A grizzly bear adorns the state flag of California, although the last surviving member of the state's historic population was killed in 1922. East of California these mighty bears roamed across the American Southwest at least as far east as central Texas.

By 1922 biologists were aware of only thirty-seven intact grizzly bear populations in the contiguous United States. In 1975, when grizzly bears in the lower forty-eight

A grizzly bear adorns the state flag of California. Grizzlies were historically present in the state, but were eliminated in the 1920s.
© ISTOCK.COM/RONNIECHUA

states received protection as a "threatened species" under the Endangered Species Act, only six of those thirty-seven populations remained.

In the north historic grizzly bear populations spanned a range from the western coastline of Alaska eastward to the western shores of Hudson Bay in Canada and everywhere in between. Grizzly bears were found in abundance in the western provinces of Canada, namely British Columbia and Alberta.

Current Range

Currently, grizzly bears are found in the greatest numbers in Alaska and western Canada. They also range across northern Canada in the Yukon and Northwest Territories and Nunavut. An estimated 30,000 or more grizzly bears inhabit Alaska. Canada's grizzly bear population is estimated at 26,000 animals, nearly half of which are found in British Columbia.

In the contiguous United States, members of this species are known to inhabit Washington, Idaho, Montana, and Wyoming. Within those four states grizzly bears definitively occupy five ecosystems identified by the USFWS. In Washington State grizzlies inhabit the north-central portion in the North Cascade Mountains. This area is known as the North Cascades recovery zone for grizzly bear management and is home to a very small population. The area includes remote, mountainous terrain in and around North Cascades National Park. Bears living in this area also inhabit contiguous habitat in southern British Columbia. Given the limited number of bears in the area, most biologists feel this remnant population of grizzly bears faces low odds of survival without intense recovery efforts, which could include population augmentation with bears transplanted from other areas. Bears in this area are widely believed to be the most "at risk" population in the United States.

Given the extremely small population of grizzlies that ranges across the 9,500-square-mile North Cascades recovery zone, efforts to observe and study the bears often meet with failure. However, random encounters with grizzlies in the area attest to their survival. In late October 2009 a hiker snapped a few photos of a grizzly bear he encountered while hiking in the upper reaches of the Cascade River drainage. The photos came to light in the public eye in 2010. At the time, some wildlife officials believed grizzly bears had abandoned the North Cascades portion of the United States. However, given the bear's location, biologists concluded it wasn't likely a transient bear from Canada, but a bruin that resided in the United States. Though precarious, the population of grizzly bears in the North Cascades is apparently still viable.

East of the North Cascades, grizzly bears are also found in Washington state in the Selkirk Mountains north of Spokane, a population area that also includes the extreme northern portion of Idaho. This grizzly bear recovery area includes 2,200 square miles, an area just smaller than the state of Delaware. Similar to the North Cascades ecosystem, grizzly bear habitat in the Selkirk Mountains runs northward into Canada.

The Selkirk ecosystem has distinct boundaries. On the north and east sides, Kootenay Lake (British Columbia) and the Kootenai River (Idaho) form natural geographic boundaries. On the south and east sides, the Selkirk ecosystem finds its limits at the Salmo River (British Columbia) and the Pend Oreille River (Washington and Idaho). The Selkirk ecosystem is home to a small, and possible slowly-growing population of grizzlies. Human-caused mortality appears to be the greatest inhibitor to growth of this grizzly bear population. Of the grizzly bear deaths recorded in the period from 1983 to 2002, for example, a full 80 percent were human caused. A small percentage of the bears were misidentified by hunters legally hunting black bears. Others were removed by wildlife managers after becoming "problem bears" that strayed into small towns, raided campsites or cabins, or engaged in other activities that threatened humans. A few bears were killed by illegal hunting activities (poaching).

Not far east of the Selkirk Mountains lies a third recovery zone for grizzly bears. Known as the Cabinet-Yaak recovery zone, this area encompasses 2,600 square miles of habitat that lies primarily in northwestern Montana, but also extends westward into the Idaho Panhandle. The Cabinet-Yaak ecosystem is divided into two distinct segments by the Kootenai River in northwestern Montana. The Yaak River segment of this recovery area lies north of the Kootenai River, the Cabinet Mountain portion to the south. The Cabinet Mountain portion of the ecosystem composes roughly 60 percent of the total area and includes the Cabinet Mountain Wilderness. Grizzly bear habitat extends from the Cabinet-Yaak portion of the United States northward into Canada.

The USFWS estimates that a few dozen grizzly bears inhabit the Cabinet-Yaak recovery zone. Human-caused mortality was lower in the Cabinet-Yaak recovery zone in the 1983 to 2002 time period than in the Selkirk zone, although around 50 percent of the bears in the research study that died were killed as a result of humans. Most of the deaths occurred within a relatively short distance of a road, a trend similarly recorded in the Selkirk recovery zone. This factor points to a key principle in maintaining grizzly bear habitat. The bears do best in areas where they're buffered from frequent encounters with people and the trappings of human civilization.

Moving eastward into northern Montana, the Northern Continental Divide recovery area includes Glacier National Park, the Bob Marshall Wilderness Complex, and adjacent areas. Grizzly habitat associated with this ecosystem (also known as the NCDE) extends northward into Canada. This area is home to one of the largest populations of grizzly bears in the contiguous United States. A five-year study completed in 2008 using DNA samples from hair-snagging stations and bear rubs in the NCDE revealed samples from 563 individual bears. Undertaken by a team of over 200 researchers and assistants from the Northern Divide Grizzly Bear Project, statistical analysis of the data to account for bears not sampled in the project indicates that slightly more than 750 bears roamed the NCDE at the close of the study. The population has been increasing, with bears moving from the recovery zone into adjacent areas. Within the recovery area, a 2014 study using radio-telemetry indicated the region was completely occupied by reproductive females (sows with offspring). Similar to other parts of the country, grizzly conflicts and mortality are highest in the NCDE where bears routinely come into contact with humans. Less than 20 percent of the land area in this recovery zone is owned by private entities. However, private land accounts for the highest percentage of human-bear conflicts and bear deaths. Dispersing juvenile bears from this population have been recorded far east of the recovery area, in prairie and mountainous regions of central Montana.

The most well-known population of grizzly bears in the contiguous United States ranges across an area encompassing Yellowstone National Park and adjacent wildlands. Known as the Greater Yellowstone Ecosystem, this region includes several wilderness areas in addition to Yellowstone National Park. Grizzly bears in this area are also found in Grand Teton National Park in Wyoming. Bears are found as far east as the northwestern portion of the Wind River Indian Reservation in Wyoming and westward along the Montana-Idaho divide to a point roughly 50 miles west of Yellowstone National Park. The bears have expanded their range from a core area around Yellowstone to the Bridger-Teton National Forest south of Grand Teton National Park in Wyoming, the Targhee National Forest on the west side of the Teton Range in Idaho, and the Beaverhead-Deerlodge National Forest west of Yellowstone National Park in Montana.

In 2007 the USFWS declared this growing grizzly population to be recovered, no longer meeting endangered or threatened status as defined by the Endangered Species Act. However, an order issued in 2009 from the federal district court in Missoula, Montana, overturned the delisting of the grizzly bears in the Yellowstone area, returning them to protection under the Endangered Species Act, a status they have carried since 1975. The bears were once again delisted by the USFWS in 2017. Regardless of the bears' position under the Endangered Species Act (which seems perpetually prone to litigation and debate), grizzly bears are doing well in the Yellowstone recovery area. When they were listed as a threatened species in the lower forty-eight states in 1975, an estimated 136 grizzly bears were found in the Yellowstone recovery area. Bears now occupy at least 48 percent more of the recovery area than when they were listed as a threatened species. Yearly population increases of grizzly bears in the Yellowstone area from the mid-1990s through 2015 measured 4 to 7 percent. Biologists from a multi-agency team of researchers have concluded that more than 650 of these great brown bears roamed the wildlands in and around Yellowstone National Park in 2017. The researchers note that their population estimate is very conservative, making it possible that the number of bears actually living in the area is significantly higher. Grizzly bears are increasingly occupying habitat on the edges of the Greater Yellowstone Ecosystem due to the fact that the core area is increasingly occupied by territorial adults.

When the grizzly bear was listed as a threatened species under the Endangered Species Act, a sixth recovery area was identified, though it was believed to be void of

The area in and around Yellowstone National Park harbors the highest number of grizzly bears in the lower forty-eight states. Yellowstone's grizzly bear population has been growing in recent years due to good cub production and survival.
JACK BALLARD

grizzly bears. The Bitterroot recovery zone spans 5,600 square miles of habitat in east-central Idaho and western Montana, including two large wilderness areas: the Selway-Bitterroot Wilderness area on the Idaho-Montana divide (west of Hamilton, Montana) and the Frank Church Wilderness (west of Salmon, Idaho). Preliminary plans to reintroduce grizzly bears into the Bitterroot recovery area were eventually abandoned by the USFWS. Although the USFWS took an official position that bears were absent from the ecosystem and proposed a reintroduction program in 1997, the reintroduction plan was withdrawn as a proposal in 2001. Opposition to the reintroduction plan came on several fronts. Some local residents opposed having grizzly bears in the area under any plan. Others believed that grizzly bears did inhabit the area and were concerned that a reintroduced population would not be afforded the same federal protections as native bears. Grizzly bears are evidently taking matters into their own hands. A black bear hunter accidentally shot a young male grizzly in September 2007 while hunting in the northern end of the Bitterroot recovery zone. Since then several other grizzly bear encounters have clearly established that bears are present in or very near the recovery zone. Many of these animals have been young males, a segment of the population much more likely to wander than older males or breeding-age females. However, many experts now believe grizzly bears will recolonize this expanse of rugged habitat on their own.

Grizzly Bear Habitat

For all living species, food, water, secure places to rest, and adequate physical space to occupy are the essential elements of habitat. The current state of habitat in relation to grizzly bears is somewhat artificial. Grizzly bears are capable of living in some habitats (such as the Great Plains) that they no longer occupy because their presence is incompatible with agriculture and human civilization.

In the lower forty-eight states, grizzly bears primarily roam across alpine and sub-alpine forests. They occupy similar habitat in the mountains of western Canada and Alaska. Where bears are present along the Pacific Coast of Alaska and Canada, they're often found near streams where they prey upon fish, primarily spawning salmon. At the northernmost portions of their range, in Alaska, the Yukon, Northwest Territories, and Nunavut, grizzly bears make their living in the open tundra.

The amount of space required as habitat for individual grizzly bears varies remarkably depending upon their gender and the geographic area in which they live. Whether it's Grand Teton National Park in Wyoming or Katmai National Park in Alaska or any other location occupied by bears, male grizzlies require much more space than females. The average home range of a boar is two to ten times larger than that of a mature sow living in the same area. Scientists believe the larger ranges of males are related to two primary factors. First, a larger space gives a male higher odds of finding and mating with females. Second, the larger body size of males necessitates a higher protein and caloric intake to maintain, requiring males to range over a more expansive area in search of food. It is important to remember that grizzly bears technically occupy a home range, not a territory. In biological terms a "territory" refers to a

Grizzly bear females, with or without cubs, require a smaller home range than males.
JACK BALLARD

segment of land occupied by an animal where other animals of the same species or gender are expelled. Grizzly bears are not territorial in this sense. The range of several males and females may overlap, even though individual bears have preferred areas.

Just how large is a grizzly bear's home range? One research study involving twelve female bears on Admiralty Island, Alaska, showed an average size of slightly more than 9 square miles. Another study that recorded the movements of nineteen male bears in the central Northwest Territories of Canada yielded an average home range occupying just over 3,150 square miles, a land area significantly larger than the state of Delaware. Individual grizzly bear males in the open tundra of north-central Canada are believed to have ranges as large as 10,000 square miles, an area 100 miles wide by 100 miles long, or slightly larger than the state of Vermont. A grizzly bear's home range is highly correlated to forage. Bears occupying areas with access to abundant, high-quality food sources (such as salmon) have much smaller ranges than those living in areas where forage is less plentiful.

FORAGE AND NUTRITIONAL REQUIREMENTS

Basic Food Sources and Digestive Biology

The sheer size of a grizzly bear demands a considerable intake of nutrition to maintain. Large bears feeding actively may consume eighty to ninety pounds of forage per day. Grizzly bears newly emerged from their dens in the spring don't consume as much forage as they do in the fall prior to denning in the winter. After hibernation it takes the digestive system of a bear a period of time to reaccustom itself to food intake after a long period of dormancy.

Contrary to the beliefs of many people, grizzly bears are not primarily meat-eaters. However, it's difficult to make sound generalizations about the diet of grizzly bears

Plants, particularly young, tender grasses and leafy plants, make up a high percentage of the diet of a grizzly bear.
JACK BALLARD

Along the coast of Alaska and some other locations, grizzly bears consume a high percentage of their diet in meat, most of it spawning salmon. This grizzly sow has caught a silver salmon at Lake Clark National Park in Alaska.
© ISTOCK.COM/STUCKREED

because their eating habits vary drastically based on the time of year and the region of the continent in which they live. Like other carnivores (including humans), bears have a digestive system that includes a single stomach. Their intestines are fairly short. The digestive system of a grizzly bear processes food quite quickly. Meat clears the digestive tract in about 13 hours, while tender plants such as clover may be digested in as little as 7 hours. Although most grizzly bears eat plant matter as a high percentage of their diet, they are very selective herbivores. Lacking the ability to digest plant stalks efficiently, bears favor young, tender grasses and leafy plants that break down more easily than mature grasses or woody plants.

The mouth and teeth of a grizzly bear facilitate its eclectic diet. Their canine teeth are sharp enough to aid them in catching and killing prey. However, their molars are much more developed for chewing than those of carnivores from the feline and canine families, allowing them to efficiently eat and digest plant material.

Grizzly bears are highly omnivorous, meaning they eat both plants and animals. Compared to polar bears, grizzlies eat less meat and more plants. Compared to black bears, grizzlies eat more meat, making them the most omnivorous of the North American bears. However, the percentage of meat in a grizzly bear's diet is highly variable. In general, grizzly bears that inhabit the coastal regions of Alaska or have access to spawning salmon consume a much higher percentage of meat than those living in the interior of the continent. Research indicates that bears with access to salmon may consume as much as 75 percent or more of their diet in meat. By contrast, bears roaming areas without salmon, such as Montana's Glacier National Park, may live on a diet consisting of less than 10 percent meat.

So what do all grizzly bears eat? The best answer to that question is "Whatever is edible and available." A grizzly bear's digestive system can handle about anything, from wasps to mushrooms to the decaying carcass of a winter-killed bison to a simple blade of grass.

Following the system of humans eating from four food groups, the diet of grizzly bears can be similarly analyzed. Let's call the first category vegetables. This would include some grasses that bears commonly eat in the springtime by grazing. Bears also eat forbs (leafy plants), along with portions of plants that grow beneath the soil: roots, corms, and bulbs. Biscuitroot, glacier lily, sweetvetch, and yampa provide grizzlies in some areas with important sources of nutrition that come from the below-ground portions of the plants. The long claws of grizzly bears enable them to efficiently excavate large patches of soil in search of these root crops.

A second category of grizzly food is fruit. This includes primarily berries. These high-calorie fruits are gleaned from shrubs. Huckleberries, blueberries, buffaloberries, rose hips, and bearberries are all important fruits for grizzly bears. In some areas they may eat chokecherries and raspberries as well.

Nuts are a third category of grizzly grub. One nut in particular comprises this food group. Where available, grizzly bears feed voraciously on the nuts of the whitebark pine tree. Whitebark pine cones are loaded with nuts and the trees are loaded with cones in years with good precipitation. Whitebark pine nuts are most important to grizzly bears in the northern Rocky Mountain region of the contiguous United States in such places as Grand Teton and Yellowstone National Parks. Although many grizzlies in these areas feed extensively on whitebark pine nuts, they don't do the work of harvesting them. Bears most commonly raid the extensive caches of pine nuts gathered by red squirrels.

The final category included in the grizzly diet is meat. This category includes the normal creatures people expect grizzly bears to prey upon, such as elk, moose, deer, and caribou. However, grizzly bears are also known to expend considerable energy and effort to dig voles and small ground squirrels from their burrows. They will also eat earthworms and wasp nests. In certain locations in Glacier and Yellowstone National Parks, moths are an extremely important source of meat (can you imagine seeing "moth meat" on a menu?) for grizzly bears. Grizzly bears acquire their "moth meat" from hundreds of thousands of moths that sometimes roost in rockslides in remote, high-elevation locations. Rounding out the meat category is fish. While salmon are the fish species most commonly consumed by grizzly bears, they will also happily dine upon trout and other species when available.

Forage Preferences by the Seasons

Nature's yearly cycle of seasons significantly affects the types of foods available to grizzly bears no matter where they live. Before the advent of refrigeration and modern transportation, the diets of humans were also more significantly influenced by seasonal cycles than they are today. Americans can pop into a grocery store for a bag of apples whether it's January or June, though the natural production of apples occurs in the fall. Grizzly bears have no way of storing or preserving food from season to season except as fat reserves. Thus, grizzly bears must eat what's available and in season.

When bears emerge from hibernation in the springtime, the annual foliage cycle is just beginning. Plants are starting to green up. The greening begins at lower elevations where the snow retreats more quickly, then moves upward to higher elevations as the season progresses. In spring and early summer, grizzly bears are usually found at the lower elevations within their range. They graze heavily upon newly emerging grasses. In most places bears recently arisen from their dens also scavenge the carcasses of winter-killed mammals. This food source and the species it involves vary

Winter-killed animals are an important food source for grizzlies in some locations in early spring. Here a trio of bears feeds upon a bison carcass.
JACK BALLARD

depending on the area. In Yellowstone and Grand Teton National Parks, bison and elk carcasses are the two major sources of winter-killed carrion, although dead antelope, moose, and mule deer may also be found by a wandering bruin. In Alaska and Canada moose and caribou become increasingly important sources of after-winter carrion for grizzly bears.

From late May through June, grizzlies exploit another source of protein. This period represents the birthing season for ungulates such as elk, deer, caribou, and moose. Grizzly bears are often very adept at discovering and killing newborn ungulates. Elk calves are especially prone to predation by bears in some areas. Cow elk tend to birth their young in the same places year after year in areas known as "calving grounds." Grizzly bears learn to frequent the calving grounds. Although elk calves are nearly scentless and well camouflaged, persistent grizzly bears consistently discover and dine upon the young in certain areas, especially in the northern Rocky Mountains, where elk are plentiful.

During the summer several seasonal trends affect the diet of grizzly bears. In the northern Rockies their access to meat declines as carrion is eaten and ungulate calves become too athletic to be easily captured. However, summer normally sprouts a robust and varied crop of plants. Grizzly bears typically ascend to alpine and subalpine meadows where they feed heavily upon plants and their roots. Bears inhabiting the coastal areas of British Columbia and Alaska descend to streams in midsummer where they dine enthusiastically upon spawning salmon. However, not all bears within traveling distance of spawning streams become fish-eaters. Some remain at high elevations, obtaining the highest percentage of their nutrition from alpine plants.

Locally, certain sources of what might best be described as "niche nutrition" become available to bears during the summer. In Yellowstone and Glacier National Parks, this includes the moths of the army cutworm. The moths show up during the summer among very high mountain slopes. Cutworm moths burrow into rockslides to avoid sunlight. Literally millions of moths may inhabit rockslides in the high country. Although they might not seem too appetizing to a human, moths pack a high punch of nutrition for bears, especially in the form of fat. Each moth contains around a half calorie of fat. It is estimated that an ambitious bear may consume in excess of 10,000 moths per day, with some estimates ranging as high as 40,000 moths per day. Thus, a moth-munching grizzly might easily consume 5,000 to 10,000 calories in a single day. Some biologists believe an enterprising grizzly that finds a bumper moth crop could account for nearly half of its yearly caloric requirements in a single month. However, the moth crop is highly variable. Some years they're abundant; at other times they're not.

In Yellowstone National Park spawning cutthroat trout were once an important summer protein source for several dozen grizzly bears in the Yellowstone Lake area. When the cutthroat trout moved upstream from Yellowstone Lake into spawning tributaries, they were preyed upon by bears that would stand in the small spawning streams. The bears usually caught the fish by squashing them against the stream bottom with their front paws. A researcher once observed a female grizzly catch and consume over one hundred cutthroat trout in a single day. Then in 1994 a fisherman caught a trout of a different species in Yellowstone Lake. Nonnative lake trout had evidently been illegally planted in the lake by humans. In a short period of time, the predatory lake trout decimated the cutthroat trout population in Yellowstone Lake. Currently, few cutthroats make the spawning run into Yellowstone Lake tributaries. This once-abundant source of early-summer protein for bears has all but vanished. Lake trout love deep water and do not require streams to spawn. Thus, the fish that now dominates Yellowstone Lake is inaccessible to grizzlies.

Spawning cutthroat trout were once an important food source for grizzly bears in Yellowstone National Park, but have been displaced by nonnative lake trout.
JACK BALLARD

Late summer provides a caloric boost to foraging grizzly bears in many areas. At this time huckleberries, raspberries, chokecherries, rose hips, and other berries begin to ripen. Grizzly bears often descend to somewhat lower elevations at this time of year because berry bushes lower on the mountains produce their crop before those at higher altitudes.

In the fall grizzly bears enter a period in their yearly life cycle known as "hyperphagia." Hyperphagia is a term used to describe overeating in humans. In relation to people chronic hyperphagia commonly leads to obesity and its related health problems. However, for grizzly bears hyperphagia isn't a dietary problem; it's a necessity. In late summer and autumn, bears enter a stage of hyperphagia where they eat ravenously. Weight gains by large bears during this feeding frenzy are impressive. A mature bear with access to abundant, high-calorie food sources can gain three to six pounds per day.

Grizzly bears commonly consume large quantities of fat- or sugar-laden foods during the fall, such as nuts and berries. The fall feeding strategy of a grizzly bear is very simple. Gorge on as much high-calorie food as possible to gain the fat reserves needed to maintain its body during several months of winter hibernation.

For grizzlies like this one in Denali National Park, fall is a critical, but sometimes unpredictable, season in the yearly forage cycle.
© ISTOCK.COM/

In years of plenty nature provides grizzly bears with all they need to satisfy their appetite during fall hyperphagia. However, in areas where berry crops are sparse or whitebark pines produce few nuts, autumn becomes a stressful time for bears seeking to accumulate the needed fat for winter. Hungry bears are more likely to raid camps and cabins seeking human food at this time. The potential for conflict with human hunters also increases. In many areas hunting seasons that allow people to kill moose, elk, deer, and other ungulates for their own consumption coincide with the hyperphagia stage of the grizzly's yearly feeding cycle. Grizzly bears may scavenge gut piles or carcasses from animals killed by human hunters, which sometimes results in deadly confrontations between these two-legged and four-legged predators. Bears with empty bellies are more likely to claim berry patches or frequent other food sources in areas of heavy human use during lean years, also increasing the odds of conflict with people. During this time bears living in areas that provide consistent sources of high-calorie foods buffered from high use by humans encounter the least amount of stress bulking up for hibernation.

ABILITIES AND BEHAVIOR

Physical Abilities

For many wildlife species their appearance gives some hint of their physical abilities. The lithe, streamlined form of the cheetah betrays its speed. The oversized hind legs of a jackrabbit suggest its ability to leap great distances. However, like some human athletes who don't quite look the part, grizzly bears are much faster and more agile than they appear. As noted earlier, grizzly bears can sprint as fast as the average horse and maintain a swift gait for several miles. Despite their lumbering appearance, should nature hold a North American track and field competition for mammals, grizzlies could compete favorably as both sprinters and endurance runners. Grizzlies are also excellent swimmers and very comfortable in the water.

Along with their speed and swimming ability, grizzly bears are incredibly strong. I've watched foraging grizzly bears easily overturn rocks with a single jerk of a forepaw that I'm not sure I could so efficiently dislodge with the aid of a crowbar. Researchers in the mechanical engineering department at Montana State University

Grizzly bears are proficient swimmers and very comfortable in the water.
© ISTOCK.COM/TWILDLIFE

once tested the strength of captive grizzly bears relative to humans. Grizzly bears commonly displayed strength equivalent to that of three to five humans under normal conditions. For example, the grizzly bears could easily roll over a 700-pound dumpster that it took two humans considerable effort just to tip over. The researchers also noted that if the grizzlies were enraged, their strength would be even more dramatic. Grizzly bears are reputed to have the ability to kill a moose or elk with a single blow of a forepaw. More readily observed is their dramatic strength in moving the carcasses of such animals. An adult grizzly bear can handily drag the carcass of an elk or caribou weighing 300 pounds or more should it decide it wants a change of scenery in its dining experience.

In addition to their bodily brawn, grizzly bears possess incredibly powerful jaws, estimated to have one of the highest crushing forces of any animal on the planet. A grizzly bear can break the large bones of its prey or carrion with its teeth to eat the nutritious marrow inside. An angry grizzly bear can sever the trunk of an evergreen tree several inches in diameter with a single bite. Researchers once found the skeletal remains of a large male black bear killed by a large male grizzly bear. The black bear's skull had been crushed by the jaws of the grizzly.

A certain amount of confusion surrounds the grizzly bear's ability to climb trees. Many people believe that black bears can climb trees but grizzly bears cannot. While it's true that black bears are much more efficient and agile tree-climbers than grizzlies, young grizzly bears can easily climb a tree. Adult grizzly bears seem much less inclined to climb, but most biologists believe they have the ability, especially in large trees with stout branches. Some literature erroneously claims that climbing a tree is a good way for humans to avoid a grizzly bear attack. However, grizzly bears have been known to climb trees in pursuit of humans. It's also important to remember that a standing adult grizzly bear can commonly reach 10 feet into a tree to grab an object with a front paw. In Denali National Park in Alaska, more than 10 percent of the documented bear-induced injuries to people have involved grizzlies pulling humans from trees.

Myths and misconceptions also pervade many people's understanding of grizzly bears' sensory abilities. The great brown bears are often described as creatures with a highly developed sense of smell, but possessed of poor eyesight and hearing. Only one aspect of this characterization is correct: Grizzly bears do have an incredibly developed sense of smell. The skull of a grizzly bear exhibits a notably large nasal cavity. Inside the cavity is a complex network of nasal mucus, roughly one hundred times larger than that of a human. In fact, smell is believed to be the grizzly bear's most highly developed sense. Estimates of ability vary, but many biologists feel

Grizzly bears have a highly developed sense of smell. A grizzly bear's ability to detect odors probably rivals that of any animal in the world.
KEVIN RHOADES

a grizzly bear's sensitivity to odors is thousands of times more acute and sophisticated than that of a human.

Direct comparisons are difficult to establish, but a grizzly bear's sense of smell may be several times more acute than that of a bloodhound. Coastal grizzly bears in Alaska detect the presence of clams buried along the seashore by smelling them. Grizzly bears can smell carrion from several miles away. In addition to using their noses to find food, grizzly bears perceive much about one another based upon smell. By smelling urine or footprints, a male bear can learn much about another grizzly that's entered his home range, be it a female that he may court for mating or another male that might become a rival. Like some other animals, a grizzly bear has an additional scent-detecting organ on the roof of its mouth known as a Jacobson's organ. This organ detects scents borne by moisture and aids grizzly bears in communication with one another. Subordinate males can perceive the scent of a dominant bear and avoid it. Males use their olfactory senses to detect the presence of females and their readiness for breeding during the mating season.

Although a grizzly bear's sense of smell is assumed to be the most highly developed of its five senses, that doesn't mean its other perceptual abilities are stunted. Contrary to widespread belief, grizzly bears probably see just as well as humans. Grizzlies are often observed reacting to visual stimuli at considerable distances while hunting, just like a human might react to spotting a grizzly bear from a half mile away. Like other bears, grizzlies will often stand on their hind legs to make themselves taller. This behavior is not aggressive in nature. In most instances the bear is simply raising itself farther from the ground so that it can see better.

A grizzly bear's night vision is superior to a person's. Bears have a reflective layer of tissue on the back of their eyeballs that bounces light back through the retina. This provides additional stimulation of the rods, the sensory portion of the eyeball responsible for night vision, increasing the bears' visual acuity in low light.

Little scientific information exists regarding the specific hearing abilities of grizzly bears or bears in general. It is believed by some biologists that bears have hearing abilities in the ultrasonic range, allowing them to detect sounds indiscernible to the human ear. One research project involving polar bears demonstrated their ability and willingness to react to vocalizations of ringed seals, one of their primary prey. The ears of grizzly bears usually appear quite small in relation to their massive bodies, but this does not imply that their hearing ability is underdeveloped. Based upon numerous observations of grizzly bears, experts have concluded that their hearing is at least as acute as that of humans.

Tactile proficiency, or the sophisticated use of touch, might seem an ability far removed from the paws and jaws of a creature as big and brawny as a grizzly bear. However, grizzlies can adeptly work their claws into a crack between two rocks to gain leverage for unearthing a meal of grubs (or breaking into a garbage dumpster). "Bear-proof" food containers and garbage cans give ample evidence of grizzlies' dexterity with their paws. Such containers must be carefully engineered so that an

enterprising bear can't use its dexterous paws to access what's inside. Additional evidence of the grizzly bear's sophisticated sense of touch is found in their method for munching the nuts of whitebark pines. For decades biologists wondered how such large animals could effectively feed upon such small nuts. The riddle was answered when researchers gave captive bears some cones. The bears stomped and ripped the cones with their front paws to extract the nuts, then nimbly licked them up with their tongues!

Vocal and Visual Communication

Grizzly bears rely upon a wide variety of communication strategies. They "talk" to one another in sounds, although many of their vocalizations aren't easily heard from a distance. Females and cubs exchange vocal cues of their contentment and bond. Sows may grunt softly to their cubs. Cubs sometimes make a low noise indicating their security and contentment, similar to the purring sound of a cat. Young grizzlies still in the company of their mother may emit loud noises of distress that have the quality of bawling or screaming. Bears also blow air from their lungs as a means of vocalizing and make grunting sounds. Blowing and grunting can both be signs of apprehension or disturbance.

Loud, agitated huffing sounds are among those most strongly associated with aggression. Intense growling also communicates anger. Both of these sounds are highly significant to humans who accidentally encounter grizzly bears at close range. Huffing noises occurring just before a charge are reported by a high percentage of

people who have been attacked by grizzly bears. Popping its jaws together is a similar means for a bear to communicate aggression.

Along with vocal indications, a bear's body language communicates its feelings. Grizzly bears standing on their hind legs are usually curious and merely attempting to get a better look at an object of attention. A bear that sits down is comfortable and at ease. When confronted by another bear, a human, or some other creature perceived as a threat, a grizzly bear may turn sideways or swing its head from side to side to indicate that it feels threatened but is looking for a noncombative way out of the situation. Bears that stare another bear or animal directly in the eyes and lay back their ears feel threatened and may attack. This behavior can be accompanied by barks, moaning sounds, or woofing noises.

Grizzly bears also communicate in other ways. Bears use trees to communicate their presence to others of their kind. Grizzlies will rub their backs and shoulders on these "scratching posts," leaving behind a clear message in scent to other bears that wander into the area. They also mark the trees with their claws, often reaching high onto the trunk and scoring the bark deeply. These claw marks are thought to give other bears an indication of the health and strength of the individual marking the scratching post.

Hibernation

From late fall until spring, most grizzly bears retreat to dens below ground or dug into a snowbank to hibernate. On Alaska's Kodiak Island some males do not den at all. Elsewhere, denning behaviors generally follow predictable patterns. Females den before males in the fall and emerge later in the spring, making the total denning time for sows substantially longer than that of boars. Grizzly bears inhabiting northern climates have a longer denning period than those in the south. Thus, a male grizzly bear in Yellowstone National Park (latitude 44 degrees N) may spend around 130 days in its den, while a male in central Alaska (latitude 62 degrees N) may spend about 180 days in its winter dormancy.

Is "hibernation" the best descriptor of a bear's winter activity (or lack thereof)? In the past some biologists argued that bears are not true hibernators and their winter dormancy should be called "torpor" instead. However, most wildlife biologists now accept "hibernation" as the best description of this remarkable adaptation grizzly bears possess to avoid winter starvation. During hibernation bears do not eat, drink, or expel body waste. However, they do lose lots of weight. Remember all that fat bears try to gain during their fall feeding binges? A grizzly bear commonly drops 15 to 30 percent of its body mass during hibernation.

Hibernation in grizzly bears differs in some important ways from that experienced by other animals such as ground squirrels. These creatures, sometimes known as "deep hibernators," experience drastic decreases in body temperature. The body temperature of a deep hibernator may fall from over 100 degrees F to below 50 degrees F. Grizzly bears experience a much more modest reduction in body temperature of around 10 to 12 degrees F. A grizzly bear's metabolic rate drops to about one-half the rate of energy consumption when it is active at other times. A hibernating bear's heart rate may slow from forty-five beats per minute at rest during the summer to fifteen beats per minute during hibernation. Respirations can drop from seven breaths per minute to one breath every 45 seconds. Unlike deep hibernators that cannot be easily awakened or react in a coordinated manner to danger, hibernating grizzly bears can awaken quite quickly and are able to react efficiently when they do.

In most places grizzly bears dig their own dens. Some bears will use excavated dens for more than 1 year. Others utilize natural cavities such as caves for dens. In the far north bears sometimes dig dens into snowbanks. Location of denning sites varies with geographical region. However, some general trends exist. Dens are most often found on slopes that are steeper than others in an area. Grizzly bears prefer remote, undisturbed locations for their dens and are particularly vulnerable to disturbance at denning time. A grizzly bear surprised at its den may abandon the site.

Excavation of a den may involve a grizzly moving more than a ton of earth to create a winter home. It takes a grizzly about 3 to 7 days to dig a den. In terms of winter preparation, bears are just like people. Some folks put on their storm windows in advance; others wait until the last minute. Researchers have observed a similar pattern with grizzly bears. Some dig a den well in advance, while others don't do their excavating until shortly before retreating below ground for the winter.

In the yearly life cycle of the grizzly bear, another miraculous milestone occurs during hibernation. This is the time that sows give birth to their tiny, helpless cubs. But that's a story we'll save for the next section!

REPRODUCTION AND YOUNG

The Mating Season

Grizzly bear cubs are born to hibernating females in the dead of winter. But their life story actually begins the previous summer during the mating season. In late spring or early summer, male bears that are solitary during the rest of the year begin to seek and keep company with females. How do two grizzly bears, both of which might have a home range of several hundred square miles, find each other for mating? Scientists believe females of sufficient age and fitness for breeding leave scent trails in late spring that are discovered and followed by male bears. Once a male and female meet, they get acquainted. The prospective pair may engage in a game of chase, or wrestle. During these courtship activities the female is assessing the male's health and strength. If she finds him acceptable, the two will become a pair. Evidence of a female's acceptance of her suitor may be displayed by both bears through nuzzling and licking. These pair bonds, however, are short-lived, usually lasting a few days or weeks.

The time of actual breeding varies considerably depending on the location, the age and physical state of the female, and the particular year. A research study conducted in Yellowstone National Park reported the earliest date of breeding on May 18 and the latest on July 11. In Katmai National Park in Alaska, mating occurs from late May to early July. No matter where they live, most grizzly bears probably breed during the month of June.

During this time male bears will try to hide a female away from other males, keeping her in an isolated area where she's less likely to be seen or smelled by a rival. Grizzly bears are not monogamous, which means that during any given year a female may

Grizzly sows may mate with more than one boar. "Twin" cubs might actually have different fathers.
© ISTOCK.COM/EEI_TONY

mate with more than one male and a male may mate with more than one female. Thus, a male bear will expend considerable energy trying to keep a female away from other males. In Waterton Lakes and Banff National Parks in Canada, researchers have documented boars essentially herding sows to high mountaintops. There they forcibly repel the female's attempts to return to lower elevations until breeding is complete. Evidently, some instinctual drive prompts them to isolate females in these lofty areas where their scent is much less likely to be dispersed to rival males.

In cases where a female mates with more than one male, each of the boars may father offspring in the same litter. Female grizzlies may produce up to four cubs in a litter, although one to three is most typical. In a litter of three, each of the cubs may be sired by a different father if the female mated with several different males during the breeding season. After breeding, a male may stay with a female for a short period of time. But by early August the pairs have normally broken up and bears of both sexes have gone back to their solitary ways.

Pregnancy and Gestation

For most mammals, whether a female becomes pregnant as a result of breeding is determined quickly. If the female's egg (or eggs) doesn't become fertilized and attach to the uterine wall shortly after mating, she will not become pregnant. This process, however, is much more complex for grizzly bears. Grizzly bears are one of a number of species (including other bears and animals such as weasels, armadillos, and seals) that become pregnant through a process known as "delayed implantation." Delayed implantation is an obligatory biological process for some species (such as grizzly bears), meaning it occurs all the time. In other species delayed implantation is a facultative process, referring to the fact that it occurs in response to conditions in a female's body or the environment.

After mating, fertilized eggs (embryos) float in a grizzly bear's uterus for a period of time. They remain viable during this interval, but do not absorb the nutrients from the female's body necessary for growth because they have not yet attached to the wall of the uterus. Sometime in late fall or early winter, about the time the sow enters her den, the embryos she is carrying either attach to the uterine wall, creating a pregnancy, or are simply reabsorbed by her body.

What determines whether a female bear becomes pregnant following the process of delayed implantation? Remember all that food grizzly bears eat in late summer and fall to store fat for hibernation? For female bears that mated earlier in the summer, fat reserves also play a critical role in pregnancy. If her body senses she has sufficient reserves of fat and other nutrients necessary to successfully birth and nurse young, a sow will become pregnant. If not, her embryos will be reabsorbed by her body, delaying pregnancy for at least another year. Although it is a seemingly odd process, evolutionary biologists believe delayed implantation performs a necessary and beneficial function in grizzly bears. Gestation (the process of nourishing an embryo from implantation to birth) and nursing are costly biological processes for grizzly bear sows.

By discontinuing a pregnancy when the female has insufficient physical reserves to either gestate or nurse her young, delayed implantation gives a measure of insurance to the reproductive process. In years that a female is in less than optimal body condition, she won't bear offspring, insulating both herself and her offspring from the risk of malnutrition.

If a female grizzly's body gives her pregnancy the green light, so to speak, the embryos attach to the uterine wall and begin to develop. Although the time between a female's mating and the birth of her cubs commonly spans 6 months or more, the actual gestation period is much shorter. From the time the embryo attaches to birth is about 8 weeks.

Birth

Grizzly cubs are born in January or February. Ironically, this is typically the coldest season of winter. Newborn cubs are extremely small and helpless in relation to the size and strength of an adult bear. They weigh less than a pound and enter the world blind, hairless, and without teeth. While birthing her cubs, the mother bear becomes semiconscious but quickly falls back into a deep sleep. The tiny cubs can move well enough to nurse, but are otherwise quite helpless. Growth occurs rapidly, however, due in large measure to the rich milk of the mother bear, which is more than 20 percent fat. By the time the cubs emerge from the den with their mother, their eyes are open, they have become very mobile, and their bodies are covered with fur. Although still very small, they've grown considerably, now weighing some six to nine pounds.

Nurturing Cubs to Adulthood

In general, sows with cubs are the last grizzly bears to awaken from hibernation in the spring. While the mother bear is still lethargic from her long winter's sleep, the cubs are playful and energetic. Females with young often stay close to the den site for several weeks and may sometimes temporarily return to the den for shelter.

For the first several months of life, grizzly bear cubs are highly dependent on their mother's milk for nourishment. Like adult bears, grizzly cubs are very intelligent. From an early age they are constantly observing their mother's behavior and mimic it with actions of their own. This pattern enables them to master skills they'll need in adulthood, such as feeding strategies. Cubs eat the foods their mother provides for them and quickly learn to find and harvest them on their own. Grizzly cubs also prepare for adult life with their seemingly boundless enthusiasm for play. Siblings from the same litter spend many hours wrestling on the ground or grappling while they stand upright on their hind legs. They like to chase one another or play what appears to be a game of follow-the-leader that may find them climbing on logs or scrambling over boulders.

More elaborate amusements are sometimes observed among individual cubs. In Yellowstone National Park I once observed a sow and her two yearling cubs scavenging an old bison carcass. The carcass had decomposed to just a skeleton, but the

mother and one of the cubs seemed quite content to gnaw on the bones. The other cub had a different agenda. Grasping a sizeable bone in its forepaws, it rolled onto its back and proceeded to toss the bone in the air. Thinking it a random but fascinating act, I grinned with delight at having the opportunity to observe and photograph such a unique, playful behavior. My delight turned to astonishment when the cub spent the next couple minutes deliberately tossing the bone aloft with its front paws and attempting to catch it. Such activities probably develop dexterity among young bears and also enhance their problem-solving skills. What's next? I thought as the bears finally ambled away. Is this youngster going to figure out how to juggle with bison bones?

Young grizzly bears typically stay with their mother until they are 2 years old. As they age, they become increasingly less dependent upon the sow for care, although 2-year-old offspring have been observed nursing. Separation of mothers and their young may be triggered by her readiness to mate and produce another litter. Adult male grizzly bears are a persistent threat to cubs. For their first year of life, a grizzly sow will attempt to protect her cubs from an aggressive male. Grizzly bears can efficiently climb trees in

Grizzly bears have one of the lowest reproductive rates of any North American mammal.
© ISTOCK.COM/ MATTALBERTS

their first year of life, a strategy they may use to elude the jaws of a threatening male. Scientists believe male bears may kill cubs for a variety of reasons. In some cases the cubs are eaten. Removing cubs from a female bear may also make her more apt to breed. It has also been theorized that boars kill cubs that have been sired by other males, increasing the likelihood that young in a particular area are the offspring of the dominant male. Whatever the motivation, adult males of their own kind are one of the hazards cubs must avoid in order to reach adulthood.

The fact that grizzly sows normally invest what amounts to 3 years from the time they breed until their cubs depart and they breed again is one of the reasons grizzlies have one of the lowest reproductive rates of any North American mammal. Another factor involves their slow pace toward sexual maturity. Grizzly bear females normally become capable of reproduction at between 4 and 7 years of age. Males usually reach sexual maturity at 4 to 6 years of age.

The age at which a female births her first litter and becomes part of the reproducing population of grizzly bears varies substantially by region. Nutrition plays a big factor in when a grizzly sow is able to produce her first litter. Bears on the Alaskan Peninsula, where food is abundant, often birth their first litter at 4 or 5 years of age. In Yellowstone National Park the age of first reproduction for females averages around 6 years of age. Areas that offer bears poorer access to nutritious forage may see few females reproducing until they are 7 or 8 years old. Once they reach breeding age, sow grizzlies may produce young until they are 20 years old or more. Given the grizzly bear's slow rate of sexual maturity and reproduction, the loss of even a few breeding-age females in a small population may greatly reduce its viability.

GRIZZLY BEARS AND OTHER ANIMALS

Grizzlies and Other Predators

Grizzly bears are often referred to as "top-of-the-food-chain predators." Such a characterization is correct. I've found Internet chats debating the outcome of a fight between a grizzly bear and a lion or male gorilla. But under wild, natural conditions, precious few rival predators will challenge the supremacy of a grizzly bear. In eastern Russia, Siberian tigers are known to kill members of the *Ursus arctos* species (and vice versa). Conflicts

between grizzly bears and polar bears may find the great white hunters of the north gaining the upper hand. Wolverines are believed capable of usurping or defending a carcass from a grizzly bear, primarily through a frightful display of snarling and intimidation. But with very rare exceptions, no single wild animal that shares its habitat deliberately challenges an adult grizzly bear.

Nonetheless, grizzly bears in many habitats maintain complex and important relationships with other predators. The relationship between wolves and grizzly bears is particularly intriguing. In Alaska and Canada interactions between grizzly bears and wolves have continued their natural course for centuries. In the lower forty-eight states, however, wolves were exterminated a century ago. The reintroduction of wolves to Yellowstone National Park and the natural colonization of wolves in Glacier National Park and other portions of the northern Rocky Mountains in the contiguous United States have necessitated that indigenous grizzly bear populations once again accommodate wolves in their world.

In Yellowstone researchers have had ample opportunity to observe interactions between grizzly bears and the recently returned wolves. From the standpoint of grizzlies, wolves represent both opportunity and opposition. Prior to wolf reintroduction management biologists theorized that winter wolf predation would leave fewer carcasses of winter-killed ungulates (primarily elk and bison) available for scavenging by grizzly bears in the early spring. However, they also postulated that this diminished presence of a potentially important food source might be offset by grizzly bears taking over carcasses of animals killed by wolves. Some concern was expressed regarding the possibility of wolf packs killing young grizzly bear cubs.

In general, biologists' predictions regarding wolf and grizzly bear interactions in Yellowstone were accurate and reflect the relationship between the two species in Alaska, Canada, and other places where wolves and grizzlies share the same range. Adult grizzly bears in Yellowstone are usually successful in usurping carcasses from wolves, but not always. Female bears with cubs frequently repel wolves, possibly for the cubs' protection. Wolves and grizzly bears have also been observed peaceably feeding on the same carcass.

Do the two species kill one another? The short answer is yes. In 2001, 6 years after wolves were reintroduced to Yellowstone, researchers discovered the carcasses of two grizzly bear cubs in separate locations. Both were killed near animal carcasses (one an elk, the other a bison) that had been fed upon by both grizzly bears and wolves. Laboratory analysis of the dead cubs indicated both had been killed by wolves.

Undisputed rulers of their world, grizzly bears are only in rare instances deliberately challenged by other predators.
© ISTOCK.COM/MOOSE HENDERSON

In many places such as Yellowstone National Park, wolves and grizzly bears share a complex relationship that may ultimately be very beneficial to bears.
KEVIN RHOADES

The status of interactions between wolves and grizzly bears in Yellowstone is essentially similar to those observed elsewhere. Grizzly cubs are in the greatest danger from wolves. Wolves take their greatest risk when attempting to defend a carcass from an adult grizzly bear. Den sites of wolves are vigorously protected by the pack. Wolf packs are highly successful repelling grizzlies from their denning areas. However, black bears are known to have killed single female wolves defending a den, so a similar outcome from an aggressive grizzly bear is also possible. Biologists seem to agree that where prey animals are abundant, competition between wolves and grizzly bears is negligible. Where prey is less plentiful, the presence of the two species may exert some influence on the populations of each other, but such a relationship is difficult to establish. For wildlife watchers the rare opportunity to view wolves and grizzly bears in the same setting or observe their infrequent interactions with each other is a thrill not soon to be forgotten.

Interactions between wolves and grizzly bears are not commonplace. But due to the fact that both of these predators frequent open country, these interactions are more easily observed by humans than interactions between grizzlies and more seldom seen predators, such as mountain lions (cougars). Mountain lions are rarely viewed by humans in the wild. As they prefer habitats with timber or shrub cover and are highly nocturnal creatures with incredible eyesight, the odds of a person sighting a mountain lion in uncontrolled outdoor settings is very low. Thus, directly observing behavioral exchanges between grizzly bears and mountain lions is like uncovering a needle in the proverbial haystack.

Nonetheless, researchers have discovered a potentially very important relationship between mountain lions and grizzly bears. Researchers in the northern Rocky Mountains of the United States have documented grizzly bears displacing cougars from their kills with a surprising frequency. In one study researchers found that of fifteen cougar-killed elk in the Kintla Lake region of Glacier National Park, grizzly bears visited 33 percent, or five of the kills. Mountain lions in several study areas routinely lost carcasses to grizzly bears. Grizzlies usurping cougar kills happens most frequently in the fall and early spring, when the two animals both tend to live in proximity to elk and deer, two of the most common prey species of mountain lions.

At least in some locations, it appears that stealing carcasses from cougars may be a significant way for grizzlies to access high-protein, nutritious forage at times when they most need it. Prior to denning and just after emergence are two times of the year when discovering abundant food sources is very beneficial to bears, and these are the times when they're most likely to obtain carcasses from mountain lions. However, the situation isn't so advantageous for the cats. When a grizzly bear moves in on a mountain lion's kill, the cat is forced to attempt a defense of its prey or make another kill. Predation is a high-risk endeavor for cougars. A study in Alberta, Canada, indicated that almost 30 percent of the natural deaths to cougars were a result of wounds sustained while attempting to kill prey. Researchers once observed an exceptionally skilled team of mountain lion hunters consisting of a female and her two large cubs. In

23 days this hunting team killed four elk, two cows, and two large calves. Grizzly bears displaced the cougars from one of the kills and fed on two others. Biologists estimated that the bears gleaned nearly 350 pounds of food from these carcasses. Where grizzly bears and cougars share the same range, the bears may receive substantial benefit from the mountain lions. The cougars, by contrast, may experience more risk and adversity from the bears.

Grizzlies also share their world with other bears, polar and black. Interactions between grizzly and polar bears occur on the fringes of the animals' range in Alaska and Canada. Research concerning specific behavioral interactions between the species is lacking. However, it is known that grizzly and polar bears can and do interbreed. Crossbred animals have been killed by hunters in Canada, and at least one instance of a hybrid mating with a grizzly bear has been recorded. As warming continues to occur in northern latitudes interactions and interbreeding between these two massive species of bears will likely become more common, the results of which remain uncertain.

In general, black bears give grizzly bears a wide berth. Large male black bears may effectively compete with subadult grizzly bears, but otherwise the dominance of grizzlies over their smaller, black cousins is obvious and rarely challenged. Grizzly bears may attempt to kill black bears, but in these infrequent instances the black bears' climbing ability gives them an advantage. An adult grizzly bear is unlikely to expend the effort to try to dislodge a black bear from a tree it has climbed for protection. However, researchers have documented black bear deaths at the jaws of grizzlies.

Parasites and Diseases

Grizzly bears, like other free-roaming mammals, commonly encounter a range of parasites. These include external parasites (such as ticks and fleas) and internal parasites (such as tapeworms and roundworms). The role of parasites in relation to grizzly bears' health and reproductive efficiency is not clearly understood. But researchers believe that the nutritional stress caused by parasites that has been well documented with other species also affects grizzly bears. Various habitats and locations determine the extent to which grizzly bears might be exposed to parasites. Some parasites are common in certain portions of grizzly bear range but absent in others.

A survey of grizzly bears in western Montana and Yellowstone National Park discovered nine various parasites afflicting grizzlies, from wood ticks to hookworms. It is assumed that grizzlies inhabiting similar habitats in Idaho, Washington, and the Canadian Rockies would be exposed to similar parasites. Roundworms were the mostly commonly occurring parasite, followed by trichina worms, tapeworms, and hookworms. Most of these are intestinal parasites, except for the trichina worm, which invades its host's tissue. Forty percent of the cubs surveyed were host to parasites, a figure that climbed to over 90 percent in 6- to 9-year-old bears. Grizzly bears surveyed in the Northwest Territories of Canada were also commonly afflicted with intestinal parasites, especially roundworms and tapeworms.

Healthy, adult grizzly bears probably don't experience severely negative effects from internal parasites in low concentrations. However, in high concentrations intestinal parasites may rob significant levels of nutrition from grizzly bears. Some species of tapeworms absorb high quantities of vitamin B12 from humans, resulting in anemia, but the extent to which this occurs in bears is unknown. Large numbers of intestinal parasites rob nutrition from their host, an occurrence that may influence the health of infected grizzly bears. In 2010 a female grizzly bear killed one camper and injured two others at a campground near Cooke City, Montana. She fed upon the individual she killed. The attack was most probably motivated by hunger. The sow was accompanied by three cubs and in very poor physical condition, her small intestine loaded with parasites. It is impossible to explain the exact reason for such a deadly attack, but experts believe her severe malnutrition, exacerbated by parasites, probably prompted the attacks.

Predation

Grizzly bears consume a mostly vegetarian diet in most places, yet their ability as predators is considerable. In certain areas of Yellowstone National Park, grizzly bears prey upon a higher percentage of elk calves than any other predator, including wolves. In a 2003 to 2005 study in Yellowstone, bears (black and grizzly) accounted for around 55 to 60 percent of the entire mortality of tagged calves in the study. The keen noses of grizzly bears and their intelligence and stamina make them very effective predators of elk calves. Elk birth their young in the same areas year after year. Grizzlies remember these places and use their hunting skills in several strategies to kill young elk. When elk calves are very young, grizzlies will cover a known calving area in a zigzagging pattern.

Grizzly bears are capable predators, commonly targeting the young of species such as elk, deer, moose, and caribou, but are also capable of killing adult animals.
JACK BALLARD

They use their keen sense of smell to locate the nearly scentless calves, but also periodically rear on their hind legs to visually search for calves. Grizzlies also ambush bands of elk cows and calves in open areas, seeking to confuse and separate young calves from the herd. The young elk are often caught by a bear that cuts them off when they attempt to rejoin the herd. Ambush tactics are also used by grizzly bears that stalk within close range of elk calves using timber or other cover, then rush quickly to make their kill. Finally, grizzlies will occasionally use their speed and stamina to capture young elk. Researchers once observed a grizzly bear chasing a herd of elk for over 30 minutes in a chase that covered almost 2 miles, killing three elk calves in the process. Newborn caribou, moose, and deer are likewise primary prey animals for grizzlies in areas where they exist.

Young ungulates aren't the only ones killed by grizzlies. Under the right circumstances grizzly bears can

and do prey upon adult animals. Grizzly predation on mature ungulates usually occurs in the spring, when bears are able to target animals weakened by the winter. They also opportunistically hunt hoofed animals that have been injured or are otherwise vulnerable. In rare instances grizzly bears successfully hunt and kill healthy adult ungulates, even bison, the largest hoofed animal in North America. In the fall of 2000, a researcher observed a sow grizzly bear successfully bring to earth a 3-year-old bull bison.

The predation efforts of grizzly bears aren't always targeted on large animals. They routinely dig small, burrowing animals such as pocket gophers from the earth. Grizzlies have been observed chasing ducks, geese, and sandhill cranes. To my knowledge, no one has seen a grizzly bear actually catching a bird, but such an outcome isn't outside the realm of possibility, given the remarkable physical abilities of these great, athletic predators.

GRIZZLY BEARS AND HUMANS

Grizzly Bears in History

The awe, fear, and fascination that modern people find in the grizzly bear were shared by many ancient peoples. Evidence of the dominant place the grizzly bear held in the lore and legends of our historical predecessors is amply illustrated in stories concerning stars. The name of the constellation Ursa Major means "great bear." Ancient Greeks identified the stars of this constellation forming the shape of a bear. A legend concerning Zeus, the ruler of the gods, accompanied it. Zeus fell in love with a nymph, Callisto, who bore him a child. Zeus's wife, Hera, was jealous and transformed Callisto

Various American Indian legends equate the Big Dipper with a grizzly bear.
© ISTOCK.COM/
IGORKOVALCHUK

into a bear. Later Callisto's child, who had become a hunter, was about to inadvertently kill his mother. Zeus intervened, tossing both the bear-mother and her son into the sky, where they became the constellations Ursa Major and Ursa Minor. In the two constellations the "bears" have very long tails, unlike flesh-and-blood grizzly bears on earth. Evidently, Zeus used the long tails as handles for casting the bears into the sky.

Independently of the Greeks, American Indian peoples generated their own legends of a great bear in the sky. While the Greeks identified the bear with the entire constellation of Ursa Major, American Indians saw the bear in the stars of the Big Dipper. Technically speaking, the Big Dipper is not a constellation, but an obvious grouping of stars, known in the astronomical world as an "asterism." An asterism is a smaller, more easily recognized portion of a constellation. Various American Indian tribes viewed the Big Dipper as a great bear (most likely a grizzly) being pursued by three hunters. The four stars composing the "cup" portion of the Big Dipper are the bear; the three stars composing the "handle" part of the asterism are the hunters. Throughout the seasons the movements of the Big Dipper across the northern sky recount a story of the interactions between the hunters and the hunted. The hunters discover the bear in the spring. All summer they pursue the bear across the night sky. In the fall they catch up to it and pierce it with their arrows. The bear rises on its hind feet, staining the earth with its blood, which corresponds to the red coloration in autumn foliage. All winter it is laid low in death, but as hibernating bears of the earth disappear below ground in late fall only to reappear in the spring, the great bear in the sky is also reborn. The story of the hunt is replayed every year in the movements of the Big Dipper across the night sky. Various tribes told differing versions of the story. Some replaced humans hunting the great bear with birds. Of the birds pursuing the grizzly bear, it was the robin that killed it, forever staining the feathers on its breast with the blood of the bear. This is why robins have a red breast.

In addition to the dramatic story staged in the heavens, American Indian tribes recounted numerous other legends regarding the grizzly bear, stories that involved the grizzly bear in relation to other animals as well as humans. Throughout the legends one dominant theme persists. The grizzly bear is the mightiest of the animals and very intelligent as well. Both humans and other animals are wise to remember this and give the bear its due respect.

The American Indians' reverence toward the grizzly bear showed in activities other than their legends. Plains Indians felt that the powers of the grizzly bear, if appropriated by people, could guard warriors in battle and cure or insulate individuals from illness. Native peoples of the Pacific Northwest commonly adorned totem poles, dishes, and other items with images of bears. Hunters from some tribes pursued and killed grizzly bears as a sign of a warrior's exceptional courage and skill. Grizzly bear claws and hides decorated the clothing of some tribes, and the meat of a grizzly bear would be consumed as well. Other groups left bears alone, prohibiting the eating of bear meat.

Grizzly Bears in Modern Times

As described earlier in this chapter, the arrival of European immigrants to North American and their settling of the West dramatically reduced the range of grizzly bears. A few bears persisted in places as far south as California in the 1920s, but bears were eliminated from all but a few areas shortly thereafter. One of the strongholds of the grizzly bear was Yellowstone National Park, a place whose history with bears suggestively illustrates changing attitudes of Americans toward grizzly bears and the natural world over time. When Yellowstone was created in 1872 through an act of Congress, it preserved a large region of habitat from logging, agriculture, settlement, and other human activities that brought people in conflict with grizzlies. However, human interactions with grizzlies in the early decades of Yellowstone weren't always in the bears' best interest. By the early 1890s grizzly bears had joined black bears in scavenging garbage from open-pit dumps adjacent to lodging facilities and campgrounds, developing an association with humans and food. In 1916 the first documented human fatality occurred in the park. A grizzly bear killed a wagon driver and raided his load of oats and hay. In response, associates of the teamster baited a barrel filled with dynamite. When the bear came to the trap, the charge was detonated, blowing up the bear.

People viewing captive grizzly bears can falsely conclude that they're oversized pets. This grizzly was photographed as part of a streetside animal act in Moscow, Russia, in 2000. Such portrayals have become less common in the United States in the past several decades and are highly discouraged by grizzly bear experts.
JACK BALLARD

By the 1950s bears begging along the park's roadsides, both grizzly bears and black bears, were a major tourist attraction in Yellowstone. Visitors hand-fed bears from their vehicles, sometimes getting clawed in the process. Bears damaged automobiles and camps. While most visitors viewed Yellowstone's food-scavenging bears as a novelty, others saw them as a nuisance. Cartoon portrayals, circus acts, and other uses of bears for entertainment purposes during this time (and sometimes persisting into the present) often portrayed bears more along the lines of overgrown pets or cuddly characters than wild and potentially dangerous animals that are never truly tamed.

Recognizing the need for greater self-sufficiency in the grizzly bear population and charting a new management course to return bears to their natural mode of living, Yellowstone National Park enacted a series of management plans from the 1960s to the mid-1980s that closed dumps, vigorously enforced prohibitions on bear feeding, and created food storage regulations for campers. At first grizzly bears had a difficult time readjusting. However, conflicts and necessary removal of "problem bears" began to diminish as new generations of grizzlies, no longer dependent upon human food

A grizzly bear researcher snapped this photo of a sow grizzly and three cubs raiding a dumpster at night. Such instances led to the development of bear-proof storage for garbage and food in national parks and other areas.
KEVIN RHOADES

sources, were born. Although the specifics varied in different locations, a similar evolution of bear management and conservation also occurred in such locations as Glacier National Park, Canadian parks, and popular bear-viewing areas in Alaska.

In 1975 grizzly bears in the contiguous United States were designated a threatened species under the provisions of the Endangered Species Act. As such, grizzly bears are protected from hunting in the lower forty-eight states. Land-use practices in grizzly bear habitat must also conform to certain measures of conservation for bears.

In Alaska and Canada grizzly bears are protected in some areas, but can be hunted by humans in others. Grizzly bear hunting is closely regulated and monitored, with quotas intended to protect populations from decline due to overhunting. Although some advocacy groups believe grizzly bears should never be hunted, wildlife managers in Alaska and Canada believe that regulated hunting does not represent a significant risk to grizzly bear numbers.

Humans and Bears: Current Interactions and Precautions

The thought of being attacked by a grizzly bear is enough to keep some people from recreating in bear habitat or may leave them shivering in their sleeping bag or constantly looking over their shoulders for a ghost bear when hiking. However, statistics reveal that this fear, while potentially a strong motivator for taking precautions that protect both bears and people, is unfounded. As many outdoor folks are fond of quipping, you're probably at greater danger from dying in an automobile accident on the way to the trailhead than encountering the jaws of an enraged grizzly while on the trail. Dogs and lightning strikes both kill more people per year, on average, than grizzly bears. Nonetheless, grizzly bears do occasionally attack and kill people. In some years several deaths have occurred in the contiguous United States in a single season of grizzly activity, from the time of their emergence from their dens in the spring until they hibernate in the winter.

Certain scenarios greatly increase the odds of a grizzly attacking a human. Hunters are often at much higher risk than hikers or other backcountry users. The tactics used by human hunters to control their scent, walk quietly to avoid detection by their quarry, and hide from sight up the odds of surprising a grizzly bear at close range. In some areas grizzly bears seem to have associated rifle shots and human activity in the fall with food in the form of discarded entrails and carcasses. A hunter returning to a kill site to retrieve meat from an animal may come upon a grizzly bear that has claimed the carcass and aggressively defends it. While human hunters encounter risk from inadvertently provoking a grizzly bear, bears are also at risk from hunters. In many places legal black bear hunting takes place in grizzly habitat. Grizzly bears being misidentified and downed by black bear hunters is a common occurrence.

The same behavior (defending a carcass) that may provoke conflict between hunters and grizzly bears also puts other recreationists at risk. Hikers or backcountry anglers may accidentally stray close to a carcass being eaten by a grizzly bear, triggering an aggressive response. When in grizzly bear habitat, if you see or smell carrion, it's wise to back out of the area the way you came and either give the location a wide berth or take your recreation elsewhere.

Females with cubs are considered the grizzly bears most likely to attack people, and such defensive measures by sows account for a high percentage of injurious or fatal conflicts. The typical scenario involves a person (or persons) who unexpectedly encounters a sow with cubs at close range or comes between a sow and her cubs. Making noise while hiking or recreating in grizzly habitat, avoiding heavy cover, and being especially vigilant while entering areas (such as ridgetops) where you might have trouble sensing bears and vice versa will greatly reduce the possibility of encountering this potentially deadly scenario.

Despite people's best attempts to avoid a confrontation with a grizzly bear, attacks may still occur. Experts offer several suggestions for surviving a grizzly attack. Bear-pepper spray, a substance derived from the stinging oil of hot pepper, has a proven record as a bear repellent. The spray is contained in pressurized canisters. During an attack the user sprays the contents of the canister in the bear's face at close range. The spray causes a burning sensation to the membranes of the bear's face and nasal passages, similar to the effects in a human struck with tear gas (or pepper spray).

In the absence of bear-pepper spray or if it fails to repel a charging bear, experts advise individuals to "play dead." This involves lying facedown on the ground, using your arms and hands to shield your head and neck. If wearing a pack, leave it on. The pack helps protect your back from bites or clawing. In most cases an aggressive grizzly is simply attempting to show a human who is boss or eliminate a perceived threat from its environment. Many biologists feel that even in fatal attacks, the grizzly's actions aren't specifically designed to kill a person, just to rough it up a bit to send a message. However, even a "disciplinary" swat or bite from an animal that can kill a large ungulate with a single snap of its jaws or blow from its paws can be fatal to a human. By playing dead you're communicating to the bear that you aren't a threat. After the bear leaves remain on the ground as long as you can. If you move too soon, the bear might renew the attack if it hasn't left the area.

Grizzly bears need personal space and habitat protection to thrive in the world they share with humans.
LISA BALLARD

While the prospect of being mauled by a grizzly is terrifying, bear experts believe the vast majority of attacks can be avoided. In addition to the precautions noted above, individuals should take extreme care to store food and other items that might draw grizzly bears when camping in bear country. Most developed or backcountry campsites in national parks offer bear-proof containers for storing food or elevated poles that allow food to be hung out of reach of bears. No matter where you camp in grizzly country, food and other items potentially attractive to bears should never be kept in a tent and should be stored well away from your campsite. These items include toothpaste, skin creams, some soaps, and other items not normally perceived as food.

Magnificent icons of wilderness, grizzly bears afforded their proper respect are far less likely to claim the life of a human than many other creatures and occurrences that we don't normally regard as dangerous. Grizzly bears need both personal space and large expanses of untrammeled habitat to healthily coexist with humans. In offering it to them, it seems we improve our own world as well.

AUTHOR'S NOTE: The above suggestions about how to avoid and survive a grizzly bear attack are provided only as very general guidelines. For more specific details please refer to information provided by the national parks or other government agencies. Or pick up a copy of the FalconGuide *Bear Aware* by Bill Schneider, an excellent book with comprehensive information for individuals in grizzly and black bear country.

CHAPTER 11
MOUNTAIN LIONS

The cry was startling and chilling. Laden with a backpack and grinding up a wilderness trail with my older brother in late November, we heard what sounded like a woman screaming in a grove of quaking aspens adjacent to the path. Although the noise was new to my ears, I recognized it immediately as the scream of a mountain lion. We camped about a mile up the trail. Remembering that spine-tingling wail, we had a hard time falling asleep that night.

In all likelihood we witnessed the call of a female looking for a mate, as mountain lions may mate at any time of the year. The unnerving experience lingered in my consciousness for the duration of our outing, but I knew we were in little danger from the vocalizing cat. Mountain lions infrequently attack humans. Such incidences are very rare—so much so that we were at greater risk of a fatality in an automobile accident while driving to the trailhead than succumbing to the claws and jaws of a cougar.

Beyond hearing that eerie call, my experiences with mountain lions, in four decades of tramping the wildlands of America, have been surprisingly few. I have

The concolor portion of the mountain lion's scientific name refers to the uniform color of its coat. This cat was photographed in Wyoming's Grand Teton National Park.
NPS

discovered the tracks of cougars on several occasions. I have sighted a mountain lion but twice. A friend and I observed a large male dart in front of my pickup on a mountain road at dawn. The animal paused in the evergreens for a few moments, giving us a clear, but brief view of its massive paws and muscular body. Another time, I caught the outline of four animals on the highway in my headlights before daylight. They appeared about the size of wolves. I slowed in anticipation of a pack sighting. Instead, my headlights illuminated a female mountain lion with three nearly grown kittens. The youngsters continued to romp for a moment, their presence and antics bringing a broad smile to my face. But their mother quickly shepherded them to the roadside then into the timber, a matron apparently not quite ready to leave her offspring unsupervised.

As I write this while sitting at Chicago's O'Hare Airport, the image of a seated mountain lion greets me from the tail of a Frontier Airlines plane. It appears a sub-adult, its intelligent amber eyes seemingly captivated by my typing form. Here's hoping this chapter will similarly captivate the reader with the secret lives of mountain lions, and enhance, if even in small measure, our society's respect and toleration for these enigmatic cats.

NAMES AND FACES

Names and Visual Description

Mountain lion is the name given to a large wild member of the cat family in North America. The name, however, is somewhat misleading. Members of this species can thrive in deserts and woodlands as well as the mountains. Historically, and in various regions of the country, the mountain lion has been given many other names, including *cougar*, *puma*, *catamount*, and *panther*. Less frequently the mountain lion has been called the *mountain screamer* or *painter*. There is perhaps no other species in America described by so many monikers. The *Guinness Book of World Records* claims that the mountain lion has the most number of names of any species on Earth. More than forty different names have been given to this feline hunter. In this book, the names mountain lion and cougar will be used interchangeably for variety and in acknowledgment that both terms are often used in scientific and popular literature.

Even the cat's scientific name can be confusing. Mountain lions were scientifically named *Felis concolor* by Carl Linnaeus, the father of modern taxonomy, in the late 1700s. In the 1970s, researchers concluded that mountain lions were not part of the *Felis* genus, which includes housecats and other small wildcats. The mountain lion now shares the *puma* lineage with the cheetah and jaguarundi and is scientifically known as *Puma concolor*, although the former name, *Felis concolor*, still occurs in some scientific and popular literature. The change in the scientific name from *Felis concolor* to *Puma concolor* was officially recognized by the American Society of Mammologists in 1993.

One of the mountain lion's physical characteristics can be inferred from its scientific name. *Concolor* refers to something that exhibits a uniform color. A mountain lion's coat displays a range of hues, depending on where the cat is found, but mountain lions are notably uniform in color. The cat's shades may range from tawny red to tawny gray to a rich medium brown. Lighter fur typically adorns its ears and cheeks and the inside of its legs and belly. A small black patch of fur is found at the tip of the tail, and the animal sports black stripes or irregular spots on the muzzle, sometimes referred to as a moustache.

Mountain lions look somewhat like an enormous, lean, athletic housecat. Their eyes are large and usually appear yellowish or hazel in color, although very young mountain lions have blue eyes. A cougar's ears are fairly short and rounded at the tips. The animals sport a nose pad that may vary from pink to brown (sometimes with black spots) and long, pale whiskers. In relation to its body, the legs of a mountain lion are quite long. Its legs appear rather thick and muscular. One of the most distinguishing physical characteristics of the mountain lion is its very long, full tail. It often accounts for nearly 40 percent of the animal's total length, and the cat carries its tail in a drooping or lowered position while walking or standing motionless.

The terminology used to describe the genders and ages of cats in the cougar family varies. It is sometimes similar to that used to describe housecats. Domestic male cats are called *toms*, female housecats are officially known as *mollies*, or *queens* if they are nursing young. Baby or immature housecats are dubbed *kittens*. In scientific literature, the genders of mountain lions are usually referred to simply as *males* and *females*. The young are often called *kittens*, although scientific literature may also refer to them as *cubs* or simply *young*. Some researchers occasionally call male mountain lions *toms* and the folks who live in cougar country frequently call the animals *tom*. The term *molly* or *queen*, however, does not appear to be part of the common or scientific verbiage associated with mountain lions. Thus, the terminology used to identify the ages and genders of mountain lions can be quite variable, depending on the purpose (scientific versus popular discussion) and place.

Related Species in North America

Mountain lions are one of seven species of wildcats found north of Mexico on the North American continent. They are joined in many places by populations of feral (domestic animals gone wild) housecats that prey upon native birds and small mammals in destructively high numbers.

Genetically, mountain lions are most closely related to the jaguarundi, a small cat whose range occurs from Central America, through Mexico, and is rarely found in the extreme southeastern portions of Texas and New Mexico. Like the mountain lion, the jaguarundi displays solid coloration across its body. The jaguarundi exhibits three distinct colors: black, gray, and reddish. Jaguarundis have long tails, but it is unlikely that a competent observer would confuse them with a mountain lion. An adult jaguarundi weighs from around fifteen to eighteen pounds, roughly

Cougars are slightly smaller than jaguars, although their size overlaps considerably. The spotted jaguar is nearly extinct in the United States.
© ISTOCK.COM/PHOTOCECH

seven to ten times smaller than the typical adult mountain lion.

The other five species of wildcats found north of Mexico are all readily distinguished from the mountain lion in appearance as well as size. All of these are spotted to some extent, in contrast to the uniform coloration of the mountain lion and jaguarundi. The largest of these is the jaguar, a stocky spotted cat that may be infrequently found in Texas, New Mexico, and Arizona. The jaguar is the third-largest cat in the world behind the lion and tiger. It is somewhat larger than a mountain lion (perhaps 20 percent larger, on average), although the size of adult mountain lions and jaguars includes considerable overlap. Like cougars, jaguars have a long tail. However, the intense dark spotting on their yellowish-gold coats (observable at close range even on the minority population of jaguars with black coats) easily differentiates them from mountain lions.

Two other spotted cats, the margay and the ocelot, are native to the extreme southwestern portions of the United States. The margay is exceedingly rare in the United States if it exists at all. Margays are small cats (around fifteen to twenty pounds) with pronounced spots and long tails. Ocelots range in a limited area in south Texas and are infrequently sighted in southern Arizona. The ocelot is a medium-size wildcat that weighs from twenty to forty pounds. Skilled climbers, ocelots may kill birds roosting in trees. They are beautifully spotted, have fairly long tails, and have been described at times as dwarf leopards.

The paw prints of mountain lions comingle much more frequently with the final two species of North American cats found in the United States: the bobcat and the lynx. Along with their sometimes-spotted coats, bobcats and lynx have other physical characteristics that easily distinguish them from mountain lions. While the grayish lynx may exhibit few distinct spots, its tail is much shorter than the mountain lion's, appearing as a stubby appendage rather than a long, elegant adornment. The ears of lynx are pointed, with distinct tufts of black hair extending from the tip of each ear. Lynx are much smaller than mountain lions. The largest male lynx weighs only around 50 percent of a small mountain lion female. Lynx share habitat with cougars in much of Canada and portions of the northern Rocky Mountains in the United States.

Bobcats are more brownish in color and more heavily spotted than lynx. Like lynx, they have a short stubby tail that looks very different from the long, obvious tail of the mountain lion. Bobcats have pointed ears with black tufts on the tips that are much smaller than those found on the lynx. Bobcats are pint-size in comparison to mountain lions. While some very large males may weigh forty pounds, most bobcats weigh less than thirty pounds, making them much smaller than mountain lions. Bobcats range across most of the contiguous United States, so they are the cat with which the cougar shares the most extensive part of its range.

Subspecies

Categorizing the various subspecies of mountain lions is fraught with the same questions and controversies that surround attempts to classify the subspecies of many other animals. A subspecies is generally defined as a geographically isolated population of a particular species that displays physical and/or behavioral characteristics that distinguish it from other members of its kind. During the eighteenth and much of the nineteenth centuries, wildlife biologists seemed happy to identify as many subspecies for a particular animal as possible. These were often determined not only on the basis of geography, but on physical attributes such as overall size or variations in skull measurements. Subsequent analysis has questioned many subspecies definitions. For example, the size of an animal is largely determined by the amount and quality of the food sources it has available during its growth years. Thus, a population of bobcats in one vicinity may be 20 percent larger on average than those from a population 100 miles away. In the heyday of subspecies classification, this might constitute the designation of the two as separate subspecies. However, if one population has access to a larger and more stable prey base, the difference in size simply may be a function of nutrition, not true variation in the animals' characteristics. The current trend has thus been toward reducing rather than increasing the number of subspecies identified within a particular animal species.

Another factor at work in present-day "subspecies theory" is the use of DNA analysis. Many biologists feel that genetic kinship established through DNA analysis is more definitive in classifying a subspecies than variation in physical or behavioral characteristics. Thus, subspecies designations based on extensive DNA research usually undergo a reclassification that more closely aligns with the animals' genetic similarities than with the characteristics formerly used to identify the subspecies.

These trends are readily apparent in subspecies classifications for mountain lions. Various biologists from the eighteenth to the twentieth centuries identified as many as thirty-four different subspecies of cougars ranging across North, Central, and South America. Thirteen of those subspecies were identified in North America north of Mexico.

More recently many leading mountain lion biologists, informed by the most current DNA analysis, have reduced the number of subspecies from over thirty to six. Defined genetically, these six subspecies have much larger geographical ranges than previous designations. Of the six subspecies, four are found in South America, a single subspecies exists in Central America, and all of the cougars in North America are grouped together as a single subspecies.

However, as late as 2011 the US Fish & Wildlife Service (USFWS) was still managing mountain lions under the 1946 subspecies classifications proposed by researchers Young and Goldman, who identified fifteen subspecies of mountain lions in North America. Although the USFWS has acknowledged problems with Young and Goldman's subspecies definitions (at least one subspecies was identified on traits associated with the analysis of the skulls of just eight animals), it has yet to formally accept a more recent paradigm of mountain lion subspecies.

Florida panthers roam the forests and swamps of south Florida. They are the only population of cougars that has survived since presettlement times east of the Mississippi River.
USFWS

The Florida panther, *Puma concolor coryi*, is one of the subspecies of mountain lions in the United States still recognized by the USFWS and many biologists. Prior to European settlement, mountain lions left their fuzzy paw prints across most of the southeastern United States. By 1900, cougars had been widely eliminated, primarily due to direct eradication through hunting and trapping or indirectly by habitat destruction. However, a small population of the cats persisted in undeveloped areas of south Florida.

The Florida panther was given protection under the Endangered Species Act (ESA) in 1973. At that time the animal's total population in the wild was estimated at just a few dozen individuals. Intensive conservation efforts in the following decades failed to bolster the population. By the 1990s it became apparent that the critically small population was suffering from inbreeding, which caused genetic and physical defects that decreased reproduction. After considerable debate, the population was augmented with eight female mountain lions from Texas in 1995 to promote genetic diversity.

The introduction of genetically dissimilar females appears to have been perhaps a lifesaving measure for the Florida panther. Current population censuses indicate some 100 to 180 of the elusive cats now track the swamps and forests of south Florida, with several refuge areas containing the cat that was designated as the state animal in 1982. Major refuges harboring these mountain lions include Big Cypress National Preserve, the Florida Panther National Wildlife Refuge, and Everglades National Park.

Did the introduction of the eight females (which essentially doubled the number of females in the population) from a different subspecies effectively nullify the Florida panther's status as a subspecies? The USFWS argues it did not. Many independent biologists believe otherwise, some suggesting the Florida panther has never been a legitimate subspecies, simply an isolated population of North American mountain lions that developed genetic and physical peculiarities (such as a kinked tail and cowlick on the back) due to inbreeding. The American public, I suspect, doesn't care. We're just happy these notable animals have maintained a stronghold in the southeast from which, perhaps, their kind may expand into other areas.

Physical Characteristics

Mountain lions inhabit an astonishingly large range from northern British Columbia in North America to the southernmost regions of South America. Due to the variety of habitats over which they roam, mountain lions vary considerably in size. In biological circles, Bergmann's Rule states that within a species, animals are larger on average as one moves from the equator toward the poles. Although this postulate does not apply to all species, it appears to generally hold true for cougars. On average, the cats are larger in the colder, more extreme climates toward the northern reaches of their range in North America and in the southern parts of their range in South America.

What accounts for this trend? Greater body mass is advantageous in maintaining warmth in the winter, although it also takes more fuel to sustain a larger body. Many of the mountain lion's major sources of food are large ungulates such as mule deer, whitetail deer, and elk. All of these animals tend to follow Bergmann's Rule, with body size for both species of deer increasing substantially toward the northern portions of their range. For predators such as the mountain lion, Bergmann's Rule may simply be a function of killing efficiency. Where prey is larger, predators possessing greater size and strength have an advantage. Thus, mountain lions in the north may simply be larger because they routinely prey on larger animals than their southern cousins do.

Mountain lions display a high degree of sexual dimorphism, a term that refers to species in which there is considerable difference in size between males and females. Adult males (animals older than two years of age) are generally around 40 percent heavier than equivalent females. In some smaller populations the variation in average male and female weights may be even more extreme. Researchers in the San Andres Mountains of New Mexico who studied cougars over a ten-year period found that males in the study area were 70 percent heavier on average than females.

Adult female mountain lions typically range from around 75 to 135 pounds. Males normally weigh from 115 to 200 pounds. Occasionally males reach heavier weights. An eviscerated (internal organs removed) male in Arizona was recorded in 1926 as weighing 275 pounds. President Theodore Roosevelt shot a tom weighing a reputed 227 pounds northwest of Meeker, Colorado, in February 1901. Suffice it to say that any male weighing over 200 pounds is on the extreme end of the scale. Female mountain lions are generally 5 to 6 feet in body length with tails measuring from 21 to 32 inches. Males measure from 5.5 to 9 feet in body length, with tails ranging from 26 to 35 inches. Height measured at the top of the front shoulder typically ranges from 21 to 30 inches for males. Female shoulder height varies from 17 to 26 inches.

A mountain lion's claws are retractable. Claw marks are not visible on mountain lion tracks.
NPS

Like housecats, mountain lions have very sharp retractable claws. This feature helps skilled observers distinguish their paw prints from other species, such as bears and wolves. Viewed in snow, mud, or soft soil, cougar prints lack the noticeable claw and toenail marks accompanying the spoor of bears and canines.

RANGE AND HABITAT

Historic Range

The mountain lion's historic range is larger than that of any other land-dwelling animal in the Western Hemisphere (except for humans). Prior to European settlement, cougars were found from northern British Columbia to the southernmost reaches of South America. Their range spanned from the Atlantic Ocean to the Pacific Ocean on both the North and South American continents. In North America, the mountain lion's historic range found its northern limits at a line drawn from roughly the northern border of British Columbia to the southern end of Hudson Bay, then directly eastward to the Atlantic Ocean. South of that line, cougars are thought to have occupied essentially the entirety of both continents.

However, the existence or abundance of mountain lions in certain parts of this extensive range is uncertain. Cougars are very flexible predators, but a viable prey base is essential to their survival. Even where a prey base is present, competition with other, more formidable predators such as wolf packs or grizzly bears may limit mountain lion numbers. Thus, it is doubtful that mountain lions were ever abundant on the open prairies, where they would no doubt come into conflict with wolves and grizzly bears. Areas that likely contained the greatest number of cougars on the plains included river corridors and other habitat niches that offered trees and cover where mountain lions could elude rival predators and females could safely hide young.

Mountain lions require terrain and cover allowing them to successfully stalk prey. This cat was photographed hunting in Glacier National Park, Montana.
NPS

Current Range

The mountain lion's historic range in the Americas has been reduced by nearly half over the past 200 years. South American mountain lions still roam over much of the continent. Their range on the southern continent has retracted to the greatest extent in areas of intense agriculture and where urbanization has occurred. For the most part, these areas include coastal regions on the east and west sides of the continent. The mountain lion's range has also diminished in Central America. The status of mountain lion populations in South and Central America, however, is uncertain. Some biologists have estimated that up to 40 percent of the mountain lion's historic habitat has been negatively altered by urbanization and deforestation. Government management and monitoring of cougar populations are variable. Mountain lions have no legal protection in Ecuador. They are hunted in Mexico and Peru. In other South and Central American countries, they are legally protected, although it is believed they are often still killed in rural areas where they may be a real or perceived threat to livestock.

In the United States, the distribution of cougars has been cut by about two-thirds since prior to European settlement. The mountain lion's range now occurs primarily in the western portion of the United States. The exception to this rule is the Florida panther (the isolated population of cougars in Florida discussed in the beginning of this chapter), which is found in the extreme southern portion of Florida. More precisely, Florida panthers are found in portions of nine counties, with Collier County and Miami-Dade Counties claiming the largest segments of habitat.

Mountain lions, like this one lounging in the shade in Big Bend National Park, Texas, thrive in arid environments where prey is present.
NPS/REINE WONITE

The mountain lion's range in Florida can generally be described as the part of the state south of a line drawn from Fort Myers (Lee County) to the southern end of Lake Okeechobee (Palm Beach County) and west of a line sketched from the south end of Lake Okeechobee to the point at which Highway 1 passes from the mainland to the Florida Keys (Miami-Dade County). The central portion of this approximate distribution holds the highest numbers of Florida panthers.

The rest of the mountain lion's range in the United States occurs far west of Florida, with most of the cougar's range occurring west of the eastern front of the Rocky Mountains. The eastern edge of the mountain lion's range occurs roughly at a boundary drawn from the Canadian border traveling south through the western half of Montana, continuing south through the western two-thirds of Wyoming and Colorado, south along the eastern border of New Mexico, and from the southeastern corner of New Mexico to the Mexico border about 100 miles southeast of Laredo, Texas.

Although the portion of the country that lies west of the boundary outlined here is typically described as mountain lion range on a map of the United States, the extent to which cougars actually inhabit this area is quite variable. For example, the foothills ranching and farming community west of Three Forks, Montana, in which I grew up is included as mountain lion range. However, cougars were unknown to the area in my childhood some forty years ago. Today, mountain lion scat or tracks are rarely sighted in the area, and when they are, they probably come from young cats dispersing from occupied habitat. There really is no resident population. The situation is similar in Washington State and elsewhere. The entire state of Washington is included in current mountain lion range, yet the odds of cats actually colonizing places like the eastern portion of the state, with its intensive agriculture and absence of forests or other cover, are unlikely. Of that massive range through which mountain lions may occasionally travel, perhaps 50 percent is continuously inhabited by these secretive tawny cats.

Beyond the western range described here, mountain lions occupy several areas to the east. In Montana, cougars have reclaimed and continue to expand into other areas of their historic range in a region known as the Missouri Breaks. The Missouri Breaks are an extensive system of badlands, often sprinkled with ponderosa pine trees and junipers along the Missouri River in eastern Montana. Lewis and Clark regularly encountered grizzly bears and bighorn sheep on their epic westward journey in the Missouri Breaks. And it was here that they made their first observation of a mountain lion. The region is currently home to substantial herds of elk and mule deer, with smaller numbers of whitetail deer and bighorn sheep also tracking the deep coulees and forested benches above the river. All of these ungulates represent favored prey for mountain lions.

By the 1930s, mountain lions were eradicated from the Missouri Breaks, their population in Montana restricted to mountainous regions west of the Continental Divide and in the Absaroka-Beartooth region of southwestern Montana. Cougars began expanding their range in the state by 1950, primarily in an eastward direction. The Missouri Breaks were naturally recolonized by the mobile felines by 1990. Mountain lions are also now found in southeastern Montana, primarily in remote timbered areas where deer and elk are also present.

Another nuclear population of mountain lions is located to the east of their primary western range in North Dakota. These animals roam a rugged area in the far western portion of the state often referred to as the "Badlands." The Badlands are found in the south to south-central part of North Dakota, just east of its border with Montana. Cougars were never officially listed as extinct in North Dakota, although the status of the cats in the state throughout most of the twentieth century was uncertain. By 1990, mountain lion observations had become more common, and in 2005 the state began a hunting season for cougars. North Dakota's small mountain lion population has declined in recent years, most likely as a result of too many adult animals being killed during the hunting season.

Some 150 miles to the south, a nuclear population of mountain lions occurs in the Black Hills of South Dakota. The mountainous, timbered topography of the Black Hills provides fine habitat for mountain lions, replete with a diverse array of prey including elk, deer, and many smaller mammals. Mountain lions were listed as a threatened species by the state of South Dakota in 1978. Their numbers increased through the latter part of the 1900s, with the first confirmed kitten born in 1999. Researchers have documented breeding male mountain lions in the Black Hills that have immigrated considerable distances from the Bighorn Mountains (northwestern Wyoming) and the Laramie and Snowy Mountains (southeastern Wyoming). Like the isolated population in North Dakota, it appears that overhunting is currently the most serious threat to the Black Hills population.

Two other very small populations of mountain lions persisting east of the major portion of their North American range are worthy of note. A tiny, but reproducing number of mountain lions occurs in the Pine Ridge region of northwestern Nebraska. This small community of cats may hold as few as twenty adults. About 50 miles north of the Montana-Canada border, a breeding population of mountain lions has reestablished itself in the Cypress Hills Interprovincial Park that straddles the Saskatchewan-Alberta border. Mountain lions appeared in the park around the dawn of the third millennium. A viable, slowly expanding population is now found in the park, where they are protected from hunting.

The successful recolonization of areas such as the Badlands of North Dakota and the Black Hills of South Dakota has many mountain lion enthusiasts speculating about if and when *Puma concolor* might reclaim range even farther east. Questions of cougars in the East have engaged the minds of many. Hundreds of mountain lion sightings are reported in states from Wisconsin to New York each year. Is it possible that a remnant population of the subspecies *Puma concolor couguar* remains in existence?

It appears not. In 2011 the USFWS declared the Eastern cougar extinct and recommended the subspecies be removed from the Endangered Species List under which it had been protected since 1973. The USFWS's review of purported evidence of mountain lions east of the Mississippi River concluded that the vast majority were actually sightings of other creatures such as bobcats or domestic dogs. In cases where mountain lions were actually discovered, the USFWS concluded via DNA analysis that the animals were dispersers from western populations or domestic cougars (typically from South or Central America) that had escaped or been set free by their owners.

Nonetheless, multiple instances of young mountain lions wandering from western enclaves (typically the Black Hills) have been documented in locations such as Wisconsin, Illinois, Nebraska, and Missouri. What are the odds of the cats establishing a breeding population east of their current range?

In terms of habitat, there are numerous places where mountain lions might find a home in the Midwest and eastern regions of the nation. However, several factors decrease the likelihood of it occurring anytime soon. First of all, a reproducing population obviously requires a male and female cat. While young females have journeyed away from the Black Hills, most of the dispersers are young males. At the present time the prospects of two dispersers meeting and mating in suitable habitat to the east are quite small. Perhaps more important, many states in which mountain lions might become established east of their current range have minimal or no legal protection for the animals. A considerable number of dispersers have been shot in states where both cougars and legal protection for them are absent. Along those lines, the dispersing cats would most likely move through eastern North Dakota and South Dakota. In neither state are mountain lions sufficiently protected outside their current range to ensure wandering adolescents could make the eastern journey in large enough numbers to up the odds of males and females crossing paths in viable habitat. While many wildlife advocates would like to see mountain lions established in habitats to the east of their range, current conditions make the odds of a natural recolonization very small.

Mountain Lion Habitat

Along with their distinction of occupying the largest range of any terrestrial (land-dwelling) mammal in the Western Hemisphere, it might also be argued that mountain lions occupy the most diverse types of habitat. Historically, mountain lions were found at elevations stretching from sea level to around 15,000 feet. Schoolchildren in both the United States and Europe are introduced to the concept of separating various geographic areas that support different types of plant and animal life into units. In America these are known as *biomes*. In Europe they are usually referred to as *major life zones*. Biomes may be labeled as temperate deciduous forests, interior grasslands, tropical rain forests, alpine tundra, and the like. It is believed that as late as 1900, mountain lions inhabited every biome in North, Central, and South America, except the arctic tundra.

Mountain lions are flexible predators capable of living in nearly any ecosystem in North, Central, and South America.
© ISTOCK.COM/JOHN PITCHER

Two factors dictate where mountains lived historically and continue to persist. Their habitat must support a sufficient prey base that provides sustenance for adult mountain lions, females raising kittens, and sub-adult individuals learning to hunt on their own. This normally includes hoofed animals such as elk and deer, but mountain lions may also rely on other types of prey, including bighorn sheep, wild pigs, porcupines, various types of rabbits and hares, and a host of other small mammals and birds. Mountain lions sometimes thrive in harsh environments that hold good numbers of potential prey species. They are currently abundant in many areas classified as desert in the American Southwest. Wilderness areas in central Idaho are often characterized by steep terrain and cold winters with deep snow, yet mountain lion populations remain healthy in these daunting environments as well.

Along with a reliable prey base, mountain lions need habitat that supports their hunting techniques and buffers them from competitive predators. Cougars are often described as a "spot and ambush" predator, meaning they habitually sneak close to a potential prey animal, then rush in to catch it from a close distance. This is easiest to accomplish where forest cover, shrubbery, desert scrub, and geological features such as rocks, cliffs, and gullies provide mountain lions with ideal places in which to approach and ambush prey undetected. They also use trees and cliffs to elude competitive predators, which include grizzly and black bears, wolves, and coyotes. Mountain lions are at a serious disadvantage on flat expanses of unbroken prairie, both from the standpoint of successfully ambushing prey and keeping themselves and their kills safe from other predators.

Human disturbance is another factor that currently dictates mountain lion habitat. Areas used extensively for agriculture, especially large expanses of cleared croplands, are unsuitable to mountain lions. Some of the enterprising cats have taken up residence in suburban areas, but they are often lethally removed as a potential threat to people, pets, and livestock. Additionally, mortality from vehicle collisions claims many cougars each year. Even if a semi-urban area contains a robust population of whitetail deer (a favorite prey of many mountain lions), if it is riddled with roads, mountain lions may not survive.

The best home for a mountain lion occurs where large expanses of native habitat remain intact. In such locations, cougars play a valuable role in balancing the populations of their prey species and creating a healthier ecosystem for other animals.

Mountain lions may use cliffs and stone outcroppings for stalking prey, but these features may also help them avoid other predators. This cougar is traversing a rock face in Lake Mead National Recreation Area in Nevada.
NPS

ABILITIES AND BEHAVIOR

Physical Abilities

An ambush predator such as the cougar must rely on stealth and skillful use of cover to get close to its prey. Once within range, the cat's success is highly dependent on the speed of its attack. What adaptations allow the mountain lion to successfully hunt deer and other ungulates that can run 30 miles per hour or faster?

Mountain lions have very long, muscular hind legs, proportionately longer than those of other members of the cat family. Their spine is also long and flexible, similar to that of the cheetah. Muscles along the spine, as well as those found on the legs, are used to propel the mountain lion's body in a chase. These physical characteristics facilitate some of the cougar's most amazing athletic abilities. Estimates vary, but it is commonly reported that mountain lions can sprint from 40 to 50 miles per hour over short distances. The exceptional length and strength of their hind legs, coupled with a spine that allows the hind feet to reach far under the body for leverage in making a bound, give the cats a remarkable ability to accelerate in as few as two leaps. Mountain lions may cover as much as 40 feet in a single bound. It is often reported that they can clear up to 15 feet in a single vertical leap.

However, when compared to most of their prey and other predators such as wolves that often use long-distance chases to tire their victims, mountain lions have a notably limited lung capacity. This diminishes the distance over which they can effectively pursue prey, and also makes them susceptible to attacks from rival predators with more stamina if caught in the open. Thus, when chased by other dangerous animals, such as wolves or a pack of hunting dogs, mountain lions typically climb a tree or flee to other

cover where the pursuers are unable to follow, such as elevated rock ledges or stony spires. Mountain lions seem very aware of the limits of their endurance in relation to their prey. If a fleet of foot prey animal such as a whitetail deer is not caught within a short distance, an adult cougar will very quickly abandon the chase.

The large paws of a mountain lion are outfitted with large, very sharp retractable claws. The mountain lion's flexible, expansive paws and soft, furry underbelly allow it to crawl almost silently across nearly any terrain in approach of prey. Five claws are found in each of the front feet, one of which is associated with the dewclaw (thumb). The dewclaw and its claw do not bear any weight and are not used in running. They are very instrumental, however, in the lion's ability to grasp and hold prey. Each rear paw has four claws, which may be used in subduing prey and in self-defense, though their function is certainly secondary to the claws on the forepaws. Mountain lions are very adept at climbing trees. The sharp, curved claws on their hind feet allow them to propel themselves quickly up a tree trunk, while the claws on the front feet are used to grasp bark and branches. Like ordinary house cats, mountain lions are very comfortable in moving about in trees, an ability directly related to the shape and strength of their claws.

The mountain lion's retractable claws are one of the features that help naturalists distinguish the cats' paw prints from those of canines, including coyotes, foxes, and wolves. Any track that shows claw marks along with pad prints does not belong to a mountain lion (or any other member of the cat family in North America). Claw marks left by a coyote's foot may be hard to pick out on bare ground or in vegetation. In snow, mud, or soft ground, they are usually quite evident and serve as one of the distinguishing features separating canine tracks from cougar prints.

Their oversize paws also help make mountain lions capable swimmers. Contrary to some portrayals, cougars are very comfortable around water and cross sizeable bodies of water with ease.

Incredible sprinting speed and sharp claws enable mountain lions to catch and hold their prey. Specialized teeth, bones, and jaw muscles are the lethal weapons the cats

Mountain lions, like this one photographed in Grand Teton National Park, are good swimmers and at ease around water.
NPS

then use to kill those animals. Compared to many other predators, mountain lions have fewer teeth. The mouth of an adult cougar contains just thirty teeth, while dogs, foxes, and other North American canines have forty-two, as do black, polar, and grizzly bears. The bite of a raccoon includes forty teeth, while wolverines have thirty-eight teeth.

Having fewer teeth is not a disadvantage to a mountain lion's killing methods. It means greater force is exerted on each tooth. The cougar's four canine teeth (fangs) are stout and long and do not bend in any direction. They are responsible for the penetrating wounds usually directed at the back of the neck or throat of the cat's prey. Smaller animals are often killed with a single bite to the back of the neck, where the fangs slide between the vertebrae to cut the spinal cord. Behind the canine teeth are premolars and molars, comparatively longer and sharper than those of bears and canines. These allow mountain lions to easily slice through flesh and may aid them in delivering a suffocating bite to the throat of their prey. However, these teeth are not as efficient for crushing and chewing. Unlike bears and wolves, which often crack surprisingly large bones to eat the marrow, mountain lions' teeth are not adapted for chewing or crushing bones.

Strong specialized teeth allow mountain lions to kill much of their prey with a single bite to the back of the neck.
© ISTOCK.COM/ JOHNPITCHER

The muscles that close a mountain lion's jaws are highly developed and attached to the lower jaw in a manner promoting leverage, which results in very powerful bite force. Such strong muscles and large teeth exert massive force on the jaw. Both the upper and lower jaws have reinforcement-like portions of bone, rendering the jaws highly resistant to bending or breaking.

Mountain lions commonly hunt and travel at night or in the low-light hours of dawn and dusk. Their eyes are equipped with oversize pupils that allow abundant light to reach the retina on the rear side of the eyeball. The retina contains a preponderance of rod cells, which facilitate vision in low light. A layer of reflective tissue common to nocturnal (active at night) animals, called the *tapetum lucidum*, enhances light transmission within a mountain lion's eyes. It is this tissue that also causes the cat's eyes (and those of other nocturnal animals) to glow when struck by headlights or other bright light sources. In addition to having superior light-gathering properties in the dark, the mountain lion's eyes also have corneas (the clear front windows of the eyes) that provide a very broad field of binocular vision and acute depth perception. These sensory abilities are thought to assist the cat in delivering precise bites and blows to its prey. The cougar's daylight vision is at least as good as that of a human. Biologists theorize the cat's night vision is six times better than that of people. This is based on the fact that mountain lions require just 17 percent as much light to detect details in the visual world as humans do at night. The long whiskers on a cougar's nose also help it to avoid obstacles in night navigation and are thought by some biologists to guide the cat's teeth when biting prey.

The mountain lion's vision is probably the sense most responsible for its hunting skill. However, the animals also rely on a keen sense of hearing equal to or better than that of humans to detect prey, sense danger, and communicate with members of their own kind. In fact, mountain lions are capable of hearing high-frequency sounds undetectable to the human ear.

The role of smell as a hunting tool for mountain lions is poorly understood. Some research indicates the olfactory (smelling) sensitivity of a cougar is roughly thirty times greater than that of a human. In comparison to hoofed animals like deer and elk, or other predators such as coyotes and bears, a mountain lion's sense of smell is quite weak. (Scientists estimate wolves and grizzly bears have a sense of smell that is perhaps one thousand times more sensitive than a human's.) Nonetheless, observational studies of hunting mountain lions support the notion that they do use their noses when hunting. Researchers have documented mountain lions approaching bedded prey animals that the cat likely did not locate by sight. Mountain lions most often approach their prey from downwind, a tactic necessary to keep their own scent from drifting to their potential victim, but a method perhaps also favored by their ability to smell their prey.

Vocal and Visual Communication

Humans rarely observe the lives of wild mountain lions. Some evidence of their vocalizations is available, but exactly how and why mountain lions make sounds under natural conditions is not clearly understood.

The most dramatic noise uttered by the cougar is its scream, a call some researchers describe as the "caterwaul." This call is likened to the mating call a domestic female cat produces when she is ready to mate, and it probably serves the same purpose. In comparison to a housecat's cry, the caterwaul of a mountain lion is very loud and high-pitched, often described as the sound of a woman screaming in distress. Researchers believe this call is normally issued by female mountain lions to attract males when they are ready to mate. While the high-pitched screaming aspect of the caterwaul is most readily heard from a distance, the call may also contain lower-pitched and less voluminous pieces, including purring and mewing.

Other sounds mountain lions emit are also similar to those heard from domestic cats. Very young cougars (under two weeks old) emit a bleating or sharp, high-pitched mewing sound indicating distress. Both mother and young mountain lions purr as a sound of contentment, and a female cougar may purr as a means of communicating assurance to her entire litter.

Spitting, hissing, and growling are common ways housecats indicate their displeasure. Mountain lions make equivalent vocalizations for similar purposes. Numerous researchers have been confronted by hissing and growling as they approached a mountain lion confined in a cage-trap or snare. Hunters using dogs to "tree" mountain lions also report hearing these "do not approach" type of sounds.

A vocalization occasionally used by both male and female mountain lions is sometimes dubbed the "ouch" call, for its similarity to the iconic noise uttered by a human who drops a cup on his bare toes. Its purpose isn't clearly understood. Some researchers have witnessed it as perhaps a vocal indication of frustration after an unsuccessful predation attempt. Others believe it may be used to announce a mountain lion's presence to others.

A yowling call is common to both genders of adult mountain lions. It is thought other cats may be able to discern the sex, age, and stature of the yowler. This call may help cougars avoid surprise encounters with other animals, or perhaps it aids in the maintenance of a territory.

Social Structure and Dynamics

Mountain lions are notoriously solitary creatures. They rarely hunt cooperatively as African lions do. The exception to this rule may be a female in the company of her sub-adult young. In fact, females with young are the only group of mountain lions known to regularly exist together as a social unit.

Both male and female mountain lions utilize home ranges, expanses of habitat that might be seen as an animal's neighborhood from which it rarely strays. Male cougars also claim territories, specific geographical areas that they defend against other males. Researchers have documented some overlap in the ranges of both sexes, with females showing a tolerance for other females within their home range. Studies have indicated that the home ranges of female mountain lions sometimes overlap by over 50 percent. However, within the home range most females occupy a core area that is less regularly encroached upon by other females. While male territories often overlap on the fringes, studies conducted with radio collars indicate adult male mountain lions seldom deliberately penetrate the core of another male's territory, typically with hostile intent.

Home ranges among female mountain lions in North America have been documented to cover as little as 21 square miles and as much as 300 square miles. Research

Female cougars caring for young may temporarily reduce their home range to provide security for their offspring.
© ISTOCK.COM/ JOHNPITCHER

indicates that females sometimes occupy two seasonal home ranges where their primary prey base (such as mule deer) is migratory. Deer and other ungulates frequently move from summer to winter range, necessitating a shift in a mountain lion's range as well. The range of female mountain lions shrinks considerably when they are raising young, particularly in the first two months after birth.

Adult male cougars are aggressively territorial. On average the territories of male cougars are considerably larger than those of females. Normally the range of a single male mountain lion will overlap those of several females. Their territories are usually 50 percent to 300 percent larger than those of adult females. Researchers have discovered male mountain lion territories in North America ranging from 58 square miles to more than 300 square miles. Despite some overlap in territories, males monitored by researchers have shown an uncanny ability to avoid areas of overlap currently occupied by a rival.

Male cougars make scrapes within their territories, often on ridges or other well-frequented travel routes. Scrapes are created when the males scratch the ground with their hind legs. Unlike some other species of cats that leave scent on a scrape via urination, male cougars create their scrapes by scratching alone. Biologists theorize the scrapes are used as territorial markings to announce the presence of the local tom to others. Evidence of this theory is found in the fact that researchers have seldom documented scrapes made by females or immature adults.

Large, combative male mountain lions are the most successful at claiming a territory and producing offspring. Oftentimes they are also the number one reason other cougars die in nonhunted populations. Adult male mountain lions are known to aggressively kill cubs sired by another male. Many biologists believe death at the fangs of an adult male is the leading cause of mortality to young cougars. Eliminating the offspring of another male accomplishes two purposes. First, it rids the population of rival genes to the dominating male. More important, perhaps, females who are not caring for cubs become reproductively active. By killing a female's kittens, a male may incite her to mate.

Males also kill females, especially if the two have not been engaged in a previous breeding relationship. Adult males often kill females that are attempting to defend their young. They may also fatally attack a female to claim the carcass of killed prey. Some researchers have recorded instances where female mountain lions have been killed and eaten by males for food.

Battles between male mountain lions are usually fierce and unforgiving. In the absence of human-caused mortality, such as hunting or vehicle collisions, fatal interactions between male cougars are the primary source of survival risk. Both female and male cougars tend to disperse (move to a different territory than the one used by their mother) as they reach adulthood. Males tend to disperse farther than females. Dispersing males must either claim a territory uninhabited by another male or fight with an established tom to conquer its range. Dominant males may also fight to enlarge their territory or when they encounter one another where their geographical spheres of influence overlap.

Interactions between toms in any of the above scenarios frequently leads to the death of one of the males. Depending on the severity of the wounds sustained by the victor, it is possible that both males may eventually die as a result of the battle. A study of mountain lions in New Mexico recorded thirty-five interactions between male cougars. Nearly 30 percent of those encounters resulted in the death of one of the males. A few of the fatalities occurred at carcasses, but most of them involved males vying for territory or directly competing for breeding rights to a female.

The mountain lion's social web is characterized by a generally solitary life and extreme strife and violence instigated by males. However, a handful of recent observations by researchers indicate that rarely encountered social dynamics exist and paint a somewhat different picture of cougar interactions. For example, researchers in the Jackson, Wyoming, area (home to Grand Teton National Park) have documented amicable social interactions between adult mountain lions, including two unrelated females with kittens that often shared kills. Within the mostly solitary, often violent world of mountain lions, there appears to be a range of more peaceful and perhaps cooperative behaviors biologists have yet to observe and understand.

MOUNTAIN LIONS AND OTHER ANIMALS

Mountain Lions and Their Prey: Prey Species

The mountain lion's diet consists almost entirely of other animals that it obtains through predation and occasionally by scavenging or stealing a kill from a less formidable predator. Mountain lions normally focus on prey species that weigh 50 percent as much as they do or larger. The efficiency of cougars in killing large prey is extraordinary. Of all the large cats in the world, mountain lions bring down the largest prey in relation to their own size. It is not uncommon for mountain lions to prey upon animals whose weight is more than twice their own.

However, mountain lions are known to dine on smaller animals as well. The extent to which they utilize smaller prey is somewhat unclear. Biologists who study mountain lions most often rely on tracking data from radio collars to ascertain a cougar has made a kill. The site is then investigated, and data—including the species, gender, approximate age, and weight of the prey—are recorded. However, a cougar nabbing a cottontail rabbit while on the move won't register on a radio collar (researchers often know a cat has made a larger kill when it remains in one place for a period of time). Furthermore, the carcasses of smaller creatures may be completely consumed by a mountain lion, leaving nothing behind for a biologist to analyze. Remains of rodents, birds, and other little creatures may show up in mountain lion scat. The presence of a prey item in scat, however, doesn't provide definitive information about the extent to which it occurs in the cougar's diet and its significance to its overall nutrition.

What types of animals will mountain lions target for prey? Researchers have recorded them consuming reptiles, birds (such as ruffed grouse and wild turkeys), and mammals. Amphibians, fish, and other aquatic creatures may be eaten as well, although the frequency with which this happens is unclear. In South America some cougars consume iguanas and caiman (an alligator-like reptile) on a somewhat regular basis and are also known to prey upon bats. A general rule appears to govern mountain lion predation in relation to latitude: Those in tropical and subtropical regions rely on smaller prey to a greater extent than those in northern regions.

Ground squirrels and marmots are among the smaller prey sometimes taken by mountain lions. The cats are also known to kill opossums and moles. Rabbits and hares are another source of pint-size prey and may be a very important food source in some habitats, especially when the bunnies are at the peak of their population cycle. Research projects in Utah, Washington, and Florida indicate rabbits and hares may represent over 10 percent of some cougars' annual diet.

Slightly larger prey taken by mountain lions include beavers and porcupines. In fact, some mountain lions become very adept at killing porcupines. Where they are abundant in the Rocky Mountains, porcupines comprise up to 20 percent of a mountain lion's annual diet, according to some studies. Biologists have documented a young male mountain lion killing thirty-five porcupines in the span of three months in Colorado. A young female in Wyoming took twenty-four in two and a half months. Cougar predation on porcupines may substantially impact local numbers. A small population of porcupines in Nevada was reduced by over 90 percent in three years due to mountain lion predation.

However, preying upon porcupines isn't without risk. It is not clearly known how mountain lions kill porcupines, although evidence indicates at least some cats learn to harass them into falling from trees, where they are killed or sustain debilitating injuries on contact with the ground. Some folklore claims cougars reach a paw under the porcupine's quill-less belly and flip it over, though there is no biological evidence of which

I am aware to support this theory. Regardless of the method, mountain lions are sometimes impaled with quills when preying upon porcupines. The results can be fatal.

The sharp quills of porcupines have a barb on the end. When driven into the muscle of an attacker, the quill works itself deeper into the flesh as the muscle expands and contracts. Heat from the attacker's body enlarges the barb, making it even more tenacious. Interestingly, quills do not carry infection. These specialized hairs are covered with a peculiar compound possessed of antibacterial characteristics, evidently an adaptation that protects porcupines from infection when they're accidentally stuck with their own quills.

Over time quills may migrate from the skin and outer tissues of an impaled aggressor into the body cavity, puncturing vital organs or causing wounds susceptible to infection. Young mountain lions learning to hunt apparently kill porcupines by leaping upon them, at least in some cases. Researchers have recorded multiple instances in which mountain lions have been killed by porcupines. In one well-documented case in Wyoming, an autopsy of the dead young female showed one lung completely destroyed by the aftermath of a quill invasion, the other severely lacerated. Mountain lions are among a very tiny handful of North American predators fearless enough to prey on porcupines. Sometimes the porcupine wins in the end.

Collared peccary (javelina), a type of pig-like animal found in the southwestern United States, are an important prey species to some mountain lions. Weighing from thirty-five to sixty pounds, an adult peccary represents a substantial meal, especially to a sub-adult or small female cougar. Mountain lions also prey upon armadillos. Some studies indicate armadillos make up 10 percent or more of the diet of some Florida panthers.

Mountain lions also have a taste for feral hogs. Domestic pigs turned wild have become a significant problem in many parts of the country due to their damage of crops and wildlife habitat. Some cougars regularly prey upon feral hogs in Texas and California. One study of Florida panthers indicated that feral hogs may comprise up to 59 percent of the annual diet of some cats. Mountain lions in some places in the Southwest also prey upon feral horses. In both cases the native cats are eliminating potentially destructive nonnative species (neither domestic hogs nor horses are native to North America) from native ecosystems.

However, in most habitats in North America, ungulate prey species of the deer family compose the "lion's share" of a cougar's diet. Evolutionary biologists theorize that the mountain lion's solitary and specialized hunting strategies are most efficient when targeted at the largest animals they can reasonably subdue. For example, stalking and rushing a 250-pound mule deer may require the same amount of time and skill as sneaking up on and snatching a 4-pound rabbit. Although the deer may represent more risk of bodily harm to the predator, it also enables the cat to feed for several days, providing enough energy for the mountain lion to turn its attention to other critical biological tasks such as defending a territory, searching for mates, or rearing young.

The types of ungulates mountain lions routinely prey upon differ by geographic region and abundance, but in most places, mule and whitetail deer make up the bulk of the typical cougar's diet, especially in winter. Numerous research projects throughout the northern and southern Rocky Mountains have found deer represent 85 percent or more of mountain lions' diet in places where they are abundant. However, the cat regularly preys upon other ungulates as well. In one study in British Columbia, researchers recorded elk comprising as high as 69 percent of the annual predation of a sample of mountain lions. Prior to the reintroduction of wolves into Yellowstone National Park, researchers found that elk were the number one source of prey for mountain lions in the northern part of the park, which held an exceptionally large elk population. Mountain lions also kill moose with some frequency in Alberta, British Columbia, and Idaho. Adult elk and moose are infrequently targeted by mountain lions, unless they are weakened. Immature animals of both species are those most routinely killed by cougars.

Bighorn sheep are also a mountain lion's preferred prey in some local areas; so much so that reintroduction of bighorns in some places in the southwestern United States has been hampered by cougar predation. Mountain lions are also known to feed on pronghorn (antelope) and mountain goats, although these animals typically inhabit terrain in which the hunting skills of cougars are not usually effective.

Studies of mountain lion predation on ungulates reveal some interesting tendencies. As might be expected, larger mountain lions tend to target larger prey. A robust male cougar weighing 150 pounds is far more likely than a 90-pound female to make a predation attempt on an adult elk. One study in Alberta reported that nearly 70 percent of the kills made by male cougars were moose, mostly calves. By contrast, moose represented less than 5 percent of the kills made by female mountain lions. Regardless of gender, some mountain lions appear to specialize in taking certain prey species more frequently than others. Several studies have documented specific lions downing an unusually high percentage of the bighorn sheep preyed upon by the big cats in local areas. For example, one team of researchers studying mountain lions in New Mexico recorded four bighorn sheep kills by mountain lions. Of those, three were made by the same male cougar.

Mountain lions also have the ability to readily switch between prey sources, depending on abundance or scarcity. As mentioned previously, hares and rabbits are regularly targeted in seasons of abundance. One study in Idaho found mountain lions dining heavily on ground squirrels in the summer, when they are plenteous. Researchers in British Columbia found snowshoe hares made up around 25 percent of the mountain lions' diet during the peak of the bunnies' reproductive cycle. Following a crash in the mule deer population in Big Bend National Park in Texas, biologists observed cougars switching from deer to rabbits, hares, and collared peccaries as their primary sources of prey.

Mountain Lions and Their Prey: Hunting Strategies
Mountain lions and wolves commonly prey upon many of the same species of animals where their range overlaps, yet their predation strategies are very different. Whereas

wolves often test the fitness of a single animal or animals within a herd through an extended chase or harassment, cougars appear to make up their minds about attacking an animal in advance. Wolves often chase their prey for long distances before bringing it down. Mountain lions abandon the chase very quickly if unsuccessful. Wolves thus belong to the family of coursing (chasing) predators, while cougars are aligned with other meat eaters who stalk their prey.

As mentioned earlier, mountain lions can run very fast, but they sustain their blinding speeds only over short distances. Thus, they attempt to get very close to their prey before rushing to seize it. One study concluded that mountain lions were most successful when they stalked within less than 10 feet of mule deer and contacted the targeted animal within less than 35 feet.

Cover plays an important role in the mountain lion's hunting techniques. Their hunting is most successful where ground cover (rocks, trees, brush, and so on) is heavy enough to aid in their concealment as they approach their prey, but open enough to allow a fairly unobstructed field of vision. Mountain lions are very adept at advancing slowly on their bellies, their soft fur and padded feet allowing them to move nearly soundlessly. Like housecats, their ability to remain motionless for long periods of time is remarkable. Similar to domestic cats, the tip of a mountain lion's tail might twitch slightly in anticipation as it closes the distance on potential prey.

Much is made of wolves' ability to detect and exploit weakness among ungulates. Packs frequently kill older animals or those weakened by disease or injury. The canines are evidently able to perceive vulnerabilities as they harass or chase elk and deer, motivating them to sustain the attack until successful.

Cover is essential for mountain lions to approach prey closely enough for a successful ambush.
© ISTOCK.COM/RICK DUBBS

Research involving mountain lion predation reveals a nearly identical pattern. Ungulates killed by mountain lions are typically older or weaker than their counterparts. In the case of a bull elk blinded in one eye and weakened by an antler wound to its head from fighting a rival during mating season, a mountain lion can obviously perceive vulnerability that would also be obvious to a human. But older animals do not often appear weak or out of shape to a person's eye. Yet mountain lions have an uncanny ability to mark them for predation. They evidently sense other weakness as well. Chronic wasting disease (CWD) is a malady often affecting mule and whitetail deer in various regions of the country. Prior to its final stages, animals infected with CWD show no visible signs of the infection. However, one study in a mule deer population where CWD was present discovered that mountain lions preyed upon infected animals four times more often than those that were uninfected. Some biologists believe mountain lions have a remarkably sophisticated ability to observe very subtle aspects of behavior and appearance in their prey that indicate greater vulnerability to a predatory attack.

After stealthily closing the distance to their prey, mountain lions bound swiftly to catch the animal, normally contacting it within a few leaps. The cats use their curved, exceedingly sharp claws to grasp and control the fleeing animal. Smaller prey is normally killed with a fatal bite directed to the neck, just behind the skull, or a bite to the back of the skull that pierces to the brain. Larger prey, such as deer-size animals, may be dispatched with a bite to the neck. However, mountain lions often kill creatures larger than themselves by directing their fangs to the animal's throat, crushing its airway and strangling it. Larger animals killed by mountain lions often have extensive claw marks on the nose and cheeks. Mountain lions use their powerful forelegs and claws to cling to struggling prey. Sometimes cougars kill ungulate prey swiftly, at other times the struggle may span several minutes and cover considerable distance, occasionally up to 100 yards.

Once a kill has been made, mountain lions normally drag their prey to a sheltered location to feed. This behavior evidently decreases the odds of the cat losing its meal to a wolf pack, bear, or other rival predators. Some biologists also theorize cougars transport prey to more secretive locations to avoid the attention of scavenging birds such as ravens and magpies, which might more easily attract the attention of a larger scavenger like a grizzly bear.

A deer-size ungulate will normally keep a cougar at the carcass for twelve hours to three days, sometimes up to a week. After the kill, most mountain lions feed heavily on the carcass, first consuming the heart, liver, lungs, and diaphragm. These organs are easily obtained once the body cavity is torn open, and they are highly nutritious. The cats then turn their attention to other digestive organs and fats. Afterward they consume muscle tissues, but they do not attempt to eat or gnaw on bones. Between feeding sessions, mountain lions "cache" the carcass, covering it with sticks, grass, or soil. Some research indicates male cougars may consume from twenty to thirty pounds of flesh from a carcass in the initial feeding.

The extent to which a mountain lion fully consumes a prey animal depends on the size of the prey and the cougar. Smaller prey are normally eaten in full. Larger prey are often consumed relative to the cat's size and gender. On average, big toms eat the smallest percentage of a carcass, lightweight females consume the highest percentage. This is likely due to the disparity of effort in making a kill between the two classes of cougars. A large male has an easier time bringing down a deer than a small female and thus has the luxury of dining on only the choice parts of the carcass, or so many biologists assume.

As noted previously, mountain lions often attack prey more than twice as large as themselves. Ungulate prey are equipped with hard, sharp hooves. Depending on the time of the year, male ungulates may also sport dangerous antlers. Cougars are amazingly effective predators, but their carnivorous lifestyle comes with many risks. In rare instances mountain lions may be directly killed in a predation attempt. For example, researchers in Yellowstone National Park once found the body of a bighorn ram and a mountain lion that had tried to kill it at the base of a cliff from which both animals had fallen. The robust five-year-old male cougar died from the impact of the fall. Injuries sustained in predation attempts can prove indirectly fatal, too. Mountain lions gored by an antler tip may later succumb to infection. Dislocated joints or other injuries sustained in predation may render the cat unable to hunt, leading to starvation.

Mountain Lions and Other Predators

The number of prey species that are themselves predators recorded in the diets of mountain lions is astonishing. Raccoons are commonly killed and consumed by Florida panthers. Ringtails and coatis, relatives of the raccoon that live in the desert Southwest, are also sometimes eaten by mountain lions. Mountain lions often dine upon skunks, with some evidence indicating that some sub-adult cougars perhaps specialize in killing skunks as they mature. Incidences of mountain lions in North America eating weasels, gray foxes, badgers, bobcats, coyotes, wolves, otters, and black bears have also been recorded. As already noted, mountain lions may also kill and eat other mountain lions. In the case of the previously mentioned predators, they are sometimes eaten after being killed by a mountain lion, sometimes not. Whether a cougar eats another predator it has dispatched is possibly determined by how hungry the cat is at the time. How can a mountain lion stand to eat something as foul-smelling (and tasting) as a skunk or weasel? Mountain lions have far fewer taste buds than humans and many other creatures. Perhaps this is why they sometimes gladly chow down on a stinky skunk.

Mountain lions have been documented killing coyotes, wolves, and bears. However, these creatures also infrequently end the lives of mountain lions. Kittens and sub-adults are at the greatest danger from coyotes, although packs of coyotes can

Young mountain lions are at risk from other predators. This young cougar was trapped on a fence on the National Elk Refuge in Jackson Hole, Wyoming, by a pack of aggressive coyotes.
USFWS/LORI IVERSON

capably drive some adult mountain lions from their kill. On the other hand, an adult lion can handily chase a coyote from a carcass. Coyotes and similar-size predators are typically killed by a mountain lion with a crushing bite to the back of the skull or the neck.

The interactions among mountain lions, wolves, and bears are oftentimes complex. Under the right circumstances, each of these creatures can be a lethal threat to one another, although cougars are typically at a disadvantage due to the superior size of a mature black or grizzly bear and the overwhelming numbers of a wolf pack. However, mountain lions are not always on the losing side of the confrontations. Researchers in the Jackson, Wyoming, area documented a female mountain lion killing and eating a young wolf that was apparently part of a pack. Canadian researchers have also found evidence of cougars lethally interacting with single wolves.

In most situations, however, a wolf pack is a much greater threat to a mountain lion than the converse. Studies in Yellowstone National Park and Banff National Park (Canada) concluded wolves usurped (stole by force) between 6 percent and 14 percent of cougar kills in the study areas. Research in the parks and other areas, including central Idaho and Glacier National Park in northwestern Montana, indicated wolves visited mountain lion kill sites quite frequently (up to 33 percent), although the extent to which wolves drove the cat from the carcass is unknown.

Grizzly bears commonly usurp carcasses from cougars. The keen nose of the grizzly bear is exceptionally suited for smelling and can likely detect the scent of a freshly killed carcass from over a mile away. One study of grizzly bears in Yellowstone and Glacier National Parks found the bears displaced mountain lions from 50 percent (Glacier) and 37 percent (Yellowstone) of the observed carcasses. Other research in the Glacier National Park area has indicated routine usurpation of mountain lion prey by grizzly bears and wolves may exert considerable stress on cougars, perhaps leading to malnutrition or, in extreme cases, starvation. Taking down an elk or deer is an energy intensive, physically dangerous task for a mountain lion. If the cat loses its bounty to a competing predator, it must soon kill again. It appears that this equation can become very costly to mountain lions, especially in habitats where they must contend with both wolves and grizzly bears.

Parasites and Diseases

Mountain lions are often described as being largely free of parasites and diseases, although such a conclusion may be in error due to the very limited research that has been conducted on these conditions in wild cougars. The cats sometimes harbor intestinal parasites such as roundworms and tapeworms. Mountain lions sometimes deliberately consume grass, a behavior some biologists believe may aid in expelling such parasites. External parasites such as ticks, fleas, and mites may also infest cougars.

Documented deaths of mountain lions due to disease are rare. On just two occasions have cougars been confirmed dying from rabies: one of those cases occurred in 1909, the other more recently in Florida. A California mountain lion was diagnosed with feline leukemia and was euthanized (killed to prevent suffering). One expert familiar with the case believed the cougar contacted the disease from preying upon domestic cats.

At the present time it is believed that parasites and diseases are not a significant factor in mountain lion mortality or health. As the lives of these elusive cats become more thoroughly understood through research, a more precise understanding of the role of these maladies may alter current perceptions.

REPRODUCTION AND YOUNG

The Mating Season

In contrast to animals with a defined mating and birthing season (wolf pups in the wild, for example, are always born in the spring), mountain lions may mate during any season of the year. However, in North America most cougars mate from late fall to early spring. Mountain lions are polygamous, meaning one male may mate with multiple females, and a single female may mate with several toms.

When a female enters estrus and is prepared to mate, she seeks scrapes made by male cougars and calls to announce her presence and readiness to breed. The advertising female may attract the attention of more than one male, resulting in heated combat between the males.

Courtship rituals between wild mountain lions are rarely observed by humans. However, it is known that mating usually occurs over a period of several days in which the pair may mate as many as fifty times per day. After mating with one male, a female may mate with another. Mating appears to develop peaceful relationships between male and female cougars. Females are less likely to be attacked by males with which they have mated, giving themselves and their offspring a higher chance of survival when encountering a male.

Pregnancy and Gestation

Because female mountain lions sometimes mate with more than one male, it is possible that kittens in the same litter may have different fathers. This phenomenon has been observed in other polygamous species, but the extent to which it occurs in mountain lion populations is unknown. The gestation period (the time from mating to birth) for mountain lions averages around ninety-two days. Thus the female gives birth three months after becoming pregnant.

Birth

Female mountain lions give birth to their young in a den of sorts, typically a protected space under a rock ledge, between overlapping boulders, or in a patch of very dense vegetation providing cover from the sides and overhead. Unlike the den sites of wolves and coyotes that often enlarge or modify a hole through digging, female mountain lions are not known to alter natural den sites. Many biologists thus prefer

Depressions under overhanging rocks or crevices are used by mountain lions as birthing and nursery sites.
© ISTOCK.COM/TWILDLIFE

to call the site in which a mountain lion births and cares for her young in the first weeks of life a *nursery* as opposed to a *den*. If the nursery is threatened before the young are ready to leave, the mother may move them to an alternate rearing site, carrying each kitten carefully in her mouth.

Baby cougars are tiny, with average birth weights scarcely exceeding one pound (around eighteen ounces). Mountain lion kittens are quite helpless at birth. They are covered in fur at birth with coats ranging from reddish brown to grayish brown. Black spots adorn their coats, black rings are found on their tails. Stripes, or a series of continuous spots that nearly form a stripe, sometimes run along the kitten's back. The eyes and ears of newborn mountain lions are shut. Newborn mountain lions instinctively suckle and nurse soon after birth.

Mountain lion females normally give birth to multiple offspring, but single births can also occur. Litter sizes range from one to six kittens, with three representing the average. At one time biologists speculated younger females birthed fewer kittens on average than older mothers. Recent research, however, indicates females birthing their first litter of kittens do not have significantly fewer offspring on average than older females.

Kittens may be born at any time of the year, but in their western range in North America most births (over 70 percent) take place during the seven-month period from May to October. However, within local and regional populations, a "birth pulse" may occur, a biological term used to describe a significant concentration of births within a longer birthing season. Birth pulses among cougars uncannily coincide with prey abundance, which provides mother mountain lions with a readily available food source with which to nourish herself, provide for milk production, and meet the nutritional demands of her litter. Such spikes in mountain lion births typically occur in relation to the birth of ungulate prey, which are normally produced in late May and early June across much of their range in the Rocky Mountains. One study showed mountain lions in Wyoming experienced a birth pulse from August to November, a phenomenon some biologists attribute to the fact that growing kittens and their mothers can take advantage of high numbers of ungulate prey concentrated on winter range about the time the young begin eating larger quantities of meat on their own. Among Florida panthers, a birth pulse occurs from March to July, coinciding with the peak of the fawning period for whitetail deer.

Nurturing Kittens to Adulthood

Within just a few weeks, the helpless kittens change dramatically. Their eyes and ears open by two weeks of age. In contrast to the yellowish eyes of adults, the eyes of baby mountain lions are strikingly blue. By the time they are one month of age, the young have grown mobile and playful, interacting with their siblings through wrestling matches and chasing.

When the kittens are around six to eight weeks of age, the mother cougar leads them from the nursery into a larger and more dangerous world. The cubs follow the female to kill sites, where they learn to feed on the flesh of other animals along with their mother's milk. They have developed quickly. Even at this young age, they are now able to navigate difficult terrain as they accompany their mother. For the next few months their teeth and jaw muscles will develop more fully, allowing them to increasingly ingest larger and less-tender portions of their mother's prey. This development coincides with a decrease in their mother's milk production. Most cougar kittens are weaned from their mother's milk by three months of age, the timing of which is determined in substantial measure by the nutritional health of the female.

At five months of age, mountain lion kittens have changed dramatically from the tiny, helpless creatures born to their mother. Their eyes have transitioned from baby blue to the amber orbs of adulthood. The black spots on their coats and the dark rings on their tails have faded considerably and will all but disappear by the time they reach their first birthday. Five-month-old cougars can skillfully climb trees, allowing them to flee other antagonistic predators. The kittens have now grown from just over a pound at birth to sixteen to thirty-five pounds, depending on their sex and access to sufficient nutrition.

Mountain lion kittens face a host of hazards in the first six months of life. In some populations, over 50 percent of the kittens born will not likely survive to reach six months of age. Studying the survival rates of mountain lion kittens is difficult. Even in areas undergoing intensive research, it is possible that some young die before investigators discover them.

Of the cubs that fail to survive six months, many are killed by male cougars. In one study in New Mexico, researchers found that 44 percent of the mortalities that occurred in young kittens from birth to 13 months of age, for which a cause was known, were attributed to male mountain lions. Another 37 percent starved to death. Of these, half succumbed to malnutrition because their mother was killed by an adult male. Other kittens starved due to the fact that their mother died in a predation attempt or was taken by illness. Cougar kittens also met their end in accidents (falling from a cliff) and at the jaws of rival predators (coyotes).

For the next six to twelve months, young mountain lions will remain with their mother until they achieve independence. During this time they will still be dependent on their mother for food, especially during the first few months.

By five months of age, mountain lions can easily climb trees, a skill necessary to avoid other predators such as wolves and coyotes.
© ISTOCK.COM/GKUCHERA

Research indicates female mountain lions with sub-adult kittens around the age of six months are required to kill a mid-size ungulate such as a whitetail deer about every four days. In preparation for independence, the growing cubs must learn to avoid potentially dangerous predators (including adult male cougars) and obtain their own hunting skills, behaviors they will largely acquire from their mother. At one year of age, a young mountain lion has lost its spots, although faint dapples on the coat can often still be detected by researchers or individuals very familiar with cougars. The year-old cougar is approaching its adult weight, although most individuals will continue to grow, sometimes increasing their weight by nearly 50 percent between their first and second birthdays. Occasionally, groups of mountain lions are seen together, perhaps three or four adult-looking cats traveling together in a group. Such sightings sometimes prompt people to report a "pack" or "pride" of mountain lions. In all likelihood these observations include female mountain lions and their nearly grown young. By the time it reaches the age of independence, a sub-adult male cougar may weigh more than its mother.

Young mountain lions typically separate from their mothers at eleven to eighteen months of age. Their independence is usually triggered by an adult female deliberately abandoning her young, perhaps from a kill site or failing to return to her cubs at a site at which they are resting. Oftentimes the female's separation from her kittens is triggered by her mating or association with a prospective mate. At this point the kittens are on their own, now entering a life stage biologists often describe as the *sub-adult* stage. Newly independent siblings often stay together for a period of time, normally from one to seven weeks, occasionally longer.

The life histories of females and males take different courses during the sub-adult stage. Around half of the females will establish a home range that differs from, but overlaps with, the range of their mother. The other sub-adult females will disperse (travel) away from their mother's home range and take up residence in new territory. Research suggests sub-adult females typically disperse from 10 to 30 miles from their mother's home range.

MOUNTAIN LIONS AND HUMANS

Mountain Lions in History: Native Peoples of North America

For many centuries prior to the arrival of Europeans, indigenous peoples of North America interacted with mountain lions. Cougars occasionally killed American Indians, and native peoples sometimes hunted and killed mountain lions.

Attitudes toward the cats varied from tribe to tribe. While most tribes held mountain lions in esteem, some peoples of the Pacific Northwest thought they were generally a mysterious, contemptible animal. Mountain lions were also viewed with suspicion by some tribes dwelling on the plains. In his book, *Red Hunters and the Animal People*, published in 1904, Charles Eastman recounts the attitudes of Sioux Indians (his ancestral people) toward various animals. The feelings are illustrated in one chapter as a conversation between an elder and younger men. In it the elder describes *igmu-tanka*, the cougar, in the following way: "They are unsociable, queer people. Their speech has no charm. They are very bashful and yet dangerous, for no animal can tell what they are up to. If one sees you first, he will not give you a chance to see so much as the tip of his tail. He never makes any noise, for he has the right sort of moccasins."

However, other tribes afforded the mountain lion great respect. The Hopi tribe, indigenous to the American Southwest, revered the mountain lion as a god and the protector of the tribe. An intriguing petroglyph (stone art) featuring a mountain lion was discovered in Arizona in 1934. Displayed at Petrified Forest National Park in Arizona, the rock art is thought to be around one thousand years old. It was created by the Anasazi, ancestors of the Pueblos.

Native hunters sometimes killed cougars. It was thought by many that ending the life of such a predator would mystically pass some of its spirit (and hence hunting skills) to the one who made the kill. Mountain lion claws and skins were used as adornments by some tribes. Lewis and Clark recorded in their journals that some native peoples were very fond of mountain lion robes and noted it took the skins of four cougars to create such an article of clothing.

Numerous American Indian legends involve the mountain lion. One explains how the mountain lion came to have such a long, lean shape. A mountain lion, at the time a more stocky creature with a short tail, stole a meal of small rodents (variously identified as squirrels or prairie dogs) from Old Man, the creator. Old Man followed the mountain lion and caught it as it slept on a rock, gorged from its stolen dinner. He was so angry he stretched its husky body into a lean shape, also seizing and pulling its

This petroglyph of a mountain lion in Arizona is thought to be around one thousand years old. NPS

short tail into a long one in his anger. Ever since, the mountain lion has been a long, lean creature, ever in search of prey.

Mountain Lions in History: European Settlers in North America

European settlement in North America afforded the mountain lion the same fate as other larger predators. Farming cleared forests, depriving the cats of cover for hunting and rearing young, and also eliminated prey species such as deer and elk. Mountain lions sometimes preyed upon domestic livestock. Most settlers viewed them as a nuisance and threat to human life and livestock, and they sought to eliminate cougars from the landscape where possible.

Cleared land, previously forests, is estimated by some experts to have covered over 50 percent of the landscape in the eastern United States by 1850. In many locations the ratio of land converted from native woodlands to agricultural lands was even higher. The resulting loss of habitat for wild creatures, along with unregulated hunting, led to the rapid decline of both predators and ungulates alike. Historical records indicate mountain lions were essentially eliminated from most locations east of the Mississippi River by the close of the nineteenth century. The cats may have persisted longer in a few isolated locations, but the remnant population of Florida panthers is the only known population to persist until modern times.

The mountain lion ultimately fared better west of the Mississippi River, but not because settlers in that portion of the country looked more kindly upon the cats. Rugged, mountainous regions became strongholds for cougars after decades of deliberate extermination eliminated them from more accessible areas, especially where livestock was involved. By 1930, mountain lion populations were absent from most of their historic habitat in the United States.

The rapid plunge in mountain lion numbers from the late 1800s to 1930 was accelerated by government efforts to rid them from the landscape. Many states enacted bounties (payments for killing a certain type of animal) on mountain lions in response to the perception that cougars were dangerous to people and livestock. During the same period, the federal government employed professional hunters who attempted to eliminate mountain lions and other predators from federal lands.

In Montana, for example, a bounty on mountain lions was enacted in 1884. Interestingly, the original bounty offered for mountain lions (eight dollars) was eight times greater than that paid for an adult wolf (one dollar). A record 177 bounty payments were made for mountain lions in 1908. From 1925 to 1930, fewer than five bounty payments were made for mountain lions, though the bounty had increased to twenty-five dollars by 1930. Montana's bounty system for mountain lions was dropped in 1962. Records of the system from 1932 to its termination were lost, but some sources suggest fewer than five payments per year were made for mountain lions from 1932 to 1950, an indication of their scarcity. Mountain lion numbers began to increase in the state around 1950. One source indicates 167 bounty payments were made in 1961 and 1962, the final two years of the system.

Mountain Lions in Modern Times

The elimination of bounty payments and the enactment of legal protection of the mountain lion as a game animal that could be taken by hunters and trappers but not killed indiscriminately allowed cougar populations in western states to expand dramatically from 1950 to 2000.

The early portion of this period also coincided with a rise in ungulate numbers in many locations in the West, a further boon to mountain lions. Experts believe mountain lion numbers in some areas in the Rocky Mountains may actually be higher at the present time than they were historically. Mountain lion populations surged during the late 1980s and 1990s in many places for reasons not fully understood. Cougar populations are thought to be stable or increasing in most regions of the West. Their future expansion into suitable habitat currently unoccupied will be dependent on human toleration for these notable carnivores.

A large cougar visits a water tank on the Sevilleta National Wildlife Refuge in New Mexico. Cougar populations expanded across much of their range in the final decades of the twentieth century.
USFWS

Humans and Mountain Lions: Current Interactions and Challenges

The development of better techniques to census (estimate population numbers) mountain lions in recent years has contributed to refined estimates of local populations. However, one of the continuing challenges to mountain lion research and management involves the largely solitary and secretive nature of the big cats.

In the past few decades, wildlife managers have witnessed booming deer (and in some cases elk) herds taking up residence in suburban areas in numerous locations. At the same time, development of land for human residence at or within the edges of rural wildlife habitat have increasingly found people and wild animals attempting to live together. These two factors, along with a growing mountain lion population, have led to dramatically rising numbers of human-cougar interactions in some areas. Mountain lions living at the edge of human society sometimes prey upon pets. They may be lured to suburban backyards and parks by robust numbers of ungulate prey. Such events dramatically up the odds of negative interactions between mountain lions and humans.

At least two dozen fatal mountain lion attacks have been confirmed in North America since 1890. Other nonfatal attacks have also occurred. According to records compiled by the California Department of Fish and Wildlife, fourteen attacks happened in California from 1986 to 2014, three of which were fatal. Although mountain lions mauling humans is very rare (domestic dogs kill far more people on an annual basis than cougars), experts offer several pieces of advice on countering an aggressive encounter.

In most situations, mountain lions appear to ambush people in a predatory attempt, meaning the cougar plans to feed on its victim. If the animal perceives the person is not an easy meal, it will usually back off. Experts thus coach people to stand tall and spread their arms or raise them above their head to appear larger. Confronting the cat with eye contact and shouting is also advised. If sticks or stones are handy, hurl them at the cat or use a stout branch in self-defense. Back away slowly. Should the cat initiate physical contact, fight back. Blows to the end of the nose or a finger in the eye may convince the cougar to break the attack. Above all, do not turn your back to the mountain lion or run.

A mountain lion crosses prairie habitat at dawn. The future of this great cat depends on how much of the world humans are willing to share with this powerful predator.
© ISTOCK.COM/ JOHNPITCHER

Most cougars that get into "trouble" with humans are sub-adults, many of which may have been orphaned by their mothers. These "teenagers" may not have learned from their mothers to distinguish domestic dogs or humans from wild prey and are essentially experimenting with new prey based on their lack of knowledge. Protecting female mountain lions with young may thus reduce the number of negative human-cougar interactions.

In mountain lion country, it's wise to hike with another person or in a group. Most mountain lion attacks are directed at a solitary human. Parents should also be aware that children make up a high percentage of cougar attack victims. Keep the family together when hiking or recreating in mountain lion country. Carrying pepper spray, the kind used by biologists and recreationists in bear country, is also an excellent preparation for deterring a cougar attack.

Increasing mountain lion numbers in some areas may also lead to a reduction of ungulate species highly valued by hunters, whose expenditures fund state wildlife agencies and contribute to many local economies. Currently hunting is the greatest single cause of cougar mortality in most western states where it is allowed. The extent to which mountain lions pose real threats to human safety, game populations, and livestock is not as thoroughly understood as many commentators (both pro- and anti-predator) suggest. Mountain lions are not endangered in the US, nor is the average citizen in any significant danger from a cougar. The extent to which *Puma concolor* is allowed to thrive in the future will depend as much on public perception as on scientific management.

CHAPTER 12
WOLVES

My consciousness as a youngster encompassed two divergent worlds when it came to predators. On the family ranch in western Montana, my father trapped and killed predators—coyotes in particular—that infrequently attacked newborn calves during severe winters. I well remember a tiny calf we discovered one frigid February morning. A coyote had bitten its hindquarter. Through torn flesh I could see the shiny white bone of its hip joint. At that moment I hated coyotes. By fall the calf's wound healed, leaving only a ragged scar on its tough black hide.

Although antagonistic toward most predators and certain other species, my dad was possessed by an overall fascination with wildlife, an attitude that rubbed off on his children. Wildlife stories were among my favorite books I plucked from the shelves of the Three Forks School library. I especially loved tales of predators. I read with passion *Yellow Eyes*, a book about a mountain lion, and *Old One Toe,* a story of a fox. But my very favorite was *The Black Wolf of Savage River*, a 1959 fictional tale of an Alaskan wolf. When reading the books, I found myself rooting for the predators and against

Gray wolves may be black and nearly white, as well as their typical gray color.
KEVIN RHOADES

the hunters and trappers. In those moments I loved them all: coyotes, mountain lions, wolves, foxes, and bears.

While cross-country skiing in Yellowstone National Park in late winter 2000, I first heard the howl of a wolf, mournful, deep, and very strong. Less than an hour later, my companions and I spotted three wolves at a distance. Since then I have observed wolves on numerous occasions, both in Yellowstone and other remote areas of Montana. They are fascinating and sometimes fearsome creatures. Neither the antipathy held by many ranchers and hunters toward wolves, nor the near-religious devotion many wolf advocates carry toward the creatures, can be justified, at least not in my mind.

In this chapter I hope to present a picture of wolves from the standpoint of natural history that focuses minimally on the social controversies surrounding these creatures. Informed management and conservation do not tolerate villains or celebrities in the world of wildlife. It is not appropriate to view wolves in either light. It is my hope that the future of wolves and humans in the United States will soon enter an era where these iconic predators are afforded no more or no less respect than other carnivores and their prey.

NAMES AND FACES

Names and Visual Description

Wolf is the English name given to the largest species in the dog-like family of mammals, the canines. In the case of wolves, the common and scientific names are essentially equivalent, although they are derived from different languages. The common name, *wolf*, is Germanic in origin. The scientific, or Latin, name for the wolf is *Canis lupus*. *Canis* refers to the animal's family, the canines. *Lupus* is the Latin word for "wolf." Thus, in reference to wolves, the common and scientific names are the same terms derived from different languages.

In North America, members of the *Canis lupus* species are most often described as wolves. However, in field guides and scientific literature, the species is more technically referenced by the term *gray wolf*. To a lesser extent these animals might also be known as timber wolves.

Gray wolves have the overall appearance of a large dog, somewhat similar to an oversize German shepherd or a malamute. When it comes to coloration, the name *gray wolf* is somewhat deceiving. Although most wolves have an overall grayish appearance, individual animals within various geographic regions and gene pools may be almost completely white to completely black. The "typical" gray wolf sports a grizzled gray coloration over its entire body, with darker highlights on the back, neck, and shoulders that yield to lighter tones on the lower rib cage, belly, and legs. Some wolves exhibit slightly reddish highlights in the lighter portions of their coats. On most animals, however, the paler part of their pelage is whitish or cream colored.

A wolf's legs appear long in relation to its body. This characteristic is more prominent in the summer, when the animal wears its shorter coat, than in the winter, when its fur is much longer. A wolf's tail is bushy and roughly one third the length of its body from the tip of its nose to the end of its rump, or slightly longer. A wolf with the common gray-grizzled appearance most often has a black tip on the end of its tail. When it is on the move, the wolf carries its tail straight out from its body.

A wolf's ears are erect and slightly rounded at the tips. Its black nose pad is more prominent than that observed on other canines; it measures more than 1 inch wide. A wolf's eyes are often described as orange or hazel in color with a distinct greenish cast. Framing a wolf's head is a ruff of longer hair that makes the face of the animal appear much larger than the underlying skull.

Unlike many other animal species that are given special terms for the two genders, terminology for the wolf sexes is very simple. Male wolves are referred to as males, and female wolves are called females. Their offspring, like the babies of domestic dogs, are known as pups.

Related Species in North America

Gray wolves share temperate and arctic regions of North America with six other canine species: coyotes, red foxes, swift foxes, kit foxes, gray foxes, and red wolves. Given the extreme difference in size between wolves and foxes, it's unlikely that a reasonably educated observer would ever mistake a fox for a wolf. Tiny kit foxes usually weigh a mere five pounds or less. Even the largest fox species, the red fox, is much small than the wolf. At around fifteen pounds, large red foxes are still four times smaller than a small adult wolf. What's more, all the North American fox species exhibit a coloration that is very different from gray wolves.

Differentiating gray wolves from coyotes and red wolves, however, isn't quite as simple. Despite their smaller size, each of these two species can be easily confused with gray wolves.

The most obvious difference between a coyote and a gray wolf is its size. In terms of weight, coyotes usually weigh from twenty-five to forty-five pounds, roughly half the size of an adult wolf of modest proportions. An adult wolf stands about 2.5 feet tall at the shoulder; a coyote is only 1.5 feet tall. But unless the two species are observed in proximity to one another (an unlikely occurrence) or the observer has had ample opportunities to view both species separately, the untrained eye can easily confuse a coyote for a wolf.

Beyond size, what's the best way to tell the two species apart? In some cases identification is quite obvious.

Red foxes and coyotes are smaller canines that share ranges with wolves in some areas.
LISA BALLARD

Red wolves that live in the southeastern United States are midway in size between gray wolves and coyotes.
USFWS/STEVE HILLEBRAND

Gray wolves that sport black coats or are nearly white can be distinguished from coyotes based on color. But trained observers can positively identify animals of the two species that are similar in color by paying attention to differences in size and other physical features.

When it runs, a wolf carries its tail straight out behind its body. A coyote, by contrast, keeps its tail low, sometimes between its legs. In relation to the rest of its face, the black nose pad appears smaller on a coyote than on a wolf. A coyote's ears appear slightly larger and more pointed than those of a gray wolf. However, this feature is somewhat variable depending upon the time of year, the latitude in which the animal lives, and individual variations. Viewed head-on, a wolf's face is described by some biologists as more blocky and square, while a coyote's face is narrow and triangular.

Gray wolves also share the North American continent with red wolves, a species aptly described by some naturalists as appearing as a cross between a gray wolf and a coyote. In both size and appearance, red wolves have the look of a gray wolf–coyote intermediary. It is believed that red wolves became extinct in the wild by 1980. In 1973 the US Fish & Wildlife Service began a captive breeding program for the species. Since 1987, red wolves have been reintroduced in the southeastern United States, with the highest concentration of animals occurring in North Carolina. Because current red wolf and gray wolf ranges in the United States are separated by many hundreds of miles and geographical obstacles, it's not likely to confuse the species, at least not yet. However, the interactions between gray wolves, coyotes, and red wolves represent a fascinating, yet puzzling peek into the workings of nature, our next topic of discussion.

Subspecies

Worldwide, gray wolves have been separated into at least thirty-two subspecies by biologists at various times in history. Of those subspecies, twenty-four have historically been identified in North America. Most of the subspecies are associated with particular habitats and regions in which they live (or have lived). For example, the Alaskan tundra wolf, *Canis lupus tundrarum*, roams along the Arctic coast of northern Alaska. An extinct subspecies, the Mogollon mountain wolf, *Canis lupus mogollensis*, is named for the native Mogollon people of New Mexico and Arizona, the region it inhabited until its extinction in the early part of the twentieth century.

Many wildlife biologists in recent times have proposed reducing the number of North American subspecies of gray wolf from two dozen to five.

The Mexican gray wolf, *Canis lupus baileyi*, is the most easily identifiable, due to its current isolation from other wolves. According to the US Fish & Wildlife Service, the Mexican gray wolf "is the smallest, southern-most occurring, rarest, and most genetically distinct subspecies of gray wolf in North America." Prior to the settlement of the American Southwest by Europeans, Mexican gray wolves occupied vast regions of Texas, New Mexico, Arizona, and Mexico. Conflict with livestock interests prompted widespread killing of these wolves in the early 1900s. By the middle of the twentieth century, Mexican gray wolves had been essentially extirpated from the United States and severely reduced in Mexico.

The smallest subspecies of gray wolf, Mexican gray wolves range in weight from approximately fifty to eighty pounds, are 5 to 6 feet in length (including the tail), and about 2.5 feet tall at the shoulder. Mexican gray wolves are quite similar in size to German shepherd dogs. Unlike other gray wolf subspecies, Mexican gray wolves do not exhibit nearly white or nearly black color phases. Rather their coats are a mix of gray, black, buff, and reddish brown. The primary prey species of Mexican gray wolves include elk, mule deer, and whitetail deer, along with other smaller mammals. Like larger subspecies of gray wolves, the Mexican gray wolf is capable of, and sometimes does, kill livestock, such as young calves and sheep.

In 1977 the United States and Mexico began a cooperative captive breeding program with Mexican gray wolves. Because this wolf was listed as an endangered species in the United States in 1976, the goal of this program was to reestablish a viable population in the American Southwest. In 1998, Mexican gray wolves bred and reared in captivity were released in the Blue Range Wolf Recovery Area in the Apache National Forest in eastern Arizona. Offspring from this initial reintroduction, and captive-reared wolves released in subsequent years, now roam across mountainous portions of southeastern Arizona and southwestern New Mexico in the Apache and Gila National Forests. The White Mountain Apache Tribe became a formal partner in Mexican gray wolf recovery efforts in 2002. Wolves have been released and now occupy portions of the Fort Apache Indian Reservation. A decade after the recovery program for the Mexican gray wolf began, approximately fifty wolves were living in New Mexico and Arizona.

Another subspecies, the eastern wolf or eastern timber wolf, *Canis lupus lycaon,* occupies southeastern Canada. These wolves are also known as eastern Canadian wolf, eastern Canadian red wolf, eastern gray wolf, and Algonquin wolf. These wolves are found in Algonquin Provincial Park, Ontario, and other adjacent regions. Historically the eastern wolf ranged across the northeastern United States and westward toward the Great Lakes.

West of the range of the eastern wolf, the plains wolf or Great Plains wolf, *Canis lupus nubilis*, historically occupied a massive range consisting of the interior portions of the United States, westward through the Rocky Mountains to the northern Pacific Coast. The plains wolf also ranged along the mountains of Canada's Pacific Coast and into northeastern Canada toward Hudson Bay. Currently the plains wolf is found in the Great Lakes area of northern Minnesota, Wisconsin, and Michigan. At the present time the plains wolf is the most abundant subspecies inhabiting the continental United States. This subspecies is sometimes called the buffalo wolf, in reference to one of its historic prey species on the Great Plains.

To the north and west of the plains wolf's historic range lies the range of the northwestern wolf or Rocky Mountain wolf, *Canis lupus occidentalis*, also known as the Alaskan wolf or Mackenzie Valley wolf. The historic and current range of this wolf lies primarily in the mountainous areas of western Canada and Alaska. Its historic and current range also juts southward into the contiguous United States in northern Montana, Idaho, and Washington. When wolves were reintroduced into Yellowstone National Park and central Idaho from Canada in 1995 and 1996, members of the northwestern subspecies were chosen. Wolves transplanted in 1995 were captured in an area east of Jasper National Park near Hinton, Alberta, a region roughly 550 miles north of Yellowstone National Park. Animals relocated from Canada in 1996 came from the Williston Lake area of British Columbia, about 750 miles north of the Yellowstone release site. Northwestern wolves were chosen from these areas because of their excellent health and occupation of habitat that closely resembles that of Yellowstone Park and central Idaho.

Given ample prey, northwestern wolves grow quite large. Members of this subspecies range in weight from around 85 to 115 pounds and stand nearly 2.5 feet at the front shoulder, which is considerably larger than the three subspecies previously described. Exceptionally large northwestern wolves may weigh up to 145 pounds. In Alaska, northwestern wolves may inhabit territories as large as 600 square miles. Northwestern wolves are usually gray or black in color, with some animals exhibiting an intermediary pelage between gray and black with a markedly bluish appearance.

Arctic wolves, *Canis lupus arctos,* occupy the northernmost dwelling of any gray wolf subspecies. Sometimes called polar wolves or white wolves, this species roams barren, frozen environments primarily north of the Arctic Circle. Several adaptations help these wolves survive in one of the harshest environments on the planet. Their muzzles, legs, and ears are fairly short, helping them retain body heat. Fur between the pads of their feet and exceptionally long, thick fur further insulate them from extremely cold temperatures that may plunge to -70 degrees Fahrenheit. Arctic wolves have white coats that blend with their snowy surroundings, enhancing their ability to stalk prey. They primarily prey upon musk oxen and arctic hares. They also consume caribou, birds, lemmings, and sometimes seals. Prey is much less abundant in the Arctic than in other places gray wolves live, which means arctic wolves may maintain territories in excess of 1,000 square miles.

Physical Characteristics

Like other species that occupy a wide range of latitudes and habitats, wolf sizes vary considerably. Small members of the southern-dwelling Mexican wolf subspecies may weigh a modest fifty pounds, while exceptionally weighty specimens of the northwestern subspecies occasionally triple them in bulk. How large can wolves become? A wolf weighing 175 pounds was killed in Alaska in 1939.

Wolves have very large feet compared to similar-size domestic dogs. According to the National Zoo in Washington, DC, a captive wolf weighing sixty pounds has paws similar in size to a one hundred-pound domestic dog. Adult wolf tracks average about

4.5 inches long by 3.5 inches wide, with prints of larger animals being notably bigger. The oversize feet of wolves allow them to run more easily in snow, serving somewhat like snowshoes.

RANGE AND HABITAT

Historic Range

The regions inhabited by herbivores and carnivores follow different, but highly related patterns. Herbivores are found only where there are plants they find palatable and that meet their nutritional requirements. Carnivores, on the other hand, live only where prey species they can kill in sufficient numbers to sustain their existence are found. In some cases the range of its primary prey species largely determines a particular carnivore's range. The Canada lynx, for example, preys heavily on snowshoe hares. Snowshoe hares may constitute as much as 97 percent of a lynx's diet. Rarely does a lynx garner more than one third of its diet from prey species other than hares. Thus the snowshoe hare's range largely determines the Canada lynx's range.

The ranges of less selective predators may overlap or correspond with numerous types of prey. Such is the case with wolves. Wolves generally glean most of their sustenance from mid-size to large ungulates such as moose, elk, caribou, musk ox, whitetail deer, mule deer, and bighorn sheep. Wherever a sufficient prey base of one or more of these herbivores exists, wolves are also likely to be found.

Describing the historic range of wolves in North America yields two interesting conclusions. First, one's estimation of historic ranges depends on whether or not the red wolf's range is included in the southeastern United States. Second, not all sources and the maps they produce of historic range agree. Assuming "historic range" refers to an animal's distribution prior to the European settlement of North America (around AD 1500), sources for determining historic range are highly variable. Archaeological materials, journals of trappers and other early explorers who encountered various animals, Native American histories, and other data all come into play when assessing the historic range of a particular creature. It is not an exact science.

Disagreement regarding the wolf's historic range is most prominent along areas of the Pacific Coast, most specifically California. Most sources exclude central and southern California from the historic range of wolves. Others show wolves absent from portions of Nevada, Arizona, Washington, and Oregon as well. However, historical records indicate wolves were found in the Sacramento Valley of central California. In 1918 a wolf killing was recorded in Los Angeles County, a county that lies along the Pacific Coast in the southwestern portion of the state.

When it comes to wolves, biologists agree that essentially every habitat in North America that contains large ungulates was inhabited by wolves, from mid-Mexico to the ice pack of the Arctic. Thus, if the historic range of "wolves" in North America includes both gray wolves and red wolves, these adaptable carnivores essentially roamed across the entire continent with very few exceptions.

Historically wolves roamed the deciduous forests of the central and eastern United States as well as the mountains and the plains.
JACK BALLARD

Historically, habitats that the public now perceive as being marginally associated with wolves held some of the greatest concentrations of these formidable predators. The seemingly innumerable herds of bison that grazed and galloped across the Great Plains, along with vast numbers of plains-dwelling elk, supported exceptionally large numbers of wolves. Many people today do not associate wolves with prairie habitats. However, given the enormous ungulate population on the prairies prior to European settlement, the rolling grasslands of the plains also held very high numbers of wolves.

Current Range

For the average person, determining the current range of wolves in North America involves some of the same problems as assessing the historic range. All sources do not agree. Even range maps from government agencies don't always show the same range. Wolves themselves are also making the endeavor more difficult. The animals are rapidly expanding their range in the western United States. Populations continue to disperse in the Great Lakes region as well. Some biologists believe wolves are also moving into the extreme northern regions of the Northeast.

When describing current wolf ranges, it's helpful to separate Alaska and Canada from the contiguous United States. Wolf populations in those areas have varied throughout modern history but are relatively stable, at least compared with the situation in the Lower 48. Wolves range across all of Alaska, inhabiting most of the major islands in the southeastern part of the state as well as the mainland. Most of Canada also holds wolves, from the frozen islands of the far north to the lush, coastal forests of British Columbia, including Vancouver Island. Wolves are not present on the Island of Newfoundland in eastern Canada. They are also absent in the southern portion of Saskatchewan, southeastern Alberta, and southwestern Manitoba.

In the contiguous United States, aggressive efforts by individuals and government agencies in the late 1800s and early 1900s eliminated wolves from virtually all of their historic range. Bounties (cash payments for killing a wolf) were instituted in many states as early as the 1840s. These bounties originally amounted to just a few dollars, but in a time when workers might toil for a dollar a day, the monetary incentive for hunting or trapping wolves was considerable.

The bounties offered by states were not a new invention. In 1630 the Massachusetts Bay Colony provided a bounty for settlers who killed wolves. Bounties were a very effective means of wolf elimination. For example, Montana's bounty law was enacted in 1884. In its first year, 5,450 wolf hides were presented to government officials as proof of wolf kills and processed for bounty payments. From 1900 to 1931, all but three counties in Montana reported bounty payments. With the exception of perhaps a few lone individuals, wolves were thought to be eliminated in the Treasure State in the 1930s. The timing of the wolf's demise in other states varied somewhat, but due to bounties, government-sponsored trapping and poisoning, along with incidental killing by ranchers and homesteaders, wolves were essentially eliminated from the Lower 48 by 1940.

However, one small segment of the gray wolf population persisted, despite such widespread elimination efforts. Wolves were never completely eliminated from the dense woods of northeastern Minnesota, although it is believed their population dropped to as low as a few hundred animals in the 1960s. During the extremely cold winter of 1948–1949, wolves actually recolonized a tiny portion of the United States. Isle Royale, Michigan, is the largest island in Lake Superior, measuring some 45 miles long by 9 miles across at its widest point. In the depths of this exceptional winter, an ice bridge formed between the island and the mainland of Canada, 15 miles away. Wolves crossed the ice, discovering a population of moose that had established itself on the island sometime after 1900. The moose probably came from Canada as well, perhaps swimming to the island.

Previously caught in a boom-and-bust population cycle in the absence of predators, moose populations on Isle Royale are now balanced by wolves. From a conservation standpoint, the timing of the wolves' arrival on Isle Royale was fortuitous. The island had been authorized as a National Park in 1931 by President Herbert Hoover "to conserve a prime example of North Woods Wilderness." Nine years later, Isle Royale National Park was established under the administration of Franklin Roosevelt. Arrival of the wolves less than a decade later indeed enhanced the "North Woods Wilderness" character of the national park.

Since its low point in the 1960s, when gray wolf numbers in the contiguous United States numbered a few hundred animals in northern Minnesota and around two dozen animals on Isle Royale, the population has now expanded to an excess of 6,200. The wolves of northeastern Minnesota, along with transients from Canada, have expanded their range to northern Wisconsin and Michigan's Upper Peninsula. Growth of wolf numbers in Wisconsin and Michigan has been very rapid. In the five years from 2005–2006 to 2010–2011 (winter population counts), the US Fish & Wildlife Service reported an increase in Wisconsin from 467 to 782 wolves and an increase in Michigan from 434 to 687 wolves. In both states, wolf numbers rose more than 50 percent in the five-year period. In Minnesota, gray wolf numbers rose steadily in every decade from 1960 to 2010, but their population has since stabilized and is now prone to fluctuations in areas as is the case with wolves in other intact habitat.

Minnesota wolves range across the northeastern third of the state, with their population expanding slightly south and westward. Large, lightly populated regions of national forest land comprise much of northeastern Minnesota and offer excellent habitat for wolves. As a rough estimate wolves are found northeast of a line beginning at the Minnesota–Wisconsin border approximately 60 miles north of Minneapolis, extending to the Minnesota–Canadian border about 30 miles east of the Minnesota–North Dakota border.

In Wisconsin, wolves are present mainly across the northern third of the state, an area with significant areas of State Forest and National Forest lands. A line drawn from Green Bay west and slightly north to the Governor Knowles State Forest on the Minnesota border roughly marks the southern boundary of Wisconsin's northern wolf population. Another population of wolves, located in the west-central portion of the state, ranges primarily throughout several protected areas in the region of the Necedah National Wildlife Refuge and Black River State Forest.

Michigan's wolves are primarily found in the Upper Peninsula, although wolf sightings in the lower portion of the state have increased in recent years. Wolves have been recorded in every county of the Upper Peninsula, with numbers typically higher in the west than in the east. The northernmost reaches of the Upper Peninsula, with their extreme winters and deep snows, limit whitetail deer densities, making it difficult for wolves to establish year-round territories during cycles of severe winters.

Where will Midwest wolves wind up next? One wolf traveled from Wisconsin to eastern Indiana. Another moved from Michigan to north-central Missouri. At least two lone wolves from the upper Midwest have made their way into Nebraska. Wandering wolves are most often young loners. If two of these individuals of mating age and differing sexes meet, it's possible they may mate and form a pack, leapfrogging a wolf population to a new area.

Since the reintroduction of gray wolves to Yellowstone National Park and central Idaho in 1995 and 1996, wolf numbers have grown rapidly in the northern Rocky Mountains.

The wolves reintroduced to central Idaho were released primarily at the edge of the Frank Church–River of No Return Wilderness. A total of thirty-five wolves were released in Idaho; thirty-one were released in Yellowstone. However, these were not the only wolves colonizing the Rockies in the 1990s. Wolves from Canada had moved into Montana's Glacier National Park and were slowly establishing themselves southward by the time wolves from Canada were transplanted to central Idaho and Yellowstone National Park. In more recent years other wolves from Canada have crossed into the contiguous United States and have been responsible, at least in part, for the establishment of a small population in Washington.

Currently around 1,800 wolves roam the wild lands in portions of Wyoming, Montana, Idaho, Washington, and Oregon. Populations are variable to due the abundance of prey species, hunting and other factors, such as disease. Wyoming's wolves are found primarily in the northwestern part of the state, in the mountains of and around Yellowstone National Park. For an approximation of Wyoming's wolf range, draw a line from the Montana border directly north of Cody to Lander. From Lander extend the line west and slightly south to the point where the borders of Wyoming, Idaho, and Utah intersect. The vast majority of Wyoming's wolves are found northwest of these lines.

In Montana, wolves are found in the greatest numbers in the mountainous areas in the western third of the state. For the purposes of approximation, a line can be sketched from the eastern boundary of Glacier National Park southward to Helena, then southwestward to Red Lodge. West of the line is where most of Montana's wolves roam. However, packs have also been established in several mountain ranges lying east of the line, including the Little Belt and Crazy Mountains.

Wolves range across most of central and northern Idaho, with additional packs claiming territories in the east-central portion of the state west of Yellowstone and Grand Teton National Parks. Roughly speaking, wolf range in Idaho lies north of a line drawn from Jackson to Boise, with the agricultural and flatter areas northwest of Idaho Falls containing few wolves.

Recently wolves have also come to occupy Washington and Oregon. Several packs have been established in the extreme northeastern corners of both states. In Washington, packs have also colonized a few areas farther west.

Dispersals of lone wolves, usually young animals in search of a mate and new territory, have taken these creatures to locations far beyond their currently established range in the northern Rockies. A young male split from a pack in northeastern Oregon, traveled to the southern Cascade Range in southwestern Oregon, then crossed into California in 2011. The animal was photographed on a hunter's trail camera. It is presumed that prior to this incident a wild wolf had not made tracks in California since the 1930s. The last confirmed wolf sighting in southwestern Oregon was in 1946. In 2009 a young female wandered from Paradise Valley north of Yellowstone National Park to Colorado. Biologists believe her trip covered around 3,000 erratic miles and took about six months. Another wolf moved from the Yellowstone area to the Black Hills of South Dakota, where it was killed by a vehicle. Given the increasing population of gray wolves and the frequent dispersals of young animals, it's reasonable to predict that wolves will continue to expand their range into the southern Rocky Mountains and remote areas in western Washington, Oregon, and northern California. Many experts anticipate that gray wolves will continue to disperse east of the Rockies, but limited

Red wolves were reintroduced to the Alligator National Wildlife Refuge in North Carolina in 1987.
USFWS/STEVE HILLEBRAND

habitat and social conditions will prohibit the establishment of viable populations. However, wolf numbers in the northern Rocky Mountains may fluctuate significantly in the future due to hunting, trapping, disease, and changes in habitat conditions.

Mexican wolves (the gray wolf subspecies described in the beginning of this chapter) range over parts of New Mexico and Arizona. The wolves are currently found primarily on mountainous National Forest lands in southeastern Arizona and southwestern New Mexico. They also roam on the eastern portions of the White Mountain and San Carlos Apache Reservations in Arizona.

Red wolves are currently found in northeastern North Carolina. Animals from a captive breeding program were first released in the Alligator National Wildlife Refuge in 1987. Their population has expanded to cover roughly 1.5 million acres in northeastern North Carolina, including additional national wildlife refuges, a Department of Defense bombing range, and other private and public lands.

Wolf Habitat

Wolves can occupy essentially any type of habitat in which they can find sufficient prey. Although individual wolves can subsist on smaller quarry such as ground squirrels, hares, beavers, and birds, in most places the presence of wolf packs is dependent upon mid-size to large ungulates. Elk, moose, caribou, musk oxen, whitetail deer, and mule deer are primary prey species of wolves. They may also feed on other species such as bighorn sheep, pronghorn, and mountain goats.

Wolf habitat thus mirrors the range of their prey. From arid regions of the southwestern United States to the frozen tundra of northeastern Canada, wolf numbers tend to be highest in areas that hold the most abundant prey. They also tend to be the lowest in areas of high human population and activity. Wolves have lived and successfully reared young in a variety of areas including missile ranges and livestock pastures and near dumps. However, they're most comfortable in areas where they have limited contact with people.

ABILITIES AND BEHAVIOR

Over most of their range, gray wolves prey primarily on ungulates—large, hoofed animals. Thus, wolves require the speed, strength, and intelligence to effectively hunt and kill such creatures. If wolves were fleeter of foot than their prey species, it seems nature's balance would tip too much in favor of the predators and prey would become scarce. Compared to most of the creatures they hunt, wolves are evenly matched or slightly slower. A healthy whitetail deer can normally outrun a wolf, as can a mature elk.

Physical Abilities

That said, wolves are still quite fleet of foot. How fast are they? While researching this book, I encountered highly divergent estimates of wolf speed even from apparently credible sources. It appears that some "wolf fans" are as likely to inflate their favorite animal's abilities as is the admirer of a professional athlete. One source asserted wolves can run up to 45 miles per hour, a speed well in excess of reasonable estimates of any of their prey, with the exception of pronghorn, the fastest animal in North America. Most credible sources place the speed of wolves between 30 and 35 miles per hour, generally on par or slightly slower than their normal prey. One nationally recognized biologist notes that wolves seldom pursue their prey at speeds exceeding 25 miles per hour.

Within their territory wolves often move at speeds of 5 miles per hour or slightly faster for hours on end. Wolves are sometimes reputed as covering more than 100 miles per day when hunting, but such claims are exaggerated and are certainly based on extreme examples. Wolves with large territories have been recorded traveling 35 miles in a single night and 50 miles in a full day (twenty-four hours). Wolves with smaller territories, such as those on Michigan's Isle Royale, normally travel less than 10 miles per day while hunting in the winter.

Wolves may sprint over 30 miles per hour in pursuit of prey.
NPS/JIM PEACO

In soft snow the narrow, pointed hooves of ungulates are more efficient than the broad pads on the feet of wolves. However, if the snow develops even a moderate crust, the wolf's spreading pads allow it to run efficiently on the surface, while the hooves of its prey break through the crust. This adaptation of gray wolves greatly enhances their predatory abilities in late winter, when freezing and thawing are most likely to create a crust on the surface of the snow. The sharp claws on a wolf's feet are not used as tools for grasping prey like those on a mountain lion, but they do serve an important purpose. They give the animal extra traction on hard soil, ice, and crusted snow.

Interestingly, the average pace of a hunting wolf can be easily matched by a fit, athletic human. American Indians of some groups ran down wolves in a game of endurance. Historical records also verify Europeans doing the same. In 1865 a Canadian in Saskatchewan ran down a wolf in a 100-mile effort that terminated when the worn-out wolf was killed by the pursuer's knife. Wolves possess both formidable speed and reasonable endurance, but in comparison to their prey, they excel at neither. Hunting success is more often a product of strategy and cooperation rather than speed or endurance, an aspect of wolf biology discussed in a later section.

Several features of the wolf's skull and dental structure are highly instrumental to its success as a predator. The teeth of a gray wolf are especially suited to delivering injurious bites to prey, then ripping and tearing at the meat once an animal has been killed. Wolves also have teeth that are specialized for crushing and cracking bones, which allows them to extract the nutritious marrow inside. From a hunting standpoint, the fangs or canine teeth of wolves are most important for subduing their prey. These teeth measure about 1 inch in length. They are very strong, sharp, and curved slightly backward to aid in holding prey. Toward the back of the wolf's mouth are another set of extremely important teeth known as the carnassials. These large, sharp teeth are used for slicing meat much like a pair of scissors shearing cloth. The function of these teeth is so critical that a wolf with cracked, infected, or excessively worn carnassials is at risk of starvation due to its inability to tear meat.

Several large and powerful muscles attached to the rear of its skull and jawbone close the wolf's jaws. Although the wolf's bite is not as strong as that of the slightly larger hyena, its jaws have enough power to crack bones from its prey. It has been estimated that a gray wolf's jaws exert significantly more force than those of a similar size domestic dog.

Wolves rely on several senses for hunting and communicating with their own kind. They have keen eyes, an uncanny sense of smell, and excellent hearing. Which of these senses is most important when hunting?

Many popular notions exist that say the wolf's sense of smell is its most highly developed and important sense. However, it is imperative to note that it is nearly impossible to construct and control legitimate scientific experiments evaluating any of the wolf's sensory apparatuses. Biologists are thus forced to compare the sensory abilities of wolves with those of similar creatures, such as domestic dogs. Dogs can perceive and discriminate odors on a level that is one hundred to perhaps one million times more sensitive than that of the human nose. Wolves are presumed to have similar, if not greater, olfactory abilities than dogs. Several observations by researchers attest to the wolf's skill in detecting prey by scent. One biologist recorded wolves smelling three moose at a distance of 1.5 miles. Research on gray wolves in Minnesota indicates that they often use scent as a means of locating whitetail deer as prey. The *Canis lupus*'s sense of smell is also extremely important for communicating the territorial boundaries of packs, along with the sex and reproductive status of individual animals.

The wolf's eyes are quite different from human eyes. Wolves, like domestic dogs and various species of cats, have eyes that function well in both daylight and at night. Research on the vision of domestic dogs indicates that their eyes are more sensitive to motion and far more capable at differentiating variations in the color gray than human eyes are. Presumably the wolf's vision is likewise more sensitive. Human vision exceeds that of canines in its overall definition (clarity) and color distinction. At least one research study indicates that the wolf's vision may be sharper than that of domestic dogs. Suffice it to say that the wolf's enhanced ability to detect motion and excellent low-light vision serve it very well in detecting and pursuing prey. Research performed with captive coyotes indicates that eyesight is their most dominant sense when hunting. It is quite possible that wolves in open environments rely more heavily on their eyesight to detect prey, while those that inhabit forested regions favor their noses.

A wolf's eyes are especially suited to detecting motion and function remarkably well in low light.
KEVIN RHOADES

Wolf pups are born deaf, but they attain adult-level hearing capabilities within three weeks. The erect ears of a wolf point toward sounds the animal finds interesting. Research specific to wolves' hearing is absent, but most biologists believe they have hearing capabilities similar to domestic dogs—more acute than humans, but not exceptional in relation to other mammals. Wolves are definitely more sensitive to high-pitched noises than people are.

Compared to other clawed creatures such as bears and cats, wolves are unskilled in the use of their forepaws. Both grizzly bears and bobcats are adept at using their paws to manipulate objects or capture prey. Wolves, however, primarily use their teeth and jaws. Some researchers feel that the poor close-up vision of wolves is partly responsible for the limited use of their paws in sophisticated ways.

Vocal and Visual Communication

So varied and sophisticated are the vocal and visual communication of wolves that an entire book could be devoted to the subject. The intricate social web within a pack and between rival packs requires complex and subtle communication; without this communication, there would be excessively destructive conflict.

The wolf's iconic howl is the species' vocalization most recognized by humans. However, the actual role of howling in wolf communication is not as simple as many

Wolves communicate with body language such as bared teeth and snarls. Bared teeth may signal aggression or defensiveness.
© ISTOCK.COM/ RAMIROMARQUEZPHOTOS

people believe. For example, most folks assume that howling is a territorial behavior. When a pack howls, it tells other wolves to stay away. Biologists testing this theory have played recordings of wolf howls in the vicinity of a pack to see how it would respond. Packs that did not return the recorded howls with vocalizations of their own usually moved away. Packs that howled back stood their ground. Wolves defending a kill or protecting pups often howl aggressively. "Chorus howling," the scientific term that refers to multiple members of a pack howling at once, appears to serve an important function in maintaining a buffer between rival packs. Some theorists also believe that howling together strengthens the bond of wolves within a pack.

Lone wolves also howl, although not nearly as long or as frequently as those in a pack. Research indicates that the howls of single wolves last from around three to seven seconds. Rarely will the moan of a lone wolf last longer than twelve seconds. By contrast, the chorus of howls of gray wolves in a pack lasts from around thirty seconds to two minutes. Some biologists believe single wolves howl less frequently than packs to reduce their risk of being discovered and killed by a territorial pack.

Numerous authors have written eloquent descriptions regarding the howl of a wolf. The sound touches some people with sadness, others with strength and wildness. Despite our emotional reactions to the sound, exactly why wolves howl remains something of a mystery.

Along with howling, wolves communicate with one another (and sometimes other creatures) with noises similar to those of domestic dogs. Wolves bark, whine, whimper, and yelp as signs of submission. Barks indicate a wolf is disturbed or annoyed. They use a woofing sound to warn one another of danger. For example, a wolf may woof to announce a black bear approaching the den. Pups respond to woofs by retreating to cover or the den. Wolves may switch from a woof to a bark as a threat comes closer. Much like a barking dog, wolves may either attack or flee, depending on their perception of the danger represented by an intruder. Growls and snarls are other noises wolves make that signal aggression and conflict. These sounds are usually emitted in dominance displays and defensive situations.

Gray wolves also use body language to communicate, which provides a visual signal of their intentions. Again, much of the wolf's body language parallels that of the domestic dog. In an aggressive or defensive situation, the hairs on a wolf's neck and back may become erect. It may pull back its lips and snarl. Wolves also signal submission through body language. When approaching a dominant member of the pack, a subordinate wolf may maintain a low crouch, with its ears back and tail lowered. Submissive wolves also wag their tails and attempt to lick or nuzzle dominant animals.

Pack Structure and Dynamics

Wolf packs are generally composed of a breeding pair and their offspring. New packs are formed when lone wolves of the opposite sex become pairs and produce pups. Younger members of the pack are usually one to three years old. Typically, young wolves disperse from the pack in their first year or two of life. The dominant male and female within a pack are commonly known as alphas in the public vocabulary, although this term is rarely used by wolf biologists. In conflict with other pack members, they are dominant. As the alphas age, they may be challenged by younger members of the pack. In the case of females, an alpha that is successfully challenged by a younger wolf may stay with the pack, although displaced alphas are often driven away or even killed. In at least two cases in Yellowstone National Park, dominant females have been killed by rival females within the pack.

For the most part wolf packs behave harmoniously, like the extended family that they are. Cooperation and camaraderie are much more normal than conflict. Conflict is most likely to occur when there is a major disruption in the pack's structure. Alpha members, both male and female, may be killed when hunting, by rival packs or by humans. When this happens, a wolf from outside the pack may join and take up the role of an alpha, or a formerly subordinate member might gain the position. In either case, such disruption within a pack can cause a period of tension and conflict. Once leadership has been reestablished, the pack normally returns to its harmonious way of living.

On an early morning in May 2000, wolf observers in Yellowstone National Park found a badly mauled female wolf. The alpha female of the Druid Peak pack, she had been attacked by members of her own pack and would soon succumb to her wounds. Known as #40F, she had previously ruled the Druids with iron teeth, viciously harassing her sister and two daughters, disrupting their denning attempts, and "disciplining" the subordinates with a ferocity not normally seen in wolf packs. Researchers speculate that the aggressive, seemingly cruel behavior of #40F was instrumental in causing her mother and another sister to abandon the pack.

During the time #40F reigned as alpha female of the Druids, the pack reflected some of her super-aggressive character. The pack was responsible for killing coyotes, other wolves, and even mountain lions that trespassed in its territory. Evidently, #40F's subordinate sister and daughter finally had had enough, turning on the ruthless matriarch in an uprising that left her dead.

In the world of wolves, like humans, there are extreme personalities. Just as an individual's character cannot be completely assessed from a single act of selfishness or generosity, a species cannot be characterized by an individual or small group. Observers who saw only the Druid Peak pack might conclude that social dynamics among wolves are much more violent than they actually are. Sound biology is based on multiple observations of many animals in various habitats and contexts. The behavior and death of #40F is a good reminder of this principle and also underscores that in the natural world, individual animals sometimes exhibit behaviors that are very different from the norms for their species.

WOLVES AND OTHER ANIMALS

Wolves are considered apex predators. Yet the prey of gray wolves consists of other animals and food sources beyond the large ungulates that make up the bulk of their diet in most locations.

Wolves and Their Prey

Prey Species

Arctic wolves prey upon arctic hares. In some places, beavers represent a significant source of nutrition for wolves. Wolves may also opportunistically kill juvenile snowshoe hares and other rabbits, along with young birds and other smaller creatures, mostly in the summer. Around den sites, wolves often hunt for even smaller mammals, such as mice and ground squirrels. In Alaska, they sometimes eat spawning salmon.

Wolves may also scavenge the carcasses of dead animals. In Yellowstone National Park wolves occasionally dine upon elk and other animals struck and killed by vehicles. Wolves targeting these carcasses have also been struck and killed by vehicles. Wolves sometimes eat berries and fruits in the summer, perhaps to gain specific nutrients. Like domestic dogs, wolves will also eat grass to induce vomiting, which may assist in expelling internal parasites or hair from the digestive tract.

But across the vast majority of their habitat, wolves meet their nutritional requirements by preying on weighty ungulates, of which bison are the largest. Bison represent occasional prey for wolves in Yellowstone and Grand Teton National Parks in the contiguous United States and in a few isolated areas in Canada. Wolves seldom attempt to kill a healthy adult bison. Instead, in the winter they actively target old and weak animals. In the summer they harass groups of bison in an attempt to separate vulnerable young from the herd. Bison represent a very small percentage of wolf prey, even where they are abundant.

Wolves also prey upon moose, another large ungulate. Moose roam over most of Alaska and Canada, where they are an important prey species for wolves. In the contiguous United States, wolves prey upon moose in the northern Rocky Mountains and the Great Lakes region. Most biologists believe that moose pose the greatest risk to attacking wolves of any of their prey. Moose are surprisingly quick and agile. A wolf struck by a direct or incidental blow from a moose's hoof during a predation attempt may be severely injured or killed.

Large and clumsy-looking, musk oxen are an important source of prey for arctic wolves. Musk oxen use their herds as a defensive tactic against wolves. The young are bunched toward the middle, with adults facing outward in a circle. The long, curved horns of the musk oxen on the outside of the circle can impale an attacking wolf. Wolves can most efficiently kill musk oxen by creating enough confusion in the herd that the oxen run, making it possible for wolves to target a single animal.

Elk and caribou are middle-size prey animals for wolves. Wolves prey upon caribou in Alaska and Canada. Although animals may occasionally drift into the northern

United States from western Canada, few, if any, caribou are prey for wolves in the Lower 48. Elk roam the Rocky Mountains of the contiguous United States and western Canada, with some animals also present in Alaska. Elk and caribou are the favorite prey of wolves in many of the areas they inhabit.

Of the smaller ungulates that wolves target, whitetail deer are the most common. Wolves in much of southern Canada, the Great Lakes region, and the Rocky Mountains frequently prey upon whitetail deer. Other smaller ungulates wolves prey upon are mule deer and bighorn and Dall sheep. Wolves also may occasionally kill mountain goats and pronghorn.

In agricultural areas and where ranchers graze livestock in mountainous regions, wolves sometimes kill domestic animals such as cattle, horses, sheep, and goats. Wolves that learn to prey upon livestock, whether individual animals or packs, often develop a preference for this prey. They chase and test domestic animals for signs of weakness and vulnerability, just like they do with wild animals. Individuals or packs that repeatedly kill livestock may be shot by ranchers or wildlife agents to protect the livelihood of agricultural families.

Hunting Strategies

Wolves use a variety of hunting strategies to take down their prey. Their methods may change in relation to the number and skill of wolves in the pack, the size of the prey and the habitat, and the conditions of the day.

The first thing hunting wolves must do is locate their prey. Scent, sight, and sound are all important means of finding a meal. Although sound is a less obvious method than scent and sight, vocal clues to the location and type of prey can greatly enhance a wolf's chances of making a kill. For example, the bleating of a young elk separated from a herd not only alerts wolves to its whereabouts, but also gives a strong indication of its vulnerability. Biologists also note that like human hunters, wolves sometimes have lucky encounters with their intended prey. For example, a wandering wolf may happen upon a mother grouse with a clutch of a half-dozen, easy-to-catch chicks or fortuitously encounter a lame elk while returning to a den site.

Locating prey that they can successfully kill occupies much of a wolf's life. Researchers have found that during winter, 25 to 50 percent of a wolf's time is spent in search of prey. Wolves on the hunt generally walk or trot in a single file, but they may spread out in forested or brushy areas, a strategy that increases their odds

Wolves stalk as close as they can to their prey before making a rush to attack.
KEVIN RHOADES

of discovering or flushing creatures in places where it is difficult for them to see at a distance.

Usually when wolves spot prey, they attempt to get as close to it as possible before attempting a chase. They use trees, vegetation, ravines, rocks, and other natural sight barriers to approach their prey without being detected. Wolves become very excited while stalking prey, moving more quickly and wagging their tails. They may approach small prey uneducated to the wiles of predators and thus easily captured, such as very young ungulates and hares, more directly once they spot them.

After closing the gap as much as possible, wolves sprint forward in a rush toward their prey. However, not all members of a pack may participate in the rush. Wolves sometimes use an ambush strategy, where some members of the pack circle behind the prey and wait to intercept it while other wolves make the rush.

An animal's reaction to the rush of hunting wolves often determines its survival. Large, strong creatures such as moose and elk may stand their ground. If they do, wolves often spend some time harassing them, attempting to bite at their flanks and haunches. Animals that respond with vigorous, well-aimed kicks or sweeping antlers are normally left alone after a short period of testing. Bison and musk oxen may refuse to run and may even become aggressive in driving wolves away. Whitetail deer are much smaller than moose or bison, but deer that stand their ground may also repel the attack of a wolf pack.

Whether targeting a single animal or a herd, wolves want to make their prey run. Oftentimes a fleet creature, such as a deer, will simply outrun the wolves. If the wolves can keep up with a single animal, they usually attempt to bite at its hindquarters and sides. Puncture and slashing wounds caused by a wolf's fangs slow and weaken the animal due to a loss of blood. During chases that follow a zigzagging course, some members of the wolf pack may run diagonally to cut off the flight of their prey. Wolves may also attempt to bite and hold the nose of a fleeing animal, hoping to bring it down. Not all animals that lose their footing during a chase are doomed, however. In Yellowstone National Park, I once saw a cow elk pulled down by two wolves regain her footing. Although badly wounded, she managed to outrun the wolves to a river where she found safety standing in deep water between two strong currents that the wolves were unable to swim without being swept downstream. Did she get away? Although I didn't see the final outcome, a very large grizzly bear was walking along the riverbank in the direction of the elk, about a quarter of a mile away. I suspect that the job begun by the wolves may have been finished by the bear.

When targeting a herd of creatures, wolves normally single their efforts upon young, weak, or wounded animals. Sometimes wolves will simply run alongside the herd, a strategy that biologists believe is designed to identify easier targets. Wolves do not always prey on just the young, weak, and injured, however. In areas of high wolf densities, where more vulnerable animals are often eliminated from the herds, wolves can and do kill healthy adult animals.

Despite gray wolves' position as apex predators, their percentage of success in predation attempts is quite low. Many factors influence these predators' success rates as hunters. A study of wolf predation attempts in a national park found that their success was almost twice as high during a severe winter than during the subsequent mild one. Research on Isle Royale indicates that wolves are successful in less than 10 percent of their predation attempts on moose. Interestingly, on a per-wolf basis, wolves hunting singly, in pairs, or in small packs are more successful hunters than members of large packs. Packs with numerous individuals often contain many young members, whose hunting skill and strength are inferior to adult wolves.

Wolves and Other Predators

Wolves share their range with numerous other predators, yet the number of other carnivores with which they compete directly for prey is quite small. Grizzly bears sometimes hunt the same prey as wolves, yet with the exception of targeting young animals in the spring, grizzly bears are seldom in direct competition with wolves. The same is true of coyotes. Packs of coyotes infrequently kill adult deer, but they can easily take down fawns, prey also prized by wolves. However, for most of the year coyotes are after much smaller prey. Mountain lions may be the predator with which wolves compete most directly for food. These large cats routinely prey upon deer and elk, two species that also comprise a significant portion of the wolf's diet in many habitats.

Grizzly bears are the only predator in North America that can successfully dominate a pack of wolves in a physical confrontation on a regular basis. In Alaska and Canada, and locations in the contiguous United States such as Glacier and Yellowstone National Parks, grizzly bears and wolves may regularly come into conflict. Most confrontations occur at kill sites, where a grizzly bear attempts to steal a carcass from wolves or vice versa. Researchers in Yellowstone National Park have concluded that adult grizzly bears are usually successful in defending or usurping a kill from wolves. When grizzlies investigate den sites, wolves are most often successful in driving them away. Wolves kill grizzly bear cubs on rare occasions, and adult grizzlies have also been known to kill wolves.

With the exception of grizzly bears, wolf packs dominate in conflicts with other predators, sometimes actively seeking and killing competitors within their territory. Wolf packs are known to kill mountain lions and black bears, occasionally attacking the bears in their dens. However, there are also documented instances of both mountain lions and black bears killing wolves.

Adult grizzly bears are large and strong enough to chase wolves from a kill.
LISA BALLARD

Smaller carnivores are also at risk from wolves. Prior to their reintroduction into Yellowstone National Park, packs of coyotes were "top dogs." The fourteen wolves released in Yellowstone in 1995 were documented killing at least thirteen adult coyotes in their first winter. In the first three years after the return of the wolf, the territories of coyote packs shifted and splintered. Dominance hierarchies were disrupted due to the elimination of alpha members by wolves, causing some coyote packs to disintegrate and others to contract in numbers. The northern portion of Yellowstone, often referred to as the northern range, saw a 50 percent reduction in the coyote population within three years of the wolf's reintroduction. In some places representing core areas inhabited by wolf packs, coyote numbers plummeted by 90 percent. For some species of ungulates, the change was positive. The park's pronghorn numbers increased, as fewer fawns were killed by coyotes.

Wolves are also known to kill other small carnivores such as red foxes. Researchers in Denali National Park, Isle Royale, and Wood Buffalo National Park in Alberta have documented red fox kills by wolves. However, although smaller canines like red foxes and coyotes may die at the jaws of wolves, they also benefit from their larger cousins. Coyotes routinely scavenge on carcasses of animals killed by wolves, as do other creatures such as foxes, ravens, and magpies.

Parasites and Diseases

Parasites and diseases that infect domestic dogs often afflict wolves, too. Internal parasites, such as roundworms, tapeworms, and hookworms are commonly found in wolves. Heartworms have also been documented in wild wolves. Generally, wolves can tolerate low to moderate infestations of these parasites without negative effects. However, severe cases of intestinal parasites can weaken wolves, diminishing their ability to hunt.

External parasites, including ticks and fleas, are also often found on wolves. Mange, a skin affliction caused by a mite, can cause wolves to lose their hair, creates scabs, and causes intense itching. Researchers have documented wolf deaths due to mange in Yellowstone National Park, Minnesota, Wisconsin, and elsewhere. The hair loss caused by mange can be so severe that infected animals are unable to hunt and die from starvation and exposure during the winter.

Wolves are also susceptible to a number of diseases, including rabies. A severe rabies outbreak once infected a number of wolf packs in Alaska, causing a severe reduction in their population. While rabies may cause temporary setbacks to wolf numbers in local areas, its effect on long-term populations is probably minimal. Parvovirus (parvo), another canine virus that is most devastating to pups, can also temporarily inhibit wild wolf populations. Canine distemper is yet another disease contracted by gray wolves. Yellowstone wolves have suffered from bouts of distemper that have seasonally reduced their numbers.

REPRODUCTION AND YOUNG

The Mating Season

The mating season of wolves normally occurs from January to April, depending on the latitude where the animals are found. Wolves living in southern locations breed sooner than those living in the north. In Montana, and similar latitudes in the contiguous United States, gray wolves mate from mid- to late February. Red wolves in North Carolina begin mating around the first of February, but females may conceive a litter of pups in March as well. The Mexican wolves of New Mexico and Arizona breed from late January to early March. Arctic wolves breed the latest. The breeding season for this northern subspecies generally occurs in April.

Courtship and mating among wolves follow one of several patterns. In the most typical scenario, the alpha male and female mate to produce young within a pack. However, subordinate females may also mate with the alpha male and produce a litter. Young produced by two females within the same pack is uncommon. This rare occurrence usually happens in places where prey is abundant, making it possible for members of the pack to nourish two litters of pups. In most cases when two females within a pack produce offspring, the mothers are either sisters or an older alpha female and her daughter. Wolf researchers have documented at least one occurrence among arctic wolves where an alpha female that advanced past reproductive age stayed with the pack while her daughter became the alpha male's mate and pup producer. Two sisters mating with the alpha is a temporary situation that seldom lasts more than a year or two. Eventually one of the females becomes dominant and the pack reverts to the normal pattern of one female birthing one litter of pups per year.

In captive wolves another male member of the pack may also mate with a female. However, the observed incidences of this behavior have occurred in packs that were highly disrupted (lacking one or both parent wolves), a situation that infrequently occurs in wild populations. Although it has been documented that subordinate males among wild wolves sometimes also breed, it is exceedingly rare. Under normal

Courtship and breeding for gray wolves occur in late winter or early spring.
© ISTOCK.COM/MIRCEAX

circumstances the alpha female interferes aggressively with subordinate females' attempts to court or mate with the alpha male. The alpha male is similarly intolerant of the mating behaviors of subordinate males.

Sometimes, however, these interference efforts are unsuccessful. On Isle Royale, after the dominant male of a pack disappeared, the alpha female accepted another mate. The new alpha male not only mated with the alpha female, but also with a subordinate female, even though she was chased from the pack by the alpha female several times.

How long do dominant male or female wolves retain their breeding status within a pack? Generally wolves that attain breeding status produce offspring for three to four years. However, researchers have observed wolves that have sired or birthed pups for as few as one year or as many as eight.

The mating season is the time when young females and males that have dispersed to new territories are most likely to meet and form a pair. If lone wolves meet, form a pair, and produce a litter of young, a pack is born. The meeting and mating of unrelated single wolves of the opposite sex is the most common means by which a new wolf pack is established. A male and a female that are unattached and become a breeding pair have an extremely difficult time establishing a territory and producing offspring in an area where wolves are already abundant. Under normal conditions packs are most readily formed in places where there is a robust prey base and few or no wolves to compete with the newly mated pair.

Prior to mating, reproductively capable wolves engage in a variety of territorial and courtship behaviors. Lone wolves of the opposite sex may meet and become associated as a pair at any time of the year. However, their courtship and mating behavior will wait until late winter, the time at which other mated wolves in packs also prepare for breeding.

Territory marking via scratching the ground and urination increases among paired wolves before mating. Interestingly, newly mated wolves spend more time scent marking than established pairs. In packs the alpha male and female spend more time in close proximity, sometimes in seclusion from the rest of the pack. Researchers have observed that just prior to mating, wolf mates sleep within a yard of each other, much closer than they do after mating or at any other time of the year.

For some days prior to breeding, wolf pairs engage in other behaviors that are sometimes likened to the flirting between humans of the opposite sex who find one another attractive. The female may nuzzle the male, or the male may prance playfully toward the female. Prancing, nuzzling,

Scent marking of territory increases with paired wolves during the mating season.
NPS

playing, and sniffing are common courtship activities among wolves. But like courtship among people, a wolf of the opposite sex may be "turned off" or uninterested in the advances of another, sometimes playing hard to get. Another interesting parallel exists between human courtship and that of wolves: It is not always the most flirtatious female or the most aggressive male that is of most interest to wolves of the opposite sex. Wolves sometimes pay no attention to, or actively avoid, the overly enthusiastic advances of an animal of the other sex.

Pregnancy and Gestation

The gestation period (the amount of time between breeding and the birth of offspring) for wolves is not sharply defined. Most sources place the gestation period from sixty to sixty-five days. Looking for a figure easier to remember? If you define the gestation period of a wolf at nine weeks, you're right on target.

Once conceived, the pups' development proceeds rapidly. Within about three weeks, heartbeats of the developing pups can be detected. By the end of seven weeks, the fetuses have skeletons.

Pregnant females normally stay near the den where the pups will be birthed for several weeks before their arrival. At this time other members of the pack deliver food to the expectant mother. Den sites and construction follow some predictable patterns, but they exhibit a wide range of diversity depending on latitude, habitat, and the behavior of individual packs. Wolves often dig dens four to five weeks before the birth of a litter, but researchers have documented den digging as early as the previous autumn. All members of a pack may help with digging a den. Dens are excavated with their sharp, strong claws, much like a dog digging a hole in an attempt to burrow under a fence.

Of all the similar characteristics of wolf dens, proximity to water is perhaps the strongest. Wolf dens are typically located within 100 yards of a creek, river, or lake. Another highly predictable factor in the location of a den site is its position in the pack's home range. Wolves usually locate their dens in the interior of the pack's territory, where the pups have the least potential of encountering hostile individuals from a rival pack. Only rarely are dens found within half a mile of a pack's territorial boundary, the zone at which wolves are most likely to fight and be killed by members of competing packs.

Riverbanks and bluffs that afford southern exposure are often used as den sites. Wolves in many locations seem to prefer areas of soft or sandy soil, where it is easier to dig a den than in hard, stony ground. Dens may be dug under the roots of trees, too. Excavated dens may consist of a short tunnel that connects to a larger chamber or a simpler depression in the earth. In the far north, wolves sometimes dig a den in or through snowpack. Naturally occurring "dens" occasionally afford wolves the luxury of not digging a den at all. Arctic wolves often use caves or crevices in rocks as denning sites. Wolves in other areas may also use caves, along with hollow logs and abandoned

Wolf dens are often dug in soft, sandy soil near water.
KEVIN RHOADES

beaver lodges. They might also simply enlarge a badger hole or another hole previously excavated by some other mammal.

Within a wolf pack's territory, there are often multiple den sites. Do females use the same den for birthing their pups every year? The short answer is no although female wolves generally prefer a known den. Packs may use a traditional denning site for over ten years. One wolf researcher has observed the traditional use of a den for fifteen consecutive years. While they may den in different sites from one year to the next, female wolves seem to prefer a known den. In a study of wild wolves in Minnesota, researchers found that most females (more than 80 percent) returned to a traditional denning site to birth their pups.

Birth

Wolf pups are birthed in a manner similar to domestic dogs. Many observers have likened the appearance of newborn wolf pups to the whelps of a German shepherd. Newborn wolves have fine, dark fur. They are born with their eyes closed and are deaf, presumably due to closed ear canals. Wolf pups arrive with small ears and blunt noses. Very shortly after birth they instinctively nuzzle their mother's belly. Upon encountering a nipple, their innate sucking reflex prompts them to nurse.

The average number of pups born in a litter is around five or six. Litters ranging from one to eleven have been observed. Several factors affect litter size. The age and health of the mother wolf is one of these. Females nearing the end of breeding age (around ten years old) tend to have fewer pups than younger females, as do those who are nutritionally stressed. In general, females tend to have larger litters where prey is abundant versus areas where the wolf pack must work much harder to sustain itself. Some experts believe that packs living in areas with a surplus of ungulate prey are more likely to have two young-producing females.

Compared to smaller wild canines such as coyotes and foxes, wolves birth fewer, larger pups. They range in weight from around ten ounces to slightly over one pound, with an average weight of fifteen ounces. Such creatures seem quite tiny, yet newborn wolf pups are at least four times larger than the newborn kits of a red fox.

Nurturing Pups to Adulthood

Biologists sometimes break the development from newborn to adult canine into four stages, a theory that is helpful in describing the maturation of young wolves. The *neonatal stage* refers to the period of time from birth until the pups open their eyes at roughly two weeks or a few days before. During this period the pups spend much of their time sleeping and nursing, often jumbled in a furry pile. Upon opening, the eyes of wolf pups are often blue, later transitioning to the greenish hazel common to grown wolves. However, a small number of wolf pups retain their blue eyes into adulthood.

The next period of development is known as the *transition stage*. This is a relatively short segment of development that occurs from the time wolf pups open their eyes until they gain enough strength and coordination to leave the den. During this

Female wolves may retrieve pups that wander from the den in their mouth. Pups may also be moved in this way from one den to another.
KEVIN RHOADES

stage their senses develop rapidly, especially those of touch and smell. Their muscles become stronger and more coordinated, allowing them to walk or stumble about. The transition stage technically lasts from the time of eye opening until about three weeks of age.

At the end of the transition stage, wolf pups emerge from the den, where they encounter other members of the pack. This begins the *socialization stage,* when pups learn the correct ways to interact with the pack, their extended family. This stage ends when the pups reach about eleven weeks of age, at which time they are weaned from their mother's milk.

From three to five weeks of age wolf pups are still quite weak and uncoordinated, although their physical abilities develop quickly during this time. Pups learn to nurse their mother from a standing position. They seldom wander more than a few hundred yards from the den. If they do, the mother often retrieves them by carrying them in her mouth. By five weeks, pups have learned to follow their mother and other adult wolves in the pack. They may be moved from their birthing den to other dens within the pack's territory. Pups of this age have also learned to retreat to the den during bouts of nasty weather and to avoid potential predators.

After five weeks of age, wolf pups can generally digest small bits of solid food in addition to their mother's milk. Solid food is delivered to the pups through a unique behavior known as "lick up." When members of the pack return to the den after a successful hunt, they are met by pups that lick and nuzzle around the adults' mouths.

Most wolves leave the pack to find their own territories before they reach three years of age.
LISA BALLARD

This action prompts the adult wolf to regurgitate a portion of the contents of its stomach, which is then eaten by the pups. Both male and female members of the pack contribute to the pups' care in this way. As they age, young wolves learn to cache extra pieces of meat around the den site, which they may eat at a later time.

During the socialization period wolf pups become increasingly mobile and playful, often wrestling and chasing one another in strength- and coordination-building exercises. They learn that bashing into a sibling from the side is more likely to knock it from its feet than attacking from the front. Skills such as these not only prepare the pups to interact (perhaps aggressively) with members of their own kind, but also serve as training for hunting as adults.

The final stage of development for wolf pups is the *juvenile stage,* which lasts from twelve weeks until the youngsters become adults. At around three months of age, young wolves begin chasing small creatures such as grasshoppers and mice. They also learn to leap and pounce in an attempt to capture small rodents. Sometime, at about three to four months of age, they may accompany adult wolves on a hunt. However, it takes some time for pups to become aggressive toward prey. At first they might be scared of the animals they're supposed to attack. A researcher on Ellesmere Island, a Canadian island near Greenland, witnessed a litter of pups accompanying the alpha male from a pack of arctic wolves as it caught and killed an arctic hare. Rather than rushing over to investigate the meal, the pups were so frightened by the dying wails of the hare that they took cover in a nearby rock pile.

Although wolf pups will continue to grow after four months, by this time they are fully capable of following the pack as it moves and hunts. For the next several months they will hone their hunting skills as members of the pack. Some young wolves will remain with the pack for up to three years, while others may disperse to find their own territories as early as nine months of age.

WOLVES AND HUMANS

Wolves in History

World Cultures

Since prehistoric times, the relationship between humans and wolves has been chronicled in artwork and legend. Paintings from caves indicate prehistoric artists were inspired by wolves, along with numerous other creatures. Roman folklore recounts the story of Romulus and Remus, the founders of Rome. According to the legend, the twin baby boys were ordered to be executed. Instead, the executioner, a servant, left them in a cradle on the banks of the Tiber River. A flood ferried the cradle downstream. The infants were discovered and reared by a female wolf. From this legend came the Lupercalia Festival, or "Wolf Festival." The she-wolf who nursed Romulus and Remus was named Lupa. The festival occurred in the spring and was thought to bring fertility and health to the celebrants.

Norse mythology recounts the tale of Fenrir, a monstrous creature in the form of a wolf. The gods feared Fenrir, so they put him in chains. The immense wolf creature easily broke the chains. The gods conferred with the dwarves who made magic ribbons of six mysterious elements. When the gods challenged Fenrir's strength against the wispy ribbons, he ignored the challenge, saying there was no pride in breaking such feeble bonds. Fenrir agreed to the test, only if one of the gods would place a hand in his mouth. Tyr, the god of war, finally accepted Fenrir's condition. Discovering he couldn't free himself from the magic cords, Fenrir bit off Tyr's hand. One day, predicts the legend, Fenrir will finally break free. He will pursue and kill Odin, the father of the gods. Fenrir will then die at the hand of Vadir, Odin's son.

Wolves have been characters in the legends and religions of other various peoples at different periods in history. Sometimes wolves have been portrayed positively. At other times they have been viewed quite negatively. In Turkish tradition, a mother wolf, Ashina Tuwu, rescued an injured boy. They later had ten half-wolf, half-human children. Bumin Khayan, the oldest of their offspring, became the ruler of the Turkish tribes. Turkish culture still generally regards the wolf as a positive symbol of leadership.

Gaelic mythology from Scotland and Ireland includes legends of Cailleach, sometimes referred to as "the hag," or queen of winter. She works to keep spring from coming and prolongs the cold and hardship of winter. Cailleach can take the form of a wolf. Some traditions assert she summons fierce wolf storms in the middle of January when the days lengthen, indicating spring is on its way. These storms coincide with the coldest portion of winter. One line of Cailleach lore recounts a story similar to Groundhog Day that occurs on February 2. If the first day of February is sunny, Cailleach has fine weather for gathering firewood, which means she can keep herself warm for more nights and winter will be longer. If February 1 is cloudy, Cailleach sleeps and will run out of firewood soon, resulting in a shorter winter. Along with taking the shape of a wolf and unleashing wolf storms on the world, the feared Cailleach is sometimes portrayed as riding on a wolf, bringing destruction and death to people in the darkness and cold of winter.

Wolves have been the subject of human folklore and legends since ancient times.
KEVIN RHOADES

Native Peoples of North America

Like other peoples of the world, the native peoples of North America did not universally view the wolf positively or negatively. Wolves were held in esteem by many tribes for their hunting skills and intelligence. The Cherokee, Chippewa, Algonquin, and several other tribes had clans known as the Wolf Clan. Wolves were thought to be "medicine" animals by numerous tribes, creatures capable of giving special powers to humans. Indian names often included wolves, suggesting a positive link between the person and the presumed spiritual power of the creature. Nonetheless, wolves were killed through trapping and hunting by many of the North American native peoples. Wolf skins might be worn as ceremonial decorations. Scouts from tribes inhabiting the Great Plains often wore wolf skins. In their sign language, *scout* and *wolf* were the same. Young hunters and warriors were encouraged to mimic the habits of hunting wolves, such as being aware of potential danger behind them and not solely focusing on what was ahead.

The Nunamiut people of central Alaska believed wolves were exceptional hunters from which human hunters could learn much. They were also skillful hunters of wolves. Nunamiut hunters would lure wolves by howling or creeping up on them as they slept. They also devised various traps for wolves, including snares and deadfalls. Deadfalls are a type of trap in which a heavy object such as a log is held in place by a support connected to some type of trigger. When an animal trips the trigger by accidentally coming into contact with it or purposefully taking an attached bait, the "deadfall" drops and kills the creature. Nunamiut hunters, while very skilled in taking wolves, refrained from bragging about their accomplishments. Such activity was thought to bring bad luck. The Nunamiuts did not fear wolves, but they took precautions to prevent wolf attacks.

The oral history of some Athabascan tribes of Alaska and western Canada indicates they deliberately killed wolves (primarily pups at den sites) to decrease predation upon the big game animals the Indians relied on for food.

European Settlers in North America

European settlers in North America took a dim view of wolves. The animals not only proved a perceived threat to human life and livestock, but they were also vilified in certain religious traditions. Sparse biblical references attribute negative wolflike characteristics to evil people, yet the Bible does not judge the creatures evil themselves. Nonetheless certain Christian traditions eventually condemned wolves as animals with an evil nature. Wolves were thought to be gluttonous and cruel. Early immigrants to North America brought with them these negative perceptions. Coupled with real and imagined dangers to people and livestock, these notions inspired settlers with a strong motivation to rid their world of wolves.

As early as 1630, colonists and Indians were offered incentives in cash or commodities to kill wolves. In the early to mid-1800s, many states developed bounty systems for wolf extermination. States paid a cash bounty to residents who brought in hides or

carcasses as proof of eliminating a wolf. During the mid- to late 1800s, market hunters wiped out extensive herds of bison and elk on the Great Plains and across the West. These vast herds were replaced with domestic livestock. Attacks on cattle and sheep prompted intense government-sponsored efforts to eliminate wolves. The federal government created a division of Predator and Rodent Control within the Bureau of Biological Survey in 1915. Part of this agency's charge was ridding Bureau of Land Management and National Forest lands of wolves. Other predators were targeted as well. Both the public and most professional biologists welcomed these predator sup-pression efforts. Even in Yellowstone National Park, a refuge created in part for the protection of wildlife, wolf extermination efforts were pursued with enthusiasm. With the exceptions of northern Minnesota and Wisconsin, wolves were essentially elimi-nated from the contiguous United States by 1940. The 1960s probably represent the low point in wolf numbers in North America in recorded history.

Wolves in Modern Times

As early as the 1940s, a handful of conservationists suggested wolves should be restored to Yellowstone National Park. Among these was Aldo Leopold, considered by many to be the "father" of modern conservation and wildlife management in the United States. An avid hunter, Leopold recognized the value of wolves as creatures and to ecosystems. In subsequent decades field studies of wolves in Alaska, Canada, and Isle Royale provided more objective information about the creatures than most biological treatments of the past.

The 1970s advanced gray wolf conservation on several fronts. Both the gray wolf population in the Great Lakes region and Mexican wolves received protection under the Endangered Species Act (ESA). Gray wolves were listed under the ESA in 1974 and Mexican wolves in 1976, with several revisions and reclassifications that expanded wolf protection under the ESA to all the contiguous United States by 1978. From 1978 to 1982, recovery plans were developed for wolves in the Great Lakes area, the northern Rocky Mountains, and the Southwest. Wolves also took a hand in recovery. Animals from Canada began moving southward in the 1980s. Wolves denned in Glacier National Park in 1986. This fledgling population grew quickly, expanding the range of wolves southward into other parts of Montana in the subsequent decade.

After several years of controversy, wolves were reintroduced to Yellowstone National Park and central Idaho in 1995 and 1996. These populations encountered an abundant prey base and grew rapidly. By 2002 wolves had exceeded the recovery goal of thirty breeding pairs and 300 animals in Montana, Idaho, and Wyoming set by the US Fish & Wildlife Service (USFWS) that would allow them to be removed from the endangered species list in these states. However, repeated legal challenges by environmental groups and other legal maneuvering forestalled the "delisting" of wolves until 2011, when Congress intervened directly to remove the animals from federal protection in Montana and Idaho and transferred their management to the states. At the time of this delisting, the USFWS estimated a minimum population of 1,700 wolves and one hundred breeding pairs in Montana, Wyoming, and Idaho. Gray wolf populations are healthy in Alaska and Canada, where the animals are often hunted as a game animal.

Wolves captured in Canada were transplanted to Yellowstone National Park in 1995.
USFWS/LURAY PARKER

In the past decade wolf populations have grown substantially in the contiguous United States.
YELLOWSTONE NATIONAL PARK

Current Interactions and Challenges

Despite the overwhelming success of recovery efforts in the contiguous United States, gray wolves remain a controversial species whose presence and protection evoke extreme emotional reactions from certain segments of the human population. Many ranchers hold extremely hostile attitudes toward wolves and their actual and perceived threats to livestock. Viewed on a national scale, wolf depredation comprises a small percentage of livestock losses in comparison to other factors such as disease and natural disasters. However, livestock depredation, according to the USFWS, may substantially impact individual ranchers. For example, cattle reared as breeding stock represent an asset worth thousands of dollars per animal. As such, wolf losses represent far more than an incidental cost to livestock producers in some areas.

Some hunters also harbor excessive ill will toward wolves, blaming them for any imagined or real decrease in big-game populations. Most biologists believe wolf predation can locally decrease the numbers of such species as elk, moose, caribou, and deer. In and around Yellowstone National Park, rising wolf numbers have coincided with substantially decreased elk numbers. Although the latest addition to the predation and habitat equation in portions of the contiguous United States (along with other predators, hunting, drought, habitat quality and winter severity), wolves are simply one of a myriad of factors that affect big-game populations.

The "wolf haters'" extreme and often unfounded emotional reactions toward wolves are mirrored as strongly on the opposite side by the "wolf lovers." An intense period of public involvement over several years resulted in the Environmental Impact Statement (EIS) that charted the course for wolf reintroduction to the northern Rocky

Mountains. Specific recovery goals, viewed by many as essentially a contract between the federal government and local residents most affected by wolf populations, was developed. However, long after the recovery goals were met, wolf advocacy groups fought their delisting under the ESA. Many of these groups vocally opposed wolf hunting seasons enacted in Montana and Idaho in 2011, attempting to sway the public into believing wolf hunting threatened the entire population. However, leading wolf biologists report wolf populations can normally experience 30 to 50 percent mortality per year without significant declines to the population. States are required to manage wolves in such a way that their numbers do not dip below federal requirements that would trigger relisting under the ESA.

Looking forward it seems reasonable to predict that wolves will continue to expand their range in the contiguous United States, particularly in remote regions of the southern Rocky Mountains and the Pacific Northwest. Like most wolf biologists and researchers, I hope citizens of the United States will develop a more balanced view of the wolf. Wolves are intriguing apex predators, carnivores that deserve no greater or less respect and protection than other species of wildlife. The natural world and human society are healthiest when we view them as such.

INDEX

names, 280, 281, 282–84
nurturing cubs to adulthood, 302–3
parasites and diseases, 305–6
physical abilities, 293–96
physical characteristics, 280–81, 284–85
polar bears and, 281
populations. *See* habitat; range (current/
    historic)
predation, 306–7
predators (other) and, 303–5
pregnancy and gestation, 300–301
pronghorn, 270
range (current), 286–88
range (historic), 285–86
related species in North America, 281–82
reproduction and young, 300–303
subspecies, 282–84
wolves and, 304–5, 405
blacktail deer. *See* mule deer
bluetongue virus (BTV), 65, 98, 134, 170,
    271–72, 277
bobcats
    mountain goats and, 238
    mountain lions and, 354, 355
    mule deer and, 96
    pronghorn and, 267–68, 269, 270
    whitetail deer and, 133
bovine tuberculosis, 28, 134, 202
brainworms. *See* meningeal worms

brucellosis, 28, 188, 201–2, 271
buffalo. *See* bison

C

Caprocks State Park, 189
capture myopathy, 170
caribou, 3–4, 39–40, 105–6, 307, 328, 402–3
cattle
    bison and, 180, 182–83, 200, 201–2, 205
    black bears and, 307
    elk and, 27, 28
cattle guards, 191
chronic wasting disease (CWD), 28–29, 97, 134,
    271, 373
communication
    bighorn sheep, 159–60
    bison, 192–93
    black bears, 296–97
    elk, 19–21
    grizzly bears, 334
    moose, 55–56
    mountain goats, 229–30
    mountain lions, 366–67
    mule deer, 87–88
    pronghorn, 262
    whitetail deer, 124–25
    wolves, 399–400
contagious ecthyma, 170, 241
cougars. *See* mountain lions
coyotes
    bighorn sheep and, 168
    bison and, 200
    elk and, 30
    moose and, 63
    mountain lions and, 375–76, 379
    mule deer and, 91, 95, 96
    pronghorn and, 267–68, 269–70
    whitetail deer and, 132–33
    wolves and, 387–88, 405–6

development stages, 410–12

elk and, 30

European settlers and, 414–15

gender names, 387

grizzly bears and, 341–42, 405

habitat, 396

in history, 412–15

humans and, 412–18

legal protection for, 415–16, 418

mating season, 406–9

in modern times, 415–16

moose and, 61–62, 402

mountain goats and, 239–40

mountain lions and, 376, 405

names, 386, 387, 388–90

nurturing pups to adulthood, 410–12

pack structure and dynamics, 401

parasites and diseases, 406

physical abilities, 397–99

physical characteristics, 386–87, 390–91

predators (other) and, 405–6

pregnancy and gestation, 409–10

prey hunting strategies, 403–4

prey species, 402–3

pronghorn and, 269–70

range (current), 392–96

range (historic), 391–92

related species in North America, 387–88

reproduction and young, 406–12

subspecies, 388–90

whitetail deer and, 132, 403

world cultures and, 412–13

Y

Yellowstone National Park

    bighorn sheep and, 149, 152, 156, 162, 171

    bison and, 177, 182, 186–87, 188, 190, 192, 197–200, 201–2, 206

    black bears and, 304, 305, 309, 311, 312

    elk and, 1, 10, 12, 27, 28, 30, 34

    grizzly bears and, 199–200, 323, 327, 328, 329, 338–39, 341–42, 344, 347–48

    moose and, 45, 50, 51

    mountain goats and, 236, 237, 238

    mountain lions and, 376, 386, 390

    mule deer and, 83, 84, 85, 94

    pronghorn and, 249, 252, 260, 269–70

    wolves and, 394–95, 401, 402, 404, 405–6, 415–16, 417

young animals. *See* reproduction and young

ABOUT THE AUTHOR

A writer, naturalist and photographer, Jack Ballard is a frequent contributor to numerous regional and national publications. He has written hundreds of articles on wildlife natural history, conservation, and other wildlife-related subjects. His photos have appeared in over one hundred regional and national magazines in the past two decades, along with posters, billboards, and other media. He works as an assignment photographer for educational institutions, conservation groups, and other entities. His photos have been published in numerous books. Jack has received multiple awards for his writing and photography from the Outdoor Writers Association of America and other professional organizations. He is the author of a dozen books. Jack lives in Red Lodge, Montana with his wife, Lisa, and English Setter, Percy. See more of his work at jackballard.com.

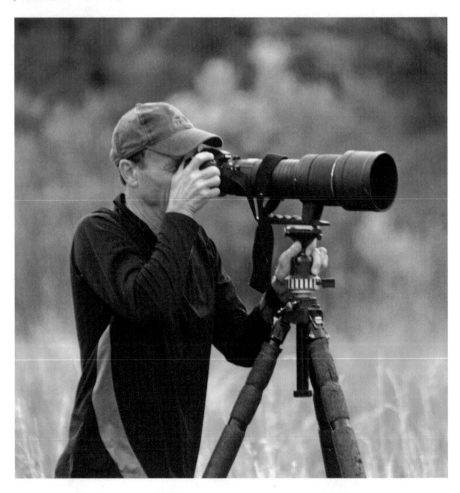